Sermon
On The
Mount

Sermon On The Mount

Arthur W. Pink

Sovereign Grace Publishers, Inc.
P.O. Box 4998
Lafayette, IN 47905

Contents

CHAPTER   PAGE

INTRODUCTION 9
I THE BEATITUDES: MATTHEW v, 3-11 15
II THE BEATITUDES—CONTINUED 22
III THE BEATITUDES—CONTINUED 29
IV THE BEATITUDES—CONCLUDED 36
V THE MINISTERIAL OFFICE: MATTHEW v, 13-16 . . 43
VI CHRIST AND THE LAW: MATTHEW v, 17, 18 . . 49
VII CHRIST AND THE LAW—CONTINUED . . . 55
VIII CHRIST AND THE LAW—CONCLUDED 61
IX THE LAW AND MURDER: MATTHEW v, 21-26 . . 67
X THE LAW AND MURDER—CONCLUDED . . . 73
XI THE LAW AND ADULTERY: MATTHEW v, 27-32 . . 79
XII THE LAW AND ADULTERY—CONTINUED . . . 85
XIII THE LAW AND ADULTERY—CONCLUDED . . . 91
XIV THE LAW AND OATHS: MATTHEW v, 33-37 . . 97
XV THE LAW AND OATHS—CONCLUDED . . . 103
XVI THE LAW AND RETALIATION: MATTHEW v, 38-42 . 109
XVII THE LAW AND RETALIATION—CONTINUED . . 115
XVIII THE LAW AND RETALIATION—CONCLUDED . . 121
XIX THE LAW AND LOVE: MATTHEW v, 43-48 . . . 127
XX THE LAW AND LOVE—CONTINUED . . . 133
XXI THE LAW AND LOVE—CONCLUDED 139
XXII THE GIVING OF ALMS: MATTHEW vi, 1-4 . . . 145
XXIII PRAYER: MATTHEW vi, 5-8 152
XXIV PRAYER: MATTHEW vi, 9-13 159
XXV PRAYER: MATTHEW vi, 14, 15 166
XXVI FASTING: MATTHEW vi, 16-18 172
XXVII FASTING—CONCLUDED 179
XXVIII COVETOUSNESS CORRECTED: MATTHEW ix, 19-21 . 185
XXIX COVETOUSNESS CORRECTED—CONCLUDED . . 192
XXX THE SINGLE EYE: MATTHEW vi, 22, 23 . . 198
XXXI THE SINGLE EYE—CONCLUDED 205
XXXII SERVING GOD: MATTHEW vi, 24 212
XXXIII ANXIETY FORBIDDEN: MATTHEW vi, 25 . . 219
XXXIV ANXIETY FORBIDDEN—CONTINUED . . . 226
XXXV ANXIETY FORBIDDEN: MATTHEW vi, 28, 29 . . 233
XXXVI ANXIETY FORBIDDEN: MATTHEW vi, 30, 31 . . 239
XXXVII ANXIETY FORBIDDEN: MATTHEW vi, 32-34 . . 246
XXXVIII ANXIETY FORBIDDEN—CONCLUDED . . . 253
XXXIX UNLAWFUL JUDGMENT: MATTHEW vii, 1 . . 260

8 CONTENTS

CHAPTER   PAGE

XL JUDGING OTHERS: MATTHEW vii, 1 267

XLI DISSUASIVES FROM JUDGING OTHERS: MATTHEW vii, 2-4 274

XLII HELPING ERRING BRETHREN: MATTHEW vii, 5 . . 281

XLIII UNLAWFUL LIBERALITY: MATTHEW vii, 6 . . . 288

XLIV SEEKING GRACE: MATTHEW vii, 7, 8 295

XLV SEEKING GRACE—CONTINUED 302

XLVI SEEKING GRACE: MATTHEW vii, 9-11 . . . 309

XLVII THE GOLDEN RULE: MATTHEW vii, 12 . . 316

XLVIII THE WAY OF SALVATION: MATTHEW vii, 13, 14 . 323

XLIX THE WAY OF SALVATION: MATTHEW vii, 14, 15 . 330

L FALSE PROPHETS: MATTHEW vii, 15 . . . 337

LI FALSE PROPHETS—CONTINUED 344

LII FALSE PROPHETS—CONTINUED 350

LIII FALSE PROPHETS—CONTINUED 357

LIV FALSE PROPHETS: MATTHEW vii, 15-20 . . 363

LV FALSE PROPHETS—CONCLUDED 370

LVI PROFESSION TESTED: MATTHEW vii, 21-27 . 377

LVII PROFESSION TESTED—CONTINUED . . . 384

LVIII PROFESSION TESTED—CONTINUED . . . 392

LIX PROFESSION TESTED—CONTINUED . . . 400

LX PROFESSION TESTED—CONTINUED . . . 407

LXI PROFESSION TESTED—CONTINUED . . . 414

LXII PROFESSION TESTED—CONTINUED . . . 422

LXIII PROFESSION TESTED—CONCLUDED . . . 429

LXIV CONCLUSION: MATTHEW vii, 28, 29 . . . 436

Introduction

MATTHEW'S Gospel breaks the long silence which followed the ministry of Malachi, the last of the Old Testament prophets. The silence extended for four hundred years, and during that time God was withdrawn from Israel. Throughout this period there were no angelic manifestations, no prophet spoke for Jehovah, and though the Chosen People were sorely pressed, yet were there no Divine interpositions on their behalf. For four centuries God shut His people up to His written Word. Again and again had He promised to send the Messiah, and from Malachi onwards there was a believing remnant who anxiously awaited the appearing of the predicted One. It is at this point that Matthew picks up the thread dropped by the last of the Old Testament prophets. The first purpose of Matthew's Gospel is to present Christ as the *Fulfiller* of the promises made to Israel and the prophecies which related to their Messiah. This is why the word "fulfilled" occurs in Matthew fifteen times, and why there are more quotations from the Old Testament in his Gospel than in the remaining three added together.

The *position* which Matthew's Gospel occupies in the Sacred Canon indicates its character and scope. Standing immediately after the Old Testament and at the beginning of the New, it is therefore the connecting link between them. Hence it is *transitional*, and also more Jewish than any other book in the New Testament. Matthew reveals God appealing to and dealing with His Old Testament people. The numerical place of Matthew in the Divine library confirms this, for being the *fortieth* book it shows us the nation of Israel in the place of *probation*, being tested by the presence of Jehovah in their midst. Matthew presents the Lord Jesus as Israel's Messiah and King, as well as the One who shall save His people from their sins. The opening sentence gives the key to its contents: "The book of the generation of Jesus Christ, the Son of David, the Son of Abraham." Seven times over Christ is addressed as "the Son of David" in this Gospel, and ten times altogether is this title found there. "Son of David" connects Christ with the *throne*, while "Son of Abraham" associates Him with the *altar*.

This opening Gospel explains how it is that in the later books of the New Testament Israel is viewed as cast off by God, why it is Christendom has superseded the Jewish theocracy—the result of rejecting their Messiah. A striking foreshadowment of this is found in the second chapter, where a significant incident—passed over by the other Evangelists—is recorded, namely the visit of the wise men who came from the East to worship the Christ child. In the

9

attendant circumstances we may perceive a prophetic anticipation of what is recorded throughout this Gospel and the New Testament. First, Christ is seen *outside* of Jerusalem. Then we have the *blindness* and indifference of the Jews to the presence of their Messiah: unaware that He was now among them, undesirous of accompanying the Magi. Next there are the *strangers* from a far country with a heart for the Saviour, seeking Him out and worshipping Him. Finally, we behold the civil head, so filled with hatred, determined to put Him to death—presaging His crucifixion by the Jews.

Not until the middle of his fourth chapter does Matthew tell us, "From that time Jesus began to preach, and to say, Repent: for the kingdom of heaven is at hand" (verse 17). The time-mark here is, in the light of its context, most significant, emphasizing the same solemn aspect of truth as was adumbrated in chapter ii. First, we are told that our Lord's forerunner had been "cast into prison" (verse 12). Second, we are informed that Christ "leaving Nazareth" came "and dwelt in Capernaum" (verse 13), for Nazareth (where He had dwelt so long: ii, 23) had openly rejected Him (see Luke iv, 28-30). Third, it is here emphasized that the Saviour had gone "beyond Jordan" into "Galilee of the Gentiles," where "the people which sat in darkness saw great light" (verse 16)—another illustrative anticipation of His rejection by the Jews and His turning to the Gentiles.

The fourth chapter closes by telling us, "And His fame went throughout all Syria: and they brought unto Him all sick people that were taken with divers diseases and torments, and those which were possessed with devils, and those which were lunatick, and those that had the palsy: and there followed Him great multitudes of people from Galilee, and from Decapolis," etc. (verses 24, 25). Some have wondered why our Lord performed these miracles of healing upon the bodies of the people *before* He delivered His great Sermon on the Mount for the nourishing of their souls. First, it should be noted that these miracles of healing *followed* His "teaching in their synagogues and preaching the gospel of the kingdom" (iv, 23). Second, these miracles of healing were an essential part of His Messianic credentials (Isaiah xxxv, 4-6). Third, these miracles of healing made way for His fuller preaching, by disposing the people to listen unto One who manifested such Divine power and mercy.

The preface to the Sermon is a very short one: "And seeing the multitudes, He went up into a mountain, and when He was set, His disciples came unto Him; and He opened His mouth, and taught them" (v, 1, 2). Yet brief as these verses be, there are several things in them which call for careful consideration. First, we must notice *the place* from which this Sermon was preached. "As in other things, so in this, our Lord Jesus was but ill-accommodated: He had no convenient place to preach in, any more than to lay His head on. While the scribes and Pharisees had Moses' chair to sit in, with all possible ease, honour, and state, and there corrupted the

Law; our Lord Jesus, the great Teacher of truth, is driven out to the desert, and finds no better place than a 'mountain' can afford.

" Nor was it one of the *holy* mountains, nor one of the mountains of *Zion,* but a common mountain; by which Christ would intimate that there is no distinguishing holiness of place now, under the Gospel, as there was under the Law; but that it is the will of God that men should pray and praise everywhere, anywhere, provided it be decent and convenient. Christ preached this Sermon, which was an exposition of the Law, upon a mountain, because upon a mountain the Law was given: and this was also a solemn promulgation of the Christian Law. But observe the difference: when the Law was given the Lord came down upon the mountain, now the Lord ' went up ' into one; then He spoke in thunder and lightning, now in a still small voice; then the people were ordered to keep their distance, now they are invited to draw near—a blessed change!" (Matthew Henry).

We believe there is yet a deeper significance in the fact that Christ delivered this Sermon from a mountain. Very often the noting of *the place where* a particular utterance was made supplies a key to its interpretation. For example, in Matthew xiii, 36, Christ is seen entering "into the house," where He made known unto His own the inner secrets of His kingdom. In Luke's Gospel Christ is seen as man (the perfect Man) among men, and there He delivers a sermon " in the plain " (vi, 17)—descending as it were to a common level. But in Matthew His royal authority is in view, and consequently He is seen again in an elevated place. In the seventeenth chapter we behold Him transfigured on the mount. In xxiv, 3, He delivers His great prophetic discourse from a mount. Then in xxviii, 6, we see the Conqueror of death commissioning His disciples from the mount. So here in v, 1, He ascends the mount when about to give forth the manifesto of His kingdom.

Next we would notice that our Lord was *seated* when He preached this Sermon. It seems to have been His usual manner to preach sitting: "I *sat* daily with you teaching in the temple " (Matt. xxvi, 55). This was the custom of the Jewish teachers: " The scribes and the Pharisees *sit* in Moses' seat " (Matt. xxiii, 2). Nevertheless, we are persuaded that the Spirit's notice of our Lord's posture on this occasion intimates something more important and significant than that He accommodated Himself to the prevailing mode of the day. In this Sermon Christ enunciated the laws of His kingdom and spoke with an authority infinitely transcending that of the Jewish leaders; and therefore His posture here is to be regarded as emblematic of the King sitting upon His throne, or the Judge upon the bench.

"And he opened His mouth and taught them." Here the Spirit of God has noted the great Prophet's *manner of speaking.* First, it is to be understood naturally, and carefully emulated by all His servants. The first essential of any public speaker is that he open his mouth and articulate clearly, otherwise, no matter how good may be his matter, much will be lost on his hearers. Alas, how many preachers mutter and mouth their words, or employ a pious whine which elderly people cannot catch. It is most desirable that the young preacher should spare no pains to acquire a free and clear delivery: avoiding shouting and yelling on the one hand, and sinking his voice too much on the other.

Second, we may also behold here the perfections of our blessed Redeemer. So far as Scripture informs us, from the age of twelve till He reached thirty, Christ maintained a steady silence, for the time appointed by His Father to deliver His great message had not then arrived. In perfect submission to the One who had sent Him, the Lord Jesus *waited* the hour which had been set Him—"There is a time to keep silence, and a time to speak" (Eccles. iii, 7). To one of His prophets of old God said, "I will make thy tongue cleave to the roof of thy mouth, that thou shalt be dumb, and shalt not be to them a reprover" (Ezek. iii, 26). Later, He said, "now the hand of the Lord was upon me in the evening . . . and my mouth was opened, and I was no more dumb: then the word of the Lord came unto me" (Ezek. xxxiii, 22, 23). So it was here with the supreme Prophet: the time had come for Him to enunciate the laws of His kingdom: the hand of God was upon Him, and He "opened His mouth."

Third, as Scripture is compared with Scripture, this expression will be found to bear yet another meaning. "Supplication for all saints; and for me, that utterance may be give unto me, that I may *open my mouth boldly*, to make known the mystery of the Gospel" (Eph. vi, 18, 19). The apostle was referring to a special kind of speech, upon far more weighty matters than his ordinary conversation. So when we are here told that Christ "opened His mouth and taught them" we are to understand that He spoke with liberty and authority, with faithfulness and boldness, delivering Himself upon matters of the deepest weight and greatest importance. It means that, without fear or favour, Christ openly set forth the truth, regardless of consequences. That this is the meaning appears from what we read of at the finish of the Sermon: "The people were astonished at His doctrine: for He taught them as one *having authority*, and not as the scribes" (vii, 28, 29).

Let us now observe *the persons* to whom our Lord here addressed Himself. There has been considerable difference of opinion concerning the ones to whom this Sermon really applies: the saved or the unsaved. Extreme positions have been taken on both sides, with a good deal of unnecessary dogmatism. Personally, we regard this Sermon as a forecast and an epitome of the entire oral ministry of Christ, that it summarizes the general tenor of His whole teaching. The older we grow, the less do we approve the drawing hard and fast lines through the Scriptures, limiting their application by insisting that certain parts belong only to such and such a class, and under the guise of "rightly dividing" the Word, apportioning segments of it to the Jews only, the Gentiles only, or the Church of

God only. Man makes his canals rigidly straight, but God's rivers wind in and out. God's commandment is "exceeding broad" (Psalm cxix, 96), and we must be on our guard against placing restrictions thereon.

A careful study of the four Gospels reveals that Christ's ministry had, first, a special application to the afflicted people of God; second, it evidently had a peculiar reference to His own immediate disciples; and third, it had a general bearing upon the people at large. Such we take it was also the case with the Sermon on the Mount, embodying and illustrating these three distinctive features of Christ's public ministry. First, its opening section (the "Beatitudes") is most evidently addressed to those who were afflicted in their souls—those deeply exercised before God. Second, its next division referred to His public servants, as will be shown (D.V.) when we take it up in detail. Third, its larger part was a most searching exposition of the spirituality of the Law and the refutation of the false teachings of the elders, and was meant mainly for the people at large.

We do not think that W. Perkins went too far when he said of the Sermon on the Mount, "It may justly be called the key of the whole Bible, for here Christ openeth the sum of the Old and New Testaments." It is the longest discourse of our Lord's recorded in the Scriptures. He began His public ministry by insisting upon repentance (Matt. iv, 17), and here He enlarges upon this vitally important subject in a variety of ways, showing us what repentance really is and what are its fruits. It is an intensely *practical* sermon throughout: as Matthew Henry expressed it, "There is not much of the credenda of Christianity in it—the things to be believed; but it is wholly taken up with the agenda—the things to be done, for 'If any man will do His will, he shall know of the doctrine' (John vii, 17)."

Though we are told at the beginning of chapter v that it was His "disciples" whom Christ here taught, yet it is equally clear from the closing verses of chapter vii that this Sermon was spoken in the hearing of the multitudes. This must be steadily borne in mind throughout, for while it contains much instruction for believers in connection with their living a good, honest, and blessed life, yet not a little in it is evidently designed for unbelievers, particularly those sections which contain a most searching setting forth of the spiritual nature of His kingdom and the character of those who enter and enjoy its privileges. Romish teachers have greatly erred, for they insist that Christ here propounded a *new* Law—far more perfect than the Law of Moses—and that He delivered now entirely *new* counsel to His disciples, which was never given in the Law or the Prophets; whereas His intention was to clear the true meaning of the Law and the Prophets, which had been greatly corrupted by the Jewish doctors. But we will not further anticipate what we shall (D.V.) contemplate more fully in the studies to follow.

CHAPTER ONE

The Beatitudes

" Blessed are the poor in spirit : for theirs is the kingdom of heaven. Blessed are they that mourn : for they shall be comforted. Blessed are the meek : for they shall inherit the earth. Blessed are they which do hunger and thirst after righteousness : for they shall be filled. Blessed are the merciful : for they shall obtain mercy. Blessed are the pure in heart : for they shall see God. Blessed are the peacemakers : for they shall be called the children of God. Blessed are they which are persecuted for righteousness' sake : for theirs is the kingdom of heaven. Blessed are ye, when men shall revile you, and persecute you, and shall say all manner of evil against you falsely, for My sake." (Matt. v, 3-11.)

AT the close of our Introduction it was pointed out that Christ's public ministry had first a special application to the afflicted people of God; second, a peculiar reference to His immediate disciples, considered as His apostles or ministers; third, to the people at large. Such is clearly the case with His Sermon on the Mount, as will be made evident (D.V.) in the course of our exposition of it. Herein Christ is seen discharging His prophetic office, speaking as never (uninspired) man ever spoke. A careful study of the Sermon reveals that it has twelve divisions—the number of Divine *government*—varying considerably in length. It is the first of them which is now to engage our attention. In it our Lord makes known wherein true happiness or blessedness consists, disclosing to us a secret which is hidden from the unregenerate, who suppose that outward comforts and luxuries are absolutely indispensable to contentment of mind and felicity of life. Herein too He strikes at the root of the carnal conceit of the Jews, who vainly imagined that *external* peace and prosperity were to result from a receiving of the Gospel.

It is indeed blessed to observe how this Sermon opens. Christ began not by pronouncing maledictions on the wicked, but benedictions on His people. How like Him was this, to whom " judgment " is a " strange work "! Nevertheless, later, we also hear Him pronouncing " woe " after woe upon the enemies of God: Matthew xxiii. It was not to the multitude at large that the Redeemer first spoke, but to the elect, who had a special claim upon Him, as given by the Father's love to Him (John xvii, 9, 10). Nor was it to the favoured apostles He addressed His opening remarks, but rather to the poor of the flock, the afflicted in soul, those who were conscious of their deep need. Therein He has left an example for all His under shepherds: "Strengthen ye the weak hands, and confirm the feeble knees"; Comfort ye, comfort ye My people, saith your God" (Isaiah xxxv, 3; xl, 1).

"Blessed are the poor in spirit: for theirs is the kingdom of

15

heaven " (Matt. v, 3). In these words Christ began to draw a picture of those characters upon whom the Divine benediction rests. It is a composite picture, each line in it accentuating some distinct spiritual feature; and with the whole we should honestly and carefully *compare ourselves*. At what complete variance is this declaration of Christ's from the popular view among men! The idea which commonly obtains, the world over, is, Blessed are the rich, for theirs is the kingdom of the world. But Christ says the flat contrary: "Blessed are the poor in spirit: for theirs is the kingdom of heaven," which is infinitely better than all the kingdoms of the earth; and herein we may see that the wisdom of this world is foolishness with God (I Cor. i). Who before Christ ever regarded the poor in spirit as the blessed or happy ones of the earth? And who, except genuine Christians, do so today? How this opening word struck the keynote of all the subsequent teaching of Him who was Himself born in a stable: not what a man does, but what he *is* in the sight of God.

" Blessed are the poor in spirit." There is a vast difference between this and being hard up in our circumstances. There is no virtue (and often no disgrace) in financial poverty as such, nor does it, of itself, produce humility of heart, for anyone who has any real acquaintance with both classes soon discovers there is just as much pride in the indigent as there is in the opulent. This poverty of spirit is a fruit that grows on no merely natural tree. It is a spiritual grace wrought by the Holy Spirit in those whom He renews. By nature we are well pleased with ourselves, and mad enough to think that we deserve something good at the hands of God. Let men but conduct themselves decently in a civil way, keeping themselves from grosser sins, and they are rich in spirit, pride filling their hearts, and they are self-righteous. And nothing short of a miracle of grace can change the course of this stream.

Nor is real poverty of spirit to be found among the great majority of the religionists of the day: very much the reverse. How often we see advertised a conference for " promoting the higher life," but who ever heard of one for furthering the *lowly* life? Many books are telling us how to be " filled with the Spirit," but where can we find one setting forth what it means to be spiritually emptied—emptied of self-confidence, self-importance, and self-righteousness? Alas, if it be true that, " That which is highly esteemed among men is abomination in the sight of God" (Luke xvi, 15), it is equally true that what is of great price in His sight is despised by men—by none more so than by modern Pharisees, who now hold nearly all the positions of prominence in Christendom. Almost all of the so-called " ministry" of this generation feeds pride, instead of starving the flesh; puffs up, rather than abases; and anything which is calculated to search and strip is frowned upon by the pulpit and is unpopular with the pew.

" Blessed are the poor in spirit." And *what is* poverty of spirit?

It is the opposite of that haughty, self-assertive and self-sufficient disposition which the world so much admires and praises. It is the very reverse of that independent and defiant attitude which refuses to bow to God, which determines to brave things out, which says with Pharaoh, "Who is the Lord that I should obey His voice?" To be " poor in spirit " is to realize that I have nothing, am nothing, and can do nothing, and have need of all things. Poverty of spirit is a consciousness of my emptiness, the result of the Spirit's work within. It issues from the painful discovery that all my righteousnesses are as filthy rags. It follows the awakening that my best performances are unacceptable, yea, an abomination to the thrice Holy One. Poverty of spirit evidences itself by its bringing the individual into the dust before God, acknowledging his utter helplessness and deservingness of hell. It corresponds to the initial awakening of the prodigal in the far country, when he " began to be *in want.*"

God's great salvation is free, "without money and without price." This is a most merciful provision of Divine grace, for were God to offer salvation for sale no sinner could secure it, seeing that he has nothing with which he could possibly purchase it. But the vast majority are insensible of this, yea, all of us are until the Holy Spirit opens our sin-blinded eyes. It is only those who have passed from death unto life who become conscious of their poverty, take the place of beggars, are glad to receive Divine charity, and begin to seek the true riches. Thus " the *poor* have the Gospel preached to them " (Matt. xi, 5): preached not only to their ears, but to their hearts!

Poverty of spirit may be termed the negative side of faith. It is that realization of my utter worthlessness which precedes the laying hold of Christ, the eating of His flesh and drinking His blood. It is the Spirit emptying the heart of self that Christ may fill it: it is a sense of need and destitution. This first Beatitude, then, is foundational, describing a fundamental trait which is found in every regenerated soul. The one who is poor in spirit is nothing in his own eyes, and feels that his proper place is in the dust before God. He may, through false teaching or worldliness, leave this place, but God knows how to bring him back; and in His faithfulness and love He will do so, for it is the place of blessing for His children. How to cultivate this God-honouring spirit is revealed in Matthew xi, 29.

He who is in possession of this poverty of spirit is pronounced " blessed." He is so because he now has a disposition the very opposite of what was his by nature, because he has in himself the first sure evidence that a Divine work of grace has been wrought in his heart, because he is an heir of the " kingdom of heaven "—the kingdom of grace here, the kingdom of glory hereafter. Many are the gracious promises addressed to the poor in spirit. " I am poor and needy: yet the Lord thinketh upon me: Thou art my help and my deliverer " (Psalm xl, 17), " The Lord heareth the poor" (Psalm lxix, 33), " He shall spare the poor and needy, and shall save the

souls of the needy" (Psalm lxxii, 13), "Yet setteth He the poor on
high from affliction" (Psalm cvii, 41), "I will satisfy her poor with
bread" (Psalm cxxxii, 15), "To this man will I look, even to him
that is poor and of a contrite spirit, and trembleth at My word"
(Isaiah lxvi, 2). Let such favours as these stir us up to pray earnestly
for more of this poverty of spirit.

"Blessed are they that mourn; for they shall be comforted"
(verse 4). Mourning is hateful and irksome to poor human
nature: from suffering and sadness our spirits instinctively shrink.
It is natural for us to seek the society of the cheerful and joyous.
The verse now before us presents an anomaly to the unregenerate,
yet is it sweet music to the ears of God's elect: "if "blessed" why
do they "mourn"? If they mourn, how can they be blessed? Only
the child of God has the key to this paradox, for "happy are they
who sorrow" is at complete variance with the world's logic. Men
have, in all places and in all ages, deemed the prosperous and the
gay to be the happy ones, but Christ pronounces blessed those who
are poor in spirit and who mourn.

Now it is obvious that it is not every species of mourning which
is here referred to. There are thousands of mourners in the world
today who do not come within the scope of our text: those mourning
over blighted hopes, over financial reverses, over the loss of loved
ones. But alas, so far from many of *them* coming beneath this Divine
benediction, they are under God's condemnation; nor is there any
promise that such shall ever be Divinely "comforted." There are
three kinds of "mourning" referred to in the Scriptures: a *natural*,
such as we have just referred to above; a *sinful*, which is a disconso-
late and inordinate grief, refusing to be comforted, or a hopeless
remorse like that of Judas; and a *gracious*, a "godly sorrow," of
which the Holy Spirit is the Author.

The "mourning" of our text is a *spiritual* one. The previous verse
indicates clearly the line of thought here: "Blessed are the poor
in spirit, for theirs is the kingdom of heaven." Yes, "Blessed are the
poor," not the poor in purse, but the poor in heart: those who
realize themselves to be spiritual bankrupts in themselves, paupers
before God. That felt poverty of spirit is the very opposite of the
Laodiceanism which is so rife today, that self-complacency which
says, "I am rich, and increased with goods, and have need of
nothing." In like manner it is *spiritual mourning* which is in view
here. Further proof of this is found in the fact that Christ pronounces
these mourners "blessed." They are so because the Spirit of God has
wrought a work of grace within them, and hence they have been
awakened to see and feel their lost condition. They are "blessed"
because God does not leave them at that point: "they shall be
comforted."

"Blessed are they that mourn." The first reference is to that
initial mourning which ever precedes a genuine conversion, for
there must be a real sense of sin before the remedy for it will even

be desired. Thousands acknowledge that they are sinners, who have never *mourned over* the fact. Take the woman of Luke vii, who washed the Saviour's feet with her tears: have you ever shed any over your sins? Take the prodigal in Luke xv: before he left the far country he said, " I will arise and go unto my Father and say unto Him, Father, I have sinned against heaven, and before Thee, And am no more worthy to be called Thy son "—where shall we find those today with this sense of their sinnership? Take the publican of Luke xviii: why did he " smite upon his breast " and say " God be merciful to me a sinner "? Because he felt the plague of his own heart. So of the three thousand converted on the day of Pentecost: they were " pricked in their heart, and *cried out*."

This " mourning" springs from a sense of sin, from a tender conscience, from a broken heart. It is a godly sorrow over rebellion against God and hostility to His will. In some cases it is grief over the very morality in which the heart has trusted, over the self-righteousness which has caused such complacency. This " mourning" is the agonizing realization that it was *my* sins which nailed to the Cross the Lord of glory. When Israel shall, by faith, see Christ, " they shall mourn for Him" (Zech. xii, 10). It is such tears and groans which prepare the heart to truly welcome and receive the " balm of Gilead," the comfort of the Gospel. It is, then, a mourning over the felt destitution of our spiritual state, and over the iniquities that have separated between us and God. Such mourning always goes side by side with conscious poverty of spirit.

But this " mourning" is by no means to be confined unto the initial experience of conviction and contrition, for observe the tense of the verb: it is not " have mourned," but " mourn "— a present and continuous experience. The Christian himself has much to mourn over. The sins which he now commits—both of omission and commission—are a sense of daily grief to him, or should be, and *will* be, if his conscience is kept tender. An ever-deepening discovery of the depravity of his nature, the plague of his heart, the sea of corruption within—ever polluting all that he does—deeply exercises him. Consciousness of the surgings of unbelief, the swellings of pride, the coldness of his love, and his paucity of fruit, make him cry, " O wretched man that I am." A humbling recollection of past offences: "Wherefore remember that ye being *in time past*" (Eph. ii, 11).

Yes, " Ourselves also, which have the firstfruits of the Spirit, even we ourselves *groan* within ourselves" (Romans viii, 23). Does not the Christian groan under the disciplining rod of the Father: " No chastening for the present seemeth to be joyous, but grievous" (Heb. xii, 11). And is he not deeply grieved by the awful dishonour which is now done to the Lord Jesus on every hand? The fact is that the closer the Christian lives to God, the more will he mourn over all that dishonours Him: with the Psalmist he will say, " Horror hath taken hold upon me because of the wicked that forsake Thy law" (Psalm cxix, 53), and with Jeremiah, "My soul shall weep in secret places for your pride; and mine eyes shall weep sore and run down with tears, because the Lord's flock is carried away captive" (xiii, 17). But blessed be God, it is written, "Go through the midst of the city, through the midst of Jerusalem, and set a mark upon the foreheads of the men that sigh and that cry for all the abominations that be done in the midst thereof" (Ezek. ix, 4). So too there is a sympathetic mourning over the sufferings of others: "Weep with them that weep" (Romans xii, 15).

But let us return to the primary thought of our verse: "Blessed are they that mourn" has immediate reference to the convicted soul sorrowing over his sins. And here it is most important to note that Christ does not pronounce them "blessed" simply because they are mourners, but because they are *such* mourners as "shall be *comforted*." There are not a few in Christendom today who glory in their grief and attempt to find comfort in their own inward wretchedness—as well seek health from our sicknesses. True comfort is not to be found in anything in self—no, not in perceiving our own vileness—but in *Christ* alone. Distress of soul is by no means always the same thing as evangelical repentance, as is clear from the case of Cain (Gen. iv, 13). But where the Spirit produces in the heart a godly sorrow for sin, He does not leave him there, but brings him to look away from sin to the Lamb of God, and then he *is* "comforted." The Gospel promises no mercy except to those who forsake sin and close with Christ.

"They shall be comforted." This gracious promise receives its fulfilment, first, in that Divine consolation which immediately follows a sound conversion (i.e. one that is preceded by conviction and contrition), namely the removal of that conscious load of guilt which lies as an intolerable burden on the conscience. It finds its accomplishment in the Spirit's application of the Gospel of God's grace to the one whom He has convicted of his dire need of a Saviour. Then it is that Christ speaks the word of power, "Come unto Me all ye that labour and are heavy laden, and I will give you rest" (Matt. xi, 28)—observe that His language clearly presupposes the feeling of sin to be a "burden" as that which impels to Him for relief; it is to the *sin-sick* heart that Christ gives rest. This "comfort" issues in a sense of a free and full forgiveness through the merits of the atoning blood of Christ. This Divine comfort is the peace of God which passeth all understanding, filling the heart of one who is now assured that he is "accepted in the Beloved." First God wounds and then heals.

Second, there is a *continual* "comforting" of the mourning saint by the Holy Spirit, who is the Comforter. The one who sorrows over his departures from Christ is comforted by the assurance that "if we confess our sins, He is faithful and just to forgive us our sins, and to cleanse us from all unrighteousness" (I John i, 9). The one who mourns under the chastening rod of God is comforted by the promise, "afterward it yieldeth the peaceable fruit of righteousness unto them which are exercised thereby" (Heb. xii, 11). The one who grieves over the awful dishonour done to his Lord in the religious world is comforted by the fact that Satan's time is short, and soon Christ will bruise him beneath His feet. Third, the *final* "comfort" is when we leave this world and are done with sin for ever. Then shall "sorrow and sighing flee away." To the rich man in hell, Abraham said of the one who had begged at his gate, "now he is *comforted*" (Luke xvi, 25). The best wine is reserved for the last. The "comfort" of heaven will more than compensate for all the "mourning" of earth.

From all that has been before us learn, first, the folly of looking to the wounds which sin has made in order to find consolation; view rather the purging and healing blood of Christ. Second, see the error of attempting to measure the helpfulness of the books we read or the preaching we hear by the degree of peace and joy they bring to our hearts. Yet how many there are who say, We have quite enough in the world, or in the home, to make us miserable, and we go to church for comfort. But it is to be feared that few of them are in any condition of soul to receive comfort from the Gospel: rather do they need the Law to search and convict them. Ah, the truth is, dear friend, that very often the sermon or the article which is of most benefit is the one which causes us to get alone with God and *weep* before Him. When we have flirted with the world or indulged the lusts of the flesh the Holy Spirit gives us a rebuke or admonition. Third, mark then the inseparable connection between godly sorrow and godly joy: compare Psalms xxx, 5; cxxvi, 5; Proverbs xiv, 10; Isaiah lxi, 3; II Corinthians vi, 10; I Thessalonians i, 6; James ii, 13.

CHAPTER TWO

The Beatitudes—Continued

"BLESSED are the meek: for they shall inherit the earth" (Matt. v, 5). There has been considerable difference of opinion as to exactly what meekness consists of. When we wrote upon this verse some twelve years ago, we defined it as *humility*, but it now appears to us that that is inadequate, for there is no single term which is capable of fully expressing all that is included in this virtue. A study of its usage in Scripture reveals, first, that it is linked with and cannot be separated from *lowliness*: "Learn of Me: for I am meek and lowly in heart" (Matt. xi, 29); "Walk worthy of the vocation wherewith ye are called; with all lowliness and meekness" (Eph. iv, 1, 2). Second, it is associated with and cannot be divorced from *gentleness*: "I beseech you by the meekness and gentleness of Christ" (II Cor. x, 1); "To speak evil of no man, to be no brawlers, but gentle, shew- ing all meekness unto all men" (Titus iii, 2). Third, "receive with meekness the engrafted word" is opposed to "the *wrath* of man worketh not the righteousness of God" (James i, 20, 21). Fourth, the Divine promise is "the meek will He guide in judgment, and the meek will He teach His way" (Psalm xxv, 9), intimating that this grace consists of a *pliant* heart and will.

Additional help in determining for us the meaning and scope of the word "meek" is to be obtained from duly noting our present verse in the light of the two preceding ones. It is to be kept steadily in mind that in those Beatitudes our Lord is describing the orderly development of God's work of grace as it is experientially realized in the soul. First, there is a poverty of spirit: a sense of our insufficiency and nothingness, a realization of our unworthiness and unprofitableness. Next, there is a mourning over our lost condition, sorrowing for the awfulness of our sins against God. And now we have meekness as a by-product of self-emptying and self-humiliation; or, in other words, there is a broken will and a receptive heart before God. Meekness is not only the antithesis of pride, but of stubborn- ness, fierceness, vengefulness. It is the taming of the lion, the making of the wolf to lie down as a kid.

Thomas Scott rightly points out that "There is a *natural* meek- ness of spirit, springing from love of ease, defect in sensibility and firmness, and the predominancy of other passions, which should be carefully distinguished from evangelical meekness. It is timid and pliant, easily deterred from good, and persuaded to evil; it leads to criminality in one extreme, as impetuosity of spirit does in another; it is often found in ungodly men; and it sometimes forms the grand defect in the character of pious persons, as in the case of Eli, and of Jehoshaphat. Divine grace operates in rendering such men of an opposite temper more yielding and quiet. The meekness to which the blessing is annexed is not constitutional, but *gracious*: and men of the most vehement, impetuous, irascible, and implacable dispositions, by looking to Jesus through the grace of God, learn to curb their tempers, to cease from resentment, to avoid giving offence by injurious words and actions, to make concessions and forgive injuries."

Meekness is the opposite of *self-will* toward God, and of *ill-will* toward men. "The meek are those who quietly submit themselves before God, to His Word, to His rod, who follow His directions and comply with His designs, and are gentle toward men" (Matthew Henry). As pointed out above, this is not constitutional, but gracious —a precious fruit of the Spirit's working. Godly sorrow softens the heart, so that it is made receptive to the entrance of the Word. Meekness consists in the spirit being made pliant, tractable, submissive, teachable. Speaking prophetically through Isaiah the Saviour said, "The Lord hath anointed Me to preach good tidings unto *the meek*" (Isaiah lxi. 1), for *they* have bowed to the authority of the Law. And again it is written, "For the Lord taketh pleasure in His people: He will beautify the meek with salvation" (Psalm cxlix, 4).

A word or two on the fruits of meekness. First, *Godwards*. Where this grace is in the ascendant, the enmity of the carnal mind is subdued, and its possessor bears God's chastenings with quietness and patience. Illustrations thereof are seen in the cases of Aaron (Lev. x, 3), Eli (I Samuel, iii, 18), and David (Psalm xxxix, 9). Supremely it was exemplified by Christ, who declared, "I am a worm, and no man" (Psalm xxii, 6), which had reference not only to His being humbled into the dust, but also to the fact that there was nothing in Him which resisted the judgments of God: "The cup which My Father hath given Me, shall I not drink it?" (John xviii, 11). He was "led [not dragged] as a lamb to the slaughter": when He was reviled, He reviled not again; when He was buffeted, He threatened not. He was the very King of meekness.

Second, *manwards*. Inasmuch as meekness is that spirit which has been schooled to mildness by discipline and suffering, and brought into sweet resignation to the will of God, it causes the believer to bear patiently those insults and injuries which he receives at the hands of his fellows, and makes him ready to accept instruction or admonition from the least of the saints, moving him to think more highly of others than of himself. Meekness enables the Christian to endure provocations without being inflamed by them: he remains cool when others get heated. "Brethren, if a man be overtaken in a fault, ye which are spiritual, restore such a one in the spirit of meekness: considering thyself, lest thou also be tempted" (Gal. vi, 1). This means, not with a lordly and domineering attitude, not with a harsh and censorious temper, not with a love of finding fault and desire for inflicting the discipline of the church, but with gentleness, humility and patience.

But meekness must not be confounded with weakness. True meekness is ever manifested by yieldedness to God's will, yet it will not yield a principle of righteousness or compromise with evil. God-given meekness can also stand up for God-given rights: when God's glory is impeached, we must have a zeal which is as hot as fire. Moses was "very meek, above all the men which were upon the face of the earth" (Num. xii, 3), yet when he saw the Israelites dancing before the golden calf, in zeal for Jehovah's honour, he broke the two tables of stone, and put to the sword those who had transgressed. Note how firmly and boldly the apostles stood their ground in Acts xvi, 35-37. Above all, remember how Christ Himself, in concern for His Father's glory, made a whip of cords and drove the desecrators out of the temple. Meekness restrains from private revenge, but it in nowise conflicts with the requirements of fidelity to God, His cause, and His people.

"For they shall inherit the earth" or "land," for both the Hebrew and Greek words possess this double meaning. This promise is taken from Psalm xxxvii, 11, and may be understood in a threefold way. First, *spiritually*, as the second half of that verse intimates: "The meek shall inherit the earth, and shall delight themselves in the abundance of *peace*." The spirit of meekness is what enables its possessor to get so much enjoyment out of his earthly portion, be it small or large. Delivered from a greedy and grasping disposition he is satisfied with such things as he has: "A little that a righteous man hath is better than the riches of many wicked" (Psalm xxxvii, 16). Contentment of mind is one of the fruits of meekness. The haughty and covetous do not "inherit the earth," though they may own many acres of it. The humble Christian is far happier in a cottage than the wicked in a palace: "Better is little with the fear of the Lord, than great treasure and trouble therewith" (Prov. xv, 16).

Second, *literally*. The meek inherit the earth in regard of *right*, being the members of Christ, who is Lord of all. Hence, writing to the saints, Paul said, "For all things are yours; whether ... *the world*, or life, or death, or things present, or things to come, all are yours" (I Cor. iii, 21, 22). Right or title to the earth is twofold: civil and spiritual. The former is that which holds good—according to their laws and customs—before *men*, and in regard thereof they are called lords of such lands they have a right unto in the courts. The latter is that which is approved before *God*. Adam had this spiritual right to the earth before he fell, but by his sin he forfeited it both for himself and his posterity. But Christ has regained it for all the elect, hence the apostle said, "As having nothing, and yet possessing all things" (II Cor. vi, 10). Third, *mystically*. Psalm xxxvii, 11, is an Old Testament promise with a New Testament meaning: the land of Canaan was a figure of heaven, of which meekness proves the possessor to be an heir, and for which it is an essential qualification.

From what has been before us let us learn, first, the value of this spiritual grace and the need of praying for an increase of the same: " Seek ye the Lord, all ye meek of the earth, which have wrought His judgment: seek righteousness, *seek meekness* " (Zeph. ii, 3). As a further inducement to this end, mark these precious promises: " The meek shall eat and be satisfied " (Psalm xxi, 26), " The Lord lifteth up the meek " (Psalm cxlvii, 6), " The meek also shall increase their joy in the Lord " (Isaiah xxix, 19). Second, see the folly of those who are so diligent in seeking earthly possessions without any regard to Christ. Since all right to the earth was lost by Adam and is only recovered by the Redeemer, until they have part in Him none can, with the comfort of a good conscience, either purchase or possess any mundane inheritance. Third, let the fact that the meek. through Christ, inherit the earth serve for a bridle against all inordinate care for the world: since we are members of Christ the supply of every need is certain, and an infinitely better portion is ours than the perishing things of time and sense.

" Blessed are they which do hunger and thirst after righteousness: for they shall be filled " (Matt. v, 6). In the first three Beatitudes we are called upon to witness the heart exercises of those who have been awakened by the Spirit of God. First, there is a sense of need, a realization of their nothingness and emptiness. Second, there is a judging of self, a consciousness of their guilt and sorrowing over their lost condition. Third, there is an end of seeking to justify themselves before God, an abandonment of all pretences to personal merit, a taking of their place in the dust before God. And here, in the fourth, the eye of the soul is turned away from self to Another: there is a longing after that which they know they have not got and which they are conscious they urgently need. There has been much needless quibbling as to the precise import of the word " righteousness " in this verse, and it seems to us that most of the commentators have failed to grasp its fullness.

In many Old Testament passages " righteousness " is synonymous with " salvation," as will apear from the following. " Drop down ye heavens from above, and let the skies pour down *righteousness*: let the earth open, and let them bring forth *salvation*, and let righteousness spring up together; I the Lord have created it " (Isaiah xlv, 8); " Hearken unto Me, ye stouthearted, that are far from righteousness: I bring near My *righteousness*; it shall not be far off, and My *salvation* shall not tarry: and I will place salvation in Zion " (Isaiah xlvi, 12, 13); " My *righteousness* is near. My *salvation* is set forth, and Mine arms shall judge the people: the isles shall wait upon Me, and on Mine arms shall they trust " (Isaiah li, 5): " Thus saith the Lord, Keep ye judgment and do justice: for My *salvation* is near to come, and My *righteousness* to be revealed " (Isaiah lvi, 1); " He hath clothed me with the garments of *salvation*, He hath covered me with the robe of *righteousness* " (Isaiah lxi, 10). Yet after all, this does not bring us much nearer in that "salvation" is one of the most comprehensive terms to be found in the Scriptures. Let us, then, seek to define its meaning a little more closely.

Taking it in its widest latitude, to "hunger and thirst after righteousness" means to yearn after God's favour, image, and felicity. "Righteousness" is a term denoting all spiritual blessings: "seek ye first the kingdom of God and His righteousness" (Matt. vi, 33). More specifically, "righteousness" in our text has reference, first, to the righteousness of faith whereby a sinner is justified freely by Divine grace through the redemption that is in Christ Jesus. As the result of his Surety's obedience being imputed to him, the believer stands *legally righteous* before God. As sinners who have constantly broken the Law in thought, word, and deed, we are utterly destitute of righteousness. "There is none righteous, no not one" (Romans iii, 10). But God has provided a perfect righteousness in Christ for all who believe: it is the best "robe" put upon each returning prodigal. The merits of Christ's perfect keeping of the Law is reckoned to the account of every sinner who shelters in Him.

Second, this "righteousness," for which the awakened sinner longs, is to be understood of *inward and sanctifying* righteousness, for as we so often point out, justification and sanctification are never to be severed. The one in whom the Spirit graciously works desires not only an *imputed* righteousness, but an *imparted* one too; he not only longs for a restoration to God's favour, but to have God's image renewed in him. For this twofold "righteousness" the convicted "hunger and thirst," expressive of vehement desire, of which the soul is acutely conscious, for as in bodily hunger and thirst there are sharp pangs and an intense longing for their appeasement, so it is with the soul. First, the Spirit brings before the conscience the holy and inexorable requirements of God. Next, He convicts the soul of its destitution and guilt, so that he realizes his abject poverty and lost condition, seeing there is no hope in and from himself. And then He creates a deep hunger and thirst which causes him to look unto and seek relief from Christ, "The Lord our righteousness."

Like the previous ones, this fourth Beatitude describes a *dual* experience: an initial and a continuous, that which begins in the unconverted, but is perpetuated in the saved sinner. There is a repeated exercise of this grace, felt at varying intervals. The one who longed to be saved by Christ now yearns to be made like Him. Looked at in its widest aspect, this hungering and thirsting refers to that panting of the renewed heart after God (Psalm xlii, 1), that yearning for a closer walk with Him, that longing for more perfect conformity to the image of His Son. It tells of those aspirations of the new nature for Divine blessings which alone can strengthen, sustain and satisfy it. Our text presents such a paradox that it is evident that no carnal mind ever invented it. Can one who has been brought into vital union with Him who is the Bread of Life and in whom all fullness dwells be found *still* hungering and thirsting? Yes, such is the experience of the renewed heart. Mark carefully the tense of the verb: it is not "Blessed are they which have," but "Blessed are they *which do* hunger and thirst." This has ever been the experience of God's saints (Psalm lxxxii, 4; Phil. iii, 8, 14).

"They shall be filled." Like the first part of our text, this also has a double fulfilment: an initial, and a continuous. When God creates a hunger and thirst in the soul, it is that He may satisfy it. When the poor sinner is made to feel his need of Christ, it is that he may be drawn to and led to embrace Him. Like the prodigal who came to the Father as a penitent, the believing sinner now feeds on the One figured by the "fatted calf." He is made to exclaim, "Surely in the Lord have I righteousness." "They shall be filled" with the peace of God which passeth all understanding. "Filled" with that Divine blessing to which no sorrow is added. "Filled" with praise and thanksgiving unto Him who has wrought all our works in us. "Filled" with that which this poor world can neither give nor take away. "Filled" by the goodness and mercy of God, till their cup runneth over. And yet, all that is enjoyed now is but a little foretaste of what God has prepared for them that love Him: in the day to come we shall be "filled" with Divine holiness, for we shall be made "like Him" (I John iii, 2). Then shall we be done with sin for ever: then shall we "hunger *no more,* neither thirst *any more*" (Rev. vii, 16).

As this fourth Beatitude has been such a storehouse of comfort to many a tried and troubled believer, let us point out the use which may be made of it by Satan-harassed believers. First, by those whose faith is little and weak. There are not a few in God's family who sincerely long to please Him in all things and to live in no sin against their conscience, and yet they find in themselves so much distrust and despair of God's mercy that they are conscious of much more doubting than faith, so that they are brought seriously to question their election and state before God. Here, then, is Divine consolation for them: if they genuinely hunger and thirst after righteousness, Christ Himself pronounces them *blessed.* Those who are displeased with their unbelief, who truly desire to be purged from distrust, who long and pray for increased faith and assurance —evidencing their sincerity by diligently using all proper means— are the subjects of God's approbation.

Second, by those whose sanctification is so imperfect. Many there be who are most anxious to please God and make conscience of all known sins, yet find in themselves so much darkness of mind, activity of rebellious corruption, forwardness in their affections, perverseness in their wills, yea, a constant proneness to all manner of sins; and, on the contrary, they can perceive so little of the fruits of sanctification, so little evidence of spiritual life, so few signs of Divine grace at work within, that they often seriously doubt if they have received any grace at all. This is a fearfully heavy burden, and greatly casts down the soul. But here is Divine consolation. Christ pronounces "blessed" not those who *are full* of righteousness, but those who "hunger and thirst" *after it*. Those who mourn over their depravity, who grieve over the plague of their hearts, who yearn for conformity to Christ—using the means constantly—are accepted of God in Christ.

Third, by the more extreme case of one who has grievously departed from God and long been a backslider, and now, conscious of his wickedness, is in despair. Satan will tell him that his case is hopeless, that he is an apostate, that hell is prepared for him and he must surely be damned; and the poor soul is ready to believe that such must really be the case. He is destitute of peace, all his evidences are eclipsed, he cannot perceive a ray of hope. Nevertheless, here is Divine comfort. If he truly mourns over his departure from God, hates himself for his backsliding, sorrows over his sins, truly desires to repent of them and longs to be reconciled to God and restored to communion with Him, then he too is among the blessed: "Blessed are they which do hunger and thirst after righteousness: for they shall be filled."

CHAPTER THREE

The Beatitudes—Continued

IN these Beatitudes the Lord Jesus delineates the distinguishing characteristics and privileges of those who are " His disciples indeed," or the birthmarks by which the true subjects of His kingdom may be identified. This is only another way of saying that His design was to make known the character of those upon whom the Divine benediction rests, or that He here revealed who are the truly happy. Looking at these Beatitudes from another angle, we may regard them as furnishing a description of the nature of true happiness, and as propounding sundry rules by which it is attained. Very different indeed is Christ's teaching here from the thoughts and the theories which obtain in the carnal mind. Instead of attributing genuine felicity unto the possession of outward things, He affirmed that it consists in the possession and cultivation of spiritual graces. It was God incarnate pouring contempt on the wisdom of this world and showing how radically opposed are its concepts to the Truth.

" Blessed are the merciful: for they shall obtain mercy " (Matt. v, 7). Grossly have these words been perverted by merit-mongers. Those who insist that the Bible teaches salvation by works appeal to this verse, among others, in support of their pernicious error. But nothing could be less to their purpose, for there is not a word in it which affords the slightest support to their fatal delusion. Our Lord was not here describing the foundation on which rests the sinner's hope of receiving mercy from God, but is tracing the spiritual features of His own people, among which mercifulness is a prominent one. His evident meaning was: mercy is an indispensable trait in that holy character which God has inseparably connected with the enjoyment of that happiness—both here and hereafter—which is the product of His own sovereign kindness.

The place occupied by this particular Beatitude in the series furnishes a sure key to its interpretation. The first four may be regarded as describing the *initial* exercises of heart in one who has been awakened by the Spirit, whereas the next four treat of the *subsequent* fruits. In the preceding verse the soul is seen hungering and thirsting after Christ, and then filled by Him, whereas here we are shown the first effect and evidence of this. Having received mercy from the Lord, the saved sinner now exercises mercy unto others. It is not that God requires us to be merciful in order to obtain His mercy—that would be to overthrow the whole scheme of grace—but having been made the recipient of His wondrous grace,

I cannot now but act graciously toward others. That which is signified by "they shall obtain mercy" will come before us in the sequel.

"Blessed are the merciful: for they shall obtain mercy." First, let us endeavour to define the nature of this mercy. This mercifulness upon which the Divine approbation rests is a holy compassion of soul, whereby one is moved to pity and go to the relief of another in misery. In saying that it is a compassion of soul, we mean that it causes its possessor to make the case of another his own, so that he is grieved by it, for when our heart is really touched by the state of another, we are stirred within. "It is an aversion to everything harsh, cruel, oppressive or injurious; a propensity to pity, alleviate or remove the miseries of mankind; an unwillingness to increase personal emolument or indulgence by rendering others uneasy; a willingness to forgo personal ease, interest or gratification to make others easy and happy" (Thomas Scott).

Mercifulness, then, is a gracious disposition toward our fellow creatures and fellow Christians. It is a spirit of kindness and benevolence which sympathizes with the sufferings of the afflicted, so that we weep with those that weep. It ennobles its possessor so that he tempers justice with mercy, and scorns the taking of revenge. But it is a *holy* disposition in contrast with that foolish sentimentality which flouts the requirements of justice, and which inclines many to sympathize with those in deserved misery. That is a false and unholy mercy which petitions the powers that be to cancel or modify a just and fully merited sentence which has been passed upon some flagrant offender. Therefore are we told, "And *of some* have compassion, making a difference" (Jude 22)—king Saul defied this principle when he spared Agag. It is also a holy compassion as opposed to that partiality which is generous to some and harsh to others.

This mercifulness has not its roots in anything in the natural man. True, there are some who make no profession of being Christians in whom we often find not a little kindliness of disposition, sympathy for the suffering, and a readiness to forgive those who have wronged them, yet is it merely instinctive, and though amiable there is nothing spiritual in it—instead of being subject to Divine authority it is often opposed to God's law. That which Christ here inculcated and commended is very different from and vastly superior to natural amiability: it is such compassion as *God* approves of, which is a fruit of His Holy Spirit and is commanded in His Word. It is the result of Christ living in us. Was He moved with compassion? Did He weep with the mourner? Was He patient with the dull-witted? Then if He indwells me, that same disposition, however imperfectly manifested, must be reproduced.

This mercy is something more than a feeling: it is *an operative principle*. It not only stirs the heart, but it moves the hand to render help unto those in need, for the one cannot be severed from the other. So far from it being a well shut up or a fountain sealed, this mercy is a copious source of acts of beneficence, from which issue streams of blessing. It does not exhaust itself in profitless words, but is accompanied by helpful deeds. " But whoso hath this world's goods, and seeth his brother have need, and shutteth up his bowels of compassion from him, how dwelleth the love of God in him?" (I John iii, 17): this verse makes it clear that no work of mercy is shown to those in misery except that it proceeds from inward compassion. Thus we see what is the " mercy " which is here mentioned: it is that which exerts itself in doing good, being a fruit of the love of God shed abroad in the heart.

This mercy may, through walking after the flesh, for a time be checked and choked, but taking the general tenor of a Christian's character and the main trend in his life, it is seen to be an unmistakable trait of the new man. " The wicked borroweth, and payeth not again; but the righteous showeth mercy, and giveth " (Psalm xxxvii, 21). It was " mercy" in Abraham, after he had been wronged by his nephew, which caused him to go after and secure the deliverance of Lot. It was " mercy" on the part of Joseph, after his brethren had so grievously mistreated him, which moved him to freely forgive them. It was " mercy" in Moses, after Miriam had rebelled against him and the Lord had smitten her with leprosy, which moved him to cry, " Heal her now, O God, I beseech Thee " (Num. xii, 13). It was " mercy" in David which caused him to spare the life of his arch-enemy when the wicked Saul was in his hands. In solemn contrast, of Judas we read " he remembered not to shew mercy, but persecuted the poor and needy man " (Psalm cix, 16).

Were we sermonizing Matthew v, 7, our next division would be *the duties* of mercy, which are answerable to the miseries of those we should relieve, as the form and degree of its manifestation is regulated by our own station and circumstances. This mercy regards not merely the bodies of men but also their *souls,* and here again it is sharply distinguished from that natural and instinctive kind which pities and ministers to the temporal needs of sufferers, but has no concern for their eternal prospects. The preacher needs to carefully heed this fifth Beatitude: so, too, the employer and the tradesman. But we must dismiss this branch of our subject by calling attention to " he that sheweth mercy *with cheerfulness* " (Romans xii, 8), which is what gives chief value to the service rendered. If God loves a cheerful giver, it is equally true that He takes notice of the spirit in which we respond to His precepts.

A word now on *the reward*: " for they shall obtain mercy," which, as the older theologians pointed out, is not the reward of condignity (wholly deserved), but of congruity. This gives not the least countenance to the horrible error of Rome, that by alms deeds we can make satisfaction to God for our sins. Our acts of mercy are not meritorious in the sight of God: had that been the case, Christ had said, " Blessed are the merciful, for they shall obtain *justice*," for what is meritorious is due reward by right. Our text has nothing to do with salvation matters, but enunciates a principle pertaining to the governmental ways of God, by which we reap what we sow and have measured again to us according as we have meted out to others (Matt. vii, 2). "He that followeth after righteousness and mercy findeth life, righteousness, and honour" (Prov. xxi, 21).

"For they shall obtain mercy." First, there is an *inward benefit*. The one who shows mercy to others gains thereby: "the merciful man doeth good to his own soul" (Prov. xi, 17). There is a personal satisfaction in the exercise of pity and benevolence, which the fullest gratification of the selfish man is not to be compared with: "he that hath mercy on the poor, *happy* is he" (Prov. xiv, 21). Second, he reaps mercy at the hands of his *fellows*: the overruling providence of God causes him to be dealt with mercifully by others. Third, he receives mercy from *God*: "with the merciful Thou wilt show Thyself merciful" (Psalm xviii, 25)—contrast "he shall have judgment without mercy that hath showed no mercy" (James ii, 13). Mercy will be shown to the merciful in the Day to come (see II Timothy i, 16, 18; Jude 21). Then let us prayerfully heed the exhortations of Romans xii, 10; Galatians vi, 2; Colossians iii, 12.

"Blessed are the pure in heart: for they shall see God" (Matt. v, 8). This is another of the Beatitudes which has been grossly perverted by the enemies of the Lord: those who have, like their predecessors the Pharisees, posed as the champions of the Truth and boasted of a superior sanctity to that confessed by the true people of God. All through this Christian era there have been poor deluded souls who have claimed an entire purification of the old man, or have insisted that God has so completely renewed them that the carnal nature has been eradicated, and in consequence they not only commit no sins, but have no sinful desires or thoughts. But God tells us, "If we say that we have no sin, we deceive ourselves, and the truth is not in us" (I John i, 8). Of course, such people appeal to the Scriptures in support of their vain delusion, applying to experience verses which describe the legal benefits of the Atonement, or by wresting such a one as that which is now before us.

That purity of heart does *not* mean sinlessness of life is clear from the inspired record of the history of all God's saints. Noah got drunk, Abraham equivocated, Moses disobeyed God, Job cursed the day of his birth, Elijah fled in terror from Jezebel, Peter denied Christ. Yes, perhaps someone will exclaim, but all these were before Christianity was established. True, but it has also been the same since then. Where shall we go to find a Christian of superior attainments to those of the apostle Paul? And what was *his* experience? Read Romans vii and see. When he would do good, evil was present with him (verse 21); there was a law in his members warring against the law of his mind, and bringing him into captivity to the law of sin (verse 23). He did, with the mind, serve the Law of God, nevertheless with the flesh he served the law of sin (verse 25). Ah, Christian reader, the truth is, one of the most conclusive evidences that we *do* possess a pure heart is to be conscious of and burdened with the impurity which still indwells us.

"Blessed are the pure in heart." Here again we see the Lord exposing the thoughts of the natural man, who errs greatly in his ideas of what constitutes real blessedness. Therein He refutes the Pharisees, who contented themselves with a species of external ceremonialism or mere outward holiness, failing to realize that God requires "truth in the *inward* parts" (Psalm li, 6). Very solemn and searching is this sixth Beatitude, for it equally condemns most of that which now passes current for genuine religion in Christendom. How many today rest satisfied with a *head* religion, supposing that all is well if their creed be sound; and how many more have nothing better than a *hand* religion—busily engaged in what they term "Christian service." "But the Lord looketh on the *heart*" (I Samuel xvi, 7), which includes the mind, conscience, affections and will.

How is purity of heart effected? for by nature the heart of fallen man is totally depraved and corrupt, deceitful above all things and desperately wicked (Jer. xvii, 9). How can it be otherwise when each of us must make the humiliating confession, "Behold, I was shapen in iniquity; and in sin did my mother conceive me" (Psalm li, 5)? This purity of heart is by no means to be restricted to inward chastity or simplicity—being without guile and deceit—but has a far more comprehensive meaning and scope. The heart of the Christian is made pure by a fourfold operation of the Holy Spirit. First, by imparting a holy nature at the new birth. Second, by bestowing a saving faith which unites its possessor to a holy Christ. Third, by sprinkling him with the precious blood of Christ, which purges his conscience. Fourth, by a protracted process of sanctification so that we, through His aid, mortify the flesh and live unto God. In consequence thereof, the believer has a sincere desire and resolution not to sin against God in thought or word or deed, but to please Him in all things.

In what measure is the heart of the Christian now made pure? Only in part during this life, relatively and not absolutely. "The believer's understanding is *in part* purified from darkness, his judgment from error, his will from rebellion, his affections from enmity, avarice, pride, sensuality" (T. Scott). The work of Divine grace in the soul is begun here, but it is only completed hereafter (Phil. i, 6). We are not wholly perfected, having received only "the *firstfruits* of the Spirit" (Romans viii, 23). Observe carefully the tense of the verb in Acts xv, 9: it is not "purified their hearts by faith," but "purifying their hearts by faith"—a continuous experience. So again "He saved us by the washing of regeneration and (not "renewal" but) *renewing* of the Holy Ghost" (Titus iii, 5). Consequently it is written "in many things we *all* stumble" (James iii, 2, R.V.). Yet it is our bounden duty to use every legitimate means of purification: the daily denying of self, sincere confession of our sins, walking in the paths of righteousness.

What is this purity of heart? a question which requires a some-what more definite answer than has been given above, where we have intimated that this sixth Beatitude contemplates both the new heart or nature received at regeneration and the transformation of character which is the effect of a Divine work of grace in the soul. Spiritual purity may be defined as undivided affections, sincerity and genuineness, godly simplicity. It is the opposite of subtlety and duplicity, for genuine piety lays aside not only hatred and malice, but guile and hypocrisy. It is not sufficient to be pure in words and outward deportment: purity of desires, motives, intents, is what should, and in the main does, characterize the child of God. Here, then, is a most important test for each professing Christian to apply to himself: Have I been freed from the dominion of hypocrisy? Are my motives pure and intentions genuine? Are my affections set upon things above? Do I meet with the Lord's people to commune with Him or to be seen of men?

A " pure heart " is one which has a pure Object before it, being attracted by " the beauty of holiness." It is one in which the fear of the Lord has been implanted and the love of God shed abroad, and therefore it hates what He hates and loves what He loves. The purer the heart be, the more conscious it becomes of, and the more it grieves over, indwelling filth. A pure heart is one which makes conscience of foul thoughts, vile imaginations, and evil desires. It is one that mourns over pride and discontent, unbelief and coldness of affection, and weeps in secret over unholiness. Alas, how little is this *inward* purity esteemed today: the great majority of professors content themselves with a mere form of godliness, a shadow of the reality. The heaviest burden of a pure heart is the discovery that such an ocean of unclean waters still indwells him, constantly casting up mire and dirt, fouling all that he does.

Consider now the attendant blessing: the pure in heart " shall *see God.*" Once again we would remind our readers that the promises attached to these Beatitudes have both a present and a future fulfilment; notably is this the case with the one now before us. Corresponding to the fact that the Christian's purity of heart is only in part in this life, but perfected in the life to come, is the experience that " Now we see through a glass, darkly; but then face to face; now I know in part; but then shall I know even as also I am known (I Cor. xiii, 12). To " see God " is to be brought nigh to Him (for we cannot see an object which is a vast distance from us), to be introduced into intimate intercourse with Him, which is the consequence of having the thick cloud of our transgressions blotted out, for it was our iniquities which separated us from Him (Isaiah lix, 2). We need scarcely say that it is a spiritual sight and not a corporeal one, a heart knowledge of and communion with God.

The pure in heart possess spiritual discernment and with the eyes of their understanding they obtain clear views of the Divine character and perceive the excellency of His attributes. When the eye is single, the whole body is full of light. It is by faith God is beheld. To "see God" also has the force of *enjoy* Him, as in John iii, 36, and for that a pure heart is indispensable. That which pollutes the heart and beclouds the vision of a Christian is unjudged evil, for when any sin is "allowed" communion with God is broken, and can only be restored by genuine repentance and unsparing confession. Since, then, the privilege of seeing God is dependent upon the maintenance of the heart purity, how essential it is that we give earnest heed to the exhortations of Isaiah i, 16; II Corinthians vii, 1; I Peter iii, 15. Oh to be able to say "I have set the Lord always before me" (Psalm xvi, 8).

"In the Truth, the faith of which purifies the heart, they 'see God,' for what is that Truth but a manifestation of the glory of God in the face of Jesus Christ—an illustrious display of the combined radiance of Divine holiness and Divine benignity! ... They who are pure in heart 'see God' in this way, even in the present world; and in the future state their knowledge of God will become far more extensive and their fellowship with Him far more intimate. To borrow the words of the Psalmist, we shall 'Behold His face in righteousness, and shall be satisfied when we awake in His likeness' (Psalm xvii, 15). Then, and not till then, will the full meaning of these words be understood, 'the pure in heart shall see God'" (J. Brown).

CHAPTER FOUR

The Beatitudes—Concluded

"BLESSED are the peacemakers: for they shall be called the children of God" (verse 9). "The Jews, in general, regarded the Gentile nations with bitter contempt and hatred, and they expected that, under the Messiah, there should be an uninterrupted series of war-like attacks made on these nations, till they were completely destroyed or subjugated to the chosen people of God (an idea based, no doubt, on what they read in the book of Joshua concerning the experiences of their forefathers—A.W.P.). In their estimation, those emphatically deserved the appellation of 'happy' who should be employed under Messiah the Prince to avenge on the heathen nations all the wrongs these had done to Israel. How different is the spirit of the new economy! How beautifully does it accord with the angelic anthem which celebrated the nativity of its Founder: 'glory to God in the highest, and on earth peace, good will toward men!'" (J. Brown).

This seventh Beatitude has to do more with conduct than with character, though, of necessity, there must first be a peaceable spirit before there will be active efforts put forth to make peace. Let it be remembered that in this first section of the Sermon on the Mount, the Lord Jesus is *defining the character* of those who should be subjects and citizens in His kingdom. First, He described them according to the initial experiences of those in whom a Divine work is wrought. The first four may be grouped together as setting forth the negative graces of their hearts. They are not self-sufficient, but consciously poor in spirit; they are not self-satisfied, but mourning because of their spiritual state; they are not self-willed, but meek; they are not self-righteous, but hungering and thirsting after the righteousness of Another. In the next three, the Lord names their *positive* graces: having tasted of the mercy of God, they are merciful in their dealings with others; having received a spiritual nature, they now hate impurity and love holiness; having entered into the peace which Christ made by the blood of His Cross, they now wish to live in amity with all.

"Blessed are the peacemakers." This takes note of the horrible contention and enmity which sin has brought into the world, for where there is no strife there is no need for peacemakers. The world is "living in malice and envy, hateful and hating one another" (Titus iii, 3): though attempts are often made to conceal this by the cloak of hypocrisy yet it soon peeps forth again in its hideous nakedness, as the history of the nations attests. And let not writer and reader forget the solemn fact that such was once our own sad case, as the opening words of Titus iii, 3, declare—"for we *ourselves* also were." But on the other hand, our text also brings into view the triumph of God over the Devil: grace has brought in that which even now in measure, and in the future completely, displaces the vile works of the flesh.

To be a lover of and worker after peace is one of the distinguishing marks of those who are followers of the Prince of peace. That miracle of grace which has made them at peace with God causes them to regard their fellows with sincere benevolence, desiring to promote their best interests, both here and hereafter. It is their care, so much as in them lies, to live peaceably with all men, and therefore do they abstain from deliberate injury of others. In each relationship they occupy—domestic, social, ecclesiastical—it is their desire and endeavour to prevent and allay strife. They are lovers of concord, promoters of unity, healers of breaches. They delight to pour oil on troubled waters, to reconcile those who are estranged, to right wrongs, to strengthen the kindly ties of friendship. As the sons of peace they bring into the fetid atmosphere of this world a breath from the pure and placid air of heaven. How much the world is indebted to their presence, only the Day to come will show.

Let it be pointed out that this lovely Christlike disposition is a vastly different thing from that easy-going indolence which is so often naught but cowardice or selfishness. It is not a peace at any price which the Christian loves and aims to promote. No, indeed, that is a false peace, unworthy to be called peace at all. "The wisdom that is from above is first pure, then peaceable, gentle, easy to be intreated, full of mercy and good fruits, without partiality, and without hypocrisy" (James iii, 17): note well the words "first pure"—peace is not to be sought at the expense of righteousness. Hence it is important that we lose not the thread of connection between our present Beatitude and the one which precedes it: as the "pure in heart" modifies the "mercy" of verse 7, so also it qualifies the "peace" of verse 9—it is *such* mercy and peace as God Himself approves of. The same qualification is seen again in "follow peace with all men *and* holiness" (Heb. xii, 14). We are to avoid all needless occasions of contention, yet not to the point of sacrificing the Truth, compromising principle, or forsaking duty—Christ Himself did not so: Matthew x, 34.

"If it be possible, as much as lieth in you, live peaceably with all men" (Romans xii, 18). The very terms of this exhortation denote that so far from compliance therewith being a simple task, it is one which calls for constant vigilance, self-discipline, and earnest prayer. Such is the state of human nature, that offences must needs come, nevertheless it is part of Christian duty to see to it that we so conduct ourselves as to give no just cause of complaint against us. It is for our own peace we do so, for it is impossible to be happy in broils and enmities. Some believers are of a naturally contentious disposition, and doubly do *they* need to beg God to hold His restraining and calming hand upon them. When disturbance and turmoil is aroused, we should diligently examine ourselves before the Lord as to whether the cause for it lie *in us*, and if so, confess the sin to Him and seek to reconcile those offended. If we be innocent, we must meekly submit to it as an affliction.

If it be true that "Blessed are the peacemakers," it necessarily follows that cursed are the peacebreakers. Then let us be diligently on our guard against bigotry, intemperate zeal, and a quarrelsome spirit: the things of God are too sacred for wrangling. Highly important is it that we give earnest heed to the exhortation of "Endeavouring to keep the unity of the Spirit in the bond of peace" (Eph. iv, 3). Let it be carefully noted that the preceding verse specifies the chief *aids* to this. In order to the development of a peaceful disposition we must first cultivate the grace of "lowliness," which is the opposite of pride, for "only by pride cometh contention" (Prov. xiii, 10). Second, there must be the cultivation of "meekness," which is the opposite of self-assertiveness, the determination to press my will at all costs: remember "a soft answer turneth away wrath." Third, the grace of "long sufferance," which is the opposite of impatience. Finally, "forbearing one another in love," for the queen of the graces "endureth all things."

See here the blessedness of that work to which the ministers of God are called: not merely to effect peace between man and man, but to reconcile men to God. What a contrast is this from the task allotted to Joshua and his officers under the Mosaic economy, of taking up the sword to slay the enemies of the Lord! In this dispensation the servants of Christ are commissioned to seek the reconciliation of those who are at enmity with God. The heralds of the Cross are the ambassadors of peace, bidding sinners throw down the weapons of their warfare and enter into amnesty with God. They know there is no peace for the wicked, and therefore do they exhort them to acquaint themselves with God and be at peace (Job xxii, 21). Of them it is written, "How beautiful are the feet of them that preach the gospel of peace, and bring glad tidings of good things!" (Romans x, 15).

There is still another way in which it is the holy privilege of believers to be peacemakers, and that is by their *prayers* averting the wrath of God from a guilty nation. In the day when the Lord's anger is kindled against a sin-laden people and the dark clouds of providence threaten an impending storm of judgment, it is both the duty and the privilege of God's remembrancers to stand in the breach and by their earnest supplication stay His hand, so making peace. Moses did so (Exodus xxxii, 10); so too Aaron (Num. xvi, 47, 48), and David (II Samuel xxiv, 14). When a fearful plague visits our country, or another nation threatens it with war, we are to behold God raising His rod, and entreat Him to be merciful: see Jeremiah xii, 11; Ezekiel xxii, 30, 31. This is indeed a blessed work of peace:

to stay the Lord from the work of destruction, as Abraham's intercession had done for Sodom if there were but ten righteous persons in it. Once more we say, only the Day to come will show how the wicked gained by the presence of the righteous remnant in their midst.

A word now upon the reward: "for they shall be called the children of God," which is a decisive proof that these Beatitudes contemplate not the moral virtues of the natural man, but rather the spiritual graces of the regenerate, To be *made* a child of God is to be renewed in His image and likeness; to be *called* so is to be esteemed and regarded as such. The Lord Himself is "the God of peace" (Heb. xiii, 20), and where this holy disposition is manifested by His people He *owns* them as His children—compare Hebrews ii, 11, and xi, 16, for this force of the word "called." Futhermore, holy peacemakers are recognized as children of God by their spiritual brethren. Have you received this grace of the Spirit, so that you sincerely desire and endeavour to live at peace with all men? Then that is an evidence you are a child of God, a pledge of your adoption. Labour to maintain it. Ultimately, God will make it manifest to all the universe that we are His children (Romans viii, 19).

"Blessed are they which are persecuted for righteousness' sake: for theirs is the kingdom of heaven" (verse 10). The Christian life is one that is full of strange paradoxes which are quite insoluble to human reason, but which are easily understood by the spiritual mind. God's saints rejoice with joy unspeakable, yet do they mourn with a lamentation to which the worldling is an utter stranger. The believer in Christ has been brought into contact with a source of vital satisfaction which is capable of meeting every longing, yet does he pant with a yearning like unto that of the thirsty hart. He sings and makes melody in his heart to the Lord, yet does he groan deeply and daily. His experience is often painful and perplexing, yet would he not part with it for all the gold in the world. These puzzling paradoxes are among the evidences which he possesses that he is indeed blessed of God. But who by mere reasoning would ever conclude that the persecuted and reviled are "blessed"! Genuine felicity, then, is not only compatible with but is actually accompanied by manifold miseries in this life.

"It is a strong proof of human depravity that men's curses and Christ's blessings should meet on the same persons. Who would have thought that a man could be persecuted and reviled, and have all manner of evil said of him for righteousness' sake? And do wicked men really hate justice and love those who defraud and wrong their neighbours? No; they do not dislike righteousness as it respects *themselves*: it is only that species of it which respects God and religion that excites their hatred. If Christians were content with doing justly and loving mercy, and would cease walking humbly with God, they might go through the world, not only in peace, but with applause; but he that will *live godly* in Christ Jesus shall suffer persecution (II Tim. iii, 12). Such a life reproves the ungodliness of men and provokes their resentment" (Andrew Fuller). It is the enmity of the Serpent—active ever since the days of Abel (I John iii, 12)—against the holy seed.

"Blessed are they which are persecuted for righteousness' sake." The connection between this and all that has been before us must not be overlooked. It is not every sufferer, nor even every sufferer for religion, who is entitled to appropriate such consolation. This antagonism is not in return for wrong-doing or in response to what has given just cause for offence. They who are morose, haughty, selfish, or evil-speaking, have no right to seek comfort from this Beatitude when people retaliate against them. No, it is where Christ-liness of character and conduct is assailed, where practical godliness condemns the worldly ways of empty professors and fires their enmity, where humble yet vital piety cannot be tolerated by those who are devoid of the same. The wicked hate God's holy image and those who bear it, His holy Truth and those who walk in it. This pro-nouncement of Christ's signifies, Blessed are the spiritual which the carnal detest; blessed are the gentle sheep, whom the dogs snap at.

How many a Christian employee who has refused to violate his conscience has suffered at the hands of an ungodly master or mistress! Yet such persecution, painful though it may be, is really a blessing in disguise. First, by means of the opposition which they encounter, the Lord's people become the better acquainted with their own infirmities and needs, for thereby they are made conscious that they cannot stand for a single hour unless Divine grace upholds them. Second, by persecution they are often kept from certain sins into which they would most likely fall were the wicked at peace with them: the rough usage they receive at the hands of worldlings makes impossible that friendship with them which the flesh craves. Third, such persecution affords the believer opportunity to glorify God by his constancy, courage, and fidelity to the Truth.

This searching word "for righteousness' sake" calls upon us to honestly examine ourselves before God when we are being opposed: "But let none of you suffer as a murderer, or as a thief, or as an evildoer, or as a busybody in other men's matters" (I Peter iv, 15). The same qualification is made in the verse which immediately follows the last quoted: "Yet if any man suffer as a Christian, let him not be ashamed; but let him glorify God on this behalf": this is a most necessary caution, that the believer see to it that he is buffeted for *right doing* and not on account of his own misconduct or foolish behaviour. It is to be observed that persecution is often so speciously disguised that those guilty thereof are not conscious of the same, yea, so deceitful is the human heart, they imagine they are doing God a service (John xvi, 2). But "Blessed are they that are persecuted for righteousness' sake: for theirs *is* [not "shall be"] the kingdom of heaven"; its privileges and blessings (Romans xiv, 17) are theirs even now: though hated by men, they are "kings and priests unto God" (Rev. i, 6).

" Blessed are ye, when men shall revile you, and persecute you, and shall say all manner of evil against you falsely, for My sake " (Matt. v, 11). In verse 10 the Lord enunciates the general principle; here He makes special application of it to His servants. Note carefully the change from " them " throughout verses 5-10 to " ye " and " your " in verses 11 and 12: opposition is the general lot of God's people, but it is the special portion of His ministers. If faithful to their calling, they must expect to be fiercely assailed. Such has ever been the experience of the Lord's servants. Moses was reviled again and again (Exodus v, 11; xiv, 11; xvi, 2; xvii, 2; etc.). Samuel was rejected (I Samuel viii, 5). Elijah was despised (I Kings xviii, 17) and persecuted (I Kings xix, 2). Micaiah was hated (II Chron. xviii, 17). Nehemiah was oppressed and defamed (Neh. iv). The Saviour Himself, the faithful witness of God, was put to death by the people to whom He ministered. Stephen was stoned, Peter and John cast into prison, James beheaded, while the entire course of Paul was one long series of bitter and relentless persecutions.

" Blessed are ye, when men shall revile you, and persecute you, and shall say all maner of evil against you falsely, for My sake. Rejoice and be exceeding glad, for great is your reward in heaven; for so persecuted they the prophets which were before you " (verses 11 and 12). In these words the Lord Jesus faithfully warns His servants what they may fully expect to encounter, and then defines how they are to respond thereto, how they are to conduct themselves under the fire of their enemies. That blessedness which worldly leaders value and crave is to be flattered and feted, humoured and honoured; but the felicity and glory of the officers of Christ are to be made conformable to the Captain of their salvation, who was " despised and rejected of men." Yet instead of being downcast over and murmuring at the hostility they meet with, ministers of the Gospel are to be thankful to God for the high honour He confers upon them in making them partakers of the sufferings of His Son. Because that is so difficult for flesh and blood to do, the Lord here advances two reasons as encouragements.

It is true that persecution of both ministers and saints is today in a much milder form than it assumed in other ages; nevertheless, it is just as real. Through the goodness of God we have long been protected from legal persecution, but the enmity of the Serpent finds other ways and means for expressing itself. The words of Christ in John xv have never been repealed: " If ye were of the world, the world would love his own; but because ye are not of the world, but I have chosen you out of the world, therefore the world hateth you. Remember the word that I said unto you, The servant is not greater than his Lord. If they have persecuted Me, they will also persecute you; if they have kept My saying, they will keep yours also " (verses 19 and 20). Let it be carefully noted that it was the professing and not the profane " world " that Christ was alluding to: it was from religious leaders, those making the greatest spiritual pretensions, that the Redeemer Himself received the worst treatment. And so it is now: members and officers of the "churches" stoop to methods and use means of opposition which those outside would scorn to employ.

Let us carefully note the qualification made by Christ in the verses we are now considering. This benediction of His is pronounced only on them who have all manner of evil spoken against them *falsely*: they have themselves given no just occasion for the same. No, far from it, it is not for any lawful ground of accusation in themselves, but for "My sake"—for their loyalty and fidelity to Christ, for their obedience to His commission, for their refusal to compromise His holy Truth. To be "reviled" is to suffer personal abuse: said Paul, "We are made as the filth of the world, and are the offscouring of all things" (I Cor. iv, 13). "Persecution" may involve acts of ill-treatment or ostracism. To have "all manner of evil said against" us is to suffer defamation of character: I Thessalonians ii, 2, clearly implies that even the moral reputation of the apostle was attacked. All these are efforts of the Devil to destroy the usefulness of God's ministers.

The Lord Jesus here pronounced blessed or happy those who, through devotion to Him, would be called upon to suffer. They are "blessed" because such are given the unspeakable privilege of having fellowship with the sufferings of the Saviour. They are "blessed" because such tribulation worketh patience, and patience experience, and experience hope, and such a hope that will not make ashamed. They are "blessed" because they shall be fully recompensed in the Day to come. Here is rich comfort indeed. Let not the soldier of the Cross be dismayed because the fiery darts of the wicked one are hurled against him. Remember that "The sufferings of this present time are not worthy to be compared with the glory which shall be revealed in us" (Romans viii, 18).

"Rejoice and be exceeding glad": this too is spoken specially to ministers. Those afflictions which faithfulness to Christ brings upon them are to be endured not only with patience and resignation, but thanksgiving and gladness, and that for a threefold reason. First, that they come upon them for Christ's sake: if He suffered so much for them, should they not rejoice to suffer a little for Him? Second, they shall be richly recompensed hereafter: "great is your reward in heaven"—not as of merit, but purely of grace, for there is no proportion between them. Third, they bring them into fellowship with a noble company of martyrs: "for so persecuted they the prophets which were before you"—they too were ill-treated by members of the outward Church: what an honour to share, in our measure, the lot of those holy men! Verily there is cause to rejoice, no matter how fierce the conflict may be. Oh, to emulate the apostles in Acts v, 41, and xvi, 25. May Divine grace enable all the oppressed servants and saints of God to draw from these precious words of Christ the comfort and strength they need.

CHAPTER FIVE

The Ministerial Office

" Ye are the salt of the earth : but if the salt have lost his savour, wherewith shall it be salted ? it is thenceforth good for nothing, but to be cast out, and to be trodden under foot of men. Ye are the light of the world. A city that is set on an hill cannot be hid. Neither do men light a candle, and put it under a bushel, but on a candlestick ; and it giveth light unto all that are in the house. Let your light so shine before men, that they may see your good works, and glorify your Father which is in heaven." (Matt. v, 13-16.)

" YE are the salt of the earth." These words (and those which follow to the end of verse 16) are frequently regarded as being spoken of God's people at large, but this we think is a mistake. First, because such an interpretation is out of harmony with the immediate context. In our last chapter we called attention to our Lord's changing of the pronoun in verse 11 from the " they " in verses 1-10 to the " ye." In verse 10 Christ enumerated the general principle that " blessed are they which are persecuted for righteousness' sake," but in verse 11 He made particular application to His own ministers: persecution is the usual experience of God's people, but it is the *special* portion of His *servants*. Clear confirmation of this distinction is found in verse 12, where the maligned ministers of Christ are bidden to rejoice because " so persecuted they the *prophets* which were before you "—not " the saints," but the official servants of God.

Thus, the " Ye are the salt of the earth " obviously has reference to those who now occupy the same position as did the " prophets " of old, namely those called of God to act as His mouthpiece and interpret His will. Additional proof is found in what immediately follows, where after further designating them the " light of the world " Christ added, " A city that is set on a hill cannot be hid "— a figure fitly pertinent to the *officers* of Christ, who are made a spectacle to the world. Finally, what is said in verse 15 plainly pertains to the ministers of God rather than to their hearers, for the candle on a candlestick again speaks of official dignity, and the giving " light to all that are in the house " is plainly the one man ministering to the many.

Matthew Henry begins his comments on these verses by pointing out, " Christ had lately called His disciples and told them they should be ' fishers of men ' (iv, 19); here He tells them further what He designed them to be—the salt of the earth and light of the world: that they might be indeed what it was expected they should be." It is only in recent generations, when the spirit of socialism has invaded

43

the religious realm, that this passage has been promiscuously applied to Christians. The two emblems which Christ here employed are very striking, and their *order* significant. He resembles His ministers to " salt " to *humble* them, for salt is cheap, common, and insignificant; to "light" to *encourage* them, for light is illuminating, conspicuous, elevated.

The passage we are now to ponder forms the second section of our Lord's Sermon on the Mount. In it Christ touches upon the office of the apostles, and therein (according to their measure) that of all His ministers. It was a distinct division of His address, yet there is a manifest relation between it and the last one: only those whom the Lord pronounces " blessed," whose characters correspond to that which He portrayed in verses 1-11, are called by Christ to witness publicly for Him. The ministers of God must themselves first be seasoned by the Word: how could they fittingly apply salt to the consciences of others who had never felt the bite of it on their own? The design of these verses, then, is to stir up Christ's servants to diligence and fidelity in declaring the will of God unto saint and sinner alike.

Thus, the first two sections of this Sermon are closely connected. The coherence of our present portion with the former stands thus: Christ had declared that there is a company on earth upon whom the Divine benediction rests. Anticipating the question, How do they attain to and maintain this felicity by such graces of the Spirit, which fits them for that estate? He answers, the preaching of God's Word is the principal means to work in the heart those graces to which true happiness is promised. Because this is a high and holy privilege to bring men to this estate, Christ exhorted His ministers unto earnestness in their service by two weighty reasons, drawn from the properties of their work, and propounded by two similitudes.

"Ye are the salt of the earth" (verse 13). "Ye," that is those whom I have called to be apostles and set apart for the work of the ministry. Ye are "salt," not literally, yet by resemblance; yet not in regard of their persons, but of their *labours*. They are here likened to "salt": they were to season souls for God by making them savoury in heart and life. From this emblem both ministers and people may learn their respective duties. Ministers are to dispense the Word, both Law and Gospel, in such a way as to express *the qualities of salt*. Now the properties of salt as applied to raw flesh or fresh meats are principally these: first, it will fret and bite, being of a hot and dry nature; second, it makes meat savoury to our taste; third, it preserves meat from putrefaction by drawing out of it superfluous moisture.

Salt is an indispensable necessity of life. It is God's great antiseptic in a sphere of decay. It is wrought into the very rocks and soil of earth so that the waters filtering through them become purified thereby. It is a necessary element of the blood, which is the life of our bodies. How well suited is it then as a figure of the Truth, by which means the soul is sanctified, for as salt arrests natural corruption, so the Word of God militates against moral corruption. This figure, then, furnishes clear direction to every minister of God as to his *manner* of preaching. Since the Word alone be the savoury salt whereby souls are seasoned for the Lord, then it ought to be dispensed purely and sincerely. If salt be mixed with dust and rubbish it loses its pungency and efficacy, and if the Word be mingled with levity or exciting anecdotes its power is nullified.

This figure plainly warns the minister of his pressing *need of fortitude*. It is "salt" and not sugar candy he is to employ: something which the ungodly will be more inclined to spit out than swallow with a smile, something which is calculated to bring water to the eyes rather than laughter to the lips. The minister, then, must not expect faithful preaching to be acceptable and popular. It is contrary to nature for those whose consciences are pricked to be pleased with those who wound them. Christ's servants must be prepared for their hearers to fret and set themselves against what searches out their corruptions. Such displeasure and opposition is a testimony that their ministry *is* "salt," that it has bitten into the depravity of their people. Instead of being discouraged and dismayed they are to persevere, endeavouring to season their congregation more and more with the pure salt of God's Word.

The hearer also is to receive instruction from this figure. Hereby each one may see what he is in himself by nature: depraved and corrupt, as unsavoury flesh and stinking carrion in the nostrils of God, or else what need of *salt*? How this should humble and cause us to lay aside all pride and self-righteousness. Again, every one must learn hereby to suffer the word of reproof, whereby his secret sins are discovered and denounced. When our conscience is searched we must be willing for salt to be rubbed into it, for mortification precedes salvation. The hearer must give all diligence to be seasoned with this heavenly salt so that the thoughts of his heart, the words of his mouth, and the actions of his life may be acceptable to God (Col. iv, 6). If we sit under the ministry of the Word (oral or written) and be not seasoned thereby our case is doubly evil (Judges ix, 45).

"But if the salt have lost his savour, wherewith shall it be salted? It is thenceforth good for nothing but to be cast out, and to be trodden under foot of men" (verse 13). This was brought in by Christ to move His servants unto fidelity and diligence in their ministry by the danger attending the opposite. Infidelity in the ministry is like unsavoury salt: ineffectual, worthless, despicable, subject to a fearful curse. This is the great danger of the pulpit: to become menpleasers, to yield unto the demand for smooth speaking, to tickle the ears of their auditors with novelties. Such preachers become unsavoury salt, unprofitable in their ministry, failing to season souls so that they are acceptable to God. Salt is useless when it loses its virtue and acrimony. Ministers become such when through lack of prayer and continuous study they fail to increase in spiritual knowledge, or when adopting false doctrine they preach error, or when they cease to denounce sin, or when they fail to practise what they preach.

The greatness of the danger attending ministers who become unfaithful and unprofitable is here pointed out by Christ in His words "wherewith shall it [i.e. the salt—cf. Mark ix, 50] be salted." Those who depart from fidelity are very seldom, and then only with great difficulty, recovered and restored. Read what is recorded of the false prophets in the Old Testament and of false apostles in the New and where is there an instance that any *repented*? The same solemn principle is exemplified in the case of almost all those preachers who have forsaken Protestantism and gone over to Rome. How diligently, then, do ministers need to take to heart that injunction, "Meditate upon these things; give thyself wholly to them; that thy profiting may appear to all. Take heed *unto thyself,* and unto the doctrine; continue in them: for in doing this thou shalt both save thyself and them that hear thee" (I Tim. iv, 15, 16); and again, "But thou, O man of God, flee these things [cf. verse 10]; and follow after righteousness, godliness, faith, love, patience, meekness" (I Tim. vi, 11).

The *unprofitableness* of unfaithful ministers is expressed in the words "it is thenceforth good for nothing": just as unsavoury salt is become worthless to season meat, so unfaithful ministers are valueless to God and man. The curse resting upon such is, "it is cast out and trodden under foot of men," that is, such preachers are condemned both by the Lord and by their fellow men. "Therefore have I also made you contemptible and base before all the people, according as ye have not kept My ways, but have been partial in the law" (Mal. ii, 9), such was the fate pronounced upon the renegade priests of old. No doubt Christ was here making an oblique reference to the scribes and Pharisees of His day, affirming their unprofitableness and announcing the impending doom of Judaism. Solemn beyond words is this verse, and prayerfully should it be laid to heart by all Christian ministers.

"Ye are the light of the world" (verse 14). Here Christ likens His ministers unto "light," and that with the object of stirring them up to preach the will of God. It was as though He said, Your position and condition is such that your sayings and doings are open to the cognizance of man, therefore be careful to please God therein. Spiritually the world is in darkness (II Peter i, 19) and sits in the shadow of death (Matt. iv, 16), because in Adam it turned away from Him who is Light. But ministers of the Word carry with them a Lamp of Truth, and by the illumination of their ministry are they to shine upon the benighted souls of men. By their preaching ignorance is to be exposed, that their hearers may be "turned from darkness to light" (Acts xxvi, 18).

By this figure Christ shows *how* the Word is to be *handled*: it is to be so applied to the minds and consciences of men that they may be made to see their sins and their woeful wretchedness thereby, then bringing before them the remedy for their misery, which is the person and work of the Lord Jesus; and then to make plain that path of obedience in all good duties to God and men which He requires in the life of a Christian. Preachers may display great homiletical skill and deliver flowery discourses, but only that is true preaching which conveys the light of spiritual knowledge to the heart and leads souls to God. So, too, since the ministers are the light of the world it is incumbent upon all who hear them to raise the blinds of carnal prejudice and open the windows of their souls so that the illuminating message may receive due entrance.

"A city that is set on an hill cannot be hid. Neither do men light a candle and put it under a bushel, but on a candlestick; and it giveth light unto all that are in the house" (verses 14, 15). Such is the case with God's ministers by virtue of their calling. Christ has denominated His servants "the light of the world," and they may be inclined to regard themselves as men of some renown, and therefore He informs them with His *intent therein*. It was not to give them titles of praise, to puff them up, but to acquaint them with the demands of their office: by reason of their high calling they would be public spectacles—heard and scrutinized by men—and therefore it doubly behoved them to see to it that their message was acceptable to God and their walk blameless before men, for if by their fidelity they might "turn many to righteousness," infidelity would involve souls in eternal destruction.

Hereby God's ministers must learn not to think it strange if they lie more open to manifold reproaches and abuses of the world than do the rank and file of God's people, and the more godly their conduct be the more distasteful to the unregenerate. Hence it follows that God's servants cannot without great sin hide the gifts and talents which He has bestowed upon them, for they are as lighted candles which must not be put under a bushel. That may be done in various ways: by refusing to humble themselves and speak in terms suited to the capacity of the most simple, by refusing to give out the Truth of God, by toning it down through the fear of man, by flirting with the world and adopting its ways.

"Let your light so shine before men, that they may see your good works, and glorify your Father which is in heaven" (verse 16). By "so shine" is signified ministerial teaching, whereby God's will and grace are made known to His people, backed up by a godly example. Seeing that by your calling you are so conspicuous in the world, look well to the holiness of your lives and the fruits of your labours, so that God's people may not only hear your doctrine but also perceive your good works, and thereby be moved to follow the same, and thus bring honour and praise to the Lord. These two things must never be separated: sound doctrine and holy deportment are ever to be conjoined in a minister. He who teaches to write will give rules of writing to the scholars, and then set before them a copy to

follow. God will have men learn His will in two ways: by hearing
and seeing (cf. I Timothy iv, 12).

In regard of this double charge which lies on every minister, his
hearers (or readers) must, for their part, remember in their prayers
to crave of God that their pastors may be Divinely enabled to preach
to them by lip and life. It is striking to note how often Paul required
the churches to which he wrote to *pray* for him in regard of his
ministry (see Romans xv, 30; II Cor. i, 11; Eph. vi, 19). If, then, the
chief of the apostles had need to be prayed for, how much more so
the ordinary minister of God! Great reason is there for this, for the
Devil stood at the right hand of Israel's high priest to resist him
(Zech. iii, 1). Though he opposes every Christian, yet he aims especially at the minister to cause him to fail, if not in his teaching, then
in his conduct.

"That they may see your good works": your sincerity, fidelity,
love, self-sacrifice, perseverance, zeal, etc. "And glorify your Father
which is in heaven": this is the chief though not the whole end of
good works—subordinately, they enrich ourselves and benefit our
fellows. As regards God they serve, first, as means whereby we give
evidence of our homage by obeying His commands. Second, they
serve as tokens of our gratitude for all His mercies, both spiritual
and temporal, for thankfulness is to be expressed by life as well as
lip. Third, they serve to make us followers of God. who hath bidden
us to be holy as He is holy (I Peter i, 16) and to put into practice
the duties of love to our neighbour. This must be the main aim of
the minister: to bring men to glorify God. Though the unregenerate
are quite capable of perceiving the minister's failures, it is only real
Christians who can discern his spiritual graces and the fruit thereof,
as it is they alone who will glorify the Father because of the same.
Probably the Day to come will reveal that few things have evoked
so much genuine praise to God as His people's returning thanks for
the piety, integrity, and helpfulness of His servants, who untiringly
sought their good.

CHAPTER SIX

Christ and the Law

" Think not that I am come to destroy the law, or the prophets: I am not come to destroy, but to fulfil. For verily I say unto you, Till heaven and earth pass, one jot or one tittle shall in no wise pass from the law, till all be fulfilled." (Matt. v, 17, 18.)

THE manifestation of Christ in Israel's midst was sudden and startling. The first thirty years of His life on earth had been lived in private, and outside His own immediate circle He seems to have attracted little attention. But as soon as He appeared on the stage of public action this was altered: the eyes of all were fixed upon Him and the leaders of the nation were compelled to take notice of Him. His meekness and lowliness at once distinguished Him from those who sought the praise of men. His miracles of healing soon became heralded far and wide. His call to repentance and proclamation of the Gospel (Mark i, 15) made people wonder what was the real character and design of His mission. Was He a revolutionary? Was it His purpose to overthrow the existing order of things? What was His attitude towards the Scriptures, and particularly to the Law of Moses? Did He disavow their Divine authority? These were questions agitating the minds of men, and calling for clear answers.

Christ's preaching was so entirely different from that of the Pharisees and Sadducees (which was supposed to be based on the Old Testament), that the people were inclined to imagine His intention was to subvert the authority of God's Word and substitute His own in its place. Because Christ despised " the traditions of the elders," the religious leaders supposed Him to be a deceiver, going about to destroy the very foundations of piety. Because He threw far more emphasis upon great moral principles than upon ceremonial institutions, many were ready to imagine that He repudiated the entire Levitical system. Because He was the Proclaimer of grace and the Dispenser of mercy, the "Friend of publicans and sinners," the idea became current that He was opposed to the Law. The balance of Truth had been lost, and because the Lord Jesus did not echo the prevailing theology of the day, He was regarded as a heretic. Christ had refused to identify Himself with any of the sects of His time, and because He was outside them all, people wondered what was His real attitude to the Law and the prophets.

For a long time past the view had more or less obtained that when the Messiah appeared He would introduce radical changes and

49

entirely overthrow the ancient order of religion. Therefore did Christ here assure the people that so far from being antagonistic to the Old Testament Scriptures, He had come to fulfil them. He strongly disavowed any hostile design in regard to the Word of God, and proceeded to confirm its authority. The verses we are now to ponder begin the third and longest section of the Sermon on the Mount: from verse 17 to the end of chapter v, Christ treats of the most important subject of *the moral Law,* showing its true meaning, which had been much corrupted by the Jewish teachers. First our Lord refuted the erroneous ideas which the people had formed of Him by three emphatic declarations, the force of which we shall now endeavour to bring out.

"Think not that I am come to destroy the law, or the prophets" (verse 17). The Old Testament Scriptures were comprehensively summarized under the title, "the law and the prophets" (Matt. vii, 12; Luke xvi, 16): thus the first and widest meaning of our Lord's words is, Suppose not that My mission is to repudiate the authority of Holy Writ; rather is it to establish and enforce the same. This will be the more evident when we examine the verses which immediately follow. The entire record of His ministry furnished clear proof of what He asserted on this occasion. Christ venerated the sacred Scriptures, was regulated by them in all His actions, and definitely set His imprimatur upon their Divine inspiration. No fouler calumny could be laid to His charge than to accuse Him of any antagonism to or disrespect for the Divine oracles.

We must next duly note that Christ did not here speak of "the law *and* the prophets," but "the law, *or* the prophets," a distinction we are required to weigh and understand, for it presents quite a different concept. The Law and the prophets are not here associated in such a way as to comprise a unity, or as indicating the spirit of the Law by another word. No, the two terms are here put together by the disjunctive particle "or," and therefore each of them must represent a distinct idea familiar to the Jews. Christ was here referring to the prophets not so much as the commentators upon the Law, but as those who had foreannounced His person, mission, and kingdom. His obvious design, then, was to intimate that the Old Testament in all its parts and elements—ethical or predicative—referred to Himself and was accomplished in Himself.

It is also to be observed that no further reference is made to the prophets throughout this Sermon (let those who have such a penchant for prophecy take due note!), and that from verse 18 onwards it is the Law which Christ treats of. Before proceeding farther we must next inquire, Exactly what did Christ here signify by "the law"? We answer, unhesitatingly, The whole Jewish Law, which was threefold: ceremonial, judicial, and moral. The ceremonial described rules and ordinances to be observed in the worship of God; the judicial described ordinances for the government of the Jewish commonwealth and the punishment of offenders: the former was for the Jews only; the latter primarily for them, yet concerned all people in all times so far as it tended to establish the moral Law. The moral Law is contained in the Ten Commandments.

While the entire Jewish Law was comprehended by our Lord's expression "the law," yet it is clear that He alluded principally to the moral Law, for the subsequent parts of the Sermon refer directly and mainly to it. But we must add that this term here also included the types, the law of sacrifice, and especially the sin-offering; for the question might well be asked, If there had been no real accomplishment of the sacrificial emblems, what then became of all the references in Moses to the propitiatory offerings and to the entire typical system? If Christ had not accomplished them by presenting to God the substance which they shadowed forth, then they would have been an unfulfilled prophecy or pledge, for they manifestly pointed to Him. Christ, then, came to present the reality of which they were the pledge.

" I am not come to destroy, but to fulfil " (verse 17). We must now carefully inquire what our Lord here meant by "fulfil." We understand Him to signify that so far from its being His purpose to annul the moral Law, He had come with the express design of meeting its holy demands, to offer unto God what it justly required—to magnify it by rendering to it a perfect obedience in thought and word and deed; and that so far from despising the prophets His mission was to make good their predictions concerning Himself by performing the very work they had announced He should do. In a word, we regard this statement of Christ's as a definite declaration that He had entered this world with the object of bringing in a perfect righteousness, which should be imputed to all His believing people. But this vital and glorious truth is now blankly repudiated by some who pose as being orthodox, and therefore they viciously wrest this passage.

Unwilling to admit that Christ rendered to the Law any vicarious obedience on behalf of His people, Socinians contend that the word "fulfil" in this passage simply means to "fill out" or "fill full." They imagine that in the remainder of the chapter Christ partly cancels and partly adds to the moral Law. Even Mr. Grant, in his Numerical Bible, rendered it "complete," and in his notes says, "What would the Old Testament be without the New? Very much like a finger pointing into vacuity." As quite a number of our readers have more or less come under the influence of this error, we deem it necessary to expose such a sophistry and establish the true meaning of Christ's declaration. In essaying this we cannot do better than summarize the arguments used by George Smeaton.

First, that " usage of language is opposed to such an interpretation which here adopts the rendering ' to fill out ' in preference to fulfil. No example of such a usage can be adduced when the verb is applied to a law or to an express demand contained in the spirit of the law; in which case it uniformly means ' to fulfil.' Thus it is said, 'He that loveth another hath fulfilled the law' (Romans xiii, 8). The inflexible usage of language rules the sense in such a phrase, to the effect that Christ must be understood to say that He came not to fill out or to supplement the Law by additional elements, but to *fulfil* it, by obeying it or by being made under it."

Second, "fill out" is inadmissible as applied to the second term or object of the verb: Christ did not come to fill out or expound the prophets, but simply to *fulfil* their predictions. Whenever the word here used is applied to anything prophetical, it is always found in such a connection that it can only mean "to fulfil," and hence we must not deviate from its uniform signification. Third, verse 18 must be regarded as giving a reason for the statement made in verse 17. But what sort of reason would be given if we were to render the connected verses thus: "I came to fill out or to supplement the Law, for verily I say unto you, Till heaven and earth pass, not one jot or tittle shall in any wise pass from the Law till all be *fulfilled*"?

To these arguments we would add this forcible and (to us) conclusive consideration: the term "fulfil" was here placed by Christ in direct antithesis from "destroy," which surely fixes its scope and meaning. Now to "destroy" the Law is not to empty it of meaning, but is to rescind, dissolve or abrogate it. But to "fill out" or complete the Law obviously presents no proper contrast with "destroy" or render void. "To fulfil," then, is to be taken in its prime and natural sense, as meaning to perform what they (the Law and the prophets) required, to substantiate them, to make good what they demanded and announced. Merely to rescue the Law from the corrupt glosses of the Jews and to explain its higher meaning was business which could have been done by the apostles, but to bring in an "everlasting righteousness" no mere creature was capable of doing. Law can only be "fulfilled" by perfect obedience.

If we take "fulfil" here in its widest scope, then we gladly avail ourselves of the compound definition of W. Perkins. First, Christ fulfilled the Law by His *doctrine*: both by restoring to it its proper meaning and true use, and by revealing the right way in which the Law may be fulfilled. Second, in His *person*: both by performing perfect and perpetual obedience unto its precepts, and by suffering its penalty, enduring death upon the Cross for His people. Third, *in men*: in the elect by imparting faith to their hearts, so that they lay hold of Christ who fulfilled it for them, and by giving them His own Spirit which imparts to them a love for the Law and sets them on endeavouring to obey it; in the reprobate when He executes the curse of the Law upon them.

Taking our verses as a whole, we may perceive how that though the Law and the Gospel vary in some respects very widely, yet there is a perfect consonance and agreement between them. Many now suppose that the one is the avowed enemy of the other. Not so. There is a sweet consent between the Law and Gospel, for Christ came to fulfil the former and is the substance of the latter, and therefore are we informed through His chief apostle that "by faith we *establish* the law" (Romans iii, 21), and that when Moses had given the Law unto the people of Israel he offered sacrifices and sprinkled the blood thereof upon the book and the people (Heb. ix, 19, 20)—type of the shedding of Christ's blood and which thus did notify the perfect harmony of the Law and the Gospel.

What that blessed consonance is between the Law and the Gospel no regenerate soul should have any difficulty in perceiving. Let us briefly present it thus. The Law required perfect obedience and pronounced death on the least breach thereof, and does not propose any way of fulfilling the same in our own persons. But the Gospel directs us to Christ, who, as the believer's Surety, fulfilled the Law for him, for which reason Christ is called "The end of the law for righteousness to everyone that believeth" (Romans x, 4). And through Christ it is that "the righteousness of the law might be fulfilled in us, who walk not after the flesh, but after the Spirit" (Romans viii, 4).

"For verily I say unto you, Till heaven and earth pass, one jot or one tittle shall in no wise pass from the law, till all be fulfilled" (verse 18). In these words our Lord advances a conclusive argument for clearing Himself from the false imputation that He had come to destroy the Law, as the opening "For" (following His statement in verse 17) clearly indicates. His argument is drawn from the very nature of the Law, which is immutable. Since the Law is unchangeable, it must needs be fulfilled—that its Author be vindicated and glorified; and since fallen man was incapable of rendering perfect obedience to it, it was essential that Christ Himself should perform and bring in that everlasting righteousness which God required. Christ's argument, then, may be stated thus: If the Law be inviolable and for observance eternal, then I could not have come to destroy it. Because the Law *is* immutable and eternal it necessarily follows that He came not to annul but to *accomplish it.*

"Verily I say unto you" was a form of speech employed by the Saviour when He would solemnly avouch any weighty truth, propounding it in His own name. Herein He evidences Himself to be the grand "Amen," the "faithful and true Witness," the antitypical Prophet, the Divine Teacher of His Church, to whom we must hearken in all things, for He cannot lie. In saying "till heaven and earth pass away"—the most stable of all created objects—Christ affirmed the unchangeableness of the Law, and that this might be rendered the more emphatic He made reference to the minutiae of the Hebrew alphabet, that not so much as its smallest part shall pass from the Law—the "jot" being the tiniest letter, and the "tittle" the smallest curve of a letter.

The ceremonial law has not been destroyed by Christ, but the substance now fills the place of its shadows. Nor has the judicial law been destroyed: though it has been abrogated unto us so far as it was peculiar to the Jews, yet, as it agrees with the requirements of civic justice and mercy, and as it serves to establish the precepts of the moral law, it is perpetual—herein we may see the blasphemous impiety of the popes of Rome, who in the " canons " have dared to dispense with some of the laws of consanguinity in Leviticus xviii. While the moral law remains for ever as a rule of obedience to every child of God, as we have shown so often in these pages.

Let us learn from Christ's declaration of the immutability of the Law that, first, the Scriptures are the very Word of God, and therefore a sure resting place for our hearts. A Christian is subject to many doubts of the truth of God's promises in times of trial and temptation, but this should ever be remembered: not one jot or tittle can pass till all be accomplished. Second, that no part of the inspired Scriptures, still less any whole book of it, can be lost: neither man nor devil can destroy one jot of it. Third, this immutability of the Law shall stand against them for ever. Fourth, Christ's setting His seal upon the inviolable authority of the Law intimates its perfections: every part of it is needed by us, every sentence evidences its Divine authorship, every precept calls for our loving obedience.

CHAPTER SEVEN

Christ and the Law—Continued

"Think not that I am come to destroy the law, or the prophets: I am not come to destroy, but to fulfil. For verily I say unto you, Till heaven and earth pass, one jot or one tittle shall in no wise pass from the law, till all be fulfilled. Whosoever therefore shall break one of these least commandments, and shall teach men so, he shall be called the least in the kingdom of heaven: but whosoever shall do and teach them, the same shall be called great in the kingdom of heaven. For I say unto you, That except your righteousness shall exceed the righteousness of the scribes and Pharisees, ye shall in no case enter into the kingdom of heaven." (Matt. v, 17-20.)

WE are not unmindful of the fact that the passage now before us is one which will possess little attraction for the great majority of professing Christians in our degenerate age, and possibly some of our own readers would be better pleased if we superficially summarized its teaching rather than endeavoured to give a detailed exposition of its weighty contents. Those verses which contain God's *promises* are far more acceptable in this day of self-pleasing and self-gratification than those which insist upon our obedience to the Divine *precepts*. But this ought not to be, for the one is as truly a part of God's Word as the other, and just as much needed by us. If any vindication of our present procedure be required, it is sufficient to point out that the words we are to examine are those of Christ Himself, and He ever sought the glory of God and the good of souls, caring not for either the praise or the criticism of His hearers.

Healthy Christianity can only be maintained where the balance is properly preserved between a faithful exposition of the holy Law of God and a pressing of its claims upon the conscience, and by tenderly preaching the Gospel and applying its balm to stricken hearts. Where the former predominates to the virtual exclusion of the latter, self-righteous pharisaism is fostered; and where the proclamation of the Gospel ousts the requirements of the Law, antinomian licentiousness is engendered. During the past hundred years Christendom has probably heard fifty Gospel sermons or addresses to one on the Law, and the consequence has indeed been disastrous and deplorable: a light and backboneless religion, with loose and careless walking. Therefore when a servant of God is expounding, consecutively, any portion of the Scriptures, and in the course thereof arrives at a passage upon the Law, it is now (more than ever before) his bounden duty to tarry there and press its claims upon his hearers or readers.

Such a verse as the one which is to be particularly before us ought indeed to search all our hearts, especially those of us who have been called by the Lord to His service. Taken at its surface meaning Matthew v, 19, emphasizes the deep importance of obedience to the Divine commandment, and most solemnly warns against disobedience. Yet it is at this very point that modern Christendom errs most grievously, and the pulpit is chiefly to be blamed for this sad state of affairs. Not only do many who pose as ministers of Christ themselves break the commandments, but they publicly teach their hearers to do the same; and this not with regard to the "least" of the Divine precepts, but in connection with the most fundamental of God's laws. Should these lines catch the eyes of any such men, we trust that it may please the Lord to use the same in convicting them of the enormity of their sin.

Our Lord was on the point of correcting various corruptions of the Law which obtained among the Jews of His day, and He prefaced what He had to say by cautioning them not to misconstrue His design, as though He were opposing either Moses or the prophets, neither of whose writings were at any variance with the kingdom He had come to establish. So far from setting Himself against Moses, He, with the most solemn asseveration, declared the Law to be of perpetual obligation (verse 18), and such was His regard for it that if anyone posing as a minister in His kingdom should break the least of the Law's precepts and teach others to make light of it, he should be as little in the eyes of the Lord as the precept was in his eyes (verse 19); while those practising and inculcating the Law should have His highest approval.

Our passage begins at v, 17, in which our Lord made known in no uncertain terms *His* attitude toward the Divine Law. False conceptions had been formed as to the real design of His mission, and those who were unfriendly toward Him sought to make the people believe that the Lord Jesus was a revolutionary, whose object was to overthrow the very foundations of Judaism. Therefore in His first formal public address Christ promptly gave the lie to these wicked aspersions and declared His complete accord with the Divine revelation at Sinai. Not only was there no antagonism between Himself and Moses, but He had come to earth with the express purpose of accomplishing all that had been demanded in the name of God. So far was it from being His design to repudiate the holy Law, He had become incarnate in order to work out that very righteousness it required, to make good what the Levitical institutions had foreshadowed, and to bring to pass the Messianic predictions of Israel's seers.

"Think not that I am come to destroy the law, or the prophets: I am not come to destroy, but to fulfil" (Matt. v, 17). Well did Beza say upon this verse, "Christ came not to bring any new way of righteousness and salvation into the world, but to fulfil that in deed which was shadowed by the figures of the Law: by delivering men through grace from the curse of the Law; and moreover to teach the true use of obedience which the Law appointed, and to grave in our hearts the force of obedience." On the dominant word "fulfil," Matthew Henry pertinently pointed out, "The Gospel is 'The time of reformation' (Heb. ix, 10)—not the repeal of the Law, but the amendment of it [i.e. from its pharisaical corruptions, A.W.P.] and, consequently, *its re-establishment*."

"For verily I say unto you, Till heaven and earth pass, one jot or one tittle shall in no wise pass from the law, till all be fulfilled" (verse 18). In these words our Lord affirmed the perpetuity of the Law, insisting that it should never be abrogated. The grass withereth and the flower fadeth, but the Word of God endureth for ever: the Old Testament as much as the New, the Law as truly as the Gospel. The "verily I say unto you" was the solemn asseveration of the Amen, the faithful and true Witness. Everything in the Law must be fulfilled: not only its prefigurations and prophecies, but its precepts and penalty: fulfilled, first, personally and vicariously, by and upon the Surety; fulfilled, second and evangelically, in and by His people; and fulfilled, third, in the doom of the wicked, who shall experience its awful curse for ever and ever. Instead of Christ's being opposed to the Law of God, He came here to magnify it and render it honourable (Isaiah xlii, 21); and rather than His teachings being subversive thereof, they confirmed and enforced it.

"Whosoever therefore shall break one of these least commandments, and shall teach men so, he shall be called the least in the kingdom of heaven; but whosoever shall do and teach them, the same shall be called great in the kingdom of heaven" (verse 19). This afforded proof of what Christ had declared in verses 17 and 18, for the language He here employed manifestly implies the perpetual and inflexible obligation of the Law throughout the entire course of the kingdom of heaven—this Christian era. Not only so, but the words of Christ in this verse make unmistakably clear the inestimable value which He placed upon the Divine commandments, and which esteem He would strictly require and exact from all who taught in His name: His disapproval falling on the one who slighted the least of the Law's requirements, and His approval resting on each who by his example and teaching honoured the same.

"Whosoever *therefore* shall break one of these least commandments," namely the "jot and tittle" of the previous verse—the smallest part of the Law. Weigh carefully the word we have placed in italics: it denotes two things. First, Christ is here illustrating or exemplifying what He had so expressly affirmed in the previous verses and insists that instead of encouraging His followers to disregard the Divine Law He upheld its claims in the most certain manner, for the King Himself would frown upon any of His officers who dared to disesteem its smallest requirements. Second, Christ drew an obvious conclusion from what He had laid down in the foregoing. If the Master Himself came not to destroy the Law but rather to fulfil it, then it manifestly followed that His servants too must keep the commandments and teach others to do the same. It is in this way the ministers of Christ are to be identified: by their following the example which He has left them.

Let us take notice of how what immediately follows the "therefore" clinches the interpretation we gave of the "destroy" and the disputed but simple "fulfil" of verse 17. To "destroy" the Prophets would be to deny their validity, to repudiate their inspiration, to annul their authority, so that they would then possess no binding power on the people of God. In like manner, to "destroy" the Law is not simply to break it by transgression, but also to abolish it: it is such a destruction as would rob it of all virtue and power so that it would be no law at all. This is why the Lord added, "break one of these commandments and *teach* men so." The order is significantly the same in both verses: "destroy . . . fulfil" (verse 17), "break . . . do and teach them" (verse 19).

Let us further observe how the contents of this verse establish the definition we gave of "the law" in the preceding verses—a matter on which there has been some difference of opinion among the commentators. We pointed out that, while it is clear from the later parts of the Sermon that Christ alluded principally to the moral law, yet in view of the circumstances under which this Discourse was delivered and in view of Christ's allusion to the "jot and tittle" of the Law, the ceremonial and judicial aspects of it must not be excluded. Throughout this passage "the law" is to be understood in its widest latitude, as embracing the Mosaic Law. This is clear from our Lord's reference to "one of these *least* commandments," for surely we cannot think of the Ten Commandments in such a connection; for they one and all belong to the fundamental statutes of the kingdom

Should anyone demur at what has just been said and insist that "the law" is to be understood as here referring to the Ten Commandments only, we shall not quarrel with him. It may indeed be pointed out, inasmuch as the Divine Decalogue is a unit, and therefore all of its commands possess equal authority, that no part of it can be of slight obligation; yet some parts of it respect matters of, relatively, more importance than do others. Transgressions of the first table are far more heinous than those against the second: to take the Lord's name in vain is much more sinful than stealing from a fellow creature. So too there are degrees of criminality in offences against the precepts of the second table: to murder is a graver crime than to bear false witness against my neighbour. Thus, while none of the Ten Words is trivial, some respect more momentous objects than the others. Nevertheless, let not the solemn fact be forgotten that "whosoever shall keep the whole law, and yet offend in *one* point, he is guilty of *all*" (James ii, 10).

Ere passing on it should be pointed out that the verse now before us also definitely confirms our explanation of the "ye" in verses

13-16—a point which is disputed by many of our moderns. When treating of that passage we called attention to our Lord's change of the pronoun in His second division of the Sermon. In verses 3 to 10 the Saviour throughout used "theirs" and "they," but in verses 11 to 16 He employed "ye" and "you." We insisted that this second section has exclusive reference to Christ's official servants—the New Testament successors of the "prophets" (verse 12), for they are, ministerially, the salt of the earth and the light of the world. That Christ continued to have in mind the same class, and was addressing Himself not to the rank and file of His people, but to His official servants, is clear from His "Whosoever shall do and *teach* them."

"Whosoever therefore shall break one of these least command- ments, and shall teach men so, he shall be called the least in the kingdom of heaven." The "kingdom of heaven" here, as in the great majority of places, has reference to the sphere of profession. It is wider than the Church which is Christ's body, for none but the elect of God are members of *that*. The "kingdom of heaven" takes in all who claim to own the sceptre of Christ, and therefore it includes the false as well as the real, as is clear from our Lord's parables: the tares growing in the same field as the wheat, the bad fish being enclosed in the net with the good; though at the end there shall be a severance of one from the other. This at once removes any difficulty which may be felt over a minister who teaches others to break God's commands having any place at all therein. This kingdom was announced by Christ's forerunner (iii, 2), and since that time has been preached (xi, 12).

Two different explanations have been given by the commentators as to the meaning of "he shall be called the least in the kingdom of heaven." First, that one is called "the least" because he is not deemed worthy to have any part at all or any real inheritance in the kingdom of Christ and of God: this is negatived by the Lord's own words. Second, and strange to say the one adopted by the best writers: this person shall be held in such low esteem by his fellow citizens as to be called *by them* the least in the kingdom. But we see nothing in our verse which indicates that the reference is to the judgment of men. Personally, we believe something far more solemn than *that* is in view: the evil minister shall be judged "the least" by the King Himself. Does not our verse look back to, "The ancient and the honourable, he is the head; and the prophet that teacheth lies, he is *the tail*" (Isaiah ix, 15)? It was Christ's con- demnation of the unfaithful servant.

Not only does our present verse solemnly condemn Dispensation- alists (who repudiate one of the greatest of all God's commands: the Sabbatic-statute), but it announces the disapproval of Christ upon another class of errorists. Not a few Calvinists have pitted the Gospel against the Law, and instead of showing the one as the handmaid of the other, have represented them as being irreconcilable enemies. These men have disgraced Divine grace, for they fail to show that grace works through righteousness, and have taken from the Christian his rule of life. Their conception of what Christian liberty consists of is altogether wrong, denying that the believer is under Divine bonds to walk in obedience to the Decalogue. Failing to see that Romans vi, 14, has reference to our justification and not our sanctification, they repudiate the moral law, teaching that in no sense are we under its authority. But though such men be held in high esteem by many of the churches, they are the very "least" in the sight of Christ, and must yet answer to Him for engaging in the very practice which He here denounces.

Antinomianism (the repudiation of the moral law as the Christian's rule of life) is as reprehensible and dangerous as papal indulgences. If on the one hand we need to guard against legality (seeking to keep the Law in order to merit something good at the hands of God), on the other hand there is just as real a danger of dwelling so exclusively on the grace of the Gospel that we lose sight of the holy living required. "Let us then beware equally of antinomian licentiousness and of pharisaical self-righteousness; these are Scyalla and Charybdis, the fatal rock and whirlpool: most men in shunning the one fall into the other, and we need the Lord the Spirit to pilot us between them. But the clear and full exposition of the holy Law of God, and the scriptural application of it to the heart and conscience, forms one most important preservative from these fatal extremes" (T. Scott).

"But whosoever shall do and teach them, the same shall be called great in the kingdom of heaven." Note well the order here: "do and teach." As Paul exhorted his son in the faith, "Take heed unto thyself, and unto the doctrine" (I Tim. iv, 16): Christ requires integrity of life and soundness of doctrine from His servants. The Lord is both mocked and grievously insulted by ministers who practise one thing and preach another: far better to quit preaching entirely if our lives be opposed to our sermons. Furthermore, there will be *no power* in the preaching of the man whose own walk clashes with his talk: his words will carry no conviction to the hearts of his hearers—as one quaintly but solemnly said to his minister, "I cannot hear what you say, from seeing what you do." Finally, a minister cannot with any clearness of conscience and joy of heart teach others their duty, unless he first be a practiser of what he preaches.

CHAPTER EIGHT

Christ and the Law—Concluded

"FOR I say unto you, That except your righteousness shall exceed the righteousness of the scribes and Pharisees, ye shall in no case enter into the kingdom of heaven" (verse 20). We purpose to expound this verse by supplying answers to the following questions. First, who or what were the scribes and Pharisees? Second, what was the character of their righteousness? Third, what is the nature of that superior righteousness which Christ requires from His subjects? Fourth, how is it obtained? Fifth, how is it manifested? Sixth, wherein does it exceed the righteousness of the scribes and Pharisees? Seventh, what is signified by "ye shall in no wise enter into the kingdom of heaven? Eighth, what is the relation of verse 20 to the context?

Before seeking an answer to the above questions, let us point out what a startling effect this statement of Christ's must have produced upon His hearers. The scribes were the most renowned teachers of the Law, and the Pharisees had the reputation of being the most exemplary models of Judaism; and for our Lord to have solemnly affirmed that such righteousness as *they* possessed was altogether inadequate for entitling them to an entrance into the kingdom which He had come to set up must have seemed a most radical and startling declaration. The Pharisees were looked up to as those who had attained to the very pinnacle of personal piety, and the common people supposed that such heights of spirituality were quite beyond their reach. Men in general imagined that they could not be expected to equal *their* attainments. It was a proverb among the Jews that "If but two men were to enter heaven, the one would be a scribe and the other a Pharisee."

First, who were the scribes and Pharisees? The word "scribe" is a name of *office*, whereof there were two sorts among the Jews: civil and ecclesiastical. The former were public notaries, registering the affairs of state: such a one was Shimshai (Ezra iv, 8). The latter were employed in expounding the Scriptures: such a one was Ezra (vii, 1, 5, 6). It was to the latter Christ referred in this Gospel: see xiii, 52; xxiii, 2—interpreters of the Law of Moses. They were of the tribe of Levi. The name "Pharisee" betokens a *sect*, and not an office. They differed from the scribes inasmuch as they formed a code of morals and of ceremonial acts more rigid than the Law of Moses enjoined, basing it on the traditions of the fathers: and were held in highest esteem among the Jews: see Acts xxiii, 6;

61

xxvi, 5. The scribes, then, were the doctors of the Law; the Pharisees professing the purest practice of it.

Second, what was the character of their righteousness, and wherein lay its defectiveness? First, the righteousness of the scribes and Pharisees was an *external* one only, consisting of certain outward observances of the Law. They were strict in abstaining from such gross sins as adultery, theft, murder and idolatry; but they made no conscience of impure thoughts, covetousness, hatred, and coldness of heart toward God; and therefore did Christ say unto them, "Woe unto you, scribes and Pharisees, hypocrites! for ye make clean the outside of the cup and of the platter, but within they are full of extortion and excess," etc. (Matt. xxiii, 25, 27, 28). Second, their observance of God's Law was a *partial* one: they laid far more stress upon its ceremonial precepts than upon its moral requirements; and therefore did Christ say unto them, "Ye pay tithe of mint and anise and cummin, and have omitted the weightier matters of the law, judgment, mercy, and faith" (Matt. xxiii, 23). Third, their actions proceeded from unsound principles: *self-interest*, rather than the glory of God, was their ruling motive. They were forward in fasting, praying at street corners, and giving alms ostentatiously; but it was all done to enhance their reputation among men (Matt. xxiii, 5-7).

Righteousness of soul, purity of heart, the scribes and Pharisees had no regard for. In their religion we have an exemplification of what is the natural persuasion of men the world over, namely, that a religion of external performances will suffice to ensure a blissful eternity. True, there are many who would deny this in words, but in works they substantiate it. They bring their bodies to the house of prayer, but not their souls; they worship with their mouths, but not "in spirit and in truth." They are sticklers for immersion or early morning communion, yet take no thought of keeping their hearts with all diligence (Prov. iv, 23). Multitudes of professing Christians abstain from external acts of violence, yet hesitate not to rob their neighbours of a good name by spreading evil reports against them. Thousands who would not dare to rob openly, yet misrepresent their goods and cheat their customers; which shows they have more fear of breaking man's laws than they have of breaking those of God.

Third, what is the nature of that righteousness which Christ requires from His subjects? There are three kinds of righteousness spoken of in the Scriptures. First, *inherent*, which Adam had when he left the hands of his Maker (Eccles. vii, 29), which none possess by nature today. Second, *imputed* righteousness (Romans iv, 6), which is the whole of our justification before God. Third, *imparted* righteousness (Eph. iv, 24), when God the Spirit makes us new creatures. Most of the older writers concluded that it was the second of these which Christ referred to here in Matthew v, 20, but we are satisfied that this was a mistake. It is true that the sinner's title for heaven can consist only of the perfect righteousness of

Christ being imputed to him upon his believing, yet there must be an experimental meetness for the inheritance of the saints in light as well as a legal right, and this we obtain through our regeneration and sanctification.

We fully agree with Mr. J. C. Philpot when he pointed out on Matthew v, 20, "Christ did not mean an external righteousness wrought out by His obedience to the Law *for* them, but an internal righteousness wrought out by the Holy Spirit *in* them. Thus, we read of the inward as well as the outward apparel of the Church: 'The King's daughter is all glorious *within;* her *clothing* is of wrought gold' (Psalm xlv, 13). Two kinds of righteousness belong to the queen: her imputed righteousness is her outward robe, the 'clothing of wrought gold'; but imparted righteousness is her inward adorning, which makes her 'all glorious within.' This inward glory is the new man in the heart, with all his gifts and graces." This must be so if the Church is conformed to her head, for He was "without spot" externally, and "without blemish" internally.

As this is a point which is much disputed, we must labour it a little further. That righteousness which will bring men to heaven is not a bare imputed one, but an imputed righteousness which is accompanied by an imparted one. Justification and sanctification must never be severed: wherever the former be pronounced, the other (in its fundamental aspect) has already been bestowed. The one concerns our standing before God, the other respects our state in ourselves. Romans viii is just as vital and blessed a part of the Gospel as is Romans v, and it is to the irreparable loss of the saint if the one be emphasized to the virtual exclusion of the other. Surely righteousness alone secures for us a standing before God, but evangelical righteousness is the certain proof thereof, and as the tree is known by its fruits so imputed righteousness can be recognized in no other way than by inward righteousness with its effects in the life.

To this writer the simplest and most conclusive way of ascertaining the nature of the righteousness which Christ requires from all who shall have part in His everlasting kingdom is to observe that it is placed in direct antithesis from the righteousness of the scribes and Pharisees. Now as we have pointed out, the defects of the latter lay chiefly in three things. First, their righteousness was wholly an external one, but God requires Truth in the *inward* parts: "Man looketh on the outward appearance, but the Lord looketh on the heart" (I Samuel xvi, 7). Second, their righteousness was partial, stressing certain parts of the Law which suited their tastes, while utterly ignoring or nullifying other vital features thereof. The righteousness which God requires is a universal obedience: a living by *every* word that proceeds out of His mouth. Third, their righteousness issued from a foul spring: instead of keeping the Law from a desire to please and glorify its Giver, their observance of it was only in order to promote their reputation among men.

This superior righteousness, then, consists of an obedience to the Divine Law which would be acceptable to a holy but gracious God. Such an obedience must necessarily spring from the fear of God and love to God: that is, from a genuine reverence for His authority, and from a true desire to please Him. It must comprise a strict conformity to the revealed will of God, without any self-invented and self-imposed additions thereto. It must give particular attention to the "weightier matters of the law," namely justice, mercy and faith. It must be a sincere and not a feigned obedience, a filial and not a slavish one, a disinterested and not a selfish one. It must be a symmetrical or complete one, having respect to all God's commandments. Such an obedience will not puff up or encourage self-righteousness, but will cause the one who sincerely aims thereat to walk softly before the Lord, and will produce humility and denying of self.

Fourth, how is this superior righteousness obtained? Not by the strivings of a fallen creature, but by the effectual working of Divine grace. Such an obedience as we have delineated above can only proceed from a heart that is reconciled to God, because "the carnal mind is enmity against God: for it is not subject to the law of God, neither indeed can be" (Romans viii, 7). Now as II Corinthians v, 17, 18, so plainly teaches us. God's reconciling us to Himself by Jesus Christ is the immediate outcome of our being made new creatures in Christ. *Initially* we become partakers of this righteousness at the new birth, when a holy nature is communicated by the Spirit, so that there is now a principle within us which "delights in the law of God" (Romans vii, 22) and causes us to "serve" it (Romans vii, 25). *Progressively*, this inward righteousness is developed as we "grow in grace and in the knowledge of our Lord and Saviour Jesus Christ," which is through our using the appointed means and by learning to draw our strength from the Lord. *Perfectly*, this inward righteousness will only be consummated at our glorification, when we shall be filled with all the fullness of God.

Fifth, how is this evangelical righteousness manifested? Inasmuch as this inward righteousness consists of and proceeds from a new creation to holiness it is known by the fruits it produces. A radical change is affected in the temper and life of its possessor, so that he now loathes and shuns what he formerly delighted in, and loves and seeks after the things he once disliked. It is evidenced by a real hatred of sin and an unfeigned love of God. It is known by the felt antagonism between the two natures in the believer. His indwelling corruptions continually war against this principle of righteousness, so that often he is prevented from doing the good which he desires and strives to perform. This conflict with the flesh humbles the Christian, causes him to mourn over his sad failures, and to confess he is but an unprofitable servant. Nevertheless, he continues in his efforts to mortify the old man and vivify the new. Another proof of indwelling righteousness is that its possessor has an ever-deepening appreciation of the forbearance of God and an increasing valuation of the precious blood of Christ.

Sixth, wherein does this righteousness "exceed" the righteousness of the scribes and Pharisees? The superiority of the Christian's righteousness has already been shown in some detail, but one or two other things may be pointed out in connection therewith. The Christian's righteousness springs out of love and faith, whereas theirs issued from an evil heart of unbelief. The Christian's righteousness is the result of his being made a partaker of the Divine nature (II Peter i, 4), whereas theirs was altogether human. The defects of the Christian's righteousness are covered by the infinite merits of Christ, whereas theirs has nothing to commend them unto God. Evangelical righteousness—according to the terms of the new covenant—is approved by God, but legal righteousness found no provision in the Sinaitic compact for its acceptance by the Most High. The righteousness of the Christian secures an entrance into heaven, but that of the scribes and Pharisees will exclude them therefrom.

Seventh, what is signified by "Ye shall in no case enter the kingdom of heaven," which is the Lord's verdict upon those who possess not this righteousness? In our comments upon verse 19 we pointed out that this expression, "the kingdom of heaven," is wider than the Church which is Christ's body, covering the whole sphere of profession—Christendom; thus including the counterfeit as well as the genuine. But we were careful to qualify that definition by saying this was its meaning in the "great majority of cases." There are one or two notable exceptions: as for example, "Verily I say unto you, Except ye be converted, and become as little children, ye shall not enter into the kingdom of heaven" (xviii, 3), where the kingdom of heaven must refer to the kingdom of glory. Such too is the case in our present verse: Christ was speaking of *real* righteousness, and that alone will secure entrance into heaven.

Eighth, what is the relation of our verse to its context? Let us recall that in the whole of this passage our Lord was engaged in refuting the erroneous conception which had been formed of His mission. His detachment from the religious leaders of His day, His disregard of the "traditions of the elders," and His proclamation of *grace* in the synagogue at Nazareth (Luke iv, 16-22), had inclined many to regard Him as the opponent of Moses. True, He had come to bring in something new, something vastly superior to that which then obtained in Israel, nevertheless there was no real conflict between Christianity and Judaism: though differing much in incidentals, there is really perfect accord in fundamentals. Alas, that the spiritual unity of the two economies is now so little perceived, yea, is emphatically denied by most of the much-advertised "Bible teachers" of our day.

First, Christ plainly and emphatically declared He had not come to destroy the Law or the prophets, but to "fulfil" them (verse 17):

in what ways He was to "fulfil" them we have endeavoured to show. Second, He solemnly affirmed the perpetuity and immutability of the Law (verse 18), asserting that not the smallest part thereof could pass away till all was fulfilled. Third, He insisted that His own servants must maintain the integrity of the Law, both by practice and by preaching (verse 19), otherwise they would not receive His approval. Fourth, so far was He from being antagonistic to Moses, He demanded of His subjects a righteousness which surpassed that of the scribes and Pharisees. Hereafter there was not the slightest occasion for any of His hearers to have any doubt of Christ's attitude toward the Law of God.

It is most important that we perceive clearly our Lord's *design* in verse 20. It was not there His purpose to state the terms on which men might obtain the Divine favour, rather was He describing the character of those who already possessed the same. No doubt many of the multitude which had there flocked around Him supposed—such is poor human nature—that by attaching themselves to His cause they would obtain greater latitude to indulge their lusts: it must therefore have been a real shock for them to learn that the morality and spirituality which was to distinguish the genuine citizens of His kingdom would be of a far more exalted character than that taught by the scribes and exemplified by the Pharisees: He would not regard anyone as His subject unless *his* righteousness exceeded *theirs*. Thus, the nature and demand of His kingdom was proof positive that He honoured and maintained the Law.

With regard to the relation of our passage to its yet wider context, we may note how that one of the principal designs of Christ throughout this Sermon was to awaken His hearers to feel their deep need of that which alone could satisfy the requirements of a holy God. It was ignorance of the Law which permitted pharisaism to flourish, for they claimed to fulfil it in the outward letter, and consequently Christ here aimed to arouse conscience by enforcing its true import and requirements. It will be found that this Sermon returns again and again to one main idea: that of awakening men to a sense of their wretchedness, and shutting them up to the righteousness of God. That object could only be obtained by a spiritual application of the Law and by enforcing its inviolable exactions: thereby alone could they be prepared to appreciate and embrace the Gospel.

CHAPTER NINE

The Law and Murder

" Ye have heard that it was said by them of old time, Thou shalt not kill ; and whosoever shall kill shall be in danger of the judgment : But I say unto you, That whosoever is angry with his brother without a cause shall be in danger of the judgment : and whosoever shall say to his brother, Raca, shall be in danger of the council : but whosoever shall say, Thou fool, shall be in danger of hell fire. Therefore if thou bring thy gift to the altar, and there rememberest that thy brother hath aught against thee ; Leave there thy gift before the altar, and go thy way ; first be reconciled to thy brother, and then come and offer thy gift. Agree with thine adversary quickly, while thou art in the way with him ; lest at any time the adversary deliver thee to the judge, and the judge deliver thee to the officer, and thou be cast into prison. Verily I say unto thee, Thou shalt by no means come out thence, till thou hast paid the uttermost farthing." (Matt. v, 21-26.)

THE discourse which our Lord delivered on this occasion entirely corresponds with the new era which it marked in the history of God's dispensations. The revelation from Sinai, though grafted on a covenant of grace (i.e. the Abrahamic: Galatians iii, 19—" added "), and uttered by God as the Redeemer of Israel, was emphatically a promulgation of law. Its direct and formal object was to raise aloft the claims of the Divine righteousness, and meet, with repressive and determined energy, the corrupt tendencies of human nature. The Sermon on the Mount, on the other hand, begins with blessing. It opens with a whole series of beatitudes, blessing after blessing pouring itself forth as from a full spring of beneficence, and seeking, with its varied and copious manifestations of goodness, to leave nothing unprovided for in the deep wants and longing desires of men. Yet here also, as in other things, the difference between the New and the Old Testament is relative only, not absolute. There are the same fundamental elements in both, but these differently adjusted, so as fitly to adapt themselves to the ends they had to serve, and the times to which they respectively belonged.

" In the revelation of law there was a *substratum* of grace, recognized in the words which prefaced the ten commandments, and *promises* of grace in blessing also intermingled with the stern prohibitions and injunctions of which they consist. And so, inversely, in the Sermon on the Mount, while it gives grace the priority and the prominence, it is far from excluding the severer aspect of God's character and government. No sooner, indeed, had grace poured itself forth in a succession of beatitudes, than there appear the stern demands of righteousness and law—the very same law proclaimed from Sinai—and that law so explained and enforced as to bring

67

fully under its sway the intents of the heart, as well as the actions of the life, and by men's relation to it determining their place and destinies in the Messiah's kingdom " (P. Fairbairn).

It is with these " stern demands of righteousness " that we are now to be engaged. The transition point is found in verse 17, though in the verses preceding our Lord had intimated the trend of what was to follow, by likening the ministry of His servants to the nature and action of " salt." Verses 17-20 contain the preface of all that follows to the end of chapter v. In affirming that He had come to " fulfil " the Law, Christ signified, first, that it was His mission as the faithful Witness of God and the Teacher of His Church to expound the Law in its purity and spirituality, and to rescue it from the corruptions of the false teachers of that day. Second, to exemplify its righteousness in His own conduct by rendering to it a personal, perfect, and perpetual obedience, in thought and word and deed. Third, to endure its curse in His people's stead.

To understand a discourse, nothing is of greater importance than a clear grasp of its object and design. If this be not definitely understood, then the plainest statements may appear obscure, the most conclusive arguments unsatisfactory, and the most pertinent illustrations irrelevant. A great deal of the obscurity which, in most men's minds, rests on many passages of the Scriptures is to be accounted for on this principle. They do not distinctly perceive, or they altogether misapprehend, the *purpose* of the inspired writer, consequently they fail to understand his arguments and true meaning. Considerable misapprehension has obtained in reference to those sections of our Lord's Sermon which we are about to consider, in consequence of mistakes as to their *object* or design. Yet there is no excuse for this: by carefully weighing verses 17-20 the scope of what follows is obvious.

The words of Christ in verse 17 make it plain that He had not come here to antagonize or annul the Law of God, as they equally exclude the idea that it was His design to replace it with a new law. Is it not strange, then, to find Mr. Darby (in his " Synopsis "), after giving an outline of the contents of the Sermon, subjoining a footnote to verses 17-48 in which he says, " In these the exigencies of the law and what Christ required are *contrasted*," which would be to pit the Son against the Father! In verse 20 the Lord Jesus enunciated a general principle, and from verse 21 onwards He was engaged in illustration, by varied examples, how and wherein the righteousness of those whom He would own as subjects of His kingdom exceeded the righteousness of the scribes and Pharisees.

It should be self-evident that the distinctions which Christ proceeded to draw between what had been said by the ancients on certain points of moral and religious duty, and that which He Himself solemnly affirmed, must have respect, not to the *real* and actual teaching of the Law and the prophets, but rather to the erroneous conclusions which had been drawn therefrom, and to the false notions founded thereon, which were currently entertained at His advent. It were blasphemy to imagine that Christ was so inconsistent as to contradict Himself on this occasion. After so definitely asserting His entire accord with the Law and the prophets and His own dependence upon them, we cannot believe for a moment that He would immediately afterwards set Himself in opposition to them. This must be settled at the outset if we are to have hearts prepared to weigh what follows.

"The scribes and Pharisees of that age had completely inverted the order of things. Their carnality and self-righteousness had led them to exalt the precepts respecting ceremonial observances to the highest place, and to throw the duties inculcated in the ten commandments comparatively into the background, thus treating the mere appendages of the covenant as of more account than its very ground and basis" (P. Fairbairn). Therefore it was that when He proceeded to expose the inadequacy and hollowness of "the righteousness of the scribes and Pharisees," our Lord made His appeal to the testimony engraved on the two tables, and most commonly, though not exclusively, to the precepts of the second table, because He had to do more especially with hypocrites, whose defects might most readily be revealed by a reference to the duties of the *second* table (cf. Matt. xix, 16; Luke x, 25 and xviii, 18).

The first commandment brought forward by Christ on this occasion was the sixth of the Decalogue: "Thou shalt not kill." All that the Pharisees understood by this was a prohibition of the act of murder; but our Lord insisted that the commandment in its true import prohibited not only the overt act but every evil working of the heart and mind which led to it, such as unjust anger, with contempt and provoking language. Such an interpretation should not stand in need of any argument. The spiritual mind would rightly reason from such a law: if He who desireth truth in the inward parts (Psalm li) condemns murder, then it is evident we must abstain from all that might lead to that culmination of wickedness; and so it would be discovered that "Thou shalt not kill" really signifies "Thou shalt not hate."

"Ye have heard that it was said by them of old time, Thou shalt not kill; and whosoever shall kill shall be in danger of the judgment" (Matt. v, 21). To what, or rather to whom, did our Lord refer in His "them of old time"? Certainly not to Moses, nor to His Father, as the plural "them" unequivocally shows. Then to whom? In answering this question, let us also show wherein lay the special need for Christ here to expound and enforce the Law. Unfortunately for the nation, there was ample opportunity for the scribes and Pharisees to corrupt God's Law, for the rank and file of the people were unable to read the Scriptures in their original tongue. When the Jews returned from the Babylonian captivity they had largely forgotten their own language, and therefore could not read the Hebrew text.

Obviously, it was the duty of the learned to supply the people with a plain and simple translation of God's Word into the Chaldee or Aramaic. But the proud and selfish rabbis were concerned not with the glory of God and the good of the people, but with the exaltation of their own order. Therefore, instead of preparing a translation which could be read by the masses at large, they were accustomed, in the synagogues, to read off a loose rendering of the sacred text (alleged to be simpler than the original), intermingled with their own explanatory remarks. It was this ancient paraphrase of the Law with the comments of the rabbis that the scribes and Pharisees reiterated, and to which our Lord alluded when He here mentioned "them of old time."

God's commandment, "Thou shalt not kill," was capable of expansion into the widest spiritual meaning, prohibiting all hatred against our fellows. But the scribes and Pharisees restricted it to the bare act of murder as an external crime, as is quite clear from the next verse, where it is referred to as a crime for the consideration of the judicial courts of earth. Thus they were guilty of restricting the scope of God's command, and by connecting it with earthly courts both suggested to their hearers that only external deeds are sinful, and also removed the very wholesome fear of the judgment to come, when God shall lay bare not only the actual deeds of men, but even their innermost thoughts, and account the murderer in desire and intention equally guilty with the actual slayer of his fellow.

Ere passing on, let us make three remarks. First, how strangely has history repeated itself! If the religious leaders of Israel refused to make a plain translation of the Hebrew Scriptures into the speech used by the people upon their exodus from the Babylonish captivity, keeping them in ignorance of the pure Word of God, determining to retain matters in their own hands and exalting their own order; so the papacy (after the desolating persecution of the early Church by the Roman emperors) refused to make an accurate translation of the Scriptures (clinging instead to the faulty rendition of the Vulgate version), corrupting her dupes by the additions, restrictions, and alterations she made to Divine revelation; her present-day prelates and priests reiterating what was said by their predecessors "in old time."

Second, how worthless is antiquity as such! As there is a class of people who make a fetish of what is modern and despise anything of the past, so there is a certain type of mind which is strongly attracted by the antique and which venerates hoary traditions. But antiquity is no infallible mark of true doctrine, for this exposition of the sixth commandment had obtained among the Jews for centuries past, yet Christ, the great Doctor of the Church, rejected it as false, and therefore the argument which the papists use for the establishment of some of their dogmas and practices drawn from antiquity is of no effect. Equally worthless are the appeals of Protestants to the Reformers and the Puritans unless they can show that their teachings rested upon a clear "Thus saith the Lord."

Third, how thankful we should be that we have the pure Word of God reliably translated into our mother tongue! To the multitudes of His day Christ said, "Ye have *heard* that it was said by *them* of old time"; but to us He can exclaim, "Ye may *read* what God hath said." This is a wondrous and inestimable privilege—purchased by the blood-shedding of many of our forefathers—that the Holy Scriptures are no longer confined to the learned and the abbot of the monastery. They are accessible to the unlearned and the poor, everywhere, in simple English. But such a privilege carries with it, my reader, a solemn responsibility. What use are we making of this precious treasure? Do we search it daily, as did the noble Bereans (Acts xvii, 11)? Are we nourishing our souls thereby? Is our conduct governed by its teaching? If not, double guilt lies at *our* door.

"But I say unto you, That whosover is angry with his brother without cause, shall be in danger of the judgment; and whosoever shall say to his brother, Raca, shall be in danger of the council: but whosoever shall say, Thou fool, shall be in danger of hell fire" (verse 22). This is far from being the easiest verse of Matthew v to interpret, and the commentators vary in their explanations of its details; yet its general meaning is plain enough. With His royally authoritative "I say unto you," the Lord Jesus at once swept aside the rubbish of the rabbis and placed the Law of God before His hearers in all its majesty and holiness, propounding the true interpretation of the sixth commandment. No matter what you may have heard the scribes and Pharisees teach—whether from themselves or from the ancients—it was but the bluntings of the sharp edge of God's precept. I, the incarnate Son of God, who seekest only the glory of the Father and the good of souls, declare unto you that there are three degrees of hatred, falling short of the actual deed of murder, which expose a man to the judgment of God as a violator of the sixth commandment.

First, "Whosoever is angry against his brother without cause"; "brother" would be one Jew against another; for us, against a fellow Christian; but in its widest scope, against a fellow man, for by creation all are brethren. It is not anger simply which Christ here reprehends, but unwarrantable and immoderate anger. There is a holy anger, as appears from the example of Christ (Mark iii, 5) and the apostolic precept, "Be ye angry and sin not" (Eph. iv, 26). It may be asked, How are we to distinguish godly anger from that which is unlawful? The former proceeds from love or righteousness, has in view the good of him against whom it is exercised, and looks to the glory of God, whereas unholy anger issues from pride and desires the injury of the one against whom it is directed. Anger is lawful only when it burns against sin, and this is equivalent to zeal for the Divine honour.

In His first singling out of unjust anger when expounding the sixth commandment, Christ did hereby teach us in general that whenever God forbids one sin He at the same time forbids all sins of the same kind, with all the causes thereof; and in particular that specific passion from which most murders proceed. Since, then, un-justified and immoderate anger is a breach of the Decalogue deserving of Divine punishment, how diligently and constantly we should be on our guard, lest this headstrong affection break forth, seeking grace to restrain and nip it in the bud. Now in order that we may subdue this lust that it prevail not, lay to heart this commandment which forbids rash anger, and frequently call to mind how patiently and mercifully God deals with us every day, and that therefore we ought to be likeminded toward our brethren (Eph. iv, 31, 32).

The second branch of the sin here condemned is, "whosoever shall say to his brother, Raca," or, as the margin renders it, "vain fellow." What is here prohibited is that scorn, arising from un-controlled temper, which leads to speaking contemptuously. All abusive language is forbidden by the sixth commandment, all expressions of malignity issuing from a bitter heart, for as Matthew Henry rightly pointed out, "all malicious slanders and censures are 'adders' poison under their lips' (Psalm cxl, 3), and kill secretly and slowly." The Spirit of God refers to Ishmael's jeering at Isaac as "persecution" (Gal. iv, 29), and the same may be said of all bitter speaking. Yea, the prohibition here extends to the gestures of our body—a sneer, the wagging of our head (Matt. xxvii, 29). Therefore are we required to make conscience of every gesture, every casting of the eye (Gen. iv, 6), as well as every passionate word.

The third degree of murder mentioned by Christ is censorious reviling or calling our brother a "fool." It is not the simple use of this English word which renders us guilty of this crime, as is clear from Luke xxiv, 25; I Corinthians xv, 36. A benevolent desire to make men sensible of their folly is a good work, but the reviling of them from an ungovernable rage is wickedness. With the Jews "fool" (moren) signified a rebel against God, an apostate, so that the one using this term arrogated to himself the passing of judicial sentence, consigning his fellow to hell. This was the very word Moses used (in the plural form) in Numbers xx, 10, and for which he was excluded from Canaan. It is to be observed that never once does the Lord designate His people "rebels," though on several occasions He charges them with being rebellious.

One other thing remains to be mentioned. In the different degrees of penalty mentioned by Christ, He alluded unto the various courts of judgment in vogue among the Jews for punishment, which He applied to the Divine judgment which should fall upon those guilty of the sins He here condemned. And let us say in conclusion, there is no way of escaping the Divine curse upon these sins except by humbling ourselves before God, penitently confessing the murderous passions of our hearts, and the manifestation of the same in gesture and speech; suing for His pardon through the atoning blood of Christ.

CHAPTER NINE

The Law and Murder—Concluded

"THEREFORE, if thou bring thy gift to the altar, and there remember-est that thy brother hath aught against thee; leave there thy gift before the altar, and go thy way; first be reconciled to thy brother, and then come and offer thy gift" (verses 23, 24). Christ here drew a practical conclusion from what He had declared in the preceding verses, in which He enforces the duty of preserving Christian love and peace between brethren. First, He held up to view the false interpretation of the sixth commandment given by the ancient rabbis and perpetuated by the scribes and Pharisees (verse 21). Second, He gave the true meaning of it (verse 22). And third, He here propounded certain rules of concord between those that be at variance. If even a secret feeling of anger, and much more so a contemptuous or maledictory reproach, constitutes in God's sight a breach of His Law, and that He will not accept the worship of those guilty of such a crime, we must, without delay, remove every root of bitterness that might spring up and produce so deadly a fruit.

Our Lord here spoke in the language of the dispensation then in force, but the principles He enunciated on this occasion apply equally to Christian ordinances, especially the Lord's supper: the maintenance of righteousness and amity between one another is indispensable to fellowship with the thrice holy God. "It was the doctrine of the scribes, and the practice of the Pharisees corresponded with it, that anger, hatred, and the expression of these, if they did not go so far as overt acts of violence, were among the minor faults; and that God would not severely judge men for these, if they were but regular in presenting their sacrifices, and observing the other external duties of religion. In opposition to this, our Lord teaches that, according to the righteousness of His kingdom, having one's mind not subject to the law of justice and love, would render all external religious services unacceptable to God" (J. Brown).

Under the Mosaic law various gifts and sacrifices were presented to Jehovah, some of them being absolutely obligatory, others optional—"freewill offerings." Broadly speaking, those gifts were of two kinds; propitiatory and eucharistic: the one for obtaining Divine forgiveness, the other as expressions of thanksgiving. Christ alludes here only to the latter, but under it He comprehended all manner of true outward worship, whether legal or evangelistic. The Lord Jesus had not yet offered Himself to God as the great anti-typical sacrifice, and therefore He conveyed His lesson through the

73

terms of the ceremonial law; but we have no difficulty in transfer-
ring what He then affirmed unto ourselves. It was as though He said,
If thou comest to worship God in any way, either by prayer, hearing
His Word, offering sacrifices of praise, or celebrating the Lord's
supper, you must live in peace with your brethren, or your worship
will be rejected.

It is indeed solemn and searching to ponder the important practical principle which our Lord here enunciated. How deceptive is the
human heart, and what numbers impose upon themselves in this
matter. But we cannot impose upon that One before whom everything is naked and open. Of old the Jews were guilty of this very
thing. "To what purpose is the multitude of your sacrifices unto
Me? saith the Lord: I am full of the burnt offerings of rams, and
the fat of fed beasts; and I delight not in the blood of bullocks. . . .
And when ye spread forth your hands, I will hide Mine eyes from
you: yea, when ye make many prayers, I will not hear" (Isaiah
i, 11, 15). Why? "Your hands are full of blood." While they cruelly
oppressed their brethren, the worship they offered unto God was an
abomination unto Him. So again in Isaiah lviii, 5, 6, we find
Jehovah despising the religious fasts of Israel because they omitted
those acts of mercy which He required, and instead were guilty of
evilly treating their fellows.

The Lord charged the people with the same sins in the time of
Jeremiah: "Will ye steal, murder, and commit adultery, and swear
falsely . . . and come and stand before Me in this house, which is
called by My name?" (vii, 9, 10). Other passages might be quoted,
but these are sufficient if we duly lay them to heart. From them we
may learn that the performance of any outward service unto God
is displeasing to Him if it be separated from unfeigned love of the
brethren. To serve God acceptably we must perform not only the
duties of the first table of the Law, but also those of the second.
Make no mistake, my reader, the Holy One abhors all professions of
piety from those who make no conscience of endeavouring to live
in peace with their brethren.

"Therefore, if thou bring thy gift to the altar, and there rememberest that thy brother hath aught against thee; leave there thy gift
before the altar" (verses 23, 24). The words "thy brother hath aught
against thee" clearly signify, "If you have done him some injury"
or he has cause of complaint (either real or fancied) against you. If
you have treated him in some way inconsistent with the fraternal
relationship, if he be conscious that you have wronged him, then
you must promptly seek to right that wrong, no matter what the
cost may be to your pride or interests. It may be that you were guilty
of what some would lightly dismiss as "only an outburst of temper,"
which you regretted afterwards; nevertheless, peace has been
disrupted, and God requires you to do everything in your power to
lawfully restore it.

Does not failure to heed this rule go far to explain why the supplications of so many of the Lord's people remain *unanswered*? What numbers fondly imagine that so long as they are regular in their attendance at the house of prayer, and maintain a reverent demeanour therein, their petitions will prevail, even though they be at enmity with some of their brethren. Not so; the words of the Psalmist on this are much too pointed to be misunderstood. " If I regard iniquity in my heart, the Lord will not hear me " (Psalm lxvi, 18). Before bending the knee in prayer, let us call to mind that we are about to draw near unto Him who is as much the Father of the offended brother as He is ours, and that He cannot receive us while we continue casting a stumbling-block in the way of the other. No worship or service can be acceptable to God while we are under the influence of a malicious spirit.

" Leave there thy gift before the altar, and go thy way; first be reconciled to thy brother." This means there must be a sincere and penitent acknowledgment of the offence committed and proper restitution made for any injury done, so that by all proper means and reasonable concessions we seek forgiveness from the one offended. " In this case the person, instead of offering his gift, is to go immediately to his brother, and to be reconciled to him; dismissing all malignant feeling from his mind, he is to repair the injury he has done to his brother. If he has deprived him of his property, he is to restore it; if he has calumniated him, he is to do all that lies in his power to counteract the effect of his calumny, and acknowledge his regret for having acted so unbrotherly a part. In this way he is likely to be reconciled to his brother, that is, to be restored to his brother's favour " (J. Brown).

The question may be raised, What can be done in a case where the one whom I have offended is no longer accessible to me?—one perhaps who has moved to far-distant parts. Answer: every effort must be made to obtain his or her address, and then write them a confession of your fault and your grief for the same, as frankly as though you were speaking to them. But suppose their address be unobtainable? Then in such a case you are hindered by Divine providence and God will accept the will for the deed, if there be a willing mind, providing you have done all you can to right the wrong, and have humbly confessed the same unto God and sought *His* forgiveness.

It should be pointed out that in this rule concerning reconciliation with an aggrieved brother, the Lord furnished a third direction for the expounding of God's commandments. First, He showed that under any *one* sin prohibited in the commandment God forbids *all* sins of the same kind, with all the causes thereof (verse 22). Second, that to the breach of any commandment there is annexed a curse, whether it be specifically expressed or not (verse 22). And now, third, that where any vice is forbidden, there the contrary virtue is enjoined; and on the contrary, where any virtue is commanded, the opposite vice is reprehended. Herein the Divine laws evidence their superiority to human, for man's laws are satisfied by abstaining from the crime prohibited, though the contrary virtue be not practised; so long as we abstain from murder, it matters not though we fail to love our brethren. But God requires not only abstention from vice, but also the practice of virtue.

Another general principle is brought out in the verses before us, one which is of considerable importance in the correct interpreting of many New Testament passages, namely that to be "reconciled" to another does not signify so much to cherish kindly feelings towards one with whom we have been offended, as to be restored to the favour of one we have offended. This throws light on such a statement as, "For if, when we were enemies, we were reconciled to God by the death of His Son, much more, being reconciled, we shall be saved by His life" (Romans v, 10), the primary reference in which is to the Redeemer's propitiating God and obtaining for us His blessing—the same holds good equally of Ephesians ii, 16, and Colossians i, 21. In like manner, "Be ye reconciled to God" (II Corinthians v, 20) means not only throw down the weapons of your warfare against Him, but, primarily, be restored to His favour.

One other important principle enforced by Christ in our passage is that there are degrees of value in the several duties of Divine worship: all are not equal, but some are more and some less necessary. The highest degree of holy worship is prescribed in the first commandment: to love, fear, and rejoice in God above all, trusting Him and His promises. The second degree is to love our neighbours as ourselves, living in accord with them, and seeking reconciliation when any division exists. The third degree consists of the outward ceremonial duties of God's worship: and that these are inferior to the other is clear from Christ's "*first* be reconciled to thy brother." Even the outward solemnities of Sabbath keeping are to give place to the works of love. God esteems mercy above sacrifice. Alas, how many today are sticklers for the details of baptism and the Lord's supper who will not even speak to some of their brethren!

"First be reconciled to thy brother, and then come and offer thy gift" (verse 24). This is far from implying that the regaining of his brother's esteem is a good work which entitles him to the favour of God. No; the man who rests his hope of the acceptance of his religious services on the consciousness that his brethren have nothing against him is leaning on a broken reed; the only valid ground of hope for the acceptance of either our persons or our worship is the free grace of God. But it means that, when peace has been restored, he must not forget to return and offer his gift; for although God will not receive our worship unless—so far as in us lies—we are on loving terms with our neighbours, yet the performance of our duty to men in nowise frees us from obligation of direct service to God.

"Agree with thine adversary quickly, while thou art in the way with him; lest at any time the adversary deliver thee to the judge, and the judge deliver thee to the officer, and thou be cast into prison. Verily I say unto thee, Thou shalt by no means come out thence, till thou hast paid the uttermost farthing" (verses 25, 26). This is one of the passages appealed to by the papists in support of their Christ-insulting dogma of purgatory: that they have to apply to such verses as these in order to bolster up their error shows how hard pressed they are to find anything in the Scriptures which even appears to favour their vile tenets.

The Roman expositors are not even agreed among themselves. Some take the "adversary" to be the Devil, and the "judge" God Himself; but others among them suppose the "adversary" to be God administering His Law, the "judge" they regard as Christ, the "officer" an angel, and the "prison" to be purgatory; "the way" the span of our life on earth. Agree with God while thou art in this life, lest thou come before Christ in judgment, and He cause His angels to cast thee into purgatory, and there thou remainest till thou hast made full satisfaction for all thy venial sins. But such a concept utterly ignores the context, where Christ lays down a rule of reconciliation between man and man, and not between God and man. Moreover, such an interpretation (?) pits the Father against the Son. Finally, it denies the sufficiency of Christ's atonement, making the sinner himself the one who provides satisfaction for his venial sins.

Many Protestant commentators regard verses 25 and 26 as a parable which portrays the grave peril of the sinner and his urgent need of believing the Gospel. Injurious conduct toward our fellow men renders us noxious to the wrath of God, who is our Adversary-at-law. We are in the way to the judgment-seat and our time here is but short at best. But a way of reconciliation is revealed in the Gospel, and of this we should avail ourselves immediately. If it be neglected and despised, then we forsake our own mercies, and close the door of hope against us. If we die with our sins unpardoned, then nothing awaits us but a certain judgment, and we shall be cast into the prison of hell, and being unable to offer any satisfaction to Divine justice we must there suffer the due reward of our iniquities for ever and ever. Such a concept may evidence the ingenuity of the commentator, but where is the slightest hint in the passage that Christ was speaking parabolically?

Personally, we see no reason whatever for not understanding our Lord's words here *literally*. Christ had exhorted the party doing wrong to seek to be reconciled with his brother, by acknowledging the offence and making reparation according to the injury inflicted. In support thereof, He had advanced the solemn consideration that until this be done communion with God is broken and our worship is unacceptable to Him. Here (knowing how proud and obstinate the human heart is, and how slow men are to yield and submit to this duty) Christ descends to a lower level, and points out another reason why it is highly expedient for the offending believer to put matters right with him whom he has wronged, namely lest the aggrieved one *go to law*, and this involve him in costly litigation, or even procure his imprisonment.

"Agree with thine adversary" is just the same as " be reconciled to thy brother," for " adversary " is a general name applied to all persons in common who have a controversy or are at variance with each other. " Agree with " the one you have provoked, seek restoration to his favour, by repairing the injury you have done him. An injured one, or a creditor, might at any time sue him, demanding that his case be tried in a magistrate's court. While on their way thither, there was still time to come to an amicable agreement between themselves, but once they appeared before the magistrate the matter would pass out of their hands, and be subject to the decision of the court, whose business it is that strict justice be impartially enforced.

The view given above was held by the renowned Calvin, " If in this place the judge signify God, the adversary the Devil, the officer an angel, the prison purgatory, I will readily subscribe to them (the Papists). But if it be evident to everyone that Christ thus intended to show to how many dangers and calamities persons expose themselves, who prefer obstinately exerting the rigour of the law to acting upon the principles of equity and kindness, in order the more earnestly to exhort his disciples to an equitable concord, pray where will purgatory be found?" Verses 26 and 27 are to be regarded as a warning of what may befall those who heed not the command in verses 24, 25. If we refuse to humble ourselves and strive to preserve peace, we must not be surprised if others deal harshly with us and sue us at law. In closing, it may be observed, that Christ here approves of the magisterial office, his proceeding against the guilty and of imprisonment.

CHAPTER ELEVEN

The Law and Adultery

" Ye have heard that it was said by them of old time, Thou shalt not commit adultery: But I say unto you, That whosoever looketh on a woman to lust after her hath committed adultery with her already in his heart. And if thy right eye offend thee, pluck it out, and cast it from thee: for it is profitable for thee that one of thy members should perish, and not that thy whole body should be cast into hell. And if thy right hand offend thee, cut it off, and cast it from thee: for it is profitable for thee that one of thy members should perish, and not that thy whole body should be cast into hell. It hath been said, Whosoever shall put away his wife, let him give her a writing of divorcement: But I say unto you, That whosoever shall put away his wife saving for the cause of fornication, causeth her to commit adultery: and whosoever shall marry her that is divorced committeth adultery." (Matt. v, 27-32.)

LET us begin by pointing out once more that the several distinctions drawn by Christ in this discourse between what had been said in ancient times upon a number of matters of moral and religious duty, and what He now affirmed, must have respect not to the real teaching of the Law and the prophets but to the inadequate and erroneous views entertained of their teaching by the rabbis and the false notions founded upon them. After so solemnly and expressly declaring His entire harmony with the Law and the prophets (v, 17-20), we must regard with abhorrence the idea that Christ, immediately after, proceeded to pit Himself against them, affirming that Moses taught one thing and He quite another. No, in every instance where a commandment is quoted as among the things said in former times, it was the understanding and views entertained thereof against which the Lord directed His authoritative deliverances. It is not the Law *per se* which is under consideration, but the carnal interpretations of it made by the Pharisees.

It should prove a real help to the reader if he looks upon Matthew v, 20, as the text of this third division of the Sermon, and all that follows to the end of chapter v as an enlargement thereof. That verse enunciated a most important practical truth, and the verses which immediately follow contain a series of illustrative examples of how and wherein the righteousness of the citizens of the kingdom of heaven must exceed the righteousness of the scribes and Pharisees. First, the Law-giver Himself had freed the sixth commandment from the rubbish which carnal men had heaped upon it (verses 21-26), and now He proceeded to restore the seventh commandment to its true sense and meaning, and therefore to its proper use, purging it from the false interpretation of the Jews. Thus, in the verses which are now to be before us, we have the Saviour contrasting the righteousness of His kingdom with the righteousness of the religious leaders of His day respecting the all-important matter of chastity.

"Ye have heard that it was said by them of old time, Thou shalt not commit adultery" (verse 27). Again we would carefully note that Christ did not say, "Ye know that God said at Sinai," but instead, "ye have heard that it was said by *them* of old time." This makes it quite clear that He was continuing to refute the injurious traditions which the Jews had accepted from their elders: "them of old time" referring to the ancient teachers—compare our comments on verse 21. "Thou shalt not commit adultery"; those were indeed the actual words of the Holy Spirit, but the preceding clause makes it plain that our Lord was alluding to them in the sense in which the scribes and Pharisees understood them. They saw in the seventh commandment nothing more than the bare injunction, "No man shall lie with another man's wife," and hence they thought that so long as men abstained from that particular sin, they met the requirements of this precept.

The ancient rabbis, echoed by the Pharisees, restricted the scope of the seventh commandment to the bare act of unlawful intercourse with a married woman. But they should have perceived, as in the case of the sixth commandment, that the seventh spoke specifically of only the culminating crime, leaving the conscience of the hearer to infer that anything which partook of its nature or was calculated to lead up to the overt deed was also and equally forbidden, even the secret thought of unlawful lust. That the Pharisees did narrow the meaning of the seventh commandment to the mere outward act of impurity is evident from our Lord's contrastive exposition of it in the next verse, where He insists that its true intent had a much wider scope, reaching also to the inward affections, prohibiting all impure thoughts and desires of the heart.

Once more we are shown the vast difference there is between the spiritual requirements of a holy God and the low standard which is deemed sufficient by His fallen creatures. The religion of carnal and worldly men is merely *political*; so far as good and evil affect society, they are in some measure concerned; but as to the honour and glory of God, they have no regard. So long as the outside of the cup and of the platter be clean, they are indifferent to whatever filth may exist within (Matt. xxiii, 25, 26). So long as the external conduct of its citizens be law-abiding, the State is satisfied, no matter what iniquity may be seething in their minds. Different far is it with the Judge of all the earth: "The Lord seeth not as man seeth; for man looketh on the outward appearance, but the Lord looketh on the heart" (I Samuel xvi, 7). That which the world pays no attention to, God regards as of first importance, for "out of the heart are the issues of life" (Prov. iv, 23). It is only "the pure in heart" who shall ever see—commune with and eternally enjoy—God (Matt. v, 8).

In what has just been before us we may see a very real warning against a *slavish literalism*, which has ever been the refuge into which not a few errorists have betaken themselves. In this instance the Pharisees kept themselves close to the letter of the Word, but sadly failed to understand and insist upon its *spiritual purport*. Papists seek to justify their erroneous dogma of transubstantiation by an appeal to the very words of Christ, "this is My body," insisting on the literal sense of His language. Unitarians seek to shelter behind His declaration, "My Father is greater than I" (John xiv, 18), arguing therefrom the essential inferiority of the Son. In like manner, the ancient rabbis took the words of the seventh commandment at their face value only, failing to enter into the full spiritual meaning of them. Let pre-millenarians heed this warning against a slavish literalism or a being deceived by the mere sound of words, instead of ascertaining their *sense*.

The great Teacher of the Church here supplied us with an invaluable canon of exegesis or rule of interpretation by teaching us that God's commandment "is exceeding broad" (Psalm cxix, 96), and that human language becomes invested with a far fuller and richer meaning when used by God than it has on the lips of men. This of itself should be sufficient to silence those who condemn the servants of God when they spiritualize Old Testament prophecies, objecting that they are reading into those prophecies what is not there, and unwarrantably departing from their plain sense. When the Lord Jesus affirmed, "But I say unto you, That whoso looketh on a woman to lust after her, hath committed adultery with her already in his heart," had not the Pharisees as much occasion to demur, and say, "The seventh commandment says nothing about lustful *looks*: You are reading into it what is not there"?

Ere passing on, a few words need to be said on the special heinousness of this particular crime. Adultery is the breach of wedlock. Even the Pharisees did condemn it, for though they made light of disobedience to parents (Matt. xv, 4-6), yet they clamoured for the death of the woman guilty of this sin (John viii, 4, 5). The grievousness of this offence appears in that it breaks the solemn covenant entered into between husband and wife and God, it robs another of the precious ornament of chastity, it defiles the body and ruins the soul, it brings down the vengeance of God upon the posterity, which Job called "a fire that consumeth to destruction" (xxxi, 12). "Be not deceived; neither fornicators, nor idolators, nor adulterers . . . shall inherit the kingdom of God" (I Cor vi, 9, 10). "Whoremongers and adulterers God will judge" (Heb. xiii, 4).

"But I say unto you, That whosoever looketh on a woman to lust after her, hath committed adultery with her already in his heart" (verse 28). Here we have an exposition of the seventh commandment by the supreme Prophet of God, wherein He reveals the height, depth, and breadth of the spirituality of the Divine Law. That commandment not only forbids all acts of uncleanness, but also the desire of them. The Pharisees made it extend no farther than to the outward and physical act, supposing that if the iniquity was restricted to the mind, God would be indifferent. Yet their own Scriptures declared, "If I regard iniquity in my heart, the Lord will not hear me" (Psalm lxvi, 18), and Christ here made it known that if a man allows himself to gaze upon a woman till his appetites are excited and sexual thoughts are engendered, then the holy Law of God judges him to be guilty of adultery and subject to its curse; and if he indulges his licentious imagination so as to devise means for the gratification thereof, then is his guilt that much greater, even though providence thwart the execution of his plans.

Our Lord here declared that the seventh commandment is broken even by a secret though unexpressed desire. There is, then, such a thing as *heart adultery*—alas, that this is so rarely made conscience of today. Impure thoughts and wanton imaginations which never issue in the culminating act are breaches of the Divine Law, All lusting after the forbidden object is condemned. Where the lascivious desire is rolled under the tongue as a sweet morsel, it is the commission of the act so far as the heart is concerned, for there is then lacking nothing but a convenient opportunity for the crime itself. He who weighs the spirits judges the going out of the heart after that which is evil as sin, so they who cherish irregular desires are transgressors of the law of impurity.

"But I say unto you, That whosoever looketh on a woman to lust after her, hath committed adultery with her already in his heart." It is not an involuntary glance which constitutes the sin, but when evil thoughts are thereby prompted by our depraved natures. The first step and degree, then, of this crime is when lust stirs within us. The second stage and degree is when we deliberately *approach unto*— a feeding of the eye with the sight of the forbidden fruit, where further satisfaction cannot be obtained. Then if this lust be not sternly mortified, the heart swiftly becomes enthralled and the soul is brought into complete bondage to Satan, so that it is fettered by chains which no human power can break. Such was the deplorable condition of those mentioned by the apostle, "Having eyes full of adultery, and that cannot cease from sin" (II Peter ii, 14).

Well did Matthew Henry point out, "The eye is both the inlet and the outlet of a great deal of wickedness of this kind; witness Joseph's mistress (Gen. xxxix, 7), Samson (Judges xvi, 1), David (II Samuel, xi, 2). What need have we, therefore, with holy Job, to ' make a covenant with our eyes' (xxxi, 1) to make this bargain with them: that they should have the pleasure of beholding the light of the sun and the works of God, provided that they would never fasten or dwell upon anything that might occasion impure imaginations or desires; and under this penalty, that if they did, they must smart for it in penitential tears. What have we the covering of our eyes for, but to restrain corrupt glances and to keep out defiling impressions?" How much sorrow and humiliation would be avoided if such wholesome counsel was duly laid to heart and carried out in practice.

By clear and necessary implication, Christ here also forbade the using of any other of our senses and members to stir up lust. If ensnaring looks be reprehensible, then so much more unclean conversation and wanton dalliances, which are the fuel of this hellish fire. Again, if lustful looking be so grievous a sin, then those who dress and expose themselves with desires to be looked at and lusted after—as Jezebel, who painted her face, tired her head, and looked out of the window (II Kings ix, 30)—are not less, but even more guilty. In this matter it is only too often the case that men sin, but women tempt them so to do. How great, then, must be the guilt of the great majority of the modern misses who deliberately seek to arouse the sexual passions of our young men. And how much greater still is the guilt of most of their mothers for allowing them to become lascivious temptresses.

As looking to lust is here forbidden, so by proportion are all other like occasions unto adultery. The reading of books which make light of immodesty and indecency, and that cater to those who relish the suggestive and questionable, are therefore prohibited. So too is the use of light and wanton talk and the jesting about loose morals: "But fornication, and all uncleanness, or covetousness, let it not be once named among you, as becometh saints; neither filthiness, nor foolish talking, nor jesting" (Eph. v, 3, 4). Many who are given to this think it a trifling matter, but in reality they are double offenders, for not only have they a wanton eye, but a lascivious tongue also. In like manner, promiscuous dancing and mixed bathing are most certainly condemned by the seventh commandment, for in both there is additional provocation unto lust.

How solemnly do these words of Christ in Matthew v, 28, condemn us, for even though (by preserving grace) our bodies have not been defiled by the outward act of adultery, yet who can say "My *heart* is clean"? Who is free from a wanton eye, from evil desires, from impure imaginations? Who can truthfully affirm that he has never been guilty of questionable jesting and unchaste conversation? Must we not all of us lay our hands upon our mouths and condemn ourselves as offenders in the sight of God? Surely we have ample cause to humble ourselves beneath His mighty hand and acknowledge our breach of the seventh commandment. And if our repentance and confession be sincere, shall we not be doubly on our guard against a repetition of these sins, seeking to avoid temptations and taking heed of every occasion which may incite us? Surely it is evident that if our hearts be honest before God we cannot do less. Yea, shall we not with increased earnestness pray, "Turn away mine eyes from beholding vanity; and quicken Thou me in Thy way" (Psalm cxix, 37)?

Again, if the lust of the heart be adultery in the sight of God, then with what diligence and care should we respond to that injunction, "Having therefore these promises, dearly beloved, let us *cleanse* ourselves from all filthiness of the flesh and spirit, perfecting holiness in the fear of God" (II Cor. vii, 1); that is, labour to keep our hearts and minds as pure as our bodies. Unless they do so Christians themselves will be deprived of a comforting assurance of their personal interest in the love of God, for when they defile their minds by harbouring impure thoughts the Spirit is grieved, and withholds His witness to our sonship. Nay, if we truly realize that the Holy One has taken up His abode within our hearts, must we not put forth every effort to keep the guest-chamber clean? As the best way to keep down weeds is to plant the garden with vegetables and flowers, so the most effective means of excluding from the mind those foul imaginations is for it to be filled with thoughts of spiritual things, to have our affections set upon things above. If we give God His proper place within, Satan will be defeated.

We feel that we cannot do better in closing this article than by quoting here the salutary counsels of another: "To temptations to impurity in some of its forms we are commonly exposed, and it requires constant vigilance to avoid falling before some of them. There are a few advices which, on this subject, I would affectionately urge on the attention of the young. Be on your guard against loose and unprincipled companions. 'Be not deceived: evil communications corrupt good manners.' It is impossible to associate intimately with the profligate without danger. Abstain from the perusal of books tainted with impurity. These are scarcely less mischievous—in many cases they are more so—than the company of the wicked. The deliberate perusal of such books is a plain proof that the mind and conscience are already in a deeply polluted state. Keep at a distance from all indelicate and even doubtful amusements—I allude chiefly to theatrical amusements—where the mind is exposed, in many instances, to all the evils at once of depraved society and licentious writing. Seek to have your mind occupied and your affections engaged with 'things unseen and eternal.' Habitually realize the intimate presence of that God, who is of purer eyes, than to behold iniquity. Never forget that His eye is on your heart, and that 'all things are naked and opened' to Him: and, as one of the best and most effectual methods of mortifying your members which are on the earth—crucifying the flesh with its affections and lusts—'Seek the things which are at God's right hand.' Never tamper with temptations, but flee youthful lusts" (J. Brown).

CHAPTER TWELVE

The Law and Adultery—Continued

FROM what has been before us in Matthew v, 21-26, and still more
so from the searching and pride-withering declaration of Christ in
verse 28, we may perceive again how deeply important is a right
understanding of the Divine Law, and what fatal consequences must
inevitably follow from inadequate and erroneous views thereof. It
is at this point, more than anywhere else, that the orthodoxy and
helpfulness of the preacher must be tested, for if he fails here—in
his interpretation and enforcement of the strictness and spirituality
of the Decalogue—the whole of his teaching must necessarily be
fundamentally faulty and injuriously misleading. This is evident
from the method followed by Christ in His first public sermon. No
matter how deplorable and general be the failure of the modern
pulpit, let it be said emphatically that all of us are bound and must
yet be judged by the holy Law of God, and no repudiation thereof,
no modifying of its high demands by unfaithful preachers, can in
any wise justify our disobedience to God's commands.

"Whilst we therefore view the strictness, spirituality, and reason-
ableness of the precepts which we have been reading, as expounded
by our Divine Teacher; let us impartially compare our past and
present lives, our tempers, affections, thoughts, words, and actions,
with this perfect rule; then we shall find every self-confident hope
expire, and plainly perceive that, ' by the works of the Law no flesh
shall be justified in the sight of God'; then will Christ and His
salvation become precious to our souls. Whether we look to our
conduct towards those who have injured us, or those whom we have
offended; towards our superiors or inferiors, relatives, friends, or
servants; the state of our heart or the government of our passions;
to what we have or what we have not done; we shall see cause for
humiliation and need of forgiveness; and when we consider that we
must be made holy according to this standard, in order to the enjoyment of God and heaven; we shall as evidently perceive our need
of the powerful influences of the Holy Spirit, and learn to value the
ordinances of God, through which that sacred assistance is
obtained " (T. Scott).

"And if thy right eye offend thee, pluck it out, and cast it from
thee: for it is profitable for thee that one of thy members should
perish, and not that thy whole body should be cast into hell " (Matt.
v, 29). In this and the following verse our Saviour furnishes heavenly
instruction for the avoiding of those offences against which He had

just spoken. It is supplied by Him in the way of answer to a secret objection to the exposition He had given of the seventh commandment, wherein He had condemned adultery of heart. Corrupt human nature would be ready to at once murmur, It is impossible to be governed by so exacting a law, it is a hard saying, who can bear it? Flesh and blood cannot but look with pleasure on a beautiful woman, and it is inevitable that there should be lusting after so attractive an object. What, then, shall we do with our eyes, if an unchaste look be so evil and fatal? It was to just such risings up of the depraved heart against the spiritual requirements of a holy God that Christ here made reply.

"And if thy right eye offend thee, pluck it out, and cast it from thee." Here again the language of Christ is not to be taken at its proper sense, i.e. it is not to be understood literally. One of the rules in expounding Scripture is that where the literal sense of a verse is against any of the commandments of the Law, then its words must be regarded figuratively, for obviously one part of the Word must not be made to contradict another. Now just as the seventh commandment not only prohibited the physical act of adultery, but also all mental impurity, so the sixth commandment not only forbade the taking of life, but also reprehended any deliberate maiming of either our own body or that of our neighbour. Therefore, no man can without sin pluck out his eye or cut off his hand.

By the "eye" we are to understand, first, the eye of the body, yet not that only but any other thing that is dear to us—the "eye" being one of the most precious of our members. The word "offend" does not here signify to displease, but to hinder: the reference is to anything which occasions us to commit this sin, whatever would cause us to stumble. Thus the figure is easily interpreted: whatever in our walk or ways exposes the soul to the danger of unholy desires must, at all costs, be abandoned. There must be the uncompromising excision of everything hurtful to the soul. To pluck out the right eye means that we are to rigidly restrain and strictly govern our senses and members, deny ourselves, even though it involves present hindrance, financial loss, and personal pain. No matter how pleasant and dear the presence and use of certain things be to us, yet if they are occasions of sin they must be relinquished and avoided.

Since the Lord Jesus so pointedly condemned unlawful desires and the exercise of impure imaginations, then it is our bounden duty to suppress and disallow them, to strive earnestly against the same, to subdue the lusts from which they spring. Though the senses and members of our bodies be the instruments of evil, yet the sin itself proceeds from the lusts of our hearts, and if *they* be subdued, if every idolized object be renounced within, then there will be no need either to flagellate or mutilate our bodies. On the other hand, if we crucify not the flesh with its affections and lusts, the mere plucking out of an eye or the cutting off of a hand will profit the soul nothing. The root of sin lies much deeper than the physical: "cleanse first that which is *within* the cup and platter, that the outside of them may be clean also" (Matt. xxiii, 26). Make the tree good, and the fruit will be good (Matt. xii, 33).

"Mortify therefore your members which are upon the earth; fornication, uncleanness, inordinate affection, evil concupiscence," etc. (Col. iii, 5), not the mortification of our physical "members," but the appetites and passions of the soul. This expresses the same idea as our Lord was propounding. But the subjugation of sexual appetites, the obtaining of victory over such strong desires of the heart, is no easy matter, especially in cases where both constitution and habit have united to enslave in these sins. No, the mortification of such lusts cannot but be attended with most painful exercises and the sacrifice of what has been delighted in and held dear. Nevertheless, though it be as painful as the plucking out of an eye, it must be done. We are obliged to choose between mortification and damnation, and therefore the strongest corruptions are to be mastered and all that is within us brought into subjection to God and subordinated to the eternal good of our soul.

It is to be observed that this is one of many passages in the Gospels in which we find the Son of God making definite reference to a future state. How often did He refer to the resurrection of the body, and of a hell into which the wicked shall be cast! He was continually bringing these things to the attention of men and pressing them upon their serious and solemn consideration. No flesh-pleasing sycophant was He: the glory of God and not the praise of men was ever the object before Him. And herein He has left an example to be followed by all whom He has called to be officers in His kingdom; not to lull to sleep by "smooth speaking," but to declare "the wrath of God is revealed from heaven against all ungodliness and unrighteousness of men (Romans i, 18). If men and women could be persuaded to weigh with due deliberation the vast importance and endlessness of eternity, and the brevity and uncertainty of this life, they would cease trifling away so many of their swiftly passing hours and prepare to meet their God.

"For it is profitable for thee that one of thy members should perish, and not that thy whole body should be cast into hell." Christ here emphasizes the fact that lustful looks and wanton dalliances are so disastrous and destructive to the soul that it is better to lose an eye than to yield to this evil and perish eternally in it. This, as we have pointed out, is in reply to the objection that heart adultery is something no man can prevent, that it is beyond his power to resist temptations to gaze with longing eyes upon an attractive woman. Rightly did Matthew Henry point out: "Such pretences as these will scarcely be overcome by reason, and therefore must be argued against with the terrors of the Lord, and so they are here argued against." Alas, that this powerful deterrent to evil and incitement to holiness is so rarely made use of in our degenerate times, when little else than honey and soothing-syrup is being handed out from the pulpit.

Different far was the course followed by the chiefest of the apostles. When he stood before Felix, he "reasoned of righteousness, temperance, and judgment to come," and we are told that the governor "trembled" (Acts xxiv, 25): but what is there in modern preaching—even that known as "Calvinistic"—which is calculated to make sin-hardened souls to tremble? Little wonder that the rising generation defy their parents with such impudence, when their elders are unrestrained by fear of the hereafter. "Knowing therefore the terror of the Lord [in the previous verse he had spoken of the judgment-seat of Christ], we persuade men" (II Cor. v, 11), said the apostle, and so will every faithful servant of God today. Ministers of the Gospel are required to conduct their hearers to Sinai before they lead them to Calvary, to make known the "severity of God" (Romans xi, 22) as well as His goodness, to declare the reality and awfulness of hell as well as the blessedness of heaven; and if they do not so, then they are unfaithful to their trust, and God will require at their hands the blood of their hearers" (Ezekiel xxxiii, 6; Acts xx, 26).

"And if thy right hand offend thee, cut it off, and cast it from thee: for it is profitable for thee that one of thy members should perish, and not that thy whole body should be cast into hell" (verse 30). This is the same exhortation as was before us in the preceding verse, the same stern and startling argument to restrain us from the sin of heart adultery. Nor is this to be regarded as a needless multiplying of words, for such repetitions in the Scripture have a particular use, namely to signify that things thus delivered are of special importance and worthy of our most careful observation and obedience. There is indeed a slight variation, and what strikes us (though the commentators seem to have missed it) as a designed gradation. As the "eye" was a figure of what is *dearest* and most cherished by us, so the "hand" is to be understood as what is most *useful* and profitable. Many have wondered why our Lord did not mention the plucking out of an eye last, as being the severer loss of the two; but it must not be overlooked that He was not here addressing a company of the rich and learned, but the common people, and to a *labouring* man the loss of the right hand would be a far more grievous deprivation than the loss of an eye!

Nor is it to be overlooked that Christ was here more immediately speaking to His own disciples. This well may startle some today, yet as Andrew Fuller rightly pointed out: "It is necessary for those whom the Lord may know to be heirs of salvation, in certain circumstances, to be threatened with damnation, as a means of preserving them from it." Such passages as Romans xi, 18-20; Galatians vi, 7, 8; Hebrews x, 26-30; are addressed to believers! "Mature reflection on our situation in this world will reconcile us to that self-denying and painful mortification of our sins to which we are indispensably

called; we shall see tender mercy crouch under the apparent harshness of the requirement; that our safety, advantage, and felicity are
consulted; and that the grace and consolations of the Spirit will
render it practicable and even comfortable. And would we be
preserved from gross iniquities, our hearts must be kept with all
diligence, and our eyes and all our senses and faculties forbidden to
rove after those things which lead to transgression: the strictest
rules of purity and self-denial will be found, by experience, the
most conducive to true and solid comfort while in this world."
(T. Scott).

By these exhortations, then, the Lord Jesus teaches us that we
must keep a strict watch over the senses and members of our body,
especially the eye and the hand, that they become not the occasions
of sinning against God: "Neither yield ye your members as instruments of unrighteousness unto sin; but yield yourselves unto God,
as those that are alive from the dead, and your members as instruments of righteousness unto God" (Romans vi, 13). We must use
our sight in obedience to God. "Let thine eyes look right on, and
let thine eyelids look straight before thee" (Prov. iv, 25): that is,
we are to order our sight according to the rule of the Word, for that
is the way wherein we are to walk. The necessity of heeding this
Rule appears from many solemn examples. Eve's looking on the
forbidden fruit, contrary to the Divine commandment, was the door
of that sin into her heart. Ham was cursed for looking upon his
father's nakedness (Gen. ix); Lot's wife was turned into a pillar of
salt for looking back toward Sodom (Gen. xix); over fifty thousand
men of Beth-shemesh were slain for looking into the ark of the Lord
against His revealed will (I Samuel vi). Do not these cases tell us
clearly that before we look at anything we should pause and ask
whether the same will be for God's glory and our good?

Again, these exhortations of Christ teach us plainly that we must
seek diligently to avoid all the occasions of every sin, though it be
most painful to ourselves and attended with great temporal loss.
As one old writer expressed it: The fallen nature of man is like
unto dry wood or tow, which will quickly burn as soon as fire
touches it. As mariners at sea set a constant watch to avoid rock and
sands, so should we most warily avoid every occasion to sin. Self
must be denied at all costs, constant watch kept over the heart, the
first risings of corruption therein suppressed, temptations to sin
shunned, the company of those who would be a snare unto us
avoided. So there must be a constant seeking unto God for His grace,
that we may be enabled so to walk in the Spirit that we will not
fulfil the lusts of the flesh.

The task unto which the Lord Jesus here calls us is that of
mortification, the putting to death of our evil lusts. That this is
a most unwelcome and painful work, He warns us by the figures He
employed. Unto those who object that the keeping of their hearts
free from unlawful desires and lustful imaginations is a task utterly

beyond their powers, Christ replies: If as you say it is impossible, if there be no other way of governing your appetites [which, blessed be God, through His grace, there is], then pluck out and cut off your offending members rather than use them to the eternal undoing of your souls. Who is there among us who would not consent to the amputation of a gangrened limb, no matter how painful the operation and heavy the loss, if persuaded that this was imperative in order for life itself to be preserved? Then why refuse painful mortifications which are essential to the saving of the soul? When tempted to shrink therefrom, seriously consider the only other alternative—in hell both body and soul will be tormented for ever and ever.

Not only must there be the uncompromising avoidance and refusal of all that is evil, but we must abridge ourselves in or totally abstain from things lawful in themselves if we find they are occasions of temptation to us. "Take a familiar illustration. A person is fond of wine; it is agreeable to his taste; it is useful in refreshing him after severe exertion. But he finds that this taste has seduced him into intemperance; he finds that there is constant danger of its doing so. He has fallen before the temptation again and again. What is such a person's duty? According to our Lord, it is obviously to abstain from it entirely—on this plain principle, that the evil he incurs by abstaining, however keenly felt, is as nothing to the evil to which the intemperate use of wine subjects him, even everlasting punishment in hell: and to make this abstinence his duty, it is not necessary that he should know that he will fall before his temptation: it is enough that he knows that, as he has repeatedly fallen before it, he may fall before it again" (John Brown).

CHAPTER THIRTEEN

The Law and Adultery—Concluded

MOST writers regard Matthew v, 32, 33, as forming a separate sub-division of our Lord's sermon, but really it belongs to the same section as verses 27-31, treating of the same subject and reprehending the same sin, though a different aspect thereof. Under the general head of adultery occurred another evil, namely the use and misuse of divorce, concerning which the Law of Moses had been grossly corrupted. Having shown the strictness and spirituality of the seventh commandment, Christ here took occasion to condemn the lax views and practices which then obtained in connection with the annulment of marriages. The Jews had fearfully perverted one of the political statutes of the Law, so that divorces were granted on the most frivolous pretences, and it was this our Lord here condemned. Thus, in reality, He was continuing to restore the seventh commandment to its proper place and perfections.

In the passage which is to be before us, we are supplied with a further illustration of the vast superiority of the righteousness of Christ's kingdom over the righteousness of the scribes and Pharisees. There is an invariable outworking of the principle that where spirituality wanes morality also deteriorates. All history bears witness to the fact that when vital godliness is at a low ebb, the sacred institution of marriage is held in light esteem. It is both solemn and sad to behold an exemplification of the same in our own times; as the claims of God are less and less regarded by those of high and low estate alike, the holy obligations of wedlock are gradually whittled down and then increasingly disregarded. When a country, avowedly Christian, begins to tamper with the institution of marriage and make more elastic its divorce laws, it is a certain proof of its ethical decadence.

Even those with only a smattering of ancient history are aware of the fact that in the last few decades before the fall of both the Grecian and Roman empires, marriage was held in such low esteem that it was a common thing for the women to keep tab on their divorces by the number of rings worn on their fingers. It may be replied, They were *heathen* peoples. True, but what our moderns would term "highly civilized." Moreover, human nature is the same the world over, and when the fear of God is lost moral corruptions quickly abound. It was not otherwise with the favoured nation of Israel, as a glance at the prophets will show. The case of the woman in John iv, to whom our Lord said, "Thou hast had *five* husbands:

and he whom thou now hast is not thy husband" (verse 18), is not to be regarded as an exception, but rather as symptomatic of a disease which had spread widely through the nation.

"It hath been said, Whosoever shall put away his wife, let him give her a writing of divorcement" (Matt. v, 31). The original statute on this matter is found in Deuteronomy xxiv, 1-4. But so perversely had that injunction been interpreted, that one of the leading schools of theology (that of Hillel) taught that a man might put away his wife for *any* cause. In the Apocryphal writings we read: " The son of Sirach saith, If she go not as thou wouldest have her, cut her off from thy flesh, give her a bill of divorce, and let her go " (Ecclus. xxv, 26), which is one of many definite indications that the Apocrypha was not inspired by the Holy Spirit. Josephus also wrote: " The law runs thus: He that would be divorced from his wife, for any cause whatever, as many such causes there are, let him give her a bill of divorce." He also confessed that he himself put away his wife after she had borne him three children, because he was not pleased with her behaviour.

Moses had indeed been Divinely directed to allow divorce in case of uncleanness, for the prevention of yet worse crimes. But that which had been no more than a temporary concession was changed by the Pharisees into precept, and that so interpreted as to give licence to the indulging of their evil and selfish desires. And yet, hypocrites as they were, they made a great parade of obeying Moses with regard to the " bill of divorcement." The Talmudical writings, though they took little trouble to describe the justice of divorce, were rigidly definite with regard to the *form of the bill*, insisting that it must be written in twelve lines, neither more nor less. Such is ever the folly of those who strain at a gnat and swallow a camel.

Let us now consider a few details in Deuteronomy xxiv, 1-4. The first thing we notice is the *kind* of statute there given. It was not a moral but a political or civil one, for the good ordering of the state. Among such laws were those of tolerance or permission, which *did not approve* of the evil things concerned, but only suffered them for the prevention of greater evil—as when the sea makes a breach into the land, if it cannot possibly be stopped, the best course is to make it as narrow as possible. Such was the law concerning usury (Deut. xxiii, 20), permitting the Jews to exact it of a stranger, but not to exercise it towards a brother; similar too was the law regulating polygamy (Deut. xxi, 15). These laws tolerated what God condemned, and that for the purpose of preventing greater evils.

Such was the Mosaic law for divorce: not approving of the giving of a bill of divorce for every trifling cause, but permitting it for the sake of preventing greater misery and crime. For instance, if a man took a strong and rooted dislike to his wife and wished to be rid of her, he would be likely to ill-treat her, until she was in danger of her very life. This law of divorce, then, was granted so as to remove the temptation for a hard-hearted husband to commit murder

Divorce is always a deviation from the original marriage institution, consequent upon human depravity. In this instance if a man found that in his wife—something short of adultery, for that was to be punished by death—which made her repulsive to him, he was permitted to divorce her. But this was not to be done verbally and hurriedly, in a fit of temper, but after due deliberation. A "bill of divorcement" had to be legally drawn up and witnessed, making the transaction a solemn and final one.

Second, we may note the *strictness* of this law. The man only was permitted to give this bill of divorcement; neither here nor anywhere else in the Old Testament was this liberty granted unto the wife. If this strikes us as being unjust or unduly severe, two things are to be taken into consideration. First, in the case of a husband being guilty of immorality, the wife could bring it to the notice of the magistrate, and relief was then afforded her by her guilty partner suffering the death penalty. Second, this statute was expressly designed for the prevention of violence and bloodshed, to protect the weaker vessel; it being taken for granted that the man could protect himself if his wife should attack him.

Third, a brief word now upon the *force* and effect of this law. It made the bill of divorcement, given for the stipulated cause, to be regular before men, and marriage thereafter lawful in human courts (Deut. xxiv, 4); and whichever guilty party under such a divorcement married again, committed adultery (Matt. xix, 9). Now this law the Pharisees had grossly perverted. They taught that it was a "commandment" (Matt. xix, 7), whereas Moses only gave a permission—as the language of Deuteronomy xxiv, 1, plainly denotes. So too they taught that for *any* cause (Matt. xix, 3) a man could divorce his wife and thereby be free from her before God, and therefore at liberty to marry another.

"But I say unto you, That whosoever shall put away his wife, saving for the cause of fornication, causeth her to commit adultery: and whosoever shall marry her that is divorced committeth adultery" (verse 32). Here Christ refutes the corrupt interpretation of the scribes and Pharisees, and positively affirms that divorce is permissible only in the case of that sin which in God's sight disannuls the marriage covenant, and even then it is only allowed, and not commanded. Many have understood (being misled by the meaning of the English word) the "saving for the cause of fornication" to refer to this sin being committed *before* marriage and concealed by her till afterwards, arguing that only a married person can be guilty of "adultery." This leads us to raise the point, Do the Scriptures make any real and definite distinction between fornication and adultery? And we answer, No. True, in Matthew xv, 19, and Galatians v, 19, they are mentioned separately, yet in Revelation ii, 20, 22, they are clearly used interchangeably, while in Ezekiel xvi, 25-28, the wife of Jehovah is said to commit *both* sins.

"But I say unto you, That whosoever shall put away his wife, saving for the cause of fornication, causeth her to commit adultery: and whosoever shall marry her that is divorced committeth adultery." These words of our Lord are too plain to be misunderstood. "According to this law, adultery is the only sufficient reason of divorce. He who for any other cause puts away his wife, is to be held an adulterer if he marry another woman; and she, by marrying him, commits adultery; while, at the same time, he becomes the guilty occasion of adultery, if the woman, who is still his wife, marry another man; for in this case she commits adultery as he also who marries her" (J. Brown). No matter how unscriptural be the laws of the land in which we live, or lax the sentiments and practices of the public today, nothing can possibly excuse anyone flying in the face of this express declaration of the Son of God—repeated by Him in Matthew xix, 9.

Something higher than the laws of man must govern and regulate those who fear God. The laws of all "civilized" countries sanction the practice of usury, but the Word of God condemns the same. The laws of our land are open for men to go to court at the first, upon every light occasion, without seeking for some means of agreement. But those who do so are guilty before God, notwithstanding the liberty given them by our political statutes. In like manner, human laws permit divorce for "incompatibility" of disposition, "mental cruelty" and various other things; but the Law of God condemns such licentiousness. Papists allow divorce for religious reasons, appealing to "every one that hath forsaken . . . father or mother, or wife . . . for My name's sake" (Matt. xix, 29), but in that place Christ refers not to divorce at all, but to a separation caused by imprisonment, banishment, or death.

Marriage is not a mere civil thing, but is partly spiritual and Divine, and therefore God alone has the power to appoint the beginning, the continuance, and the end thereof. Here the question is likely to be asked, What of the *innocent party* where a divorce has taken place: may such a one marry again with Divine sanction? To the writer it seems strange that, though there is a decided consensus of agreement, yet all Christians are not one on this matter. In seeking the scriptural answer to the question, let it first be borne in mind that infidelity on the part of either husband or wife annuls the marriage covenant, the man and woman being no longer "one flesh," one of them having been adulterously united to some other. Divorce goes yet farther, for it legally dissolves and removes the marriage relation. We are therefore in hearty accord with the Westminster Catechism of Faith which declares: "In the case of adultery after marriage, it is lawful for the innocent party to sue out a divorce, and after the divorce to marry another, as if the offending party were dead" (Chapter 24, section 5).

In his excellent piece, "Of Marriage after Divorce in Case of Adultery," John Owen pointed out that to insist that divorce simply secures a legal separation but does not dissolve the marriage relation would bring in a state harmful to men. God has appointed marriage to be a remedy against incontinence (I Cor. vii, 2), but if innocent parties lawfully divorced may not marry again, then they are deprived of this remedy and debarred from this benefit. If the divorced person has not the gift of continency, it is the express will of God that he should marry for his relief; yet on the supposition of the objector he sins if he marries again, yea is guilty of the horrible crime of adultery. Is not this quite sufficient to expose the untenability of such an anomoly?

Again, can we suppose for a moment that it is the will of a righteous God for an innocent person to be penalized *the remainder of* his or her earthly life because of the infidelity of another? Surely the very idea is repugnant to all who are really acquainted with the Divine goodness and mercy. Why, if an innocent man upon a divorce is not then at liberty to marry again, he is deprived of his right by the sin of another, which is against the very law of nature; and on such a supposition it lies within the power of every wicked woman to deprive her husband of his natural right. The right of divorce in case of adultery, specified by Christ, for the innocent party to make use of, is evidently designed for his liberty and relief; but on the supposition that he may not again marry, it would provoke a snare and a yoke to him, for if thereon he has not the gift of continence, he is exposed to sin and judgment.

But apart from these convincing considerations, the Word of God is plain and decisive upon the matter. In Matthew v, 32, Christ lays down a general rule, and then puts in an exception thereto, the nature of which exception necessarily implies and affirms *the contrary* to the general rule. The general rule is: Whosoever putteth away his wife causeth her to commit adultery, and he who marrieth her becometh guilty of the same crime. The "exception" there must be a contrary, namely that the innocent party in the divorce may lawfully marry again, and the one marrying him or her is not guilty of adultery. But *that* is the *only* exception. I Corinthians vii, 15, has been appealed to by some as warranting re-marriage in the case of total desertion: but that passage is quite irrelevant, teaching no such thing. The verse refers to an unbelieving husband deserting a believing wife: in such case (says the apostle) she is not "bound" to pursue her husband and demand support, nor to go to law on the matter; rather is she to follow a course of "peace." The verse says nothing whatever about her being free to marry again; nay, verse 39 of the same chapter says "The wife is bound by the law as long as her husband liveth."

In Matthew xix, 9, Christ declared, "Whosoever shall put away his wife, *except* it be for fornication, and shall marry another, committeth adultery: and whoso marrieth her which is put away doth commit adultery." Here again it is evident that the plain sense of these words is: He who putteth away his wife for fornication and then marrieth another is not guilty of adultery. In such a case the bond of marriage has already been broken, and the one so putting away his guilty wife is free to marry again. When our Lord condemned the putting away and marrying again for every cause, the *exception* He made of "fornication" clearly allows both divorce and re-marriage, for an exception always affirms the contrary unto what is denied in the rule, or denies what is affirmed in it. (Condensed from Owen, who closes his piece by saying, "This is the constant practice of all Protestant churches in the world.")

Prevention is better than cure. Even a temporary separation should be the last resource, and every possible effort made to avoid such a tragedy. Marriage itself is not to be entered into lightly and hurriedly, but once the knot is tied, each party should most earnestly consider the relationship which has been entered into and the serious importance of its duties. If love rules, all will be well: unselfishness and forbearance are to be mutually exercised. If the husband gives honour to his partner as unto "the weaker vessel" (I Peter iii, 7), and the wife see to it that she render unto her husband "due benevolence" (I Cor. vii, 3), much needless friction will be avoided. Let them bear with each other's infirmities, study each other's dispositions, and seek to correct each other's faults. Above all, let them often together draw near unto the Throne of Grace and seek God's blessing on their married life. The holier their lives, the happier they will be. Nothing is more honouring to God than a home which bears witness to the sufficiency of His grace and shadows forth the union which exists between Christ and His Church.

N.B. Our purpose in adverting (above) to the writings of John Owen was not because we felt our case needed the support of any human authority, but in order that our readers might know what was taught and practised by the godly Puritans.

CHAPTER FOURTEEN

The Law and Oaths

" Again, ye have heard that it hath been said by them of old time, Thou shalt not forswear thyself, but shalt perform unto the Lord thine oaths : But I say unto you, Swear not at all ; neither by heaven ; for it is God's throne : Nor by the earth ; for it is His footstool : neither by Jerusalem ; for it is the city of the great King. Neither shalt thou swear by thy head, because thou canst not make one hair white or black. But let your communication be, Yea, yea ; Nay, nay : for whatsoever is more than these cometh of evil." (Matt. v, 33-37.)

THE subject which is now to engage our attention is hardly one that is likely to appeal very strongly to the average reader, probably because it treats of matters which rarely engage his mind. Yet the very fact that the Lord Jesus gave the same something more than a passing notice in His first formal Sermon should indicate to us that it is one which we cannot afford to ignore. The Son of God did not waste time on trivialities nor make public deliverances on technicalities devoid of practical value. No, rather did He concern Himself with vital matters that directly affected the glory of God and concerned the eternal welfare of immortal souls. It is therefore a slighting of His honour and impugning of His wisdom if we refuse to attentively weigh and prayerfully consider His teaching on the subject of oaths. Nor is this the only occasion on which He brought it to the notice of His congregations; as we shall see, in Matthew xxiii He returned to the theme and spoke at great length thereon.

Someone has said, " Where ignorance is bliss, 'tis folly to be wise," but such a silly statement savours more of insanity than perspicuity and prudence. Blissful ignorance is often highly dangerous, and in connection with the things of God, fatal. " My people are *destroyed* for lack of knowledge " (Hosea iv, 6) said the Lord of old. True, knowledge itself will not always deter from sin, but often it serves as a salutary restraint. It is much to be feared that millions of the present generation, who are guilty of the crimes which Christ here condemned, are totally ignorant of their wickedness in this matter. Nothing is more prevalent today, among all classes, than cursing and swearing, and it is high time that both the pulpit and the press sounded a loud and solemn warning thereon.

The deep importance of our subject may further be intimated by pointing out that it is essentially bound up with a right understanding and observance of the third of the ten commandments. It is therefore basic and vital, for the curse of God rests upon all transgressors of His Law. If the reader will take the trouble to examine a good concordance on the words " oaths," " swear " and " vow," he

97

may be surprised to find how many scores of passages there are speaking thereof. Finally, when it is seen that the rightful taking of an oath is an act *of worship*, we may then more clearly perceive the momentousness and value of our present inquiry, for it deeply concerns us all to be scripturally regulated on anything which has to do with the worship of God, and it behoves us to spare no effort in seeing to it that our worship be performed in a manner which will meet with Divine approval and acceptance.

"Again, ye have heard that it hath been said by them of old time, Thou shalt not forswear thyself, but shalt perform unto the Lord thine oaths: But I say unto you, Swear not at all; neither by heaven; for it is God's throne: Nor by the earth; for it is His footstool; neither by Jerusalem; for it is the city of the great King. Neither shalt thou swear by thy head, because thou canst not make one hair white or black. But let your communication be, Yea, yea; Nay, nay: for whatsoever is more than these cometh of evil" (Matt. v, 33-37). This time we propose to make only a few expository and explanatory remarks on our passage, and then devote the remainder of our space unto a topical treatment of the whole subject.

"Again, ye have heard that it hath been said by them of old time, Thou shalt not forswear thyself, but shalt perform unto the Lord thine oaths." It is almost ludicrous to see what shifts many of the commentators have put themselves to in their efforts to identify this statement of Christ's with one or more of the Mosaic statutes, ending with the confession that His actual words cannot be found anywhere in the Old Testament, and supposing that He here epitomized the teaching of the Law thereon. Such confusion is inexcusable, and such an explanation most unwarrantable. The fact is that our Lord does not here refer to the Divine precepts at all, but instead to the Jews' perversion of them. He pursues identically the same order in these verses as He had followed in the preceding sections. First, He mentions the pharisaic corruption of the Divine Law, and then sets forth the character of that righteousness which He requires from the citizens of His kingdom on the matter under discussion.

"Thou shalt not take the name of the Lord thy God in vain, for the Lord will not hold him guiltless that taketh His name in vain" (Exodus xx, 7). Here is the original and fundamental law concerning oaths, with which we may also link "Thou shalt fear the Lord thy God, and serve Him, and shalt swear by His name" (Deut. vi, 13). Thus an oath was a solemn appeal to the dread name of Jehovah, which, by awaking the spirit of the swearer to a consciousness of the awe-inspiring presence and cognizance of the Most High, gave all its sanctity and power to it. And then, when anyone *had* so sworn, there was the solemn warning that the Lord would not hold him guiltless that took His name in vain. Thus it is quite clear that Israelites were permitted to swear by the name of the Lord, but having once done so they must not change their minds nor in any way fail to keep their promises.

It is striking to note that when the Psalmist delineated the character of him who was fitted to "abide in the Lord's tabernacle" and "dwell in His holy hill" (i.e. commune with God and enjoy His presence for ever), one of the marks specified was "He that sweareth to his own hurt, and changeth not" (Psalm xv, 1, 4): that is, who at no cost will go back upon his sworn word. It is therefore obvious from these passages that the Mosaic law had a strong tendency to check the practice of oath-taking and to restrict the same unto solemn occasions. The interested reader may also consult such passages as Exodus xxii, 11, 12; Leviticus v, 1; xix, 12; Numbers v, 19-21.

But the Jewish doctors had found ways of perverting the Divine statutes, and the Pharisees had perpetuated and added to their corruptions. From the language used by Christ on this occasion we have no difficulty in ascertaining the nature of their errors and evil practices. First, it is clear from verse 33 that they had unwarrantably *restricted* the Mosaic precepts upon oaths to the single prohibition against perjury. They drew the wicked inference that there was no evil in any oath, at any time, provided a man did not forswear himself. Thus they opened wide the door for men to multiply oaths on any matter and every trivial occasion.

Not only was perjury severely condemned by the Mosaic law, but any vain and *needless* use of the name of God in our ordinary communications was strictly prohibited. No man ought voluntarily to take an oath unless it be a matter of controversy and the contention cannot be settled without it: "For men verily swear by the greater: and an oath for confirmation is to them an end of all strife" (Heb. vi, 16). But the Pharisees had so wrested the law they taught that so long as men swore truthfully as to matters of fact, and performed their vows in case of promise, all was well. They seem to have had no conscience of swearing *lightly*. In order for an oath to be lawful, it requires not only that the affirmation be true and the vows performed, but that such a mode of affirmation or vowing be *necessary*.

Second, it is equally plain from Christ's words in verses 34-36 that the Jews had wrested the third commandment by inventing the idea of swearing *by the creature*. Aiming to ingratiate themselves with men by pandering to their corruptions—for it is ever the way of all false teachers to accommodate the Truth to the blindness and lusts of their dupes—the scribes devised a means whereby men might swear without the guilt of perjury although they swore never so falsely; and this was to swear not by the name of God, but by the heavens or the earth, by Jerusalem or the temple. They made a distinction between oaths: according to them, some were binding, others were not—the obligation of an oath depending upon the nature of the object by which the person swore (Matt. xxiii, 16).

It is not difficult to see why such a device was resorted to by the leaders, or why it should be so popular with their followers. The Law was very definite, "Thou shalt fear the Lord thy God, and serve Him, and shalt swear by His name" (Deut. vi, 13). To swear in the

name of the Lord was ordained not only for the placing of a solemn
bridle upon fallen man's proneness to lying, but also to restrain the
act itself unto serious matters and important occasions. Hence, this
invitation of swearing by some inanimate object removed the very
awe with which an oath should be invested and surrounded. Yet one
can readily perceive how easily those hypocrites could cloak their
wickedness—pretending such veneration for God that His name
must not be used by the people. Philo taught, " It is a sin and a vanity
presently to run to God or the Maker of all things, and to swear *by
Him*: it is lawful to swear by our parents, by heaven, and the stars."

Third, it is equally obvious from our Lord's words in verse 37 that
the Jews had been encouraged and permitted to make use of oaths
lightly and commonly in their ordinary conversation. This would
logically and inevitably follow upon the second evil to which we
have just referred, for such a device was not only dishonest and
demoralizing in itself, but it was sure to bring about an utter disregard of the third commandment, for since such oaths (where the
name of God was omitted) would be lightly esteemed, men would be
inclined to resort unto oaths upon any matter or occasion. " With
the exception of oaths by the gold of the temple and by the sacrifices of the altar—which, for some selfish or superstitious reason,
they held to be binding—they appear to have thought that to swear
by any created thing was of very little consequence, involved no
obligation, and might be done in common conversation without
sin " (J. Brown).

" But I say unto you, Swear not at all; neither by heaven; for it is
God's throne: Nor by the earth; for it is His footstool; neither by
Jerusalem; for it is the city of the great King " (verses 34, 35). In
these verses and in the two which immediately follow our Lord
inveighs against the erroneous teachings and corrupt practices of
the scribes and Pharisees. Let it be clearly understood that all of
the things prohibited by our Saviour in this Sermon were in themselves and also by virtue of the Law of God antecedently *evil* and
unlawful. Most certainly He is not here pitting Himself against any
of the Mosaic precepts; rather was He restoring them to their original
place, purity and power. It was the pharisaic veil of religious
hypocrisy which Christ rent asunder, exposing the corruptness of
their traditions and denouncing the soul-ruining sins into which
the great body of people had been drawn.

Let any of the immediately preceding sections of this Sermon be
considered, and it will at once be found that the particulars there
mentioned by Christ were things which were wrong in themselves,
and declared so in the positive Law of God. Was it not gross wickedness to be angry with a brother without cause, and to call him " raca
and fool "? Was it not exceedingly sinful to look upon a woman so
as to lust after her? In like manner, what is here prohibited by
Christ in His " Swear not at all " is not the legitimate taking of an
oath in law courts, nor even between man and man so as to end a

controversy; but rather that which was directly opposed to the Mosaic statutes, yet practised and supported by the false interpretations of the Law by the Pharisees.

"But I say unto you, Swear not at all." This injunction of Christ's supplies another example of the need for careful *interpretation* of the language of Scripture. Not a few good men have been misled here by the mere sound of words, failing to ascertain their real sense. By taking the prohibition absolutely, instead of relatively, they have certainly erred. This verse also shows us the importance of comparing scripture with scripture, for it is quite clear, not only from the Old Testament but from many passages in the New, that in certain circumstances, and when they are ordered by the rules of God's Word, oaths *are lawful*, yea, necessary—we shall discuss this at more length in our next (D.V.). But we do not have to go outside the bounds of our present passage to find that Christ did not intend His prohibition to be taken without any limitations. He Himself qualified it, first, by forbidding us to swear by any creature; and second, by reprehending all oaths in our ordinary conversation.

Had His "Swear not at all" meant that He here forbade all oaths, in any form and under every circumstance, it was needless to add anything more, and in such a case what is found in the next two verses would simply be a multiplying of words to no purpose. Instead, Christ proceeded to amplify and explain His prohibition, and at the same time expose the sophistry of the Pharisees' devices and show wherein lay the sinfulness of the same. They had invented a method which they supposed would clear the oath-taker from incurring the guilt of breaking the third commandment, and that was to swear by some creature, instead of doing so in the sacred name of the Lord God. *This* it was which Christ was here reproving, and in so doing He once more discovered to us the exceeding "breadth" of the Divine commandments (Psalm cxix, 96).

"Swear not at all; neither by heaven; for it is God's throne: Nor by the earth; for it is His footstool; neither by Jerusalem; for it is the city of the great King." Here Christ made it plain that by no subtle subterfuge can men escape the solemn responsibility of an oath. Though they may omit mentioning the fearful name of God, yet let them know that His is the name of Creator and Owner of all things, and therefore it is invoked in all the works of His hands. If men swear by "heaven," as the Pharisees recommended, let them duly bear in mind that *that* is God's "throne," and so it is really Himself that they summon as a witness to their integrity. If men swear by "the earth," that is God's "footstool," and he who swears by it swears by the God whose footstool it is; if by "Jerusalem," that was the capital, the seat of His worship.

"Neither shalt thou swear by thy head, because thou canst not make one hair white or black" (verse 36). A swearing by any creature necessarily implies an appeal unto God Himself, because of its relation to Him. The whole universe is the Lord's and therefore to swear by any part of it is a reference to its august Maker and Ruler. If we swear by our "head" that too has been given us by God, and is *His* far more than it is ours. God has made it and has the sole disposing of it—a statement easy of proof, for you are incapable of changing the colour of a single hair on it! An oath by your head, if it have any meaning at all, is an oath by the universal Proprietor. Every oath, because it is an oath, is an ultimate reference to Deity. Man's inability really to change the colour of his hair is here brought in by Christ to demonstrate that he has no power over his head. If man has no power over the least creature (a hair!), then how unlawful and ridiculous it is for him to swear by any creature!

"But let your communication be, Yea, yea; Nay, nay: for whatsoever is more than these cometh of evil" (verse 37). In these words Christ makes further amplification of His "Swear not at all," and lays down an important rule which is binding upon all. "Your communication" means your everyday dealings with your fellows, particularly your own common speech or conversation. Thousands of things are true, which yet it would be profaning the name of God to swear to. Christ was not here referring to judicial transactions at all, but to the ordinary intercourse of men with each other. "He did not censure His followers for what was said before a magistrate, but for what passed in their ordinary communications: that is, light and unnecessary oaths. This was a sin so prevalent among the Jews that even Christians who were called from among them stood in need of being warned against it (James v, 12)" (Andrew Fuller).

"Swear not at all . . . but let your communications be, Yea, yea; Nay, nay." In its particular application to His own people, Christ here struck at the root of the special evils He was now condemning, by demanding from His followers veracity in every word. It was as though He said, I not only forbid you to swear falsely, but to swear at all—in your common speech. What need should there be for *you* to swear?—you who are disciples of Him who is "the Truth"! As the followers of the Holy One, you must speak the truth in *every* utterance of your lips. Your character and conduct are to be such that all acquainted with you have the assurance that your word is your bond. If your communications are "yea" in the promise and "yea" in the performance, then there will be no need for you to appeal to God in witness of your veracity. Alas that the standard now set by the vast majority of professing Christians is so very far beneath this, and that the word of many of them is often worth less than that of those who make no profession at all. "Whatsoever is more than these, cometh of evil": that is, savouring of an oath; or even extravagant avowals in our ordinary conversations are sinful in the sight of God.

CHAPTER FIFTEEN

The Law and Oaths—Concluded

"AGAIN, ye have heard that it hath been said by them of old time, Thou shalt not forswear thyself, but shalt perform unto the Lord thine oaths: But I say unto you, Swear not at all; neither by heaven; for it is God's throne: Nor by the earth, for it is His footstool; neither by Jerusalem; for it is the city of the great King. Neither shalt thou swear by thy head, because thou canst not make one hair white or black. But let your communication be, Yea, yea; Nay, nay: for whatsoever is more than these cometh of evil" (Matt. v, 33-37). In the preceding article we gave an exposition of these verses, in which we showed how our Lord here condemned the wicked devices of the scribes and the evil practices of the Pharisees and their followers. Now we propose to treat the subject topically, for there is real need today for a scriptural enforcement of the whole subject.

"Thou shalt not take the name of the Lord thy God in vain; for the Lord will not hold him guiltless that taketh His name in vain" (Exodus xx, 7). This is the fundamental precept of God upon the matter of oaths, and the scope of its prohibition and the range of its meaning are far more extensive than is now commonly supposed. "Thy commandment is exceeding broad" (Psalm cxix, 96), declared David of old, and clearly was it made manifest in Christ's teaching. Those who have followed us closely in the previous chapter will remember that in this Sermon the Saviour has furnished us with some most important and invaluable rules for interpreting the ten commandments. First, that when God forbids one sin He at the same time prohibits all sins of the same kind, with all the causes and occasions thereof. Second, that to the breach of any commandment there is annexed a curse, whether it be expressed specifically or not. Third, that where any vice is condemned the opposite virtue is enjoined.

When God said, "Thou shalt not kill," He not only prohibited the overt deed of murder, but also condemned every evil working of heart and mind which had a tendency to lead up to it: all hatred, anger, provoking language or gestures. When He said, "Thou shalt not commit adultery," He not only forbade the actual act of immorality, but also all unlawful lustings and desires, all impure thoughts and imaginations. In like manner, when He said, "Thou shalt not take the name of the Lord thy God in vain," He not only reprehended the vile sin of using any of His sacred titles in cursing, He not only prohibited the crime of perjury, but He also forbade us

103

both to swear by any of His creatures or take any unnecessary oaths, as well as condemned all extravagant expletives.

Scholars tell us that an oath in the Hebrew is called *shebuah*, and that there are two things observable about it. First, that the verb "to swear" is used only in the niphal—a passive conjugation—which implies that we should be passive in swearing; that is, we should not take an oath unless called upon to do so, or at least unless circumstances morally oblige us thereunto. Most significantly the Hebrew word is taken from a root that signifies "seven," which perhaps implies that it should be taken before many witnesses, and seven being the sacred and complete number, the name of an oath may be derived from it because it is appointed to put a complete end to differences. The Greeks called it *horkos*, most probably from a root signifying "to bind or strengthen," for by an oath a man takes a bond on his soul which cannot be loosed ordinarily. The Latin *juro* and *jus jurandum* are plainly derived from "*jus*," that is "right and law."

Let us now consider, first, the *nature* of an oath. An oath is a religious and necessary confirmation of things doubtful by calling God to be a Witness of truth and a Revenger of falsehood. That it is confirmation is clear from Hebrews vi, 16, where the Holy Spirit expressly affirms the same. That it is a religious confirmation appears from the fact that it is a part of Divine worship, God Himself being invoked therein: in Isaiah xix, 18, "swear to the Lord of hosts" is used for the whole of His worship. It must be a necessary confirmation, because any oath is unlawful which concerns only trifling matters or things which need no solemn settlement. That God is called in both as Witness and Revenger is self-evident, because therein consists the form and all the force of an oath. The one who thus swears acknowledges the Divine perfections, appealing to Him as the God of truth and the hater of lies.

Properly speaking, then, in an oath there are four things. First, a formal *asseveration* of the truth, which should always be spoken even when no oath be taken. Second, a *confession* of the omnipotent presence of the thrice holy Lord God, whereby we do most solemnly acknowledge Him as Witness, Judge, and Revenger of falsehood. Third, an *invocation* whereby God is called upon to bear witness to our conscience that what we swear to is nothing but the truth. Fourth, an *imprecation*, in which the swearer asks God to be the Revenger of all lies, binding himself to Divine punishment if he swear falsely. Therefore it clearly follows that an oath is not to be lightly entered into, that one is not to be taken at all except in matters of real importance, and that it must be taken in the most solemn manner, otherwise we violate the third commandment and are guilty of the awful sin of taking the holy name of the Lord God in vain.

Second, the *design* of an oath consists in a solemn confirmation of what we affirm or deny by a religious invocation of the name of

God, as One that knoweth and owneth the truth. So far as God is thus invoked in an oath, it is part of His worship, both as required by Him and as ascribing glory to Him. When a man is admitted under oath he is, as it were, discharged from an earthly tribunal, having betaken himself to the Lord as the only Judge in the case. By what particular expression this appeal unto God and invocation of Him is made is not absolutely necessary unto the nature of an oath to determine. It is sufficient that such expressions be used as are approved and received signs of such an invocation and appeal among those that are concerned therein. The placing of one hand upon a copy of God's holy Word while we are being sworn in appears to us eminently desirable, while the other hand might well be raised toward heaven; but the kissing of the Book afterwards strikes us as both needless and unsuitable.

Third, a word now upon the *qualifications* or characteristics of lawful oaths. These are clearly expressed by the prophet, so that nothing needs to be added to them, and nothing must be taken from them. "Thou shalt swear, The Lord liveth, in truth, in judgment, and in righteousness" (Jer. iv, 2). "Truth" is required in it, in opposition unto guile and falsehood; for where this obtains not, God is called to be Witness unto a lie, which is to deny His very being. It must be "in judgment" we swear: not lightly, not rashly, not without a just and sufficient cause. There must be discernment and careful discretion in exercise, both in connection with the thing in question which is to be confirmed, and also of the solemn nature of an oath and of the issue of the same. "In righteousness" we must swear, namely that it be equity which we wish to confirm, tending to the glory of God and the good of our fellows.

When the above qualifications are complied with and where matters are in controversy among men and the peace of human society in general or particular depends upon the rightful determination of them, it is meet and proper for a believer, being lawfully called, to confirm the truth which he knows by the invocation of God, with the design of putting an end to strife. Oath-taking is a part of the natural worship of God, which the light of nature leads unto. This is evident from the example of the Lord Himself, who at sundry times took an oath both before the Mosaic law (Gen. xxii, 16) and afterwards. Now it is obvious that if men had not had from the light of nature an understanding of the legitimacy and obligation of an oath, this would have had no significance for them and would have been of no use to them.

In earliest times God often enlightened and more fully instructed men by His own example. In compliance therewith we find that those who walked the closest with Him, centuries before the giving of the Law at Sinai, did solemnly swear one to another when occasion did require it, and when they were legitimately warranted in so doing. Thus Abraham swore to Abimelech (Gen. xxi, 23, 24), and required an oath to be taken by his servant (Gen. xxiv, 8, 9). In like manner

Jacob swore with Laban (Gen. xxxi, 53). And so too Joseph swore to his father (Gen. xlvii, 31). Let it be duly noted that these instances had no respect unto the legal institutions of Moses, and therefore there is no reason to think there would be anything in the Gospel which condemned such a practice today.

One would think the above was quite simple and clear, but alas, such is man that he will discover difficulties where none exist and twist and wrest the plainest statement. Though the great majority of professing Christians have rightly understood and acted upon the teaching of Scripture on this subject, there have been a number that err therein. The Society of Friends and a few others consider that the New Testament expressly forbids the use of any oaths. They appeal to Christ's saying, "Swear not at all" and to "But above all things, my brethren, swear not, neither by heaven, neither by the earth, neither by any other oath: but let your Yea be yea; and your Nay, nay; lest ye fall into condemnation" (James v, 12), supposing these passages prohibit us swearing under any circumstances whatever; and therefore they refuse to bear witness upon oath even when called upon to do so by the rulers of the land.

It is evident that the verse quoted from James is derived from and has respect to the words of our Saviour in Matthew v, 33-37, it being an exhortation inculcating His precept and directions on the same matter. The same answer will therefore serve both places, nor will it be at all difficult to expose and refute the errors based thereon. First of all, it must be pointed out that there is nothing in the essential nature of an oath which can make it criminal, or it would never have been enjoined by Divine authority (Deut. vi, 13). An oath is simply an appeal to the Omniscient One (who searches the heart and is the great Governor of the world, punishing fraud and falsehood) as to the truthfulness of our testimony and the sincerity of our promises. As this is a dictate of the light of nature no mere change of dispensation could make right to be wrong.

Second, the prophecy of Isaiah xlv, 23, belongs and is expressly applied to believers in the New Testament. "I have sworn by Myself, the word is gone out of My mouth in righteousness, and shall not return, That unto Me every knee shall bow, every tongue shall swear"—see Romans xiv, 11. This had respect to what God had of old prescribed (Deut. vi, 13). This now, says the prophet, shall in the days of the Gospel be observed throughout the world, which certainly could not be the case if it were unlawful to swear under any circumstances by that holy Name. In like manner Jeremiah predicted concerning the calling and conversion of the Gentiles under the new covenant, "It shall come to pass, if they will diligently learn the ways of My people, to swear by My name, The Lord liveth . . . then shall they be built in the midst of My people" (xii, 16). But that could be no direction or encouragement to converts of the Gentiles if it be unlawful for them to swear and if it be not their duty when duly called upon.

Third, as we have fully shown in our exposition of Matthew v, 33-37 (in the previous chapter), Christ was there condemning only those oaths which were contrary to the Law, prohibiting things which were essentially evil in themselves. It was the errors of the Jews He was exposing, the wicked perversions of the Pharisees He was refuting. That this *must be* the right way of understanding our Lord's teaching in this passage appears plain from the principles which He had laid down so emphatically at the beginning of this section of His Sermon: "Think not that I am come to destroy the law, or the prophets: I am not come to destroy, but to fulfil. For verily I say unto you, Till heaven and earth pass, one jot or one tittle shall in no wise pass from the law, till all be fulfilled (verses 17, 18). If oaths pertain to "the law" or "the prophets" (and they did), then it most certainly was not Christ's purpose to annul them. The Giver and Fulfiller of the Law is not also its Destroyer.

Fourth, in the matter of judicial oaths Christ Himself has left us an example (which we should follow—I Peter ii, 21), for when He stood before the Sanhedrin, though He had previously refused to answer either His accusers or the high priest, He immediately responded to Caiaphas when he said, "I adjure Thee by the living God" (Matt. xxvi, 63, 64). Fifth, Paul, the greatest of the apostles, confirmed his testimony again and again by calling God for a Witness (II Corinthians i, 23; Galatians i, 20; Philippians i, 8; etc.). In such passages he most solemnly swears to the truth of his own affirmations concerning himself and his sincerity therein (cf. Romans ix, 1). It was not respecting any doctrine he taught that he did swear to, for it needed no confirmation of an oath, deriving as it did all its authority and assurance from Divine revelation. But it was concerning his own heart and purpose, whereof there might be some doubt, and when it was of great concern to the Church to have the Truth emphatically stated.

Sixth, Hebrews vi, 16, tells us, "For men verily swear by the greater: and an oath for confirmation is to them an end of all strife." In this verse Paul, the apostle to the Gentiles, addressing the holy brethren who are "partakers of the heavenly calling" (iii, 1), not only urges the common usage of mankind, but lays down a certain maxim and principle of the law of nature, whose exercise was to be approved among all. And if the practice thereof had not been lawful unto those to whom he wrote, namely Christians, those who obeyed the Gospel, then he had exceedingly weakened the whole design of his discourse there concerning the oath of God, by shutting it up with this instance, which could be of no force to them if it were unlawful for them to practise the same or have an experience of its efficacy. Finally, if oaths had become unlawful under the New Testament, then God would not have continued their use in any kind, lest His people be encouraged to act contrary to His command. But He *did* so, commissioning an angel to "swear by Him that liveth for ever and ever" (Rev. x, 4-6).

From what has been before us in Matthew v, we may perceive the importance and need of heeding two particular rules when interpreting Scripture. First, that universal affirmations and negations are not always to be universally understood, but are to be limited by their occasions, circumstances, and the subject-matter treated of. Things expressed in universal language must be regarded according to the thing in hand. Thus, when the apostle declared, " I am made *all* things to *all* men, that I might by *all* means save some " (I Cor. ix, 22), if his language were taken without limitation it would signify that he became a blasphemer to blasphemers, etc., whereas his statement must be restricted to things indifferent and innocent, in which he yielded to the weakness of others. In like manner, when Christ said, "Swear not at all," His obvious meaning (according to what follows) is swear not blasphemously, needlessly or by any mere creature.

Second, it is a rule of real use in the interpreting of Holy Writ that when anything is prohibited in one passage, but allowed in another, not the thing absolutely considered is spoken unto in either case, but rather some particular mode, cause, end, or reason is intended. So here, in Matthew v, 34, swearing is forbidden, whereas in other passages we find it is allowed and that examples thereof are proposed unto us. Wherefore it cannot be swearing absolutely that is intended; but evil and needless swearing is condemned by the one, and swearing in right causes or for just ends is approved in the other.

Nor is the taking of an oath to be restricted to law courts only (Exodus xxii, 11), and the instances of Paul and his epistles prove otherwise. In certain cases *private* oaths, between man and man, are perfectly legitimate. "Boaz was a private person, who confirmed by an oath his promise of marriage to Ruth (Ruth iii, 13). Obadiah was a private person, a righteous man, and one that feared the Lord, who declared with an oath the fact of which he wished to convince Elijah (I Kings xviii, 10). I can find, therefore, no better rule than that we regulate our oaths in such a manner that they be not rash or inconsiderate, wanton or frivolous, but used in cases of real necessity" (John Calvin). The awful solemnity of an oath appears from I Kings viii, 31, 32. So too we should duly lay to heart the fearful judgments of God which came upon Israel of old when they were guilty of breaking the third commandment (Jer. v, 7-9; Zech. v, 4).

CHAPTER SIXTEEN

The Law and Retaliation

" Ye have heard that it hath been said, An eye for an eye, and a tooth for a tooth : But I say unto you, That ye resist not evil : but whosoever shall smite thee on thy right cheek, turn to him the other also. And if any man will sue thee at the law, and take away thy coat, let him have thy cloke also. And whosoever shall compel thee to go a mile, go with him twain. Give to him that asketh thee, and from him that would borrow of thee turn not thou away." (Matt. v, 38-42.)

IN what is now to be before us we may perceive once more the deep importance of observing the *scope* of a speaker or writer, of ascertaining the meaning and relation of the context, before attempting to expound a passage. We will not enlarge any further here upon this, having already done so in the introductory paragraphs of one or more of the preceding chapters. It is failure at this very point which has resulted in some commentators of renown quite missing the force of our present portion. They suppose that our Lord here announced a higher standard of spirituality than Moses did, that He introduced a more merciful code of conduct than that which was required during the Old Testament economy. Yet, incredible as it may sound, these same men insist that other verses in this very chapter do not belong to us at all, but pertain only to some " Jewish remnant " of the future.

It does seem strange that men who have no slight acquaintance with the letter of Scripture should err so flagrantly. Yet nothing is more blinding than prejudice, and when a pet theory is allowed to dominate the mind everything is twisted and forced to conform to it. Surely it is perfectly plain to every unbiased soul that, as the same God is the Author of old and new covenant alike, there can be no vital conflict between them, that the fundamental principles underlying the one and the other must be and are in full accord. If those who are so desirous of being looked up to as men who "rightly divide the word of truth " would cease their grotesque efforts to illustrate what they suppose are "dispensational distinctions," and would rather seek to display the wondrous and blessed *unity* of the Old and New Testaments, they would be rendering a more profitable service and God would be far more honoured.

A few of our own readers imagine that in our contending for the doctrinal and practical unity of the entire Scriptures we confound two of its principal objects and subjects, and deny that there is any radical difference between the Law and the Gospel. This is quite an unwarrantable conclusion. Yet do not such mistakes have their roots in the supposition that the Gospel is peculiar to the New Testament? But we ask, Does the Old Testament contain nothing more than typifications of the Gospel in the ceremonial law and predictions of it in the prophecies of Isaiah? Surely it does. Galatians iii, 8, tells us expressly that the Gospel was preached unto Abraham, and Hebrews iv, 2, insists that it was proclaimed unto Israel in the wilderness. Does not the whole of Hebrews xi make it very plain that the Old Testament saints were saved in precisely the same way and on exactly the same ground as we are? Assuredly it does.

" Ye have heard that it hath been said, An eye for an eye, and a tooth for a tooth. But I say unto you, That ye resist not evil: but whosoever shall smite thee on thy right cheek, turn to him the other also. And if any man will sue thee at the law and take away thy coat, let him have thy cloke also. And whosoever shall compel thee to go a mile go with him twain. Give to him that asketh thee, and from him that would borrow of thee turn not thou away" (Matt. v, 28-42). Christ is not here pitting Himself against the Mosaic law, nor is He inculcating a superior spirituality. Instead He continues the same course as He had followed in the context, namely to define that righteousness demanded of His followers, which was more excellent than the one taught and practised by the scribes and Pharisees; and this He does by exposing their error and expounding the spirituality of the moral law.

" Ye have heard that it hath been said, An eye for an eye, and a tooth for a tooth" (verse 38). These words are found three times in the Pentateuch. They occur first in Exodus xxi, a chapter which opens thus, "Now these are the judgments." The word "judgments" signifies judicial laws. The statutes recorded therein were so many rules by which *the magistrates* were to proceed in the courts of Israel when trying a criminal. The execution of these statutes was not left to private individuals, so that each man was free to avenge his own wrongs, but they were placed in the hands of the public administrators of the law. This is further borne out by the third occurrence of our text in Deuteronomy xix, for there we read, "And the *judges* shall make diligent inquisition . . . and thine eye shall not pity; but life shall go for life, eye for eye, tooth for tooth, hand for hand, foot for foot" (verses 18, 21).

A century or so ago such verses as those last quoted were made the object of bitter attacks both by atheists and infidels, but today not a few who profess to be Christians denounce them as inhuman. In this flabby age, when sentiment overrides principle, the doctrine of an eye for an eye and a tooth for a tooth strikes many as being cruel and barbarous. We shall not waste time in replying to such rebels: in due course the Lord Himself will deal with them and vindicate His honour. Nor is there anything in His Holy Word which requires any apology from us: rather does it strengthen our faith when we find so many cavilling at its contents. Nevertheless, there may be a few of the saints who are somewhat disturbed by the barkings of these dogs, so for their sake we would call attention to one or two details.

First, this Divinely prescribed rule was a *just* one: "And if a man cause a blemish in his neighbour: as he hath done, so shall it be done to him; Breach for breach, eye for eye, tooth for tooth: as he hath caused a blemish in a man, so shall it be done to him again" (Lev. xxiv, 19, 20). What is more equitable than an exact *quid pro quo?* Surely it is a most elementary and unchanging principle of sound jurisprudence that the punishment should be made to fit the crime—neither more nor less. So far were the ancients in advance of our moderns that we find a heathen owning the righteousness of such a law: "But Adoni-bezek fled; and they pursued after him, and caught him, and cut off his thumbs and his great toes. And Adoni-bezek said, Threescore and ten kings, having their thumbs and great toes cut off, gathered their meat under my table: as I have done, so *God* hath requited me" (Judges i, 6, 7). If it be objected that in this Christian era justice is far more tempered with mercy than was the case in Old Testament times, then we would remind the objector that "Whatsoever a man soweth that shall he also reap" (Gal. vi, 7) is found in the *New Testament.* "With what measure ye mete, it shall be measured to you again" (Matt. vii, 2) are the words of Christ Himself.

Second, this Mosaic statute was a most *merciful* one. It is to be observed that in Exodus xxi, both before and after the rule recorded in verses 23-25, legislation is given concerning the rights of "servants" or, as the word really means, "slaves." If their masters, out of brutality or in a fit of rage, maimed them, then the magistrates were required to see to it that they in turn should be compelled to take a dose of their own medicine. Who can fail to see, then, that such a law placed a merciful restraint upon the passions of the owners and made for the safeguarding of the persons of their slaves. Moreover, this statute also curbed any judge who in righteous indignation at the cruel injury of a slave was inclined to punish his master too severely: he was not allowed to demand a *life* for an eye, or a limb for a tooth!

Third, such an arrangement was a *beneficent* one for society as a whole, for this law applied not only to masters and servants but to all Israelites in general. It was designed to protect the weak against the strong, the peaceful from lovers of violence. It was a wise and necessary means for preserving law and order in the community. This is clear from the closing verses of Deuteronomy xix: "Then shall ye do unto him as he had thought to have done unto his brother: so shalt thou put the evil away from among you. And those which remain shall hear, and fear, and shall henceforth commit no more any such evil among you" (verses 19, 20). The fear of punishment—providing that punishment be severe and summary—would deter the passionate and vicious. Thus, so far from this law being a cruel and barbarous one, it was a most just, merciful and beneficent one, calculated to remove "evil" and produce that which is good.

Ere passing on let it be pointed out that this law of judicial retaliation ought to be upon our statute books today and impartially and firmly enforced by our magistrates. Nothing would so effectually check the rapidly rising tide of crimes of violence. But alas, so foolish and effeminate is the present generation that an increasing number are agitating for the abolition of capital punishment and the doing away with corporal punishment, and this in the face of the fact that in those countries where capital punishment is most loosely administered there is the highest percentage of murders, and that as corporal punishment is relaxed crimes of brutal violence are greatly increasing. Those who have no regard for the persons of others are very tender of their own skins, and therefore the best deterrent is to let them know that the law will exact from them an eye for an eye and a tooth for a tooth.

"No man needs to be more merciful than God. The benefit that will accrue to the public from this severity will abundantly recompense it. Such exemplary punishment will be warning to others not to attempt such mischiefs" (from Matthew Henry's comments on Deuteronomy xix, 19-21). Magistrates were never ordained of God for the purpose of reforming reprobates or pampering degenerates, but to be His instruments for preserving law and order, and that by being "a terror to the evil" (Romans xiii, 3). The magistrate is "the minister of God," not to encourage wickedness, but to be an "avenger to execute wrath upon him that doeth evil" (Romans xiii, 4). Let it not be forgotten that Christ Himself affirmed of the judge who refused to "avenge" the poor widow of her adversary that he was one "who feared not God neither regarded man" (Luke xviii, 2).

Of course we do not expect to carry all our readers with us, and we shall be rather surprised if we receive no letters condemning us for such "harshness." But let us point out what we are firmly convinced are the causes of the moral laxity and the immoral sentimentality which now so widely prevails. We unhesitatingly blame the pulpit for the present sad state of affairs. The unfaithfulness of preachers is very largely responsible for the lawlessness which is now so rife throughout the whole of Christendom. During the last two or three generations thousands of pulpits have jettisoned the Divine Law, stating that it has no place in this dispensation of grace. And thus the most powerful of all restraints has been removed and licence given to the lusts of the flesh.

Not only has the Divine Law been repudiated, but the Divine character has been grossly misrepresented. The attributes of God have been perverted by a one-sided presentation thereof. The justice, the holiness, and the wrath of God have been pushed into the background, and a God that loves everybody thrust into the foreground. In consequence, the masses of church-goers no longer fear God. For

the past fifty years the vast majority of pulpits have maintained
a guilty silence on Eternal Punishment so that few now have any
dread of the wrath to come. This logically follows from the former,
for no one needs to stand in any terror of One who loves him. The
repercussions have been unmistakable, drastic, and tragic. Sickly
sentimentality regulated the pulpit until it dominated the pew, and
this evil leaven has so spread that it now permeates the whole nation.

Conscience has been comatose: the requirements of justice
are stifled: maudlin concepts now prevail. As eternal punishment
was repudiated—either tacitly or in many cases openly—ecclesiastical punishments were shelved. Churches refused to enforce sanc-
tions, and winked at flagrant offences. The inevitable outcome has
been the breakdown of discipline in the home and the creation of a
"public opinion" which is mawkish and spineless. School-teachers
are intimidated by foolish parents, so that the rising generation
are more and more allowed to have their own way without fear of
consequences. If some judge has the courage of his convictions and
sentences a brute to the "cat" for maiming an old woman, there
is an outcry raised against him. But enough. Most of our readers are
painfully aware of all this without our enlarging any further: but
few of them realize the *causes* which have led up to it—an unfaithful
pulpit, the denial of eternal punishment, the misrepresentation of
God's character, the rejection of His Law, the failure of the churches
to enforce a scriptural discipline, the breakdown of parental
authority.

"Ye have heard that it hath been said, An eye for an eye, and a
tooth for a tooth." This Divine statute, like those which were
before us in the previous sections, had been grossly perverted by the
scribes and Pharisees. They had wrested its purport and design by
giving it *a false application*. Instead of confining it to the
magistrates in the law courts, they had made the statute a promiscuous one. The Jewish leaders had so expounded this precept as
though God had given permission for each individual to take the
law into his own hands and avenge his own wrongs. They intimated
that it allowed each person to take private revenge upon his
enemies: if thy neighbour smite thee and destroyeth one of thine
eyes, then go thou and do likewise to him. Thus a spirit of resistance
was cherished and the act of retaliation condoned.

Should it be asked, How came it that the scribes and Pharisees so
glaringly wrested this law which was manifestly designed for the
guidance of magistrates only? we would point out first that it is a
natural opinion that a man may avenge himself in private when
wrong has been done to him personally; second, answerable thereto
there is a very strong desire for revenge in everyone's heart by
nature; and as the Jewish leaders sought to ingratiate themselves
with the people rather than to please God, they pandered to this
evil lust. In this we may see the workings of the Devil; for in all
ages his policy has been directed to the overthrowing of the Divine

order. The great enemy of God and man has ever sought to move corrupt leaders, both civil and religious, so to temper things to the depraved inclinations and popular opinions of the people that true piety may be overthrown.

Perceiving the earthly-mindedness and materialistic outlook of the Jews, the Devil moved their teachers to dream about a Messiah who should dispense mundane rather than spiritual blessings, so that when Christ came preaching salvation from sin and exhorting men to lay up treasure in heaven, they despised and rejected Him. The Italians had ever been greatly addicted to sorcery and idolatry, as ancient writers testify; and though God vouchsafed them the true Gospel at the beginning of the Christian era, yet the Devil, knowing their natural disposition to superstition, soon corrupted the Truth among them, so that in a short time their church abounded as much in idolatry as ever they did when they were heathen. The like malicious tactics has the Devil used among Protestants, for when he was unsuccessful in corrupting doctrine in the mouths of its leaders, he has greatly weakened it among the rank and file, by causing them to receive in their hearts only that which accords with their evil proclivities.

It is at this very point that the true ministers of God stand out in sharp contrast with the Devil's hirelings. The latter are unregenerate men, with no fear of God in their hearts. "They are of the world, and the world heareth them" (I John iv, 5). They trim their sails to the winds of public opinion. They accommodate their preaching to the depraved taste of their hearers. Their utterances are regulated by a single motive: to please those who pay their salaries. But the servants of Christ shun not to declare all the counsel of God, no matter how distasteful and displeasing it may be to the natural man. They dare not corrupt the Truth and refuse to withhold any part of their God-given message. To glorify their Master and be faithful to the trust He has committed to them is their only concern. Consequently, they share, in their measure, the treatment which was meted out to Him.

"But I say unto you, That ye resist not evil: but whosoever shall smite thee on thy right cheek, turn to him the other also" (verse 39). In this verse and the three which follow Christ confutes the false application which the scribes had made of the Mosaic statute, and it is in *this* light that His exhortations here must be understood. To say He is exhorting His followers absolutely to a passive endurance of any and every injury they may receive at the hands of wicked and unreasonable men is to give a meaning to our Lord's words which the context does not warrant, and which other passages and important considerations definitely forbid. That which He was refuting was the taking of *private* vengeance on those who wrong us. Further proofs in support of this must be left for our next.

CHAPTER SEVENTEEN

The Law and Retaliation—Continued

" BUT I say unto you, That ye resist not evil: but whosoever shall smite thee on thy right cheek, turn to him the other also " (verse 39). In order to properly understand and rightly apply this injunction due regard must be paid to its context, and the whole interpreted in harmony with the general Analogy of Faith, otherwise we are in imminent danger of making Scripture to contradict itself. As we sought to show in our last, Christ was not here repealing an important Mosaic statute and substituting in its place a milder and more merciful rule for His followers to observe, but was (as in the preceding sections of His Sermon) refuting an error of the scribes and reprehending the evil practice of the Pharisees. They had given a promiscuous application to a judicial regulation for the use of magistrates, a regulation which placed strict bounds upon the punishment to be meted out unto those guilty of deeds of maiming.

The statute pertaining to magistrates only had been given a general application, so that the people were allowed to take the law into their own hands, each individual being free to avenge his wrongs privately, which not only condoned but encouraged the spirit of malice and revenge. It was in view of this wicked perversion of the Divine Law that our Saviour said "Resist not evil." More literally it is "Resist not the evil one," that is, the evil individual who has injured you. Resist not: think not of taking the law into your own hands, requiting the adversary as he has done to you. Cherish not against him the spirit of revenge, but be actuated by nobler principles and more spiritual considerations. Such is plainly the general purport of this precept: its particular implications must now be considered.

Even Mr. F. W. Grant (a leader among the " Plymouth Brethren ") agreed that, " The righteousness of the law of course remains righteousness, but it does not require of any that they exact for personal wrongs. There is no supposition of the abrogation of law or of its penalties. The government of the world is not in question, but the path of disciples in it. Where they are bound by the law, they are bound, and have no privileges. They are bound, too, *to sustain it in its general working,* as ordained of God for good. Within these limits there is still abundant room for such practice as is here enjoined. We may still turn the left cheek to him that smites the right, or let the man that sues us have the cloak as well as the coat which he has fraudently gained: for that is clearly within our rights. If the cause were that of another, we should have no right of this kind, nor to aid men generally in escape from justice or in slighting it. The Lord could never lay down a general rule that His people should allow lawlessness, or identify themselves with indifference to the rights of others" (The Numerical Bible).

"Resist not evil." That which Christ here forbade was not the resisting of evil by a lawful defence, but by way of *private revenge.* Public reparation is when the magistrate, according to the justice and mercy of the Divine Law, sentences an evil person who has injured his fellow. Private revenge is when those who are not magistrates take matters into their own hands and retaliate against those who have wronged them. The former is clearly permitted, for an apostle declared the magistrate is "the minister of God" for executing judgment upon evil-doers, the same apostle as expressly forbids retaliation: "Recompense no man evil for evil" (Romans xii, 17).

"But I say unto you, That ye resist not evil." There are many who err in supposing that such a precept as this is peculiar to the New Testament. A comparison of the two Testaments will show that identically the same rule of duty obtained in both economies. "If thine enemy be hungry, give him bread to eat; and if he be thirsty, give him water to drink: For thou shalt heap coals of fire upon his head" (Prov. xxv, 21, 22); Therefore if thine enemy hunger, feed him; if he thirst, give him drink: for in so doing thou shalt heap coals of fire on his head" (Romans xii, 20). Rightly did one of the older writers say, when commenting upon this passage in Proverbs xxv, "The law of love is not expounded more spiritually in any single precept either by Christ or His apostles than in this exhortation." Its obvious meaning is, seize the moment of distress to show kindness to him that hateth thee.

Living in a sinful world, we must expect to meet with injustices and unprovoked injuries. How, then, are we to conduct ourselves under them? The answer is, first, God forbids us, both in the Law and in the Gospel, to recompense evil for evil. The taking of private revenge, either inwardly or outwardly, is expressly prohibited. "Say not thou [no, not even in thine heart] I will recompense evil" (Prov. xx, 22). I must not so much as allow the thought that some day I shall have an opportunity to get my own back: I am not even to hope it, still less resolve the same. The Christian should not desire or determine anything which he cannot in faith ask God to assist him in; and most assuredly he would have no ground whatever to expect the Lord to help him in the execution of a malicious revenge.

We may not requite evil for evil in thought, word, or deed to those who mistreat us, but rather suffer injury and refer our cause to Him who is the Judge of all the earth. Because this duty goes against our natural inclinations, let us mention one or two persuasives thereto. First, it is the expressly revealed will of God for us, and His commands are not grievous. Second, vengeance belongeth unto the Lord, and if we take it upon ourselves to avenge our wrongs privately, then we rob Him of His right. Third, Christ has left us an example that we should follow *His* steps, and "When He was reviled, reviled not again; when He suffered, He threatened not; but committed Himself to Him that judgeth righteously" (I Peter ii, 23); yea, when He was cruelly and unjustly crucified, He prayed for His persecutors. Finally, Christ has plainly warned us that if we forgive not men their trespasses, neither will God forgive ours (Matt. vi, 15).

But now we must face the question of *how far* this precept "Resist not evil" is binding upon us. Is it to be regarded absolutely? Does it recognize no limitation and make no allowance for exceptions? Is the Christian passively to endure *all* wrong? Here is where we must seek guidance from the Analogy of Faith, or in other words, ascertain the teaching of collateral passages. If this be done, it will be found that while our text enunciates a principle of general application, it is not a universal one. To deduce from it the doctrine of unlimited non-resistance to evil is to pervert its teaching, and to exalt the letter above the spirit; just as to insist that the plucking out of a right eye which offends or the cutting off of an offending right hand (verses 29, 30) must be understood and obeyed literally, would be to miss entirely our Lord's meaning in those verses.

First, the teaching of Christ elsewhere manifestly forbids us to understand "Resist not evil" in an unqualified and universal sense. He gave explicit directions to His disciples concerning their duty toward those who wronged them: "If thy brother shall trespass against thee, go and tell him his fault between thee and him alone: if he shall hear thee, thou hast gained thy brother. But if he will not hear thee, then take with thee one or two more, that in the mouth of two or three witnesses every word may be established. And if he shall neglect to hear them, tell it unto the church: but if he neglect to hear the church, let him be unto thee as a heathen man and a publican" (Matt. xviii, 15-17). Now that is very definite resistance to evil: it challenges the wrong done, examines the offence, and punishes the wrong-doer. There are more ways of resistance to evil than the employment of physical force.

Second, the idea of an unqualified non-resistance to evil is contrary to the example of Christ. He resisted evil, attacked wrong-doers, and when smitten did not turn the other cheek. When He went up to Jerusalem and found His Father's house turned into a house of merchandise and a den of thieves, He made a scourge of small cords and cast out of the temple both sheep and oxen. He scattered the money of the desecrators and overthrew their tables (John ii, 13-17). On another occasion He drove them out, stopped the service, and refused to let any man carry a vessel through the temple (Mark xi, 15-17). That was not passive resistance, but vigorous aggression. In the judgment-hall of Caiaphas one of the officers struck the Saviour with his hand, but instead of turning the other cheek Christ challenged the smiter (John xviii, 22, 23). He did not answer force with force and return blow for blow, but He exposed and rebuked the wrong.

Third, were we to offer no resistance whatever unto injuries inflicted upon us, no matter what their nature, or who their perpetrators, then we should fail in supporting and co-operating with the Divine ordinance of the magistrate, and be guilty of abetting evildoers. The magistrate is God's lieutenant, His minister for vindicating the oppressed and punishing criminals. Under certain circumstances it would be our bounden duty to seek the protection and help of the officers of the law, for they are one of God's means for preserving order in the community. If it be right for me to bring an offending brother before the church—the well-being of the church requiring that it should be purged if he be rebellious ; then by what principle can it be wrong for me to summon a law-breaker before the magistrate, in cases where the good of the community obviously requires it?

"This command of our Lord, illustrated by the examples He brings forward, plainly does not forbid us to defend ourselves when we are in danger. To do so is one of the strongest instincts of our nature, the law of God written on our hearts. But with regard to personal injuries, when there is no hazard of life, as in the case specified, it is our duty to repress resentment and to abstain from violence. In like manner, there are cases in which it is plainly a man's duty to avail himself of the protection which the law gives to property. Justice to his creditors, to the public, to his family, may require him to defend his estate, though even this must not be done under the impulse of private revenge. But we ought to have resort to the tribunals of justice only when the cause is important and the call urgent ; we are to prosecute our claims with humanity, moderation, and a spirit of peace; we are to be content with reasonable satisfaction " (John Brown).

When the injury received is a personal and private one it is the Christian's duty to bear it in the spirit of meekness, so long as by so doing he is not encouraging evil-doers and thereby rendering them a menace to others. If I am walking on the pavement and a drunken motorist mounts the kerb, knocks me down, and then drives off, it is plainly my duty to take the number of his car, report the offence to the police, and if required bear witness in the court. So too when a wrong is done to others for whom we are responsible, resistance becomes a duty. If a man's child is in peril at the hands of some human fiend, is he to stand by and see it outraged or murdered? Did not Abraham, the friend of God and the "father of all them that believe," arm his servants, smite those who had taken his nephew prisoner, and free him (Genesis xiv, 14-16)?

As we have so often pointed out in these pages, every truth of Scripture has a balancing one, and it is only by heeding the same that we are preserved from going to an unwarrantable extreme. Examples of those guilty of lopsidedness, not only in doctrine but in practice, are numerous. As there are those who put to false use Christ's " Swear not at all " (verse 34), so there are not lacking others who place an unjustifiable interpretation upon His " resist not evil." They suppose that in this dispensation of grace it is the will of God that His children should allow the principle of grace to regulate all their actions. But certainly it is not God's will that the principle of grace should override and swallow up all other principles of action. The requirements of justice and the demands of holiness are also to be honoured by the Christian. Here too grace is to reign " through righteousness" (Romans v, 21) and not at the expense of it.

The same rule applies to other matters. Abstention from going to law is a sound rule of life. It is a man's wisdom, generally speaking, to keep free of litigation. The apostle condemned the Corinthians because they took their contentions before the civil courts. But is a man, is a Christian, never to resort unto law? What right have we to enjoy the social and civil privileges of a community if we ignore its obligations? Even though we may forgive an offence against our property, have we no responsibility to our neighbours? If I corner a burglar in my house am I at liberty to turn loose upon society one who will plunder its property and imperil its security? There are times when it is the clear duty of a Christian to hand a law-breaker over to the law.

But exceptions do not nullify a rule, rather do they prove it. Care must be taken, then, lest in turning from the letter we lose the spirit of those precepts. " Resist not evil" is a plain command of Christ's and as such it is binding upon us. His follower is to be a man of peace, meekness, enduring wrong, suffering loss, accepting hardship, full of compassion and simple faith. A contentious spirit is evil: to be ever wrangling and always on the defensive is not Christian. Going to law as a rule is neither seemly nor wise. But all of that pertains to the *negative* side: as we shall yet see, there is a positive one too. Good must be returned for evil, for only by good can evil be overcome. Our business is not the punishment of sinners, but the desiring and seeking after their salvation. Such was the life of our Lord, and such also must be ours.

The very fact that the Lord Jesus here designated the evil-doer " the evil one " makes it clear to us that it is the characteristic of an evil man to inflict injury upon others. The giving of this title to the wrong-doer gives us to understand that if we retaliate in the same wicked spirit then we necessarily place ourselves in the same class to which he belongs. We are therefore to suffer wrong patiently. There are but two classes in the world, the good and the evil, and it is the mark of the former that they do good unto all. They who do evil evidence their likeness to the evil one; whereas the prosecution of that which is good is Godlike. If we set ourselves to do harm unto others, either by word or deed, we are in the sight of God evil men: such are usurers and extortioners, profiteers, fraudulent traders, those engaged in any enterprise which subverts morality, underminers of health, Sabbath breakers. The Christian, then, must separate himself from all such callings, and (though it entails a smaller salary) engage in that which is pleasing to God.

Although by nature fallen men be likened unto untamed beasts and fierce animals, resembling the "wild ass's colt" (Job xi, 12), the lion, the leopard, the wolf, the cockatrice (Isaiah xi, 6-8), whose nature it is to hurt and devour other creatures, yet when God in His infinite mercy is pleased to work in them a miracle of grace, bestow upon them spiritual life and reconcile them to Himself, then they lay aside their enmity and ferocity and live in peace with one another, so that the ancient saying is fulfilled: "They shall not hurt nor destroy in all My holy mountain" (Isaiah xi, 9). It is a property of Christ's kingdom that His subjects shall "beat their swords into plowshares and their spears into pruninghooks" (Micah iv, 3)— weapons of bloodshed being transmuted into instruments of usefulness. When men are truly converted, they lay aside malice and wrath and become the doers and promoters of good. This was notably exemplified in the case of Paul, who, from a fierce persecutor, was transformed into a preacher of the Gospel of peace.

CHAPTER EIGHTEEN

The Law and Retaliation—Concluded

THE section of our Lord's Sermon which we are now considering has been misunderstood and wrested by not a few, fanatics attributing to it a meaning which is flatly contradicted by other passages. For this reason we deemed it necessary to enter into a detailed examination of its terms. Two chapters have already been devoted thereto, but as these appeared in the 1939 volume,* it is requisite for us to present a brief summary of the ground therein covered, that new readers may the better grasp what we now write. First, it has been shown that Christ is not here repealing a Mosaic statute and substituting in its place a more merciful and spiritual rule, but that He was engaged (as in the previous sections of this Sermon) in refuting a serious error of the scribes and Pharisees and in presenting the high requirements of the Law.

The words, " An eye for an eye and a tooth for a tooth " (verse 38), occur three times in the Pentateuch. They enunciated one of the judicial laws which the Lord gave to Israel. That law was prescribed solely for the guidance and use of *magistrates*. Its design was threefold: to protect the weak against the strong, to serve as a salutary warning unto evil-doers, to prevent the judge from inflicting too severe a punishment upon those guilty of maiming others. As such it was a just, merciful and beneficent law. If the principle of this statute—the infliction of corporal punishment on those convicted of crimes of violence—was universally and strictly enforced today, it would make this world a much safer place to live in. But this law had been greatly perverted by the Jewish leaders, for instead of confining it to the magistrates they had made a general application of it, teaching that it gave to each person the right to avenge his wrongs privately; and thereby they fostered the spirit of malice and condoned deeds of violence.

" But I say unto you, That ye resist not evil " (verse 39). This signifies that we are forbidden to take the law into our own hands, and requite an adversary as he has done to us: nobler principles and spiritual considerations are to actuate us. Nor is this precept in any wise peculiar to the New Testament: such passages as Proverbs xx, 22; xxiv, 29; xxv, 21, 22, expressly prohibit the taking of private vengeance. Our Lord, then, was continuing to press the high requirements of the moral law. It is to be duly noted, however, that neither

* *Studies in the Scriptures.*

the Law nor the Gospel requires from us an unqualified and universal non-resistance to evil. There are times when an ignoring of wrongs done to us or of injuries inflicted upon us would obviously be a failure to perform our duty. We must never connive at the guilty escaping from justice nor in the slighting of it. Righteousness is to mark us in all our ways.

Graciousness and lawlessness are widely different things. Though gladly willing to forgo our own rights, we must not neglect the rights of others by turning loose on society those who would imperil its security. When a brother trespasses against us he must be challenged and not winked at: if he be unreasonable and impenitent, the matter must be brought before the Church: should he still prove to be defiant and rebellious, then he is to be punished by being disfellowshipped (Matt. xviii, 15-17). Christ Himself resisted evil in the temple, when He found His Father's house had been turned into a house of merchandise and a den of thieves (John ii, 13-17). The office of the magistrate is a Divine ordinance, and we are morally bound to support and co-operate with it. Notwithstanding, we must never appeal to the law in a spirit of malice and revenge, but only because God has appointed and the good of society requires it.

But, on the other hand, exceptions do not nullify a rule, rather do they serve to prove it. In turning from the strict letter of the precept, we must beware of losing its spirit. The disciple of Christ, the Prince of peace, is to be a man of peace, meekly enduring wrong, patiently suffering loss, accepting hardships graciously. Not only are we to refrain from the act of retaliation, but even the desire itself must not be allowed, for God requires holiness of heart as well as of life. All malice and bitterness, wrath and clamour, evil speaking and unkind gestures are to be put off: and bowels of mercy, compassion, and long-suffering put on—anything less is a falling short of the Christian standard. Not only are we to refrain from returning evil for evil, but we must return good for evil, blessing those who curse us and praying for those who despitefully use us.

In what immediately followed, Christ amplified His "Resist not evil" by three examples, wherein He shows how men are to behave themselves when they are wronged. First, "But whosoever shall smite thee on thy right cheek, turn to him the other also" (verse 39). Under these words are expressed all injuries done to men's *bodies*, not only by words and blows, but also in the contempt of their persons, which is intimated by the reference to the "right cheek." Usually, men strike with the right hand and the blow falls on the left cheek, so that if the right cheek be smitten it is commonly with the back of the hand—a blow of contempt, which is even more provoking of retaliation than one given in anger. Nevertheless, says Christ, even such a blow must not be returned, for the taking of private revenge is strictly prohibited. Let the old saying be remembered: it takes two to make a quarrel—though the aggressor be guilty of provocation, yet it is the second party who gives consent to a quarrel if he hits back.

" But whosoever shall smite thee on thy right cheek, turn to him the other also. There has been some controversy in certain quarters as to whether or not these words are to be considered literally. The question may be answered more readily by asking, Are they to be regarded absolutely or comparatively? Obviously, it must be the latter. First, were we to turn the other cheek to the smiter we should be tempting him unto sin, by inviting him *to repeat* the offence, which is manifestly wrong. Second, the example of Christ Himself refutes such an interpretation, for when He was smitten upon the cheek He did not turn the other unto the smiter. Third, the second half of this verse must not be detached from the first. Resist not evil: no matter how provoking be the occasion: revenge not thyself, but rather "give place unto wrath" (Romans xii, 19). Rather than be guilty of malice and violence, be willing to submit to further insults.

Our Lord certainly did not mean by these words, "Whosoever shall smite thee on thy right cheek, turn to him the other also," that we should *court* further wrongs, or that in all cases we must meekly submit to such without any kind of resistance. When He was smitten before the high priest, He did not return blow for blow, but He did remonstrate against it. In so doing Christ was not actuated by a spirit of retaliation, but of justice to His own character, and what He said had a tendency to convict the offender and the assembly. This precept is expressed in the strongest possible form to teach us that we must not render evil for evil, but rather suffer wrong, and submit to a repetition of an injury rather than go about to avenge ourselves. It is the principle rather than the act which is inculcated, yet in certain circumstances a literal compliance would be right, which instead of disgracing us would raise us in the esteem of the godly.

Christ here condemned the common practice of fighting and quarrelling. Even though sorely provoked by another, He will not allow us to strike back. There is nothing to intimate that He disallowed the apostles from carrying swords for self defence, but as soon as Peter drew his to *resist* the officers who came to apprehend Him in the garden, He bade him sheathe it again. In like manner, this precept reprehends the challenging unto a duel, and also the acceptance of such: better be dubbed a coward by our fellows than disobey and displease the Lord. If it be said that it is a disgrace to show the white feather, the reply is that it is true grace to abstain from sinning. Mark it well that a slap in the face is a vastly different thing from life itself being endangered: where *that* is the case, flight or calling for the help of the law is our duty; yea, we must seek to defend ourselves rather than be killed.

"And if any man will sue thee at the law and take away thy coat, let him have thy cloke also" (verse 40). The first example cited by Christ concerned insults to our *persons*, this one has to do with

wrongful attacks upon our *possessions*. It sets forth another
characteristic of evil men, namely to prey upon the goods of their
fellows, either privately or under cover of the law. Such a one was
Zacchaeus, before his conversion, for he had enriched himself by
"false" or fraudulent methods (Luke xix, 8). But know thou, that
all who resort to what are called "tricks of the trade," all who trade
upon the ignorance of their fellows by means of "shady" devices,
all who are successful in the courts as the result of employing crafty
lawyers, are—no matter what be their reputation for shrewdness in
the world—in the sight of God *evil* men; and therefore the Christian
must have no fellowship with such.

It is to be duly noted that this second example respects one of *a
trifling character*. As the former concerned not the severance of a
limb by the sword, but only a slap in the face, so this relates not to
the seizure of our property but merely the loss of a garment. Unless
this be duly noted, we are likely to miss the force of our Lord's
exhortation and make an entirely unwarrantable application. That
which Christ here condemned was not the legitimate use of the courts,
but the going to law over mere trifles. The doing so evidences a contentious spirit and a heart that is anxious for revenge, which ill
becomes a Christian, as the apostle shows in I Corinthians vi, 1-8;
yet it is all too common a practice among men in general. Rather
than enter into litigation over the loss of a coat—the costs entailed
in such a procedure often being more than the purchasing of a new
garment—far better to suffer the loss of it.

"In cases of great importance, other duties may require him to
avail himself of the protection of the law: justice to his creditors,
and to the public, and even to his family, may require him to defend
his estate and to give a check to the exorbitancy of unreasonable
men; and a Christian may prosecute a criminal out of love to public
justice, though not from private revenge. Yet there will generally
be men of the world enough to deal with such depredators; and a
disciple of Christ will seldom have occasion to waste his time or
lose his temper about them" (Thomas Scott). Thus, on the one hand
we must guard against anything which would encourage evil in the
wicked; and on the other, conduct ourselves as those whose affections
are set upon things above. Divine wisdom and grace are necessary if
we are properly to preserve the balance here.

The ruling of our own spirit is far more important than the
clothes which we wear. The preservation of inward tranquillity is of
greater price than a coat or a cloak. Here our Lord teaches us to set
lightly by our temporal goods, that our time and strength may be
devoted to the concerns of eternity. Nothing more surely unfits us for
the pursuit of holiness than a heart which is resentful at and contentious with others. Angry passions and the workings of a spirit of
revenge disqualify us for the worship of God. Meekness and lowliness
of heart are the graces which we particularly need to learn of Christ.
Though there may be cases where duty requires us to take legal

action against one who defrauds us, yet this must be our last resort, for it is extremely difficult to handle pitch without the fouling of our garments.

"And whosoever shall compel thee to go a mile, go with him twain" (verse 41). The actual reference is to public transport service. The Roman troops had power to requisition able-bodied men. Marching through a district, they could compel men to act as porters or guides within a certain area or limit: an illustration of which we have in the case of Simon of Cyrene being compelled to bear the cross of Christ (Mark xv, 21). Such service was not popular: often the demand was inconvenient as well as laborious, and was apt to be rendered in a reluctant and complaining spirit. Christ's command is that even when service is constrained and unreasonable, it should never be performed in a sullen and slavish spirit; but cheerfully and in excess of the demand. Happily there remain but few occasions when we are impressed into the service of the State. But in every life there are circumstances that force to unwelcome tasks; every man has duties which are undertaken not of choice but of necessity; they should be performed readily and cheerfully.

This third example cited by Christ, in which He forbids us to resist evil, has to do with the deprivation or curtailment of our personal *liberties*. It is a case where superiors are guilty of wrongdoing to their inferiors, wherein the injured one is prohibited from making resistance by way of private revenge. That which is inculcated is the abuse of authority and how the offended are to conduct themselves under the same: rather than give way unto bitter resentment, we must patiently bear the injustice, and even be ready to suffer the repetition thereof. The prohibition here made by Christ condemns all private reviling of the laws of the land, the railing of servants against what they deem to be unreasonable in their masters, and the refusal to pay our just dues.

In the example now before us we have noted a third kind of wickedness in evil men, namely those in positions of power and authority wronging those who are under them, by infringing on their personal rights and unjustly curtailing their liberties. Those who are guilty of charging exorbitant rents, overworking their employees, robbing them of their Sabbath rest, and of grinding the faces of the poor, are—no matter what their rank, wealth and honour in the world—*evil men* in the sight of God, and as such they will meet with the due reward of their iniquities in the Day to come. It is for this reason, among others, that we are forbidden to resist or retaliate: in due time the Judge of all will right every wrong, and make it manifest to the whole universe that "the triumphing of the wicked is short."

"In reference to personal liberty there can be no doubt that, next to the blessings of a good conscience and the hope of eternal life, it is one of the most valuable privileges. Every Christian and every man should be ready to do much and suffer much, in order to secure it and retain it for himself and others. Yet at the same time, he will not only patiently submit to every necessary burden and constitutional restraint, but in obedience to our Lord's precept he will bear much of the insolence of men—dressed up in a little brief authority—overlook many stretches of power, and endure even a variety of acts of oppression, rather than have recourse to violence and tumult " (J. Brown).

" Give to him that asketh thee, and from him that would borrow of thee turn not thou away" (verse 42). This supplies a further illustration of that noble and generous spirit which the righteousness of Christ's kingdom requires of its subjects. That righteousness will not only deter them from standing on every point of individual rights, but it will incline them to do good unto others. Interpreting this precept in the light of its setting, it sets forth the *positive* side of our duty: not only does Christ forbid men to requite evil for evil, but He commands them to return good for evil. It is better to give unto those who have no claims upon us and to lend unto those who would impose upon kindness, than to cause strife by a selfish or surly refusal. Our possessions are to be held in stewardship for God and at the disposal of the real need of our followers.

Unto those who object against the limitations we have placed upon the other precepts and the exceptions that have been pointed out, we would earnestly beg them to attend very closely to this one. Surely it is self-evident that the application of this particular injunction is *strictly qualified*. No one with any real acquaintance of the Scriptures can suppose that Christ here imposed an indiscriminate charity as a Christian duty: that we are to give or lend to every one who asks. One of the growing curses of modern life is the ill-advised charity of those who allow their sympathies to run away with them. Lending is to be done "with discretion" (Psalm cxii, 5). The apostolic principle is, "That if any would not work, neither should he eat " (II Thess. iii, 10): it is no part of duty—either of the individual or of the State—to maintain in idleness those who are too lazy to work. If the following passages be carefully pondered, the will of God for us in this matter may be readily perceived: Proverbs iii, 27; I Corinthians xvi, 2, 3; II Corinthians viii, 13, 14; Ephesians iv, 28; I John iii, 17.

CHAPTER NINETEEN

The Law and Love

" Ye have heard that it hath been said, Thou shalt love thy neighbour, and hate thine enemy. But I say unto you, Love your enemies, bless them that curse you, do good to them that hate you, and pray for them which despitefully use you, and persecute you ; That ye may be the children of your Father which is in heaven : for he maketh His sun to rise on the evil and on the good, and sendeth rain on the just and on the unjust. For if ye love them which love you, what reward have ye ? do not even the publicans the same ? And if ye salute your brethren only, what do ye more than others ? do not even the publicans so ? Be ye therefore perfect, even as your Father which is in heaven is perfect." (Matt. v, 43-48.)

" YE have heard that it hath been said, Thou shalt love thy neighbour, and hate thine enemy. But I say unto you, Love your enemies, bless them that curse you, do good to them that hate you " (verses 43 and 44). Few sections of the Sermon on the Mount have suffered more at the hands of expositors than has this one. Most of them, through failure to attentively weigh and rightly understand the whole context, have quite missed the scope of our passage. In con‑ sequence of such failure our Lord's design in these verses has been misapprehended, the prevailing but erroneous idea being held that they set forth the vastly superior moral standard of the New Covenant over that which obtained under Judaism. Many have wrongly defined its principal terms, giving too restricted a meaning both to " neighbour " and " love." Ludicrous indeed are the shifts made by some in the endeavours to harmonize their interpretation of these verses with the theological system to which they are committed.

How widely the commentators differ among themselves, and how ambiguous and unsatisfactory are their explanations will appear from the following quotations—taken from their remarks on " Love your enemies." " We cannot have complacency in one that is openly wicked and profane, nor put a confidence in one that we know to be deceitful; *for are we to love all alike*; but we must pay respect to the human nature, and so far honour all men; we must take notice with pleasure of that even in our enemies which is amiable and commendable; ingenuity, good temper, learning, moral virtue, kind‑ ness to others, profession of religion, etc., and love that, though they are our enemies. We must have a compassion for them, and a good will toward them " (Matthew Henry). That seems to us about as clear as mud. First, this eminent author virtually tells us that we cannot love an enemy: then he affirms we must respect any good qualities we can discern in them: and closes with the statement that we should wish them well.

127

Much to the same effect are the reflections of Thomas Scott, for though he begins by asserting it as a Christian duty to love our enemies, to regard them "with benevolence, to return good works and kind wishes to their revilings and imprecations, and beneficent acts to their injuries," yet he spoils this by adding: "As however there are various favours which He bestows only on His people, so our peculiar friendship, kindness and complacency must and ought to be *restricted to the righteous;* yea, gratitude to benefactors and predilections for special friends consist very well with this general good will and good conduct toward enemies and persecutors." Here again we are left wondering as to what our Lord really meant when He bade us "*love* your enemies."

Andrew Fuller sought to cut the knot by having recourse to the subtleties of the schoolmen, who insisted there are two different kinds of love, both in God and in man—wherein they confounded mere kindness with love. This writer said, "Much confusion has arisen on this subject from not distinguishing between benevolence and complacency. The one is due to all men, whatever be their character, so long as there is any possibility or hope of their becoming the friends of God; the other is not, but requires to be founded on character" (*On love to enemies*). The substance of which is that the love we exercise unto the enemies of God is of a totally different order from that which we bear to His children.

Stranger still is the method followed by the renowned John Gill in his effort to explain away Christ's injunction that we must love our enemies. "I apprehend, the love with which Christ exhorts His people to love their enemies is not to be understood *quoad affectus* (as respecting the internal affections of love): I cannot believe that Christ requires of me that I should love a persecutor as I do my wife, my children, my real friend, or brother in Christ; but *quoad effectus* (as to the effects), that is, I am required to do these things as they lay in my way and according to my ability, as a man would do to his neighbour whom he loves; that is, feed him when he is hungry, and give him drink when thirsty" (from *Truth Defended*).

The explanation given by Mr. Gill is the worst of them all, for it contains a most serious error, implying as it does that outward compliance with God's requirements will be accepted by Him even though the one spring from which all such actions must proceed be inactive. It is not the outward appearance, but the heart, God ever looks at. Now "love is the fulfilling of the law" (Romans xiii, 10), and love is essentially a thing of the heart. Love is the fulfilling of the Law because love to God and to man is all that it requires. Real obedience is nothing more and nothing less than the exercise of love and the directing of it to what God has commanded. Strictly speaking, there is no ground for the distinction commonly made of internal and external obedience: all true obedience is internal, consisting in the exercise of love, and external obedience is simply the expression thereof. Consequently, external conformity to the Divine commands which proceeds not from *love*—holy affections— is worthless "dead works."

"Ye have heard that it hath been said, Thou shalt love thy neighbour, and hate thine enemy" (verse 43). As we have passed from section to section of Matthew v, we have warned against and sought to repudiate the widely held mistake that Christ was here setting up a more spiritual and merciful law than the one which had been given at Sinai. In the verse just quoted we have additional proof, clear and conclusive, that our Lord was *not* engaged in pitting Himself against the law of Moses, but rather that He was concerned with the refuting and rejecting of the deadly errors of the Jewish teachers. The Pentateuch will be searched in vain for any precept which required the Israelites to entertain any malignity against their foes: thou shalt "hate thine enemy" was a rabbinical invention pure and simple.

"Thou shalt not avenge, nor bear any grudge against the children of thy people, but thou shalt love thy neighbour as thyself: I am the Lord" (Lev. xix, 18): such was the original commandment. Now our Lord was not referring to this Divine statute at all, but to the Pharisees' perversion of the same. True, they quoted the actual words, "thou shalt love thy neighbour as thyself," but they misunderstood and misapplied them. The lawyer's question to Christ, "Who is my neighbour?" (Luke x, 29), asked in order to "justify himself," revealed the error of the party to which he belonged, as our Lord's answer thereto made plain the scope of the term over which they stumbled. The Jewish rabbis restricted the word "neighbour" to friends or those closely related to them: to those of their nation and particularly those who belonged to their own party.

The term "neighbour" is used in the Old Testament in a twofold manner: a wider and more general, and a narrower and more specific. In its common usage it includes anyone with whom we may come into contact, having respect unto our fellow men. In its specific sense it signifies one who is near to us by ties of blood or habitation. But anyone who searches the Scriptures should have been left in no uncertainty as to the Spirit's meaning. "Speak now in the ears of the people, and let every man borrow of his neighbour, and every woman of her neighbour, jewels of silver, and jewels of gold" (Exodus xi, 2): the reference here is to the Egyptians among whom Israel then lived. "Strangers," equally with "neighbours," are represented as the proper objects of such love as we bear to ourselves, and that, in the very chapter where the command to love our neighbour is recorded: "If a stranger sojourn with thee in your land, ye shall not vex him; but the *stranger* that dwelleth with you shall be unto you as one born among you, and thou shalt *love him* as thyself: for ye were strangers in the land of Egypt" (Lev. xix, 33, 34).

So far from the Divine injunction, "thou shalt love thy neighbour as thyself," being restricted to those who are amiable and friendly toward us, in more than one passage in the Law even an adversary in a law-suit is described as a neighbour: "When they have a matter, they come unto me; and I judged between one and his neighbour" (Hebrew of Exodus xviii, 16). Hence the inference which the Pharisees should have drawn from the Divine statute would be, "Thou shalt love all men, even those who are seeking to injure thee." When God prohibited His people from bearing false witness against their neighbours, and when He forbade them coveting the wife of a neighbour (Exodus xx, 16, 17), the prohibition must of necessity be understood without any limitation. Thus, the commandment to love their neighbours, properly understood, bade them to love all mankind.

As, then, this Divine precept commanded the Israelites to love all men, it most certainly prohibited the harbouring of a malignant spirit against anyone. But not only did the Jewish rabbis unwarrantably restrict the injunction to *love* their neighbours, but they also drew from it the false and wicked inference "and *hate* thine enemy." How excuseless was any such conclusion appears from the fact that the command to love their neighbours was immediately preceded by the prohibition, "thou shalt not avenge, *nor bear any grudge* against the children of thy people" (Lev. xix, 18), while verse 34 bids them to love as themselves any stranger living in their midst. To cherish any ill feeling against any enemy was directly opposed to both the letter and the spirit of the morality of the Law: no such sentiment was expressed in any form of words.

How utterly opposed to the Law itself was this evil conclusion of the rabbis will appear from the following scriptures. "If thou meet thine enemy's ox or his ass going astray, thou shalt surely bring it back to him again. If thou see the ass of him that hateth thee lying under his burden, and wouldest forbear to help him, thou shalt surely help with him" (Exodus xxiii, 4, 5). "Rejoice not when thine enemy falleth, and let not thine heart be glad when he stumbleth; lest the Lord see, and it displease Him" (Prov. xxiv, 17, 18). "If thine enemy be hungry, give him bread to eat; and if he be thirsty, give him water to drink" (Prov. xxv, 21). Nor were these unqualified precepts in any wise annulled by the special instructions Israel received through Moses and Joshua to destroy the wicked inhabitants of Canaan, for in so doing they were acting as the executioners of the righteous judgments of God upon those who were so corrupt and vile that they were a public menace. Nor were they bidden to *hate* those miserable wretches. No foundation, then, was laid in those extraordinary judgments on the Canaanites for the general principle that hatred to enemies is lawful.

It may be objected to what has been pointed out above that there are some passages which seem to make against our contention. For example, we find David saying, "Do not I hate them, O Lord, that hate Thee? And am not I grieved with those that rise up against

Thee? I hate them with a perfect hatred: I count them mine enemies" (Psalm cxxxix, 21, 22). Upon these verses we may remark that first we must distinguish sharply between private and public enemies. The former is one who has done us some personal injury: even so, we must not hate him or retaliate. The latter is one who is in open and inveterate revolt against God, a menace to His cause and people: even so, though we righteously hate his evil cause and sins, we must not his person. So in the above passage, it was the public enemies of Israel and of God whom David hated.

From what has been before us we may see in the case of the rabbis two abuses of the Scriptures, dangerous and disastrous abuses, against which every teacher of the Word must most diligently guard, namely misinterpretation and the drawing of seemingly logical but false inferences. How necessary it is that terms of Holy Writ should be rightly defined, and what labour is demanded from the teacher (often the patient examination of scores and sometimes of hundreds of verses to discover how the Spirit has used a particular term) in order to achieve this; otherwise he is very liable to be guilty of causing error to pass muster for the Truth. Doubly solemn is that exhortation, "My brethren, be not many teachers, knowing that we shall receive the greater condemnation" (Greek of James iii, 1).

Again, from what has been before us we may discover an infallible mark of a *false teacher*: he is one who deliberately panders to the corrupt inclinations of his auditors, adapting his message to their perverted inclinations, wresting the Scriptures so as to secure their approbation. The teaching of the scribes and Pharisees was: Jews are required to love and do good unto their brethren after the flesh, but they are not only permitted, it is their bounden duty to cherish bitter enmity against the Gentiles. Such a doctrine was only too agreeable to the malignant and selfish principles of fallen human nature, and accordingly we find the Jews generally acted under its influence. "They readily show compassion to their own country-men, but they bear to all others the hatred of an enemy" (Tacitus); while Paul describes them as "contrary to all men, forbidding us to speak unto the Gentiles that they might be saved" (I Thess. ii, 15, 16).

Finally, we may behold here *the fruit of false doctrine,* namely evil communications corrupting good manners. The Jews have ever been a people marked by strong passions—loving their friends fervently and hating their enemies intensely; and from the Phari-sees' corrupting of the law of God so as to make it square with the prejudices of their disciples, the most evil consequences followed. Erroneous beliefs necessarily lead to erroneous conduct, for "as a man thinketh in his heart so is he." This principle is horribly exem-plified in Romanism: their evil practices resulting from their false traditions. Thus, they regard their "places of worship" as more holy than any other buildings, and consequently many of the deluded papists never-engage in formal prayer except when they enter one of their "churches" or "cathedrals."

" But I say unto you, Love your enemies." From all that has been
before us it should be quite plain that our Lord was not, in these
words, pitting Himself against any Mosaic precept, nor even making
an addition thereto: rather was He purging that Divine statute
from the corruptions of the scribes and Pharisees, and revealing the
scope and high spirituality of God's precepts. The love which the
Divine Law demands is something vastly superior to what we call
"natural affection": love for those who are nearest to us by ties
of blood is but a natural instinct or feeling—found in the heathen,
and in a lower degree among the animals. The love which the
Divine Law requires is a holy, disinterested, and spiritual one. This
is unequivocally established by the fact that our Lord linked inseparably together, "Thou shalt love the Lord thy God with all thy
heart" and "thy neighbour as thyself" (Matt. xxii, 37, 39)—our
neighbour must be loved with the very same love that God is.

" But I [God incarnate, the Giver of the original Law] say unto
you, Love your enemies, bless them that curse you, do good to them
that hate you, and pray for them that despitefully use you, and
persecute you" (verse 44). In these words Christ does three things.
First, He expressly refutes the error of the scribes and Pharisees, who
restricted the term "neighbour" unto friends and acquaintances,
and shows that it is so all-embracive as to include "enemies":
verily, God's command is "exceeding broad" (Psalm cxix, 96).
Second, He bluntly repudiates their evil teaching that an enemy
is to be hated, affirming the very opposite to be the Truth, insisting
that God commands us to love even those who hate and injure us.
Third, He makes crystal clear what is signified by "love," namely
a holy, inward, and spiritual affection, which expresses itself in
godly and kindly acts. Thus we are assured beyond any shadow of
doubt that the moral law is of Divine origin, for who among men
had ever conceived such a precept as "love for enemies"?

CHAPTER TWENTY

The Law and Love—Continued

STRICTLY speaking, the contents of the last six verses of Matthew v contain a continuation of the same subject dealt with in the section immediately preceding them (verses 38-42). There, we saw our Lord taking up the important matter of the Law and retaliation; here, He deals with the same theme, though from a different angle. There, He treated more especially with the negative side, declaring what the subjects of His kingdom *must not do* when they are provoked by personal affronts and private injuries: they are not to resist evil. But here, He takes up the positive aspect, stating what His followers *must do* unto those who hate and persecute them, namely return good for evil, love for hatred. So far from being overcome with evil, the Christian is to overcome evil with good (Romans xii, 20).

It will therefore be seen that in this concluding section of His exposition of the moral law our Lord reached the climax in His showing how far the holiness required of His subjects exceeded the righteousness of the scribes and Pharisees: as Christ had taken up one commandment after another, He had made clear the vast difference which separated the one from the other. They had systematically distorted each precept that concerned man's relations with his fellows—lowering the Divine standard and narrowing its scope, so as to comport with the depraved inclinations of their followers. Count after count the Saviour had preferred against them: over against which He had set the elevated and inexorable spirituality of God's requirements. The contrast is radical and revolutionary: it is the contrast between error and truth, darkness and light, corruption and holiness.

First, Christ had exposed their perversion of the Divine statute, "Thou shalt not kill," and had revealed how far beyond their representations this requirement extended (verses 21-26). Second, He had condemned their unwarrantable whittling down of the commandment, "Thou shalt not commit adultery," and had shown that it reached to the very thoughts and intents of the heart (verses 27-32). Third, He had rebuked their wicked tampering with the injunction, "Thou shalt not take the name of the Lord thy God in vain," and had affirmed that all unnecessary oaths of whatsoever kind were thereby prohibited (verses 33-37). Fourth, He had shown how they had corrupted the magisterial rule of "an eye for an eye" (verses 38-42). And finally, He dealt with their vile corruption of

133

the commandment, "Thou shalt love thy neighbour as thyself" (verses 43-48).

In our last chapter we intimated that the commentators are all at sea in their understanding of Christ's "But I say unto you, Love your enemies": they failed to see that His purpose was to re-enforce the requirements of the Moral Law. The "Moral Law" we say, not merely the Mosaic Law, but that which God originally implanted in man's very nature, to be the rule of his being. The requirements of that original Moral Law (renewed at Sinai), are summed up in two things: first, "Thou shalt love the Lord thy God with all thy heart, and with all thy soul, and with all thy mind" (Matt. xxii, 37), that is, thou shalt esteem and venerate Him supremely, delight thyself in His excellency superlatively, honour and glorify Him constantly.

"And the second is like unto it, Thou shalt love thy neighbour as thyself" (Matt. xxii, 39). Here are three things. First, the duty required: "thou shalt love." Second, the ground or reason of it: because he is "thy neighbour," that is thy fellow man, of the same order and blood as thyself. Third, the standard by which love to our neighbour is to be regulated: "as thyself," which defines both its nature and its measure. Such a requirement presupposes that we have a right temper of mind: an upright, impartial, benevolent temper, even to perfection, without the least tincture of anything to the contrary. This is self-evident, for without such love we shall not, we cannot, love our neighbour in a true light, nor think of, nor judge of, nor feel toward him exactly as we ought. A wrong temper, a selfish, uncandid, censorious, bitter spirit, will inevitably give a wrong turn to all our thoughts and feelings unto him.

What is it to love our neighbour as ourself? Our love to ourself is unfeigned, fervent, active, habitual and permanent: so ought to be our love unto our neighbour. A regular self-love respects all our interests, but especially our spiritual and eternal interests: so ought our love unto our neighbour. A regular self-love prompts us to be concerned about our welfare tenderly, to seek it diligently and prudently, to rejoice in it heartily, and to be grieved for any calamities sincerely: so ought our love unto our neighbour prompt us to feel and conduct ourselves with regard to his welfare. Self-love makes us take unfeigned *pleasure* in promoting our welfare: we do not think it hard to do so much for ourselves: we ought to have just the same genuine love to our neighbour, and thereby prove "it is more blessed to give than to receive."

The kind of love which God requires us to have for our neighbour is therefore vastly superior to what is commonly called human *compassion*, for this is often found in the most lawless and wicked of men; it takes not its rise from regard to the Divine authority or respect for God's image in our fellows but springs merely from our animal constitution. The same may be said of what men term *good nature*: just as some beasts are better tempered than others, so some humans are milder, gentler, humbler than their fellows, yet their amiability is not influenced by any consideration for the commands of God. The same may also be said of *natural affection*. Some of the most ungodly cherish warm affection to their wives and children, yea, make veritable idols of them—working and toiling day and night for them—to the utter neglect of God and their souls. Yet all this affection to their children does not prompt them to strive for their spiritual and eternal welfare. It is but natural fondness, and not a holy love.

Now let it be clearly grasped that our Lord's purpose, in the last six verses of Matthew v, was to purge this great and general commandment of the second table of the Law—"Thou shalt love thy neighbour as thyself"—from the corrupt interpretations of the Jewish teachers and to restore it to its true and proper meaning. And as was His method in the previous sections, Christ here specifies first the error of the rabbis, and then proceeds to enforce the rightful application of the Divine precepts. Their error was twofold: first, the unwarrantable restricting of the term "neighbour" to those who were friendly disposed towards them; second, the drawing from it of the false and wicked inference that it was lawful to hate their enemies. How closely modern Christendom approximates to degenerate Judaism in this respect we must leave the reader to judge.

Having shown, again and again, what our Lord was engaged in doing throughout the whole of this part of His Sermon (verses 17-48) let us now point out His evident *design* in the same. To make this the more obvious, let the reader endeavour to place himself among Christ's audience on this occasion and imagine that it was the first time he had ever heard such teaching. As he listened carefully to Christ's emphatic and searching words, "I say unto you, That except your righteousness shall exceed the righteousness of the scribes and Pharisees, ye shall in no case enter into the kingdom of heaven" (verse 20), as he pondered His "But I say unto you, That whosoever is angry with his brother without a cause shall be in danger of the judgment" (verse 22), as he weighed His "But I say unto you, That whosoever looketh on a woman to lust after hath committed adultery with her already in his heart" (verse 28), what would be the effect produced upon him?

Face that question fairly and squarely, my reader. Had you stood on the slope of that mount and listened to Him who spoke as never man spoke—for He was God incarnate—the Lawgiver Himself now interpreting and enforcing the demands of His holy, just, and spiritual Law; as you honestly measured yourself by such pure and exalted requirements, what had been your reaction? Had you not been obliged to hang your head in shame, to acknowledge how far, far short you came of measuring up to such a heavenly standard, to own that when weighed in such a balance you were found woefully wanting, yea, that you were lighter than vanity? If you were honest with yourself, could you say anything less than that such a Law utterly condemned you at every point, that before it you must confess yourself to be guilty, utterly undone, a lost sinner?

And then as you listened to the passage we have now reached and heard the Son of God affirm, "But I say unto you, Love your enemies, bless them that curse you, do good to them that hate you, and pray for them which despitefully use you and persecute you" (verse 44), how had you felt? Would you be filled with resentment and exclaim, Such a request is impracticable and absurd. Why, I instinctively, automatically, inevitably, resent ill treatment and feel ill-will against those who hate and injure me. I cannot do otherwise: no efforts of mine can reverse the spontaneous impulses of my heart: I cannot change my own nature? Again we ask, would the attentive weighing of this demand "Love your enemies" evoke the angry retort, Such a requirement is preposterous, it is an impossibility, no man can obey it? If so, you would be but furnishing proof that "the carnal mind is enmity against God: for it is not subject to the law of God, neither indeed can be" (Romans viii, 7).

Hearken now unto the final demand made by Christ in this connection: "Be ye therefore *perfect*," and so that there should not be the slightest room for uncertainty, He added "even as your Father which is in heaven is perfect" (verse 48). Do you say that this is too high for us to reach, that such a standard is unattainable by flesh and blood? We answer, It is the standard which God Himself has set before us, before all men. It was God's standard before the Fall, and it is His standard still, for though man has lost his power to comply, God has not lost His right to require what is due Him. And why is it that man is no longer able to meet this righteous demand? Because his heart is corrupt: because he is totally depraved. But that in no wise excuses him: rather is it the very thing which renders him thoroughly guilty and his case inexcusable.

Cannot the reader now perceive clearly the design of Christ in here pressing upon His hearers the exalted spirituality of the Divine Law and the inexorableness or immutability of its requirements? It was to shatter the vain hopes of His hearers, to slay their self-righteousness. Of old it had been said, "But who may abide the day of His coming? and who shall stand when He appeareth? for He is like a refiner's fire" (Mal. iii, 2), which was then receiving its fulfilment, as the preceding verse (concerning John the Baptist) shows. If the heart of a fallen man was so corrupt that he could not love his enemies, then he was in dire need of a *new* heart. If to be perfect as the Father in heaven is perfect was wholly beyond him, and wholly contrary to him, then his need of being *born again* was self-evident.

After all that has been before us none should be surprised to learn that during the past fifty years there has been such a strong and widespread effort made to get rid of the flesh-withering teaching of this part of our Lord's ministry. Those professing to be the towers of orthodoxy and the most enlightened among Bible teachers have blatantly and dogmatically affirmed that " the Sermon on the Mount is *not for us*," that it is " Jewish," that it pertains to a future dispensation, that it sets forth the righteousness which will obtain in " the millennial kingdom." And this satanic sop was eagerly devoured by multitudes of those who attended the " Second Coming of Christ " conferences, and was carried by them into many of the " churches," their pastors being freely supplied with "dispensational" literature dealing with this fatal error. Slowly but surely this evil leaven has worked until a very considerable and influential section of what passes as orthodox Christianity has been poisoned by it.

The fundamental error of those men claiming to "rightly divide the word of truth" is their opposition to and repudiation of the Law of God: their insistence that it is solely Jewish, that the Gentiles were never under it, and that it is not now the believer's rule of life. Never has the Devil suceeded in palming off for the Truth a more soul-destroying lie than this. Where there is no exposition of the Moral Law and no presssing of its righteous demands, where there is no faithful turning of its holy and searching light upon the deceitful heart, there will be, there can be, no genuine conversions, for " by the law is the knowledge of sin " (Romans iii, 20). It is by the Law alone we can learn the real nature of sin, the fearful extent of its ramifications, and the penalty passed upon it. The Law of God is hated by man—religious and irreligious alike—because it condemns him and demonstrates him to be in high revolt against its Giver.

Knowing full well the detestation of their hearers for the Divine Law, a large percentage of those who have occupied the pulpits during the past few decades have studiously banished it therefrom, displacing it with "studies in prophecy" and what they designate as " the Gospel of the Grace of God." But the " gospel " preached by these blind leaders of the blind was " another gospel " (Gal. i, 6): where there is no enforcing the requirements of the Law, there can be no preaching of God's Gospel, for so far from the latter being opposed to the former, it " *establishes* " the same (Romans iii, 31). Consequently, the " churches " became filled with spurious converts, who trampled the Law of God beneath their feet. And this, more than anything else, accounts for the lawlessness which now obtains everywhere in Church and State alike.

So far from the Gentiles never having received the Law of God, the apostle to the Gentiles expressly declares, " Now we know that what things soever the law saith, it saith to them who are under the law: that *every* mouth may be stopped, and *all the world* may become guilty before God " (Romans iii, 19). What could possibly be plainer? Even if the " every mouth " did not signify all without exception, it must at the very least mean all without distinction, and therefore would include Jew and Gentile alike. But as though to remove any uncertainty, it is added, " all the world," that is, the entire number of the ungodly. However much the wicked may now murmur against God's Law, in the day of judgment every one of them shall be silent—convicted and confounded. Before the Divine tribunal every sinner will be brought in guilty by the Law, to his utter confusion and eternal undoing. However far they may have previously succeeded in an attempt at self-extenuation or in vindicating themselves before their fellows, when they shall stand " before God " their own consciences will utterly condemn them.

Then how vitally important, how absolutely essential, it is that the Law should be plainly and insistently enforced *now*. Nothing is more urgently needed today than discourses patterned after our Lord's Sermon on the Mount. It is the bounden duty of His servants to press upon their hearers the Divine authority, the exalted spirituality, the inexorable demands of the Moral Law. Nothing is so calculated to expose the worthlessness of the empty profession of modern religionists. Let them be informed that nothing less than loving God with all their heart and strength, and to love their neighbours as themselves, is required of them, and that the slightest failure to render the same brings them in guilty, and thus exposes them to the certainty of everlasting woe; and either they will bow in self-condemnation before the Divine sentence or they will come out in their true colours and rail against it.

Then see to it, preachers, that you faithfully set forth the unchanging requirements of the thrice-holy God. Spare no efforts in bringing your congregations to understand *what is signified* in loving God with all the heart, and *all that is involved* in loving our neighbours as ourselves. How otherwise shall they be brought to know their guilt? Unless they are made to feel how totally contrary to God is their depraved nature, how shall they discover their imperative need of being born again? True, such preaching will not increase your popularity, rather will it evoke opposition. But remember that the Saviour Himself was hounded to death, not for proclaiming the Gospel, but for enforcing the Law! Even though *you* be persecuted, yours will be the satisfaction of knowing your skirts are clear from the blood of your hearers.

CHAPTER TWENTY-ONE

The Law and Love—Concluded

"THAT ye may be the children of your Father which is in heaven: for He maketh His sun to rise on the evil and on the good, and sendeth rain on the just and on the unjust" (verse 45). For a right understanding of this most important verse it is highly essential that it be not divorced from what is recorded in verses 43 and 44. As we have shown at length in the last two chapters, our Lord's purpose in the last six verses of Matthew v was to purge this great and general commandment—"Thou shalt love thy neighbour as thyself"—from the corrupt interpretations of the Jewish teachers, and to restore it to its true and proper meaning. That love which the Moral Law demands is something vastly superior to what we term "natural affection," which is found in the most godless, and in a lesser degree even in animals. The love which the Divine Law requires is a holy, pure, disinterested and spiritual one—exemplified perfectly by Christ. Such a love the unregenerate have not.

In these pages we have often affirmed that God's design in regeneration is to bring us back unto conformity with His holy Law. Therein we may perceive the beautiful harmony which exists between the distinctive workings of each of the three Persons in the blessed Trinity. The Father, as the supreme Governor of the world, framed the Moral Law as a transcript of His holy nature and an authoritative expression of His righteous will. The Son, in His office as Mediator, magnified the Law and made it honourable by rendering to it a personal, perfect and perpetual obedience, and then by voluntarily enduring its curse in the stead of His people, who had broken it. The Holy Spirit, as the Executive of the Godhead, convicts the elect of their wicked violation of the Moral Law, slaying their enmity against it, and imparting to them a nature or principle the very essence of which is to delight in and serve that Law (Romans vii, 22, 25).

Originally, the Moral Law was imprinted upon the very heart of man. Adam and Eve were made in the image and likeness of God (Gen. i, 26, 27), which, among other things, signifies that they were morally conformed unto their Maker. Consequently, the very "nature" of unfallen man caused him to render loving and loyal obedience to his King. But when he fell, this was reversed. The "image" of God was broken and His "likeness" was greatly marred, though not completely effaced, for, as the apostle points out, the heathen which had not the Law in its written form "did

139

by nature [some of] the things contained in the law," and thereby
they "showed the work of the law written in their hearts," their
conscience being proof of the same (Romans ii, 14, 15). At the Fall,
love for the Divine Law was supplanted by hatred, and submission
and obedience gave place to enmity and opposition.

Such is the condition of unregenerate man the world over: he is
a rebel against the Most High, trampling His commandments
beneath his feet. For this very reason he needs to be born again,
that is, be made the subject of a miracle of grace wrought in his
heart. At conversion he is "reconciled to God": his hostility
against Him has received its death-wound and he throws down the
weapons of his warfare. The new birth is a being "*renewed* in
knowledge *after the image* of Him that created him" (Col. iii, 10):
it is a new creation, a creation " in righteousness and true holiness '
(Eph. iv, 24). Thereby the regenerate recover that which they lost
in Adam—a nature which is in harmony with the Divine will. At
the new birth God makes good that promise, " I will put My laws
into their mind and write them in their hearts" (Heb. viii, 10):
putting His laws in our mind means effectually applying them unto
us, writing them in our hearts signifies the enshrining of them in
our affections.

What is the character of that righteousness which Christ requires
from the subjects of His kingdom—a righteousness which excels
that practised by the scribes and Pharisees? It is conformity in heart
and life to the Moral Law of God. What evidence do Christians give
that they have been born again? Why, the fact that they now walk
" in newness of life." Wherein lies the proof that they are now reconciled to God? In their heartily responding to His revealed will.
How may we identify those who have been renewed by the Spirit?
By seeing displayed in them the features of the Divine image. What
is the fruit of God's putting His laws into our minds and writing
them in our hearts? Surely, our running in the way of His commandments. Whereby shall the world take knowledge of us that we
have been with the Lord Jesus? By seeing that we have drunk into
His spirit and by our producing that which rises above the level of
mere nature, which can issue only from a supernatural spring.

Now it is of this very thing that Christ speaks here in Matthew
v, 45: " That ye may be the children of your Father which is in
heaven: for He maketh His sun to rise on the evil and on the good,"
etc. First, let it be pointed out, "that ye may *be* the children of
your Father" certainly does *not* denote "that ye may *become*'
such: no, they were already His regenerate people, as is clear from
Christ's contrasting them with the world—"What do ye more than
others?" (verse 47). "That ye may be the children of your Father
which is in heaven" denotes "that ye may thereby *approve* yourselves so, that ye may *manifest* yourselves to be such." Lest this
interpretation appear somewhat strained, we refer the reader to a
parallel case in II Corinthians vi: "Wherefore come out from

among them, and be ye separate, saith the Lord, and touch not the
unclean thing; and I will receive you, And *will be* a Father unto
you, and ye *shall be* My sons and daughters" (verses 17, 18). Those
exhortations were addressed to "saints" (II Cor. i, 1), and the
promise was that upon their compliance therewith God would
manifest Himself as a Father unto them and they would give proof
of being His sons and daughters.

Because it is against the nature of fallen man to love his enemies,
therefore our Saviour here encouraged His followers unto the exercise of such heavenly conduct by pressing upon them the *benefit*
therefrom: by so doing they would give demonstration that they
were the children of God. A similar inducement had been held out
by Him in an earlier section of this Sermon, when He said to the
officers of His kingdom, "Let your light so shine before men that
they may see your good works and glorify your Father which is in
heaven" (verse 16). It is not sufficient that we profess ourselves to be
the children of God: our works must declare it. If we have to wear
some button or badge on the lapel of our coats so as to evidence we
are Christians, that is a poor way of doing so—we must by our
"good *works*" glorify God (I Peter ii, 12), we must "*show* forth"
His praises in our daily lives.

The force of the first half of verse 45 is clearly established by
what follows: "For He maketh His sun to rise on the evil and on
the good, and sendeth rain on the just and on the unjust." Children
resemble their parents: there is an identifying likeness between
them. The character and conduct of God in this connection are well
known: His providences declare His benignity. Not only does God
bear with much longsuffering the vessels of wrath fitted to destruction, but He bestows upon them many favours. So far from making
a distinction in this matter, He disburses temporal blessings among
the just and the unjust alike. As the Gospel of Luke expresses it,
"He is kind unto the unthankful and to the evil" (vi, 35). Therein
He sets His people an example to follow, hence the force of the
apostolic injunction, "Be ye therefore followers [imitators] of God,
as dear children; And walk in love, as Christ also hath loved us and
hath given Himself for us" (Eph. v, 1, 2).

From this reason or inducement here given by Christ to enforce
His exhortation in verse 44, we may perceive *what are the things*
in which Christians should principally employ themselves, namely
in those things in the doing of which they may obtain evidence
that they are the children of God. How many Christians there are
who lament their lack of assurance. And in most cases this is not to
be wondered at. If they are so zealous in serving self rather than
Christ, if they run so greedily after the things the world is absorbed
with, how can it be otherwise? There is an inseparable connection
between Romans viii, 14 and 16: we must be led of the Spirit (and
not resist His motions) if we are to have Him bearing witness with
our spirit that we are the children of God. We must be more

diligent in cultivating supernatural fruit if we would have clearer evidence of a supernatural root-dwelling within us.

Ere passing on, let us note how Christ here spoke of the common gifts of God in creation and providence: "He maketh *His* sun to rise." It is not simply "the sun": it is His sun and not ours. It is His by creation and His by regulation, making it go forward or backward as He pleases. The Lord is the sole Author and Governor of this heavenly body, for He continues to give it being and determines its power and virtue. The same thing is equally true of every other creature in heaven, earth, or sea. In like manner He "sendeth the rain" on its specific mission: He has appointed where and when it shall fall, so that "one piece was rained upon, and the piece whereupon it rained not withered" (Amos iv, 7). Finally, note the terms by which Christ designates those who are the friends of God and those who are His enemies: good and just, evil and unjust—the first term relating to character, the second to conduct.

"For if ye love them which love you, what reward have ye? do not even the publicans the same?" (verse 46). In this and the following verse Christ propounded another reason to persuade His disciples and hearers to love their enemies, the force of which is only apparent when we understand who the "publicans" were. The "publicans" were those officers who collected taxes and tributes, rates and rents from the Jews for the Roman emperor, to whom the Jews were then in subjection. Some of the most degenerate of the Jews undertook this wretched work for the money they could get out of it. From Luke xix, 8, it appears that the publicans resorted to injustice and oppression in order to fatten their own purses, and consequently they were the most hated and despised of all people (Matt. ix, 11; xi, 9). Yet (says Christ), even these publicans, though devoid of conscience, would love those who loved them; and if *we* do no more, what better are we than they?

It is not that Christ here forbids us to love those who love us, but rather that He is condemning a merely carnal love: for one man to love another simply because he is loved by the other is nothing else than a man loving himself in another. In order to love our neighbour rightly and in a manner acceptable to the Lord, we must heed the following rule: all the commandments of the second table must be obeyed from the same principle as those in the first table, namely *love to God*. Parents are to be honoured in God and for God, "Children obey your parents *in the Lord*" (Eph. vi, 1), and my neighbour must be loved in God and for God, even though he be my enemy. Why? Because he is as truly God's creature as I am, and because God has commanded me to love him. *That* must be the ground of our obedience, though from other respects our love may increase for our neighbour.

"For if ye love them that love you, what reward have ye?" In this question Christ emphasizes a principle which it is our wisdom to heed in the ordering of our lives, namely that we give ourselves especially to the doing of those things to which is attached the promise of God's reward. To make this the more forcible and impressive let us ask, What was it that moved Moses to refuse to be called the son of Pharaoh's daughter, which caused him to forsake the treasures of Egypt and to suffer affliction with the people of God? The Holy Spirit has told us: it was because he had "respect unto the recompense of the reward" (Heb. xi, 25, 26). But how little is this truth believed in and the principle acted on today, or why so much trifling away of our time? What reward can they look for at God's hand who give themselves up to "the pleasures of sin?"

"And if ye salute your brethren only, what do ye more than others? do not even the publicans the same?" (verse 47). Christ's drift in these words is the same as in the previous verse, the design of such repetition being that this weighty truth may be fixed the more firmly and deeply in our minds. We are so slow in performing the duties of love, particularly unto our *enemies,* that the duty of it needs to be pressed upon us again and again. If He who spoke as never man spoke saw well to repeat Himself frequently, His under-servants need not hesitate to do the same. Not only are we to pray for those who hate and injure us, but we are to greet them when they cross our path. How wrong then deliberately to pass a brother on the street and treat him as though he were an utter stranger to us! Nor do the words, "If there come any unto you, and bring not this doctrine, receive him not into your house, neither bid him God speed" (II John 10), militate to the slightest degree against what has just been said. It is personal or private enemies that Christ had in view, whereas II John 10 refers to those who are the open enemies *of God.*

"What do ye more than others?" What a searching question is this! And note well the precise form of it. It is not "What *know* ye more than others," or "what *profess* ye more than others?" or even "what *believe* ye more than others?" but "what *do* ye more than others?" Yet care must be taken that this inquiry be not perverted. If on the one hand it is of first importance that the Gospel trumpet gives forth no uncertain sound when proclaiming the cardinal truth of justification by faith, yet it is equally essential to make it plain that saving faith always identifies itself by the works which is produces. Justification before God is by faith alone, but it is not a faith which remains alone. Saving faith is not a life-less, inoperative and sterile thing, but a living, active, fruit-producing principle. And it is by the fruit which a saving faith produces that it is distinguished from the worthless and unproductive faith of the empty professor.

Saving faith is the gift of God. It is a supernatural principle inwrought by the Holy Spirit at the new birth. And this faith is evidenced by its fruits. It is a faith which "worketh by love" (Gal. v, 6). It is a faith that "purifieth the heart" (Acts xv, 9). It is a faith that "overcometh the world" (I John v, 4). And since those who are the favoured subjects of this faith *have* more than others, they *ought* to do more, they *can* do more, yea, they *will* do more than the unregenerate. The thing which above all others has brought the cause of Christ into such general contempt in the world is because millions of those claiming to be His followers do *not* do more, but often considerably less, than many who make no such profession: they are less truthful, less honest, less unselfish, less benevolent. It is not what we say, but how we conduct ourselves, which most impresses the ungodly.

Christ has good reason to require more from His disciples than He does from the children of the wicked one. They *profess* more, but unless their profession be supported by facts, verified by works, then it is a vain and hypocritical one: dishonouring to the Saviour, a stumbling-block to His people, and an occasion of blasphemy to His enemies. They *are* more than others. They are loved with an everlasting love, redeemed at infinite cost, indwelt by the Holy Spirit, then should they not produce more than others? "Unto whomsoever much is given, of him shall much be required." It is certain that Christians *can* do more than others. Said the apostle: "I can do all things through Christ which strengtheneth me" (Phil iv, 13). A supernatural principle indwells them, the love of God has been shed abroad in their hearts, the all-sufficient grace of God is available to them, and all things are possible to him that believeth. "What do ye more than others?" Answer this question in the presence of God.

"Be ye therefore perfect, even as your Father which is in heaven is perfect" (verse 48). From all that He had said, Christ now drew this excellent consequence, exhorting His followers to perfection in all the duties of love. "Be ye therefore perfect" is the unchanging requirement of the Law, "even as your Father which is in heaven is perfect" is the exalted standard which the Gospel presents to us. The moral excellency of the Divine character is the copy and rule set before us, and nothing short of that is to be our sincere, ardent and constant endeavour. Though such an aim is never fully realized in this life, yet we must say with Paul, "Not as though I had already attained, either were already perfect: but I follow after, if that I may apprehend that for which also I am apprehended of Christ Jesus" (Phil. iii, 12). In view of such a confession by the eminent apostle, how baseless and absurd is the pretension of those claiming to have already reached sinless perfection. The fact is that the closer we walk with God, the more will it work in us self-abasement and humiliation and not self-complacency and pride.

CHAPTER TWENTY-TWO

The Giving of Alms

"Take heed that ye do not your alms before men, to be seen of them: otherwise ye have no reward of your Father which is in heaven. Therefore when thou doest thine alms, do not sound a trumpet before thee, as the hypocrites do in the synagogues and in the streets, that they may have glory of men. Verily I say unto you, They have their reward. But when thou doest alms, let not thy left hand know what thy right hand doeth: That thine alms may be in secret: and thy Father which seeth in secret Himself shall reward thee openly." (Matt. vi, 1-4.)

WE now enter upon the fourth division of our Lord's Sermon, a section which includes the first eighteen verses of Matthew vi, the general subject of which is the performing of good works so as to secure the approbation of God. As we shall see, Christ here takes up quite a different aspect of Truth, yet is it one which is closely related to what had formerly occupied His attention. There He had made it very evident that He required more from His followers than the religion of the scribes and Pharisees produced (verses 20, 47). Here He insists that a far higher quality is also absolutely necessary. There He had warned His hearers against the erroneous doctrines of the Jewish teachers, here He cautions them against their evil practices, particularly the sins of hypocrisy and worldly-mindedness.

"Take heed that ye do not your alms before men, to be seen of them: otherwise ye have no reward of your Father which is in heaven" (Matt. vi, 1). There is no doubt whatever in our mind that in this instance the rendering of the Revised Version is to be preferred: "Take heed that ye do not your *righteousness* before men to be seen of them," though the Revised Version rightly uses "alms" in verse 2. This first verse enunciates a general principle in reference to moral and spiritual duties, which in the succeeding verses is illustrated, amplified, and enforced in the three particular duties of alms, prayer and fasting—it is *acts* of righteousness which are in view. Thus it is a case where an abstract noun is given a concrete sense: it is similarly used in Matthew iii, 15, and v, 20; in all three passages it has the force of "righteousnesses" or "good works."

In verses 2-4 the general principle laid down in the opening sentence is applied manward, Godward, and selfward, and the three duties specified have to do with our estates, our souls, and our bodies. Those three good works of alms, prayer and fasting have occupied a conspicuous place in all the leading religious

systems, and have been almost universally regarded as the chief
means of obtaining salvation and the clearest proofs of righteousness and sanctity. In their most serious moments, all, except the
most abandoned, have been willing to practise some form and
degree of self-denial, or perform acts of devotion, in the hope that
they might thereby appease the great God whose wrath they feared.

In the teachings of the Koran, prayer, fasting and alms are the
chief duties required from the Mohammedan. Prayer, it is said, will
carry a man halfway to Paradise. fasting will bring him to the gates,
and alms will give him entrance. The great prominence which
Romanism assigns to almsgiving—especially when the alms are
bestowed upon herself—to the senseless repetition of prayers, and
to bodily mortifications, is too well known to need any enlarging
upon. Similar ideas obtain among other religions, especially in
Buddhism—lamaism with its prayer-wheels being a case in point.
But in our present passage Christ shows us that, as mere formal
works, these religious acts are worthless in the sight of God.

"Take heed that ye do not your alms before men, to be seen of
them: otherwise ye have no reward of your Father which is in
heaven" (verse 1). It ought to be apparent that our Lord is not
here reprehending the giving of alms as such, but rather that He is
condemning that ostentatious bestowment of charity which is done
for the purpose of self-advertisement. As a matter of fact this
particular admonition of the Saviour's takes it for granted that His
disciples were in the habit of relieving the indigent, and this notwithstanding that most of them had to labour for their own daily
bread. That against which Christ warned was the giving of unnecessary publicity in the discharge of this duty, and the making the
praise of men our ultimate object therein. Most flagrantly did the
Pharisees err at this very point. Edersheim gives the following quota-
tion as a specimen, "He that says, I give this 'sela' that my sons
may live, and that I may merit the world to come, behold, this is
the perfect righteousness."

To show pity unto the afflicted is but common humanity. It is a
great mistake to suppose that the exercise of beneficence is something peculiar to this Christian era. Under the legal economy God
commanded His people, "If there be among you a poor man of one
of thy brethren within any of thy gates in thy land which the Lord
thy God giveth thee, thou shalt not harden thine heart, nor shut
thine hand from thy poor brother; But thou shalt open thine hand
wide unto him, and shalt surely lend him sufficient for his need,
in that which he wanteth" (Deut. xv, 7, 8). "And if thy brother be
waxen poor and fallen in decay with thee, then thou shalt relieve
him: yea, though he be a stranger, or a sojourner, that he may live
with thee" (Lev. xxv, 35). Job declared, "I was a father to the
poor" (xxix, 16). Said the Psalmist, "Blessed is he that considereth
the poor: the Lord will deliver him in time of trouble" (xli, 1).

"He that despiseth his neighbour sinneth: but he that hath

mercy on the poor, happy is he" (Prov. xiv, 21)—there was the fullest room for the exercise of mercy under the Mosaic dispensation. "He that hath pity upon the poor lendeth unto the Lord; and that which he hath given will He pay him again" (Prov. xix, 17): yes, for the poor, equally with the rich, are *His* creatures, and the Lord will be no man's debtor. "Whoso stoppeth his ears at the cry of the poor, he also shall cry himself, but shall not be heard" (Prov. xxi, 13); we need hardly say that the principle of this verse is still in operation. "He that giveth unto the poor shall not lack, but he that hideth his eyes shall have many a curse" (Prov. xxviii, 27). At a time of great spiritual declension in Israel, Jehovah brought against them the following charges, "They sold the righteous for silver, and the poor for a pair of shoes. . . . For I know your manifold transgressions and your mighty sins: they afflict the just, they take a bribe, and they turn aside the poor in the gate from their right" (Amos ii, 6, and v, 12).

It is therefore a most un-Christian attitude to argue, We have enough to do to provide for our families: it is for the rich and not for the labouring people to give alms. If the love of God has been shed abroad in our hearts we shall feel for the afflicted, and according to our ability shall be ready to relieve the needy, especially such as belong to the Household of Faith; yea, if a situation requires it, shall gladly deny ourselves comforts so as to do more for those in want. And let us not overlook the fact that Christ here designates almsgiving as "righteousness." The apostle struck the same note when he pressed Psalm cxii, 9, on his hearers: "As it is written, He hath dispersed abroad, he hath given to the poor: his righteousness remaineth for ever" (II Cor. ix, 9). Those who refuse to give unto the poor are guilty of a gross injustice, for inasmuch as they are but stewards over what they possess they rob the needy of their due.

Thus, by making alms an essential branch of practical righteousness, our Lord teaches us that the succouring of the poor is not a work of freedom, left to our own choice, but something which is enjoined upon us by Divine commandment. So far from the matter of providing for the needy being left to our own option, it is one of bare justice, and failure therein is a grievous breach both of the Law of God and of nature. But the giving of alms to the poor is not only an act of righteousness, it is also the exercise of kindness. The Greek word, which is here rendered, "alms" is derived from a root which signifies to have compassion or to be merciful. This takes us behind the act itself to the spirit which prompts it: it is not the mere bestowment of goods or money which constitutes "alms," but the merciful and pitiful heart of the giver.

From what has just been pointed out we may also discover who are the ones entitled to be relieved, the kind of persons whom we may rightfully bestow alms upon, for we are not to act blindly in this matter. It is those who are in such a condition as really to draw out our pity: such as orphans and elderly widows, the maimed, the sick, and the blind. If this principle be duly heeded, we shall be guarded against indiscriminate giving, which often does a great deal more harm than good—encouraging idleness and intemperance. Obviously, healthy and robust beggars who would trade upon the generosity of others are not entitled to receive alms: "This we commanded you, that if any would not work, neither should he eat" (II Thess. iii, 10). Thus, in abetting the indolent we are partners with those who defy Divine authority.

"Take heed that ye do not your alms before men, to be seen of them." This admonition is for the avoidance of an unlawful manner of giving alms, for even a good deed may be done in an ill way. Alas, so very deceitful and desperately wicked are our hearts that our most beneficent actions may proceed from corrupt desires and thereby be rendered not only void, but evil in the sight of Him with whom we have to do. Christ's "take heed" intimates that we are in great danger of erring at this very point. Acts of charity are specially offensive in the sight of our gracious God when they are performed from a desire to procure for ourselves a reputation of sanctity or generosity among our fellows. Alas, how much of this obnoxious pride, this vaunting of charity, is there today both in the religious world and the secular.

That against which Christ here warns His disciples is the secret *pride* of their hearts. This pride is twofold: of the mind and will, and of the affections. Pride of mind is a corrupt disposition whereby a man thinks more highly of himself than he ought to do: this was the sin of the Pharisees (Luke xviii, 12) and of the Laodiceans (Rev. iii, 16). This conceit is most dangerous, especially in the matter of saving grace, for it has caused multitudes to deceive themselves by imagining they had been born again when in fact they were dead in trespasses and sins, and moving real Christians to imagine they possess more grace than they actually do. Pride of will is an inward affection which makes a man discontented with the estate in which God has placed him, leading him to hanker after a better: this was the sin of Adam and Eve (Gen. iii, 5, 6).

Now from these corrupt principles of pride of mind and pride of will issues that exercise or practice of pride in a man's life whereby he is determined to do whatever he can which will promote his own praise and glory. Such pride is not something which is peculiar to a few people only, but is found in every man by nature—the Lord Jesus alone excepted. And where this pride is not mortified and held in leash by God, it is so strong that it will not be crossed at any price, for rather than have his proud will thwarted a person will commit any sin: as Pharaoh when he asked, "Who is the Lord, that I should obey His voice to let Israel go?" (Exodus v, 2); as Absalom, who was responsible for the banishing of his father from his own kingdom; and as Ahithophel, who went and hanged himself when his counsel was rejected. It was just such pride as this which occasioned the fall of Satan himself (Isaiah xiv; I Tim. iii, 6).

Therefore, "take heed," says Christ: take every possible precaution to guard against this sin. How? First, by unsparing self-examination. The more careful we are to know the pride of our hearts, the less likely are we to be deceived by it. Second, by sincere self-condemnation: "If we would judge ourselves, we should not be judged" (I Cor, xi, 31). If we would humble ourselves before God, we must hate ourselves for our wicked pride and penitently confess it to Him. Third, by reminding ourselves of the judgments of God upon this sin. Herod was eaten up of worms because he took unto himself the glory due unto God (Acts xii, 23). "God resisteth the proud, but giveth grace to the humble" (I Peter v, 5). Fourth, by meditating upon the fearful sufferings of Christ in Gethsemane and on Golgotha: nothing will more effectually humble my proud heart than the realization that it was *my* very sins which occasioned the death of God's Lamb.

"Otherwise ye have no reward of your Father which is in heaven" (verse 1). The value of an action is determined by the principle from which it proceeds. To give to the poor simply because it is customary is merely the limitation of others. To minister unto the needy in order to increase our own influence and power is a display of carnal ambition. To give so as to advance worldly interests is a manifestation of covetousness; if to seek applause, it is to gratify pride; if to alleviate the sufferings of my fellows, it is only the exercise of common humanity. But if I minister unto the needy out of a respect to the Divine authority and with the desire of pleasing God, acting from regard for His will, to which I long to be conformed in all things, then it is a spiritual act and acceptable unto the Lord. (Condensed from John Brown.)

"Therefore when thou doest thine alms, do not sound a trumpet before thee as the hypocrites do in the synagogues and in the streets, that they may have glory of men. Verily I say unto you, They have their reward" (verse 2). "Sound not a trumpet" is a figurative way of saying, Seek not to attract the attention of other people unto thyself. The word "hypocrite" is a significant one, for it properly denotes an actor who wears a mask, playing his part behind it. The Pharisees posed as being most devout worshippers of God and lovers of their fellow men, when in reality they were self-righteous and sought only the applause of men: behind the outward appearance of piety and generosity they were the slaves of worldly and selfish passions. They performed their deeds of charity where the largest number of onlookers congregated together. Their "reward" was the admiration of shallow-minded men, as "dust" is the Serpent's meat.

The sin which Christ here reprehended is far more grievous than is commonly supposed, and, we may add, far more prevalent, many of the Lord's own people being guilty of it. It consists of making *men*, rather than God, the judges and approvers of their actions. And do not *we* often fall into this snare? When we do that which is right,

and yet incur thereby the displeasure of our fellows, are we not more
grieved than when by sin we offend God Himself? If so, does not
that clearly prove that our hearts have more regard to the censure
of men than of the Lord? Are we not deeply hurt when our fellows
dishonour *God*? Are we more afraid of offending mortal man than
the everlasting God? When in sore straits, which comforts us the
more: the assurances of earthly friends to relieve us or the promises
of the Lord?

"But when thou doest thine alms, let not thy left hand know
what thy right hand doeth" (verse 3). This Divine precept is
designed to restrain the corrupt ambition of our hearts after the
praise of men. It goes much farther than the commandment in
verse 2. There the Lord had forbidden that ostentatious giving of
alms which is done for the purpose of self-advertisement and the
procuring of the applause of our fellows; while here He prohibits
any self-satisfaction or complacency in the performing of this good
work. It is strange how the commentators see in verse 3 nothing
more than the repetition of that which is found in verse 2, quite
missing the force of "let not *thy* left hand know [approve of] what
thy right hand doeth." We are to give alms in simplicity, with the
sole intent and desire of pleasing God only. When a good work has
been done, we should dismiss it from our minds and not congratu-
late ourselves upon it, and press on to what is yet before us.

"That thine alms may be in secret" (verse 4). Here is still another
instance where the language of Christ in this discourse must not be
taken literally and absolutely, or otherwise *any* act of mercy which
came under the cognizance of our fellows would be thereby prohibited. Certainly the primitive Christians did not always conceal
their donations, as is clear from Acts xi, 29, 30. Secrecy itself may
become a cloak to avarice, and under the pretence of hiding good
works we may hoard up our money to spend upon ourselves. There
are times when a person of prominence may rightly excite his backward brethren by his own example of liberality. So we must not
understand Christ as here forbidding all charitable actions which
may be seen by others, but rather understand Him to mean that
we should perform them as unobtrusively as possible, making it
our chief concern to aim at the approbation of God therein.

"That thine alms may be in secret: and thy Father which seeth
in secret Himself shall reward thee openly" (verse 4). Though
there be nothing meritorious about our best performances, yea,
though everything we do is defiled, nevertheless "God is not un-
righteous to forget our work and labour of love, which ye have
showed toward His name, in that ye have ministered to the saints,
and do minister" (Heb. vi, 10). Nevertheless, it must be a work of
faith—for "without faith it is impossible to please Him"—and
a labour of love, if it is to receive God's commendation. In the
Divine administration it is so ordered that, in the end, the selfish
person is disappointed, while he who seeks the good of others *is*

himself the gainer. The more we truly aim at our Father's approbation, the less shall we be concerned about either the praise or contempt of the world. The Divine reward, in the day to come, will be given "openly," before an assembled universe. "Therefore judge nothing before the time, until the Lord come, who both will bring to light the hidden things of darkness and will make manifest the counsels of the heart: and then shall every one have praise of God" (I Cor. iv, 5).

CHAPTER TWENTY-THREE

Prayer

" And when thou prayest, thou shalt not be as the hypocrites are: for they love to pray standing in the synagogues and in the corners of the streets, that they may be seen of men. Verily I say unto you, They have their reward. But thou, when thou prayest, enter into thy closet, and when thou hast shut thy door, pray to thy Father which is in secret; and thy Father which seeth in secret shall reward thee openly. But when ye pray, use not vain repetitions, as the heathen do: for they think that they shall be heard for their much speaking. Be not ye therefore like unto them: for your Father knoweth what things ye have need of, before ye ask Him." (Matt. vi, 5-8.)

As we pointed out in the opening paragraphs of our last chapter, we are now in the fourth division of our Lord's Sermon, a division which includes the first eighteen verses of Matthew vi, the general subject of which is the performing of good works so as to secure the approbation of God. In order to do this His disciples must shun not only the false doctrines but also the evil practices of the scribes and Pharisees. The keynote is struck in the opening verse, "Take heed that ye do not your righteousness before men to be seen of them" (R.V.). The general principle which is expressed in this warning is enlarged upon in verses 2-18, being applied to three specific cases: in "alms" manward, in "prayer" Godward, and in "fasting" selfward. Having already dwelt upon the first, we now turn unto what Christ here had to say upon the second. By keeping in mind the connection we shall the better perceive His scope and design, and be preserved from an erroneous interpretation of the clauses which are to be before us.

"And when thou prayest, thou shalt not be as the hypocrites" (verse 5). The opening words make it quite clear that Christ takes it for granted His disciples *will pray*, and in what follows He reveals the need there is for them to be diligent to perform this duty in a way acceptable to God. When the Lord assured Ananias of the conversion of Saul of Tarsus He said, "Behold, he prayeth" (Acts ix, 11). As a "Pharisee of the Pharisees" he had made many long prayers, but not until the miracle of grace had been wrought within him could it be said that he *prayed*. Saying prayers and pouring out the heart before God are totally different things: a self-righteous Pharisee may be diligent in the former, only one who has been born again will do the latter. As another has said, "The moment a spiritual babe is born into the new creation it sends up a cry of helpless dependence toward the source of its birth."

152

That which is now to engage our attention consists of the first recorded utterance of Christ on the subject of prayer, and it is most searching and solemn to note that it opens with *a warning against hypocrisy* in the discharge of this duty. That particular species of hypocrisy which is here reprehended is ostentatiousness in our devotions, the public parading of our piety, the seeking to attract the notice of others and win for ourselves the reputation of great spirituality. Prayer is the expression of creature need and dependency and therefore it is utterly inconsistent with thoughts of pride and self-complacency. But alas, such is fallen man that he can unite these opposites, and therefore our need of this caution: " And when thou prayest, thou shalt not be as the hypocrites." A " hypocrite ' is one who assumes a character which does not belong to him. The " hypocrites " which Christ had immediately in view were the Pharisees (Matt. xxiii, 13), for their " leaven " was hypocrisy (Luke xii, 1).

" And when thou prayest, thou shalt not be as the hypocrites: for they love to pray standing in the synagogues and in the corners of the streets, that they may be seen of men. Verily I say unto you, They have their reward " (verse 5). We need hardly say that Christ is not here condemning this posture of standing in prayer (for He Himself employed it—John xi, 41), nor is He forbidding His disciples to pray in public: Paul gave thanks unto God in the presence of a whole ship's company (Acts xxvii, 35), and in his epistles gave order that " men pray everywhere " (I Tim. ii, 8). No, rather was it the *motive* and *manner* of prayer which our Lord here had in view. It is a caution against vainglory, the seeking to commend ourselves unto our fellows. And what sort of creatures are we that need this caution? Think of it—praying to *God*, in order that we may be seen of *men*! In how many ways does the evil of our hearts lead us away from godly simplicity and sincerity.

Sin defiles our very devotions, and unless we are very much on our guard it will not only render them nugatory but an offence unto God. Particularly does the minister need to place a strict watch upon himself in his public praying, lest he be guilty of praying to the congregation rather than unto God. Alas, does not a spirit of hypocrisy often creep into the pulpit prayers of those who could not justly be called " hypocrites?" It is but natural that the minister should desire to be regarded as a highly spiritual man, as one who enjoys very close communion with God, whose aspirations of soul are of a most exalted order. It is no easy matter not to be mindful that there are many critical ears which are listening to our petitions and to be affected accordingly both in the matter and manner of our supplications. Would not our public prayers often be simpler and shorter if we were alone with God?

What need there is, then, that those who are accustomed to lead in public prayer should diligently examine their hearts and cry earnestly unto God for the mortifying of their pride. What is the

good opinion of fellow sinners worth if we have not the Lord's
"Well done"? Let us be more careful in seeing to it that our
affections prompt each petition, than in giving thought to the
expressing of them in words which will charm the ears of men.
Truth and sincerity in the heart are vastly more important than
choice language or a correct demeanour. Let us seek grace to heed
that exhortation, "Keep thy foot when thou goest to the house of
God . . . Be not rash with thy mouth and let not thine heart be
hasty to utter any thing before God: for God is in heaven, and thou
upon earth, therefore let thy words be few" (Eccles. v, 1, 2). If the
Divine perfections duly impress our souls, then we shall be saved
from much folly.

"But thou, when thou prayest, enter into thy closet, and when
thou hast shut thy door, pray to thy Father" (verse 6). Having condemned the vice of hypocrisy in the former verse our Lord now
commends the virtue of sincerity, and instructs us in the right
manner of praying to God. It seems strange that some have quite
missed Christ's meaning here, a few extremists supposing that He
forbade all praying in the congregation. That which our Lord was
reprehending in the previous verse was not public prayer, but personal praying in public, which was done with the object of calling
attention to ourselves. The Lord Jesus encouraged social praying
in His memorable declaration, "where two or three are gathered
together in My name, there am I in the midst" (Matt. xviii, 20),
which was specifically a promise to praying souls, having no reference at all to the Lord's supper. That united prayer was practised
by the early Christians is clear from many passages in the Acts (see
i, 14; ii, 42; vi, 4; xii, 5; xvi, 13).

"But thou, when thou prayest, enter into thy closet, and when
thou hast shut thy door, pray to thy Father which is in secret; and
thy Father which seeth in secret shall reward thee openly." In our
exposition of Matthew v we have shown repeatedly that much of
our Lord's language in this Sermon cannot be understood literally,
and if this principle be borne in mind we shall be preserved from
unwarrantably restricting His scope and meaning in this verse.
Viewed in the light of its immediate context, we regard this verse as,
first, giving most necessary directions to the one who leads in *public*
prayer. So far from engaging therein in order to win human esteem,
we must discharge the duty in precisely the same spirit of humility
and sincerity as though we were alone, engaged in private prayer.
Entering the closet and closing the door was a figurative way of
saying, Shut out from thy mind all thoughts of the creature and
have respect unto God alone; be not occupied with those present,
but with Him who is invisible.

While we are satisfied that the first reference in verse 6 is to
public prayer, yet (as the greater includes the less) there is also
important teaching here concerning private prayer. Three things
in it are to be noted: the place of prayer, the privacy, and privilege

thereof. "But thou, when thou prayest, enter into thy closet." By the "closet" we are to understand a place of seclusion and retirement. Our omniscient Saviour knew the tendency of our minds to stray, how easily our thoughts wander away from God, and therefore He exhorts us to get away from everything which disturbs and distracts, to some quiet spot where our communion with God may not be hindered. Private prayer is to be as secret as possible, and this calls for a secluded spot, a place free from the observations and interruptions of our fellows. When Christ engaged in private prayer He withdrew from the crowd and retired to the solitude of the mountain.

Ere passing on it should be pointed out that we must be careful not to run to an unwarrantable extreme at this point, otherwise we should make this verse clash with other passages. If on the one hand we must be careful to avoid ostentation and seeking the praise of men, yet on the other we must be on our guard against intimidation and being unfaithful through the fear of men. Daniel closed not the windows of his room when praying, even though he knew that he was thereby endangering his life (vi, 10). Even when in a public place we should not allow the sneers of others to hinder us from bowing our heads and returning thanks to God at meal times, or kneeling by our bedside at night if someone else be sharing the room.

"Enter into thy closet": these words suggest not only a silent and secluded place, but also a *stated* place—whether it be in the fields, the woods, or our own dwelling. When David received tidings of the death of Absalom, we are told that he "went up to the chamber over the gate" and wept (II Samuel xviii, 33), as though that was the spot where he was accustomed to pour out his griefs unto the Lord. When the widow of Zarephath acquainted Elijah with the death of her son, the prophet "carried him up into a loft where he abode, and laid him upon his own bed," and then and *there* "he cried unto the Lord" (I Kings xvii, 19, 20). The same practice was evidently followed by our Saviour, for we read that He "went [for the specific purpose of making supplication to God] as He was wont [accustomed] to the mount of Olives" (Luke xxii, 39).

It is interesting to note that the Greek word for "closet" occurs but four times in the original New Testament—in Matthew xxiv, 26, it is translated "secret chambers." Our Lord's language was most probably adopted from Isaiah xxvi, 20: "Come, My people, enter thou into thy chambers, and shut thy doors about thee." Now what would these words "enter into thy closet" suggest to a Jew? The "closet" is simply a closed place, shut in for privacy, shut out from obtrusion. What would such a term naturally suggest to Christ's hearers? There was one place in their midst which was preeminently a *secret chamber*, namely the innermost section of the temple, where Jehovah had His special dwelling in the holy of holies. It was peculiarly a "closet," from which the people were excluded. It was a place marked by silence and secrecy, seclusion and separation.

The holy of holies in the tabernacle and temple was of unique design. It had neither door nor window, and unlike the inner courts of Orientals which are opened to the sky, this one was roofed in and had no skylight. None of the Levites were permitted to enter, save only the high priest, who went there as the representative of the nation to meet with God. Significantly enough there was in it but a single piece of furniture, namely the sacred ark covered by the mercy-seat. How unspeakably blessed: Aaron drew nigh to converse with God at a blood-sprinkled mercy-seat. There was one notable exception to what we have just pointed out: "and when Moses was gone into the tabernacle of the congregation to speak with Him, then he heard the voice of One speaking unto him *from off the mercy seat* that was upon the ark of testimony, from between the two cherubims: and he spake unto him" (Num. vii, 89). Thus the Holy "closet" was where man spoke to God and God to him.

There are two expressions in our verse which emphasize the note of *privacy* in our individual devotions: "when thou hast shut thy door" and "pray to thy Father who is in secret." The former suggests the need for seclusion and silence, the getting away from all sights and sounds which would disturb and distract. The latter means get alone with God, enter the secret place of the Most High, converse and commune with Him in the holy of holies. Let the reader carefully note the special stress which is here laid upon the singular number of the second personal pronoun: "but *thou, when thou prayest, enter into thy closet,*" etc. Here is something which is unique in all the Word of God: no less than eight times in this one verse is the second person used in the singular number. Nothing could bring out more strikingly the imperative need of aloneness with God: for this the world must be entirely shut out.

"But thou, when thou prayest, enter into thy closet, and when thou hast shut thy door, pray to thy Father which is in secret." How clear it is that both the spirit and the letter of this verse rebuke those misguided souls who clamour for churches and chapels to be kept perpetually open so that any member of the public may repair thither for private devotions either day or night, as if buildings set apart for religious exercises were any nearer to the throne of grace than our own dwellings or the open fields. The Lord of heaven and earth "dwelleth not in temples made with hands." He is "not far from every one of us" (Acts xvii, 24, 27). The localization of worship was abolished when Christ declared, "The hour cometh when ye shall neither in this mountain nor yet at Jerusalem worship the Father. . . . God is a spirit: and they that worship Him must worship Him in spirit and in truth" (John iv, 21, 24). The argument that church buildings should be kept open for the benefit of those away from home can have no

weight in the face of Matthew vi, 5, 6. Such an innovation is certain
to be abused.

"Pray to thy Father which is in secret, and thy Father which
seeth in secret shall reward thee openly" (verse 6). Here is set forth
the holy and unspeakable privilege of prayer. Here we are invited
to open our minds and hearts freely unto Him who cares for us,
acquainting Him with our needs and cares, making known our
requests with thanksgiving. "Pray to thy Father which is in secret":
He is invisible to carnal sight, imperceptible to our bodily senses,
but a living reality unto faith. We must therefore labour to come
into His conscious presence, seek to acquaint ourselves with Him,
and make Him real to our souls, for He is "a rewarder of them
that *diligently* seek Him." In order to this, after entering our closet
and before offering up any petition, we need to meditate upon
God's wondrous perfections; ponder His blessed attributes; dwell
upon His ineffable holiness, His almighty power, His unchanging
faithfulness, His infinite mercy; above all rejoice in the fact that
He is our *Father*.

"Pray to thy Father which is in secret, and thy Father which
seeth in secret shall reward thee openly." This is set over against
"they have their reward" of verse 5. Their "reward" is not the
approbation of God, but merely the worthless admiration of their
silly dupes who are imposed upon by an outward show of piety.
They "*have* their reward," for there is nothing but the gall of
bitterness awaiting them in the future: "men of the world have
their portion in *this* life" (Psalm xvii, 14). Different far is it with
the Christian. His prayers do not and cannot merit anything from
God, yet if they are offered from right principles and unto right
ends they are pleasing unto Him, and are rewarded even now by
tokens of His favour, and in the Day to come they shall be openly
approved by Him.

"But when ye pray, use not vain repetitions as the heathen do:
for they think that they shall be heard for their much speaking"
(verse 7). That which our Lord here condemned is not our asking
again and again for the same thing, but the reducing of the duty
and privilege of prayer to a mere lip labour. In Psalm cxix we find
David praying "teach me Thy statutes" no less than seven times.
Our Saviour in the garden repeatedly asked for the removal of the
cup, and Paul thrice besought the Lord for the departure of his
thorn in the flesh (II Cor. xii, 8). It is *vain* repetitions that are
prohibited, such as those used by the prophets of Baal (I Kings xviii,
26), the worshippers of Diana (Acts xix, 34), and the papists' "Pater-
nosters" and "Ave Marias," which they are taught to use without
meaning or devotion and which they number by counting strings
of beads. Cold and formal extempore prayers are equally forbidden,
for they are mere babblings.

"Be not ye therefore like unto them: for your Father knoweth
what things ye have need of, before ye ask Him" (verse 8). Here

Christ presents as an inducement to praying souls the very reason which infidels use as an argument against prayer: if God be omniscient what need is there for us to inform Him of our requirements? We do not present our requests to God in order to acquaint Him with our wants, but to render obedience unto His commandment which requireth this duty from us. We pray unto God for the purpose of honouring Him, acknowledging Him to be the Knower of our hearts and the Giver of all mercies. Moreover, prayer is a means for us rightly to receive and improve the gifts of heaven, being an indispensable preparation of our souls thereto. It should be understood that this knowledge of our Father's is far more than a bare cognition of our wants: it is such a solicitation for our welfare that ensures the supply of every needed thing.

CHAPTER TWENTY-FOUR

Prayer—Continued

" After this manner therefore pray ye: Our Father which art in heaven, Hallowed be Thy name. Thy kingdom come. Thy will be done in earth, as it is in heaven. Give us this day our daily bread. And forgive us our debts, as we forgive our debtors. And lead us not into temptation, but deliver us from evil: For thine is the kingdom, and the power, and the glory, for ever. Amen." (Matt. vi, 9-13.)

IT is only two years since we wrote a series of ten cover-page articles on what is usually designated the Lord's Prayer, and therefore we shall not now enter as fully into detail as we otherwise would have done. Before taking up its several clauses, let us make one or two general observations on the prayer as a whole. First, we would note the words with which Christ prefaced it: " After this manner therefore pray ye." This intimates that the Lord Jesus was supplying a pattern after which our prayers are to be modelled. So ignorant are we that " we know not what we should pray for as we ought" (Romans viii, 26), and therefore in answer to our oft-repeated request, " Lord, teach us to pray" (Luke xi, 1), He has graciously furnished the instruction we so sorely need, revealing the manner in which Christians should approach God, the order in which their requests should be presented, the things they most need to ask for, and the adoration which is due to the One they are supplicating.

This model prayer is also found, in condensed form, in Luke's Gospel, and there it is introduced by the words, " When ye pray, say," (xi, 2). This makes it clear that this prayer is not only a pattern to be copied, but also a form to be used verbatim, the plural pronouns therein suggesting that it is appropriate for collective use when the saints assemble together. The fact that its use as a form has been perverted is no argument why it should never be thus employed. True we need to be much on our guard against repeating it by rote, coldly and mechanically, and earnestly seek grace to recite it reverently and feelingly—in our judgment, once every public service, and always at family worship. In view of the class to whom we write it is scarcely necessary to add that many have made a superstitious use of this prayer as though it were a magical charm.

A few of our readers may have been disturbed by the foolish and harmful error that the Lord's prayer was not designed and is not suited for use in this dispensation: that instead, it is " Jewish " and intended for a godly remnant in some " great tribulation period "

159

yet future. One would think the very stating of such a phantasy quite sufficient to expose its absurdity to those with any spiritual intelligence. Neither our Lord nor any of His apostles gave any warning that this prayer was *not* to be used by Christians, or any intimation that it was designed for a future age. The fact that it is found in Luke's Gospel as well as Matthew's is clear indication that it is to be employed by Jewish and Gentile saints alike. There is nothing whatever in this prayer which is unsuited to Christians now, yea, everything in it is needed by them. That it is addressed to "our Father" furnishes all the warrant we need for it to be used by all the members of His family. Then let none of God's children allow Satan to rob them of this valuable part of their birthright.

The more this blessed and wondrous prayer be pondered—one which we personally love to think of as "the family prayer"—the more will the perfect wisdom of its Author be apparent. Here we are taught both the manner and method of how to pray, and the matter for which to pray. Christ knew both our needs and the Father's good will toward us, and therefore has He graciously supplied us with a simple but sufficient directory. Every aspect of prayer is included therein: adoration in its opening clause, thanksgiving at the close, confession of sin is implied. Its petitions are seven in number, showing the completeness of the outline here furnished us. It is virtually an epitome of the Psalms and a most excellent summary of all prayer. Every clause in it is taken from the Old Testament, denoting that our prayers cannot be acceptable unless they be scriptural. "If we ask anything according to His will, He heareth us" (I John v, 14), and God's will can only be learned from His Word.

"Our Father which art in heaven." This opening clause presents to us the Object to whom we pray and the most endearing relation which He sustains to us. By directing us to address the great God as "Our Father which art in heaven" we are assured of His love and power: this precious title being designed to raise our affections, excite to reverential fear and confirm our confidence in the efficacy of prayer. It is to a Divine person, One who has our best interests at heart, that we are invited to draw nigh: "Behold what manner of love the Father hath bestowed upon us" (I John iii, 1)! God is our "Father" first by creation: (Mal. ii, 10). Second, He is our Father by covenant-relationship, and this by virtue of our federal union with Christ—because God is His Father, He is ours (John xx, 17). Third, He is our Father by regeneration: when born again we are "made partakers of the Divine nature" (Gal. iv, 6; II Peter i, 4.) Oh, for faith to extract the sweetness of this relationship.

It is blessed to see how the Old Testament saints, at a time of peculiar trouble and distress, boldly pleaded this relationship to God. They declared, "Thou didst terrible things . . . behold Thou art wroth." They owned, "We are all as an unclean thing, and all our righteousnesses are as filthy rags." They acknowledged, "Thou hast hid thy face from us, and hast consumed us because of our iniquities." And then they pleaded, "But now, O Lord, Thou art *our Father*" (Isaiah lxiv, 3-8). Though we have conducted ourselves very undutifully and ungratefully toward Thee, yet we are Thy dear children: though Thou hast chastened us sorely, nevertheless Thou art still our Father. To Thee therefore we now in penitence turn, to Thee we would apply ourselves in prayer, for to whom should we look for succour and relief but our Father! That was the language of faith.

"*Our* Father." This teaches us to recognize the Christian brotherhood, to pray for the whole family and not for ourselves only. We must express our love for the brethren by praying for them: we are to be as much concerned about their needs as we are over our own. "Which art in heaven." Here we are reminded of God's greatness, of His infinite elevation above us. If the words "Our Father" inspire confidence and love, "which art in heaven" should fill us with humility and awe. It is true that God is everywhere, but He is present in heaven in a *special* sense. It is there that He has "prepared His throne": not only His throne of government, by which His kingdom rules over all, but also His throne of grace to which we must by faith draw near. We are to eye Him as God in heaven, in contrast with the false gods which dwell in temples made by hands.

These words, "which art in heaven," should serve as a guide to direct us in our praying. Heaven is a high and exalted place, and we should address ourselves to God as One who is infinitely above us. It is the place of prospect, and we must picture His holy eye upon us. It is a place of ineffable purity, and nothing which defiles or makes a lie can enter there. It is the "firmament of His power," and we must depend upon Him as the One to whom all might belongs. When the Lord Jesus prayed He "lifted up His eyes to heaven," directing us whence to obtain the blessings we need. If God is in heaven then prayer needs to be a thing of the heart and not of the lips, for no physical voice on earth can rend the skies, but sighs and groans will reach the ears of God. If we are to pray to God in heaven, then our souls must be detached from all of earth. If we pray to God in heaven, then faith must wing our petitions. Since we pray to God in heaven our desires and aspirations must be heavenly.

"Hallowed be Thy name." Thus begins the petitionary part of this blessed prayer. The requests are seven in number, being divided into a three and a four: the first three concerning God, and the last four (ever the number of the creature) our own selves—similarly are the Ten Commandments divided: the first five treating of our duty Godward (in the fifth the parent stands to the child in the place of God), the last five our duty manwards. How clearly, then, is the fundamental duty in prayer here set forth: self and all its needs must be given a secondary place and the Lord freely accorded the pre-eminence in our thoughts, desires and supplications. This petition must take the precedence, for the glory of God's great name is the ultimate end of all things: every other request must not only be subordinated to this one, but be in harmony with and in pursuance of it. We cannot pray aright unless the honour of God be dominant in our hearts. If we cherish a desire for the honouring of God's name we must not ask for anything which it would be against the Divine holiness to bestow.

By "Thy name" is meant God Himself, as in Psalm xx, 1, etc. But more particularly His "name" signifies God as He is *revealed*. It has pleased the Maker of heaven and earth to make Himself known to us, not only in His works, but in the Scriptures, and supremely so in Christ. In the written and in the personal Word God has displayed Himself to us, manifesting His glorious perfections: His matchless attributes of omniscience, omnipotence, and omnipresence; His moral character of holiness, righteousness, goodness and mercy. He is also revealed through His blessed titles: the Rock of Israel, Him that cannot lie, the Father of mercies, the God of all grace. And when we pray that the name of God may be hallowed we make request that the glory thereof may be displayed by Him, and that we may be enabled to esteem and magnify Him agreeably thereto.

In praying that God's name be hallowed we ask that He will so act that His creatures may be moved to render that adoration which is due Him. His name has indeed been eminently glorified in all ages, in the various workings of His providence and grace, whereby His power, wisdom, righteousness and mercy have been demonstrated before the eyes of angels and of men. We therefore request that He would continue to glorify these perfections. In the past God has in the magnifying of His name employed methods and measures which were strange and staggering to finite intelligence: often allowing His enemies to prosper for a time and His people to be sorely persecuted—nevertheless, they glorified "the Lord in the fires" (Isaiah xxiv, 15). And so now, and in the future, when we ask for God to be glorified in the prosperity of His Church, the dissemination of the Gospel and the extension of His kingdom, we must subordinate our request to the Divine sovereignty and leave it with Him as to where and when and how these things shall be brought to pass.

"Hallowed be Thy name": how easy it is to utter these words without the slightest thought of their profound and holy import! If we offer this petition from the heart we desire that God's name may be sanctified by us, and at the same time own the indisposition and utter inability to do this of ourselves. Such a request denotes a longing to be empowered to glorify God in everything whereby He makes Himself known, that we may honour Him in all situations and circumstances. Whatever be my lot, however low I may sink, through whatever deep waters I may be called to pass, get to Thyself glory in me and by me. Blessedly was this exemplified by our perfect Saviour. "Now is My soul troubled; and what shall I say? Father, save Me from this hour: but for this cause came I unto this hour. Father, glorify Thy name" (John xii, 27, 28): though He must be immersed in the baptism of suffering, yet "Hallowed be Thy name."

"Thy kingdom come: Thy will be done in earth, as it is in heaven." The first petition has respect to God's honour, the second and third indicate *the means* whereby His glory is manifested on earth. God's name is manifestatively glorified here just in proportion as His "kingdom" comes to us and His "will" is done by us. This is why we are exhorted to "seek ye first the kingdom of God, and His righteousness" (Matt. vi, 33). In praying "Thy kingdom come" we acknowledge that by nature we are under the dominion of sin and Satan, and beg that we may be the more fully delivered therefrom and that the rule of God may be more completely established in our hearts. We long to see the kingdom of grace extended and the kingdom of glory ushered in. Accordingly we make request that God's will may be more fully made known to us, wrought in us and performed by us: "in earth as it is in heaven": that is, humbly, cheerfully, impartially, promptly, constantly.

"Give us this day our daily bread." This is the first of the four petitions more immediately relating to the supply of our own needs, in which we can clearly discern an implied reference to each of the Persons in the blessed Trinity. Our temporal wants are supplied by the kindness of the Father; our sins are forgiven through the mediation of the Son; we are preserved from temptation and delivered from evil by the gracious operations of the Holy Spirit. By asking for our "daily bread" a tacit acknowledgment is made that "in Adam and by our own sins we have forfeited our right to all the outward blessings of this life, and deserve to be wholly deprived of them by God, and to have them cursed to us in the use of them; and that neither they of themselves are able to sustain us, nor we to merit, or by our own industry to procure them, but prone to desire, get and use them unlawfully; we pray for ourselves and others that they and we, waiting upon the providence of God from day to day, in the use of lawful means, may of His free gift, and as His Fatherly wisdom shall deem best, enjoy a competent portion of them, and have the same continued and blessed unto us in our holy and comfortable use of them and contentment in them" (Larger Cat.).

"And forgive us our debts, as we forgive our debtors." As it is contrary to the holiness of God, sin is a defilement, a dishonour and reproach to us; as it is a violation of His Law, it is a crime; and as to the guilt which we contract thereby, it is a *debt*. As creatures we owed a debt of obedience unto our Maker and Governor, and

through failure to render the same on account of our rank disobedience we have incurred a debt of punishment, and it is for this
latter that we implore the Divine pardon. In order to the obtaining
of God's forgiveness we are required to address ourselves unto Him
in faith and prayer. The designed connection between this and the
preceding petition should not be missed: "Give us . . . *and* forgive
us": the former cannot profit us without the latter—what true
comfort can we derive from external mercies when our conscience
remains burdened on account of a sense of guilt! But since Christ
here teaches us that He is a *giving* God, what encouragement to
look unto Him as a *forgiving* God!

"And lead us not into temptation." The "us" includes all
fellow Christians on earth, for one of the first things which grace
teaches us is unselfishness; to be as much concerned about the good
of my brethren as I am about my own—not only for their temporal
welfare, but especially for their spiritual. In the preceding petition
we have prayed that the guilt of past sins may be remitted, here we
beg to be saved from incurring new guilt through being overcome
by fresh sin. This request makes acknowledgment of the universal
providence of God, that all creatures are at the sovereign disposal
of their Maker, that He has the same absolute control over evil as
over good, and therefore has the ordering of all temptations. It is
from the *evil* of temptations we ask to be spared: if God sees fit
that we should be tempted objectively (through providences which,
though good in themselves, offer occasion to sin within us), that
we may not yield thereto, or, if we yield, that we may not be
absolutely overcome.

"But deliver us from evil." All temptations (trials and troubles)
are not evil either in their nature, design, or outcome. The Saviour
Himself was tempted of the Devil and was definitely led into the
wilderness by the Spirit for that very end. It is therefore from the
evil of temptations we are to ask for deliverance, as this final petition indicates. We are to pray not for a total exemption from
them, but only for a removal of the *judgment* of them. This is clear
from our Lord's own example in prayer: I pray not that Thou
shouldest take them out of the world, but that Thou shouldest
keep them from the evil" (John xvii, 15). To be kept from the evil
of sin is a far greater mercy than deliverance from the trouble of
temptation. But how far has God undertaken to deliver us from
evil? First, as it would be hurtful to our highest interests: it was
for Peter's ultimate good that he was suffered temporarily to fall.
Second, from its having full dominion over us, so that we shall not
totally and finally apostatize. Third, by an ultimate deliverance
when He removes us to heaven.

"For thine is the kingdom, and the power, and the glory, for
ever. Amen." Thus the family prayer closes with a doxology or an
ascription of that glory which is due unto God, thereby teaching
us that prayer and praise should always go together. It is to be

carefully noted that this doxology of the Divine perfections is made use of as a plea to enforce the preceding petitions: "deliver us from evil for Thine is the kingdom," etc.—teaching us to back up our requests with scriptural reasons or arguments. From the Divine perfections the suppliant is to take encouragement to expect a gracious answer. There is nothing in or from ourselves which is meritorious, and therefore hope must be grounded upon the character of Him to whom we pray. His perfections are not evanescent, but "for ever." The concluding "Amen" expresses both a fervent desire, "so be it," and an avowal to faith, "it shall be so."

CHAPTER TWENTY-FIVE

Prayer—Concluded

" For if ye forgive men their trespasses, your heavenly Father will also forgive you : But if ye forgive not men their trespasses, neither will your Father forgive your trespasses." (Matt. vi, 14, 15.)

"FOR if ye forgive men their trespasses, your heavenly Father will also forgive you: But if ye forgive not men their trespasses, neither will your Father forgive your trespasses" (verses 14, 15). These verses have received scant attention from most of those who have written on the Lord's prayer. This ought not to be, for they form a most important appendix to and round off the teaching of our Lord begun at verse 6. It is significant to observe that the fifth petition in the family prayer is the only one singled out by Christ for specific comment—probably because the duty enforced in it is the most painful of all to flesh and blood. But however distasteful the contents of these verses may be to our sinful hearts, that is no reason why they should be virtually shelved by most of the commentators.

Timely indeed are the brief remarks of Matthew Henry thereon: " If we pray in anger, we have reason to fear that God will answer us in anger. What reason is it that God should forgive us the talents [huge sums] we are indebted to Him, if we forgive not our brethren the pence they are indebted to us? Christ came into the world as the great Peacemaker not only to reconcile us to God, but to one another; and in this we must comply with Him. It is a great assumption and of dangerous consequences for anyone to make a light matter of that which Christ lays great stress upon. Men's passions must not frustrate God's Word." Far too weighty and momentous are these solemn and searching declarations of the Lord Jesus to be summarily dimissed with only a brief and light notice of them.

It was the comparative failure of Christian expositors in the past to adequately explain and enforce the teaching of Christ in the verses now before us which made it so much easier for modern errorists to foist their evil perversions on the uninstructed and unwary. For example, take the following footnote from the *Scofield Reference Bible*: " This is legal ground. Compare Ephesians iv, 32, which is grace. Under the Law forgiveness was conditioned upon a like spirit because we have been forgiven." This is a fair example of the vicious method followed by " Dispensationalists" who (under the pretence of " rightly dividing the

Word of Truth") delight in pitting the Old Testament against the New, and lowering the standard of Christianity, presenting a fictitious "grace" which does *not* "reign through righteousness" (Romans v, 21). Let us briefly examine this statement of Scofield's, which has misled thousands.

By saying that because our receiving Divine forgiveness is dependent upon our forgiving those who wrong us is "legal ground," attempt is made to set aside the Lord's positive declaration. In the added statement—" Compare Ephesians iv, 32, which is grace "—we are asked to believe that Matthew vi, 14, 15, pertains not at all to this Christian era. This is made quite plain in what follows where this "renowned Bible teacher" opposes the one to the other. " Under the Law forgiveness was conditioned upon a like spirit in us, under grace we are forgiven for Christ's sake, and exhorted to forgive because we have been forgiven." Such a declaration betrays the mental confusion of its author. Under no dispensation has God bestowed mercy upon any who maintained a vindictive spirit, nor does He now: were He to do so, it would not be "grace," but a disgrace to His holiness. Throughout the whole of the Old Testament economy penitent souls were pardoned for *Christ's* sake, as truly as believers are today. There is no conflict between the Law and the Gospel: the one is the handmaid of the other.

" For if ye forgive men their trespasses, your heavenly Father will also forgive you." What analogy is there between our forgiving of others and God's forgiving us? Let us begin with the *negative* side. First, it is *not* because our forgiving those who wrong us is in any sense or degree a *meritorious* act which deserves well at the hands of God. The meritorious ground on which God pardons our sins is the atonement of Christ, and that alone. Our best performances are imperfect, and in no way proportionate to the mercies we receive from God. What proportion is there between God's pardoning of us and our pardoning of others, either with respect to the parties interested in the action, the subject matter, the manner of performance or the issues of the action? God has laid a law upon us that we should forgive others, and compliance therewith is simply discharging our duty, and not something by which we bring the Lord into debt to us.

Second, it is *not a rule* so that our forgiving others should be a pattern of forgiving to God. " Thy will be done in earth *as* it is in heaven " does denote a conformity of the one to the other; but "forgive us our debts *as* we forgive our debtors " is not a pattern or rule. We are to be imitators of God, but He does not imitate us in pardoning offenders—it would fare ill with us indeed if God were to forgive us no better than we forgive one another. God is matchless in all His work and all His ways. Let it be duly noted that when He declares, " For My thoughts are not your thoughts, neither are your ways My ways, saith the Lord. For as the heavens are higher than the earth, so are My ways higher than your ways, and My thoughts than your thoughts" (Isaiah lv, 8, 9), it is specifically said in connection with His "abundant pardon" (see verse 7).

Third, nor do these words "For if ye forgive men their trespasses your heavenly Father will also forgive you" signify *a priority of order*, as though our acts had the precedency of God's, or as if we could heartily forgive others before God had shown mercy to us. No, in all acts of love God is first: His mercy to us is the cause of our mercy to others. In the great parable on forgiveness (Matt. xviii, 23-35), which forms the best commentary on the verses now before us, God's forgiving us is the motive of our forgiving: "I forgave thee all that debt, because thou desirest Me: shouldest not thou also have had compassion on thy fellowservant, even as I had pity on thee?" (verses 32, 33). So again, "Be ye kind one to another, tenderhearted, forgiving one another, even as God for Christ's sake hath forgiven you" (Eph. iv, 32)—in that manner, according to that example.

Turning now to the *positive* side. "If ye forgive men their trespasses, your heavenly Father will also forgive you." Very searching indeed are these words, constituting a severe test of discipleship, a test which excludes from the ranks of God's children those professors who cherish a spirit of malignity and revenge, refusing to forgive those who injure them. Unless our pride be truly broken by a sense of sin, so that we are not only willing to forgive others, but also rejoice in those opportunities for exercising (in some small degree at least) that loving kindness which we ourselves stand in such sore need of from God, then we are not really penitent in heart and therefore cannot be pardoned ourselves. If our prayers are to be acceptable unto God we must "lift up holy hands, *without wrath*" (I Tim. ii, 8).

First, our forgiveness of others is a *condition* or necessary qualification if we are to receive the continued pardon of God. "For if ye forgive men their trespasses, your heavenly Father will also forgive you": these two are definitely joined together and must not be sundered by us. Divine forgiveness always presupposes our repentance: it is not bestowed on that account, yet it is inseparably connected with it. Unless we forgive those who injure us we are in no moral condition ourselves to receive the mercy of God. We have no scriptural warrant whatever to expect the Divine pardon while we refuse to pardon those who have trespassed against us. It is quite wrong to limit this by saying that we cannot expect the *comfort* of God's pardon: so long as we indulge implacable resentment it is presumptuous for us to hope for Divine mercy.

Second, as intimated above, our forgiveness of others is a *mark* or sign that we ourselves have been pardoned by God. "Hateful and hating one another" (Titus iii, 3) was our condition by nature; but if by grace we have drunk of the blessed spirit of the Redeemer then shall we like Him (Luke xxiii) pray for our enemies. Said the beloved apostle, "Howbeit for this cause I obtained mercy, that in me first Jesus Christ might show forth all longsuffering" (I Tim. i, 16). Where the grace of God has wrought a miracle in the human heart graciousness is the inevitable effect. Reconciliation with God is made manifest by a conciliatory spirit to our fellows. If God has softened our hearts, how can we be hard and mercilessly exacting toward others? "There is none so tender to others as they which have received mercy themselves: that know how gently God hath dealt with them" (Thomas Manton).

Third, the joining together of our forgiving of others with God's forgiving of us is in order to show this is a *duty* incumbent upon those who are pardoned. God has laid this necessity upon us. Every time we beg His pardon we are to remind ourselves most solemnly of this duty and bind ourselves to it in the sight of God. So that when we pray "Forgive us our debts," we are required to add, "as we forgive our debtors." It is a definite undertaking on our part, a formal promise which we make to God: His showing of mercy to us will incline us to show mercy unto others. In all earnest requests we are to bind ourselves to the corresponding duties. In asking for our daily bread we pledge ourselves to labour for it. In asking that we may not be led into temptation, we agree not to place a stumbling-block before others.

Fourth, it is an argument inspiring confidence in God's pardoning mercy. We who have still so much of the old leaven of revenge left in us find that the receiving of a spark of grace enkindles in our hearts a readiness to forgive those who injure us, what may we not expect from God! Clearly this is what is urged in "Forgive us our sins, for we also forgive everyone that is indebted to us" (Luke xi, 4): if we who have so little grace find it possible to be magnanimous, how much more so shall the God of all grace exceed the creature in this! Christ employed the same kind of reasoning in His "If ye then, being evil, know how to give good gifts unto your children, how much more shall your Father, which is in heaven, give good things to them that ask Him?" (Matt. vii, 11). Since fallen man is moved with affection toward his weak and needy offspring, certainly the Father of mercies will not be indifferent to our wants.

We must next inquire what is meant by our forgiving those who trespass against us. Before answering this question in detail it should be pointed out that we can only forgive those injuries which are directed against ourselves, for none but God can forgive those which are against Himself—He alone can remit that punishment which is due to the transgressor for the violation of His Law. It should also be premised that we are not required to forgive those injuries done to us which constitute a flagrant violation of the laws of the land, whereby the offender has committed a serious crime, for it belongs not to a private person to condone evil-doing or to obstruct the course of justice. Yet if we have recourse to human courts for the redress of wrongs, it must not be in a spirit of malice, but only for the glory of God and the public good.

What is meant by our forgiving others? First, forbearing ourselves and withholding revenge. "Say not, I will do so to him as he hath done to me: I will render to the man according to his work" (Prov. xxiv, 29). Corrupt nature thirsts for retaliation, but grace must suppress it. If someone has slandered us, that does not warrant us to slander him. "He that is slow to anger is better than the mighty; and he that ruleth his spirit than he that taketh a city" (Prov. xvi, 32): we rule our spirit when we overcome our passions. "Be not overcome of evil, but overcome evil with good" (Romans xii, 21), for this will shame the offender if his conscience be not utterly calloused. When David had Saul at a disadvantage and forbore any act of revenge against him, Saul acknowledged, "Thou art more righteous than I" (Samuel xxiv, 17).

Second, Christians are required not only to forbear the avenging of themselves, but actually to pardon those who have wronged them. There must be the laying aside of all anger and hatred, and the exercise of love toward my neighbour, remembering that by nature I am no better than the offender (Gal. vi, 1). If we have genuinely pardoned the one who has injured us, we shall earnestly desire that God will pardon him too, as Stephen prayed for his enemies, "Lord, lay not this sin to their charge" (Acts vii, 60). This forgiveness must be sincere and from the heart. When Joseph's brethren submitted themselves to him, he not only remitted their offences, but "comforted them and spake kindly unto them" (Gen. l, 21).

Third, we must be ready to perform all the offices of love unto those who have wronged us; if the offending one be not a brother in Christ, yet is he still our fellow creature. Nor must we so magnify his faults as to be blind to his compensating virtues. We are required to do good unto those that hate us (Luke vi, 27) and to pray for those who despitefully use us and persecute us (Matt. v, 44). Though Miriam had wronged Moses, yet he prayed to the Lord for her forgiveness and healing (Num. xii, 13). And surely it is fitting that we who need mercy ourselves should show mercy unto others. It is a general rule that we should do as we would be done unto. How *we* need to pray for more grace if we are to be gracious unto others!

But are we required to forgive offenders absolutely and unconditionally, whether they express contrition or no? Certainly not. A holy God does not require us to condone evil-doing and countenance sin. The teaching of our Lord on this point is crystal clear: first we are bidden to seek out the offender, privately and meekly, and expostulate with him, endeavouring to make him see that he has displeased the Lord and wronged his own soul more than he has us (Matt. v, 23, 24; xviii, 15). Second, "If thy brother trespass against thee, rebuke him; and *if* he repent, forgive him. And if he trespass against thee seven times in a day, and seven times in a day turn again to thee, saying, I *repent*; thou shalt forgive him"

(Luke xvii, 3, 4). But suppose the offender evidences no sign of repentance? Even then, we must not harbour any malice or any revenge, yet we are not to act as freely and familiarly as before. Third, we are to pray for him.

"But if ye forgive not men their trespasses, neither will your Father forgive your trespasses." Unspeakably solemn is this, and each of us needs diligently to search his heart in the light of it. Let us bear in mind that other declaration of Christ's, "For with what judgment ye judge, ye shall be judged; and with what measure ye mete, it shall be measured to you again" (Matt. vii, 2). God's government is a reality, and He sees to it that whatsoever we sow that we do also reap. The same truth, in principle, is enunciated in "Whoso stoppeth his ears at the cry of the poor, he also shall cry himself, but shall not be heard" (Prov. xxi, 13). Many an earnest prayer is offered which never reaches the ear of God. Why is it that such a verse as, "For He shall have judgment without mercy, that hath showed no mercy" (James ii, 13), has no place in the preaching of our day? How much that is distasteful to flesh and blood is withheld by men-pleasers! Such will never receive the Master's "Well done, thou good and *faithful* servant."

It will be seen, then, that the passage we have been considering presents a very real test of discipleship. On the one hand it shows that if we are merciful to others we shall ourselves "obtain mercy" (Matt. v, 7). On the other hand it teaches that if we retain malice and hatred against those who injure us, then is the hypocrisy of our Christian profession plainly exposed. How necessary it is that we diligently examine our hearts and test ourselves at this point. As a guide therein, ponder before God the following queries. Do I secretly rejoice when I hear of any calamity befalling one who has wronged me? If so, I certainly have not forgiven him. Do I retain in my memory the wrongs suffered and upbraid the transgressor with it? Or, assuming he has repented, am I willing and anxious to do whatever I can to help him and promote his interests?

It is abundantly clear from all that has been before us that God's pardon of our sins and the reformation of our lives go together: the one can only be known by the other. The more our hearts and lives are regulated by a Christlike spirit, the clearer our evidence that we are new creatures in Him. It is utterly vain for me to believe that I have received the Divine pardon if I refuse to forgive those who injure me. True, it is often difficult to forget the wrongs we have forgiven, and the injuries we have received may still rankle with us. The flesh is yet in us and indwelling sin mars all the actings of grace. Yet if we honestly strive to banish ill will and seek to cherish a meek disposition toward our enemies, we may comfort ourselves that God will be gracious unto us, for His love is infinitely superior to ours. If our hearts condemn us not, then do we have confidence toward Him.

CHAPTER TWENTY-SIX

Fasting

" Moreover when ye fast, be not, as the hypocrites, of a sad countenance : for they disfigure their faces, that they may appear unto men to fast. Verily I say unto you, They have their reward. But thou, when thou fastest, anoint thine head, and wash thy face ; That thou appear not unto men to fast, but unto thy Father which is in secret : and thy Father, which seeth in secret, shall reward thee openly." (Matt. vi, 16-18.)

OUR present passage brings before us still another subject upon which multitudes of professing Christians are in much need of instruction. Personally we have never heard a sermon or " Bible reading " on fasting, and very little has come to our notice thereon which was written during the last forty years, and most of that " little " left very much to be desired. From conversations and communications with others it appears that our experience has been by no means a singular one, and therefore we do not feel it necessary to apologize for devoting two chapters to the above verses. Following our usual custom, we will first deal with our passage generally and topically, comparing with it the teaching of other sections of Scripture on this theme; and then consider our verses more specifically, seeking to expound and apply their terms.

Four hundred years ago Calvin wrote in his *Institutes,* " Let me say something on fasting: because many, for want of knowing its usefulness undervalue its necessity, and some reject it as altogether superfluous; while on the other hand, where the use of it is not well understood, it easily degenerates into superstition." Upon this matter the passing of the centuries has produced little or no improvement, for the very conditions which confronted this eminent reformer prevail extensively today. If on the one side Romanists have perverted a means unto an end, and have exalted what is exceptional to a principal part of their religious worship, Protestants have gone to the opposite extreme, allowing what was practised by primitive Christians to sink into general disuse.

Though there may have been much formality and hypocrisy in some who attended to this religious duty, yet that is no reason why the practice itself should be discountenanced and discontinued. Nowhere in our Lord's teaching is there anything to discourage religious fasting, but not a little to the contrary. Most certainly He was not reprehending this practice in the passage before us, rather was He uttering a caution against hypocrisy therein. By saying, " When ye fast, be not as the hypocrites," He takes it for granted that His disciples *will* fast—as much so as He assumes by His " when thou prayest, thou shalt not be as the hypocrites " (verse 3) that they would be men of prayer. Christ was here engaged in condemning the wicked perversion of the Pharisees, from which He also took occasion to give us valuable instruction upon our present theme.

When the heart and mind are deeply exercised upon a serious subject, especially one of a solemn or sorrowful kind, there is a dis-inclination for the partaking of food, and abstinence therefrom is a natural expression of our unworthiness, of our sense of the compara-tive worthlessness of earthly things, and of our desire to fix our atten-tion upon things above. Fasting, either total or partial, seems to have been connected with seasons of peculiarly solemn devotion in all ages. When Jonah testified to a guilty city, "Yet forty days and Nineveh shall be overthrown " (i.e. if it did not repent and turn to God), we are told, "So the people of Nineveh believed God, and proclaimed a fast, and put on sackcloth, from the greatest of them even to the least of them. For word came unto the king of Nineveh and he arose from his throne, and he laid his robe from him, and covered him with sackcloth, and sat in ashes. And he caused it to be proclaimed . . . Let neither man nor beast . . . feed nor drink water . . . and cry mightily unto God : yea, let them turn every one from his evil way. . . . Who can tell if God will turn and repent and turn away from His fierce anger, that we perish not?" (Jonah iii, 5-9).

There are a number of features about the above incident which are to be carefully noted, for they throw not a little light on several aspects of our present subject. This was no ordinary occasion when the Ninevites fasted, but a time of exceptional gravity, when the black clouds of Divine judgment hung heavy over their heads. It was not a fast undertaken by the individual, but one into which the whole populace entered. It was designed to express their deep humili-ation before God and was an appendage unto their crying " mightily " to Him. It was not a duty performed in response to any express commandment from the Lord, but was entered into volun-tarily and spontaneously. Its object was to divert the fierce anger of heaven against them, and as the closing verse of Jonah iii tells us, "And God saw their works, that they turned from their evil way, and God repented of the evil that He had said [provisionally] that He would do unto them; and He did it not."

Our first main division, then, shall be *occasions* of fasting. Let us preface our remarks thereon by pointing out that what we are about to consider particularly is extraordinary fasting in contra-distinction from ordinary. As we shall yet see, Scripture mentions partial fasting as well as total abstinence from food. There is an ordinary fasting which is required from all men, especially from the saints, namely an avoidance of gluttony and surfeiting, a making a " god " of our belly (Phil. iii, 19). This ordinary fasting consists in temperance and sobriety, whereby the appetites are restrained from the use of food and drink which exceeds moderation. We are to be temperate in all things, and at all times. Rightly did the godly Payson point out: "Fasting is not so much by total abstinence from food beyond accustomed intervals, as by denying self at *every* meal, and using a spare and simple diet at all times—a course well adapted to preserve the mind and body in the best condition for study and devotional exercises."

Now the occasion of an *extraordinary* religious fast is when a *weighty* cause thereof is offered. This is when some judgment of God hangs over our heads, such as the sword, famine or pestilence. In circumstances of grave danger the pious kings and prophets of Israel called on the people to engage in fasting as well as prayer. As examples of this we may cite the following. When the hand of the Lord lay heavily upon Israel and thousands fell in battle before the Benjamites, "Then all the children of Israel, and all the people, went up and came unto the house of God, and wept and sat there before the Lord, and fasted that day until even, and offered burnt offerings" (Judges xx, 26). When the Moabites, Ammonites and others combined against Jehoshaphat in battle, we are told that he "set himself to seek the Lord, and proclaimed a fast throughout all Judah. And Judah gathered themselves together, to ask help of the Lord" (II Chron. xx, 3, 4). In a time of national calamity Joel cried, "Sanctify ye a fast, call a solemn assembly . . . and cry unto the Lord" (i, 14).

The second general cause and occasion for fasting is when God is earnestly sought for some special and *particular blessing* or the supply of some great need. Thus on the annual day of atonement, when remission was sought for the sins of the nation, the Israelites were most expressly forbidden to do any manner of work, no not in their dwellings, but instead to "afflict their souls" (Lev. xxiii, 29-32). So too upon the exodus of the Jews from Babylon Ezra tells us, "Then I proclaimed a fast there, at the river of Ahava, that we might afflict ourselves before our God, to seek of Him a right of way for us, and for our little ones, and for all our substance" (viii, 21).

In addition to these examples of public fasting, Scripture also mentions that of many pious individuals. When his child by the wife of Uriah was smitten with sore sickness, we are told that "David therefore besought God for the child; and David fasted, and went and lay all night upon the earth" (II Samuel xii, 16). On another occasion, when sorely beset by enemies, David declared, "But as for me, when they were sick, my clothing was sackcloth: I humbled my soul with fasting" (Psalm xxxv, 13). When Nehemiah was informed that the remnant of his people left of the captivity in the provinces were "in great affliction and reproach" and the wall of Jerusalem was broken down and its gates burned with fire, he "sat down and wept and mourned certain days, and fasted, and prayed before the God of heaven" (i, 4). When Daniel ardently desired the deliverance of the children of Israel from their captivity in Babylon he "Set his face unto the Lord God, to seek by prayer and supplications, with fasting and sackcloth and ashes" (ix, 3).

It is a great mistake to suppose that either public or private fasting on the part of the pious was a practice confined to the Old Testament era. Of Anna we read, "She departed not from the temple, but served God with fastings and prayers night and day" (Luke ii, 37). When devout Cornelius ardently desired more light from God concerning the Messiah, he fasted and prayed (Acts x, 30). When the church at Antioch sought God's special blessing upon the success of His servants in the Gospel, they "fasted" (Acts xiii, 3). In like manner when Paul and Silas were about to establish local churches, they "prayed with fasting" (Acts xiv, 23), because in a matter of such importance they looked for special directions from God. In I Corinthians vii, 5, the apostle gives plain intimation that it was the ordinary and proper custom of Christians to give themselves to "prayer and fasting" when special needs called for the same.

Next, we will consider the *manner* of fasting. Fasting consists in an abstinence from meat and drink, yet not such an abstinence as would impair health or injure the body—which is forbidden in Colossians ii, 23, and would clash with Christ's directions that we should pray for our "daily bread." It is the abstinence from such meals as would interfere with an uninterrupted and earnest waiting upon God. Such fasting would primarily be a denying ourselves of all dainties, as Daniel "ate no pleasant bread, neither came flesh nor wine into his mouth, neither did he anoint himself at all, till three whole weeks were fulfilled" (x, 3). Coupled with the sparsest possible diet, there must also be an abstaining from all the delights of nature (see Joel ii, 15, 16). All of this is designed for the afflicting of ourselves, as Paul in his "I keep under my body and bring it into subjection" (I Cor. ix, 27).

Ere proceeding farther it should be pointed out that there may be a prolonged abstinence from food and yet no fasting in the scriptural sense of the term. One may observe a weekly fast, and observe it strictly, and yet not fast at all if it be no expression of an evangelical sorrow of the soul. The mere non-partaking of food is not fasting any more than the mere moving of the lips is prayer; and certainly there is nothing whatever of it in the denying to oneself meats while yet the hunger is appeased with eggs and fish. Unless our fasting be that which marks such a heartfelt sense of sin and of seeking unto God as will brook no diversion from its purpose, moving us spontaneously and for the time being with a lack of appetite for all things else, then it is but a superstition, a piece of morbid formalism.

God is not to be imposed upon by any mere outward performance, no matter how solemnly and decorously it be executed. It is at the heart He ever looks, and unless our *hearts* be in our

fasting we do but mock the Most High with an empty show. Of old
He asked Israel, "When ye fasted and mourned in the fifth and
seventh month, even those seventy years, did ye at all fast *unto Me,*
even to Me?" (Zech. vii, 5). On another occasion He refused to accept
the fasting of the people because they were flagrantly setting at
naught the precepts of the Second Table, saying, "Is it such a fast
that I have chosen? a day for a man to afflict his soul? is it to bow
down his head as a bulrush and to spread sackcloth and ashes under
him? wilt thou call this a fast, an acceptable day to the Lord? Is
not this the fast that I have chosen? to loose the bands of wickedness, to undo the heavy burdens and let the oppressed go free?"
(Isaiah lviii, 5, 6). And at a later date the Lord gave orders, "Rend
your hearts and not your garments, and turn unto the Lord your
God" (Joel ii, 13).

From the very nature of the case we should never let our minds
dwell on the act of fasting, as though we had therein discharged a
duty. Fasting is not to be undertaken for the mere sake of fasting.
It is not as the doing of penance that we are ever to abstain from
food, neither is it as though the abstaining were a process of holiness; still less must we regard it as in any wise a meritorious performance. Private fasting must issue from an urge within and not
because it is imposed from without. Private fasting should be spontaneous, the result of our being under a great stress of spirit, and
the simple act itself be entirely lost sight of in the engrossing fervour
which prompted it. There had been little or no practical difficulties
on the subject of fasting if these simple rules had been understood
and observed.

And yet, so prone are we to run to extremes, a word of caution
is needed here lest what has just been said above be put to an evil
use. It would be quite wrong to draw the conclusion, seeing I feel
no inward urge to engage in fasting, therefore I am discharged from
this duty. The Christian reader should at once perceive that such
an argument would be quite invalid in connection with other
spiritual duties. If I feel no appetite for the heavenly manna or no
desire to draw near unto the throne of grace, then it is my bounden
duty penitently to confess unto God my coldness of heart and beg
Him to stir me up afresh unto a hearty use of the appointed means.
The same principle most certainly holds good in connection with
fasting.

The particular *seasons* for fasting are to be determined mainly by
the governmental dealings of God, and therefore those who would
improve such seasons must be strict observers of the workings of
Providence: otherwise God may be calling aloud for weeping and
girding of sackcloth, while we hear not His call but indulge in joy
and feasting (Isaiah xxii, 12, 13). As to the amount of time to be
spent in either individual or corporate fasting, the duty—the
exigencies of the situation—should regulate it and not it the duty.
Various lengths of time are mentioned in different cases (see II

Samuel xii, 16; Esther iv, 16; Daniel x, 2, 3). "Wherefore I judge that none are to be solicitous as to what quantity of time, more or less, they spend in these exercises, so that the work of the time be done. Nay, I very much doubt, men lay a snare to themselves in tying themselves to a certain quantity of time in such cases" (Thomas Boston).

Let us now consider the *purpose* of fasting. Various designs are mentioned in Scripture. The first end in fasting is the denying of self, the bringing of our body and its lusts in subjection unto the will and Word of God. Said the Psalmist, "I wept and chastened my soul with fasting, that was to my reproach" (Psalm lxix, 10). Before men, yes; but not so before God. Our Lord warned us, "Take heed to yourselves lest at any time your hearts be overcharged with surfeiting and drunkenness" (Luke xxi, 34). The body is made heavy, its senses dulled, and the mind rendered sluggish by much eating or drinking, and thereby the whole man becomes unfit for the duties of prayer and hearing of the Word. That this unfitness may be avoided and that the lusts of the flesh may be mortified and subdued, fasting is to be duly engaged in.

The second end of fasting is to stir up our devotions and to confirm our minds in the duties of hearing and prayer. In this connection it is to be duly noted that fasting and prayer are almost always linked together in the Scriptures, or it would be more correct to say "prayer and fasting" (Matt. xvii, 21; Acts xiii, 3 and xiv, 23) to intimate that the latter is designed as an aid to the former, chiefly in that the non-preparation and participation of meals leaves us the freer for uninterrupted communion with God. When the stomach is full, the body and mind are less qualified for the performance of spiritual duties. For this reason we are told Anna "served God with fastings and prayers," the design of the Holy Spirit being to commend her to our notice for the fervency of her spirit, which she evidenced in this manner.

The third end in fasting is to bear witness unto the humiliation and contrition of our hearts, for the denying ourselves of nature's comforts suitably expresses the inward sorrow and grief we feel over our sins. "Proclaim a fast" is the Lord's requirement (Joel i, 14) when He would have His people testify their contrition. Surely it is obvious that the participation of creature dainties or the indulgence of self in similar ways is most incongruous at a time when we are mourning before God and declaring our repentance. When convicted of our iniquities God requires us to turn unto Him with fasting and mourning and with the rending of our hearts.

The fourth end of fasting is to admonish us of our guilt and uncleanness, to put us in mind of our utter unworthiness of even the common mercies of Providence, that we deserve not food nor drink. It is designed to make us conscious of our wants and miseries, and thereby make us the more aware of our sins. If the Ninevites were made to perceive the propriety of abstaining from food and drink when the sword of Divine judgment was hanging over their heads (Jonah iii), then how much more should we, with our vastly greater light and privileges, be sensible of the same. If we duly "consider our ways" (Haggai i, 5) must we not feel that sackcloth and ashes well become us? The main peril to guard against in our fasting will be considered in our next.

CHAPTER TWENTY-SEVEN

Fasting—Concluded

"MOREOVER when ye fast, be not, as the hypocrites, of a sad countenance: for they disfigure their faces, that they may appear unto men to fast. Verily I say unto you, They have their reward. But thou, when thou fastest, anoint thine head, and wash thy face; that thou appear not unto men to fast, but unto thy Father which is in secret; and thy Father, which seeth in secret, shall reward thee openly." These words brought to a close the fourth division of our Lord's address, a division which covered the first eighteen verses of Matthew vi, the subject of which is the performing of good works in such a manner as to secure the approval of God. Fasting is mentioned last of the three branches of practical righteousness because it is not so much a duty for its own sake as a means to dispose us for other duties.

Fasting is the abstaining from food for a religious purpose. Though there is no express commandment in either the Law or the Gospel binding us thereto, yet it is plain both from precept and practice in the Old and New Testaments alike that there are occasions when fasting is both needful and helpful. Though there is nothing meritorious in it, fasting is both an appropriate sign and a valuable means. It should be the outward sign of an inward mortification. It is the opposite of feasting, which expresses joy and merriment. It is a voluntary denying ourselves of those creature comforts to which we are ordinarily accustomed. Rightly engaged in, it should be found a valuable adjunct to prayer, particularly for afflicting our souls when expressing sorrow for sin. As to the frequency and the duration thereof this must largely be determined by our ordinary habits, our constitutions, and our vocations.

So depraved is the human heart and so prone is man to rest in externals that he changes what was originally the means or sign unto the end itself. Thus we find the Pharisee boasting that he "fasted twice in the week" (Luke xviii, 12). Thus that which was designed as a simple means to further and to testify humiliation, repentance and zeal in prayer was perverted into a meritorious performance which produced self-complacency. But what was still worse, the Pharisees made a stage-play of this holy ordinance and resorted to various hypocritical devices therein, in order to further their reputation among men for extraordinary piety and devotion. They advertised what should have been a secret between their souls and God: they employed a counterfeit sadness and ostentatious grief, and thereby reduced to a farce and a mockery what should have been held in great sanctity.

"Moreover when ye fast, be not, as the hypocrites, of a sad countenance: for they disfigure their faces, that they may appear unto men to fast." This was our Lord's first word on the subject of fasting, and like His first on prayer it consists in a warning against *hypocrisy* therein. This is very searching and should be seriously taken to heart by all of us. Every species of pride is exceedingly foolish and most obnoxious unto the Lord, but the worst form of all is spiritual pride, and especially that which aims at securing the applause of our fellows. Fasting, if it be genuine, arises from a deep sense of our utter unworthiness and is designed to express our self-loathing before God. To make the same into a pedestal from which we proclaim our humility and sanctity is indeed a turning of light into darkness.

"When ye fast, be not, as the hypocrites, of a sad countenance: for they disfigure their faces, that they may appear unto men to fast." It may be inquired, How is such a prohibition as this to be harmonized with Joel i, 13, 14, where God required the Jews to "lament" and "howl" in their fast, which could scarcely be without mournful and appropriate gestures of the body? The answer is that Christ was not here condemning a sorrowful countenance in fasting when a just occasion for the same is offered, for godly Nehemiah looked sad (ii, 2). Instead, our Lord was here engaged in reprehending the wicked deceits of the Pharisees, who deliberately feigned an appearance of great sorrow when in fact their hearts were devoid of contrition. This is quite clear from His next words.

"When ye fast, be not, as the hypocrites, of sad countenance: for they disfigure their faces, that they may appear unto men to fast." But to this it might also be objected, Did not some of God's own people in the past disfigure their faces in various ways, and that with Divine approval? For example, are we not informed that Ezra plucked off the hairs of his head and of his beard (ix, 3), and are we not told that Joshua and his fellows fell to the ground upon their faces and put dust upon their heads (vii, 6)? But all of those cases were spontaneous expressions of deep sorrow of heart—something quite different from what our Lord was here rebuking. He blames the Pharisees for disfiguring their faces, first, because this was the chief, yea, the only, thing they had respect unto in their fasts, namely the outward show thereof, which God hated. And second, because the word "disfigure" here signifies the very abolishing of their comeliness. They deliberately took means to look wan and emaciated so that they might the better advertise their fasting.

Instead of keeping to the privacy of their homes on fast days and using the time in those sacred exercises of which fasting is both the means and the sign, the Pharisees went abroad and, like stage-players, paraded all the marks of a state of mind which they did not feel, but which they desired that others should believe they experienced. They assumed a sad countenance. " They employed all the usual tokens of deep affliction and mental distress. They covered their heads with dust and ashes, vailed their countenances, neglected their dress, and deformed their features by contracting them into the most gloomy and dejected looks. They studiously exhibited all the external appearances of humiliation, while their hearts were lifted up in spiritual pride " (Brewster).

Ere passing on let it be duly noted that it was the practice of the scribes and Pharisees not only to fast but also to be very punctilious in observing all the outward rites and signs pertaining to religious fasts; nevertheless, as in the former works of almsgiving and prayer, so in this, the principal thing was lacking, namely truth and sincerity in the *heart*. Their grief-stricken faces proceeded not from broken hearts. They were whole and righteous in their own conceits and needed neither the great Physician nor regeneration of soul. In this we may see a true exemplification of the properties of natural men in matters of spiritual moment: they are more concerned with external deeds than in having the Truth in their inward parts; they content themselves with their outward performances and have little or no regard to worshipping in the spirit. In like manner, the wicked Ahab went to much trouble in humbling himself outwardly, from fear of punishment (I Kings xxi, 27), yet continued in his sins.

How often it was thus with Israel of old; they went through the form of humbling themselves and seeking God's favour, when as David said, " They did flatter Him with their mouth and they lied unto Him with their tongues. For their heart was not right with Him, neither were they stedfast in His covenant" (Psalm lxxviii, 36, 37). And thus it is generally with natural men. The whole religion of the deluded papists stands in outward ceremonial acts, partly Jewish and partly heathenish, and when they have observed them they look no farther. And it is no better with tens of thousands among the Protestants, who content themselves with the external acts of going to church, hearing the Word, and "receiving the sacrament" once or twice a year; and when these duties are scrupulously observed they imagine that all is well with them and think God is served sufficiently. Yea, let anyone set before them the *real* requirements of a thrice holy God and he will at once be sneered at by them as being too strict and precise, puritanical and fanatical.

Since our Lord here condemned the fasting of the Pharisees because they rested in the outward work and did it ostentatiously for the praise of men, then how clear it is that the fasting of the papists is an abomination in His sight, for theirs abounds with more numerous abuses. First, they reduce the practice of fasting to a ludicrous farce, by allowing fish and eggs to take the place of meats and by placing no restriction at all upon wines and other drinks. Second, they bind men in conscience to numerous days of fasting and make the omission thereof a deadly sin, thereby taking away

Christian liberty, for neither the Saviour nor any of His apostles appointed any set fast days. Third, they make fasting a meritorious performance, teaching that a man thereby renders satisfaction unto Divine justice for his sins, whereby they blasphemously derogate from the sufficiency of Christ's obedience and sacrifice. How the godly should grieve at the spread of such wicked superstitions in our midst.

It should now be quite apparent that Christ did not here forbid all fasting as such, but was engaged in correcting the abuses of this ordinance. His words, "When ye fast, be not as the hypocrites," not only take it for granted that His disciples *would* fast, but manifestly denote that the godly *ought* to do so, both in private and in public upon just occasion. Nay, if the Saviour here rebukes the Pharisees for their perversion of this holy means of grace, then much more must He blame those who fast not at all. This is not a thing indifferent, left to our option, but something which God requires from us, and for the absence of which He may often increase His judgments (Isaiah xxii, 12-14).

Sufficient has already been before us to show that God has given us many inducements to stir up our hearts to engage in this exercise. There is the worthy precedent of many holy men in the past who carefully performed this duty when occasion offered, such as David, Daniel, Ezra and Nehemiah. In like manner we have recorded examples in the New Testament of the Saviour Himself (Matt. iv), Anna, Cornelius, the apostles and elders of the churches. Moreover, we have among us pressing occasions of fasting, both in public and in private. The present state of God's cause upon earth, the withdrawal of the Spirit's unction and blessing, the drying up of the streams of vital godliness, the lack of fruit from the preaching of the Gospel, the abounding error on every side, the rising tide of infidelity, iniquity and immorality, and, above all, the national judgments of God now hanging over our heads, call loudly for humiliation, afflicting of our souls, and repentance.

"But thou, when thou fastest, anoint thine head, and wash thy face; That thou appear not unto men to fast, but unto thy Father which is in secret" (verses 17, 18). This statement is not to be taken absolutely and literally, but relatively and figuratively. These words of Christ must be understood in the light of their setting, their scope being quite apparent from the context. In oriental countries, where the air is hot and dry, it is the common custom to anoint the head and face with oil and ointments, which are there plentiful and cheap (Ruth iii, 3; Luke vii, 46; etc.)—"oil to make his face to shine" (Psalm civ, 15). That Christ is not to be here understood literally appears from His scope: He was off-setting Pharisees' practice of disfiguring their faces. Second, from the fact that He does not here command contraries: the use of such things in fasting as are more appropriate for feasting, for the anointing of the face is indicative of cheerfulness and joy.

The obvious meaning of Christ in the above words is: When thou engagest in a private fast, so conduct thyself as it may not appear unto men that thou art so engaged. Fasting is unto God, and our one and only concern must be to perform this duty in a manner which is pleasing unto Him. So far from parading this duty before men, we must take every possible precaution to conceal our private devotions from them. If we are to enter our chambers and shut to the door when engaging in private prayer, equally necessary is it that we observe the utmost secrecy in connection with our private fasting. Everything which savours of pride and ostentation is to be rigidly eschewed. Whenever we devote a portion of our time to extraordinary private devotions there should be nothing in our deportment or general appearance to indicate this unto others. So far from any show of our religious feelings, we should do all we can to hide them from the notice of others.

"But thou, when thou fastest, anoint thine head and wash thy face; that thou appear not unto men to fast." "This exhortation certainly does not mean that on these occasions men should assume a cheerfulness they do not feel, but that there should be nothing in the dress or in the appearance calculated to attract notice; that there should be no abatement in the ordinary attention to cleanliness of person or propriety of apparel; and that when, having brought the solemn services of the closet to a termination, they go out to society, there should be nothing to tell the world how they have been engaged" (John Brown). The great thing to remember and be concerned about is that it is with *God* we have to do, and not with men. It is with Him our hearts are to be occupied, it is unto Him we are praying and fasting, it is before Him we are to unburden ourselves. It is His pardon and favour we are soliciting. The opinion and esteem of fellow mortals fades into utter insignificance before the approval and reward of our heavenly Father.

"When thou fastest anoint thine head and wash thy face." In these instructions we are also taught that Christ requires us to take due care of our bodies. There are two extremes to be avoided: undue pampering and the careless neglecting of them—the former presenting the more real danger in this effeminate age. Any species of gluttony and intemperance is sinful, for it dulls the mind, stimulates our lusts, and leads to further evil. Such excesses are forbidden in "make not provision for the flesh to fulfil the lusts thereof" (Romans xiii, 14). On the other hand we are warned against the "neglecting of the body" (Col. ii, 23) under the pretence of honouring the soul: anything which produces weakness and disability is to be avoided. That care of the body which God requires is a moderate concern for its needs, a temperate use of food so as to fit it for the discharge of duty.

In the above words of Christ we may also perceive that it is a Christian duty to preserve a cheerful countenance. While on the one hand we must eschew all carnal frivolity and lightness, manifesting an habitual seriousness and sobriety; yet on the other hand we must see to it that we carefully avoid everything which savours of an affected solemnity and melancholy. If we are bidden to guard against any external displays of grief while engaged in those religious exercises which from their very nature tend to sadden the countenance, then most certainly it is our duty to manifest in our general deportment the natural symptoms of a cheerful and contented mind.

It is our duty to refute the world's lie that Christianity is incapable of making its subjects happy. Few things have done more injury to the cause of the Gospel than the sourness, sadness, and moroseness of a large class of its professors. Where Christ rules in the heart He sheds abroad a peace which passes all understanding and a joy which is unspeakable and full of glory. True we must not pretend a peace and joy we do not possess, yet we should be most diligent in opening our hearts unto the influences of that Truth which we profess to believe. God's commands are not grievous, and in the keeping of them there is great reward. Let us seek to make it evident to those around us that Christ's yoke is not a hard one nor His burden heavy. Let us make it appear that the Truth has not made us slaves, but free, and that wisdom's ways are ways of pleasantness.

" But unto thy Father which is in secret: and thy Father, which seeth in secret, shall reward thee openly" (verse 18). These words contain a warning against the one-sided idea of dispensationalists that Christ will be the *sole* Judge and Rewarder—a concept which is plainly refuted by such a passage as Hebrews xii, 23. It is just as erroneous to restrict the judicial office to the Son as to exclude the Father and the Spirit (Job xxxiii, 4, etc.) from the work of creation. The truth is that, with regard to deliberation, authority and consent, the final judgment shall be determined by the whole Trinity, yet with regard to immediate execution by Christ.

We cannot do better than conclude these remarks by quoting from Calvin. "It were far better that fasting should be entirely disused than that the practice should be diligently observed, and at the same time corrupted with false opinions, into which the world is continually falling, unless it be presented by the greatest fidelity of the pastors. The first caution necessary is 'Rend your heart and not your garments' (Joel ii, 13): that is, God sets no value on fasting unless it be accompanied with a corresponding disposition of heart, a real displeasure against sin, sincere self-abhorrence, true humiliation, and unfeigned grief; and that fasting is of no use of any other account than as an additional and subordinate assistance to these things."

CHAPTER TWENTY-EIGHT

Covetousness Corrected

" Lay not up for yourselves treasures upon earth, where moth and rust doth corrupt, and where thieves break through and steal : But lay up for yourselves treasures in heaven, where neither moth nor rust doth corrupt, and where thieves do not break through nor steal : For where your treasure is, there will your heart be also." (Matt. vi, 19-21.)

WE are now to enter the fifth division of our Lord's sermon, and as we do it is well to remind ourselves afresh of His first and primary design in this important address, namely to correct and refute the erroneous views of His hearers. The Jews held false beliefs concerning the person of the Messiah, the character of His mission, and the nature of the kingdom He would establish. As unregenerate men their views were carnal and mundane, self-centred and confined to things temporal. It requires little perspicuity to perceive that all through this Sermon the Lord Jesus makes direct reference unto the false notions which were generally entertained by the Jews respecting His kingdom, to which He constantly opposed the holy claims of God, the righteous requirements of His Law, and the imperative necessity of the new birth for all who were to be His subjects and disciples.

What has just been pointed out explains why our Lord began His Sermon with the Beatitudes, in which He described the characters and defined the graces of those who enter His kingdom. The Jews looked for great material enrichment, festivity and feasting, and supposed that those who would occupy the principal positions of honour under the Messiah's reign would be they who were fierce and successful warriors, and who, though ceremonially holy, would avenge on the Gentiles all the wrongs they had inflicted on Israel, and that henceforth they would be free from all opposition and oppression. But Christ declared blessed those who were poor in spirit, who mourned, who hungered and thirsted after righteousness, who were merciful, pure in heart, peacemakers, and were persecuted for righteousness' sake. A greater contrast could not be imagined.

So in His second division Christ announced that the officers of His kingdom would not be the destroyers of men's bodies but the preservers of their souls—the " salt of the earth"; not the suppressors of the Gentiles but " the light of the world." In like manner, in His third division Christ declared that so far from it being His mission to overthrow the ancient order and introduce radical changes, He came not to destroy the Law but to fulfil it. Thus too

185

with what is now to be before us: "Lay not up for yourselves
treasures upon earth . . . but lay up for yourselves treasures in
heaven." The Jews expected in their Messiah a temporal prince, and
the happiness they anticipated under His sceptre was merely a high
degree of worldly prosperity, to enjoy an abundance of riches,
honours and pleasures. But our Lord here exposes their error, and
declares that the happiness He imparts is not carnal but spiritual,
and that it will be found in its perfection not on earth (Palestine)
but in heaven.

Now it should be pointed out that the false notions generally
entertained by the Jews respecting the Messiah's kingdom originated
in principles which are common to unregenerate human nature,
though taking a peculiar form and colour from their special circumstances. Hence it is that the teachings of Christ in this sermon are
pertinent to all men in every age. Human nature is the same everywhere. The citizens of this world have ever devoted the greater part
of their time and energy to procuring and accumulating something
which they may call their own, and in setting their hearts steadfastly upon the same rather than upon God. So general is this
practice that, providing they are not unduly unscrupulous and do
not injure their fellows in their greedy quest, such a policy evokes
approval rather than reproach: "Men will praise thee, when thou
doest well to thyself" (Psalm xlix, 18). Those who succeed in business are called shrewd and efficient, and those who amass great
wealth "the captains of industry," "financial wizards," etc.

"Lay not up for yourselves treasures upon earth" (verse 19).
The *order* of Truth followed by Christ in Matthew vi is very striking
and blessed, and needs to be carefully heeded by us. In the first
eighteen verses we are conducted into the Sanctuary, instructed to
have our hearts occupied with Him who seeth in secret; in verse 19
and onwards we come out to face the temptations and trials of the
world. It is parallel with what we find in Leviticus and Numbers:
in the former, Israel is engaged almost entirely with the services and
privileges of the tabernacle; in the latter we have a description of
their walk and warfare in the wilderness. It is of vital importance
that we attend to this order, for it is only as we duly maintain communion with God in the secret place that we are equipped and
enabled for the trials of the way as we journey toward the heavenly
Canaan. Unless our hearts be firmly set upon the Promised Land,
they will turn back to Egypt and lust after its fleshpots.

"Lay not up for ourselves treasures upon earth." From here to the
end of the chapter Christ's design is to divert the hearts of His
hearers from a spirit of covetousness, first delivering the prohibition
and then amplifying and enforcing the same by a variety of cogent
reasons. The word for "lay up" is more expressive and emphatic in
the original than is expressed here in the English: signifying first
to gather together, and second to hoard or heap up against the
future—as in Romans ii, 5, heapeth up or "treasurest up unto

thyself." "Treasure" means wealth in abundance, costly things such as property, lands, gold and precious stones. The words "upon earth" here refer not so much to place as to the *kind* of treasures, for heavenly treasure may be laid up while we are here on earth, and therefore it is the hoarding of earthly and material treasures which is in view.

"Lay not up for yourselves treasures upon earth." There have been some fanatics who interpreted this command literally, insisting that it is to be taken without limitation as a prohibition against accumulating money or adding to our earthly possessions. To be consistent they should not stop there, but go on to "sell that thou hast and give to the poor" (Matt. xix, 21), for this is no less expressly required than the former. But such a course would mean the overturning of all distinctions between rich and poor, *any* possession of property, which is clearly contrary to the whole trend of Scripture. Let us, then, briefly point out what Christ did not here forbid. First, diligent labour in a man's vocation, whereby he provides things needful for himself and those dependent upon him: "not slothful in business" (Romans xii, 11) is one of the precepts of the Gospel.

Nor does Christ here forbid the fruit of our labours in the possession of goods and riches, provided they be acquired honestly and used aright. Let us not forget that scripure, "But thou shalt remember the Lord thy God: for it is He that giveth thee power to get wealth" (Deut. viii, 18). The Lord graciously prospered Abraham, Job and David, and so far from their possession of wealth being a mark of His disfavour it was the very opposite. Third, nor does Christ here forbid the laying up in store for our own future use or for our family. Is not the sluggard admonished to take a leaf out of the book of the ants, who gather together their winter's food in the summertime (Prov. vi, 6-8)? And has not the apostle declared that "the children ought not to lay up for the parents, but the parents for the children" (II Cor, xii, 14)? And again, "If any provide not for his own, and especially for those of his own house, he hath denied the faith, and is worse than an infidel" (I Tim. v, 8).

What, then, is it which Christ here forbids? We answer, various forms of covetousness. First, the excessive seeking after worldly wealth, wherein men keep neither moderation nor measure: although God gives them more than sufficient to supply their needs, yet they are not content, their desire being insatiable. That it is not sinful for a man to seek after the necessities of life—either for his present or future use—we have shown above. As to what constitutes necessity, this varies considerably in different cases, according to the station which providence has allotted in this world: a workman requires tools, a business man must have capital, the master of a large estate sufficient to pay his servants. No precise rule can be laid down, but the judgment and example of the godly who use the creature aright, and not the practice of the covetous, must guide us.

Second, Christ here condemns those who seek principally after worldly goods and disparage and disregard the true riches. This is clear from the opposition made in the next verse, where "lay up for yourselves treasures in heaven" is placed over against "lay not up for yourselves treasures upon earth." Thus it was in the case of Esau, who sold his birthright for a mess of pottage (Heb xii, 16). Thus it was with the Gadarenes, who upon the loss of their herds of swine besought Christ that He would depart out of their coasts (Luke viii, 37). Thus it has been throughout the ages, and so it still is, that the great majority of men spend their strength in labouring after that which "satisfieth not" (Isaiah lv, 2), seeking after almost anything or everything rather than after that which perisheth not. That is why there is so much preaching and so little profiting: the hearers' thoughts and desires are taken up with other things.

Third, Christ here condemns those who put their trust and confidence in worldly things that they have treasured up, which is idolatry of the heart. Whatever a man sets his heart upon and looks to for support is his god, and therefore his covetousness is called "idolatry" (Col. iii, 5). If we have stored up a supply against future need and this takes us from dependence upon God for our daily sustenance, then we are guilty of this sin. It is for this reason that Christ makes it so hard for a rich man to enter heaven (Matthew xix, 23, 24), because he *trusts* in his riches, and if we are close observers we shall usually find that rich men are proud-hearted and secure, neither heeding God's judgments nor attending to the means of salvation. David's counsel must therefore be followed, "If riches increase [not give them away, but] set not your heart upon them" (Psalm lxii, 10).

The fourth practice here forbidden is the selfish laying up of treasures for ourselves only, without regard to using the same for the good of our generation, the support of the Gospel, or the praise of God. This is indeed a devilish practice, for every one of us is but a steward, to dispense our portion to the glory of God and the good of his fellows. The poor are God's poor, the creatures of His hands, and therefore He requires that each steward shall be found faithful in seeing to it that each of them has his portion. God will yet call the rich to an accounting, therefore let each of us live in the light of that day of reckoning. Let us seek grace to be preserved from hoarding up riches for our own selfish use, from putting our trust in them, and from making them our chief delight.

"Lay not up for yourselves treasures upon earth, where moth and rust doth corrupt, and where thieves break through and steal." Here our Lord gives a threefold reason for the enforcing of His precept, or illustrates the corruption and uncertainty of worldly possession by three examples: showing they are liable to destruction by such creatures as moths, by the inherent decay which pertains to all earthly things, and from the fact they may be taken from us by fraud or violence. Have we procured an elaborate wardrobe, with large supplies of apparel? In secret and silence the moth may be eating it up. Have we invested in property? The ravages of time will soon wear it away. Is it gold and platinum, diamonds and pearls we have hoarded up? The hand of the marauder may soon seize them. Heaven is the only safe place in which to deposit our riches.

As we have pointed out in an earlier paragraph, the vast majority of our fellows make it their supreme aim in life to acquire as much as possible of worldly wealth. With such an example on every side, and the trend of their own hearts in the same direction, the disciples of Christ are in greater danger from this sin than from most others. To nullify this evil tendency Christ here emphasizes the relative valuelessness of mundane things. "Wilt thou set thine eyes upon that which is not? for riches certainly make themselves wings; they fly away as an eagle" (Prov. xxiii, 5). What true satisfaction can there be in the possession of things which are subject to decay and loss by violence. One of the strongest proofs of human depravity and of the diseased state of our minds is the extreme difficulty which most of us experience in the realizing of this fact in such a way that it really influences our actions.

"But lay up for yourselves treasures in heaven" (verse 20). Having shown what we must *not* do in respect of treasures here on earth, and knowing his inclination to be such that man will needs have something for his treasure, Christ here makes known what treasure we *may* lay up for ourselves. But how shall we lay up treasure in heaven? For we cannot of ourselves come there. No man can save himself: the beginning, progress and end of our salvation is wholly of God. Answer: as often in Scripture, the work of the efficient cause is here ascribed to the instrument (cf. I Cor. iv, 15; I Tim. iv, 16). To make us rich with heavenly treasure is the work of God alone, yet because we are instrumental by His grace in the use of means to get this treasure, this command is given to us as though the work is solely ours, though God be alone the Author of it.

It is of the very first moment that we form a true estimate of what is necessary for true happiness—where it is to be found and how it is to be obtained—for the tenor of our thoughts, the direction of our affections, and the pursuit of our energies will largely be regulated thereby. Therefore does Christ here bid us, "Lay up for yourselves treasures in heaven, where neither moth nor rust doth corrupt, and where thieves do not break through nor steal." That we may the better understand and practise this command two points are to be carefully and reverently considered: what this treasure is, and how a man may lay it up for himself—matters of the greatest weight, for in the practice thereof lies our salvation. As to the real treasure, which neither time nor the creature can mar, it is the true and living God, the triune Jehovah who made and governs all things: in Him alone is all genuine good and happiness to be found.

This is clear from such scriptures as the Lord's statement to Abraham, "I am thy shield, and thy exceeding great reward" (Gen.

xv, 1); the words of Eliphaz to Job, " The Almighty shall be thy gold " (xxii, 25, margin); and the declaration of David: " The Lord is the portion of mine inheritance . . . I have a goodly heritage "—i.e. He is my treasure (Psalm xvi, 5, 6). Yet let it be said emphatically that it is God as He is revealed *in Christ* who is our Treasure, for out of Christ He is " a consuming fire." God incarnate is our true treasure, for in Him are hid " all the treasures of wisdom and knowledge" (Col. ii, 3); our very life is " hid with Christ in God " (Col. iii, 3).

" Eye hath not seen, nor ear heard, neither have entered into the heart of man, the things which God hath prepared for them that love Him " (I Cor. ii, 9). To what is the apostle there referring? Why, as the previous verse shows, to that which God has treasured up for His people in a crucified Christ: the Lord Jesus is the great Fountain and Storehouse of all true blessings communicated from God to the saints, and therefore do they exclaim, " Of His fulness [as out of a rich treasure] have all we received, and grace for grace " (John i, 16). Wouldest thou have remission of sins and righteousness with God? Then Christ was " made sin for us, who knew no sin, that we might be made the righteousness of God in Him " (II Cor. v, 21). Wouldest thou have everlasting well-being? Then Christ Himself is " the true God, and eternal life " (I John v, 20). Whatever thou needest—wisdom to direct, strength to energize, comfort to assuage grief, cleansing for defilement—all is to be found in the Saviour.

How may we lay up for ourselves in heaven the Divine and durable riches which are to be found in Christ? First, by faith's appropriation: " as many as *received* Him " (John i, 12)—so that I can say " my Beloved is mine, and I am His " (Song of Sol. ii, 16). God in Christ becomes our everlasting portion when we surrender to and accept Him as He is offered to us in the Gospel. Second, by daily communion with Christ, drawing from His " unsearchable riches " (Eph. iii, 8). " Mary hath chosen that good part which shall not be taken away from her " (Luke x, 42). And what was that " good part "? Why, to sit at His feet and drink in His word (verse 39). Third, by emulating the example which Christ has left us. And what did that example consist of? Why, complete self-abnegation, living wholly in subjection to God—for which He was richly rewarded (see Phil. ii, 5-11). Fourth, by acting as His stewards and using the goods He has entrusted to us by laying them out to His glory (see Luke xii, 33; Heb. vi, 10, etc.).

Almost all will say they hope for happiness from God in the next world, but what do they *now* make their chief good? What are they most taken up with, both in the pursuit and enjoyment? It is at this point each of us must examine and test himself. What things does my soul most favour and relish, the things of the world or of God (see Romans viii, 5)? Which seasons of time do I regard as lost or as most gainful, which are my days of richest income? Of the Sabbath the wicked ask, "When will it be gone"? But the healthy saint declares, "A day in Thy courts is better than a thousand" (Psalm lxxxiv, 10)—because of the spiritual gains it brings in. What is dearest to my heart, what engages my most serious thoughts? This determines which I prize the more highly: earthly or heavenly treasures.

CHAPTER TWENTY-NINE

Covetousness Corrected—Concluded

"LAY not up for yourselves treasures upon earth, where moth and rust doth corrupt, and where thieves break through and steal" (verse 19). Let it be borne in mind that when our Lord uttered these words there were no such things as banks or government security-bonds, that the rich were chiefly distinguished by their costly wardrobes, hoards of precious metals and jewels. Nevertheless, modern life affords no real guarantee of protection: it is still true that "riches certainly make themselves wings: they fly away as an eagle" (Prov. xxiii, 5). All happiness of a worldly sort is evanescent: all carnal enjoyments are perishable in themselves: all earthly possessions are liable to theft.

"Lay not up for yourselves treasures upon earth." It should be pointed out that there is no sin in the possessing of a considerable amount of earthly riches, providing they are come by honestly. God greatly prospered Abraham in temporal things, yet He reminded him "I am thy shield, and thy exceeding great reward" (Gen. xv, 1). Job was the owner of vast herds and flocks, and though for a season he was without them, yet "The Lord blessed the latter end of Job more than his beginning: for he had fourteen thousand sheep, and six thousand camels, and a thousand yoke of oxen, and a thousand she asses" (xlii, 12). So, too, David was permitted to acquire an immense amount of material wealth, yet he regarded not his "treasure" as being in this world. On the contrary he was sharply distinguished from worldlings, who had "their portion in this life," declaring "As for me, I will behold Thy face in righteousness: I shall be satisfied, when I awake, with Thy likeness" (Psalm xvii, 14, 15). It is just as true that it is the Lord who "giveth thee power to get wealth" (Deut. viii, 18) as it is that He alone enriches the soul spiritually.

What, then, is it which Christ here prohibits, when He says "Lay not up for yourselves treasures upon earth"? Why, He forbids us making material things our chief concern, either in the pursuit or in the enjoyment of them. He forbids us either seeking or expecting our ultimate happiness in any earthly object. He forbids us setting our affections on anything seen and temporal, with the fond imagination that it is capable of satisfying the heart. It is not sinful for a man to seek after the necessities of life, either for his present or future use, but it *is* wrong for him to give way to a spirit of covetousness and strive after worldly wealth without moderation.

" Let us, therefore, receive and lawfully enjoy that portion of this life which our Father in heaven is pleased to bestow upon us, but let us not set our affections upon them" (John Brown).

In the above commandment Christ condemned those who seek principally after worldly goods, disparaging and disregarding the true riches. This is clear from the opposition made in the next verse, where "lay up for yourselves treasures in heaven" is placed over against "lay not up for yourselves treasures upon earth." Such was the sin of Esau, who is termed a "profane person" because he sold his birthright for a mess of pottage. So, too, Christ here condemned those who put their trust and confidence in the worldly things they amass, for this is idolatry of the heart. In like manner He here reprehended the making of earthly riches our chief good and delight for He warns us that where our treasure is, there will our heart be also. Christ also condemned the selfish practice of laying up for ourselves only, without regard to using the same to the glory of God and the good of our generation, which is a grievous betrayal of our stewardship. Each of us will yet be called upon to render an account unto God.

"Lay not up for yourselves treasures upon earth, where moth and rust doth corrupt and where thieves break through and steal." In the second part of this verse Christ enforced His commandment with reasons drawn from the corruptibility and uncertainty of worldly possessions. Therein He shows us the vanity of the creature, both in respect of its nature and of its abuse. Be the treasures never so pure and costly, as gold and silver, furs and silks, yet are they subject to either rust or the moth. No matter how carefully they be tended, yet the thief may come and seize them. If it be asked whence cometh this vanity of the creature, the answer is, God has subjected them unto it for the fall of man (Romans viii, 20), to let us see the grievousness of our sin and the greatness of His anger upon it, by imprinting the stamp of His wrath on the creature. Hence, when we see a moth upon our garments or rust upon our silver, we ought to be humbled over our original apostasy and taught to hold the creature with a light hand.

"But lay up for yourselves treasures in heaven, where neither moth nor rust doth corrupt, and where thieves do not break through and steal" (verse 20). This was only another way of saying, "Labour not for the meat which perisheth, but for that meat which endureth unto everlasting life, which the Son of man shall give unto you" (John vi, 27). Instead of setting our affections upon and spending our strength in the acquirement of the perishing things of time and sense, we should desire and seek our happiness in spiritual and Divine objects which are incorruptible and eternal. Our real blessedness lies in a knowledge of God, a conformity to His image. a walking in His ways, a communing with Him: then shall we have a peace and joy which the creature can neither impart nor take from us. Men are ever seeking a safe place in which they may deposit their treasures, only to find that no place and no thing in this world is secure. If, then, we would have our treasure where no marauder can reach it, it must be hid in Christ with God (Col. iii, 3).

Let us consider five things in connection with this laying up for ourselves treasures in heaven. First, the *finding* thereof. We can neither obtain nor make use of the great Treasure until it is located. This consists of God's revealing of it to us—for like Hagar of old (Gen. xxi, 19) we are blind thereto until He opens our eyes to see it; giving us to perceive our deep need of it—for until He does so we are self-complacent; and making us feel we are poor without it—for until He does so we are like the Laodiceans, "rich and increased with goods" in our own esteem. Not till then do we seek God in Christ with all our hearts. It is here we must examine and test ourselves: have we been made to realize our wretchedness and want: our filthiness and guilt, our deep need of cleansing and pardon? If so, are we truly hungering and thirsting after Christ's righteousness?

Second, having found this great Treasure, as it is exhibited in the Gospel and revealed in the soul by the power of the Holy Spirit, we must *highly prize* and value it, above all that we have or desire, regarding it as worth far more than the whole world. Such we find was Paul's estimate of this Treasure: "I count all things but loss for the excellency of the knowledge of Christ Jesus my Lord: for whom I have suffered the loss of all things, and do count them but dung, that I may win Christ" (Phil. iii, 8). The rating of Christ so highly is absolutely necessary if we are to lay Him up for our Treasure. Here too we must honestly and diligently test ourselves. Can we truly say with David, "Whom have I in heaven but Thee? and there is none upon earth that I desire besides Thee" (Psalm lxxiii, 25)? Does the general tenor of our lives bear witness to the fact that we value spiritual things above all else? Is it true of us that "The law of Thy mouth is better unto me than thousands of gold and silver . . . I love Thy commandments above gold; yea, above fine gold" (Psalm cxix, 72, 127)?

Third, having discovered this Treasure and perceived its inestimable worth, we must strive to obtain the same and *make it our own.* As said the wise man, "If thou criest after knowledge, and liftest up thy voice for understanding; if thou seekest her as silver, and searchest for her as for hid treasures; then shalt thou understand the fear of the Lord and find the knowledge of God" (Prov. ii, 3-5). We are required to use the means which God has appointed for this purpose, which are hearing, reading, praying, exercising faith. In His written Word and preached Gospel God's two hands do, as it were, hold out to us this heavenly Treasure and all spiritual blessings, and our faith is the hand of the soul reaching out to receive, and by our prayers we testify our faith.

Fourth, having obtained this Treasure we must *labour to assure* it unto ourselves. To this end we must follow Paul's charge to rich men: "Charge them that are rich in this world, that they be not highminded, nor trust in uncertain riches, but in the living God, who giveth us richly all things to enjoy; That they do good, that they be rich in good works, ready to distribute, willing to communicate; Laying up in store for themselves a good foundation against the time to come, that they may lay hold on eternal life" (I Tim. vi, 17-19). By trusting in the living God, and then by giving liberally unto the needy, we "lay up in store a good foundation." Are we saved, then, by performing such good deeds? No, for the ground of our salvation Godwards is in Jesus Christ (I Cor. iii, 11); but in our own conscience, for assurance of our interest in Christ, the fruits of faith and the works of love are our evidences. "We *know* that we have passed from death unto life, *because* we love the brethren" (I John iii, 14). Compare II Peter i, 10, and interpret "give diligence" by verses 5-7.

Fifth, being assured that this Treasure is ours, we must *use* the same as a treasure. This means that since Christ is in heaven our hearts are to be there too, and if our affections be set upon Him in desire and delight then our behaviour will be spiritual and heavenly. If our souls be earthbound and our affections set wholly or even principally on the things of time and sense, then Christ is not our "treasure" at all. To use our Treasure aright means that we turn our earthly goods into heavenly substance, which we do when we truly employ them to the glory of God and the good of our fellows. "He that hath pity upon the poor lendeth unto the Lord; and that which he hath given will He pay him again" (Prov. xix, 17). The merciful man, then, has the Lord for his Debtor, for He sends the poor man as His messenger unto the rich, to borrow of him such things as the poor man lacks; and the Lord's return of payment is in heavenly and spiritual blessings.

"The name of the Lord is a strong tower: the righteous runneth into it, and is safe. The rich man's *wealth* is his strong city, and as an high wall [affording protection], in his own conceit" (Prov. xviii, 10, 11). What a contrast is here presented between the use which the godly and the godless make of their respective "treasures," and how often we see it illustrated on the pages of Holy Writ. Take the case of Esau and Jacob. When the former lost his birthright and wept, how did he seek to comfort himself? by planning revenge (Gen. xxvii, 41). But when Jacob was "greatly afraid and distressed" (Gen. xxxii, 7) what did he do? Why, he had recourse *to God* (his "Treasure") and hoped in Him (verses 9-11). So it was with Saul and David. When the former lost his kingdom (his "treasure") he said to Samuel. "Honour *me* now, I pray thee, before the elders of my people" (I Samuel xv, 30); but when David lost all at Ziklag he "encouraged himself in the Lord his God" (I Samuel xxx, 6). "Unless Thy law had been my delights, I should then have perished in mine affliction" (Psalm cxix, 92) he exclaimed later. Whither do *you* turn in trouble? from whence do you seek relief?

"Lay up for yourselves treasures in heaven, where neither moth nor rust doth corrupt, and where thieves do not break through and steal" (verse 20). As in the preceding verse Christ backs up His precept with a weighty consideration, one which is drawn from the unchangeability and absolute security of heavenly riches. The world may deem His followers crazy and losers because of their separation from its pursuits and pleasures, but the Lord assures them they shall be the everlasting gainers: whatever we do in His name and for His sake shall turn to our account in the day to come. "Whosoever shall give to drink unto one of these little ones a cup of cold water only in the name of a disciple, verily I say unto you, he shall in no wise lose his reward" (Matt. x, 42). God will liberally reward all denyings of self for Christ's sake: "Every one that hath forsaken houses, or brethren, or sisters, or father, or mother, or wife, or children, or lands, for My name's sake, shall receive an hundredfold, and shall inherit everlasting life" (Matt. xix, 29). Let us, then, turn our earthly goods into heavenly substance and so heed our Saviour's exhortation: "Sell that ye have, and give alms; provide yourselves bags which wax not old, a treasure in the heavens that faileth not, where no thief approacheth, neither moth corrupteth" (Luke xii, 33).

Who can wish for a better increase than that: the exchange of what is temporal and precarious for that which is eternal and imperishable? What abundant cause have Christians to adore the triune God for having begotten them unto "an inheritance incorruptible and undefiled, and that fadeth not away, reserved in heaven" for them (I Peter i, 4). What reason have they to love, trust, serve and glorify their God. Surely we should rather part with all that we have than with this Treasure—friends, goods, country, liberty, yea, life itself; thus it was with the primitive saints, who "took joyfully the spoiling of their goods, knowing in themselves that they had in heaven a better and an enduring substance" (Heb. x, 34). Those who have Christ for their Treasure find such satisfaction in Him that prosperity will not lift them too high nor adversity cast them down too low.

"For where your treasure is, there will your heart be also" (verse 21). This verse contains a further reason to enforce the commandment in the two preceding: it is common to both, persuading to the obedience of each. The force of this reason may be stated thus: where your treasure is, there will your heart be also: but your heart should not be wedded to earthly objects but to heavenly, therefore lay not up for yourselves treasures in earth but in heaven. By "treasure," as we have stated before, must be understood things which are excellent and precious in our esteem, things laid up for the time to come, wherein we repose our trust and in which we take a special delight. By "heart" we must conceive not only the affections but thoughts, imagination, and will, with the effects of them in action, such as deliberation and endeavour.

Let us try and point out some of the practical uses to which verse 21 may be put. First, how it shows the vast importance of our choosing the right kind of treasure. Oh, how deeply it concerns us for time and eternity that we make a wise selection, for the temper of our minds and the tenor of our lives will be carnal or spiritual according as our treasure is earthly or heavenly. "The heart follows the treasure as the needle follows the loadstone" (Matthew Henry). Whichever way be the direction of our deepest longings, thither will follow our efforts. This from the very constitution of our nature: that which we deem our chief good will employ our principal thoughts, draw forth our fixed longings, stimulate our most earnest endeavours. If we think that happiness is to be found in anything of earth then our whole character will be "of the earth earthy," for our desires and pursuits will all correspond with the object of our supreme satisfaction. But if we be persuaded that true happiness is only to be found in knowing, loving and serving God, walking and communing with Him, then will our character be spiritual, and our thoughts, desires and pursuits will correspond thereto.

Second, since heart and treasure go together, then how important it is that we learn to search out and try the state of our own hearts. It is true that the heart of fallen man is deceitful above all things and that none of us can know it thoroughly, nevertheless if we rightly apply this dictum of Christ unto ourselves, we ought to be able to give a true judgment of our spiritual state. Consider: an earthly treasure and an earthly heart: a heavenly treasure and a heavenly heart—these cannot be severed from each other. Therefore we must diligently inquire: Whereon is my love placed, my mind fixed, my care bestowed, my labours directed, my delights found? If honesty requires me to answer upon an earthly object, then my heart is earthly, and consequently all my church attendance and religious profession is vain (Psalm x, 4; Ezek. xxxiii, 31). But if my chief love and delight and my constant concern be a conformity to His image, and my daily endeavour be seeking to please and obey Him, then is my heart heavenly (Psalm cxxxix, 17, 18; Isaiah xxvi, 9).

Third, this coupling together of the heart and treasure shows us the relative value of the two worlds (this and the one to come) and informs us which of them should be chiefly esteemed and sought after by us. In comparison with heaven, the earth and mundane life are to be despised. We say the *relative* value of the two worlds, for we must not be unthankful to God or look with contempt upon the products of His hands. As earthly creatures are the workmanship of God and temporal mercies His blessings, they are not to be hated but received with gratitude and used to His glory; nevertheless, we must not suffer them to obtain in our hearts that place which is due alone to the Creator of earth and the Giver of every blessing. As high as heaven is above the earth and as long as eternity exceeds the duration of time, so far are spiritual things to be esteemed above material; and the more our "treasure" truly is in heaven, the less disposed shall we be to amass earthly wealth and the more inclined to improve (as means to an end) the things of time and sense.

CHAPTER THIRTY

The Single Eye

" The light of the body is the eye: if therefore thine eye be single, thy whole body shall be full of light. But if thine eye be evil, thy whole body shall be full of darkness. If therefore the light that is in thee be darkness, how great is that darkness !" (Matt. vi, 22, 23.)

THOUGH there is substantial agreement among the commentators in their interpretation of these verses, yet we find considerable difference when it comes to their explanation of details, especially so in connection with the repeated mention of the " eye " and exactly what is connoted thereby. We therefore propose to examine carefully the several terms here employed by our Lord; then seek to ascertain the coherence of the passage, its relation to the context; and then look for the practical application unto ourselves.

" The light of the body is the eye," rendered " the *lamp* of the body is the eye " by both Bagster's *Interlinear* and the American R.V. We believe this a more accurate translation, for the Greek word for " light " in this clause is quite different from the one used in "full of light " at the end of the verse, it being the same as that found in Luke xii, 35, 36. In describing the eye as the " lamp " of the body Christ employed a most apt figure, since that organ has no light within itself. The great source of light to the world and of all things therein is the sun, yet such cannot illumine the body without the eye as a medium. The eye is the receptacle of its light, and by means of its rays, which flow into it, gives light to the body. The word for " if therefore thine eye be *single* " occurs again only in Luke xii, 34, yet it is found in a slightly different form in " for our rejoicing is this, the testimony of our conscience, that in *simplicity* and godly sincerity, not with fleshly wisdom, but by the grace of God, we have had our conversation in the world, and more abundantly to you-ward " (II Cor. i, 12).

Thus the meaning of our Lord appears to be something like this: the activities of the body are directed according to the light which is received through the eye. When that organ is sound and functioning properly, perceiving objects as they really are, the whole body is illumined, and we are able to discharge our duties and to move with safety and circumspection. But if the eye be blind, or its vision faulty, then we perceive objects confusedly and without distinction, and then we stumble as if in the dark, and cannot perform our task or journey properly, being continually liable to lose our way or run into danger. So far all is simple and plain. But what, we

198

may ask, is connoted by the "eye"? and what is here signified by "the whole body"? That these are figures of speech is obvious, but figures *of what*? It is at this point the commentators vary so much in their explanations.

Matthew Henry begins his exposition with, "The eye, that is, the *heart* (so some), if that be single—free and bountiful, so the word is frequently rendered as in Romans xii, 8; II Corinthians viii, 2-9, 11, 13; James i, 5; and we read of a 'bountiful eye' (Prov. xxii, 9). If the heart be liberally affected and stand inclined to goodness and charity, it will direct the man to Christian actions, the whole conversation will be 'full of light,' full of the evidences and instances of true Christianity—that pure religion and undefiled before God and the Father (James i, 27); 'full of light,' or good works, which are our light shining before man. But if the heart be 'evil,' covetous, hard, and envious, grinding and grudging (such a temper of mind is often expressed by an evil eye—Matt. xx, 15; Mark vii, 22; Prov. xxiii, 6, 7), the body will be 'full of darkness,' and the whole conversation will be heathenish and un-Christian. The instruments of the churl are and always will be 'evil,' but 'the liberal deviseth liberal things' (Isaiah xxxii, 5-8)."

Such an explanation agrees well with the context, both with the more remote as well as the immediate. As we pointed out in the opening paragraphs of chapter twenty-eight (page 185), in this fifth section of His Sermon (which runs from vi, 19, to the end of the chapter) Christ's design was to correct the erroneous views of the Jews concerning the character of His kingdom, and to divert the hearts of His hearers from a spirit of covetousness, and this by a variety of cogent reasons. Having warned them that our characters conform to that which we treasure most, He now intimates that discernment in our choice of treasure will be determined by the singleness of our eye or aim. Yet a little consideration of the above interpretation shows it is too narrow for the scope of our passage: the "eye" is here called the light of "the whole body," but clearly a liberal mind is not the regulator of *all* our affections and actions, but only of works of mercy and bounty.

Continuing his remarks, Matthew Henry went on to say, "The eye, that is, *the understanding* (so some): the practical judgment, the conscience, which is to the other faculties of the soul as the eye is to the body, to guide and direct their motions. Now if the eye be 'single,' if it make a true and right judgment, and discern things that differ, especially in the great concern of laying up the treasure so as to choose right in that, it will rightly guide the affections and actions, which will all be 'full of light,' of grace and comfort. But if the eye be 'evil,' corrupt, and instead of leading the inferior powers, is led, and bribed, and biased by them, if this be erroneous and misinformed, the heart and life must needs be 'full of darkness,' the whole conversation corrupt. They that will not understand are said to walk on in darkness (Psalm lxxxii, 5). It is said when the spirit of a man, which should be 'the candle of the Lord,' is an *ignis fatuus;* when the leaders of the people, the leaders of the faculties, cause them to err, for then they that are led of them are destroyed (Isaiah ix, 16). An error in the practical judgment is fatal: it is that which calls evil good and good evil (Isaiah v, 20), therefore it concerns us to understand things aright, to get our eyes anointed with eye-salve."

This we deem to be more satisfactory, though it is rather lacking in perspicuity, drawing no clear distinction between the "eye" and the eye being "single." We believe the "eye" in this parable of Christ's is to be taken for *the understanding,* for this is the faculty of the soul which more than any other gives direction to the whole man in all his motions. What a man believes is what largely determines how he lives—"as a man thinketh in his heart so is he." Such an interpretation differentiates more definitely between what we have in the previous verse as also in the one which follows. In verse 21 the "heart" stands principally (though not exclusively) for the affections, for *they* are what are fixed upon our "treasure." In verse 24 (the *serving* of God and mammon) it is the *will* which is primarily in view. Thus in verses 21-24 we have the affections, the understanding, and the will respectively, which together make up the inner man.

"If the eye be single" or sound in vision. The contrast presented in the next verse is that of the eye being "evil" or "wicked," so that a "single" eye is a good or holy one. And *what* is a good "eye"? Plainly it is a renewed understanding, an anointed eye, a mind illuminated by the Spirit of God, a mind which is dominated and regulated by the Truth. As the body is furnished with light for its activities by means of the eye, so the mind is fitted for its operations only as it is receptive to the influences of the Holy Spirit. A "single" eye has but one object—God, the pleasing and glorifying of Him. This is borne out by the other occurrence (in a slightly different form) of this word: "For our rejoicing is this, the testimony of our conscience, that in *simplicity* and godly sincerity, not with fleshly wisdom, but by the grace of God, we have had our conversation in the world, and more abundantly to you-ward" (II Cor. i, 12). The joyful confidence of the apostle—which sustained him in his labours—consisted of the consciousness of his sincerity, namely his "simplicity" (the opposite of duplicity) and godly sincerity of spiritual translucence.

"The eye, that is, *the aims and intentions.* By the eye we set our end before us, the mark we aim at, the place we go to, we keep that in view, and direct our motion accordingly. In everything we do in religion there is something or other that we have in our eye: now if our eye be single, if we aim honestly, fix right ends, and move rightly towards them, if we aim purely and only at the glory of God, seek His honour and favour, and direct all entirely to Him, then the eye is single. Paul's was so when he said, 'to me to live is Christ';

and if we be right here, 'the whole body will be full of light'—all the actions will be regular and gracious, pleasing to God and comfortable to ourselves. But if the eye be evil, if, instead of aiming only at the glory of God and our acceptance with Him, we look aside at the applause of men, and while we profess to honour God, contrive to honour ourselves, and seek our own things under colour of seeking the things of Christ, this spoils all—the whole conversation will be perverse and unsteady, and the foundations being thus out of course, there can be nothing but confusion and every evil work in the superstructure" (Matthew Henry).

So much then for the meaning of the principal terms of our passage. Let us next consider *its connection* with the context. This appears to be somewhat as follows: our discernment between things, our estimation of values, our practical judgment of earthly and heavenly objects is very largely determined by the condition of our understanding—whether it be Divinely illumined or still in nature's darkness. An enlightened understanding, perceiving objects according to their real nature and worth, enables its possessor to form a true judgment, to make a wise choice and to act aright respecting them. But a darkened understanding, conveying a wrong estimate of things, results in an erroneous choice and a disastrous end. In the latter case the "light which is in" a man is unaided human reason, and moved according to *its* dictates men imagine that they are acting wisely when instead they are pursuing a course of egregious folly, and then how great is their darkness!

Above we have intimated the general connection, but there was also a more particular one with special reference to the Jews. In verses 19-21 Christ had pointed out that true happiness is of a spiritual and not of a carnal nature, and that it is to be found (in perfection) not on earth but in heaven. A firm conviction of this is indispensable if our thoughts, desires and pursuits are to take that direction in which true blessedness is to be obtained. But the bulk of the Jews were expecting from their Messiah riches of a mundane and worldly nature, and therefore they despised and refused the spiritual joys He made known to them—their "treasure" being earthly (restored Palestine), their hearts were so too. And why was this? Because the light in them was darkness. They had been erroneously taught, and as unregenerate men they could not perceive their error. They must be born again before they could "enter" or even "see" the kingdom of God (John iii, 3, 5).

The false notions of the Jews respecting the Messiah's kingdom corresponded to the carnal desires of their corrupt hearts, and but served to illustrate what is common to fallen human nature, for "as in water face answereth to face, so the heart of man to man" (Prov. xxvii, 19). The Gentile no more than the Jew has any love or longing for spiritual things, nor can either the one or the other perceive the wretchedness of his condition, for the light which is in them is darkness, great darkness. Proof of this is furnished by Christ in the

verses we are now considering: in them He may be regarded as
replying to a secret objection which the hearts of men were likely
to frame against the two commandments which He had just given.
Should it be asked, If there be such a necessity of laying up treasure
in heaven and of avoiding to lay up treasure on earth, why is it that
the best educated, the shrewdest, the great men of this world commonly seek earthly riches far more than heavenly?

This is a question which, in one form or another, often exercises
young Christians and stumbles inquirers. If the true riches of the
soul are found not in the things of time and sense, why is it that our
fellows labour so hard for "that which satisfieth not" (Isaiah lv, 2)?
If the best which this world has to offer us perishes with the using
of it, why is it prized so highly by almost one and all? Here is the
explanation: because men view things through a vitiated eye, so
that the real appears but a phantom, and the shadows are mistaken
for the substance. Marvel not at this, says Christ, they lack the single
eye, the Divinely enlightened understanding, they are in nature's
darkness: they cannot discern between things that differ, they are
incapable of judging aright of the true treasure, and being ignorant
of the heavenly they seek only the earthly.

In order that we may have a better conception of what a single
"eye" consists of, we need to inquire diligently into what *true
wisdom* is. Spiritual wisdom is no common gift which every professing Christian possesses, but is a special bestowment of God in Christ
peculiar to those who are regenerated, for Christ Himself is made
wisdom unto them (I Cor. i, 30). And this, not only because He is
the matter of their wisdom—they being only truly wise when they
are brought to know Christ and Him crucified, but because He is
the root thereof. In Christ "are hid all the treasures of wisdom and
knowledge" (Col. ii, 3), and as believers are vitally united to Him
they partake of His virtues, as a branch derives vitality from its
stock.

Now this heavenly wisdom has two actions: the first is to *discern
aright* between things that differ. Thus Paul prayed for the Philippians: "that your love may abound yet more and more in knowledge and in all judgment; That ye may approve things that are
excellent," or as the margin, "try things that differ" (Phil. i, 9, 10):
that is distinguish good from evil, heavenly from earthly.
Thereby the children of God distinguish the voice of Christ, the
true Shepherd, from the voice of all false shepherds. Thereby they
put a difference between the water of baptism and all other waters,
and between the Lord's supper and all other bread—discerning the
Lord's body therein. Thereby they discern their election and calling,
perceiving more or less in themselves the marks thereof. Thereby
they see the hand of God in providence, ever making all things
minister to their ultimate good. "He that is spiritual judgeth all
things" (I Cor. ii, 15), which the natural man cannot do.

The second action of this true and heavenly wisdom is *to determine* and give sentence of things, what is to be done and what is not to be done, what is good and what is evil in behaviour. But here let it be remembered that the principal work of this wisdom is to determine of true *happiness*, whereto the whole life of man ought to be directed, which happiness is the love and favour of God in Christ. Herein David showed his wisdom to be far different from that of the godless around him: " there be many that say, Who will show us any good?"—that is the world's vain quest for happiness: " Lord, lift Thou up the light of Thy countenance upon us " (Psalm iv, 6)— wherein is the believer's true happiness. So too with the apostle Paul (Phil. iii, 8). The same should be our wisdom, for if man have all learning and an intellect developed to the highest possible point, yet if he fail rightly to determine of true blessedness his sagacity is folly. Another important part of this heavenly wisdom is the right use of means whereby we arrive at this happiness.

Now the *fruit of* this single eye is to make " the whole body full of light," that is to order the entire life aright, guiding it into the paths of righteousness and making it abound in good works. " I [wisdom—see verses 1, 11] lead in the way of righteousness, in the midst of the paths of judgment, that I may cause those that love me to inherit substance " (Prov. viii, 20, 21). How urgently it behoves us, then, to seek after and endeavour to make sure we have obtained this true wisdom: if the mind endowed thus possesses such powers of discrimination, how necessary it is that we become partakers thereof. In order to this we must be very careful to get the fear of God into our hearts, for " The fear of the Lord is the beginning of wisdom " (Psalm cxi, 10). This fear is a reverential awe of the heart toward God, whereby a person is fearful to offend and careful to please Him in all things. And this we obtain if we receive His Word with reverence, apply it to our own souls as we read it, tremble when it searches our conscience, and humbly submit ourselves unto it without repining. David could say, " Thy word is a lamp unto my feet, and a light unto my path " (Psalm cxix, 105), and therefore " Thou through Thy commandments hast made me wiser than mine enemies " (verse 98). If we would be truly wise we must cease leaning unto our own understanding and be directed by the Word in all things.

Our deep need of diligently seeking after a single eye—an enlightened understanding, a mind endued with true wisdom— appears in the solemn fact that by nature each of us possesses an eye that is *evil*, filling our whole body with darkness. In consequence of the fall we lost the power to judge aright in spiritual things, so that we mistake evil for good, things which ought to be refused for things which ought to be chosen. The natural man perceives not the presence of God, or he would be restrained from doing things which he is ashamed to do in the sight of his fellows. The natural man perceives not the sufficiency of God, or he would not trust in the creature far more than in the Creator. The natural man is blind to the justice of God, or he would not persuade himself that sin as he may yet he shall escape punishment. So too the natural man is blind self-ward: he perceives not his own darkness, his sinfulness, his impotency, his frailty, his true happiness.

Since this evil eye is in each of us by nature, we should constantly remind ourselves of our inability to judge rightly either of God or of ourselves, for it is the first step in true knowledge to acknowledge our own blindness. We must be suitably affected by such a realization, judging ourselves unsparingly, bewailing our misery, that we have a mind so corrupt that it disorders the whole of our conduct and seeks by grace to mortify the same. Since this evil eye is common to human nature, we discover therein what explains the mad course followed by the unregenerate, why they are so infatuated by sin and so in love with the world, and why the seriously inclined among them are deceived by error and captivated by false doctrines. Since human reason is now completely eclipsed, how profoundly thankful we should be for the light of God's Word, yet if that light illumine us and we fail to walk accordingly, suppressing its requirements, then doubly great will be our darkness.

CHAPTER THIRTY-ONE

The Single Eye—Concluded

"THE light of the body is the eye: if therefore thine eye be single, thy whole body shall be full of light. But if thine eye be evil, thy whole body shall be full of darkness. If therefore the light that is in thee be darkness, how great is that darkness!" In these words Christ continues to illustrate and enforce the principle which He had inculcated all through this part of His Sermon, namely the vital importance and imperative necessity of a pure motive and right aim in all we do. First, He had shown this in the matter of our "alms" or deeds of charity, if the same are to meet with God's acceptance (verses 2-4). Second, He had insisted thereon in connection with our "prayers," if they were to meet with God's approval (verses 5-15). Next, He had pointed out the same in regard to "fasting," if we are to receive anything more than the hypocrite's portion (verses 16-18). Then He had applied the same principle to the laying up of riches, pointing out that where our treasure is, there will our heart be also (verses 19-21). And how are we to obtain right views of what the true and imperishable "treasure" is, and where it is to be found? This is the question which our Lord here anticipated and proceeded to answer.

By use of a striking figure Christ proceeded to urge upon His hearers that their undivided gaze must be fixed upon the things which are above. "The light [or better, "lamp"] of the body is the eye." This refers in the first instance to the light of reason, which distinguishes man from the lower orders of creation: animals are guided by their instincts, but man was to be regulated by his intelligence, an intelligence which capacitated him for communion with his Maker, and so long as he remained in communion with Him who is Light, his mind would so inform and govern his soul that all his ways would be ordered to God's glory and meet with His approbation. But alas, man forsook the Fountain of all blessing, left the place of dependency, apostatized. As the consequence his "eye" became "evil" or, in other words, his understanding was darkened, being alienated from the life of God through the ignorance that is in him, because of the blindness of his heart (Eph. iv, 18). Hence the imperative need of his being renewed in the spirit of his mind (Eph. iv, 23).

In seeking to ponder the verses which are now before us, it needs to be carefully borne in mind that Christ was not here addressing a heathen audience or part of the profane world, but Jews who professed to be the Lord's people. As such they were far from being atheists or infidels, rather did they acknowledge the Supreme Being and perform outward worship unto Him, though for the most part their hearts were far from Him. Their aims and intentions were divided: that is why in verse 24 the Saviour warns them, "No man can serve two masters," which was the very thing they were vainly attempting. Hence it should be carefully noted that Christ did not here say "if thine eye be *good*" (which would be the most obvious antithesis from the "evil eye" in the next verse), but "if thine eye be *single*," which both anticipates and forms a link with verse 24. Yet it is also to be pointed out that our Lord used the most suitable word pathologically, for a good or sound vision is a "single" one— to see double or to look at different objects or different parts of an object with each eye is proof that our visual organs are defective, a sign of approaching blindness.

Now at regeneration the eye of the soul is renewed and its vision rectified, the eye of faith is opened, the understanding is Divinely enlightened, and God becomes its all-absorbing object and His glory the chief concern of its possessor. In consequence, the whole of the soul is now "full of light," all its faculties come under its beneficent influences: the conscience being informed, the affections warmed, the will moved to action in the right direction. An enlightened understanding and a Divinely instructed conscience are now able to distinguish between things that differ, between good and evil, things heavenly and things earthly. Thereby the child of God discriminates between the voice of Christ, the true Shepherd, and the voices of all false shepherds; between the Source of true happiness and those broken cisterns which hold no water. Thus the believer, by means of his spiritual judgment (which is informed and educated by the Word of God), determines and gives sentence of things: what is to be done and what is to be avoided; endowed with heavenly wisdom he learns the secret of real blessedness and joy unspeakable.

But let it be pointed out that it is only so long as the believer's "eye" *remains* "single" in a practical way that his whole body (soul) is "full of light." As the physical eye, the organ of sight, has no light whatever of its own, but must be illumined from without, so the renewed understanding is entirely dependent upon God for constant enlightenment. As the physical eye is the receptacle of light, and by means of its rays gives light to the body, so the understanding and conscience are the medium through which spiritual instruction is received into the soul. And as the body is left to grope its way in darkness as soon as its eye no longer takes in the light, so the soul is devoid of discernment when communion with God is broken. It is in His light, and there alone, that we "see light" (Psalm xxxvi, 9). While the glory of God be truly our aim and His word our rule, "good judgment" will be ours, so that we shall see and avoid the snares of self-will and the pitfalls of Satan; but when the gratification of self becomes our end and carnal reason be our regulator, we shall be given up to folly, confusion and disaster.

"But if thine eye be evil, thy whole body shall be full of darkness" (verse 23). The "evil eye" is the mind or understanding of the unregenerate man, having some light of intelligence in it by nature, yet terribly blinded and darkened by the corruption of sin through our fall in Adam. That the reader may have a more definite conception of the havoc which sin has thus wrought in us, it should be pointed out that man's understanding has lost the gift of discernment and judgment in spiritual things, so that he mistakes evil for good, earthly for heavenly, things to be refused for things to be chosen. This is clear from the natural man's ignorance and blindness in the real knowledge of God. It is true that the mind of the natural man possesses some knowledge of God: he believes in His existence and professes to own His supremacy. Yet such knowledge as he possesses, though rendering him accountable to his Maker, exerts no spiritual influence upon his soul and life. Proof of this appears in the following facts.

The natural man does not realize and own in a practical way the *presence* of God, that "the eyes of the Lord are in every place, beholding the evil and the good" (Prov. xv, 3): if he did, he would not, without fear and trembling, dare to commit those sins in God's sight which he is afraid and ashamed to commit before the eyes of his fellows. The natural man does not realize and own the *particular providences* of God, for in time of want and distress, when outward springs dry up, his heart is dead within him and the promise of help from man does more to cheer him than any hope he has in God. How plain it is then that he trusts more in the creature than he does in the Creator. Again, the natural man does not realize and own the *justice* of God, for he imagines that though he sins yet he shall escape punishment: by his very conduct he says, "I shall have peace though I walk in the imagination of mine heart, to add drunkenness to thirst" (Deut. xxix, 19). Though the natural man knows God must be worshipped, yet he is quite incapable of discerning the right kind of worship: the vast majority bow down before idols and images, and even those who pretend outwardly to honour the true God have their hearts far from Him while engaged in such exercises (Matt. xv, 8).

What lamentable proofs are these that sin has debased man, corrupted the very springs of his being, and blinded his understanding. What unmistakable and irrefutable evidences are these that the "eye" of the unregenerate is an *evil* one. Though blessed with rationality, though endowed with the perception that God is and that He is to be owned and worshipped, though capable of receiving intellectual instruction concerning the character and claims of God, yet such knowledge avails him nothing in a spiritual way. The unregenerate is blind to God's glory, unaffected by His majesty, unawed by His sovereignty, unsoftened by His goodness, unable to worship Him aright or do that which is acceptable to Him. How clear it is that "the natural man receiveth not the things of the

Spirit of God: for they are foolishness unto him; neither can he know them; because they are spiritually discerned" (I Cor. ii, 14). Before he can have any spiritual discernment or experiential acquaintance with God, before he can obtain an effectual and transforming knowledge of Him, he must be born again (I John v, 20)

Not only does the blindness of the natural man appear in his crass ignorance of God, but also with respect *to himself*. His mind is totally lacking in spiritual discernment. This is evident from the following facts. The unregenerate are completely unaware of the awful darkness which rests upon their understandings. They deem themselves to be wise, when in the things of God they are veritable fools: "the way of peace have they not known" (Romans iii, 17). When really awakened by the Holy Spirit they are made aware of this, for their cry then is, "What must I do to be saved?" So blind is the natural man that he cannot discern aright of his own sins nor see the vileness of them: if he did, he would not continue therein as he does. He judges wrongly of his frailty and mortality: others may be cut off in youth, but not so himself; no matter how old, he still gives himself several more years. This is why we are instructed to pray, "So *teach us* to number our days, that we may apply our hearts unto wisdom" (Psalm xc, 12).

So blind is the natural man that he is incapable of discerning aright the scope and end of his life, which is to aim at the glory of God and be a help and blessing to his fellows. But so far from this characterizing them, the unregenerate think little or nothing about these things, but seek their own praise and are a stumbling-block unto their neighbours. Nor can the natural man judge rightly of his own true happiness. So stupid and sottish is he that he measures happiness by outward things, esteeming the wealthy to be envied and the poor to be pitied. Therefore does he regard phantoms as realities and realities as phantoms, and spends his time and strength in pursuing the shadows while he misses the substance. That is why we are exhorted to set our affection "upon things above" (Col. iii, 2), for by nature they are fixed upon things below. From all of this it is unmistakably evident that the eye of the natural man is an "evil" one, that sin has debased his faculties, darkened his understanding, destroyed his spiritual perception. And unless God is pleased to perform a miracle of grace upon us, "the blackness of darkness" (Jude 13) must inevitably be our portion for ever.

"But if thine eye be evil, thy whole body shall be full of darkness" (verse 23). Here is the fruit of an evil eye: the whole man is affected. If the understanding be Divinely illumined and the aim be the glory of God, the whole soul will be rightly directed and its activities be holy; but where the mind is blinded by sin and Satan, all the faculties of the inner man are vitiated and all his actions are evil. It is a striking fact in the natural realm that an injured optic cannot bear the light, which solemnly shadows forth the awful spiritual state of the unregenerate. They cannot endure the presence of God, nor His Word which condemns them. Their eye is evil, their judgment is blinded by love of the world, and therefore their whole life is full of disorder and unrighteousness. How can it be otherwise, when their most important faculty, which should discern between good and evil and direct accordingly, is vitiated, disabled thereunto? Thus, " The way of the wicked is as darkness, they know not at what they stumble " (Prov. iv, 19).

What cause is there for humiliation and self-judgment: that by nature we are utterly unable to judge rightly either of God or of ourselves, that we have a mind which is so corrupt that it produces nothing but disorder in the whole of our life. How greatly we dread natural blindness: what horror strikes the heart when we have reason to think we are in imminent danger of being deprived of bodily vision; yet how much worse is that spiritual darkness whereby the soul is kept from God under the power of Satan! Fearful beyond words is such a state, yet the vast majority of our fellows are quite insensible of their wretched plight and indifferent when it is declared unto them. What cause for thankfulness, then, if the writer and the reader have been enabled to discover *their* blindness: in such case, how diligently should we heed that word of the great Physician, " I counsel thee to buy of Me . . . eyesalve, that thou mayest see " (Rev. iii, 18). We must seek from Him that enlightening of His Spirit, through the Word, for this is that " anointing " which " teacheth us all things " (John ii, 27).

Hereby we perceive how the course of the world, in regard to the state of their minds, is to be reproved, for on every side we behold those who are quite content with an evil eye. Even those who acknowledge, in a formal way, that God is and He is to be loved and worshipped, and that we should love our neighbours as ourselves, yet they seek no farther. They have nothing more than the mere light of nature, the remnants of intelligence left to them since the Fall. They are still in spiritual darkness, " having no hope, and without God in the world " (Eph. ii, 12). Their life is full of darkness, and they shall yet be " cast into the outer darkness " unless the Lord is pleased to have mercy upon them. A natural knowledge of Divine things will save no man. The homage of our lips and the external reformation of our lives will not secure God's favour. Nothing but a new creation in Christ, being renewed in the spirit of our minds, God commanding the light to shine " in our hearts " (II Cor. iv, 6), will avail any for eternity.

Since this " evil eye " is in each of us by nature, what care we need to take lest we be wise in our own conceits, especially in matters of salvation: herein the Word of God must be our wisdom. " Ye shall not do . . . every man whatsoever is right in his own eyes," but " all that I command thee," says the Lord (Deut. xii, 8-11). It is not for the creature to say how the Creator is to be worshipped, nor for the sinner to determine how he shall be saved, yet such is their blind presumption that men will be their own masters in such things. The Jew, the Mohammedan, the papist, has each his own different manner of worshipping God and of seeking salvation, yet though they all depart from the Truth, each is thoroughly convinced that *his* worship meets with the Divine acceptance and that heaven will be his eternal home. And so it is with the majority who have been brought up among Protestants: either they rely on their own works, trust in their own faith (such as it is), or else they persuade themselves that if they repent at the last and commit their souls unto God all will be well.

Since this evil eye is in each of us by nature, then how earnestly we should pray for and labour after the eye of faith, by which alone we look unto the mercy of God in Christ and rest in His promises, for all things needful both in life and in death. This eye looks out of self for those supplies of grace which are lacking in natural knowledge. By means of the eye of faith we are enabled to discern aright both of God and of ourselves: His holiness and claims, our vileness and wants. By this eye we are enabled to see things afar off, to be persuaded of them, to embrace the same (Heb. xi, 13). Yea, by it we are enabled to perceive things which are invisible, for " faith is the substance of the things hoped for, the evidence of things not seen (Heb. xi, 1). By it Abraham saw the day of Christ, and was " glad " (John viii, 56). This will enable us to walk in the steps of the patriarchs unto the heavenly city. Then let us earnestly beg God for this eye of faith, that by becoming the children of the promise we may be counted for the seed.

" If therefore the light that is in thee be darkness, how great is that darkness! (verse 23). Unspeakably solemn is this. " The light that is in thee " is the light of nature, the remnants of that moral and intellectual perception with which man was originally endowed. It is that knowledge of God and that discernment of good and evil which though greatly dimmed and corrupted by the Fall has not been utterly extinguished, for the veriest atheist and the most voluptuous wretch still has some stirrings of conscience left within him, some inklings that there is a God and that he is accountable to Him. But if that remaining " light " be stifled, if no use be made of it, if its promptings be constantly resisted, if the voice of conscience be deliberately silenced, until God is denied and His Word rejected as a Divine revelation, then even that " light " becomes " darkness " and its possessors are given over by God to a reprobate mind. And then " how great is that darkness ": sin is committed greedily, without remorse; there is then nothing in that man's life but brutish confusion and devilish actions.

" If therefore the light that is in thee be darkness, how great is that darkness! " These words may also be legitimately applied unto those who are led astray by religious error and given up to fanaticism. When men deem themselves to have been extraordinarily illumined, to have received some voice or vision from heaven which will not stand the test of Holy Writ, some fancied " baptism of the Spirit " which renders them independent of the Scriptures, supposing that this special light within is all that they need, "how great is that darkness." Finally, there is a yet more solemn application of these words of Christ to those who have sat under a sound ministry: the light of the Truth has shone upon their minds, only to be resisted and the Spirit quenched, and how great is their darkness! "For if after they have escaped the pollutions of the world through the knowledge of the Lord and Saviour Jesus Christ, they are again entangled therein, and overcome, the latter end is worse with them than the beginning" (II Peter ii, 20).

If then the very light of nature may be put out and the light of the Gospel quenched by us, how seriously we ought to *meditate upon* our vileness, for *we* have within us such brutish lusts and devilish desires that unless they be restrained and kept under, they will surely plunge us into the blackness of darkness for ever. How the realization of this should humble us! And hereby we should be admonished to *mortify* our corrupt desires and unruly affections. Before the Fall, the mind ruled the will and the affections, but now these inferior faculties overrule the mind, so that they lead us into folly against our better judgment. Our only safeguard is to deny our perverse wills and corrupt desires, and strive to bring them into subjection unto the Word of God. And how we need to heed that injunction, "Take heed, brethren, lest there be in any of you an evil heart of unbelief, in departing from the living God" (Heb. iii, 12). Then let us seek grace to embrace the Gospel, walk according to its precepts, and beg God to unite our hearts to fear His name.

CHAPTER THIRTY-TWO

Serving God

"No man can serve two masters: for either he will hate the one, and love the other; or else he will hold to the one, and despise the other. Ye cannot serve God and mammon." (Matt. vi, 24.)

THOSE who have read attentively the last few chapters of this series will scarcely need for us to point out the relation of this verse to the context. Its connection is obvious almost at a glance. All through this part of His sermon Christ was separating the precious from the vile, drawing a sharp line between the true and the false. He had discriminated between the two worshippers—the genuine and the hypocrite. He had distinguished between the two treasures—earthly and heavenly. He had differentiated between the two eyes or wisdoms—the single and the evil. Now He opposes the two masters—setting God over against mammon. Herein He teaches the ministers of His Word a most important lesson: that of drawing so clearly the line of demarcation between the regenerate and unregenerate, the possessor and the mere professor, that each hearer may have no difficulty in knowing which side of the line he belongs on. It is the general lack of such searching ministry, the substituting of superficial generalities, which is bolstering up formalists and encouraging multitudes in a vain hope.

But there is yet a closer link of connection between our present verse and those more immediately preceding it. As we pointed out in the introductory paragraphs of chapter twenty-eight (page 185), verse 19 to the end of chapter vi, our Lord's design was to turn the hearts of His hearers from a spirit of covetousness or setting their affections upon the things of time and sense: first He delivered the prohibition and commandment, and then amplified and enforced the same by a variety of cogent reasons. Those reasons so far as we have yet gone may be summed up thus: Make not material things thy chief good, because earthly treasure is of a perishing nature: moth, rust, and thieves of various kinds depleting it in spite of all precaution. Because earthly treasure captures the heart: men argue that it need not do so, but the Son of God declares it *will* (verse 21). Because its pursuit ends in darkness: people suppose that wealth brings light or happiness, but instead it ends in darkness and misery (verses 22, 23). Because it will enslave us: if God be not our Master, the world and its representative, mammon, will be.

More immediately, verse 24 may be regarded as Christ's refutation of a second objection which the carnal heart of man is fond of making against the commandments He has laid down in verses 19 and 20. There He had forbidden the treasuring up of worldly riches and had commanded the seeking of heavenly treasure. First, He had anticipated the objection, if there be such an urgent necessity of laying up treasure in heaven and abstaining from the laying up of treasures on earth, why is it that the vast majority of men, including the shrewdest and best educated, bend their energies to the seeking of earthly treasure rather than heavenly? He bids His hearers to marvel not nor be stumbled by this, seeing that the unregenerate lack a sound or single eye and therefore are incapable of judging aright of the true riches. Here in our text He refutes the common persuasion that it is possible for us to seek *both*, and lay up for ourselves treasures on earth and treasure in heaven as well. Men think to compound with God and the world, dividing their affections and energies between them; but Christ here exposes the utter fallacy of such an idea and the impossibility of such a course.

Once again we must bear in mind the fact that our Lord was addressing Himself more immediately to His Jewish hearers and reprehending their false conceptions of His kingdom. They entertained certain vague notions of happiness in a future regime under the Messiah, but their minds were mainly engrossed with dreams of carnal prosperity, supposing that the expectation of worldly aggrandisement and spiritual happiness were quite consistent. Our Lord informs them of their mistake: they needed to "repent" of this also—undergo a radical change of mind. But it is not the Jews only who are infected with this delusion: it is common to the Gentiles also. In every age there are multitudes who fondly hope that though they seek their happiness in earthly objects, yet it is possible for them, at the same time, to secure the enjoyment of heavenly felicity. The hypocrite has ever argued that it is well to have two strings to one's bow, but Christ here exposes this cheat and demonstrates the impossibility of the human heart being divided between God and the world.

He who has his eye partly on God and partly on self, who desires and endeavours to grasp both worlds, deceives his own soul. Such a one is in danger of losing both, and if he does not he will certainly miss the kingdom of God. Our minds must be fixed supremely upon God in Christ, and the world sought only in strict subservience to Him. Our hearts must be given to the Lord, wholly or without reserve, and the eyes of our soul be fixed upon Him alone. Here, then, is the reason why spiritual blindness must inevitably be our portion unless both our eyes are fixed steadfastly on a heavenly Object: a man's affections cannot be divided; if he attempts to love the things of the world as well as love God, he will certainly fail of the latter, for "the friendship of the world is enmity with God: whosoever therefore will be a friend of the world, is the enemy of God" (James iv, 4). The serving of two masters is absolutely opposed to the single eye, for the eye will be at the master's hand: "Unto

Thee lift I up mine eyes, O Thou that dwellest in the heavens. Behold, as the eyes of servants look unto the hand of their masters, and as the eyes of a maiden unto the hand of her mistress; so our eyes wait upon the Lord our God, until that He have mercy upon us" (Psalm cxxiii, 1, 2).

The endeavour to lay up for ourselves both treasure upon earth and treasure in heaven is an utter impossibility, for "no man can serve two masters." But to seek both earthly and heavenly riches is an attempt to serve two masters, to wit, God and mammon; and therefore no man can seek them both. Proof of this is here set forth by Christ by *the effect of* such attempts to serve, in contrary affections and behaviour: "For either he will hate the one and love the other, or else he will hold to the one and despise the other." The conclusion therefore is unmistakable: "ye cannot serve God and mammon. To "serve God" is the same thing as to "lay up treasure in heaven," for by a Divine appointment true happiness is to be found only there, and He who has made this appointment has also ordained certain means by which we may attain unto this happiness. He who makes the attainment of this happiness, by the appointed means, the chief object in life is the servant of God—for he does the will of God. Contrariwise, to "serve mammon" is the same thing as to "lay up treasure on earth."

"No man can serve two masters." The force of our Lord's declaration is more apparent in the Greek than it is here in the English. First, the word "serve" does not signify to do an occasional act of obedience, but to be a bond-servant, a slave, the property of his master, constantly and entirely subject to his will. No one can thus *serve* two masters. The same Greek word occurs in, "Knowing this, that our old man is crucified with Him, that the body of sin might be destroyed, that henceforth we should not serve sin" (Romans vi, 6). It is also found in "but now we are delivered from the law [as a covenant of works], being dead to that wherein we were held, that we should serve in newness of spirit" (Romans vii, 6). Second, there are two different words in the Greek which both mean "other," but the one signifies another of the same kind or order, while the second denotes another of an entirely different genus or sort. When Christ here declared, "No man can serve two masters, for either he will hate the one, and love the *other*," He employed the latter term—signifying a master diametrically opposed to the other. Therefore it is evident that no one can be devoted unto two different and opposing masters.

"A man may be a servant to two masters in succession, even although they should be of very different and directly opposite characters. A man may serve two masters of opposite characters—the one in profession, the other in reality. A man may serve two masters unequally—occasionally doing an act of service to the one while he usually, habitually, serves the other. A man may serve two or more masters, if they are all on one side, all subordinate to one another: a soldier may serve his king and at the same time his commanding officer and his inferior officers, for in obeying them he is obeying his prince; but no man can be at the same time, in reality, habitually the servant of two masters who are hostile to each other, and whose interests are entirely incompatible. In this sense our Lord says, 'Ye cannot serve God and mammon'" (Jay).

"No man can serve two masters, for either he will hate the one" —that is, the master commanding him, disliking that he should be his master, and displeased with his orders—" and love the other "— that is, the master in whom he takes delight and with whose orders he is well pleased. "Or else he will hold to the one and despise the other," which words are an amplification and application of the former clause, showing how it is made manifest that a servant hates one master and loves the other. His holding to—leaning toward and cleaving unto—the one declares his love unto him: that is, he applies himself to respecting his master's pleasure and doing his commandments. And his "despising the other" denotes his hatred —seen in his having no regard to his master's will. Thus our Lord shows the impracticability and impossibility of any man seeking to serve two opposing masters from the contrary affections and behaviour exercised by the servant.

"Ye cannot serve God and mammon." Mammon is a Syriac word which denotes "riches," or as men term them, the good things of this world. But it is evident that the word is used as a personification: one can scarcely be said to *serve* inanimate things. Moreover, the figure used here is that of "two *masters*," and as mammon is here opposed to God, we must understand it to signify the god of riches, the Prince of this world and the love of the world—its treasures and pleasures—which is really the service of Satan. As, then, it is impossible to serve "two masters," how much less two gods! "Love not the world, neither the things that are in the world. If any man love the world, the love of the Father is not in him" (I John ii, 15). The influence which material riches exert upon men's minds and affections, leading them to seek happiness in them and moving them to devote their time and energies to the acquiring of the same, indicate the fearful power of this prince or master, and their yielding to that influence is the "service" which multitudes render unto him. How utterly incompatible, then, are the obtaining of heavenly happiness and the means thereto, and the seeking of earthly happiness and the efforts put forth to secure the same.

"Their orders are diametrically opposed. The one commands you to walk by faith, the other to walk by sight; the one to be humble, the other to be proud; the one to set your affections on things above, the other to set them on the things that are on the earth; the one to look at the things unseen and eternal, the other to look at the things seen and temporal; the one to have your conversation in heaven, the other to cleave to the dust; the one to be careful for nothing, the other to be all anxiety; the one to be content with such

things as ye have, the other to enlarge your desires as hell; the one
to be ready to distribute, the other to withhold; the one to look at
the things of others, the other to look only at one's own things; the
one to seek happiness in the Creator, the other to seek happiness in
the creature. Is it not plain there is no serving two such masters?
If you love the one, you must hate the other; if you cleave to the
one, you must despise the other. You cannot serve God and
mammon " (Jay).

From our text we may perceive clearly what it is to *serve God*.
This is a thing much spoken of, but little known, and practised still
less. To serve God is to "love" Him and to "hold to" or "cleave
unto" Him. Alas, how very few out of the present-day multitudes
who profess to serve God manifest these marks! Love to God consists
not of words and lip patronage, but *in deed and in truth*. And it is
to be carefully noted that in this verse Christ insists God must be
loved not only as Father, but as He is a Lord and " Master," that is,
commanding us. It is in His Word, especially in the preceptive parts
thereof, that His will and pleasure are made known. It is there He
has revealed the service which He requires at our hands, and if our
service be sincere and genuine we must love God in His right of
commanding, even though He should bestow no reward upon us.
The Lord God has Himself expressly joined these two things
together: " showing mercy unto thousands of them that love Me
and keep My commandments" (Exodus xx, 6). David exemplified
this principle very clearly in Psalm cxix: " I will delight myself
in Thy commandments, which I have loved " (verse 47 and see verses
16, 54, 97, 127, 140, 159, 167).

Moreover, our text makes it crystal clear that if we are to serve
God acceptably it must be a *wholehearted* service that we render
to Him. He is a jealous God, and will brook no rival. He is a holy
God, and will tolerate no idols in the secret chambers of our souls.
His demand is stated in unmistakable language: " Thou shalt love
the Lord thy God with *all* thine heart, and with all thy soul, and with
all thy might" (Deut. vi, 5), and nothing short of that will satisfy
Him: let it be duly noted that the Lord Jesus insisted on no less
in Matthew xxii, 37. He who serves God must serve Him singly, and
his eye must be "single." God requires all our affections and will
not permit us to divide them between Him and the world. Caleb
could say, " I *wholly* followed the Lord my God " (Joshua xiv, 8)—
can we? David declared, "I will keep Thy precepts with my
whole heart" (Psalm cxix, 69)—is such our resolution? Or must
the Lord say of us, " They have *not* wholly followed Me" (Num.
xxxii, 11).

Furthermore, our text makes it plain that if we "serve" God
acceptably we must "hold to" or "cleave unto" Him, and thereby
testify our love. What is meant by cleaving to Him? This is
answered for us in Luke xv, where we are told of the prodigal son
that he " joined himself to a citizen of that country " (verse 15),

which means that he resigned and gave himself up to his service:
so to cleave unto God is for a man to resign himself unto His service,
obeying all His commands and embracing all His promises, not
suffering himself to be drawn away from any Divine precept,
either by unbelief or disobedience, even though all the world should
set itself against him. This was the policy of David: " I have stuck
unto Thy testimonies: O Lord." "Then shall I not be ashamed,
when I have respect unto all Thy commandments" (Psalm cxix,
31, 6). On the contrary, when a man leans unto his own understanding, follows the corrupt desires of his heart, gives place to self-
pleasing, or takes "the way of the heathen" (Jer. x, 2), he departs
from and despises the Lord, and if that be the general trend of his
conduct it is clear that he hates God, no matter what he professes
by his lips to the contrary (see Titus i, 16).

From what has been before us we may clearly perceive the gross
blindness and superstitious ignorance of the world. How many there
are in this so-called Christian land and day of enlightenment who
think that if they repeat the Lord's Prayer and the Apostles' Creed
they serve God well, let their lives be never so worldly and carnal.
But Christ here teaches us that in order to serve God acceptably we
must cleave unto Him both in the affections of our hearts and in
the activities of obedience of our lives. Thus did Abraham, the
father of all them that believe, for when God called him to leave
the land of his nativity he "went out not knowing whither he
went"; and when the Lord bade him slay his well-beloved Isaac,
he promptly proceeded to do so. Alas, Christendom is filled with
atheists, for to hate and despise God is rank atheism, and all who
withdraw their hearts from God, setting themselves to seek the
things of this world to the neglect of obedience to the Divine commandments, are here accounted by Christ the despisers and haters of
God, which is the very worst form of atheism.

From the fact that God and mammon are here opposed as two
"masters," we may learn that "mammon," that is earthly riches,
is a great *lord* in the world, and therefore does Christ warn us
against the same. If it be asked, How can riches be a master or god?
the answer is, They are not so in themselves, being merely creatures,
but the corrupt hearts of men make an idol of such unto themselves,
setting their love and delight upon them, and trusting in them more
than in God: for this reason is covetousness called idolatry (Col.
iii, 5), and the covetous person an idolator (Eph. v, 5). Whatever a
man sets his heart upon, making it his true happiness, *that* is his
lord and god. Proof that men *do* set up riches in their hearts as idols,
and so become servants unto that which should serve them, appears
in the following facts: they neglect the service of God for lucre and
take greater delight in earthly things than in heavenly graces: they
derive more satisfaction from them than from Divine ordinances:
their loss of earthly goods produces greater vexation and sorrow
than all the Divine promises produce comfort.

Herein we may perceive the dreadful state into which Christendom has fallen, for the vast majority in it are plainly worshippers of mammon. They are far more eager and diligent in their quest after worldly gain than they are for personal piety and conformity to the image of Christ. A spirit of covetousness possesses State and Church alike. Greedy landlords (and landladies), profiteering merchants, the cornering of commodities, on the one hand; discontented labourers, ever demanding higher wages and more and more of the luxuries of life, on the other: the rich hoarding up wealth and the poor insisting that it be divided among them are sad witnesses to the idolatry which now reigns supreme in the hearts of men. And God's professing people are infected with the same evil spirit: the denying of self and living as strangers and pilgrims here is a thing of the past, as their extravagantly furnished homes and richly laden tables only too plainly attest. And, worst of all, the rising generation of preachers, with their motor-cars and elaborately furnished parsonages and manses, are giving a lead to this wicked self-indulgence and mammon worship.

Is there any wonder, then, that the judgments of an angry God are now falling so heavily upon us? Judgment began first at the house of God: a grieved Spirit withdrew, and His power and unction are now noticeably absent from the preaching of the Word. But instead of God's people humbling themselves beneath His mighty hand, repenting of and forsaking their sins, they have in large measure "lived in pleasure on the earth and been wanton" (James v, 5). Read Amos vi, 1, 3-6, and see if the extravagance of Israel has not been duplicated in Christendom: and as God's wrath was poured out on them, so it is now being poured out on us. Many scores of church buildings and hundreds of the homes of rich and poor alike have been reduced to rubble and ashes. Why? Why has God so visited us? Because He will not be mocked with impunity. For the last fifty years Christendom has attempted to serve both God and mammon: and having sown the wind, God is now making us reap the whirlwind. "He that hath ears to hear, let him hear."

CHAPTER THIRTY-THREE

Anxiety Forbidden

"Therefore I say unto you, Take no thought for your life, what ye shall eat, or what ye shall drink ; nor yet for your body, what ye shall put on. Is not the life more than meat, and the body than raiment?" (Matt. vi, 25.)

IT will be seen from the title of our chapter that another subject of practical importance is presented to our notice in the verse we have now reached. It is a subject which immediately concerns each one of us, for in varying degrees all are guilty of the very thing which is here forbidden, namely worrying over material things, yielding to anxiety about future supplies. This is something which is highly dishonouring to God, a sin which we need to make conscience of, confessing it with shame and seeking grace to avoid any further repetitions thereof. The very fact that such anxiety is here forbidden not only exhibits once more the exalted standard of piety which is set before us in the Holy Scriptures, but also evidences their uniqueness, their Divine Authorship, for there is no other book or religion in the world which condemns inordinate solicitude over the temporal necessities of life. Proof of this assertion appears in the fact that the natural man is quite unaware that anxiety about food and clothing *is* a SIN.

Not only is such anxiety wrong, but it is a sin of great gravity. It is not simply a constitutional infirmity which we may excuse, a mere trifle we need not be concerned about, but rather is it a foul iniquity from which we should seek cleansing. To be fearful about the supply of future needs, to be worried that we may yet be left to suffer the lack of temporal necessities, is to be guilty of wicked unbelief. It calls into question the goodness and care of our Creator. It manifests a lack of faith in His wise and gracious providence. And if we be Christians, it betrays doubt of our Father's love. And surely these are evils of the deepest dye. Moreover, as we shall yet see, such disquietude and distraction of mind is, in reality, the workings of *covetousness*, the lusting after things we have not, which is a sin of great magnitude. Oh, that the Spirit may convict us of this wickedness and subdue this iniquity.

It has been pointed out in previous chapters that the main draft of our Saviour's Sermon from verse 19 to the end of chapter vi was to dissuade and deliver His hearers from the spirit of covetousness. Having forbidden the practice itself (verse 19), and disposed of those objections which the corrupt heart of man might frame to excuse himself in the committing thereof (verses 22-24), Christ now struck

219

at the very root of covetousness and sought to remove the cause thereof, namely a distrustful and inordinate care for the things of this life, especially for such things as are necessary for the maintenance thereof. This is clear from His words in verse 25, and the attentive reader will note that the same line of thought is continued by Him to the end of verse 34. Such unusual repetitions as "Take no thought for your life, what ye shall eat" (verse 25), "Take no thought, saying, What shall we eat?" (verse 31), "Take therefore no thought for the morrow" (verse 34) intimate not only the weightiness of this Divine precept, but also our slowness in heeding the same.

"Therefore I say unto you, take no thought for your life, what ye shall eat, or what ye shall drink; nor yet for your body, what ye shall put on" (verse 25). Before proceeding to amplify what has been said in the last paragraph, let us point out that there is a close connection between this verse and those preceding. It may be regarded as Christ's meeting a further objection against what He had insisted on. He had forbidden the laying up of treasures on earth, and had warned against the making of mammon our god. To this many might answer, There is no danger of *us* doing that: so little of this world's riches come our way that we can scarcely procure the bare necessities of life. Even so, says Christ, you too are in grave danger: the fear of poverty and worrying about the future as truly ensnare the souls of the poor as the love of wealth does the rich. Distrustful and distracting care about supplies of temporal needs is a sure sign that the heart is fixed on earthly things.

"Therefore I say unto you, Take no thought for your life." This is another declaration of Christ's which must not be taken absolutely or without limitation (compare our remarks on v, 34, 42). If scripture be compared with scripture, it will be found that there are two kinds of "care": a godly and moderate one, a distrustful and inordinate. The former is enjoined upon us by the Word of God. For example, in Proverbs vi, 6, wisdom sends the sluggard to the ant to learn diligence and providence for things needful. The apostle Paul points out that it is the duty of parents to "lay up" for their children (II Cor. xii, 14), and declares that "If any provide not for his own, and specially for those of his own house, he hath denied the faith, and is worse than an infidel" (I Tim. v, 8). From these passages it is quite clear that there is a lawful care to be taken even for the things pertaining to this life, nor do the words of Christ in the passage now before us conflict with this to the slightest degree.

There is a solicitude about temporal things which is a duty, varying according to a man's station in the world. God requires him to be diligent in business and prudent in its management. He is obligated to provide for himself and family so far as health and industry will permit. He is required to live within his income, so that he may "owe no man anything." He is to guard against any of God's bounty being wasted or squandered in prodigality. It is his business to look ahead and seek to provide for those demands which may be made upon him in the future—by additions to his family, by illness, by old age. He should, so far as is consistent with piety and charity, endeavour to make provision for those dependent upon him, so that if he should die first, those left behind will not become a burden upon others. It is not faith but presumption which would lead to carelessness therein, fanaticism and not spirituality which inculcates the neglect of all proper means.

Yet it should be pointed out that there is real danger lest the above-mentioned duties be extended beyond due bounds. None ought to be so occupied with the consideration of providing for the future that he be unfitted for the discharge of present obligations or the enjoyment of present privileges. None ought to attend to such duties in a way that is distrustful of Divine providence. None ought to be weighed down with anxiety over them. The following rules must regulate us therein. First, attention to the needs of the body must be subordinated to our seeking after the welfare of our souls, for temporal affairs must never crowd out spiritual and eternal concerns. Second, in diligently walking in our earthly calling we must strictly see to it that we deal uprightly and honestly with our fellows, seeking to acquire only those things which are needful and right. Third, we must leave the issue or success of all our labours and endeavours *to God*: ours is to use the means to the best of our ability and opportunity, His is to bless and prosper according as He deems best.

Let it be clearly understood then that when Christ gave commandment "Take no thought for your life" He was very far from forbidding us to look ahead and make provision against a future livelihood. Foresight and forboding are two very different things. That which our Lord here prohibits is not the making of careful preparation for what is likely to come, but the constant occupation of the mind and distraction of the heart over what will never come. It is not the foresight of the storm and the taking in of sail while there is yet time which He reprehends, but that after we have taken in the sail we continue to gaze at the horizon with such fear and unbelief that we are weakened thereby and disqualified for the discharge of far more important duties. To be tormented by anxious thoughts about the future is unworthy of our manhood, let alone of our Divine sonship, and is most dishonouring to our Creator.

"Therefore I say unto you, Take no thought for your life." Observe the force of the opening "Therefore." Seeing that they who set their hearts upon earthly treasures do neglect the true riches and do lack the single eye of spiritual wisdom to discern heavenly treasure, and are therefore the slaves of mammon, be not concerned, harbour not immoderate and distrustful thoughts about things needful to your temporal life. Because it is impossible at one and the same time to make earthly and heavenly things the principal subject of your thoughts, all anxiety about material things is improper. Note, too, the " I say unto you "—I, your Master, upon whom you depend for instruction and direction in all things needful for both soul and body—so as to command their attention and compliance. " He says it *as* the Lord and Sovereign of our hearts; He says it *as* our Comforter and Helper of our joy " (Matthew Henry).

" Therefore I say unto you, Be not anxious for your life " (Amer. R.V.), which conveys the idea better than the A.V. The " care " which is here forbidden is a tormenting one, which disquietens and distracts, which disturbs our joy in God, and destroys our peace. When concern over making provision for the future leads the heart away from God and produces distrust, it has become sinful. Foresight must not degenerate into forboding, diligence into worrying. It is carking care and distressing fear which are here reprehended. It is distrustful care we are called upon to guard against. We are guilty of this when we trouble ourselves about the issue of our labours: when having used the means and performed our duty we vex ourselves over the success, instead of relying upon God's providence for the blessing of the same. It is this distrust of God which draws the covetous hearts of men to employ unlawful means in the obtaining of worldly things—such as lying, fraud, false weights, oppression of the weak.

" Therefore I say unto you, Take no thought for your life, what ye shall eat, or what ye shall drink; nor yet for your body, what ye shall put on." To take it on its lowest ground, such things as food and clothing are not worth worrying about. In a few years at most we shall no more need the staff of life to support us and shall be where the coarsest shroud will serve as well as a royal robe. Of what worth are those things over which death has dominion? Why be so foolish, then, as to make our chief concern those things which perish with the using? And how much worse is our offence if, instead of being content with such things as a gracious God has provided us with, we lust after and bend our best efforts to acquire something of a superior quality. What will it matter a hundred years hence whether we fed on the fat of the land or the poorest of fare, whether we were dressed in silks and satins or the cheapest of garments? But it will matter everything whether or not we fed on the Lamb and were clothed with the robe of His righteousness!

But to look higher. Why is it that there is so little fruit from the preaching of God's Word? How few realize that this worldly care is one of the chief hindrances thereto. Yet, that this *is* the case is clear from the teaching of our Lord in His parable of the Sower. There He informs us that " He also that received seed among the thorns is he that heareth the word; and *the care of this world*, and the deceitfulness of riches, choke the word, and he becometh unfruitful " (Matt. xiii, 22), so that worry over poverty is as fatal to spiritual fruitfulness as is gloating over wealth. Alas, what a large percentage there is in our congregations who can neither pray, hear the Word, nor go home and meditate thereon, without their poor minds being distracted with such worldly thoughts and carnal anxieties. Our minds are so constituted that they cannot at one and the same time be stayed upon the Lord and fixed upon next winter's new coat or hat.

Having sought to show something of the sinfulness of worrying about temporal things, let us seek to point out how it may be avoided. This is to be found in following the counsel which is given to us in the Word of Truth. "Commit thy way into the Lord: trust also in Him; and He shall bring it to pass" (Psalm xxxvii, 5). "Cast thy burden upon the Lord, and He shall sustain thee" (Psalm lv, 22). "Commit thy works unto the Lord, and thy thoughts shall be established" (Prov. xvi, 3). "Casting all your care upon Him; for He careth for you" (I Peter v, 7). It is not that these passages exempt us from performing the duties of our calling and using all lawful means therein, but that in the performance of duty and after the use of means we must leave the event and issue for good success to the blessing of God. Such a course involves the exercise of faith and the complete submitting of ourselves unto the sovereign pleasure of Him with whom we have to do, and who alone can give the increase.

Thus the tradesman, whose business it is to buy and sell, must be careful and diligent in his business, disdaining all lying and deceit, misrepresentation or overcharging, and then refer the success of his trade to the blessing of God. Thus too with the farmer and crofter: he must faithfully do his part in ploughing and sowing, and then leave the harvest to God's good providence. This is the apostle's counsel: "Be careful for nothing," that is, after a distrustful and distressing sort. "But in every thing by prayer and supplication with thanksgiving let your requests be made known unto God" (Phil. iv, 6). Thus it is clear that the anxiety and worry are opposed to prayer and thanksgiving, being a hindrance thereto. Instead, after using lawful means, we are to pray God's blessing thereon, that when it comes we may give Him thanks, yea, thank Him now by faith's anticipation.

But is it not hard for flesh and blood to abstain from anxiety about success? How, then, shall we be enabled to leave it wholly with God? By laying to heart the precious promises of God which are made to those who depend upon His mercy and goodness, labouring to live by faith thereon. "It is vain for you to rise up early, to sit up late, to eat the bread of sorrows": while men trust to themselves or in the means, moiling and toiling as they will, theirs is the bread of fretfulness; but in sharp contrast therewith, "so He giveth His beloved sleep" (Psalm cxxvii, 2). In sleep there is a laying aside of care and a forgetfulness of need. Those who trust in and love the Lord are delivered from fretting and fuming, and are given rest of soul. "The young lions do lack, and suffer hunger: but they that seek the Lord shall not want any good thing" (Psalm xxxiv, 10). If we had no other promise in the Scriptures than this, it is sufficient warrant to make us rest upon God's providence, in the sober use of lawful means. "Trust in the Lord, and do good; so shalt thou dwell in the land, and verily thou shalt be fed" (Psalm xxxvii, 3). What more can we ask than that?

"He that walketh righteously, and speaketh uprightly; he that despiseth the gain of oppressions, that shaketh his hands from holding of bribes, that stoppeth his ears from hearing of blood, and shutteth his eyes from seeing evil; He shall dwell on high; his place of defence shall be the munitions of rocks: bread shall be given him, his waters shall be sure" (Isaiah xxxiii, 15, 16). No matter in what period of the world's history our lot be cast, how evil the days, or how sore and severe God's judgments upon the earth, if we fulfil His specified conditions, then (even though drought and famine be upon the land, as in the time of Elijah) our bread and water *are sure*. Nowhere has God promised that His child shall be *feasted* with dainties, but "verily thou shalt be *fed*." Such was the blessed assurance of the apostle, "But my God shall supply all your need according to His riches in glory by Christ Jesus" (Phil. iv, 19)—not all your desire or greed, but *need*. Now if faith be really mixed with these promises, then we shall be quietened from fear and our hearts will be kept in peace.

How shall we rely upon the mercy of God in the hour of death if we are afraid to trust His providence for the things of this life? But when serious losses befall us and everything seems to be against us, must we not redouble our efforts and look increasingly to the use of means? Nay, rather is that the time to cleave more closely to God and rely upon Him to undertake for us. If the blessing were in the means men would not be so often crossed in them. God knows far better than we do what is good for us, and therefore we should rest content with His providence, no matter how He may disappoint our expectations for temporal things. Lack is often better for God's child than plenty, adversity than prosperity. So David found, "Before I was afflicted I went astray: but now have I kept Thy word" (Psalm cxix, 67). And many a saint since then has had reason to exclaim, "It is good for me that I have been afflicted" (Psalm cxix, 71).

"Take no thought for your life, what ye shall eat, or what ye shall drink; nor yet for your body, what ye shall put on. Is not the life more than meat, and the body than raiment?" Observe how Christ here distinguishes between life and food, the body and the clothing, and that He does so with the purpose of showing us how senseless is our worrying over the supply of temporal things. This first reason of His to dissuade us from such anxiety may be stated thus: the life is greatly superior to food and the body to raiment, and since the Creator has bestowed the former, therefore much more will He provide the latter for their sustenance. Therein the Saviour teaches us to make good use of our creation, and by a contemplation thereof to learn confidence in God's providence for all things needful to our natural life. "Thine hands have made me and fashioned me together round about; yet Thou dost destroy me!" (Job x, 8): thus the patriarch persuaded himself of preservation because God had made him. "Wherefore let them that suffer according to the will of God commit the keeping of their souls to Him in well doing, as unto a faithful Creator" (I Peter iv, 19): because God is our faithful Creator, in death we may fully rely upon Him.

If the Christian be trusting in God and attending to duty, he need have no fear that he will be deserted by Him and left to starve. God called us into being and furnished us with a body without our care, then is He not well able to sustain the one and clothe the other? Dependence is the law of our being: we are obliged to leave unto God the size, form, colour, and age of our body: then count upon Him for its maintenance. As long as God means us to live, He will assuredly feed and clothe us. He who brought Israel out of Egypt with a high hand and delivered them from death at the Red Sea did not suffer them to perish from lack of food in the wilderness. "He that spared not His own Son, but delivered Him up for us all, how shall He not with Him *also* freely give us all things!" (Romans viii, 32): such a guarantee should be amply sufficient to quieten every fear and allay all anxiety about food and raiment.

CHAPTER THIRTY-FOUR

Anxiety Forbidden—Continued

" Behold the fowls of the air : for they sow not, neither do they reap, nor gather into barns ; yet your heavenly Father feedeth them. Are ye not much better than they ? Which of you by taking thought can add one cubit unto his stature ? " (Matt. vi, 26, 27.)

" THEREFORE I say unto you, Take no thought for your life " (verse 25). In the last chapter we pointed out that Christ was not here forbidding a diligent use of all lawful means in our earthly calling, nor a judicious laying by against a future rainy day; rather is He prohibiting that worrying about the future which evidences a distrust of Divine providence and a doubting of our Father's goodness. Yet so senseless are we, so filled with unbelief, so slow to obey this precept, that our Lord not only repeated the same in verse 31 but condescends to reason with us and enforce His injunction by a great variety of cogent arguments. This at once intimates to us the deep importance which He attaches to a heart that is free fom distrustful anxiety and distracting fear, and also makes unmistakably evident the exceeding sinfulness of such sins. Let us then seek grace to attend closely unto our Lord's reasoning in this connection and treasure up in our hearts His different arguments.

"Take no [anxious] thought for your life." As Matthew Henry tersely summarizes it: " (1) Not about the *continuance* of it: refer it to God, to lengthen or shorten as He please. (2) Not about the *comforts* of it: refer it to God, to embitter or sweeten as He pleases." Our times are in His hands. The One who communicated life to our bodies has unalterably decreed the exact length of our earthly existence: "Thou hast appointed his bounds that he cannot pass " (Job xiv, 5), so that all our fretting and fuming is needless and useless, for neither planning nor worrying can prolong our natural life a single hour. And so long as we faithfully perform our duty and trust in God we need not be the slightest bit concerned as to *how* He is going to provide for us. The Lord is not tied to ways and means, and when one source of supplies fails us He will open another —as He did for Elijah.

" Take no thought for your life, what ye shall eat, or what ye shall drink; nor yet for your body, what ye shall put on. Is not the life more than meat, and the body than raiment?" (verse 25). Here is the first of seven reasons or arguments used by Christ on this occasion to show us how foolish, how needless, how useless, how sinful, are anxious thoughts and distracting fears over the supply of our temporal needs. It is an inference drawn from the greater to the less: an argument frequently made use of in Scripture, but one, alas, that we easily forget—see the "much more" of Romans v, 9, 10, 15. It is an argument based upon the infinite goodness and unchanging faithfulness of our Creator: God Himself has given us life and a body, and He does not stop half-way in His bestowments: when He implants life, He also grants all that is needful for its sustenance. When God gives, He gives royally and liberally, honestly and sincerely, logically and completely. Therefore we may rest assured that when He bestows life itself, He is not going to stultify His own gift by withholding anything that is needful for our good and blessing.

"Behold the fowls of the air: for they sow not, neither do they reap, nor gather into barns; yet your heavenly Father feedeth them. Are ye not much better than they?" (verse 26). These words contain Christ's second reason to dissuade us from distrustful care about things needful. It is taken from the consideration of God's providing for creatures inferior to us, His supplying needful things for them. It was as though the Redeemer said, Do you want further assurance that God will provide for all your temporal needs? Then lift up your eyes to the air and mark its feathered inhabitants as they flit to and fro, free from anxiety, filling the atmosphere with their cheerful songs. Oh, how they should show us, who are so often distrustful and despondent, how much more cause have we to celebrate the goodness of our gracious God and show forth His praises. Yet it is much to be feared that He receives less acknowledgment from us, fewer expressions of gratitude, than He does from those creatures upon whom He has bestowed the feeblest endowment.

"Behold the fowls of the air:" that is, take a serious view of, thoughtfully contemplate them. From this we learn that it is our duty duly to consider the works of God, labouring to behold His wisdom, goodness, power, mercy and providence therein. This is the lesson inculcated by Solomon: "Consider the work of God" (Eccles. vii, 13), and by Eliphaz, "Remember that thou magnify His work, which men behold" (Job xxxvi, 24). God has revealed Himself through His works as truly as He has through His Word, and we are greatly the losers if we fail to examine carefully and ponder prayerfully the wonders of creation, wherein the Divine perfections are so blessedly displayed. "O Lord, how manifold are Thy works! in wisdom hast Thou made them all: the earth is full of Thy riches" (Psalm civ, 24). "The works of the Lord are great, sought out of all them that have pleasure therein . . . He hath made His wonderful works to be remembered" (Psalm cxi, 2, 4). "Marvellous are Thy works, and that my soul knoweth right well" (Psalm cxxxix, 14).

Why was it that the Lord God took six days to make one creature after another, then took a particular view of them all after their creation, beholding with pleasure the products of His hands (Gen. i, 31), and then sanctified the seventh day for a holy rest? Was it not, among other reasons, to teach us by His own example *to consider* distinctly all the works of His hands, and that among other duties we should meditate on the Lord's day upon the wondrous and glorious works of our Creator? This was David's practice, as we learn from his Sabbath Psalm: "For Thou, Lord, hast made me glad through Thy work: I will triumph in the works of Thy hands. O Lord, how great are Thy works! and Thy thoughts are very deep" (xcii, 4, 5). Oh, to be able to say with him, "I meditate on all Thy works: I muse on the work of Thy hands" (Psalm cxliii, 5). How otherwise can we intelligently discharge the duty laid upon us in "One generation shall praise Thy works to another, and shall *declare* Thy mighty acts. I will speak of the glorious honour of Thy majesty, and of Thy wondrous works" (Psalm cxlv, 4, 5).

"Behold the fowls of the air." And what is it we are specially *to learn* and take to heart in connection with them? Why, this: "They sow not, neither do they reap, nor gather into barns; yet your heavenly Father feedeth them." They use not the means of provision which man does, and therefore have not that care and anxiety which he has. They are not required to perform those labours which are demanded of us, nor commanded to eat in the sweat of their face; nevertheless, they do not starve to death. Here is a marvellous fact which few ponder. The manner in which the lower animals, the birds of the air, and the fish of the sea, are provided with their food and clothing supplies a most convincing and unbelief-rebuking demonstration of the superintendence of God over this world, displaying as it does in so many ways His manifold wisdom, His wondrous providence, His infinite goodness, His unfailing faithfulness, His tender care, His compassions which are "new every morning."

If the question be asked, Since the fowls of the air sow not, neither reap nor gather into barns, how then are they provided for? the answer is that they expect their food from God's own hand. "Who provideth for the raven his food, when his young ones cry *unto* God" (Job xxxviii, 41). "So is this great and wide sea, wherein are things creeping innumerable, both small and great beasts . . . these wait all upon Thee, that Thou mayest give them their meat in due season" (Psalm civ, 25, 27). "The eyes of all *wait upon thee*, and Thou givest them their meat in due season" (Psalm cxlv, 15). "He giveth to the beast his food, and to the young ravens which cry" (Psalm cxlvii, 9). But how can irrational creatures be said to cry unto God? They do not use prayer as men do, yet are they said to "wait on God," because by a natural instinct in creation they seek for that food which God has ordained for them and are content therewith. By such phrases as "they cry to God" He would teach us that they depend upon His providence wholly for provision and rest satisfied therewith.

Here we may see how the irrational creatures, made subject to vanity by the sin of man, come nearer to their first estate and better observe the order of nature in their creation than man does, for they seek only for that which God has provided for them, and when they receive it are content; whereas man is deeply fallen from the estate of his creation in regard to his dependency on God's providence for temporal things. Though he be endowed with reason, and has the use of means which the fowls of heaven lack, yet his heart is filled with distrustful care, whether we respect the obtaining of or the use which he makes of earthly things. This solemnly demonstrates that man is more corrupt than other creatures, more vile and base than are the brute beasts. How deeply this ought to humble every one of us under a serious consideration of our sinfulness, that we have so debased our nature that we are more rebellious to the laws of our being and more distrustful of the Divine providence than are irrational creatures!

"Behold the fowls of the air: for they sow not, neither do they reap, nor gather into barns; yet your heavenly Father feedeth them." How the consideration of this truth ought to take us off from our useless and senseless worrying. The feathered creatures of the air use not means, yet are they fed. Man is required to use means, for God has ordained them for his provision: if, then, we dutifully employ them, in obedience to and trust in God, will He suffer us to want? Birds are incapable of providing for themselves, unable to lay up a store of food against the winter's snow and cold, yet their needs are supplied. *We* are granted foresight and the means of providing for a rainy day: if we are faithful therein, will God mock our industry? Surely not: then how unnecessary, how dishonouring to God, how sinful, are our carking care, our distrustfulness, our fretting and worrying!

"Yet your heavenly Father feedeth them." Herein we may observe God's special and particular providence. The dictates of reason would lead us to conclude that those creatures which are incapable of making provision for themselves and laying up store in summertime against the winter would starve when the earth yields not such means of nourishment during the cold weather and when the ground is covered with snow; yet they do not commonly do so. Yea, experience shows that birds are for the most part fatter and fitter for human consumption in the winter than they are in the summer! What a striking and blessed manifestation of God's special providence is this: that He attends to and meets the need of His feathered creatures and feeds them in the dead of winter! Oh, how this should shame us for doubting His providence, how it rebukes our wicked distrust of His care, how it exposes the groundlessness and wickedness of our unbelief! Next time you are tempted to worry over future supplies, dear reader, and rack your poor brains over where they are going to come from, think of the birds of the air and remember that a faithful Creator feeds them even in the winter.

"Your heavenly Father feedeth them." Has He not here set before us an example which we do well to follow? "Be ye therefore followers of God, as dear children" (Eph. v, 1). If God is so merciful unto the fowls of heaven as to feed them, then must not those who are His children evidence their likeness to the Father by exercising mercy unto all His creatures? True, He is not dependent upon *our* aid, yet is He often pleased to make use of means: then next time the ground is covered with snow, fail not to place some crusts of bread or lumps of suet in your garden or back-yard, and when the ponds are frozen over put a cup of hot water within the reach ot your feathered friends. And let not your kindness be limited unto the birds, but extend it also unto the animals, the poor among men, and especially unto any indigent members of the Household of Faith. In time of stress and scarcity, refrain from profiteering and grinding the face of the poor.

"Are ye not much better than they?" (verse 26). Here is the application which Christ makes of His second argument. Considered simply as members of the human race we are creatures of a nobler order than the fowls of the air, for we are endowed with rationality and designed for an eternal destiny. If then God feeds the birds of the air, will He fail to provide for those who are created in His own image? But considered as sons and daughters of the Almighty, the objects of His special love, of redeeming grace, of the quickening operations of the Holy Spirit, as begotten unto an inheritance "incorruptible and undefiled, and that fadeth not away, reserved in heaven for us," think you that the heavenly Father will suffer any of *them* to starve to death while they pass through this wilderness of sin? If He provides for the birds in the dead of winter, is He unable or unwilling to minister to your temporal needs in sickness or old age? How small is our faith in His goodness, His faithfulness, His tender care, if we worry now about where our future bread or clothing is to come from!

"Which of you by taking thought can add one cubit unto his stature?" (verse 27). Here is the third reason advanced by Christ against carking care for worldly things. It is propounded in the way of a question, which form of speech imports the affirming of or denying of the thing spoken of with more vehemency. Here it has the force of an emphatic negative: as though Christ had said, Certainly none of you by taking care can add a single cubit to his height. This unanswerable argument is taken from man's impotency: neither the most ambitious, the strongest, nor the wisest is able to do so. We did not reach our present weight or height by any efforts of our own, but solely by the providence of God. "An infant of a span long has grown up to be a man of six feet, and how was one cubit after another added to his stature? Not by his own foresight or contrivance: he grew he knew not how, by the power and goodness of God" (Matthew Henry).

A "cubit" varies from eighteen to twenty-one inches, being the measure taken from the length of a man's arm from the elbow to the tip of his middle finger. Now in the framing of a man's body, God brings it from a span long in the mother's womb by gradual increase, adding to it cubit after cubit until he has reached the height God ordained. The exact height each man comes to, God has appointed, and no man, either by his skill, his anxiety, or his industry, can exceed the stature God has determined him. That is the work of the Creator: He who gives the body decrees the stature, and by His providence brings it thereto by daily increase. Hence, reasons Christ, since man cannot by the most diligent use of means augment his stature one cubit, neither can he by all his fretting and fuming, moiling and toiling, better his temporal estate for things needful in this life, and therefore it is needless and useless to vex our hearts therewith.

"We cannot alter the stature we are of, if we would: what a foolish and ridiculous thing it would be for a man of low stature to perplex himself, to break his sleep and beat his brains about it, and to be continually taking thought how he might be a cubit higher; when, after all, he knows he cannot effect it, and therefore he had better be content and take it is as it is. . . . Now as we do in reference to our bodily estate. (1) We should not covet an abundance of the wealth of this world. (2) We must reconcile ourselves to our state, as we do to our stature: we must set the conveniences against the inconveniences, and so make a virtue of necessity—what cannot be remedied must be made the best of. We cannot alter the disposals of providence, and therefore must acquiesce in them and accommodate ourselves to them" (Matthew Henry).

Certain it is that man's labour, care and industry are utterly vain and fruitless without the blessing of God's providence. "Except the Lord build the house, they labour in vain that build it; except the Lord keep the city, the watchman waketh but in vain. It is vain for you to rise up early, to sit up late, to eat the bread of sorrows" (Psalm cxxvii, 1, 2). "I have planted, Apollos watered; but God gave the increase. So then neither is he that planteth any thing, neither he that watereth" (I Cor. iii, 6, 7): if two such men as these could do nothing of themselves, what shall we think to do? This same truth—so much lost sight of today—is brought out again in "Ye have sown much, and bring in little; ye eat, but ye have not enough; ye drink, but ye are not filled with drink; ye clothe you, but there is none warm; and he that earneth wages earneth wages to put it into a bag with holes . . . Ye looked for much, and, lo, it came to little; and when ye brought it home, I did blow upon it" (Hag. i, 6, 9). How this should teach us to commend all the sober care and labour of our lawful callings to God by prayer for His blessing, and when He has granted the same fail not to return thanks unto Him.

No man can better his natural estate in this world either for wealth or dignity, by all his care and labour, above that which God has appointed him to reach unto. As the Creator has determined each man's bodily stature which we cannot add to, so He has fore-ordained what each man's estate shall be, whether of wealth or poverty, dignity or disgrace, and it lies not in the power of any creature to alter the same. "Lift not up your horn on high: speak not with a stiff neck. For promotion cometh neither from the east nor from the west, nor from the south. But God is the Judge: He putteth down one, and setteth up another" (Psalm lxxv, 5-7). "The Lord maketh poor, and maketh rich: He bringeth low, and lifteth up" (I Samuel ii, 7)—true alike naturally and spiritually. The grand lessons to be drawn from all of this are that we must learn to depend upon God in the sober use of lawful means, humbly seek His blessing thereon, and rest content therewith, whether it be more or less, accepting with gratitude and thanksgiving the portion He has been pleased to allot us. We are completely dependent upon God for our stature, so why not leave *all* things to Him!

CHAPTER THIRTY-FIVE

Anxiety Forbidden—Continued

"And why take ye thought for raiment? Consider the lilies of the field, how they grow; they toil not, neither do they spin: And yet I say unto you, That even Solomon in all his glory was not arrayed like one of these." (Matt. vi, 28, 29.)

"AND why take ye thought for raiment?" (verse 28). In those words Christ returns to the commandment which He had given in verse 25: "Therefore I say unto you, Take no [anxious] thought for your life, what ye shall eat, or what ye shall drink; nor yet for your body, what ye shall put on. Is not the life more than meat, and the body than raiment?" In the verse we have now arrived at our Lord restricts His remarks to the matter of "raiment," while in verse 31 He again takes up the subject of food and drink. "Why take ye [anxious] thought for raiment?" though in the form of a question—to stir up our conscience—has the force of *a prohibition*, and therefore is a repeating of the former precept. This is very solemn and humbling, for it shows how unresponsive we are to the voice of God: we have to be told again and again what we must do and what we must avoid. There is so much self-will, so much in us which is opposed to God, that a single order from Him is not sufficient. What vile and intractable creatures we are, still are, even if regenerate.

Observe, then, the method followed by the supreme Teacher of the Church and the manner in which He propounded heavenly doctrine. He not only propounded it, and then urged it by strong and forcible reasons, but He proceeded to repeat it, and urge it by piecemeal. Whenever He had a weighty truth in hand, because fallen man is unwilling to receive and practise it, Christ, in addition to propounding and confirming it, took it up in detail, pressing it upon us again and again, that thereby it might the better find place in our hearts and be the more effectual in bringing forth obedience in our lives. Herein our blessed Redeemer has left an example to be followed by all who teach God's Word to others: not only unto ministers, but unto parents. "And thou shalt teach them diligently unto thy children" (Deut. vi, 7): the margin gives "whet" or "sharpen" for "teach diligently," the Hebrew word referring to the sharpening of a dull tool or sword—that so it may more deeply enter into the heart.

"And why take ye [anxious] thought for raiment?" All care for apparel is not here forbidden. There is a lawful and godly concern,

233

whereby we may labour honestly and in a sober manner for such clothing as is meet for the station of life which Divine providence has allotted us: such as is needful to the health and comfort of our bodies. That which is here prohibited is a carnal and inordinate care for clothing, which arises either from distrust and fear of want or from pride and discontentedness with such apparel as is meet and necessary. It is the latter which is one of the crying sins of our age, when there is such a lusting after strange and costly garments, when such vast sums are wasted annually upon outward adornment, when there is such a making of a "god" out of fashion, when maids covet the finery of their mistresses and when their mistresses waste so much time on the attiring of their bodies which ought to be spent upon more profitable duties. Well may all such seriously face the question, "Why take ye [such] thought for raiment?"

And why, we may well ask, has the pulpit for so long maintained a criminal silence, instead of condemning this flagrant sin? It is not one which only a few are guilty of, but is common to all classes and ages. Preachers were not ignorant that many in their own congregations were spending money they could ill afford in order to "keep up with the latest styles"—styles often imported from countries whose morals are notoriously corrupt. Why, then, has not the pulpit denounced such vanity and extravagance? Was it the fear of man, of becoming unpopular, which restrained them? Was it the sight of *their own* wives and daughters in silk stockings, fur coats and expensive hats which hindered them? Alas, only too often the minister's family, instead of setting an example of sobriety, frugality and modesty, has given a lead to the community in worldliness and wastefulness. The churches have failed lamentably in this matter as in many others.

It may be that some preachers who read this article will be ready to say, We have something better to do than give our attention to such things, a far more important message to deliver than one relating to the covering worn by the body. But such a rejoinder will not satisfy *God*, who requires His servants to declare all His counsel and to keep back nothing which is profitable. If the Scriptures be read attentively it will be found that they have not a little to say upon the subject of clothing, from the aprons of fig leaves made by our first parents to the mother of harlots "arrayed in purple and scarlet and decked with gold and precious stones and pearls" of Revelation xvii. Has not the Most High said, "The woman shall not wear that which pertaineth unto a man, neither shall a man put on a woman's garment: for all that do so are *abomination* unto the Lord thy God" (Deut. xxii, 5)? No wonder His wrath is upon us when our streets are becoming filled with empty-headed women wearing trousers. No wonder so many church houses are being destroyed when their pulpits have so long been unfaithful!

"And why take ye thought for raiment? Consider the lilies of the field, how they grow; they toil not, neither do they spin" (verse

28). The scope of these words is wider than appears at first glance. As "raiment" must be taken to include all that is used for the adorning as well as covering of the body, so we are to learn from the "lilies" that which corrects every form of sin we may commit in connection with apparel, not only in distrusting God to supply us with what we need, but also our displeasing Him by setting our affections upon such trifles, by following the evil fashions of the world, or by disregarding His prohibitions. In sending us to learn of the flowers of the field Christ would humble our proud hearts, for notwithstanding our intelligence there are many important and valuable lessons to be learned even from these lowly and irrational creatures if only we have ears to hear what they have to say unto us.

"Consider the lilies of the field." This is brought in here to correct that inordinate care and that immoderate lusting which men and women have concerning raiment. It seems to us that part of the force of our Lord's design here has been generally missed, and this through failure to perceive the significance of His following remarks. "Wherefore, if God so clothe the grass of the field, which today is, and tomorrow is cast into the oven, shall He not much more clothe you?" (verse 30). Thus: though the lily be such a lovely flower, nevertheless it is but "the *grass* of the field." Notwithstanding its beauty and delicacy, it belongs to the same order and stands upon the same level as the common grass, which withers and dies and is used (in oriental countries, where there is no coal) for fuel. What ground or occasion then has the lily to be proud and vain? None whatever: it is exceedingly frail, it belongs to a very lowly order of creation, its loveliness quickly vanishes, its destiny is but the oven.

In what has just been pointed out we may discover a forceful reason why we should not be unduly concerned about either our appearance or our raiment. There are some who are given gracefulness of body and comeliness of feature, which, like the lilies, are much admired by those who behold them. Nevertheless such people need to be reminded that they come only of the common stock, that they are of the same constitution and subject to the same experiences as their less favoured fellows. Physical beauty is but skin deep, and the fairest countenance loses its bloom in a few short years at most: the ravages of disease and the effects of sorrow dim the brightest eye and mar the roundest cheek, and wrinkles will soon crease what before was so attractive. "For *all* flesh is as grass, and all the glory of man as the flower of grass. The grass withereth, and the flower thereof falleth away" (I Peter i, 24), and the *grave* is the "oven" to which the handsomest equally with the ugliest are hastening.

In view of the brevity of life and fleetingness of physical charm, how groundless and foolish is pride over a handsome body! That beauty upon which we need to fix our hearts and unto which we should devote our energies is "the beauty of *holiness*" (I Chron. xvi, 29), for it is a beauty that fadeth not away, is not transient and disappointing, is not destroyed in the grave, but endureth for ever.

And what is the beauty of holiness? It is the opposite of the hideousness of sin, which is likeness unto the Devil. The beauty of holiness consists in a conformity unto Him of whom it is said, "how great is His goodness! and how great is His beauty! (Zech. ix, 17). This is not creature beauty, but Divine beauty, yet it is imparted to God's elect, for "the King's daughter is all glorious within" (Psalm xlv, 13). Oh, how we need to pray, "Let the beauty of the Lord our God be upon us" (Psalm xc, 17), then shall we be admired by the holy angels.

Not only does the evanescent beauty of the lily rebuke those who are proud of their physical comeliness, but it condemns all who make an idol of costly or showy apparel. Alas, such a sorry wretch is fallen man that even when his food is assured (for the present, at any rate) he must perforce harass himself over the matter of clothes —not merely for warmth and comfort, but for display, to gratify a peacock vanity. This gives as much concern to the rich as worrying about food does to the poor. Then, "consider the lilies of the field ': they are indeed clothed with loveliness, yet how fleeting it is, and the *oven* awaits them! Does your ambition rise no higher than to be like unto them, and to share their fate? Oh, heed that word, "Whose adorning let it not be that outward adorning of plaiting the hair, and of wearing of gold, or of putting on of apparel; But let it be the hidden man of the heart, in that which is not corruptible, even the ornament of a meek and quiet spirit, which is in the sight of God of great price" (I Peter iii, 3, 4).

But let us pass on to another thought. "Consider the lilies of the field, how they grow: they toil not, neither do they spin." Here the Saviour teaches us that the irrational creatures of the field do in their kind yield more obedience unto God than man does, that we are more rebellious than they are. Isaiah called heaven and earth to hear his rebuke of the Jews for their ingratitude (i, 2). Another prophet, when rebuking Jeroboam for his idolatry, cried, "O altar, altar, thus saith the Lord" (I Kings xiii, 2). When Jeremiah condemned the king of Judah, he exclaimed, "O earth, earth, earth, hear the word of the Lord" (xxii, 29), while Ezekiel was bidden to prophesy to the mountains of Israel (vi, 3). All of these go to show that if these insensible creatures were endowed with the intelligence with which man is, they would be more obedient to the will of their Creator than he is.

Again, in bidding us take the herbs of the field for our schoolmaster Christ would signify that though we have these creatures before us daily, beholding and using them, yet partly through our blindness and ignorance and partly through neglect and inattention we do not discern in them what we should, nor learn from them those valuable lessons which they are fitted to teach us. "Because that which may be known of God is manifest in them; for God hath shewed it unto them. For the invisible things of Him from the creation of the world are clearly seen, being understood by the things that are made, even His eternal power and Godhead: so that they are without excuse" (Romans i, 19, 20). Thus the Lord Jesus here gave a check to our dullness and neglect in meditating upon the products of God's hand. And if we are so slow to learn these things which are necessary to our temporal welfare, how shall we do in those things which concern our eternal salvation!

But *what* must we learn in the lilies? "How they grow." Like all the works of God this too is wonderful and should provoke our admiration. In the winter season they lie dead in the earth, as though they were not. They are covered with frost and snow: yet in the springtime they spring up with stalks, leaves and flowers of such delicacy and loveliness as surpasses the glory of Solomon in all his royalty. And whence comes this? Is it of themselves or from man? Neither, for it is " field " or " wild " lilies our Lord speaks of. Whence then? From the original fiat of creation, uttered by God when He made these creatures, saying, " Let the earth bring forth grass, the herb yielding seed " (Gen. i, 11). From that ever-operative word of the Almighty Creator comes the earth to have power and virtue to bear the beautiful lilies and every other herb. And the same God who by the Word of His power gives being to the lilies of the field has uttered a Word of providence that if we trust Him, using lawful means moderately, we shall have raiment sufficient and everything else that is needful to this life.

"They toil not, neither do they spin." Here the Saviour bids us take note of how free from care the lilies are. They expend no labour in order to earn their clothing, as we have to do. This is proof that God Himself directly provides for them and decks them out so attractively. And how forcibly does that fact press upon us the duty of contentment, relying upon God's gracious providence without distracting care. Not only have we title to Divine providence certainly not inferior to that possessed by the herbs of the field, but God has allowed unto us for our raiment the use of means which they lack. Though no man under the pretence of relying on God's providence may live idly, neglecting the ordinary lawful means to procure things honest and needful, yet Christ here gives assurance to all who trust in Him and serve Him that even though all means should fail them He will provide things needful for them. If through sickness, injury or old age we can no longer toil and spin, God will not suffer us to lack sufficient clothing.

"And yet I say unto you, That even Solomon in all his glory was not arrayed like one of these " (verse 29). In those words Christ rebukes that folly of the vain which moves so many to make an idol of personal adornment. Before we endeavour to show the force of our Lord's remark in this verse it should be pointed out that in making mention of the splendour of Solomon's royal apparel He did not condemn the same—had that been His object, instead of mentioning the "glory" of Solomon, Christ had termed it his " vain show " or " ostentatious folly." Though the Word of God reprehends pride and superfluities in attire, yet it allows unto princes and persons of high office the use of gorgeous and costly raiment. When Joseph was advanced unto state dignity he refused not to be arrayed in "garments of fine linen" and to have "a ring on his hand and a chain of gold about his neck" (Gen. xli, 42); nor did the apostle reprove Agrippa and Bernice because they came to hear him "in great pomp" (Acts xxv, 23).

How senseless it is to be conceited over fine attire and to be so solicitous about our personal appearance, for when we have done everything in our power to make ourselves gay and attractive, yet we come far short of the flowers of the field in their glorious array. What cloth or silk is as white as the lily, what purple can equal the violet, what scarlet or crimson is comparable with roses and other flowers of that colour? The arts of the workman may indeed do much, yet they cannot equal the beauties of nature. If then we cannot vie with the herbs of the field which we trample under our feet and cast into the oven, why should we be puffed up with any showiness in our dress? All worldly pomp is but vain, for in glory and beauty it is inferior to that of the flowers, yet what is more frail and transitory than the posies of the field!

Alas, so great is the depravity and perversity of man that he turns into an occasion of feeding his vanity and of self-display what ought to be a ground of humiliation and self-abasement. If we duly considered the proper and principal end of apparel, we should rather be humbled and abased when we put it on, than pleased with our gaudy attire. Clothing for the body is to cover the shame of nakedness which sin brought upon us. It was not ever thus, for of our first parents before the Fall it is written, "And they were both naked, the man and his wife, and were not ashamed" (Gen. ii, 25). Raiment then is a covering of our shame, the ensign of our sin, and we have no better reason to be proud of our apparel than the criminal has of his handcuffs or the lunatic of his straitjacket, for as they are badges of wrongdoing or insanity so apparel is but the badge of our sin.

"Even Solomon in all his glory was not arrayed like one of these." The array of Solomon must indeed have been magnificent. Possessed of illimitable wealth, owner of a fleet of ships which brought to him the products of many foreign countries, nothing was lacking to make his court one of outstanding splendour and pomp. No doubt on state occasions he appeared in the richest and most imposing of clothes, yet deck himself out as finely as he might, he came far short of the beauty of the lilies. Rightly did Matthew Henry point out, "Let us therefore be more ambitious of the *wisdom* of Solomon in which he was outdone by none—wisdom to do our duty in our place —than the *glory* of Solomon in which he was outdone by the lilies. Knowledge and grace are the perfection of man, not beauty, much less fine clothes." To which we would add, let us seek to be "clothed with humility" (I Peter v, 5) rather than lust after peacock feathers.

CHAPTER THIRTY-SIX

Anxiety Forbidden—Continued

"AND why take ye thought for raiment?" (verse 28). As we pointed out in our last, though in the form of a question—to stir up our minds and search our hearts—these words of Christ are an express prohibition. That prohibition is twofold: against inordinate care and against immoderate desire. "Consider the lilies of the field, how they grow: they toil not, neither do they spin" (verse 28). Here Christ bids us learn of the uncultivated flower that which rebukes our sinful distrust on the one hand and which reveals the folly of our lusting after an elaborate wardrobe on the other. The first of these lessons is inculcated by the fact that they put forth no labour in order to earn their raiment: if then God graciously provides for them, much more will He do so for those who faithfully use the means He has appointed that we may obtain things honest and needful. The second lesson is expressed in, "And yet I say unto you, That even Solomon in all his glory was not arrayed like one of these" (verse 29). How foolish then to be vainglorious of our apparel when, after all our trouble and expense, it is less beautiful than that of the flowers.

"And yet I say unto you, that even Solomon in all his glory was not arrayed like one of these." Wherein lies the point of contrast? Was it merely that the lily is clothed with a robe of more delicate texture and of greater beauty than any man-made fabric? We believe there is something else, something more important for our hearts, a deeper truth adumbrated therein. All of Solomon's stately glory was but *artificial*, put on from without, whereas the adornment of the flower comes *from within*: theirs is no foreign drapery, but an essential part of themselves, namely a development and result of what they really are. So should it be, so must it be, with the Christian. That life and light which God has communicated to his heart silently but surely illumines his mind, sanctifies his affections, and brings forth the fruits of righteousness. At the resurrection that Divine life in the soul shall break through the body and envelop the whole person with splendour: "then shall the righteous shine forth as the sun in the kingdom of their Father" (Matt. xiii, 43).

Ah, my reader, it is a very profitable exercise to "Consider the lilies of the field." A spiritual meditation thereon cannot but be most instructive, for they are the handiwork of Him who is "wonderful in counsel, excellent in working." If we "consider" and take to heart "*how* they grow," we shall perceive that which will both

239

humble and encourage us. Their growth is *gradual*: first the blade, then the bud, then the flower. Their growth is one of *increasing loveliness*. Is ours? Are we gradually becoming more Christlike: more meek and lowly, more gentle and unselfish? Are we really going from "strength to strength" (Psalm lxxxiv, 7) and being changed into the same image [of the Lord] from glory to glory" (II Cor. iii, 18)? Their growth consists in an increasing development and *display of the life* with which God has endowed them. Are we so growing: making more and more manifest the principle of grace which the Holy Spirit has communicated to our hearts, "showing forth the praises of Him who hath called us out of darkness into His marvellous light"?

"Wherefore, if God so clothe the grass of the field, which today is, and tomorrow is cast into the oven, shall He not much more clothe you, O ye of little faith?" (verse 30). Here is further instruction to be derived from the flowers of the field, namely the frailty and brevity of their life. If this be duly taken to heart by us, it will correct that carnal lusting after fine clothes. Why should we set our affections upon a lavish wardrobe, be proud of our raiment, or make the putting on of apparel our "adornment," when after all we cannot compete with the flowers of the field? Such childish vanity appears still worse when we remind ourselves of the evanescence of such displays. The beauty of the flowers lasts but a few short hours, for tomorrow they are withered and cast with other rubbish into the oven. And our sojourn upon earth is only for a very short span at most: then why be so proud of our clothes, which quickly lose their gloss and shape, soon wear out, and we ourselves cast into the grave?

Not only is a lusting after showy apparel here rebuked, but also anxiety about supplies of necessary clothing. In the opening "wherefore" of verse 30 Christ applies His argument unto His disciples and hearers. He enforces His prohibition in verse 28 by a contrast drawn between men and herbs of the field. The pre-eminence of man over them consists in these things: first, the herbs were made for man's use and not man for them—besides other uses, they serve to act as fuel. Second, the herbs of the field exist today, tomorrow they are not, for being consumed they cease to be. Far otherwise is it with man, for even though his body be reduced to ashes, yet his being is not destroyed by reason of his immortal soul, which though it had a beginning yet never shall have an end. Herein he far excels them: their life arises from the matter whereof they consist and so vanishes with it, but the soul of man is a different substance from his body and perishes not when his body dies.

The vast difference between man and all the lower orders of creatures is clearly intimated by God in connection with their respective creations: God commanded the earth to "bring forth grass, the herb yielding seed and the fruit tree yielding fruit after his kind" (Gen. i, 11). But when He created man, though He made his body from the dust of the earth, yet his spirit and soul were immediately from his Creator, who "breathed into his nostrils the breath of life; and man became a living soul" (Gen. ii, 7). This pre-eminence of man Christ insisted on when reproving the sceptical and materialistic Sadducees, for He pointed out that God is "the God of Abraham," whose body had returned to its native dust long before, yet said that "God is not the God of the dead [that is, of those who had no being at all], but of the living" (Matt. xxii, 32). Now this superiority of man strongly enforces his duty to depend upon God's care and providence without distracting anxiety, for if the Creator provides such glorious array for the mere herb, surely He will not suffer the nobler creature of His hand to go naked. This is the very conclusion which Christ here draws.

"Wherefore, if God so clothe the grass of the field, which today is, and tomorrow is cast into the oven, shall He not much more clothe you, O ye of little faith?" (verse 30). Let us observe, first, how the Saviour here gave *God* His proper place and honour: He did not ascribe the loveliness of the lily to an impersonal "nature" or the outworking of the law of its being, but expressly attributed it unto its Maker—"all the excellencies of the creature flow from God, the Fount and Spring of them" (Matthew Henry). Second, weigh well the "much more." If Jehovah-Jireh supplies such lovely array for so short-lived and comparatively useless creatures as the herbage of the field, most certainly He will not suffer any of His own dear children to lack any good thing. Then how plainly is it their duty to cast all their care upon Him, knowing that He cares for them (I Peter v, 7). We have a more excellent being than they: we are made for eternity, they for but a few days; we are taken into a closer and dearer relationship to God—His beloved people. Third, ponder well our Lord's rebuke, "O ye of little faith," which reveals what is at the bottom of our inordinate care—distrust.

"O ye of little faith." Those whom our Lord here chided were His own disciples, and that for which He reproved them was not a total lack of faith, but for the small measure of it, their distrust being more powerful than their confidence in God's providence. Herein we may see how one Christian differs from another (and how the experience of the same believer varies at different times), for there are some who, like Abraham, are so strong in faith that they rely wholly on God's promise, nothing doubting when appearances are entirely against them (Romans iv, 20). But there are others with a faith so weak, so mingled with doubts, that they are like those disciples at this time. But however weak such faith may be, however excuseless and reprovable, yet the faith itself is a true and saving one, as appears plainly in their case, for in verse 26 Christ acknowledged these fearing disciples to be God's children by calling Him *their* "heavenly Father."

Let us pause for a moment and point out that such weakness of faith in no wise jeopardizes our salvation, or that because we have more unbelief than faith our unbelief will have more force to condemn than our faith to save. Not so, for we are not saved because of our faith, though we cannot be saved without it. It is not the degree or strength of faith which renders it efficacious, but the clinging to the *right Object*. Faith saves (instrumentally) when it lays hold of the mercy of God in Christ, and weak faith may do that just as truly, though not with such assurance and comfort, as a strong faith. The doubting and weakness which is in a "little faith" does not damn us if we bewail it and use the means for strengthening faith. None of God's children have a perfect faith, and few of them attain unto the full assurance which Abraham reached. To those of little faith we would say, though thy distrust is a burden and grief to thee, comfort thyself with the blessed fact that Christ will not break the bruised reed nor quench the smoking flax (Isaiah xlii, 3).

The reason why Christ chided His disciples for the littleness of their faith was because they distrusted God for raiment. They were to be blamed for this, for their heavenly Father's care of the least of His creatures should have taught them better. Herein we may see one of the properties of saving faith. It not only lays hold of the mercy of God for the pardon of sin and everlasting life in Christ, but it also relies on His promises for temporal blessings in this life. Does not the greater include the less? If God gives Christ to him who believes, shall He not also with Him freely give him all things (Romans viii, 32)? All the promises of God are "Yea, and ... Amen in Christ" (II Cor. i, 20), whether they respect eternal life or temporal life. Therefore the same faith which says God will pardon my sins and save my soul for Christ's sake will also trust Him to provide me with food and raiment while I am left here below.

Noah's heart laid hold of the Divine promise of his preservation in the ark by the same faith whereby he was made "heir of the righteousness" (Heb. xi, 7). So too Abraham by the same faith whereby he was justified believed God's promise that he should have a son in his old age (Romans iv, 18). Let this point then be duly observed and the order remembered wherein faith lays hold of the Divine promises. It first apprehends God's mercy in Christ and then His providential care for us. This is so obvious and simple that it should need no labouring. As the Christian expects to be saved by faith after death, so he must live by faith in this world: if we rely on God's mercy for our souls, we will also depend upon Him providing for our body, for how shall we cast ourselves upon God's grace for heaven if we cannot depend upon His goodness for food and raiment while He leaves us here upon earth?

It is at this point that we should *make trial* of our faith: what sort it is, true or false; and the degree of it, whether it be weak or strong. Christ here plainly intimates that the more distracted we are by worldly cares the less is our belief in and reliance upon God, for distrustful anxiety over temporal things issues from unbelief in Divine providence. Thus it follows that the less we trust God for temporal things, the less do we really believe in His eternal mercies, for the selfsame faith lays hold on both. If we truly depend on God for bodily blessings in the sober use of lawful means, then we shall rest upon Him for the salvation of our souls. Such trial can scarcely be made in prosperity, when we have abundance, but if in the day of adversity we rely upon God then is our faith genuine; but if instead we imagine that we shall starve, and hesitate not to steal in order to supply our wants, then we have great reason to suspect that our faith is spurious.

" Therefore take no [anxious] thought, saying, What shall we eat? or, What shall we drink? or, Wherewithal shall we be clothed " (verse 31). Here Christ repeats the commandment which He had given against distrustful care in verse 25. The reasons for this repetition are these. First, to set an edge upon the commandment that so it may more sharply and deeply enter into our hearts, as we pointed out before. Second, to further His disciples in the exercise of faith, for by this repetition Christ gives them occasion to meditate and think upon this duty the more frequently, whereby their faith must needs be much confirmed. It is most important that we should recognize and understand that, in order to obtain or strengthen faith in our hearts, we are not to be mere passive patients, either in the reception or development of it. Increase of faith comes not from God to us as visions did to the prophets in a dream in the night, or as the print of the seal is set into the wax, but He works this grace in His people in the use of ordinary means.

There are some professing Christians who assume the attitude that they have no reponsibility in this matter: that since faith is a supernatural principle, a Divine gift, it lies entirely outside their power and province to do anything in order to obtain an increase thereof. Such fatalistic listlessness, such senseless inertia, are neither honouring to God nor helpful to themselves. Muscles unused become flabby: faculties never exercised soon lose the strength which they had. The way to get more faith is to put to work the measure which we already have and to use the means God has appointed. Our duty is to read daily God's Word, to meditate thereon, to strive and lay the Divine promises on our hearts, to urge our souls to believe, to strive and fight against doubting and distrust, to give ourselves to earnest prayer for the working of God's Spirit within us.

Concerning Christ's commandment against distrustful care, we sought to show (when considering verse 25) how far our duty extends in the matter of securing the things needful for this life, and where it must stay. It is to extend itself unto the diligent use of lawful ordinary means to procure things needful, and there stay. There are two dangers against which we need to be constantly on our guard: atheism on the one hand and fanaticism on the other. We are so prone to fly to extremes that much care is needed in order to strike the happy medium. While diligently using means, they are not to be relied upon to the exclusion of God: His appointment therein is to be recognized and His blessing upon them definitely and humbly sought, for no means will avail us anything except the Lord is pleased to prosper them. The most industrious labours of the farmer will produce no crop unless God sends sunshine and rain, and the most assiduous study of Scripture profits not the soul unless the Holy Spirit sanctifies it unto us.

On the other side, there must be no disdaining of means under the pretence of more fully trusting the Lord. Indolence is disobedience. Scripture says, "if any would not work, neither should he eat" (II Thess. iii, 10). The farmer who prays and expects God to give him a good harvest though he has neither ploughed nor sown his fields is guilty of the wildest fanaticism. The able-bodied person who is out of employment, and lazily sits down pleading the Divine promises to supply his need instead of going forth to seek work, is tempting God and not trusting Him. When he is ill, it is both the duty and the privilege of the Christian to spread his case before the great Physician, yet if he scorns to use the helps and remedies which Divine providence sets before him, he acts presumptuously and not in faith. The parent who fails to train and teach his child as the Word enjoins, counting on Divine election to save him, is making an evil use of that precious Truth.

Our duty in regard to the obtaining of temporal supplies is fully discharged when we have diligently put forth honest endeavours, used all lawful means, and humbly sought God's blessing thereon. Self-effort is then to give place to the exercise of faith, trustfully waiting upon Divine providence to prosper our endeavours. It is corroding care and distrustful anxiety that distracts the heart which Christ here forbids, and which is a spiritual disease infecting the souls of the vast majority of our fellows. How far the reader may be affected by this evil can be ascertained by sincerely testing himself at these points: What is it which often breaks in upon your rest so that you cannot sleep peacefully? What is it that first comes into your mind when you awake? What principally engages your thoughts throughout the day? What is it over which you take the greatest pains and which gives you most delight when you are successful? If it be the things of this world, then distrustful care infests your soul and must be striven against.

In closing let us observe how Christ here describes this unlawful anxiety by the effects it produces in distrustful persons. That there may be no mistaking this God-dishonouring and soul-paralysing disease, the great Physician has plainly described its symptoms. It causes its victims to ask, "What shall we eat? or, What shall we drink? or, Wherewithal shall we be clothed?" These are the very complaints they make when losses are encountered, adversities befall them, supplies are apparently cut off. When those whose confidence and reliance are not in the living God lose their job, or their investments miscarry, or they are stricken with a disease which incapacitates their body, they at once cry out, What will become of us? How shall we exist? It is *this* which Christ is here rebuking: those unbelieving utterances (for out of the abundance of the heart the mouth speaketh!) which denote we have no faith in God's goodness and distrust His care of us. The Christian must fight against such evil thoughts and murmuring complaints, laying fresh hold on the Divine promises and assuring himself that the "Lord *will* provide."

CHAPTER THIRTY-SEVEN

Anxiety Forbidden—Continued

" (For after all these things do the Gentiles seek :) for your heavenly Father knoweth that ye have need of all these things. But seek ye first the kingdom of God, and His righteousness ; and all these things shall be added unto you. Take therefore no thought for the morrow : for the morrow shall take thought for the things of itself. Sufficient unto the day is the evil thereof." (Matt. vi, 32-34.)

LET us summarize the verses which have already been before us in that section of our Lord's Address which is completed at the end of Matthew vi. In verses 19-24 Christ forbade the practice of covetousness, and in what follows He struck at the root from which that sin proceeds, namely distrust and excessive care for the things of this life. First, He tells us that such worry is *needless*: the bounty of God assuring supplies (verse 25). Creation is a pledge of our preservation: He who gives life will maintain it, He who provides a body will not deny it food and raiment. Second, He shows us that such worry is *senseless*: the providence of God unto inferior creatures evidencing it (verse 26). If God provides for the fowls of the air, will He suffer His own children to starve? Third, He proves it is *useless*: the impotency of man demonstrating it (verse 27). Since no anxiety or industry of ours can increase our stature, much less can worrying improve our earthly estate. Fourth, He announces it is *faithless* (verses 28-30). Since God clothes the herbs of the field, will He suffer His dear people to lack suitable covering?

None but the Divine Physician could have opened up so impressively the hideous nature of this disease. In that Divine diagnosis we are given to behold the excuselessness and the heinousness of this sin which is so prevalent among professing Christians. Distressing ourselves over the obtaining of future supplies, carking care in connection with securing the necessities of temporal life, so far from being a trivial infirmity which we need not take seriously to heart, is a sin of the deepest dye which should humble us into the dust before God. Worrying over tomorrow's food and clothing is needless, useless, senseless, faithless, and therefore it is utterly excuseless. Then surely we should make conscience of it, confess it contritely before God, and seek from Him grace to mortify it. That which was spoken by Christ on the Mount is addressed unto us today: Oh, that we may be given ears to hear and hearts to improve the same.

" (For after all these things do the Gentiles seek :) for your heavenly Father knoweth that ye have need of all these things " (verse 32). In these words our Lord advances two additional reasons why His people should not be unduly solicitous about temporal supplies. First, because such anxieties are *heathenish*. This will appear more evident to the ordinary reader when we point out that the Greek word which is here rendered "Gentiles" is translated "heathen" in Acts iv, 25; Galatians i, 16, etc. At the time Christ made this statement the "Gentiles" were without any written revelation from God and were in complete spiritual darkness. In consequence, they had the most erroneous ideas of the Divine character and government. Many of them believed that all things were fixed by a blind and inexorable fate, while others went to an opposite extreme, supposing that nothing was predetermined, but that everything was left to capricious chance. Such are the philosophizings of man's much-vaunted reason when unillumined by the Spirit of Truth.

The concepts which the "Gentiles" formed of their "gods" were such that they could have no trust in them. So far from regarding their "gods" as beings of benevolence, who regarded their devotees with compassion, they were looked upon as objects of dread, whose favour could only be purchased by the most costly of offerings (appropriated by the priests) and whose ire had to be placated by human sacrifices. Of a future life beyond this vale of tears the heathen had but the vaguest and gloomiest ideas. Consequently this world meant everything to them, and therefore their whole thought was directed and their energy devoted to the obtaining of its necessities and comforts, making such their chief good. Their ambition rose no higher than to eat and drink, to have a sufficiency of material things and make merry therewith. And those of them who possessed little of this world—and only a very small number had much—were weighed down with worry as to how soon their slender resources might completely fail them.

"For after all these things do the Gentiles seek." It should be pointed out that the word in the original whereby Christ described the behaviour of the heathen is more emphatic than our translation intimates, denoting that they "set themselves to seek" or "seek with all their might." This is a detail of some importance, for the mere or simple seeking of things necessary for our welfare is a *duty*, but when we give ourselves *wholly* to the quest thereof it is a *sin*, for it proceeds from distrust of God. And this was precisely the case of the Gentiles at that time: they were without the knowledge of the true God, had not His Word and were ignorant of His providences. How vastly and how radically different is the case of the Christian: God is revealed to him in Christ, a written revelation from Him is in his hands assuring him of the supply of all his need. How shameful then, how wicked, for a child of God to come down to the level of the heathen, as he does when carking care possesses his heart.

The force of our Lord's argument (that it *is* an argument or dissuasive is clear from its opening "for") will probably be apparent if we paraphrase it thus: because on all these things do *wordlings* set their hearts—in the parallel passage it reads "For all these things do the nations of the world seek after" (Luke xii, 30). How utterly unworthy for a Christian to be regulated by a mode of thinking and acting such as governs the godless, to descend to the level of the unregenerate. Yet, alas, how many of those now bearing the name of Christ do this very thing. How grossly materialistic is this twentieth century. How close is the resemblance between what men call "Christian civilization" and the conditions which obtained in the degenerate empires of ancient Greece and Rome. Human nature is the same in every age, the same the world over, and will inevitably remain so except where the Holy Spirit is pleased to work in His transforming power.

"Solicitude for the future is at bottom *worldly-mindedness.* The heathen tendency in us all leads to an over-estimate of material good, and it is a question of circumstances whether that shall show itself in heaping up earthly treasures, or in anxious care. They are the same plant, only the one is growing in the tropics of sunny prosperity, and the other in the arctic zone of chill penury. The one is the sin of the worldly-minded rich man, and the other is the sin of the worldly-minded poor man. The character is the same turned inside out! And therefore, the words 'ye cannot serve God and mammon' stand in this chapter in the centre, between our Lord's warning against laying up treasures on earth, and His warnings against being full of cares for earth. He would show us thereby that these two apparently opposite states of mind in reality spring from one root, and are equally, though differently, 'serving mammon.' We do not sufficiently reflect upon that" (A. MacLaren).

There are some who seek to excuse their anxiety and worrying by saying it is the result of temperament or circumstances. Even so, that does not lessen their sin. Divine grace teaches its possessor to deny ungodliness and worldly lusts (Titus ii, 12) and lifts him above circumstances (Phil. iv, 11). The fact is that those who do not trust in God's goodness and count not upon His faithfulness to supply all their need are pagans, no matter what may be their profession. Pagans believe not in Divine providence, and so rely upon the means, trusting wholly in their own efforts and endeavours, and so make themselves their own god. The real reason why empty professors are so anxious about the things of this life and so troubled over future supplies is that their hearts are earthbound and their desires heathenish. A worldling is one whose anxieties and joys are both confined within the narrow sphere of the material and the visible— take *that* from him, and he has nothing left.

Observe now the ground on which this argument or dissuasive rests. Real Christians have the true God for their God which the heathen have not, and therefore they must differ from them in their behaviour. God clothed the grass of the field (verse 30)—yea, with a verdure and beauty exceeding that of Solomon's royal robes— "*therefore* take no [anxious] thought, saying [unbelievingly and petulantly], What shall we eat? or, What shall we drink? or, Wherewithal shall we be clothed?" (verse 31). "For after all these things do the *Gentiles* seek," and ye must not be like unto them. In all things the children of God should differ from the heathen. "They are not of the world, even as I am not of the world" said Christ (John xvii, 14), and as He evidenced *His* separation from and unlikeness to it, so must we. "Be not conformed to this world, but be ye transformed by the renewing of your mind" (Romans xii, 2). Sons of the King of heaven are not to conduct themselves like the Devil's beggars.

"For your heavenly Father *knoweth* that ye have need of all these things" (verse 32). Here is still another reason, the most powerful of all, for delivering believers from distressing fears and God-dishonouring anxieties about future supplies. "Your heavenly Father" is set over against the inanimate and impotent "gods" of the heathen: His knowledge or tender solicitude, against their ignorance and lack of concern. The poor pagans might well say, If we are not wholly taken up with seeking after the necessities and comforts of this life, then pray who will provide them? But it is far otherwise with the Christian. The One who made heaven and earth sustains to *him* the relation of a heavenly Father: "Like as a father pitieth his children, so the Lord pitieth them that fear Him" (Psalm ciii, 13). He knows what I have need of, and will not deny it to me. "If ye then, being evil, know how to give good gifts unto your children, how much more shall your Father which is in heaven give good things to them that ask Him?" (Matt. vii, 11). The believer need trouble himself no further than soberly to use all lawful means, calmly and confidently counting on God to bless the same: God *will provide* what is needful for him and therefore he need not vex his mind about it.

Let it be duly noted that Christ here repeats the note which He had struck in verse 26: "*your heavenly Father* feedeth them." If He provides for such inferior creatures as the fowls of the air, will He suffer the members of His own family to want? He is their Creator and so bountifully supplies their need; but He is the Christian's Father and will not forget His own child. Here is double armour against the arrows of anxiety: the intimate relation which the great God sustains to His people, and the assurance that His knowledge of them is equal to His love for them. The children of this world are indeed tormented with anxiety as to how tomorrow's supplies will be obtained, nor is it at all strange that they should be bowed down with such cares, for they have no heavenly Father to whose infinite love and faithfulness they may commit themselves. Consequently in this argument Christ is putting His disciples to the proof, as to whether or not the relation which God sustains to them be actual and counts for anything, or whether it be mere theory and lip profession.

All distrustful anxiety concerning the supplies of things needful proceeds on the assumption that God either does not know our wants or that He cares not for us, which is precisely the attitude of the worldling. But with the Christian it is very different. He has the realization that "He that spared not His own Son, but delivered Him up for us all, how shall He not with Him also freely give us all things?" (Romans viii, 32). He is assured from Holy Writ of God's special providence over him, taking notice of his case whatever it may be and making all things work together for his good. From this assurance he must learn to practise *contentment*: depending upon God by simple faith and trustfully leaving himself and all his interests in His gracious hands. This contentment or acquiescence in the Divine will is to be practised in sickness as well as in health, under trials as well as blessings, in adversity as in prosperity, realizing that whatever may be our circumstances they are according to the good pleasure of our heavenly Father, who is infinite in power and wisdom.

"But seek ye first the kingdom of God, and His righteousness; and all these things shall be added unto you" (verse 33). In these words Christ makes known the great counter-agent unto and remedy for covetousness. As in the previous verses He had been striking at the root from which that sin proceeds, namely distrust of God and excessive care for the things of this life, so here He reveals the effectual specific: that is, making the things *of God* our paramount concern. "It is of no use only to tell men that they ought to trust, that the birds of the air might teach them to trust, that the flowers of the field might preach resignation and confidence to them. It is no use to attempt to scold them into trust, by telling them that distrust is heathenish. You must fill the heart with supreme and transcendent desire after the one supreme object; and then there will be no room and leisure left for the anxious care after the lesser. Have inwrought into your being, Christian man, the opposite of that heathen over-regard for earthly things" (A. Maclaren).

The renowned Thomas Chalmers was the author of that impressive expression "The impulsive power of a new affection." God and the world, Christ and Belial, cannot possess the soul of the same person: when the love of God is shed abroad in the heart the love of the world is cast out: "If any man be in Christ, he is a new creature: old things are passed away, behold, all things are become new" (II Cor. v, 17). Man is constituted that he cannot be devoted to two different and diverse objects at one and the same time: it is utterly impossible for him to serve two masters—God and mammon. Let his affections be set upon things above and they will be detached from things below: the more real and blessed (by the exercise of faith) become the former, the less attractive will appear the latter, and the less hold will they have. The best way to get a child to drop a filthy or dangerous object is to offer it another one more satisfying. If the horse cannot be induced to trot, turn its face homewards and it will quickly improve its speed.

Having by one argument after another dissuaded His disciples from distrustful care, Christ now shows unto them what that care is which *ought* always to possess their hearts: to wit, care of the kingdom of God and His righteousness. Three questions at once suggest themselves to us. First, what is denoted by those particular terms? Second, what is imported and included in our "seeking" after the kingdom of God and His righteousness? Third, what is meant and included by the word "first"? Most of the commentators regard "the kingdom of God and His righteousness" as a comprehensive expression for Divine things in general. Thus Matthew Henry says, "It is the sum and substance of our whole duty." Thomas Scott gives, "The blessings of the Messiah's kingdom, the righteousness in which His objects are justified, the grace by which they are sanctified and the good works in which they are to walk." To us it appears that such definitions are too brief and too vague to convey any distinct concepts to the mind, and therefore we shall endeavour to examine them more closely.

Among dispensationalists the grossest conceptions have obtained concerning "the kingdom": they have literalized what is figurative and carnalized what is spiritual. Strictly speaking the Greek word *basileia* has reference to sovereignty rather than to territory, to dominion than a geographical sphere. The "kingdom of God" signifies *the rule of God* and therefore, in its widest latitude, takes in the entire universe, for the Ruler of heaven and earth governs all creatures and things: angels and demons, men elect and reprobate, animals and fishes, planets and the elements. "Thine, O Lord, is the greatness, and the power, and the glory, and the victory, and the majesty: for all that is in the heaven and in the earth is Thine; Thine is the kingdom, O Lord, and Thou art exalted as head above all" (I Chron. xxix, 11). And again, "The Lord hath prepared His throne in the heavens, and His kingdom ruleth over all" (Psalm ciii, 19). Rightly did one of the Puritans affirm, "There is no such monarch as God is, for largeness of empire, for absoluteness of power, and sublimity of His throne." By some this aspect of it has been designated "the Kingdom of Providence."

In its more contracted sense "the kingdom of God" has reference to a certain order and estate of men, namely those who profess to be in subjection unto the rule of God, who avow their allegiance to Him. As the "kingdom" of Satan (Matt. xii, 26) is found wherever we meet with those in whom the prince of the power of the air "now worketh" (Eph. ii, 2), so the kingdom of God exists wherever there be those in whose hearts He reigns. This aspect of it is denominated "the kingdom of grace." As such it is to be considered two ways: as externally administered, and as internally received. Its external administration consists of the ordinances and means of grace and the outward profession men make thereunto—hence in the parables of the kingdom Christ pictures tares as well as wheat, bad fish as well as good being included therein. When He said to the Jews, " The kingdom of God shall be taken from you, and given to a nation bringing forth the fruits thereof" (Matt. xxi, 43) Christ had reference to the external privileges of the means of grace. As internally received the kingdom of God consists in Divine grace ruling in the hearts of His elect, so that they are brought to submit themselves unto the obedience of Christ. It is *this* aspect of the kingdom which is in view in Matthew vi, 33.

CHAPTER THIRTY-EIGHT

Anxiety Forbidden—Concluded

" BUT seek ye first the kingdom of God, and His righteousness; and all these things shall be added unto you " (verse 33). The heathen set their hearts upon material necessities and comforts: be not ye like unto them, says Christ—let a nobler, more essential and infinitely more satisfying object engage *your* attention and energies. If God be given His proper place in your hearts and lives you will not be the losers even in this world, yea, only thus will you be able to form a true estimate of the things of time and sense. Ah, my reader, it is failure to make Him our portion which renders us troubled about many things. Where there is the blessed realization that God is for us, that He is all-sufficient, a spirit of contentment and rest floods the soul. Nothing but the love of God shed abroad in the heart by the Holy Spirit will cast out dark and dismal forebodings. Where faith is in exercise and there is conscious communion with God, anxiety cannot cast us down.

By the "kingdom of God" is here meant a state or condition of men in this life, a state whereby they enjoy through Christ the favour of God and a title to everlasting felicity and glory. It is thus designated because God rules in them as a king rules in his kingdom. The words "and His righteousness" are added by way of explanation, that we may know for ourselves when we have obtained this grand object: God's kingdom stands in righteousness, as it is written, "The kingdom of God is not meat and drink [material things]; but righteousness, and peace, and joy in the Holy Ghost" (Romans xiv, 17). Now by "the righteousness of God" we are to understand two things: an imputed righteousness and an imparted righteousness, one which is placed to our account or credit and one which is communicated to our souls. The former or imputed righteousness is that perfect obedience which Christ rendered to the Law of God, which is legally reckoned to each one who believes in Him. As it is written, "Even the righteousness of God which is by faith of Jesus Christ unto all and upon all them that believe," and again, "If by one man's offence death reigned by one, much more they which receive abundance of grace and of the *gift of righteousness* shall reign in life by one, Jesus Christ" (Rom. iii, 22; v, 17). Therefore may the Christian exclaim, "I will greatly rejoice in the Lord, my soul shall be joyful in my God; for He hath clothed me with the garments of salvation, He hath covered me with the robe of righteousness" (Isaiah lxi, 10).

And how is anyone to *know* when the perfect obedience of Christ has been made over to him, so that he stands justified before God, the Law no longer able to prefer a single charge against him? Answer, by that which ever accompanies it: imputed righteousness is made known by imparted righteousness. Justification is never separated from sanctification, both arising out of regeneration. All who are justified by Christ's obedience are sanctified by the Holy Spirit that henceforth they may walk in good works. "That ye put on the new man, which after God is created in righteousness and true holiness" (Eph. iv, 24). The reference is to the new birth, whereby a new nature or principle is supernaturally communicated to the soul, a principle whose character and element is righteousness and true holiness in contrast with the character and element of the corrupt principle or flesh, which is sin and wickedness. This "new man" which is created (by God) in righteousness, believers are exhorted to "put on," that is make evident, display before the world—let it appear you *are* the children of God by your character and conduct. Therefore do we read, "every one that doeth righteousness is born of Him" (I John ii, 29).

Now this kingdom and righteousness of God Christ here calls upon men to "seek," and as we pointed out in the previous verse the word is a very emphatic one, signifying to "set ourselves to seek" or "seek with all our might." We all know how worldlings seek after the things of time and sense: not reluctantly but heartily, not perfunctorily but earnestly, not spasmodically but constantly, not carelessly but diligently. In such a manner and in such a spirit are the things pertaining to our eternal welfare to be sought. God has nowhere promised that those who seek Him indolently and indifferently shall find Him: rather has He declared, "Ye shall seek Me, and find Me, when ye shall search for Me with all your heart" (Jer. xxix, 13). So that there might be no misunderstanding of His meaning, Christ added, "seek ye *first* the kingdom of God and His righteousness," by which He meant seek it chiefly, principally, above all other things in this world. Let your paramount concern be to enter into that estate whereby ye may enjoy God's favour through Christ—justified by His obedience and sanctified by His Spirit.

From this command of Christ's it is evident that by nature we are all of us *outside* of God's kingdom and destitute of His favour, otherwise we should not be bidden to seek them. We were in fact, during our unregeneracy, under the power of Satan and in his kingdom of darkness. The Devil is called "the prince of this world" (John xii, 31) and "the god of this world" (II Cor. iv, 4), because all the world are his vassals, yielding him homage in the works of sin, and therefore is he also designated "the prince of the power of the air, the spirit that now worketh in the children of disobedience" (Eph. ii, 2). And how justly has this misery come upon men: seeing they refuse to yield submission to the sceptre of God, they are righteously left to the power of the Devil, to be made his slaves and drudges. That the unregenerate *are outside* the kingdom of God is very plain from the course of their lives, for to the Almighty they say, "Depart from us; for we desire not the knowledge of Thy ways" (Job xxi, 14).

But now the important question arises, How shall those who are by nature outside of God's kingdom and destitute of His righteousness seek an entrance into the one and an interest in the other? To this a threefold answer may be returned. First, we must go to the place where the kingdom of God is to be found. Second, we must then enter into it. Third, we must wait for the full possession of it. For the first: this kingdom of God is not to be found everywhere, but only where God is pleased to manifest and reveal the same unto the sons of men. It is made known in the Holy Scriptures, and therefore are they called "the word of the kingdom" (Matt. xiii, 19), and hence it is to the Volume of Inspiration we must turn, humbly seeking instruction from the Holy Spirit. But since it has pleased God to call and equip His own servants to expound His Word we should frequent the assemblies of His saints (where such are to be found), for it is there (in normal times) the evangel of His salvation is proclaimed, and the evangel is termed "the gospel of the kingdom" (Matt. iv, 23, and cf. Acts xxviii, 31).

Second, when we have found this kingdom, that is when it has been clearly revealed to us as set forth in the Word of Truth— whether through the instrumentality of preachers or not—we must seek *to enter into it*. It is not sufficient for us to be where it is or have it presented to our view, for Christ said to the Pharisees, "the kingdom is come upon you" (Luke xi, 20), yet He declared of them, "ye neither go in yourselves, neither suffer ye them that are entering to go in" (Matt. xxiii, 13). Now it is to be pointed out that none can enter God's kingdom of themselves without the special work of the Holy Spirit. This is plain from those words of Christ's, "except ye be converted and become as little children, ye shall not enter into the kingdom of heaven" (Matt. xviii, 3). Since conversion (a right-about-face, the heart and life being turned from the world unto God) is a fruit or consequence of regeneration, we must first be born of the Spirit. "Except a man be born of water and of the Spirit, he cannot enter into the kingdom of God" (John iii, 5). This is rarely insisted upon today, yea, the very reverse is inculcated, for sinners are given to suppose that salvation lies wholly within their own power, that they can turn unto God whenever they are pleased to do so.

Now regeneration is a renewal of the soul, a rectifying of its faculties, a work of grace is then begun and continued throughout the whole process of sanctification, which is consummated in glory. At conversion, which follows upon and may be termed the reflex action of regeneration, the image of Satan in sin and corruption was thrown down (not expelled, still less annihilated) and the image of God renewed in the soul, in knowledge, righteousness and true holiness. At conversion the proud heart of man is humbled, so that instead of continuing to conduct himself as a "god"—independent and self-sufficient—he becomes as "a little child"—tractable, teachable, meek and lowly. In conversion we renounce our own lordship and submit, voluntarily and gladly, to the rule of God, subjecting ourselves to His holy will. In conversion we repudiate the filthy rags of our own self-righteousness, and put our trust in the perfect obedience and blood of Christ. Thus, experimentally, we enter into the favour and kingdom of God and an interest in His righteousness is obtained by repentance and faith, by forsaking sin and the world, taking upon us the yoke of Christ and learning of Him, endeavouring to follow the example He has left us.

Third, we must then wait for the full fruition or possession of it. In the preceding article we pointed out the distinction which exists between the Divine kingdom of providence and the kingdom of grace: the former taking in the entire universe, the latter being internally received by the elect only, in whose hearts and lives God rules by His Spirit. We must now call attention to the difference between the kingdom of grace and the kingdom of glory, the latter consisting of two degrees. The kingdom of grace is entered the moment a soul is born again, the kingdom of glory is entered by the believer upon his removal to heaven at the moment of death. It was to this aspect of it the apostle referred when he said, "the Lord shall deliver me from every evil work, and will preserve me unto His heavenly kingdom" (II Tim. iv, 18). Heaven is the upper compartment of the kingdom of grace, for it is there Christ reigns supreme in the spirits of just men made perfect—perfectly freed from sin, and admitted into the clear and open vision of God, though their bodies remain in the grave awaiting their redemption.

But the believer's entrance into heaven at the moment of death— blessed, unspeakably blessed moment!—is but the kingdom of glory begun. It is not the ideal and ultimate state, for not only does he lack his glorified body, but the Church is not yet complete, Christ is still waiting until His enemies be made His footstool, waiting to see of the full travail of His soul. When the morning of the resurrection breaks, that "morning without clouds," the last enemy shall be destroyed, mortality shall be swallowed up of life, and Christ shall "change our vile body, that it may be fashioned like unto His glorious body, according to the working whereby He is able to subdue all things unto Himself" (Phil. iii, 21). Then shall the Redeemer say unto all His redeemed, "Come, ye blessed of My Father, inherit the kingdom prepared for you from the foundation of the world" (Matt. xxv, 34). It is to this final phase of the kingdom that the following refers: "give diligence to make your calling and election sure: for if ye do these things, ye shall never fall:...For so an entrance shall be ministered unto you abundantly into the everlasting kingdom of our Lord and Saviour Jesus Christ" (II Peter i, 10, 11).

In the meantime he who has entered the kingdom of grace is left in this world, that he may be a monument of God's sovereign mercy, that he may give evidence of the transforming power of Divine grace, that he may bring forth the fruits of regeneration. He is still left in the enemy's country, surrounded by those who seek his destruction and carrying a traitor within his own breast. He needs therefore to walk with the utmost caution and circumspection, availing himself of all appointed means of grace. He must spare no pains to keep faith and a good conscience, walking in righteousness and true holiness before God, and in the practice of love, uprightness and mercy toward his fellows. When the question is asked, "Lord, who shall abide in Thy tabernacle? who shall dwell in Thy holy hill?"—that is, Who shall enter heaven?—the inspired answer is, "He that walketh uprightly, and worketh righteousness, and speaketh the truth in his heart" (Psalm xv, 2). Herein we testify that we have entered the kingdom of grace, which stands in "righteousness," and are on our way to the kingdom of glory.

It now remains for us to say a few words on "seek ye *first* the kingdom of God and His righteousness." This means, let the things of God and your own eternal interests have the *chief place* in your thoughts and desires, making the glory of God and your own spiritual blessing your paramount concern. It is not that we are required to seek them solely and exclusively to the neglect of temporal duties and responsibilities, but that we must put first things first, and not suffer them to be crowded out by matters of far less importance. Seek them first in time, for the Divine promise is, "those that seek Me *early* shall find Me" (Prov. viii, 17). Seek them first each day, for only as holy happiness be our quest are we fitted to bear bodily trials and afflictions. And after you have, by repentance and faith, by complete surrender to the authority of God, entered His kingdom of grace and righteousness, continue to seek for the evidence of your regeneration, endeavour after closer conformity to the image of Christ and the example He has left us, and strive after more fruitfulness. Seek after an enlargement of His kingdom, by praying for God's blessing on His Word, that He will raise up and thrust forth more labourers into His vineyard, and seek to encourage and help your fellow citizens in that kingdom.

We turn now to look at the reason by which Christ enforces his command: "and all these things shall be added unto you." Here is a grand and glorious promise. In the previous verses our Lord had used one argument after another to show the needlessness and folly of carking care, calling attention to a variety of facts and drawing from them irrefutable conclusions to evidence the sin of distrusting God. But here He makes a plain and positive declaration, assuring us that if we be truly concerned about God's interests He will take care of ours, that if the Divine glory be our principal aim we shall not be the losers temporally. If God be leading us to heaven, He certainly will not deny us such things as bodily sustenance and raiment. " For the Lord God is a sun and shield: the Lord will give grace and glory: no good thing will He withhold from them that walk uprightly" (Psalm lxxxiv, 11): where He gives "grace and glory" He will not withhold the good things of this life. "Godliness is profitable unto all things, having promise of the life that *now* is, *and* of that which is to come " (I Tim. iv, 8).

" And all these things shall be added unto you." This phrase is very significant in the original. It is taken from a custom which obtained between buyers and sellers when things were sold by measure: the seller adding an extra quantity or overplus so as to ensure good weight and please his customer. Even so the Lord promises to those who truly seek His kingdom and righteousness that, besides the happy fruition thereof, He will (as it were) throw in for nothing, add for good measure, all the material things needful to this life. We read that " the ark of the Lord continued in the house of Obed-edom the Gittite three months: and the Lord blessed Obed-edom, and all his household " (II Samuel vi, 11): how much more will He bless those who receive His Spirit to rule in their hearts! It may be asked, Why then are any of God's children reduced to destitution? Sometimes to correct them for their sins; sometimes to exercise their faith in the trial of patience. All promises of temporal blessings must always be understood with this qualification: so far as God sees that such bestowments will be for His glory and our highest good.

But let it not be forgotten that the above guarantee is given only to those who meet its stipulation. Which, then, are *we* seeking first: earthly or heavenly things, the things of self or of God, making good in this world or making sure of an entrance into heaven? " It is startling to see the tide of worldliness rising fast among Christians almost everywhere, with a corresponding ebb in the desire for spiritual prosperity: on all hands there are abounding symptoms of spiritual decay, which it is to be feared will be followed by increasing ambition for fleshly advantage. Our Master's question may well ring in our ears and consciences today: 'What *do* ye more than others?' Not what *know* ye more than others? We may pride ourselves on knowing the things of God, which the poor worldling cannot possibly perceive, but if we spend all our energies, crowd our minds, engage our affections, and tax our wits for present worldly advantage, do not the men of this world the same? If we content ourselves with just the Lord's Day observances and meetings, do not religious worldlings the same? If we do not bring forth the fruit of the Spirit in a godly walk, in a faithful testimony, and devoted service, what do we more than others? The most convincing book to the worldling is our manner of living, but if, withal, we are as hard in our dealing, as keen for selfish gains, as inconsiderate for others' rights in our bargains, as shrewd and tricky in running our business as the most wide-awake worldling, he will not believe the book, for its author is a living contradiction " (E. Venn, 1901).

In view of what Christ said in verse 33 we may perceive the mad course which is followed by the vast majority of our fellow men, for they either utterly neglect or only half-heartedly set their affection on the things of God, principally addicting themselves to the things of this life. They take little or no serious thought for the eternal state of their souls, but spend their time and strength in providing for their bodies, which is to grasp at the shadow and ignore the substance. That verse also teaches the Christian with what mind or spirit he should seek temporal blessings, namely with the same honesty and prayerfulness wherewith he seeks the kingdom of God, for they are but appurtenances thereunto and depend upon it, and therefore with an upright heart we must only use lawful means moderately for the getting of them. So also this verse instructs us in the right end whereunto we must use temporal mercies, namely for the furtherance of ourselves and others towards the kingdom of God. Since temporal blessings are dependent on God's kingdom, we must learn contentment in all temporal losses: God's favour remains though worldly goods be gone.

"Take therefore no thought for the morrow: for the morrow shall take thought for the things of itself. Sufficient unto the day is the evil thereof" (verse 34). By "tomorrow" is here meant the future. In the second half of this verse Christ answers a question which might be evoked by His prohibition in the first: if we must not look forward anxiously, how will it fare with us in the time to come? First, you may be wasting your last hours on earth in fretting over a morrow you may never see! But second, if you are preserved unto the morrow it will bring with it tomorrow's God, and He has promised (I Cor. x, 13)! Third, what good can your worrying do? It does not empty tomorrow of its trials, but it empties today of its strength and comfort; it does not enable you to escape future trouble, but it unfits you to cope with it when it does come. Fourth, instead of anticipating future evil, discharge present duty—in the spirit of Philippians iv, 6, 7. Cross not your bridges before you come to them, but cheerfully shoulder the burden of today and trustfully leave the future to God.

CHAPTER THIRTY-NINE

Unlawful Judgment

" Judge not, that ye be not judged." (Matt. vii, 1.)

THE verses at which we have now arrived begin a new section of our Lord's Sermon, and that it is by no means one of the simplest appears from the diverse treatment which it has received at the hands of the commentators. They are almost unanimous in allowing that our Lord's prohibition "Judge not" cannot be understood in its widest possible latitude, yet as to how far and wherein it is to be modified there is little agreement. That Christ's forbidding us to exercise and pass judgment upon others cannot be taken absolutely, few if any who are acquainted with the general tenor of God's Word would deny, yet as soon as they attempted to define its limitations a considerable variety of opinions would be expressed. This should at once warn us against coming to any hasty conclusion as to the meaning of Matthew vii, 1, and guard us against being misled by the mere sound of its words. Yea, it should drive us to our knees, begging God graciously to subdue the prejudices of our hearts and enlighten our minds, and then diligently search the Scriptures for other passages which throw light upon the one now before us.

Not only is it very necessary for our own personal good that we spare no pains in endeavouring to arrive at a right understanding of these verses, for it is to our own loss that we misapprehend any portion of Holy Writ, as it will be to our own condemnation if we transgress this Divine commandment, but unless its meaning be opened unto us we shall be at a loss to repel those who would bring us into bondage by the corrupt use they make of it. There are few verses quoted more frequently than the opening one of Matthew vii, and few less understood by those who are so ready to cite it and hurl it at the heads of those whom they ignorantly or maliciously suppose are contravening it. Let the servant of God denounce a man who is promulgating serious error, and there are those—boasting of their broadmindedness—who will say to him, "Judge not, that ye be not judged." Let the saint faithfully rebuke an offender for some sin, and he is likely to have the same text quoted against him.

"Judge not, that ye be not judged." The word which is here rendered "judge" is one that occurs frequently in the New Testament, and it is used in quite a variety of senses. It is the one found in "I speak as to wise men; judge ye what I say" (I Cor. x, 15), and in "judge in yourselves: is it comely that a woman pray unto

God uncovered?" (I Cor. xi, 13), where "judge" means weigh carefully and form an opinion or consideration. It occurs in "thou
[Simon, whom Christ asked, "Which of them will love Him most?"]
hast rightly judged" (Luke vii, 43), where it signifies inferred or
drawn a conclusion. It occurs in "If ye have judged me to be faithful to the Lord" (Acts xvi, 15), that is, "if you regard or account
me so." "Take ye Him and judge Him according to your law"
(John xviii, 31) means, "put Him on trial before your court." In
Romans xiv, 3, "judge" has the force of despise, as is clear from
the first member of the antithesis. "Doth our law judge any man
before it hear him?" (John vii, 51), where "judge" signifies condemn—its commonest signification. Which or how many of these
meanings the word "judge" has in our text must be carefully
ascertained and not hastily or arbitrarily assumed.

Now the first thing to do when prayerfully studying a passage on
which opinions vary is to examine its *context,* first the remote and
then the immediate. In this instance the "remote" would be the
particular portion of the Word in which it occurs, namely the
Sermon on the Mount. As we pass from one section to another in
this Sermon, it is very important that we bear in mind our Lord's
dominant object and design therein, which was to show that He
requires in the character and conduct of His disciples something
radically different from and far superior to that religion which
obtained among the Jews, the highest form of which they regarded
the scribes and Pharisees as possessing. The keynote was struck by
Christ when He told His hearers, "except your righteousness shall
exceed the righteousness of the scribes and Pharisees, ye shall in no
case enter into the kingdom of heaven" (v, 20). That which precedes
and all that follows to the end of His discourse is to be pondered
and interpreted in the light of that statement.

In the earlier chapters we called attention frequently to what
has last been pointed out, and it must not be lost sight of as
we enter upon the present division of our Lord's address. That
which pre-eminently characterized the Pharisees was the very high
regard which they had for themselves and the utter contempt in
which they held all who belonged not to their sect. This is evident
from the words of Christ in Luke xviii, 9, where we are told, "He
spake this parable unto certain which trusted in themselves that
they were righteous, and despised others"; in what immediately
follows we have contrasted the Pharisee and the publican. The
Pharisees took it upon them to go up and down passing censorious
and unjust judgment upon others, while blind to their own glaring
faults. The disciple of Christ is to conduct himself in a manner
exactly the reverse: unsparingly judging himself and refusing to
invade the office of God where others are concerned.

The "more immediate context" of Matthew vii, 1, is the verses
which follow it. In order to obtain a right understanding of verse 1,
it is important to recognize that the next four verses are inseparably

connected with it, that the five together form one complete section treating of the same subject. The contents of verse 2 show plainly that we have a continuation of the theme of verse 1, while the " and " at the beginning of verse 3 and the " or " at the beginning of verse 4 denote the same thing, while verse 5 contains our Lord's application of the whole. The value of preserving the link between the later verses and the opening one lies in noting the threefold mention of "thy brother" in verses 3, 4 and 5, and in observing what is there said of his state and the state of the one who takes him to task. If these details be kept in mind we shall be preserved from making an erroneous interpretation and application of verse 1. As we must not too much anticipate what is to come we will leave these suggestions with the reader for him to ponder.

After carefully weighing both the remote and immediate contexts of our verse our next task is to search the Scriptures for all other passages treating of or bearing upon the subject of judging others. It is most essential that we do so if we are to be preserved from many erroneous ideas. Some statements of Holy Writ are presented in a very terse and contracted form, but elsewhere they are amplified and filled out: others are expressed in seemingly absolute terms, but elsewhere are modified and qualified. As an illustration of the latter, take the fourth commandment. The Sabbath day is to be kept holy: "in it thou shalt not do *any* work"; yet from the teachings of Christ we know that works of piety, of mercy, and of necessity *are* lawful on that day. So it is with our present text: unless we are very careful in our interpretation of it we shall prohibit what is elsewhere required, and be found censuring that which other passages commend.

"The capacity of judging, of forming an estimate and opinion, is one of our most valuable faculties and the right use of it one of our most important duties. 'Why even of yourselves judge ye not what is right?' (Luke xii, 57) says our Lord; 'judge righteous judgment' (John vii, 24). If we do not form judgments as to what is true and false, how can we embrace the one and avoid the other?" (John Brown). It is very necessary that we have our "senses exercised to discern [Greek "thoroughly judge"] both good and evil" (Heb. v, 14) if we are not to be deceived by appearances and taken in by every oily-mouthed impostor we encounter. It must not be thought that our Lord here forbade us to act according to the dictates of common prudence and to form an estimate of everything we meet with in the path of duty, nor even that He prohibited us from judging men's characters and actions according to their avowed principles and visible conduct, for in this very chapter He *bids us* measure men by this rule, saying, "by their fruits ye shall know them" (verse 20), and many duties to others absolutely require us to form a judgment of men, with respect both to their state and their conduct.

Unless we form estimates and come to a decision of what is good and evil in those we meet with we shall be found rejecting the one and condoning the other. "Beware of false prophets, which come to you in sheep's clothing, but inwardly they are ravening wolves" (Matt. vii, 15): how shall we heed this injunction unless we carefully measure every preacher we hear by the Word of God? "Have no fellowship with the unfruitful works of darkness, but rather reprove them" (Eph. v, 11): in order to obey this we are obliged to exercise a judgment as to what *are* "works of darkness." "We command you, brethren, in the name of our Lord Jesus Christ, that ye withdraw yourselves from every brother that walketh disorderly" (II Thess. iii, 6): this compels us to decide who is "walking disorderly." "Mark them which cause divisions and offences contrary to the doctrine which ye have learned; and avoid them" (Romans xvi, 17): this requires us to determine who are guilty of such things. Thus it is abundantly clear that our Lord's prohibition in Matthew vii, 1, is by no means to be taken absolutely.

There are four kinds of judging which are lawful and required by the Word: two public and two private. First, *ecclesiastical* judgment. This belongs chiefly to the minister, who in preaching God's Word judges men by admonishing their sins, and in his private dealings he must be faithful to their souls and rebuke where necessary. The judgment of the Church is exercised when it decides upon the credibility of the profession of one applying for membership: so too in the maintenance of discipline and exclusion of those who refuse to heed its reproofs. Second, *civil government*. This pertains to the magistrate, whose office it is to examine those charged with criminal offences, giving judgment according to the laws of the land, acquitting the innocent, sentencing those proved guilty. Legitimate *private* judgment is first where one man in a Christian manner reprehends another for his sins, which is required by the Lord (Lev. xix, 17) and second where the grosser faults of notorious offenders are condemned and others informed thereof that they may be warned against them.

"Judge not:" that which is here forbidden is unlawful judging of our fellows, of which we will instance a variety of cases. First, *officiously or magisterially,* which lies outside the prerogative of the private individual: this is assuming such an authority over others as we would not allow them to exercise over us, since our rule is to be "subject one to another and be clothed with humility" (I Peter v, 5). We are required both by the law of nature (which includes rationality and prudence) and the Scriptures to judge of things, and persons too, as we meet them in the sphere of duty, but to judge whatever lies *outside* of our path and province is forbidden. "Study to be quiet and to do your own business" (I Thess. iv, 11): if we give full and proper heed to this Divine precept we shall have little or no leisure left to pry into the affairs of others. That which our text prohibits is the passing beyond our legitimate sphere, that taking upon us to judge that which is not set before us for judgment, intruding into the circle of others: "let none of you suffer . . . as a busybody in other men's matters" (I Peter iv 15).

Second, "judge not" *presumptuously*, which is done when we treat mere suspicions or unconfirmed rumours as though they were authenticated facts, and when we ascribe actions to springs which lie outside the range of our cognizance. To pass judgment on the motives of another, which are open to none save the eye of Omniscience, is highly reprehensible, for it is an intrusion upon the Divine prerogative, an invading of the very office of God. "Who art thou that judgest another man's servant? to his own master he standeth or falleth" (Romans xiv, 4) places the Divine ban upon such conduct. A notable example of what is here interdicted is recorded in Job i. When the Lord commended His servant unto Satan, saying "Hast thou considered My servant Job, that there is none like him in the earth, a perfect and an upright man, one that feareth God and escheweth evil?" the evil one answered, "Doth Job fear God for nought? Hast not Thou made an hedge about him, and about his house, and about all that he hath on every side? Thou hast blessed the work of his hands and his substance is increased in the land: but put forth Thine hand now, and touch all that he hath, and he will curse Thee to Thy face" (verses 8-11), suggesting that Job only served God for the gain thereof. Thus to judge presumptously the *motives* of another is devilish!

Third, "judge not" *hypocritically*. This form of unlawful judgment was particularly before our Lord on this occasion, as appears from the verses which immediately follow. The one who is quick to detect the minor faults of others while blind to or unconcerned about his own graver sins is dishonest, pretending to be very precise while giving free rein to his own lusts. Such twofacedness is most reprehensible in the sight of God, and to all right-minded people too. "Therefore thou art inexcusable O man, whosoever thou art that judgest: for wherein thou judgest another, thou condemnest thyself; for thou that judgest doest the same things" (Romans ii, 1). No matter what may be his social standing, his educational advantages, his religious profession, the one who is guilty of partiality, who censures in others that which he allows in himself, is inexcusable and self-condemned. That even true, yea, eminent, saints are liable to this grievous sin appears from the case of David, for when Nathan propounded the instance of the rich man sparing his own flock and seizing the one lamb of his poor neighbour's, David's anger was greatly kindled and he adjudged the transgressor as worthy of death, while lying himself under guilt equally heinous (II Samuel xii, 1-11).

Fourth, "judge not" *hastily or rashly*. Before thinking the worst of any person we must make full investigation and obtain clear proof that our suspicions are well grounded or the report we heard is a reliable one. Before the Most High brought upon the world the confusion of languages it is said that He "came down *to see* the city and the tower which the children of men builded " (Gen. xi, 5), as though He would personally investigate their conduct before He passed sentence upon them. So again, before He destroyed the cities of Sodom and Gomorrah, He said, " I will go down now, *and see* whether they have done altogether according to the cry of it, which is come unto Me" (Gen. xviii, 21). Thus God would teach us that before we pass sentence in our minds upon any offender we must take the trouble of obtaining decisive proof of his guilt. We are expressly commanded " judge not according to the appearance" (John vii, 24), for appearances are proverbially deceptive. Always go to the transgressor and give him an opportunity to clear himself: " he that answereth a matter before he heareth it, it is folly and shame unto him" (Prov. xviii, 13).

Fifth, " judge not *unwarrantably*, which is to go beyond the rule which is set before us. In God's Word certain things are commended, certain things condemned, yet there is another class of things on which the Scriptures pronounce *no* verdict, which we term " things indifferent," and to condemn anyone for using *such* things is to be " righteous over much " (Eccles. vii, 16). It was for just such offences that the apostle reproved some of the saints at Rome, who were sitting in judgment upon their brethren over different things as " meat and drink." So too he admonished the Colossians who were being brought into bondage by the " Touch not, taste not, handle not " of the " commandments and doctrines *of men* " (ii, 20-23). The Holy Spirit points out that in such cases to judge a brother is to " speak evil of the law " (James iv, 11), which means that he who condemns a brother for anything which *God* has *not* proscribed regards the Law as being faulty because it has not prohibited such things. " He who quarrels with his brother and condemns him for the sake of anything not determined in the Word of God, does there by reflect on His Word, as if it were not a perfect rule " (Matthew Henry).

Sixth, " judge not " *unjustly or unfairly*, ignoring everything that is favourable in another and fixing only on that which is unfavourable. It is often far from being an easy matter to secure all the materials and facts which in any case are necessary to form a judgment, yet to pronounce judgment without them is to run a serious hazard of doing another a cruel injustice. Many a one has rashly condemned another who, had he known all, might have approved or at least pitied him. Again, it is very unjust to censure one who has sincerely done his best simply because his effort falls short of what satisfies *us*. Much unjust judgment proceeds from a spirit of revenge and a desire to do mischief. When David sent his servants to comfort Hanun, the king of Ammon, upon the death of his father, that king suffered his nobles to persuade him that the servants of David were spies on an evil mission (II Samuel x): a horrible war was the outcome—behold how great a fire a little matter kindleth!

Seventh, " judge not " *unmercifully*. While on the one hand we

are certainly not, as far too many today appear to think, obliged to
regard one who holds fundamental error or one who is thoroughly
worldly as a good Christian, yet on the other hand the law of charity
requires us to put the best construction we can on doubtful actions,
and never without proof ascribe good ones to evil principles or
motives. God does not require us to call darkness light or evil good,
nevertheless since we are so full of sin ourselves and so prone to
err, we must ever be on our guard lest we call light darkness and
good evil. We are not to go about with our eyes closed nor wink at sin
when we see it, yet it is equally wrong for us to hunt for something
to condemn and seize upon every trifle and magnify molehills into
mountains. We are not to make a man an offender for a word, nor
harbour suspicions where there is no evidence. Many a one has condemned another, where no ground for judgment existed, out of
personal jealousy and ill will, which is doing Satan's work. May the
Lord graciously deliver both writer and reader from all these forms
of unlawfully judging others.

CHAPTER FORTY

Judging Others

" JUDGE not, that ye be not judged" (verse 1). In the previous chapter we were obliged, so as not to exceed the usual length, to confine ourselves unto the first part of this brief verse. In it we sought to show what is here not forbidden, that there is a lawful judging which God requires us to exercise, both in public and in private. Then we pointed out no less than seven forms of unlawful judging, indicating that this prohibition of Christ's is a very com prehensive one. Our apology, if such be needed, for entering into so much detail is, first, because these words "judge not" are so frequently misunderstood and misapplied; and second, because the sin which is here forbidden is a very grievous one and has become exceedingly common. Some Christians are more prone to it than others, one in one way and one in another. It is a sin which may be committed in the house of prayer. When the minister is rebuking some evil or failure in some particular duty, there are often those present who will conclude he is addressing himself to some others in the congregation, which is one reason why so many reap so little from hearing the Word preached.

Now since it be wrong for us to judge one of our brethren or even our fellows presumptuously, hypocritically, hastily, unwarrantably, unjustly or unmercifully, how much more heinous must it be for us to give audible expression to the same and transmit it to others! Equally so is it for those who listen to us to repeat the same. "Thou shalt not go up and down as a talebearer among thy people" (Lev. xix, 16): yet who among us can plead innocence therein? Alas, how many there are, now that the pulse of love beats so feebly, who take a devilish pleasure in spreading evil reports of fellow members and enlarging on the same. "A talebearer revealeth secrets: but he that is of a faithful spirit concealeth the matter" (Prov. xi, 13). Equally reprehensible is it for us to censure and hold up to scorn those of another denomination, unless the Scriptures plainly condemn them. "Speak evil of no man" (Titus iii, 2) forbids us expressing anything to the discredit or disadvantage of another to anyone but to oneself, except where duty demands it —the putting others on their guard against an evil-doer or a doctrinal corrupter.

It should be pointed out that veracity is not the only virtue which needs to be exercised whenever we make report of the character and conduct of another. To say of such and such a person, "He possesses this or that virtue, *but*—well, least said, soonest mended," is far worse than saying nothing at all, for such an utterance insinuates to our hearers that there is some grave evil in the party to whom we have alluded. We may say nothing but what is the *truth*, yet by the very manner in which we express ourselves suggest that a certain person is not to be trusted. Thus when David came to Ahimelech begging bread for his men and requesting some weapon, and the priest granted him the sword of Goliath (I Samuel xxi), Doeg, who witnessed the transaction, put his knowledge to a wicked use by reporting the same unto Saul, implying that Ahimelech had entered into a conspiracy with David against the king's life; and the telling of the truth from such an evil motive and in such a manner cost the lives of eighty-five priests (I Samuel xxii, 18): again we say, Behold how great a fire a little matter kindleth!

"Judge not, that ye be not judged." After the commandment there follows *a reason* which is designed to cause us to make conscience of forming and expressing unlawful judgments; or, more accurately speaking, the second part of the verse is *a dissuasive*, a warning against the sin forbidden at the beginning of it. But precisely what is the nature of this warning, exactly what did our Lord here have in mind? Nearly all the expositors see in it nothing more than a threat that we must be prepared for our fellows treating us just as we treat them: that if we asperse people, others will slander us; that if we be harsh and censorious in the estimates we form of our fellows, then we in turn shall receive unkind treatment, being paid back again in our own coin. On the other hand, if we be charitable and merciful, ready to think the best and slow to think the worst of any, then others will in turn deal gently and considerately with our reputation. In brief, that the words "that ye be not judged" signify lest ye be unlawfully and unfairly judged by men.

Now we do not believe this common interpretation of Christ's warning gives the full or even the principal force of it, and that for several reasons. First, because the usual sense accorded it is one which has little weight with those who are walking with God. It is true there are many professing Christians who are greatly concerned about what others think and say of them, who are most anxious to shine in their eyes, who are very jealous of their own reputations and easily hurt if anyone slights them or speaks a word against them, yet all of this has its roots in *pride* and self-esteem. But one who is walking with God, who is painfully conscious of the plague of his heart, who in some measure at least sees himself as God sees him, is so thoroughly aware of his awful corruptions, his many inward and outward defects, that he knows quite well that the worst men can say against him falls far short of the estimate he has of himself. The one who unsparingly judges himself is unruffled by the criticisms of others.

When one is truly walking with God his only concern is what his Divine Master thinks of him. If he makes conscience of all that displeases *Him*, if he daily confesses to Him every known sin and begs Him to cleanse him from sins of ignorance and omission, if he be sincerely endeavouring to walk in the path of obedience, it will trouble him very little what other worms of the dust think or say about him. He is conscious of the fact that God knows his heart, that if only he has the approbation of the Lord this is worth infinitely more than the highest esteem of all mankind. Said the apostle Paul, "But with me it is a very small thing that I should be judged *of you*" (I Cor. iv, 3): their opinion mattered nothing, his responsibility was not unto them. "Yea, I judge not mine self," he added: Christ alone is my Lord and Judge, by Him I stand or fall. Blessed liberty is it when we are delivered from being in bondage to the fickle opinions and estimates of man, who will one day cry "Hosannah" and the next day "crucify."

It is not that walking with God produces a spirit of egotism which causes one to have so high regard of himself that he considers he is outside the range of human judgment: no, far otherwise. Nor will he disdain a correction or admonition when he needs it: rather will he say with David, "Let the righteous smite me, it shall be a kindness; and let him reprove me; it shall be an excellent oil, which shall not break my head" (Psalm cxli, 5). A truly humble soul will weigh before God the reproofs of the righteous. "Rebuke a wise man, and he will love thee" (Prov. ix, 8), for he knows full well that "faithful are the wounds of a friend, but the kisses of an enemy are deceitful." "As an earring of gold, and an ornament of fine gold, so is a wise reprover upon an obedient ear" (Prov. xxv, 12): alas, how few with an "obedient ear" are now left! But while welcoming needful reproofs and being thankful for the faithful dealings of those who wish him well, this is vastly different from being the prey of public opinion, fearful of being misunderstood, wondering what one and another will say of us, even while we are doing that which is right.

Second, we find it very difficult to persuade ourselves that when the Lord said "Judge not, that ye be not judged" He had reference to nothing else, nothing more solemn and searching than, Refrain from passing unlawful judgment upon others lest you meet with the same treatment at the hands of your fellows. Such a warning has little weight with the majority of professors and none at all with those who are walking in the fear of God, for where *His* fear possesses the heart it is delivered from the fear of man. Furthermore, it seems entirely out of accord with the whole tenor of His Sermon, with the searching character of all its details, that He should introduce and make so prominent (note the following verse) what is after all but a secular motive. In a discourse, one chief design of which was to make plain the spirituality of the Christian character in contrast with the worldly character of the Pharisee, Christ would surely employ a weightier dissuasive than the mere fear of suffering from the fickle judgments of fellow mortals.

Third, and what is more decisive, the idea that "judge not, that ye be not judged" means we shall in this matter reap in this world exactly as we sow—that if we defame others we also shall be defamed, that if we refrain from rashly and censoriously censuring others we shall ourselves be spared the experience—will not stand the test of Holy Writ. Apply it to the Lord Jesus Christ and the treatment which He met with from man: He never unjustly or unmercifully censured another, yet how frequently were false and cruel charges preferred against Him. Apply the principle to the life of the apostle Paul and see how completely it breaks down; can we suppose that God had employed him to write I Corinthians xiii had he been of a censorious, carping, pharisaical spirit? Yet *he* was "defamed" on every side and accounted "the offscouring of all things" (I Cor. iv, 13)! No, such an explanation, such a theory, will stand neither the test of Scripture nor of Christian experience and observation today.

"Judge not, that ye be not judged." In view of what has been pointed out we cannot avoid the conviction that many of the commentators unwittingly toned down this solemn portion of the Truth, blunting the sharp edge of the sword of the Spirit, for it seems clear to us that some vastly more awe-inspiring motive was in our Lord's mind, a far weightier dissuasive from the sin forbidden than the treatment we shall meet with at the hands of our fellows. We are persuaded that what Christ here had reference to was not the judgments of men but the judgments of *God,* not the decisions of time but the verdicts of *eternity.* In reality it is but a sop for the conscience, a sewing of "pillows to all armholes" (Ezek. xiii, 18), to tell people if they be guilty of transgressing this precept and unlawfully judging others that all they have to fear is being unrighteously judged by their fellows. But for Christ to declare that such conduct will meet with *Divine* judgment at the Awful Assize is a warning which may well make the most thoughtless to consider and the stoutest heart to quake.

But it should be pointed out that this warning of Christ's is not to be understood as meaning: If you be generous in the verdicts you pass upon others, God will be lenient in His judgment concerning you; that if you be harsh and cruel, God will deal severely with you. No, whatever our judgments of others may be, God's judgment will be "according to truth" and that without "respect of persons" (Romans ii, 2, 11). Thus we understand our Lord to mean: Beware of forming wrong judgments of your brethren and fellow men, especially hasty and unmerciful ones, for all your judgments are to be *reviewed* in the searching light of God's throne, and by those judgments you are yourselves to be then judged. Not that the judgments we form of each other are to be the sole test by which our profession will be weighed and our character tried, but that this will be *one* of the tests. "By thy words thou shalt be justified, and by thy words thou shalt be condemned" (Matt. xii, 37) will be another; our treatment of Christ's brethren, as Matthew xxv plainly intimates, will be yet another. Take care then that your judgments of others be such as will endure the scrutiny of the Divine Judge, for if they are not they must lead to disapproval.

We are well aware of the fact that what we have said above is contrary to most of the teaching of the day even in orthodox circles. So much emphasis has been laid upon certain favourite verses that the balance of Truth has been lost here, as it has almost everywhere else. Such a statement as "He hath not beheld iniquity in Jacob, neither hath He seen perverseness in Israel" (Num. xxiii, 21) has been interpreted to mean that God looks not upon His people as they are in themselves but ever views them in Christ, and therefore sees them as without any sin. But such an idea is flatly contradicted by Holy Writ. God *does* take cognizance of our sins and plainly declares: "If His children forsake My law and walk not in My judgments; . . . If they break My statutes and keep not My commandments; . . . Then will I visit their transgression with the rod and their iniquity with stripes" (Psalm lxxxix, 30-32). Believers are required to confess their sins, and both their forgiveness and cleansing are made contingent thereon (I John i, 9). It is blessedly true that the believer has a perfect *standing* or status before God, yet that must not be made to swallow up his *state* and present case.

We would not for a moment consciously weaken the glorious force of "There is therefore now no condemnation to them which are in Christ Jesus" (Romans viii, 1), and "he that heareth My Word, and believeth on Him that sent Me, hath everlasting life, and shall not come into condemnation [Greek "judgment"]; but is passed from death unto life" (John v, 24). Yet those verses must not be understood in such a way as to clash with other portions of God's Word, such, for example, as "For the time is come that judgment must begin at the House of God" (I Peter iv, 17). No born-again soul shall ever suffer the *eternal* judgment of God, for he has for ever passed beyond the reach of penal death or the curse of the Law, Christ having suffered the curse on his behalf. But though beyond the curse of the Law, Christians are subject to the *government* of God, and that government will not make light of wrongdoing nor relinquish its righteous requirements. Sin is no less sinful when committed by a believer than by an unbeliever, and unless it be repented of or put right before God in this life it will have to be put right in the Day to come. And who that loves holiness would wish it were otherwise? Many a breach between fellow Christians is never healed in this world: must not things be put right between them before they can spend eternity together in heaven?

Both the orthodox pulpit and what is regarded as sound literature convey the impression that no matter how grievously the Christian may have failed in his duty, he has nothing to fear so far as the next life is concerned, that however careless and fruitless he has been, unclouded bliss awaits him after death. But between death and eternity proper is the Day of Judgment! But the Truth is now so watered down and so accommodated to the carnal mind that the Lord's people are led to believe complacently that so far as they are concerned that Day will be solely one of receiving rewards and words of praise. But this writer does not so read the Scriptures: he finds another class of passages which set forth quite a different aspect of the Truth, and though these passages be almost universally shelved, or "explained away" when pressed upon the attention of those claiming to be Christians, he dare not ignore them or fritter them down.

"But why dost thou judge thy brother? or why dost thou set at nought thy brother? *for* we shall all stand before the judgment seat of Christ. For it is written, As I live, saith the Lord, every knee shall bow to Me, and every tongue shall confess to God" (Romans xiv, 10-11). We merely call attention to the bare fact that the judgment seat of Christ is here set before believers as *a solemn motive* to refrain from judging their brethren, a motive which will have no force if commendation is all they are to receive there; and that this warning is immediately followed with "So then every one of us shall give account of himself to God": that this rendering of accounts will be something more than a mere formality scarcely needs to be pointed out. "Every man's work shall be made manifest: for the day shall declare it, because it shall be revealed by fire; and the fire shall try every man's work of what sort it is. If any man's work abide which he hath built thereupon, he shall receive a reward. If any man's work shall be burned, he shall suffer loss: but he himself shall be saved; *yet so as by fire*" (I Cor. iii, 13-15). This has reference to the adjudication of the labours of Christ's servants, when their work will be subjected to the searching scrutiny of Divine holiness: "saved, yet so as by fire" certainly does not suggest a happy experience—not that we understand there is anything in these verses which furnishes the slightest support to the popish "purgatory." Ministers would do well seriously to ponder this passage and turn it into earnest prayer.

"For we must all appear before the judgment seat of Christ: that every one *may receive* the things done in his body, *according to* that he hath done, whether good or bad" (II Cor. v, 10). The "we" takes in the whole election of grace, all who are redeemed by Christ. That there will be something more than the handing out of bouquets is plainly intimated in "that every one may receive the things done in the body, according to that he hath done, whether good *or bad.*" An awe-inspiring description of Christ in His office of Judge (when inspecting and passing sentence upon His churches) is given in Revelation i, where He is seen with "His eyes as a flame of fire; And His feet like unto fine brass, as if they burned in a furnace; and His voice as the sound of many waters" (verses 14, 15). "Whatsoever ye do, do it heartily, as to the Lord, and not unto men" (Col. iii, 23): observe the solemn motive given for enforcing this solemn precept: "Knowing that of the Lord ye shall receive the reward of the inheritance: for ye serve the Lord Christ. But he that doeth wrong *shall receive for* the *wrong* which he hath done: and there is *no* respect of persons" (verses 24 and 25): that some will be "*ashamed before Him*" in that Day is clear from I John ii, 28. May the Lord enable both writer and reader to live his life more and more with the judgment seat of Christ before him.

CHAPTER FORTY-ONE

Dissuasives From Judging Others

" For with what judgment ye judge, ye shall be judged : and with what measure ye mete, it shall be measured to you again. And why beholdest thou the mote that is in thy brother's eye, but considerest not the beam that is in thine own eye ? Or how wilt thou say to thy brother, Let me pull out the mote out of thine eye ; and, behold, a beam is in thine own eye ? " (Matt. vii, 2-4.)

Two chapters have already been devoted to the opening verse of Matthew vii. Following our usual custom we first dealt with it in a topical manner. There is now so much confusion and misunderstanding of what is meant by that prohibition " Judge not " that we felt it was necessary to show at length what is *not* there forbidden and then point out what *is* reprehended, seeking to set before the reader the fact that God does not forbid us making use of the critical faculty with which He has endowed us, but rather that we are required to exert it and form an estimate of whatever we meet with in the path of duty—otherwise, how else shall we escape being deceived by false appearances and imposed upon by every impostor we meet? On the other hand, there are many forms of unlawfully judging others, against which we must be much on our guard, the principal of which we sought to describe. Second, we endeavoured to explain the first reason by which Christ enforced this prohibition— " that ye be not judged." This is a far more solemn dissuasive than is commonly believed: referring not so much to the treatment we shall receive from our fellows, but of *the Divine* disapproval at the judgment seat of Christ.

" For with what judgment ye judge, ye shall be judged: and with what measure ye mete, it shall be measured to you again " (verse 2). These words contain an amplification of the dissuasive employed by our Lord against unlawful judging at the close of the preceding verse. They warn us that there is One above whose eye is ever upon us and His ear open to every word we utter. If that solemn fact were more seriously laid to heart by us, it would act as a powerful restraint upon us. If we add to that weighty consideration the yet more awe-inspiring truth that we shall yet have to render an account unto God and that His dealings with us in that Day will be regulated by how we have dealt with our fellows, well may we take heed to our ways. "Your judging of others shall afford materials for your being judged, and the measure we have dealt out to others shall be employed, in part, as the ground of determining what measure shall be awarded us. It is just as if our Lord had said, Judging is a serious

matter, for it brings after it a fearfully important consequence"
(John Brown).

Though the Christian stands in a radically and vitally different
relation to God than the reprobate, yet both the regenerate and the
unregenerate are alike the subjects of His righteous government,
and He will no more wink at the sins of the one than He will at the
sins of the other. True, the believer does not and will not suffer the
penal consequences of his sins, for those were visited upon his
gracious Substitute. True he will not have to answer for any of the
sins he committed in the days of his unregeneracy, for they have all
been "blotted out" by the precious blood of the Lamb and
removed from before the face of God "as far as the east is from the
west." Nor do we believe that those sins committed after he became
a Christian, and which he has truly repented of and confessed to
God, will come up before him at the judgment seat of Christ, for
they are "forgiven" and from their unrighteousness he is "cleansed '
(I John i, 9). Nevertheless, it seems clear to us from Scripture that
those sins which the Christian has *not* repented of and confessed,
and those wrongs against his brethren which are not put right in
this life, must be reviewed and put right in the Day to come.

"For with what judgment ye judge, ye shall be judged: and with
what measure ye mete, it shall be measured to you again." Surely
these words of Christ are very far from conveying the idea that His
people may unlawfully judge others without fear of any unpleasant
consequences attending such a course of conduct: that they may
unjustly, uncharitably and unmercifully pass judgment on their
fellows, yea, upon their brethren, and then console themselves that
they will not be called upon to give an account of such reprehensible
behaviour in the Day of Judgment. The fallacy of such a concept
should at once appear in the light of all that is revealed of the
Divine character. It is not so much a matter of appealing to specific
statements of Holy Writ, as it is of bearing in mind the general
Analogy of Faith: the ineffable holiness of God, the uniform dealings of Him who is no respecter of persons, the One whose throne
is founded upon justice and judgment. It is the basic and broad
principles of the Divine government which enable us to envisage
its particular exercise and application to any given case.

In all of God's dealings with His people grace and righteousness
are outstandingly manifested, and never one without the other. It is
by grace they are saved, yet that very salvation is the proof of Christ's
having satisfied every demand of Divine righteousness in their
behalf. Though our God be "the God of all grace" (I Peter v, 10),
yet His grace reigns and is ever exercised toward us "through
righteousness" (Romans v, 21) and never at the expense of it. Why
then should it be thought strange if *both* the righteousness and the
grace of God should be displayed when He deals with His own
people at the judgment seat of Christ? While it be blessedly true
that "grace" will be brought to us "at the revelation [second

coming] of Jesus Christ" (I Peter i, 13), yet will not the dark background of sin be needed in order that grace may shine forth the more illustriously? If the believer is confronted with his unrepented sins, will he not then perceive as never before that doom which he justly deserves and marvel at the grace which delivers him from such a doom? If his sins be *not* brought up then, what need would there be that "he may find *mercy* of the Lord in *that* Day" (II Tim. i, 18)!

In view of what has been said above it may be replied, But does not God visit upon His wayward people the governmental consequences of their sins in *this* life? Are they not made to reap here what they have sown? If they are harsh in their judgment of others does not the overruling and righteous hand of God so order things that they meet with similar treatment at the hands of their fellows? And even if that be not always the case, yet does not retribution smite them in their conscience, so that their peace is marred and their joy greatly diminished? Against this we have nothing further to say, except that God in His sovereignty may deal more gently with one than with another offender. But what we would point out is that there is nothing whatever said in this passage (nor, so far as we are aware, in any other) that the judgment which Christ announces as coming upon the offender is one that is *limited* to this life, and where He has not so qualified it, we dare not.

In reply to our last remark it may be asked what Scriptures we have which warrant the idea that the *sins* of believers are to be dealt with (or as we would prefer to express it " be reviewed and righted ") in the Day to come. Answer: In addition to those alluded to at the close of the preceding article we would cite, " I charge thee therefore before God, and the Lord Jesus Christ, who shall judge the quick and the dead at His appearing and His kingdom; Preach the word; be instant in season, out of season " (II Tim. iv, 1, 2). In this passage the apostle is urging Timothy to persevere in the work to which he had been called, warning him that the time would come when sound doctrine would be objectionable to the hearers of it, when they should turn away their ears from the Truth unto fables: nevertheless, says Paul, "But watch thou in all things, endure afflictions" (verses 3-5). That pressing injunction was enforced by the solemn consideration brought before him at the beginning of the chapter: the living and the dead should be *judged* at the appearing of his Master. But how could that judgment be a powerful persuasive unto fidelity and diligence unless his ministry was to be thoroughly *reviewed* in that Day? Wherein lay its *solemnity* unless he would have to give a full account of his stewardship?

"So speak ye and so do as they that shall be judged by the law of liberty" (James ii, 12). This is a most weighty and solemn exhortation, one which professing Christians of this heedless generation need seriously and honestly to ponder. The "Law of Liberty" is a Divine appellation of the Moral Law (the ten commandments), as is made unmistakably clear by the immediate context. In verse 9 believers are warned that if they have "respect to persons," that is, cherish and exercise a spirit of partiality, esteeming the wealthy member of the church more highly than the poorer ones (see verses 1-5), they are guilty of *sin*, being " convinced [brought in guilty] of the Law as transgressors," for the Law requires us to love our neighbour as ourselves. Those who committed this offence might deem it a trivial one, far less heinous than adultery or murder; so the apostle reminds his readers that the Law is a unit and its authority uniform, and therefore to break any part of it brings in the transgressor as guilty of breaking it as a whole (verses 10, 11).

From what had been affirmed in verses 9-11 the apostle draws a seasonable exhortation, one which would be really startling unto many today if they pondered and believed it: the Lord's people are bidden to conduct their lives now in the realization that they are yet to be *judged by the Law*, they should order their speeches and actions in the light of the Day to come if they would then survive the test of the Law. So far from the Christian having nothing to do with the Law, he is yet going to be examined by it, as to how near or how far short his behaviour has come in meeting its requirements. For though believers have been delivered from the Law as a covenant of works, yet it is still their rule of conduct; though they have been freed from its terrors (its curse), they have not been freed from its requirements—obedience. To unbelievers that Law is a Law of bondage and death, but to those who have by grace been made partakers of the nature of the Lawgiver it is one of freedom and life: said David "I will walk at *liberty: for* I seek Thy *precepts"* (Psalm cxix, 45).

Though the Law be one of liberty, it is not one of licence: so far from it, the Law will be *the rule* of the Christian's *judgment* and therefore is he bidden so to order his speech and conduct that he may endure its trial in the Day to come. Solemn indeed is it to know that our speeches, as well as our actions, shall come under the judicature of God. Still more solemn is the next verse: " For he shall have judgment without mercy, that hath shewed no mercy; and mercy rejoiceth against judgment" (James ii, 13). Those who have dealt unmercifully with others shall find no mercy with God, but they who have acted leniently and charitably shall then receive fulfilment of that promise " Blessed are the merciful: for they shall obtain mercy" (Matt. v, 7)—their having dealt mercifully with their fellows is *not the cause* why God will then extend mercy towards them but is the *evidence* they *will* receive it. They who have been merciful will endure the test of the Law, for they shall not only find judgment tempered with mercy but overcome by it, for God will rejoice to deal mercifully with those who imitated Himself.

" For with what judgment ye judge, ye shall be judged; and with what measure ye mete it shall be measured to you again " (verse 2). In this amplification of the preceding sentence it seems to us our

Lord declares that the more rigidly or strictly *we* judge others, the more strictly will *God* yet judge *us*. In other words, the more light we had, the more we expected and demanded that the conduct of others should square with our rule or measure up to the standard of our apprehension, then let us know that God will deal with us accordingly. There will be no room for us to plead ignorance, for we shall be judged by the very light we had and insisted that others should walk according to—compare Luke xii, 47, 48, for an illustration of this principle. As Matthew Henry's commentary says on James iii, 1, "Those who set up themselves for judges and censurers shall receive the greater condemnation. Our judging others will but make our judgment the more strict and severe. Those who are curious to spy into the faults of others and arrogate a power in passing censures upon them, may expect that God will be as extreme in marking what they say and do amiss."

"And why beholdest thou the mote that is in thy brother's eye, but considerest not the beam that is in thine own eye? Or how wilt thou say to thy brother, let me pull out the mote of thine eye; and, behold, a beam is in thine own eye?" (verses 3, 4). These verses contain a second dissuasive from forming unlawful censures upon our brethren. Reduced to its simplest terms the reason may be expressed thus: no one is qualified or fit to censure another while he is himself an even greater offender. One would think this so obvious that there was scarcely need to state it, still less to urge it; yet experience proves that all of us are so corrupted by sin, so prone to act the part of a Pharisee, that we have real need to be warned thereon and to translate the warning into earnest prayer. Unless we take heed of the corruptness of our nature and are constantly on our guard against indulging depravity, breaking forth in this reprehensible and vile form, we shall soon find ourselves guilty of the very species of hypocrisy which our Lord here condemned, yea, it is much to be feared that if we reviewed the past and diligently examined ourselves, not one of us could truthfully claim to be free from this fault.

The first thing taught by this parabolic utterance of Christ's is that sin exerts a *blinding influence*. Most clearly is this evidenced by the unregenerate, for though blind to their own terrible condition they are quick to perceive the faults and failings of others. And regeneration does not free the believer from this evil tendency, for sin still indwells him, and just in proportion as he fails to judge himself unsparingly will he be inclined to censure others. The second thing intimated by Christ's figurative language is that there are degrees of sin, as appears from the "mote" and the "beam," just as when He charged the scribes and Pharisees with straining at a "gnat" and swallowing a "camel" (Matt. xxiii, 34). Not that we may draw the conclusion that any sins are mere trifles, for there can be no such thing as a little sin against a great God, nevertheless there are degress of heinousness and guilt in different transgressions, as is clear from Matthew xi, 23 24; John xix, 11; Hebrews x, 29. The contrast pointed by Christ is between one who allows some lust to prevail over him and yet presumes to criticize another for some infirmity or minor offence.

Our Lord's questions "Why seest thou the mote?" and "How sayest thou to thy brother, Let me pull out" have the force of, With what face, with what honesty, can you act thus? Upon what ground do you set up yourself as a scrutinizer and critic of the actions of others? Does such a course of procedure issue from a good conscience? Here our Lord teaches us that our deeds and words, yea, our very thoughts also, must be conceived and uttered on a good ground and in a proper manner. In Ecclesiastes v, 1, 2, we are forbidden to speak rashly in the house of prayer or utter anything which has not been duly weighed, and here our Saviour extends this rule to every thought of our hearts and word of our mouths which concern our brethren. For by "brother" here we understand a fellow member of the Household of Faith, which is what makes Christ's admonition the more solemn and searching, for it is a far more serious offence to wrong a brother or sister in Christ than a worldling: in wounding the former we are wounding Christ Himself (Acts ix, 1, 4).

"And why beholdest thou the mote that is in thy brother's eye?" The majority of the commentators take the view that "brother" here has merely the force of "neighbour," for they consider it is quite inadmissible to regard as truly regenerate one whom our Lord designates a "hypocrite": whatever difficulty that may raise we shall deal with it when we come to verse 5. To us it seems clear that it is two Christians who are in view, from the circumstance that the "eye" mentioned is not altogether blind (which is spiritually the case with the regenerate) but merely contains some foreign substance which needs removing. Another thing suggested by the figure used by our Lord on this occasion is that the "eye" (the understanding or faculty of spiritual discernment) may be quite sound in itself though temporarily damaged or put out of action by the presence of an intruding particle: hence there is a tacit but real warning for us against being too ready to denounce the *inward condition* of a brother simply because of some *outward act*, which may be but the temporary result of neglect in watching and prayer, followed by a temptation from without.

The first thing which Christ here reprehends is what we may term the deliberateness and partiality of such conduct. The offender is pictured as one who is definitely on the lookout for blemishes in his brother, fixing his gaze on such: "why *beholdest* thou the mote that is in thy brother's eye?" has the force of, How can you justify this wretched practice of so eagerly searching for and so fixedly concentrating upon his infirmities?—for a "mote" in the eye of another could only be detected by one who was watching him very closely. It is as though he is determined to overlook all that is *good* in his brother, fixing his unfriendly gaze upon the tiniest fault he can discern in him. This is indeed a deplorable state of soul to get into, one which we require to watch diligently and pray earnestly against. To overlook all that which the Spirit has wrought in another and to be occupied only with that which is of the flesh is displeasing to God, unfair to the brother, and highly injurious to our own good.

Far worse is such a course of conduct when we ourselves are guilty of much greater sins than the one we condemn in our brother, which is the principal thing which Christ is here condemning. The glaring impropriety of such a wretched procedure must at once be apparent to all fair-minded people. What right have I to complain at a tiny mote in another's eye when I suffer a beam to remain in my own? To appear so very solicitous about the welfare of a brother as to be concerned over his minutest failings and anxious to correct his slightest faults, while I completely disregard my own sad and far worse state, is nothing but a species of downright hypocrisy. Thus it was with the scribes and Pharisees, who condemned Christ for healing the sick on the Sabbath and censured His disciples for plucking ears of corn on that day to appease their hunger and for eating with "unwashen hands," yet themselves were guilty of encouraging men to hold their parents in contempt. But again we must remind ourselves that we too are Pharisees by nature, and so deeply corrupted are our hearts and so prone to this sin of rashly judging others that nothing but Divine grace—definitely and daily sought by us—can preserve us from the committal thereof.

CHAPTER FORTY-TWO

Helping Erring Brethren

"Thou hypocrite, first cast out the beam out of thine own eye; and then shalt thou see clearly to cast out the mote out of thy brother's eye." (Matt. vii, 5.)

THE rule of conduct which the Word of God sets before us contains far more than a series of negative prohibitions, forbidding certain things: it also marks out a path to be walked in, setting forth positive directions of action. To be preserved from sinning is good, but to be impelled unto practical holiness is far better, the one being the means of the other. It is not sufficient for the branches of the vine to be kept free from blight and pests: they must produce fruit if they are to justify their existence. It is not enough for a garden to be clear of weeds: it must yield healthy vegetables if it is to be of service to its owner. So of the Christian: "be not overcome of evil" is only the first part of the duty laid upon him—"but overcome evil with good" (Romans xii, 21) is what is especially required of us. An illustration of this important principle, so frequently inculcated by Christ and His apostles, appears in the passage now before us. Our Lord did not stop short by merely condemning the evil habit of unlawfully judging our brethren, but went on to give instructions as to how we should deal with those needing assistance, and particularly how we must deal with *ourselves* if we are to be qualified for a ministry of helpfulness unto others.

From what our Lord has said in the opening verses of Matthew vii it might possibly be concluded that it is not permissible for us to admonish a brother or seek the amendment of his fault, yet further reflection should show us that that inference is entirely erroneous. Christ has plainly warned us, "Think not that I am come to destroy the law, or the prophets: I am not come to destroy, but to fulfil" (Matt. v, 17)—"fulfil" it not only in His mediatorial and atoning work, but in His teachings and by inspiring His followers to act according to the requirements of the Law (Romans iii, 31; vii, 22). Now the Law had expressly enjoined, "Thou shalt not hate thy brother in thine heart: thou shalt in any wise rebuke thy neighbour, and not suffer sin upon him" (Lev. xix, 17), and therefore it must not be supposed for a moment that there was anything in the teaching of Christ which set aside that statute. It cannot be insisted upon too strongly today that there is not the slightest conflict between the Moral Law and the Gospel, but rather the most perfect harmony. It cannot be otherwise, since the Author of the one is equally the Author of the other, and He "changeth not."

One of the most disastrous errors and follies of many preachers and " Bible teachers " fifty years ago, the terrible effects of which are now spread before those who have eyes to see, was their idea that during the Old Testament era God's people were under the stern regime of Law unrelieved by Divine grace, and that Christ came here to set aside that harsh regime and bring in a much milder dispensation. Not so: Christ came here to " magnify the law, and make it honourable " (Isaiah xlii, 21). That Law needed no apology and no amendment, for it is " holy and just and good," being " spiritual " (Romans vii, 12, 14). The sum of its requirements is that we love the Lord our God with all our heart, mind and strength and our neighbour as ourself: and every requirement of the Moral Law is enforced in the precepts of the Gospel. The great difference between the Mosaic and the Chistian dispensations lies not in any change in the rule of conduct set before us, but in the more effectual motives by which that rule is now enforced and the Divine enablement which is now vouchsafed. As a nation Israel was unregenerate and therefore the Law was " weak through the flesh " (Romans viii, 3); but Christians have received the spirit of " power " (II Tim. i, 6) and a holy nature which delights in the Law.

" Thou shalt not hate thy brother in thine heart: thou shalt in any wise rebuke thy neighbour, and not suffer sin upon him " (Lev. xix, 17). How different is the tenor of that from the maudlin sentimentality of this effeminate generation. Nowadays, one who seeks to be faithful to the standard of holiness and to his brethren is, in the vast majority of instances, regarded as " lacking in love." People who speak thus have no idea of what spiritual love is. Spiritual love is no sickly sentiment but a holy principle. God is love, yet that prevents Him not from using the rod on His children when they require it, but rather moves Him to employ it. That parent who follows the line of least resistance, allowing the children to do as they please and never chastising them for their faults, is lacking in love towards his offspring; but he who truly seeks their good, lays aside his own feelings and inflicts corporal punishment when it is needed, is the father who evidences the most love. Genuine love is faithful, sets aside one's own interests and feelings, and ever seeks to promote the well-being of the object of it.

Thus should it be between Christian brethren; thus it *must* be if obedience is rendered to the Divine precepts. It is not *love* which ignores a brother's failings, which refuses to perform the unpleasant duty of seeking an amendment in his ways. No, it is a species of *hatred*, as Leviticus xix, 17, plainly intimates, for there is no third quality between love and hatred, as there is no third alternative between right and wrong. If I really have my brother's welfare at heart, then love itself requires that I wink not at his sins, but rather endeavour to save him from them—just as much as it would demand me warning him when I perceive the first wisp of smoke issuing from one of his windows: why wait till his house be half burned down before giving the alarm? Furthermore, to ignore the sins of one with whom I am intimate makes me (in some measure at least) a "partaker of them" (I Tim. v, 22), as is intimated by the alternative rendering of the last clause of Leviticus xix, 17: "that thou bear not sin for him" (margin).

There was therefore nothing in Christ's teaching in Matthew vii which in any wise conflicted with Leviticus xix, 17, but rather that which threw light thereon. It was not the act of admonishing a brother which He here forbade, but the wrong manner in which it may be done. This is clear from the verse at which we have now arrived: "Thou hypocrite, first cast out the beam out of thine own eye; and then shalt thou see clearly to cast out the beam out of thy brother's eye." Here our Lord makes known the course which we must follow if we are to be of real help to those in whose case the old saying is likely to prove true, "a stitch in time saves nine"— helping to correct a man's fault often saves from having to go to him about a much graver offence. But even here, the removing of a tiny particle from the eye of another is not one which any careless hand can successfully undertake, rather will such a hand irritate the other's eye and make bad matters worse.

First a word needs to be said on the epithet used by Christ on this occasion. It looks back to the case described in verses 3 and 4, where this evil habit of rashly censuring others, to which we are all so prone, is represented as one steadily fixing his unfriendly gaze upon the mote that is in his brother's eye while indifferent to the beam which is in his own—undertaking to correct some lesser fault in him while allowing a much graver sin in himself. What else could our holy Lord designate such a despicable person but a "hypocrite," that is, the actor of a part, one pretending to be very zealous as to the requirements of holiness while himself living in neglect of and violating its plainest dictates? Uncompromising faithfulness would not permit of Christ's using any milder term. Yet there is no more reason why we should conclude from this word that the one to whom it is applied was unregenerate than from His declaring to Peter "thou art an offence to Me" (Matt. xvi, 23) or His terming two of His disciples "fools" (Luke xxiv, 25).

Had the one whom our Lord here addressed been an unregenerate soul, not only would He have refrained from designating the one whom He censured as "a brother," but we can scarcely conceive of Him going to the pains of instructing one who was still dead in trespasses and sins what he must first do in order that he might "*see clearly* to cast out the mote out of his brother's eye." No, it appears to us that the Lord designated this careless believer who failed to judge himself unsparingly (though seeking to correct another) a "hypocrite" to express His detestation of such conduct, to let us know how it appears in *His* eyes, and therefore to bring home to our hearts the gravity of a practice which we are so ready to tolerate in ourselves. Nothing is more hateful to God than play-acting, and we are guilty of this very thing when we pose as faithful guardians of our brother's interests while we are faithless in our personal dealings with God Himself; while nothing is more pleasing in His sight than honesty and sincerity, which is the opposite of hypocrisy.

"First cast out the beam out of thine own eye" means be faithful in dealing with yourself, unsparingly judging yourself before God, putting away out of your heart and life whatsoever you know to be displeasing unto Him. This is the grand remedy for the disease of unlawfully judging others, as it is the chief requirement if you are to be of any real help in ministering to your erring brethren. Not only is it utterly incongruous for one who is allowing and indulging in some flagrant lust to pose as being grieved over some infirmity in another, but one who is almost totally blinded spiritu-ally (by arrogance and hypocrisy) is utterly incapable of performing such a difficult and delicate operation as the removal of a mote from his brother's eye: one who is under the influence of any gross sin not only has his spiritual discernment obscured, but his spiritual sensibilities are so blunted that he is unable to sympathize with a suffering one: such a one is not only unfit to judge others, but thoroughly disqualified as a critic and censor of their minor failings.

Casting the beam out of my own eye signifies unqualified judging of myself before God (I Cor. xi, 21). My first responsibility is to diligently examine my own heart, carefully consider my own ways, critically measure myself by the unerring standard of Scripture and honestly and constantly confess my many sins to God (Lam. iii, 40). If I am sincerely desirous of pleasing God in all things, I shall beg Him to show me what there is in my own life which is displeasing to Him (Psalm cxxxix, 23, 24). If I truly long to show forth His praises (I Peter ii, 9), I shall not excuse my fleshly conduct, but shall condemn it and earnestly seek grace to forsake the same. And if I genuinely wish to be of real spiritual help unto my erring brethren, I shall rigidly purge myself of everything which would defeat such efforts. Only as I am unflinchingly faithful with myself can I hope to be of any assistance to others. Clear vision is needed to locate and remove a "mote" from the eye of another, and clear vision comes only from my own close walking with Him who is light (Psalm xxxvi, 9; John viii, 12). How much longer are we going to suffer the beam in our own eye?

One principal reason why we are so slow in casting the beam out of our own eye is that we fail to "perceive" it, as is intimated by Christ in verse 3. Obviously this does not mean that we are totally unaware of its presence, but rather that we fail to make conscience of the same. The expression "perceive it not" has reference to an act of the mind which follows upon the bare sight of anything, consisting of serious consideration and prolonged meditation. It is the word used in "consider the lilies" of the field (Luke xii, 27): that is, not only look upon them but ponder them over in your mind. It is the word used in "a man that *beholdeth* his natural face in a glass" (James i, 23): that is, who gazes steadily at it and considers each feature. Thus, "perceive not" in Matthew vii, 3, means a failure to consider and regard attentively. If we are truly to "perceive" the beam in our own eye, with the purpose of casting it out, we must make conscience of the same, seriously considering its heinousness in God's sight, labouring to have our hearts affected by it.

It should be obvious that we shall never voluntarily and deliberately eject from our hearts and lives that which we still love and cherish, and therefore we must labour to have our hearts so affected by our lusts and sins that we shall sorrow over and hate them. The converse of this is that awful deadness of soul and security in sin, which if undisturbed is certain to lead to the most fearful if not fatal consequences. Proof of this appears in the case of the antediluvians, of whom Christ declared they "knew not until the flood came and took them all away" (Matt. xxiv, 29): though they may have had some consciousness of their carnality and madness, yet they thought not seriously thereon, and so remained secure in their wickedness. A similar state of affairs existed in Israel in the days of Jeremiah: the Lord complained that the people made no conscience of their sins, remaining secure therein: "No man repented him of his wickedness, saying, What have I done?" (viii, 6). Nothing is more serious and fatal than to commit sins and refuse to be humbled by them, but instead to remain unconcerned. Sins must be laid to heart and sorrowed over before they will be forsaken and expelled.

In order to be helpful at this point, it is necessary to be explicit, so let us mention one or two things which are so often a "beam" in the eyes of God's people. First, *hypocrisy*, which whenever it dominates the heart prevents all spiritual growth and fruit. Christians are guilty of allowing this vile weed to flourish far more than they are aware of. This is the case where we are more anxious to please men than the Lord; where we are more diligent in seeking to perform the external requirements of the first table of the Law than of the second—note how Christ pressed the commandment of the *second* table on the rich young ruler (Luke xviii, 20)—where we are more careful to please God in the outward action than we are with the strength of our hearts. Another great "beam" is *spiritual pride*, which also is most abhorrent unto Him with whom we have to do. This it is which makes us pleased with ourselves, self-confident, and to look down upon others. It is an inward poison which prevents the health of grace within. It is that which marks Laodiceans (Rev. iii, 17). Finally, any particular besetting sin or lust which is not resisted and mortified soon assumes the proportions of a "beam" and effectually blinds our judgment.

An important practical question which needs to be answered at this stage is, What course should be followed in order that we may feel *the weight* of these "beams" pressing upon our hearts? Surely it must be by counteracting that tendency within us to regard our sins lightly, to look upon our own constitutional faults as mere "motes,' and that must be done by faithfully examining them in the light of God's Word. More particularly we ought to compare the sins of which we are guilty with the original transgression of Adam. Are we not tolerating things in our hearts and lives which are even greater evils than Adam's eating of the forbidden fruit considered in the act? Yet by that sin he not only brought death upon himself, but also upon all his posterity! Again, if we would perceive and feel the exceeding sinfulness of our sins we must view them in the light of Calvary, and observe the fearful price which had to be paid for the atonement of them. Finally, we must contemplate the heinousness and guilt of our sins in view of the lake of fire and brimstone, for nothing short of everlasting suffering is what they deserve.

It is only as we feel the dreadful weight of our sins and their enormity in the sight of the Holy One that we shall really cry out, " Hide Thy face from my sins and blot out all mine iniquities. Create in me a clean heart, O God, and renew a right spirit within me " (Psalm li, 9, 10). But it is not sufficient that we sorrow over our sins and seek God's forgiveness of them: we must labour to break them off and amend our evil ways, striving by all means that sin may be weakened in us more and more. It is the one who confesses and forsakes his sins who finds mercy (Prov. xxviii, 13): on the other hand, " If I regard iniquity in my heart the Lord will not hear me " (Psalm lxvi, 18). Unless I cast the beam out of my own eye, how can I attend to the mote in another's? Unless I disallow and mortify my lusts I am totally disqualified to rebuke sin in my brother. "Create in me a clean heart, O God. . . . *Then* will I teach transgressors Thy ways " (Psalm li, 10, 13); *when* thou art converted, [recovered] strengthen thy brethren " (Luke xxii, 32)!

" And then shalt thou see clearly to cast out the mote out of thy brother's eye." In order to remove a " mote " from another's eye one must be *close to him*! Therein Christ intimates who are the ones we should seek to help by correcting their faults, namely those who are near to us and not strangers: those who are members of our own family, intimate friends, and those with whom we are in close church fellowship. Much harm has been done through ignoring this obvious and simple rule. My responsibility is first unto myself, then unto those bearing intimate ties: alas, not only do many think highly of themselves, but they allow sentiment to hinder faithful dealings with those dear unto them. But this necessity of closeness to one from whose eye I would remove a mote not only connotes a nearness of relationship, but also *a moral nearness,* winning a place in his affections and esteem; I cannot get close to another while standing on a lofty pedestal of assumed self-superiority!

No service calls for more prayer, delicacy of feeling, spiritual wisdom and meekness, than does this one. The motive impelling it must be love: the end in view the glory of God: our aim the recovery of an erring one. The eye is the most sensitive organ of the body and the most easily damaged. A steady and gentle hand is required to extract the foreign substance from it. Care should be taken in selecting the *best time* to approach an erring brother, so that the reproof is likely to be effectual: before Abigail admonished her husband for his churlish conduct unto David, she waited till the wine had gone out of his head (I Sam. xxv, 36, 37)—never correct one while he is in a towering rage. The nature of the fault in the erring one must be weighed: whether it proceed from human frailty or be some deliberate and high-handed sin, if we are to speak to him " a word in season." Pains should be taken to make him see that he *is* at fault, that he has acted contrary to God's Word, for we are required to reprove and rebuke " with all longsuffering *and doctrine* " (II Tim. iv, 2) and thereby deliver the admonition not in our own name but in *God's*.

" Brethren, if a man be overtaken in a fault, ye which are spiritual, restore such an one in the spirit of meekness; considering thyself, lest thou also be tempted " (Gal. vi, 1). Only he who is " spiritual "—who allows not sin in himself, walks softly with God— is fit to approach a fellow believer for this necessary and difficult task. We are to remember that we are so united together in one family and fellowship that the wrongdoing of one concerns all, and that it is in the interests of the whole household of faith to seek the restoration of the erring one. Such restoration can only be performed " in the spirit of meekness "—gentleness and lowliness of heart—for harshness and arrogance repel, not win. Whatever fault he has committed, let us not forget that but for Divine grace we too would fall in the same way, as we acknowledge to God whenever we pray " lead *us* not into temptation." What we say to him must not only be " a word in season " but " *fitly* spoken " (Prov. xxv, 11)!

Finally, it should be pointed out that if we are to remove the mote from another's eye *he* must be *willing* for us to do so—any spirit of resistance makes the operation impossible. The very figure used by Christ here plainly connotes that each of us should freely submit ourselves to brotherly correction—" submitting yourselves one to another in the fear of God " (Eph. v, 21). It is very reprehensible and evidences a sad state of soul when we resent and oppose the faithful admonitions of our Christian friends, like the Israelite said to Moses when he reproved him, " Who made thee a prince and judge over us?" (Exodus ii, 14). " Poverty and shame shall be to him that refuseth instruction: but he that regardeth reproof shall be honoured " (Prov. xiii, 18). " He that refuseth instruction despiseth his own soul: but he that heareth reproof getteth understanding " (Prov. xv, 32). " It is better to hear the rebuke of the wise than for a man to hear the song of fools " (Eccles. vii, 5): though the song of fools may be more *pleasant* to our ears, yet the reproofs of the wise are more *profitable* to our souls, if we heed the same.

CHAPTER FORTY-THREE

Unlawful Liberality

" Give not that which is holy unto the dogs, neither cast ye your pearls before swine, lest they trample them under their feet, and turn again and rend you." (Matt. vii, 6.)

OUR present verse brings before us the seventh and shortest division of our Lord's Sermon, for it manifestly treats of a different branch of the Truth from any which has been dealt with in the previous sections. Though Christ's language here be figurative (as so often in this address), it is far from being ambiguous, yet its force and purport were probably more easily perceived by His immediate audience than by us. With few exceptions it is the state of our hearts rather than the obscurity of its language which prevents our understanding the meaning of some portion in Holy Writ. Such is certainly the case here. It is greatly to be feared that there are many in Christendom today who are much averse from heeding this Divine precept, and therefore they pretend it is hard to be understood. None so blind as those who refuse to see. How many smug professors in the churches today would be highly offended if the minister dealt with them in the same way as the Saviour did with the Canaanitish women, telling them, " It is not meet to take the children's bread and to cast it to *dogs*" (Matt. xv, 26). Such discrimination does not at all suit this latitudinarian age.

" Give not that which is holy unto the dogs, neither cast ye your pearls before swine, lest they trample them under their feet, and turn again and rend you" (Matt. vii, 6). It must be admitted that most of the commentators appear to have experienced difficulty with this verse, not because they found its terms obscure, but in the fixing of their precise reference. It was not its interpretation which troubled them so much as its application. The method we propose to follow in our exposition of it is the following. First, to ascertain its precise relation to the context. Second, to ponder it in the light of our Lord's own example, for most assuredly He ever practised what He preached, and as we are called upon to " follow His steps " it is most necessary for us to examine the path He trod—here as everywhere. Third, to point out its application to the ministers of Christ, for it enunciates an important rule to regulate them in their dispensation of the Word. And fourth, to show how this rule applies to the private Christian. May the Spirit of Truth deign to guide our pen.

In examining the relation of our text to the context, we must take into account both its more remote and nearer context. As we have so often pointed out in this series of expositions, the principal key which unlocks to us the contents of this Sermon is found in our Lord's words, "Think not that I am come to destroy the law, or the prophets: I am not come to destroy, but to fulfil" (v, 17). It therefore behoves us to inquire, What was the teaching of the Law and the prophets concerning the subject treated of in our text? The first thing we learn there is that under the Law "dogs" and "swine" were *unclean and unholy* animals, the Israelites being prohibited from using them either for food or as sacrifices unto God, yea, they were not permitted to bring "the price of a dog [the money from selling one] into the house of the Lord" (Deut. xxiii, 18). Second, we should observe that the term "dog" was applied to persons of worthless character (I Samuel xvii, 43; II Samuel xvi, 9; II Kings viii, 13; etc.).

The sons of Aaron were required to "put difference between holy and unholy, and between clean and unclean" (Lev. x, 10), to maintain the line of demarcation which God had drawn between the sacred and the profane. They were commanded to exclude the heathen from participating in any of the religious privileges of God's covenant people (Deut. xxiii, 3). In the days of Israel's degeneracy God complained that "her priests have violated My Law and have profaned Mine holy things: they have *put no difference* between the holy and profane, neither have they shewed difference between the unclean and the clean" (Ezek. xxii, 26): they had dealt with a latitude or "liberality" such as God had expressly forbidden. He had ordered that His priests should "teach My people the difference between the holy and profane, and cause them to discern between the unclean and the clean" (Ezek. xliv, 23). A most discriminating ministry was appointed unto Jeremiah, for the Lord required him to "take forth the precious from the vile" (xv, 19): that is, draw the line between the godly and ungodly, addressing to each their distinctive and needed message. To Malachi it was promised, "Then shall ye return, and discern between the righteous and the wicked, between him that serveth God and him that serveth Him not" (iii, 18).

Now, says Christ, "Think not that I am come to destroy the law, or the prophets." I have received no commission from My Father to break down the barriers He has erected, to obliterate the lines He has drawn. Rather am I come "to fulfil" (Matt. v, 17): to magnify the Law and render it honourable, to vindicate the prophets and make good their declarations. I am come to bring in the substance for the shadow, the reality for the typical, the vital for the ceremonial. I too shall discriminate between the clean and the unclean and place a fence between the holy and the unholy. Did Moses prohibit the people of God from intermarrying with idolators? Did he exclude the heathen from the sacred temple? Did he declare that the food of the priestly family was "most holy"

(Lev. x, 12-15) and their exclusive portion or property? Then I likewise command you, "Give not that which is holy unto the dogs, neither cast ye your pearls before swine."

Coming now to the closer context. Is there not clearly a link between our present text and what immediately precedes it? Did not Christ here intimate that something more than clear vision and a kind and steady hand was required if we are to succeed in removing a "mote" from another's eye? As we pointed out at the close of the previous chapter, the one with an injured eye must be agreeable to submit if you are to help him; the one at fault be willing to receive an admonition. But many are not so: so far from it; they will resent your well-meant overtures and revile you for them—treading your admonitions under their feet and venting their fury upon you. "Speak not in the ears of a fool, for he will despise the wisdom of thy words" (Prov. xxiii, 9). Thus, having shown *how* to admonish, the Saviour now makes known *who* are to be admonished, or rather who are *not* to be. To reprove a son of Belial is wasted breath (I Samuel xxv, 17).

In verse 5 the Lord had shown how an erring "brother" is to be dealt with—meekly and gently: the rebuke is to be given in a loving and humble spirit. But here in verse 6 Christ intimates that love must discriminate: all are not "brethren" and will not suffer a rebuke, no matter how graciously given. It is not sufficient then that we take care to be spiritually qualified for reproving another, but we must seek to make sure that there is some probability at least that our efforts will not be worse than lost upon the one we desire to help. Thus, after prohibiting evil-minded censures, Christ here warns against imprudent ones. "Reprove not a scorner lest he hate thee" (Prov. ix, 8). Here, then, is a necessary caution: zeal must be directed by knowledge and holy prudence. Not every person is a fit subject for reproof. Unreasonable men will scoff at the mildest criticism of their evil ways, and to quote Scripture to them only incites them to blasphemy and is casting pearls before swine.

But we may discover a further connection between our text and the verses preceding. In seeking to guard against hasty and harsh judgments we must also beware of abusing grace. If on the one hand we should watch against unjust and unmerciful censuring, on the other we must not be guilty of judging laxly and loosely. There are not only the "sheep" of Christ, but the "dogs" and "swine" of the world, and they are to be treated as such. When an open worldling or obviously carnal person applies for church membership, it would be quite wrong to silence God-fearing objectors with "Judge not, lest ye be judged." Grace must not be allowed to override the requirements of holiness so that the unclean are permitted to enjoy those privileges reserved for those who are washed in the blood of the Lamb. It is through failure at this very point, through a false "charity," by refusing to heed this command of Christ, that the grossest of evils have been tolerated in the House of God, until the mystical Babylon is "now a cage of every unclean and hateful bird."

Yet it must not be supposed that our text is to be restricted unto a prohibition against imprudent reproving: rather does it enunciate a *general principle* which is of wide application, for the better perception of which we now turn to ponder it in the light of our Lord's own personal example. A very wide field is here open for investigation, yet we can only now call attention to a few of its most distinctive features. If the reader will examine the four Gospels afresh from this particular angle, he is likely to meet with some surprises and find there the reverse of what the teaching he has imbibed would lead him to expect. For example, would not the ordinary churchgoer of today suppose that the Lord Jesus spent most of His time in preaching the Gospel to the unsaved; that He sought out the unchurched masses, endeavouring to arouse them from their unconcern; that He made it His business to go after the giddy worldling and convince him of the folly of his ways; that He proclaimed the love of God to every soul He could possibly make contact with? Then turn to the first four books of the New Testament and see whether or not this was so.

We do indeed read frequently that Christ taught both in the synagogue and in the temple, yet even there He never so much as once mentioned the love of God to sinners—though He had much to say about the Father's love when He was alone with "His own." He frequently spoke of His approaching death unto His disciples, but where did He ever preach the atonement in the hearing of the multitude? It is true that He spoke often in the open air (though never on the streets!), yet it was to those who *sought unto* Him (Mark ii, 13; Luke vi, 17)—He never pressed His company on them (Mark vii, 17). He spoke many things unto the multitudes in parables, yet the interpretation of them was reserved for God's elect (Matt. xiii, 8, 9, 11, 36). Our Lord was not transfigured before the gaze of the vulgar crowd, but only in the sight of a favoured few. Nor was He seen by the unbelieving world after His resurrection. The grand prophecy of Matthew xxiv and xxv was delivered in the hearing of none but believers. He never cast pearls before swine: even when Pilate *asked Him,* "What is truth?" (John xviii, 37), He did not say, "I am the Truth," nor did He explain to him the way of salvation.

But let us not be mistaken at this point. God forbid that we should be found writing anything which would deter *exercised* souls from seeking Christ, and giving them the impression that they would be unwelcome did they come to Him in their deep distress. Nothing is made plainer in the four Gospels than the glorious fact that the Lord Jesus is accessible to every poor sinner who feels his need of Him and that He is willing and ready to heal his soul. "All that the Father giveth Me shall come to Me; and him that cometh to Me I will in no wise cast out" (John vi, 37) is His own blessed declaration. He declined not an invitation to eat with publicans and sinners, nor did He turn His back upon the leper who sought Him. But what we have directed attention to above is His attitude towards those who *sought him not,* to those who evidenced no interest in Him, to those who opposed Him. Read again the many recorded cases where the Pharisees antagonized Him: is there a single instance where He preached the Gospel to them? So with the Sadducees and lawyers who endeavoured to ensnare Him: He closed their mouths, but He never opened His heart to them or gave that which was holy unto dogs!

Third, our text enunciates an important principle for the minister of Christ to be regulated by—it is to be borne in mind that the first application of this Sermon is to ministers (Matt. v, 1, 2). That rule may be stated thus: *discrimination is to be exercised* when dispensing the Word of God. Nothing is more urgently needed and seldom found today than a discriminating ministry, by which we mean a "taking forth the precious from the vile" (Jer. xv, 19). In our congregations both of those classes are represented: those who are dear to God and those abhorred by Him. Now though you cannot distinguish by *name* yet you can by *character*. When addressing yourself to the people of God you should make it quite plain that the unregenerate have "no part or lot in the matter." When preaching from the Divine promises it is necessary to describe the spiritual marks of those to whom such Divine dainties really belong —to those who are not conformed to this world, who deny themselves, take up their cross and follow Christ. The line of demarcation must be drawn so plainly that each hearer knows to which side of the line he belongs.

The Word of God has to be "rightly divided" (II Tim. ii, 15) if each hearer is to obtain his legitimate portion. When the pulpit seeks to expose the hypocrite care needs to be taken lest Christ's little ones are stumbled, and when the minister seeks to comfort the distressed saints, the cordial must be expressly labelled so that the ungodly are not bolstered up in a false peace. Unless the minister exercises the most prayerful caution, he will be unable to escape that solemn charge, "with lies ye have made the heart of the righteous sad, whom I have not made sad; and strengthened the hands of the wicked, that he should not return from his wicked way, by promising him life" (Ezek. xiii, 22). Again, Matthew vii, 6, is woefully contravened when those with the most barren profession are received into a church fellowship: the "judgment of charity" does not require of us to call darkness light. Laxity is as much an evil as censoriousness. Admitting to the Lord's table open worldlings is a flagrant violation of our text. And how often is it disregarded in "funeral services and sermons"!

It is very necessary that this precept, "Give not that which is holy unto the dogs" should be pressed upon the *rank and file* of God's people. In certain circles it has been taught that as soon as a person has experienced the saving grace of God ·in his heart it is his bounden duty to preach Christ to all his acquaintances, to endeavour to become a "soulwinner," and that if he declines such "personal work" and evangelistic endeavour, it is because he is cold and selfish, indifferent to the eternal welfare of those around him. But where did Christ or any of His apostles bestow such a commission on any young convert? "Come and hear, all ye that *fear God*, and I will declare what He hath done for my soul" (Psalm lxvi, 16). That qualification warns us against publishing the most sacred experiences of our hearts to all and sundry, for the unregenerate have no more capacity to appreciate the sovereign operations of the Spirit than swine have to rate pearls at their true value. But is not the young convert to "witness for Christ"? Assuredly, but how? "Ye should *shew forth* the praises of Him who hath called you out of darkness into His marvellous light" (I Peter ii, 9): a changed life, an unworldly walk, is the most effective "witness" of all! (see Matt. v, 16).

Zeal needs to be tempered with knowledge. The holy things of the Gospel are not to be bandied about indiscriminately: the precious secrets of His love which the Lord has revealed to us are not to be communicated to His enemies. If believers defy this Divinely imposed restriction, they must not be surprised at meeting with insults and incurring the ire of those upon whom they attempt to force the holy mysteries of the faith. Of the Pharisees Christ said, "Let them alone" (Matt. xv, 14), not attempt to convert them from the error of their ways. "Of *some* have compassion, making a difference" (Jude 22): what a discriminating word is that! We are bidden to "Go from the presence of a fool" (Prov. xiv, 7), and not lower our Christian dignity by arguing with him. But are we not bidden to "Be ready always to give an answer to every man that asketh a reason of the hope that is in us"? Yes, when "asked" (cf. Prov. xxii, 21), and then "with meekness and fear" (I Peter iii, 15) and not with bombast and impudence. The epistles of the New Testament are to be read to "holy brethren" (I Thess. v, 27), but we know of no warrant to read them to worldlings.

It has long impressed the writer that that which takes place in the secular sphere is but a shadowing forth of what has first happened in the spiritual realm. For many years past the majority of the preachers jettisoned the Divine Law, and in the utter lawlessness which fills the world today we have the inevitable repercussion. They concentrated on the promises but ignored the precepts, and in their failure to urge upon God's children an obedient walk we have reaped the disobedience and uncontrollableness of the modern child. Women were given the place in the churches which Scripture prohibits (I Cor. xiv, 34), and in consequence a generation of self-assertive "he women" has arisen who ape men in almost everything. Today we have a *plague of dogs*—over three million in Great

Britain—making the night hideous with their howls, befouling the pavements and consuming vast quantities of food, while human beings are strictly rationed. In the cities they have become a curse, and we believe that this is a Divine judgment upon the general disregard of Matthew vii, 6. It is a common sight to behold a child leading about a huge mastiff and silly women accompanied by two or three poodles. "Beware of dogs" (Phil. iii, 2). "For without are dogs" (Rev. xxii, 15)—excluded from the Holy City.

In conclusion let us note the practical instruction hinted by the figure of the "pearls." First, it intimates what we should regard as our *true riches,* namely the contents of God's Word, for they constitute the Christian's precious treasure. "Happy is the man that findeth wisdom and the man that getteth understanding. For the merchandise of it is better than the merchandise of silver and the gain thereof than fine gold. She is more precious than rubies, and all the things thou canst desire are not to be compared unto her" (Prov. iii, 13-15). Second, it intimates wherein we should *content* ourselves in the calamities and casualties of this life. We may lose our health and wealth, our friends and fame, yet this treasure remains. Here is a lamp for the darkest night (Psalm cxix, 105): here is to be found comfort in the sorest affliction (Psalm cxix, 50): here are to be obtained songs for our pilgrimage (Psalm cxix, 54). Third, it intimates how we are to *use* the Word. A person possessed of valuable pearls is at great pains to secure them; how much more so should we be with this Pearl of pearls—storing it in our memories, locking it in our hearts: "Holding the mystery of the faith in a pure conscience" (I Tim. iii, 9). This was David's practice (Psalm cxix, 11), and Mary's (Luke ii, 51): may it be ours too.

CHAPTER FORTY-FOUR

Seeking Grace

" Ask, and it shall be given you; seek, and ye shall find; knock, and it shall be opened unto you ; For every one that asketh receiveth ; and he that seeketh findeth ; and to him that knocketh it shall be opened." (Matt. vii, 7, 8.)

VERSES 7 to 11 contain the eighth division of our Lord's Sermon. Every commentator we have consulted thereon regards the passage as dealing solely with the subject of *prayer*: personally we deem such a view to be an undue narrowing of its scope. While the supplicating of God be undoubtedly the principal duty enjoined therein, it is not the only one. It seems to us that its theme is the seeking supplies of grace to enable the believer to live a spiritual and supernatural life in this world, and though such enablement is to be sought from the throne of grace, yet that does not render needless or exempt the Christian from diligently employing the other means of grace which God has appointed for the blessing of His people. Prayer must not be allowed to induce lethargy in other directions or become a lazy substitute for the putting forth of our energies in other duties. We are called upon to watch as well as pray, to deny self, strive against sin, take unto us the whole armour of God, and fight the good fight of faith.

What has been suggested above concerning the *scope* of our present passage will be the more apparent by viewing it in relation to its whole context. From v, 20, onwards, Christ had presented a standard of moral excellence which is utterly unattainable by mere flesh and blood. He had inculcated one requirement after another, which it lies not in the power of fallen human nature to meet. He had forbidden an opprobrious word, a malignant wish, an impure desire, a revengeful thought. He had enjoined the most unsparing mortification of our dearest members (v, 29, 30). He had commanded the loving of our enemies, the blessing of those who curse us, the doing good unto those who hate us, and the praying for those who despitefully use and persecute us (v, 44). In view of which the Christian may well exclaim, "Who is sufficient for these things?" Such demands of holiness are beyond my feeble strength: yet the Lord *has* made them—what then am I to do?

Coming nearer still to our passage we find that in the opening verses of chapter vii Christ gave two apparently contradictory commands. First, He says, " Judge not, that ye be not judged ": abstain from forming harsh estimates and passing censorious censures on your fellows. Second, "Give not that which is holy unto the dogs":

discriminate sharply between the clean and the unclean, that you may not be guilty of obliterating the line which God has drawn between the righteous and the wicked. But to steer safely between such rocks as these requires not only spiritual strength but spiritual wisdom, such wisdom as the natural man possesses not. What then is the poor believer to do? The Lord here anticipates this difficulty and meets this perplexity. He is well aware that, in our own wisdom and strength, we are incapable of keeping His commands, but He at once reminds us that the things which are ordinarily impossible to men can be made possible to them by God.

Divine assistance is imperative if we are to meet the Divine requirements. The Divine assistance is to be sought prayerfully, believingly, diligently and persistently, and if it be thus sought it will not be sought in vain. It was then for the obtaining of supplies of Divine grace and heavenly strength that our Lord now exhorted and encouraged His disciples. " Ask, and it shall be given you; seek, and ye shall find; knock, and it shall be opened unto you " (vii, 7). In the foregoing chapter Christ had touched upon the subject of prayer in a way of warning, but here He refers to it as the appointed channel for obtaining supplies of grace to obey those precepts which are so contrary to flesh and blood. First He had given instructions concerning the *duty* of prayer, but now He supplies gracious *encouragements* for the exercise of it. Nevertheless, it is clear from the general tenor of scripture that every other legitimate means must be employed if we are to obtain the strength and help we so much need.

" Ask, and it shall be given you." Few texts have been more grossly perverted than this one. Many have regarded it as a sort of blank cheque which anybody, no matter what his state of soul or manner of walk may be, can fill in just as he pleases, and he has only to present the same before the throne of grace and God stands pledged to honour it. Such a travesty of the Truth would not deserve refutation were it not trumpeted about so extensively. James iv, 3, expressly affirms, " Ye ask, and receive not, because *ye ask amiss*." Such are those who seek this world first and then hope to make sure of the world to come. Such are those who beg for mercy but refuse to forsake their sins (Prov. xxviii, 9), who seek salvation in a way of their own devising—by a more flesh-pleasing method than that of the holy Gospel; or who come in their own name in contempt of the appointed Mediator. They " ask amiss " and receive not who make request for what God has not promised, or who seek formally and hypocritically without any deep-felt need of what they ask for.

Thus our text provides the minister of the Gospel with an admirable opportunity for heeding the exhortation of the previous verse and seeing to it that, in his interpretation and application, he refrains from giving that which is holy unto the dogs or casting pearls before swine. " Ask, and it shall be given you " is very far from affording *carte blanche* to all and sundry. It is a supplicating supplies of Divine grace which is here in view, and, moreover, there must be a *right asking* (and not an asking "amiss") if such are to be obtained; but this right asking is impossible for the unregenerate, for not only are they totally incapable of asking in faith, but to seek for Divine grace is diametrically opposed to their very nature and disposition. Grace is the antithesis of sin, a holy principle, and since the natural man is wholly in love with sin, it is impossible that he should have any love for or desire after that which is radically opposed to sin. The thistle cannot bear grapes, nor can a heart at enmity with God pant after conformity to Him.

It needs then to be made unmistakably clear that *right seeking* after grace presupposes *right desires* for it, but the unregenerate are, in the habitual temper of their heart, strangers to all spiritual aspirations. To have genuine desires after the thing and an entire contrariety to it in the whole soul and at the same time is a direct contradiction. To that it may be rejoined, How then will you explain the anomaly of some worldlings having at times an apparently hearty desire after grace, so that they even persuade themselves they sincerely and earnestly long for it? Easily: it is because they are ignorant of the true nature of grace, unaware that it is a *holy* principle, and therefore they have framed a false image of it in their fancies, and for this fictitious "grace"—which makes light of sin, which grants an indulgence for the lusts of the flesh—they *have* a relish, for *it* is thoroughly in accord with their corrupt nature.

Many who sit under antinomian preaching are led to believe that God is willing to save sinners *without* them forsaking their idols, throwing down the weapons of their warfare against Him; without repentance. They know not that salvation is not only a passport to heaven, but that it is a first deliverance from the love and dominion of sin, that the grace of God which brings salvation is a holy principle that effectually teaches its subjects to "*deny* ungodliness and worldly lusts, and to *live* soberly, righteously, and godly in this present world" (Titus ii, 11, 12). Did these deluded people but distinctly apprehend the true character of grace, then their native contrariety thereto would be no longer hid from them. Did not the Pharisees verily believe they loved God and revered His Law? Yet they hated the Son of God, who was the express image of the Father, and came into the world to honour His Law; they must therefore have held *erroneous* notions of God and His Law, as many now do of His grace.

But if we plainly announce that no unregenerate person can lay claim to the promise of our text, will not such teaching take from the poor sinner all motive to pray unto God and do anything else? Such a question betrays either a woeful ignorance or else a declination to face the facts of the case. So long as the sinner remains in his natural condition he cares not one jot for God, nor will he engage in any religious duty except for what he thinks he will gain thereby. Let such a creature have a hundred motives to pray (excruciating pain of body, the suffering of a loved one, the approach of death, or pleadings of friends who assure him he has merely to ask God for mercy and he will receive it) and he will only serve *self* and not God at all. To tell the ungodly that such a promise as Matthew vii, 7, 8, belongs to them is to throw dust into their blind eyes, hiding from them the desperateness of their plight, glossing over the solemn truth that while they are wedded to their lusts they are the objects of God's holy abhorrence and can have no access to Him.

Alas, where shall a faithful physician of souls be found today? The vast majority of those who occupy the modern pulpit, instead of using the lancet and knife and the Divine Law, please their unregenerate hearers with soothing syrup or anaesthetics, preaching smooth things to them and crying "Peace, peace" when there is none. What encouragement can the thrice holy God, consistently with His honour, give to those who live solely for the pleasing of themselves? At most this: "Repent, and pray God . . . *if perhaps* the thought of thine heart may be forgiven thee" (Acts viii, 22). The wickedness of man's heart is such as no human language can depict, and unless man sincerely repents of the same there is no hope for him. The business of God's servants is not to bestow false comfort, but to slay false confidence: not to persuade those who lie under the wrath of God that they may be delivered therefrom by betaking themselves to prayer, but faithfully and honestly to let their unsaved hearers know *the worst* of their case.

It is not without good reason that we find Matthew vii, 6, 7, in juxtaposition. The Saviour with His Divine omniscience foresaw the misuse which would be made of this precious promise, "Ask and it shall be given you," and therefore He placed this emphatic warning *immediately before it*: "Give not that which is holy unto the dogs, neither cast ye your pearls before swine." Thus they are without excuse who have so sadly perverted this blessed promise of God's Word. That which needs to be pressed upon promiscuous congregations today is the very same as *Christ* proclaimed in the hearing of "the multitudes" (v, 1; vii, 28), namely the spirituality of God's Law, the searching nature of its requirements, the breadth and depth of its holy demands as set forth in Matthew v, 17—vii, 5. Not until the hearer is humbled beneath the mighty hand of God, not until he sees how completely he has failed to meet the Divine requirements, not until he feels he is both "without excuse" and "without strength," is he a fit subject for the comfort of our text.

And now we must address ourselves to the genuine Christian, the one in whom a miracle of Divine mercy and power has been wrought, the one whose self-complacency and self-sufficiency have been shattered, the one who has been given "repentance unto life." Such a one has had his eyes opened to see that the Law of God is "holy, just and good" (Romans vii, 12), that though it condemns and curses him yet it is righteous and excellent. Such a one has had communicated to him a love for that Law (Psalm cxix, 174) and therefore a longing to live in full conformity thereto. Yet such a one still finds himself utterly unable to measure up to the exalted standard set before him. Nay, he discovers to his grief that there is still a principle within him which is directly opposed to the Law, that when he would do good evil is present to prevent him. He finds to his perplexity and sorrow that indwelling corruption is stronger than all his resolutions not to yield thereto, that his lusts rage more fiercely than ever, that iniquities prevail over him. He is bewildered, staggered.

It is to such a one as we have just described, and to none other, that Christ says, "Ask, and it shall be given you; seek, and ye shall find; knock, and it shall be opened unto you." You need Divine power to subdue your raging lusts, you need Divine quickening to animate your feeble graces, you need Divine wisdom to solve your perplexities, you need Divine ointment for your wounds, so address yourself to "your Father which is in heaven" (verse 11), spread before Him your need, acquaint Him with the longings of your soul, beg Him to relieve your wants, and you will not supplicate Him in vain. Ah, *this* is what genuine prayer, real prayer, is, my reader. It is not merely the formal or mechanical performance of a religious exercise; it is not simply the stringing together of pious expressions couched in eloquent language: rather is it looking outside of ourselves and seeking help from above. True prayer is artless, spontaneous, the irrepressible cry of a soul in need. Prayer is the voicing of urgent longing of soul; it is the heart turning to the Author of those longings for the satisfying of them.

"Ask." How Divinely simple! Ask, as the hungry child does for its mother's breast. Ask, as the starving beggar does for a crust of bread. Ask, as the lost traveller does the first one whom he meets. "Ask, and it shall be given you." How Divinely encouraging! Ask of God, for He "giveth to all liberally and upbraideth not." Ask, for He "is able to do exceeding abundantly above all that we ask or think" (Eph. iii, 20). But "let him ask *in faith*, nothing wavering: for he that wavereth is like a wave of the sea driven with the wind and tossed. Let not that man think that he shall receive anything of the Lord" (James i, 6, 7). To "ask in faith" is to ask with confidence in God, with reliance upon His veracity, laying hold of His promise, pleading it before *Him* and expecting an answer of peace. To "ask in faith" is to say humbly but boldly unto the Lord, Thou hast promised Thy child, "Ask, and it shall be given you": I beg to remind Thee of that promise, now "do as Thou hast said" (II Samuel vii, 25).

But we hear more than one of our readers saying, I *have* asked, yet, alas, I have *not* received. Yea, my case is worse than it was before. So far from having more grace I have less; so far from increased strength I am weaker; so far from being granted victory over my lusts I am more frequently and woefully defeated than ever. Be it so, is that proof your prayers have not been heard? You prayed for more grace, may not the answer have been given in the form of increased *light,* so that instead of your case being worse now than it was formerly you perceive your sinfulness more clearly? And if that be so, is it not something to be thankful for? You prayed for overcoming grace, but possibly God saw you were in far greater need of *humbling* grace, and if He has granted you a measure of the latter so that you are farther out of love with yourself and brought more into the dust before Him, surely that is proof that your asking has not been in vain!

Yes, says the reader, that may be true, and God forbid that I should despise small mercies, but surely you would not have me rest content with such a Christ-dishonouring experience. Answer, you must not look upon humility and mourning over your corrup-tions as "small mercies": they are distinguishing favours which mark you as belonging to another family than the self-righteous Pharisees and self-satisfied Laodiceans. It is much to be thankful for if God hides pride from you and keeps you low before Him. And what do you mean by your "Christ-dishonouring experience"? Are you aware that there is still a spirit within you which lusts after independence and self-sufficiency? Would you, if you could, attain to some experience wherein you would feel less deeply your dire need of Christ? They that are whole need not a physician, but they that are sick! Christ is most honoured when we prize most highly His sacrifice, when we avail ourselves most gladly of His cleansing blood, when we come to Him for healing and strength.

But is not Christ able to impart spiritual *health* as well as bestow spiritual healing? Assuredly He is. Then is it not my privilege to ask Him for spiritual health? Certainly, yet in subordination to His sovereign pleasure, for He knows the degree of health which will be best for you. But observe the terms of our text: something more than "asking" is required of thee—"seek, and ye shall find." That word "seek" may be regarded two ways. First, as a higher degree of the former, an intensification of the "asking." There must be an earnest and fervent asking if we are to obtain: "ye shall seek Me, and find Me, when ye shall search for Me with all your heart" (Jer. xxix, 13). Second, it enlarges its scope: seeking is more exten-sive than praying. He who sincerely longs for grace to equip for spiritual duties must leave no stone unturned. The Word must be read, studied, memorized, meditated upon. The Word must be heard if a faithful minister be accessible. The writings of godly men of the past are often a great help. "While I was musing the fire burned."

"Knock, and it shall be opened unto you." The thought suggested to us by this clause is that grace is not to be come at easily. It is as though the earnest asker and diligent seeker is now confronted by a closed door. Even so, says Christ, be not discouraged and dismayed, continue your quest, "knock." There are times when it seems as though God turns away from us, hides Himself, and we have no access to Him. This is to test our sincerity, to try our earnestness, to put us to the proof as to whether we long for His grace as much as we imagine. If we do, discouragements will only serve to redouble our efforts. When the four men who bore one sick of the palsy could not come near Christ because of the press, they broke through the roof and let down the bed whereon the man lay, and so far from Christ being displeased with their importunity, when He "saw their faith" He said unto the sick of the palsy "Son, thy sins be forgiven thee" (Mark ii, 4, 5). Faith refuses to be deterred and continues asking, seeking, knocking until its requests be granted.

CHAPTER FORTY-FIVE

Seeking Grace—Continued

IT is often helpful to compare passages with each other, for the very variations in them are found to be complementary and supplementary to one another. Markedly is this the case in connection with the four Gospels. The passage which is now before us in Matthew vii is found also in Luke xi. There the context is a different one, and it is instructive to ponder the same. Luke xi opens with one of the disciples asking the Lord "Teach us to pray." This request is not made by a stranger but by one of His own followers, signifying that believers need to be Divinely *taught* this sacred art if they are to supplicate aright. This is a very humbling truth for the proud heart of man. Prayer, which is the simplest and most spontaneous exercise of a Christian's soul, is nevertheless an art which he is not by nature competent to perform. Nor can any human school qualify him for this holy task. None but the Lord can teach him—experimentally and effectually—how to obtain the ear of God and call down showers of blessing upon himself and others. Oh, that both writer and reader may be able to feel their deep need in this matter.

Nor let it be supposed that this request "Lord, teach us to pray' is suited only to the case of a babe in Christ. True it is a most appropriate and necessary petition for young believers to present, yet there is the less need of *urging it upon them* than there is upon some of their older brethren. Alas, how often added years are accompanied by increased pride and self-sufficiency. How many who have the gift of the gab, a ready flow of language, and are quick to memorize the expressions which others use in their devotions, would be hurt if you suggested that *they* had need to cry "Lord, teach us to pray." Yet such is the case: the oldest and most experienced saint has need to be shown the way of the Lord more perfectly: "If any man think that he knoweth any thing, he knoweth nothing yet as he ought to know" (I Cor. viii, 2). Growth in grace is not evidenced by growth in haughtiness, but in increased humility. The most deeply taught believer is the one most conscious of his need of teaching: a large part of wisdom consists of consciousness of ignorance.

The Lord answered this request of His disciple by graciously furnishing a brief directory and pattern, which we like to think of as the family prayer. Then He appeared to anticipate the questions: Will God really answer us? What is the actual design of this holy exercise: is it only designed for our inward good or does it really bring down blessings from above? Does it end with the benefit it works in us or does it truly move the hand of God? The reply, though in the form of a parable, is expressed with great clearness and force. As importunity does most surely affect men, so earnestness and persistency are sure to gain an answer from God. It is not a vain thing to supplicate the mercy seat: our prayers are not lost on the air or expended merely upon ourselves. Asking is attended with receiving, seeking with finding, and knocking leads to opening. There is a connection established between Divine decree and believing prayer, between the requests that ascend from earth and the mercies which descend from heaven.

It seems strange that so many have missed the meaning of that plain parable in Luke xi. "And He said unto them, Which of you shall have a friend, and shall go unto him at midnight, and say unto him, Friend, lend me three loaves; For a friend of mine in his journey is come to me and I have nothing to set before him? And he from within shall answer and say, Trouble me not: the door is now shut, and my children are with me in bed; I cannot rise and give thee. I say unto you, Though he will not rise and give him because he is his friend, yet because of his importunity he will rise and give him as many as he needeth " (verses 5-8).

Now there is something more taught us in that parable than the need for and value of perseverance in prayer, namely *encouragement* to be earnest therein. Let us analyse its details. Why was the one sought unto displeased at the request presented to him? Because it was made not by a close relative, but simply a friend. Because the supplicant was not asking on his own behalf, but for someone else. Because it was presented at a most inopportune and inconvenient hour. Because it concerned not an urgent and pressing need, but simply a matter of some bread. Who would think of knocking up someone at midnight in order to borrow food for another? Christ shows us the natural disposition of our selfish hearts under such circumstances: "Trouble me not . . . I cannot rise and give thee "; yet because the request was repeated and the suppliant would not accept a refusal, for the sake of importunity and not that of friendship the petitioner gained his request.

Though the specific conclusion was not here formally drawn by Christ—as it is in verse 13—how blessed it is for faith to do so. The One whom the Christian supplicates is more than a "friend," namely his heavenly Father. So far from there being any reluctance in Him to supply the varied needs of His children, He "giveth liberally to all and upbraideth not" (James i, 5). Nor can we come to Him at any inopportune season, for He "slumbereth not, neither is weary": at all times we may address the throne of grace. Moreover, it is our privilege to spread before Him our smallest needs. We would hesitate to ask a man of prominence and importance for a mere trifle, knowing he would be loath to be bothered therewith, but "*in everything* by prayer and supplication let your requests be made known unto God" is the royal invitation issued to the saint. Nor is it only our own needs we are to be concerned with: those of our friends also we may beg the Lord to relieve: thereby we honour Him, acknowledging Him to be Ruler over all, the universal Supplier.

Then our Lord plainly declared, "Ask, and it shall be given you; seek, and ye shall find; knock, and it shall be opened unto you: for every one that asketh receiveth, and he that seeketh findeth, and to him that knocketh it shall be opened," which is precisely the same as our present portion in Matthew's Gospel. If the going to a mere friend, at an opportune time, asking for material bread for another, received a favourable answer, how much more will our heavenly Father, to whom there are no inconvenient seasons, grant spiritual succour to His own dear children! Here is the heart of God revealed as the ready and bounteous Giver, whose fullness cannot be exhausted and whose word to His people is "open thy mouth *wide* and I will fill it" (Psalm lxxxi, 10). A wide door is here opened to the whole family of God, possibilities of blessing which we can scarcely conceive, free leave to covet earnestly the best things. No matter how enlarged our expectations may be, they cannot exceed the bounty of the Lord. But does this mean that the Christian may ask for anything he pleases and that God stands pledged to grant the same? Are those absolute promises, without any qualification? No. First, they are limited by our own unbelief, by the meagreness of our faith, which we impose upon them. And second, they are restricted by God's benignity: the only guard He has placed upon those promises is that He will give us naught save that which is really for our "good" (verse 11). And how thankful we should be for this. In our ignorance and shortsightedness we often ask God for that which would be for our ill, but in His mercy God withholds it. Not so does He act with the wicked. Unbelieving Israel asked for flesh in the wilderness and God granted their request, "But while their meat was yet in their mouths, the wrath of God came upon them" (Psalm lxxviii, 30, 31). A later generation desired a king and he was given them "in His anger" (Hosea xiii, 11). So too the demons had their request granted that they might enter into the herd of swine (Matt. viii, 31, 32).

It is most important that the above-noted qualification be kept in mind, for in some quarters the crudest ideas obtain on this subject. Taking Matthew vii, 7, 8, at its face value, some have deduced the absurd principle that we may have anything we please from God for the mere asking, providing we ask in faith, and by "asking in faith" they signify only a working themselves up to a firm persuasion that they shall have their petitions granted. But that one word "give *good* things to them that ask Him" at once disposes of such fanaticism. To "ask in faith" requires that we lay hold of and plead before God one of His own promises: it is not an expectation that He will grant everything we may demand, but an assurance that He will bestow whatsoever He is pledged to give. "If we ask anything according to

His will [not our will, but His, as it is revealed in Holy Writ], He heareth us" (I John v, 14), and we only ask "according to His will" when we ask in faith for these things He knows will be for our good.

"Prayer is a simple, unfeigned, humble, ardent opening of the heart before God, wherein we ask things needful or give thanks for benefits received" (John Bradford, the martyr). And what is it which the Christian, every Christian, is most urgently and constantly in need of, without which it is impossible to improve or use aright all other benefits and privileges? Is it not *Divine grace*: renewing grace, enlightening grace, empowering grace, sanctifying grace? What is knowledge worth unless it be sanctified to us? What do talents amount to unless they be spiritually directed? And for this grace we are to "ask": ask from a felt sense of want, trustfully supplicating God for the supply thereof. For that grace we are to "seek": seek with care and diligence, as that which is missing and lacking, and which is felt to be of great value. For that grace we are to "knock": that is, ask and seek, with earnestness and constancy, pressing our suit with fervour and persistency, persevering notwithstanding delays, oppositions and disappointments. Continuing in prayer till our request be granted.

There is an "asking" which is mere formality and accomplishes nothing: if the suppliant himself is scarcely able to remember an hour afterwards that which he petitioned for, how can he expect to receive answers? If an experienced mother knows the difference between a child's asking for the mere sake of asking and making request out of a sense of urgent need, how infinitely less can we impose upon the Omniscient One. So also there is a "seeking" which is merely mechanical and obtains not: half-heartedness and slothfulness are not likely to be successful. We take very little pains in seeking for something we regard as a mere trifle, but when an object is valued highly and prized dearly then we hunt for it with real diligence. Yet something more than earnest asking and diligent seeking is required: "knocking" suggests an intensification of the one and a continuation of the other. If at first we don't succeed, then try, try again. What a word is that: "Ye that make mention of the Lord, keep not silence, And *give Him no rest*" (Isaiah lxii, 6, 7)!

"Praying always with all prayer and supplication in the Spirit, and watching thereunto *with all perseverance*" (Eph. vi, 18). The walls of Jericho did not fall down the first time they were encompassed, nor did the beloved apostle obtain comforting assurance from the Lord the first or the second time that he besought Him for the removal of the thorn in his flesh. So far from its being a wrong thing for a Christian to make repeated request for the same object, it is required of him that he be importunate. If it be inquired, *Why* does God require such importunity from His people? several answers may be given. First and negatively, it is not that we have to overcome any reluctance on God's side, for He is more ready to give than we are to seek blessings from Him, yea, to do for us far more exceeding abundantly above all that we ask or think. Still less is it because He would tantalize us: "therefore will the Lord wait, that He may be *gracious*" (Isaiah xxx, 18).

Second, from the positive side, that we may give *proof of our earnestness*. When someone makes request of us for anything and we find that a single refusal is sufficient to get rid of him, we conclude he was not very eager for it. But suppose a business man arrives late at his office and his chief clerk announces that a stranger has sought an interview, that he could not put him off, that he has waited for hours determined to gain his quest; then it is clear that he is eager and intent. Such intensity and perseverance are pleasing unto the Lord: when a soul can say with Jacob, "I will not let Thee go, except Thou bless me" (Gen. xxxii, 26), success is sure. "Ye shall seek Me, and find Me, when ye shall search for Me with all your heart" (Jer. xxix, 13).

Such importunity is required for *the testing of our faith*. An unbelieving heart is soon discouraged: either opposition from man or delay on the part of God, and the spirit of prayer is speedily quenched. Not so with the trusting one: faith reassures the soul, bidding it, "Wait on the Lord: be of good courage, and He shall strengthen thine heart: wait, I say, on the Lord" (Psalm xxvii, 14). How the faith of the Canaanitish woman was tried. First, she cried, "Have mercy on me O Lord," and we are told, "He answered her not a word." Then His disciples interposed and besought Him to send her away. Next He said, "I am not sent but unto the lost sheep of the house of Israel." But, nothing daunted, she renewed her petition, "Lord, help me": to which Christ replied, "It is not meet to take the children's bread and cast it to the dogs." Yet even that did not dismay her: having asked and sought, she continued knocking, begging for the "crumbs." "O woman, great is thy faith: be it unto thee even as thou wilt" (Matt. xv, 28) was the triumphant outcome.

Such importunity is necessary for *the developing of our patience*. How sadly impatient we are! How angry when our wills are crossed! What fearful rebellion lurks and works in our hearts! Truly we are "like a bullock unaccustomed to the yoke," fretful and resentful at every restriction placed upon the fulfilment of our desires. But patience must have her perfect work, and it is the trying of our faith which "worketh patience" (James i, 3). Real faith is not destroyed by God's delay: it knows He waits to be gracious, and therefore its possessor is enabled to "both hope and quietly wait for the salvation of the Lord" (Lam. iii, 26). When Elijah had prayed that the long drought should be ended, he bade his servant go and look for the first portent of the coming rain, and when he returned saying, "there is nothing," his master replied, "go again seven times" (I Kings xviii, 43). Thus, by the proving of our earnestness, the testing of faith and the developing of patience, our souls are the better fitted to receive and can the more appreciate the Lord's answer when it is vouchsafed.

But it is not for himself only that the Christian is earnestly, diligently and persistently to seek Divine grace, but *for his brethren* also. That is one reason why we referred to the parallel passage in Luke xi, where these Divine promises are immediately prefaced by the parable of one seeking the loaves on behalf of a needy friend. The lesson should be too plain to miss: because he was unable personally to supply that need, even though it was midnight, he went out and supplicated another on his friend's behalf. Immediately following this Christ says: " Ask [on the behalf of your friend] and it shall be given you." Be just as earnest in asking, just as diligent in seeking, just as importunate in knocking for grace to be given unto your needy brethren and sisters in Christ as you are in seeking it for yourself. They are bought with the same precious blood, and are members of the same family, and thus they have pressing claims upon your affections; and their need of Divine grace —to cleanse, to illumine, to fructify and sanctify—is as real, as great, and as urgent, as yours.

Ah, is it not at this very point we fail so lamentably! Is not our praying far too self-centred? Is there any wonder it is so ineffectual? If I am so little concerned about the spiritual well-being of my brethren and sisters at large, need I be surprised that the Lord refuses me the grace which I seek for my own soul? God will not put a premium upon selfishness. " Praying always with all prayer and supplication in the Spirit, and watching thereunto with all perseverance and supplication *for all saints*" (Eph. vi, 18). Yes, not merely for myself and family, or for my own church and denomination, but for all the children of God which are scattered abroad. And this not in a mere general way, and only once a week, but as definitely and diligently, fervently and constantly, as I present my own personal needs before the throne of grace. This is one of the chief lessons inculcated by the prayer Christ taught His disciples: " When ye pray, say, *Our* Father which art in heaven . . . give *us* . . . forgive *us* . . . deliver *us*"!

" We know that we have passed from death unto life because we love the brethren " (I John iii, 14). And how can our love be better expressed than by making *their* case and cause *our own* case and cause before the mercy seat! " Epaphras . . . always labouring fervently for you in prayers, that ye may stand perfect and complete in all the will of God " (Col. iv, 12). Ah, if we had more like Epaphras Zion would not long remain in its present languishing condition! If each of God's people earnestly, trustfully and daily cried unto heaven on behalf of the whole household of faith, that feeble knees might be strengthened, backsliders reclaimed, graces quickened, fruitless branches purged, half-dead preachers revived, we should soon witness showers of blessing descending on the parched vineyard. God has not changed: His arm is not shortened: the promises

of Matthew vii, 7, 8, are as available to faith now as they were on
the day of Pentecost. It is affections that have waned, the footstool
of prayer which has been neglected. " Ye have not, because ye ask
not."

Was there ever a time when prayer for the Church collectively
and its members individually was more urgently needed than now?
We need frequently to remind ourselves that the most striking
deliverances wrought in the past for God's people are recorded
chiefly as monuments of prevailing prayer. Such were the salvation
of Israel at the Red Sea, wrought in response to the supplication of
Moses (Exodus xiv, 15), the victory over Amalek at Rephidim
(Exodus xvii, 12), the discomfiture of the Philistines in the days of
Samuel—the " Ebenezer" then erected was less a monument of
victory over powerful enemies than of the prophet's prevailing
prayer (I Samuel vii, 5, 9, 12)—the overthrow of the Moabites and
Ammonites in the days of Jehoshaphat (II Chron. xx, 1-13, 17,
22-24), the remarkable deliverance from Sennacherib king of Assyria
(Isaiah xxxvii, 15-20, 35, 37). Such examples of Jehovah's readiness
to show Himself strong on the behalf of those who count upon His
intervention are recorded for our encouragement. Then ask, seek,
knock.

CHAPTER FORTY-SIX

Seeking Grace—Concluded

" Or what man is there of you, whom if his son ask bread, will he give him a stone? Or if he ask a fish, will he give him a serpent? If ye then, being evil, know how to give good gifts unto your children, how much more shall your Father which is in heaven give good things to them that ask him?" (Matt. vii, 9-11.)

EVERY Christian will grant that prayer is a bounden *duty*, that it is obligatory upon us to own our dependence upon the Giver of all good and perfect gifts, to seek from Him those things which we are in need of both temporally and spiritually, to acknowledge the Lord's goodness and lovingkindness and render thanks for His manifold mercies. To fail at such a point is inexcusable, making us like unto those who live as though there were no God, rendering not unto Him that which is His undoubted due. Prayerlessness is not to be looked upon as an innocent infirmity, but as a sin of the deepest dye, which is to be penitently confessed. Christians will also grant that prayer is a precious *privilege*, for by this ordinance they may obtain an audience with the Majesty on high, delight themselves in the Lord, commune with the Beloved of their souls, unburden their hearts before Him and prove Him to be " a very present help in trouble." Alas, that we prize this privilege so little and treat it so lightly.

Though it be freely allowed that prayer is a bounden duty and a precious privilege, yet the fact remains that many professing Christians are woefully slack in performing that duty and in availing themselves of that privilege. Why is this? Let them not add to the sin of prayerlessness the wickedness of seeking to throw the blame upon God, by saying that He has withheld from them the spirit of prayer, that He refuses them liberty of approach unto Him. That were to add insult to injury. We make an evil use of it when we appeal to God's sovereignty in order to excuse ourselves from discharging our responsibilities. If we are not enjoying the light of God's countenance it is because our sins have come in between as a thick cloud (Isaiah lix, 2). If we are not receiving good things at His hands, it is because our iniquities have withheld them (Jer. v, 24). If our hearts are cold and prayerless it is because we have grieved the Holy Spirit. The fault is wholly ours, and we must honestly own it.

Among the things that hinder a free and regular approach unto the throne of grace we may mention *the workings of pride*. Pride begets a spirit of independence and self-sufficiency. It goes against the natural grain to take our place in the dust and come before God as empty-handed beggars. True we did so at the beginning of our Christian experience, for then we had been emptied of self and brought to look entirely outside of self for deliverance. But alas, increased years are rarely accompanied by increased humility. As we become better versed in the letter of Holy Writ and more acquainted with the mysteries of our faith, a sense of self-sufficiency is apt to possess us. "Knowledge puffeth up," and the more puffed up we are the less our sense of need and the more formal and infrequent our seeking after Divine grace.

A spirit of sloth is paralysing to the prayer life. The soul loves its ease as well as the body, that is why we are exhorted to "watch unto prayer" (I Peter iv, 7). And how forceful that word from the pen of such a one! It was at that very point Peter had first failed. The Lord had bidden him to "watch and pray"; instead, he went to sleep. Prayer is likened unto "striving" (Romans xv, 30), "labouring fervently" (Col. iv, 12) and "wrestling" (Eph. vi, 12, 18), and such exertions are not possible when lethargy has overcome us. *The power of unbelief* quenches the spirit of prayer. Unbelief raises objections, is occupied with difficulties, and leaves God entirely out of its considerations. Only where faith is in healthy operation can we expect any success in this holy exercise. But flirting with the world, yielding to the lusts of the flesh or heeding the lies of Satan stifles the breath of faith, and then the soul is left to gasp in the foul atmosphere of unbelief.

Now in that section of the Sermon on the Mount which we are here considering, our Lord sets before His disciples one inducement after another to stimulate them unto prayer. First, He gives them a gracious invitation: "Ask, and it shall be given you; seek, and ye shall find; knock, and it shall be opened unto you" (verse 7). Second, He assures them of an answer, by giving them a sure promise: "For every one that asketh receiveth, and he that seeketh findeth, and to him that knocketh it shall be opened" (verse 8). Third, He draws an infallible inference from the Fatherhood of God: "Or what man is there of you, whom if his son ask bread, will he give him a stone? Or if he ask a fish, will be give him a serpent? If ye then, being evil, know how to give good gifts unto your children, how much more shall your Father which is in heaven give good things to them that ask Him?" (verses 9-11).

In order to get the full force of Christ's conclusion let us observe its premise: "If ye then, *being evil*." First of all, observe how that brief sentence expresses the Divine estimate of fallen mankind. How those words abase the pride of man, affirming as they do the depravity and corruption of human nature. Philosophers and poets, preachers and politicians may prate all they please about the dignity and divinity of man, the nobility and grandeur of human nature, but they fly in the face of this solemn and inerrant verdict of the Son of God. Christ was not deceived by the fair profession and religious pretensions of those He met with, for when "many believed in His name when they saw the miracles which He did," yet, "Jesus did not commit Himself unto them . . . for He knew *what was in man*" (John ii, 23-25). This "if ye then, being evil" is yet more solemn and striking when we note that our Lord said it not to those who were open enemies, but unto His own disciples (see Luke xi, 1, 2, 9, 13)—by nature they were polluted.

"If ye then, being evil, know how to give good gifts unto your children." Notwithstanding the fact that you not only *do* that which is evil but *are* yourselves evil—the fountain itself, from whence all actions issue, being poisoned—yet you are kind to your offspring. Parental love, by the wise and gracious arrangement of God, is one of the most powerful of all the active principles of the human heart and mind. No parent worthy of the name would refuse to supply the genuine needs of his little ones when he had it in his power to do so. He would neither turn a deaf ear to their cries nor mock them by bestowing what was useless and noxious instead of that which was requisite and beneficial for them. No, despite the ruin which the Fall has entailed, men and women still respond to the instincts of affection when they perceive that their offspring are in need, and use their best judgment to relieve the same; certainly those who are regenerate do so.

In what follows Christ drew a conclusion from this filial relationship: "If ye then, being evil, know how to give good gifts unto your children, how much more shall your Father which is in heaven give good things to them that ask Him?" It is an argument deduced from the less to the greater, a species of reasoning frequently met with in the Scriptures. "Like as a father pitieth his children, so the Lord pitieth them that fear Him" (Psalm ciii, 13). "Can a woman forget her sucking child, that she should not have compassion on the son of her womb? yea, they may forget, yet will not I forget thee" (Isaiah xlix, 15). "I will spare them, as a man spareth his own son that serveth him" (Mal. iii, 17). If godly parents respond to cries of need from their bairns, what may we expect from Him who is supremely excellent and kindly disposed unto His children? In knowledge, in wisdom, in benevolence, in power, in resources, our heavenly Father infinitely surpasses all earthly parents, and therefore we may petition Him with the fullest assurance that He will supply all our need. What conclusive reasoning is this! What persuasive appeal is here!

But let us attend next to *the connection* between this gracious and grand encouragement to seekers after Divine grace and that which immediately precedes. As we sought to point out in our last, there is a gradation or progressive development here in our Lord's teaching on prayer—especially is this observable in Luke xi. First, there is the invitation (verse 7), and then a reassuring promise (verse 8). And now Christ disposes of an objection—a most foolish and wicked one, yet one which is nevertheless raised by some. A grave doubt is apt to arise in the distressed mind. True, God hears the petitions of His people, and as a general rule makes responses of mercy to them; but I am such an unworthy one, is He not therefore likely to be displeased at my prayers and so answer me in wrath instead of love? Certainly I should deserve it: if confessing my vileness, God should judge me out of my own mouth and condemn me, what could I do? Ah, if we are afraid that God will give us something evil when we have asked Him for that which is good, then we *are* "evil" indeed.

A sense of sinfulness and the workings of unbelief cause you to fear that if you ask something good at the hands of God He will mock you with something evil, that instead of being gracious He will send you something in righteous judgment. Does the reader deem this far-fetched and suppose we are describing a very extreme and exceptional case? Then we ask, Have you never prayed about a certain matter, prayed earnestly, and the sequel has been that instead of things being improved they grew worse, instead of relief being granted difficulties increased and the pressure became more acute, until you were afraid to pray any further for such a thing? Have you begged God again and again to make you more patient, and the sequel has been such that it appeared the Lord had mocked you by taking away what little you had? If such has not been your experience, we can assure you that not a few know something like unto it.

"Or what man is there of you, whom if his son ask bread, will he give him a stone? Or if he ask a fish, will he give him a serpent?" (verses 9, 10). Here is our Lord's *refutation* of such an objection. He bids us ponder the conduct of earthly parents. Does a godly father deliberately mock his son when a reasonable request is made of him? Of course not. Then is that son afraid to come to his parent and acquaint him with his need? No, he is assured that his parent is the very one above all others who has his interests most at heart and is more likely than anyone else to minister unto him. He has confidence in his father's goodness; he trusts in his love, and therefore he hesitates not to apply unto him. True, in his ignorance the child may ask for something which is harmful, and then it is the wisdom and love of his parent which withholds it; but if he asks for that which is needful and beneficial, he will not receive that which is injurious in lieu of it.

The spiritual application is obvious. As the child trusts his parent, so must you your heavenly Father. "If ye then, being evil, know how to give good gifts unto your children, how much more shall your Father which is in heaven give good things to them that ask Him?" As high as God is above us, so high is the certainty that He will not fail His beloved children. But to be more specific. You have perhaps been earnestly beseeching God for guidance, to lead you in a plain path, to make His way plain before your face. The result has been most discouraging. Difficulties have increased, you seem more hedged in than ever, you are now at your wits' end to know what to do. Well, do not judge God harshly and conclude He has given you a stone instead of bread! Your present lot is from the Lord, your circumstances are ordered by Him who is too wise to err and too loving to be unkind. As Spurgeon says, "It may seem hard perhaps; but may it not be the *crust* of the bread for all that? Believe it to be so, but never suspect you are being treated ungenerously by your Father."

Yet it appears to us that it is not so much of temporal mercies and providential blessings as of spiritual things our passage treats. We would therefore suggest that the "bread" stands for vital and indispensable graces, and the "fish" for comforting ones. Bread is the staff of life, and the graces of repentance and faith are necessary unto salvation. Here is a soul that has prayed definitely and sincerely for repentance. But he reads that Judas repented, yet perished nevertheless. He hears some faithful servant of God draw the line between legal bondage and evangelical repentance, between the sorrow of the world and "godly sorrow which worketh repentance" (II Cor. vii, 10), and he is deeply concerned, wondering whether he has so renounced sin, so detested it, so loathed it from the very bottom of his heart, as to warrant him concluding that he has indeed been granted "repentance unto life" (Acts xi, 15). He therefore applies to the throne of grace crying, "Create in me a clean heart, O God, and renew a right spirit within me."

So far so good; but now let us take the sequel. That individual becomes better acquainted with the plague of his own heart and in the light of God discovers corruption within such as he was not conscious of before. Nay, indwelling sin now asserts itself with increasing power and iniquities prevail. He seeks deliverance, but it comes not, for the flesh remains unchanged to the end. He confesses his sins to God, but so frequently that it appears to become mechanical. It seems that his heart is as hard as a stone and he is ready to believe that he was deceived, that after all he is a stranger to genuine repentance. Here, then, is the remedy for such a case. Where did you seek repentance? At the throne of grace, you answer. From whom, we ask; from some creature? No, you reply, from God. Then has He mocked you? If you sought simply, definitely, sincerely, from a sense of need, has He given you a stone? Perish the thought. It is Satan who seeks to persuade you that God has suffered you to be deluded. Believe not his lie.

Take *the grace of faith*. We begged God for saving faith in His Son and believed that He answered us. We renounced all our own doings and trusted in the Lord Jesus. We saw Him in the glass of the Gospel dying, the just for the unjust, and we cast ourselves on His atoning sacrifice as the alone ground of our acceptance with God. But at times the question is raised in our minds, Is mine true saving faith or would it not be presumptuous for me to affirm that in Christ I am pardoned? There is an historical faith: is mine no better than that? I read that "the devils also believe" (James ii, 19): may not my faith be of that sort? Do I have the genuine grace of faith or am I only deluding myself? Come back to this touchstone, my friend: where did you seek your faith? Did you ask your heavenly Father to give it you? Have you not said to Him, If my faith be worthless, graciously work in me the faith of Thine elect? Then dare you conclude that instead of imparting faith by the Spirit's operation He has put into your heart a carnal presumption and allowed you to be deluded? Even a godly human parent would not act thus: how much less so the heavenly Father!

Take *the grace of personal piety*. You have longed for more holiness. You have asked God for more purity of heart. You have sought earnestly for a closer conformity to the image of His Son. You have knocked again and again at the throne of grace, beseeching that you might be sanctified wholly in spirit and soul and body. Great now is your dismay, for you find yourself more sinful than ever, indwelling corruption is increasingly active, and evil thoughts continually harass you. Even so, once more we must bring you back to this: for what did you ask? *where* did you seek this blessing? If from some pretended priests and mediators, such as the poor papists have recourse to, you would indeed be deceived and disappointed. But if you sought from the great High Priest, the alone Mediator between God and men, it is impossible that He should have palmed off on you something which is evil. He *has* granted your request, though you perceive it not: the holier He makes you, the more dissatisfied you will be with yourself; the purer your heart, the more sensitive to the foulness which invades it.

Take *the grace of hope*. This is a virtue which stays the heart in seasons of distress, enabling the soul to look forward with firm expectation to better things in the future. "For we are saved by hope: but hope that is seen is not hope: for what a man seeth, why doth he yet hope for? But if we hope for that we see not, then do we with patience wait for it" (Romans viii, 24, 25): the fulfilment of the promise is not yet visible, but hope causes us to wait confidently for the same. It was the grace of hope which moved Job to say, "When He hath tried me, I shall come forth as gold" (xxiii, 10). The furnace might be hot, its flames most unpleasant to the flesh, the dross might sizzle (as when he cursed the day of his birth), but he had no doubt of the ultimate outcome. Ah, says the reader, I dare not cherish such an assurance: it would be presumptuous of *me* to do so! What, presumption to expect your heavenly Father to answer your prayers? Presumption to expect Him to make good His promise: "He which hath begun a good work in you *will perform it*" (Phil. i, 6)? Oh, insult Him not with such mock humility, but trust Him to act like a *Father* unto you.

It is to be observed that in Luke xi a third thing is mentioned: "Or if he shall ask for an egg [something which only the wealthy ate

in those days], will he offer him a scorpion?" (verse 12). This seems
to carry the thought beyond asking for necessary or even comforting
graces, even for what we might term *spiritual luxuries*, as faith
grows and becomes bolder in seeking the highest enjoyments and
enrichments of the Spirit. The application is not difficult. The
mature Christian covets earnestly the best gifts. He begs that he
may be drawn closer to Christ and enjoy more intimate communion
with Him. And what form does the answer take? More persecution
from the world, more opposition from friends, more unkind treatment from brethren, which stirs up the flesh and casts down the
soul. Ah, but do not your heavenly Father the injustice of concluding He has given you a scorpion instead of an egg: malign not His
character thus! Rather charge yourself with ignorance and folly
because you fail to realize that communion with Christ in this life
consists largely in "the fellowship of His sufferings" (Phil. iii, 10),
which is the highest honour grace confers on His followers.

In closing let us point out that if we are to enter into the comfort
and assurance of our passage faith must lay firm hold of the
fatherly character and relation of God. So long as we view Him
only as the stern Judge or as the most high Sovereign, we may
expect little liberty of approach or assurance of answers. There
must be a childlike confidence in His fatherly goodness and love,
a believing He will give good things unto the members of His dear
family. There must be a reliance upon His sufficiency. An earthly
parent may "*know how* to give good gifts unto his children," but
straitened circumstances often prevent him carrying out his
desires. Not so our heavenly Father: He not only "knoweth how,"
but *actually gives* unto His children. Then doubt Him not and
cease supposing He has substituted something worthless for genuine
grace.

CHAPTER FORTY-SEVEN

The Golden Rule

" Therefore all things whatsover ye would that men should do to you, do ye even so to them : for this is the law and the prophets." (Matt. vii, 12.)

" THEREFORE all things whatsoever ye would that men should do to you, do ye even so to them: for this is the law and the prophets." This single verse forms a distinct section, the ninth in this discourse of our Lord's. Its theme is that of equity and justice, which must regulate us in our dealings with one another. Its very brevity evidences the Divine wisdom of Him who spoke as never man spoke, for who else could have condensed so much into so few words? The manner in which this rule is enforced manifests the fundamental unity of the two economies: so far from the Gospel setting aside the requirements of the Law it establishes the same (Romans iii, 31). Analysing our present verse we find it contains three things. First, a conclusion drawn from the context: " therefore." Second, a commandment which presents to us a standard of complete unselfishness: " whatsoever ye would that men should do to you, do ye even so to them." Third, a commendation of that standard: " for this is the law and the prophets."

The opening " therefore " looks back to what Christ had said in the previous section (verses 7-11). In it we behold the Divine Teacher making a practical application of what He had just said upon prayer, intimating that privilege and duty are never to be divorced, that blessings from God are to enable us the better to discharge our responsibilities unto men. " Fitly is the law of justice subjoined to the law of prayer, for unless we be honest in our conversation, God will not hear our prayers (Isaiah i, 15, 17; lviii, 6, 9; Zech. vii, 9, 13). We cannot expect to receive good things from God if we do not fair things and that which is lovely and of good report among men. We must not only be devout, but honest, else our devotion is but hypocrisy" (Matthew Henry). Alas, that this is so little insisted upon by the pulpit today; alas, that the impression is generally created that we may expect an answer to our petitions regardless of how we treat our fellows: God requires a conscientious performance of all the duties of civil righteousness as well as that we be earnest in acts of piety.

" How much more shall your Father which is in heaven give good things to them that ask Him? *Therefore* all things whatsoever ye would that men should do to you, do ye even so to them." The connection between these two things, then, shows that in the practice of this golden rule Christians are to consider not only how they would be dealt with by men, but by God Himself, thereby elevating the precept high above the ethics of the heathen. Whatever usage we expect to meet with at the hands of God, the same in our measure must we dispense to others. How can we expect God to be merciful to us if we be merciless unto our neighbour? How can we expect Him to deal liberally with us if we are eaten up with selfishness? Let us not forget that whatever need others have of us, the same need have we of God. According as we sow sparingly or bountifully, so will our reaping be (II Cor. ix, 6). I am therefore to consider how God will deal with me if I am rigid, severe, and demand the uttermost farthing from those in my power.

It is also to be observed that a due regulation of our prayer life is indispensable if we are to be fitted for dealing properly with our fellows. All inordinate affection toward the world, which is the impulse that moves men to over-reaching practices, has its root in a distrust of God. "Were we daily to ask for all we want of Him, seeking first the kingdom of God and His righteousness, and relying upon His promise to add other things as He sees them to be best for us, we should have no inclination to covetousness or injustice. But if instead of depending like sheep on the care of their shepherd we set off like beasts of prey to forage the world for ourselves, we shall often judge it to be wise and necessary to seize on that which equity forbids" (Andrew Fuller). It is only by dwelling in (not paying an occasional visit to) the secret place of the Most High that my heart will be prepared to act becomingly toward my neighbour. It is only by constant communion with Him who is both light and love that a spirit of righteousness and grace will actuate me in my relations with men.

"How much more shall your Father which is in heaven give good things to them that ask Him? *Therefore* all things whatsoever ye would that men should do to you, do ye even so to them." Consider the connection also in this manner: since your Father in heaven gives good things to you when you ask Him, make it your care to do good unto all who come within the sphere of your influence. "Be ye therefore followers [imitators] of God, as dear children" (Eph. v, 1). Since God has dealt bountifully with you, practise generosity and liberality unto men. Let not your conduct be determined by how your fellows treat with you, but rather by how *God* treats with you. How immeasurably does this holy and gracious standard from Christ exceed "the righteousness of the scribes and Pharisees" (v, 20)! How far had they departed from the Law and the prophets! Nor need we fear that the unregenerate will take such an unfair advantage of our magnanimity that we shall be the losers thereby: "Knowing that whatsoever good thing any man doeth, the same shall he receive of the Lord" (Eph. vi, 8).

But how am I to determine what will be for the good of my

neighbours? Thus: "all things whatsoever ye would that men should do to you, do ye even so to them." This commandment consists of two parts: that which is to be ordered, namely our actions unto other men; the rule which is to regulate this, namely the law of justice and equity which is in every man by nature. Whatever you would desire and deem best for yourself were you in *their* place, that is what *you* must do unto others. Nothing less than such a standard of unselfishness is our rule of righteousness. "Christ came to teach us not only what we are to know and to believe, but what we are to do: what we are to do, not only toward God, but toward men; not only toward our fellow disciples, those of our own party and persuasion, but toward men in general, all with whom we have to do" (Matthew Henry). It is utterly vain to speak like angels when on our knees before God, if we act like devils in our transactions with men.

"The meaning of this rule lies in these three things. (1) We must do that to our neighbour which we ourselves acknowledge to be fit and reasonable, that the appeal being made to our own judgment, and the discovery of our judgment is referred to that which is our own will and expectation when it is our own case. (2) We must put other people upon the level with ourselves, and reckon we are as much obliged to them as they to us. We are as much bound to the duty of justice as they are, and they are as much entitled to the benefit as we. (3) We must in our dealing with men suppose ourselves in the same particular case and circumstances with those we have to do with, and deal accordingly. If I were making such a one's bargain, labouring under such a one's infirmities and afflictions, how would I desire and expect to be treated? And this is a *just* position, for we know not how soon their case may really be ours; indeed we may fear, lest God by His judgments should do to us as we have done to others, if we have not done as we would be done by" (Matthew Henry).

This golden rule is God's witness in every human heart. Each one has so much regard for himself as quickly to feel when he is wronged, and to pass censure on the one injuring him. He has only then to apply this principle to his conduct unto others and the right or wrong of his actions must instantly appear. Hereby we are taught to abstain from everything which would injure our neighbour, either in his body, estate or good name—such as lying, slandering, dishonesty, oppression. Nature itself teaches men this, for would they have men defame, rob or oppress *them*? Then let them avoid such reprehensible practices toward *others*. For the rule is not treat with men according as they deal with you, but act toward them as you would *desire* them to act toward you. It is the corruption of nature, the yielding to sinful inclinations, which moves men to seek their own temporal advantage and advancement by the loss and debasing of others. Alas, how far, far away is the world from God and His righteousness.

How this precept cuts at the very root of all the pretensions and
sophistries used by men in their endeavours to justify crooked ways
and practices. How often they plead, "We must live," though they
like not to think that in a short time they also must die—"and after
death, the judgment"! Here these selfish creatures are reminded
that their fellows also must live, and have rights equal to their own.
However the unscrupulous may seek to excuse their dishonest
tricks of the trade, unmerciful employers grinding the faces of their
employees, harsh tyrants demanding their full pound of flesh from
widows and orphans under the plea of "business is business," let
them come nearer home and inquire whether they would like to be
dealt with thus were the positions reversed. "The money-lender
may pretend he pleases the poor, but his help is no better than he
is, that gives a draught of cold water to one that is in a burning
fever, which seems pleasant at the first but after increases his
sufferings" (W. Perkins). Were this rule heeded, the light weight,
short change, and adulterated commodities would be unknown.

This rule applies not only to giving, but *forgiving,* for as long as
we are in this world there will be infirmities and offences, and thus
the mutual need of forgiving and receiving forgiveness. "Forbearing one another, and forgiving one another, if any man have a
complaint against any: even as Christ forgave you, so also do ye"
(Col. iii, 13). If we resent the idea that others should require flawless perfection from us, then we must not demand it from them. If
we desire that our fellows view our unwitting failures with the eyes
of charity, then we must cultivate the same attitude. If we refuse to
forgive those who trespass against us, God will not forgive us our
trespasses (Matt. vi, 15). "Take no heed unto all words that are
spoken; lest thou hear thy servant curse thee: For oftentimes also
thine own heart knoweth that thou thyself likewise hast cursed
others" (Eccles. vii, 21, 22). The meaning is, be not over affected
when others speak evil of you, for you know that you are not guiltless of that very thing; therefore, meekly forbear. The realization
that the flesh is still in us, and the knowledge that we are compassed
about with infirmities, should make us pardon those who wrong us.

Let us mention another direction in which this precept needs to
be applied: where there are differences of religious opinion. Had
this principle been acted upon, then persecution in all its manifold
and cruel forms would have been unknown. Where is the man who
would acknowledge it to be right and proper to persecute him for
his conscientious convictions or for that conduct which is the necessary result of them? Then if he deems such punishment to be un-
merited and unjust in his own case, by what principle can he regard
such punishment as being deserved by his fellows? Religious
controversies will obtain while ever men differ in their views, and
regard the Truth as valuable, but they would be conducted very
differently from what they are if those who engaged in them acted
according to this golden rule. Imputation of unworthy motives,

scurrilous language, personal abuse, malignant insinuations, and all the unworthy resorts by which polemical discussions are so generally marred would be thrown to the winds, and clear statement and fair argument take their place.

By this precept we are taught the secret of how to preserve a good conscience in all our dealings with men in the world. If we are regulated by this rule in our actings with others, our hearts will condemn us not. For many particulars, express precepts are given in the Scriptures telling us what to do and what not to do, and they are strictly to be observed by us. But where we lack any specific command from God, then we are to fall back upon this general rule and search our conscience as to how we would have men deal with us in a similar case or circumstance, and act accordingly with them. This will make us jealous of the reputation of our neighbour, prevent us making false and injurious statements and cause us to be cautious of heeding and circulating any evil reports. We should then treat others with the same courtesy and kindness as we would wish to be treated by them. We should refrain from subjecting them to those slights and neglects which, were we in their place and they in ours, we should feel unpleasant and undeserved.

" It is a peculiar excellence of this rule of our Lord that it not only shows us our duty, but its obvious tendency is to *persuade* us to perform it. It brings duty before the mind in a peculiarly inviting form. It not only enlightens the mind, but inclines the heart. Self-love is the great obstacle in the way of doing our duty to our neighbour. Our Lord makes even self-love become, as it were, the hand-maid of justice and charity. Having led us to change places with our neighbour, to feel what are our rights, and how unreasonable it would be to withhold them, He then says, These are *his* rights, and you will be the unreasonable person to deprive him of them. We are made, as it were, to declare what is our neighbour's due, when we suppose we are only considering what was our own; and we cannot, without the shame of conscious inconsistency, refuse to him what we clearly see, were we in his place, we should account it unreasonable and unjust to be deprived of " (John Brown).

From all that has been pointed out it follows that the breach of this rule is more evil in the case of one who has tasted personally the bitterness of unmercifulness and injustice at the hands of others than those who have not done so, because experience gives a truer and closer knowledge of things than a bare concept of them imparts. He who knows things by mere contemplation knows them at hand and feels the smart of them. Therefore conscience should work more in them by way of restraint because they know what it is to be oppressed or disgraced and remember how grievous it was when they lay under a wrong. " Thou shalt neither vex a stranger, nor oppress him: for *ye* were strangers in the land of Egypt " (Exodus xxii, 21): the Hebrews knew from painful experience what it was to be friend-less under heavy yoke and cruelly afflicted, and therefore should be the last people to oppress any strangers who came into their hands. Servants who have groaned under heavy tasks ought to make the kindest and most considerate masters and mistresses if Providence raises their station in the world.

It should also be pointed out that this rule, like all the Divine precepts, is spiritual, and concerns the inward man as well as the outward: bearing upon our thoughts as well as our words and actions. The whole Law of God is spiritual (Romans vii, 14). "The law of the Lord is perfect, converting the soul" (Psalm xix, 7): it is a guide not only for the motions of the body, but also for the intents and workings of the heart. As is the first table, so is the second: "the second is like unto it" (Matt. xxii, 39). How so? It is as spiritual as the first, and therefore not only what I "do" but also what I think and purpose to do unto others is comprehended in it. As we saw in Matthew v, Christ speaks of murder and adultery committed in the heart, by spiteful anger and revengeful thoughts, by wanton desires and imaginations. Thus secret grudgings in our hearts against others are forbidden, that our affections be not alienated from them. Our neighbour is to be loved as ourselves, and therefore the justice and equity required by this rule is a righteousness which proceeds from a principle of love.

It will thus be seen that this golden rule is not only a guide to conduct but *a revealer of sin* to the saints, for who that knows his own heart will say that he measures up to it? Yet "Let all who habitually neglect or violate this law recollect that whatever be their profession they are not Christians. Even now Christ is saying to them 'Why call Me, Lord, Lord, and do not the things that I say?'" (John Brown). How few real Christians there are, then, in the world. How many are most resolute in standing up for their own rights, yet have no regard for the rights of others; who are very strict in demanding prompt payment from their debtors, yet are exceedingly slack in meeting the dues of their creditors; who hotly resent being slandered, yet care nothing of other men's names; who are very hurt when friends fail to sympathize with them in their trouble, yet are callously indifferent to the sorrows of their neighbours. It is vain to parade our orthodoxy in doctrine and prate about the communion we enjoy with Christ, while we pay little or no attention to this important precept. God will not accept our worship if our conduct unto our fellows contradicts our Christian profession.

"*For* this is the law and the prophets." This clause contains a commendation of the preceding commandment. It is no strange and harsh task which I am setting before you, says Christ, but one which God has required from His people since the beginning. That golden rule is in fact a remarkable epitome of the second table of the Moral Law, an abridgment of the duties there demanded by it. "Whatsoever ye would that men should do to you, do ye even so to them" is a gathering up into one compendious maxim of all that the Old

Testament teaches concerns our converse and commerce with men.
That golden rule is the sum of what the Law and the prophets
taught about the law of equity and justice between man and man.
In this declaration " For this is the law and the prophets " Christ
placed His *imprimatur* upon the authenticity and authority of the
Old Testament scriptures, for our Lord had never backed up His
own teaching with anything less than an appeal unto that which was
and is the very Word of God. The doctrine of Moses and the
prophets is of equal weight and worth as the doctrine of Christ.

Perhaps a brief amplification is called for by the last sentence
above. If we compare Christ and Moses and the prophets, we must
distinguish between their doctrine and their persons. The doctrine
of Moses and the prophets is equal to the doctrine of Christ in two
ways: first in certainty of Truth, for they spoke nothing other than
the very Word of God, and Christ did no more. Second, in efficacy
and authority for the binding of conscience, theirs being thus equal
with His. Yet the person of Christ is infinitely above the persons of
Moses and the prophets, for He is God incarnate, whereas they were
but holy men; He is the Author and Fountainhead of Truth,
whereas they were only the amanuenses and channels thereof.
Therefore Christ's doctrine more binds us to obedience than the
doctrine of the Old Testament because the Person delivering it is
of more excellency: this is forcibly argued in Hebrews i, 1, 2; ii, 1
(" we ought to give the more earnest heed "); xii, 25 (" much more.").

The Old Testament taught the imperative duty of seeking the
good of our neighbour as emphatically and clearly as does the New.
It plainly and repeatedly forbade the doing of anything which
would in any wise injure him. " Thou shalt not avenge nor bear any
grudge against the children of thy people, but thou shalt love thy
neighbour as thyself: I am the Lord " (Lev. xix, 18). " If thou meet
thy neighbour's ox or his ass going astray, thou shalt surely bring it
back to him again " (Exodus xxiii, 4): clearly that was enunciating
the principle, do unto others as you would like them to do unto
you. " Thou shalt not harden thy heart nor shut thine hand from
thy poor brother; but thou shalt open thine hand wide unto him,
and shalt surely lend him sufficient for his need, and that which he
wanteth " (Deut. xv, 7, 8). " Rejoice not when thine enemy falleth,
and let not thine heart be glad when he stumbleth " (Prov. xxiv, 17).
" If thine enemy be hungry, give him bread to eat; and if he be
thirsty, give him water to drink " (Prov. xxv, 21). Thus we may
perceive the error and senselessness of those who claim that the New
Testament contains a higher morality and spirituality than the Old.

CHAPTER FORTY-EIGHT

The Way of Salvation

" Enter ye in at the strait gate : for wide is the gate, and broad is the way, that leadeth to destruction, and many there be which go in thereat : Because strait is the gate, and narrow is the way, which leadeth unto life, and few there be that find it." (Matt. vii, 13, 14.)

THE verses to which we have now come are closely connected with the previous sections of the Lord's Sermon, in which He had described the character of those who were the subjects of His kingdom and had laid down the rules by which they must walk. Such teaching as He had given out was at direct variance with the popular views entertained by His hearers. The Jews supposed that they were all to be the subjects of the Messiah, simply from being the natural descendants of Abraham and because they bore in their flesh the mark of the covenant. But throughout this discourse the Lord Jesus had made it abundantly clear that something more essential than physical lineage and submission to ceremonial rites was required to make them spiritual heirs of the patriarch. There was a straiter gate which had to be entered than any privilege which natural birth gave admittance to, a narrower way to be traversed than that religious life mapped out by the scribes and the Pharisees. Only those are accounted the true children of Abraham who have his faith (Romans iv, 16), who do his works (John viii, 39), and who are vitally united to Christ (Gal. iii, 29).

If the teaching of Christ was radically different from that in which the Jews of His day had been brought up, it is in equally sharp contrast with most of the concepts which now prevail in Christendom. If the Jews were completely ignorant of the high and searching requirements of God's holiness it cannot be said that our own generation is any better informed. If they plumed themselves on being the children of Abraham, a large percentage of our people complacently assume that they are members of a " Christian nation." If they believed that the rite of circumcision secured for them the favour of God, multitudes in our churches imagine that the sprinkling of water on the brow of an infant obtains for it a passport to heaven. And even in those circles which are better instructed, for the most part salvation is offered on much easier terms, far more acceptable to the natural man, than those prescribed by the incarnate Son of God. The analogy may be extended still farther, for if it was the religious leaders of Israel who most strenuously opposed our Lord, it is those now making the loudest claims to orthodoxy that are the bitterest antagonists of the Truth.

In support of our assertion that the doctrine of Christ is directly contrary to the ideas now so prevalent in Christendom, take His solemn and express declaration that *few* there be that find life, which, we shall see as we proceed, means that only a few will reach heaven. But who is there today that really believes this? Where is the place in which such a truth is boldly and plainly uttered? We know of none. On the contrary it is generally assumed, yea, said openly, that many, that "millions," that the greater part of the human race will obtain eternal felicity. Let any man who "attends church" die, and no matter how worldly his life or how crooked his business dealings, do not his friends say with one consent "he is now at rest," and is not the preacher expected to declare in his funeral sermon that the deceased is "better off"? If anyone should dare to dissent is he not at once condemned for being "harsh and uncharitable"? The tree, forsooth, is not to be known by its fruits but by the label some parsonic gardener has attached to it.

The unwelcome but faithful objector may call attention to our Lord's statement that His flock is a "little"—Greek "very little"— one (Luke xii, 32), but the religious world will not listen to him. He must not challenge the Christian profession of his fellows. He must not look for perfect people in this world. We all have our failings, and though some believe differently from himself, yet their hearts are right, and though others may be slack in performing certain duties, let him remember that they claim to be trusting in the finished work of Christ, and therefore it is highly reprehensible for anyone to doubt them. So far from believing that only a *few* will reach heaven, the vast majority in Christendom today hold that somehow, in some way, the greater part of our fellows will get there. Hell, if there be such a place, is reserved for arch-criminals and villains, just as our prisons house only a small fraction of the population—the "unfortunates" and "misguided" ones.

And why is it that there are scarcely any left among us who really believe that only the *few* will reach heaven? There can only be one answer: because it is now generally held that heaven can be obtained on much easier terms than those prescribed by Christ. The adulterous generation in which our lot is cast are quite sure that heaven can be reached without treading the only way which leads there, that the kingdom of God can be entered *without* passing through "much tribulation" (Acts xiv, 22), that we may be disciples of Christ *without* denying self, taking up our cross and following Him (Matt. xvi, 24). They do not believe that if their right eye offends it *must* be plucked out and if their right hand offends it *must* be cut off (Matt. v, 29, 30). They do not believe that if they live after the flesh they shall die, and that only if through the Spirit they mortify the deeds of the body they shall live (Romans viii, 13). They are fully persuaded that a man can serve two masters and succeed in

" making the best of two worlds." In short, they do not believe the
gate is as "strait" nor the way as "narrow" as Christ declared it to
be.

All we have to do in order to be saved is to respond to Christ's
gracious invitation and "come unto Him." Ah, but that "all" is
by no means the simple matter that many think and that so many
evangelists falsely represent it to be. We have to turn our back upon
the world and forsake our cherished sins in order to turn our face
unto Christ, as the prodigal had to leave the far country, where he
had spent his substance in riotous living, before he could come to the
Father. Christ is the Holy One of God and will not be the minister
of sin. Love for the things of this world closes the heart against Him.
What caused the young man to go away from Christ sorrowing, after
some fair show of willingness to be His disciple, but love of possessions? What restrained the invited guests from accepting the invitation to the marriage feast, but immoderate affection to the husband-
ing of a farm and proving of oxen (Matt. xxii, 5)? "Whosoever is
under the government of this lust (covetousness) can no more believe
in Christ than a man lying under a heap of rubbish or at the bottom
of the sea can see the glory of the heavens. The intentness of the
eye on one object hinders it from the view of another" (S. Charnock).

When the Philippian jailer asked "What must I do to be saved?"
all the apostle answered was "Believe on the Lord Jesus Christ, and
thou shalt be saved, and thy house." Waiving now the fact that
that was not the idle inquiry of one who was still in love with the
world and taking his fill of its pleasures, but instead the distressed
cry of one who was desperate, let it be pointed out that while
believing in Christ is a simple and easy act considered in itself, yet
it becomes a very hard and difficult thing to us by reason of the
opposition made thereto by our inward corruptions and the temptations of Satan. To forgive our enemies and love those who persecute
and despitefully use us is, considered as a notion of the mind, easy to
be performed, but try and bring your heart to do the same and you
will discover it lies beyond your own unaided powers. As a motion
of the mind it is both simple and delightful to cast all our care upon
Him who careth for us (I Peter v, 7), yet a poor man, in ill health
and the father of a big family, does not find it easy to perform. No
heart can tear itself away from the world and hate beloved lusts
without first experiencing the mighty operations of the Holy Spirit."

"Enter ye in at the strait gate" says Christ at the beginning of
our passage, and that this is far from being an easy thing to do
appears from His word on another occasion: " *Strive to* enter in at
the strait gate" (Luke xiii, 24). That He should employ such an
expression clearly implies the slothfulness and carelessness which
characterize mere nominal professors, as it also denotes that there are
real difficulties and formidable obstacles to be overcome. The Greek
word there used for "strive" (*agonizomai*) is a very expressive and
emphatic one, meaning "agonize." It occurs again in I Corinthians

ix, 25, "and every man that striveth for the mastery is temperate in all things:" the reference is to the athletes who took part in the marathon races, willing to undergo the most self-denying discipline to be at their fittest, thereby hoping to win an earthly crown. This word rendered "strive" is translated "labouring fervently" in Colossians iv, 12, and "fight "in I Timothy vi, 12! Ah, my reader, becoming a Christian is not done simply by holding up your hand in a religious meeting or signing some "decision" card. Alas, that such multitudes have been deceived by these satanic catch-pennies.

"The kingdom of heaven suffereth violence and the violent take it by force" (Matt. xi, 12), like an army storming a city and capturing the same. We have often read of earthly kingdoms being obtained by violence, but it seems surprising to hear of such means being used upon the kingdom of heaven. How are we to understand this? Why, thus: "violence" here does not signify unlawful assaults, but earnest deliberation. It is not an injurious violence like that which seizes earthly prizes, but a holy and industrious violence, intensity of desire and endeavour, persevering zeal which refuses a denial. It is a determination to master all difficulties, to break through all impediments and surmount every obstacle. Such violence was necessary then: "Woe unto you scribes and Pharisees, hypocrites! for ye shut up the kingdom of heaven against men: for ye neither go in yourselves, neither suffer ye them that are entering to go in" (Matt. xxiii, 13), but did all they could to oppose them. So now: godless relatives and worldly companions will seek to deter the earnest seeker after Christ, but he must not be deterred if he would find. "The kingdom of heaven was never intended to indulge the ease of triflers, but to be the rest of them that labour" (Matthew Henry).

"Enter ye in at the strait gate." It is not enough to listen to preaching about this "gate," nor to study its structure or admire the wisdom of its appointment: it must be *entered*. Sermons on repentance and faith in Christ avail us nothing unless they move our hearts to comply therewith. The Greek word here rendered "strait" signifies restrained, cramped, or better "narrow" as it is rendered in the R.V. And what is meant by this strait or narrow gate? A "gate" serves two purposes: it lets in and shuts out. This gate is the only avenue of admittance to that "way" which leads unto life, and all who enter not by it are eternally barred from the presence of God and the realm of ineffable bliss. The second use of this "gate" is solemnly illustrated at the close of the parable of the virgins. The foolish ones lacked the necessary "oil" (the work of the Spirit in the heart), and when they sought to obtain it the Bridegroom came and "the door was *shut*" (Matt. xxv, 10), and though they besought Him to open it unto them, He answered "I know you not."

What is denoted by entering this narrow gate? Chiefly three things. First, *the acceptance of those teachings* of truth, of duty, of happiness, which were unfolded by Christ: the honest and actual receiving into the heart of His holy, searching and flesh-withering instructions. Those teachings may be summed up in His emphasis upon the righteous claims and demands of God upon us and His insistence upon our depraved state and wicked enmity against Him. No one can become a Christian while he entertains any doubt upon the Divine inspiration and authority of the Scriptures, or while he refuses to bow to the verdict which God has pronounced upon him. We must know ourselves to be utterly lost before there can be any desire for salvation, and we must accept God's sentence of condemnation upon us ere we know how guilty we are in His sight. There can be no traversing the narrow way itself until we set to our seal that God is true when He declares we are "all as an unclean thing," that there is "no soundness" in us. It is by relinquishing error, the lies of Satan, and receiving the Truth that we pass through the strait gate.

Second, *the exercise of true repentance.* "From that time Jesus began to preach and to say, Repent" (Matt. iv, 17). It was announced of His forerunner that he should "prepare the way of the Lord." And how did he do so? By making ready a people to receive Him when He appeared before them as "the Lamb of God." And in what did that readiness consist? This, that they repented, confessed their sins, and owned that death was their due by being buried in baptism in the Jordan by him (Luke iii, 1-6). The Gospel is not less holy than the Law and therefore it requires that our hearts bewail our former transgressions of the Law and be firm and sincere in its resolution against all future sin. "You and your sins must separate, or you and your God will never come together. No one sin may you keep. They must all be given up: they must be brought out like the Canaanitish kings from the cave and hanged up before the sun. You must forsake them, abhor them, and ask the Lord to overcome them" (C. H. Spurgeon). It is by abandoning our idols and the pleasures of sin that we pass through the strait gait.

Third, *the complete surrender of ourselves* to God in Christ. This will anticipate an objection which some may be ready to make: is not the Lord Jesus "the Door" (John x, 9)? Yes, and He is so according to the three principal functions of His mediatorial office: He is "the Door" into God's presence as He is Prophet, Priest and King. To believe savingly in Christ is to receive Him as Prophet to instruct us, as Priest to atone for us, and as King to rule over us. Only as His holy teachings are really accepted by a contrite heart is any soul prepared to place any value on His cleansing blood, and the sincerity of our acceptance of Him as Priest is evidenced by our readiness to submit to His royal sceptre, for like His types He is *first* the King of righteousness and *after that* the King of peace (Heb. vii, 2). Christ's cleansing blood is available to none who are unwilling to throw down the weapons of their warfare against God: they must forsake *their* way if they would be pardoned (Isaiah lv, 7). Only by a serious dedication of ourselves unto God through Christ can we become enjoyers of the riches of His grace. It is by a complete surrender of ourselves unto God that we pass through the strait gate.

"Enter ye in at the strait gate." Here were "duty repentance" and "duty faith" with a vengeance, for this exhortation is obviously addressed unto the unsaved: "Enter ye in" definitely implies they were yet outside. And unto whom was Christ speaking? Not to heathen idolaters, who were without any knowledge of the true God. No, it was to those who believed in Jehovah and who received the Scriptures as His very Word. It was to those who averred "we have one Father, even God" (John viii, 41). Nevertheless, despite all their knowledge of the Truth and enjoyment of external privileges, they had never entered that gate which alone admitted to the only way which leadeth unto life This same exhortation is equally applicable and pertinent today unto multitudes of church members who, notwithstanding their profession and performances, have never been born again. In this exhortation Christ makes it plain to His ministers that He would have them recognize the responsibility of their hearers, and call upon the unregenerate to discharge their duties.

"*For* wide is the gate and broad is the way that leadeth to destruction, and many there be which go in thereat." In those words our Lord advanced a reason or argument to enforce His previous exhortation. There is another gate than the "strait" one, altogether different therefrom, for it is "wide" and gives entrance into a broad way, but it leads to the bottomless pit. It is "the course of this world" (Eph. ii, 2), in which all its unregenerate citizens are found. It is the path of self-will and self-gratification. It is "wide" because those in it own no restrictions. They have broken down the commandments of God which were designed to be a hedge about them. It is therefore a pleasant and *easy* way to the flesh, for no inquiry or diligent search has to be made in order to find it, no resolution and perseverance are called for in order to continue treading it, no self-denial has to be practised to remain therein. A dead fish can float with the stream, but only a living one can swim against it: so the unregenerate mechanically follow this road, for there is nothing in them to resist the law of gravity. The going is smooth and easy bceause it is all *downhill*!

It is a *crowded* road, for "many there be which go in thereat." It is the very width of it which renders it so attractive to the carnal mind. Here there are no "quota" limitations, no barring of "aliens," no restrictions of colour, caste or creed. There is plenty of room for all. Men may walk in the ways of their hearts and in the sight of their eyes, give rein to their lusts and full indulgence to their inclinations, and none shall hinder them. This broad road is thronged because all mankind are in it by nature, birth admitting them into the same; nor has anyone the slightest desire to desert it unless a miracle of grace be wrought upon him. Like Lot and his wife in Sodom every last one of us is so loath to leave the city of destruction that the Christian too had preferred to remain there and

THE WAY OF SALVATION

perish, unless the Lord had sent His messengers to " pluck " him as a brand from the burning. " Woe to the multitude of many people " (Isaiah xvii, 12) says God to this densely packed road.

It is a *deceptive* road, for few upon it have any idea of whither it is taking them. Those upon it believe they are following the wise course, for they regard as fools those who differ from them. We are only young once, life is short, let us have a gay time while it lasts; let us eat, drink and be merry seems to them the very dictates of common sense. Ah, it is " the way which *seemeth right* unto a man, but the end thereof are the ways of death " (Prov. xiv, 12). So sure are its travellers they are right that they conclude anyone is afflicted with " religious mania " who prefers the narrow way. Yet it is a *fatal* road, for it " leadeth to destruction," hopeless and eternal destruction. It conducts to the bottomless pit, the unquenchable fire, and the undying worm. It is the way of the ungodly, and Scripture expressly declares that " the way of the ungodly shall *perish*" (Psalm i, 6). And, my reader, that fatal way can only be abandoned by conversion, by a radical right about face, by turning from sin and self-pleasing and turning unto God and holy living.

CHAPTER FORTY-NINE

The Way of Salvation—Concluded

" Because strait is the gate, and narrow is the way, which leadeth unto life, and few there be that find it. Beware of false prophets, which come to you in sheep's clothing. but inwardly they are ravening wolves." (Matt. vii, 14, 15.)

As Christ was the antitype of Melchizedek and Aaron, the antitype of David and Solomon, so also was He the antitypical Moses (Deut. xviii, 18) and Samuel, and therefore in the fulfilment of His commission He could say unto His hearers, " I set before you the way of life, and the way of death " (Jer. xxi, 8). This is precisely what He did in the verses before us: He likens our passage through life to a journey, a journey from time unto eternity. There are but two possible destinations unto which each of us is travelling, for we are treading the path which leads to heavenly bliss or the road which conducts to the eternal torments of hell. That we may ascertain which of those ways we are on, Christ gave a brief and clearly identifying description of each of them, defining the entrance thereto, the breadth thereof, and the numbers thereon. God has ordained two distinct places to be the final abodes of men after this life, and between them He has fixed a great gulf so that none can pass from the one to the other (Luke xvi, 26), and equally great is the distance and the difference between the ways leading to them and the character and conduct of those walking along the one and the other, for the former are the children of God, whereas the latter are the children of the Devil.

This drawing such drastic lines of discrimination, this definite and circumscribed classification, is not at all acceptable to those who traverse the spacious road leading to destruction. They pride themselves on their broadmindedness and liberality and resent anything which suggests that all is not well with them. They know their characters are not white, yet would not allow for a moment they were black, so persuade themselves they are a shade midway between. They may not be good enough for heaven, but they are quite sure they are not bad enough for hell. That is why the papish invention of a " purgatory " is so popular with multitudes of people, and just as they would fondly believe there is another *place* besides heaven and hell, so they like to think there is another *class* besides saints and sinners. But if our thoughts be formed according to the teaching of Holy Writ we are shut up to this inevitable and sole alternative, light or darkness, truth or error, Christ or Belial, holiness or sin, salvation or damnation.

Christ began this solemn and searching portion of His Sermon with the exhortation, "Enter ye in at the strait gate," which we understand to mean: first, jettison all your own ideas and receive the Truth as a little child (Matt. xviii, 3), bowing to its sentence of condemnation. Second, abandon your course of self-pleasing, bewail your rebellion against God and set your heart firmly against sin. Third, surrender yourself to God's righteous claims and yield yourself unreservedly to the Lordship of Christ. That exhortation is enforced by the following reason: "*for* wide is the gate, and broad is the way, that leadeth to destruction, and many there be which go in thereat." All who are unconverted proceed along it. "It hath in it various paths suited to men's different humours and inclinations. The covetous and the spendthrift, the profligate and the hypocrite, the Antinomian and the Pharisee, the sons and daughters of pleasure and the grave designing politicians and proud philosophers, decent moralists and infamous debauchees, have their several paths and their select companies; they mutually despise and condemn each other, yet they all keep one another in countenance by agreeing to oppose the holy ways of the Lord" (Thomas Scott).

Yet pleasant as the broad way may be to the flesh and popular as it is with the masses, it ends in unutterable woe and everlasting torments. How necessary it is then, that each of us should give heed to that injunction, "Ponder the path of thy feet" (Prov. iv, 26). Men are ready enough to do so in temporal matters, why not so in spiritual? They do not enter a train or even a bus without first ascertaining where it is bound for: then why not pause and ask, Whither will this godless mode of life take me? In which direction are my feet pointed: heavenward or hellward? So immeasurable is the distance betwixt those two bodies, so vast is the difference between life and destruction, that we are called upon to exercise the utmost care and conscience in using every Divinely prescribed means for attaining the one and escaping the other. In the verses we are now considering Christ faithfully warns us that if we are to have a well-grounded hope of attaining the home of the blessed we must give heed to that commandment, "Thou shalt not follow a multitude to do evil" (Exodus xxiii, 2).

There appears to have been some uncertainty in the minds of our translators concerning the exact relation between verse 14 and its immediate context, for it will be observed that they have suggested "How" as an alternative to its opening "Because." In the preceding verse our Lord had given a brief but emphatic exhortation which He had followed with a solemn reason to enforce the same. What then is the precise force of verse 14, which obviously returns to the original exhortation? If we take the marginal rendering, then verse 14 constitutes an *exclamation*, occasioned by what has been said of the broad way and the multitudes which choose to tread it. But if we take it as it reads, and which we regard as preferable, then verse 14 contains an *amplification*. First, informing us that entering in at the strait gate is not the end itself, but only a means thereto, for it gives entrance to the "narrow way" which has to be traversed if life is to be obtained. Second, it plainly announces that the walk thereon will be both difficult and lonely, for only the "few" succeed in finding it. And third, it offers encouragement or presents a powerful incentive by assuring its travellers that life lies at the end of it.

It seems to us there is yet another way of ascertaining the relation of verse 14 to its context, and that is by linking it not with the whole of the preceding verse but with its last clause, thus: "and many there be which go in thereat, *because* strait is the gate and narrow is the way which leadeth unto life." Considered thus it is a word of *explanation,* informing us *why* the multitudes prefer the road which leads to destruction: the only alternative path repels them. The straitness of its entrance and the narrowness of its course present no attraction for the lovers of fleshly licence and worldly pursuits and pleasures; on the contrary, the way which leads unto life is diametrically opposed to their ideas and inclinations. They may offer a hundred excuses why they seek not the narrow way, but the real one is that they have no heart for it. As a fish is out of its native element when brought from the water and placed on the land, so the unregenerate have no relish for godliness. None but those who have communicated to them a new nature will desire to tread the highway of holiness.

"Because strait [or "narrow"] is the gate." We have already pondered this expression in the preceding article, yet so little is it understood and so much is it contradicted by the claptrap evangelism of our day that a further word on it is called for. Place by the side of it another of our Lord's sayings: "That a rich man shall hardly enter into the kingdom!" (Matt. xix, 23). How far removed is that from the idea now so prevalent! Do not thousands who take the lead in tract distribution, open-air work, Gospel hall and mission hall services, suppose it is just as easy for a rich man to be saved as a poor one, seeing that all which either of them has to do is "simply believe the record which God has given of His Son." Ah, my reader, the devils believe the whole of that record (James ii, 19): believe in His deity (Matt. viii, 29), His virgin birth, His atoning death, His triumphant resurrection, but does their belief make them any less devilish in character? So of the vast majority of those who profess to have received Christ as their personal Saviour; has their believing of the Gospel made them less carnal and worldly, more truthful with their fellows, more honest in their business dealings, less selfish; if it has not, what is such "believing" worth? Less than nothing.

If saving faith were nothing but an act of the mind, an assent to the Divine testimony, then it *would be* just as easy for a millionaire to be saved as a pauper. But it is "with the *heart* man believeth unto righteousness" (Romans x, 10) and the heart is the seat of the *affections,* and how can a person hate what he loves or love what he hates? Can he do so by a mere "act of the will"? Of course not: it is contrary to nature. A miracle of grace has to be performed within him first, his heart must be "renewed," radically changed, before its affections will move in a different direction. We are told that "the disciples were astonished at His words," so they too were labouring under the delusion that salvation was a simple matter for anybody. "But Jesus answered again and saith unto them, Children, *how hard* is it for them that trust in riches to enter into the kingdom of God!" Faith is an attitude of heart Godward, and where material wealth is made the heart's sufficiency in connection with temporal supplies, how can it reverse its entire trend and trust God for spiritual and eternal things?

"It is easier [continued Christ] for a camel to go through the eye of a needle than for a rich man to enter into the kingdom of God." Now face the issue frankly, dear reader: does that declaration of the Lord Jesus denote that salvation is to be obtained cheaply, that anyone may be saved any time he is willing to be? Should it be answered, This is not a "salvation" passage, we reply, It most certainly is, for the disciples at once asked, "Who then can *be saved*?" (Mark x, 26). To which our Lord said, "With men it is impossible, but not with God, for with God all things are possible." How utterly erroneous then is the teaching that the matter of his salvation rests entirely with man's will. They are deceivers of souls, blind leaders of the blind, who go around telling the ignorant and unwary that getting saved is an easy and simple thing. Not so, it is the most difficult thing of all; nay, with men it is *impossible*, and the sooner this be recognized the sooner we are likely to get down on our knees and cry to God in earnest for the supernatural operations of His Spirit.

Trusting in riches is far from being the only thing which hinders man from seeking God's salvation. "How can ye believe," said Christ on another occasion, "which receive honour one of another and seek not the honour that cometh from God only?" (John v, 44): the love of fame, seeking the approbation of our fellows, is another fatal obstruction. If the first three Gospels be read attentively (John's Gospel is for Christians—i, 16) it will be seen that the Lord Jesus was very far from teaching that the attainment of heaven is a simple matter. He insisted that right eyes have to be plucked out (cherished lusts mortified) and right hands cut off (beloved idols destroyed)— Matt. v, 29, 30. He likened the Christian unto a "house" which has to withstand "floods" and "winds" beating upon it (Matt. vii, 25). He declared that in order to be His disciple a man must deny himself and take up his cross and follow Him (Matt. xvi, 24). Instead of promising His followers a smooth voyage through this world, He said, "If they have called the Master of the house Beelzebub, how much more shall they call them of His household?" (Matt. x, 25). Instead of teaching that a single and isolated act of faith was sufficient to secure heaven, He said, "But he that shall endure unto the end, the same shall be saved" (Matt. xxiv, 13). Instead of seeking to rush men into believing, He bade them "sit down first and count *the cost*" (Luke xiv, 28).

The gate or entrance then is a "strait" one, for it will not admit those who are loaded with the weapons of rebellion against God, nor can they squeeze through who are walking arm in arm with the world. To enter that gate the heart has to be humbled, sinful pleasures have to relinquished, worldly companions abandoned, Christ has to be received in all His offices. And mark it well, this "gate" is but the entrance, giving admittance to the one and only path which leadeth unto life. That path Christ described as a "narrow way," to intimate that it is no easier, wider or more pleasant than the gate itself. In I Thessalonians iii, 4, the cognate term is rendered "suffer tribulation." It is not on flowery beds of ease that the pilgrim is conducted to the Father's house: rather does he have to force his way through briars and thorns which cut and tear the flesh. There is not one path for the Redeemer and another for the redeemed (John x, 4). His was a path of affliction and ours cannot be otherwise if we follow the example He has left us; and if we do not we shall not join Him on high.

"Narrow is the way which leadeth unto life." As this way is entered by the heart's sincere acceptance of Christ's holy teaching, so it is traversed by the heart and life being constantly regulated thereby. They who tread this narrow way heed not the counsel of the ungodly (Psalm i, 2), lean not unto their own understanding (Prov. iii, 5), and follow not "the customs of the people" (Jer. x, 3). Rather are the believer's thoughts formed by the Scriptures and his conduct directed by its statutes, so that God's Word becomes to him in fact and experience "a lamp unto his feet and a light unto his path." The narrow way is strictly marked and exactly defined in the Divine Charter, and along it the Christian must go without turning aside either to the right hand or the left (Prov. iv, 27). When he meets with an enemy that enemy must be overcome, or he will be overcome by him. The going is strenuous and arduous, for the whole of it is *uphill*. Let anyone who thinks otherwise read Bunyan's *Pilgrim's Progress* and see if that deeply taught soul pictured pilgrim's course to the celestial city as all smooth sailing. Alas, that so much of the modern preaching is the very reverse of what is contained in that faithful and helpful work.

And why is the way such a "narrow" one? Because it is a single path, whereas the way of death is manifold, containing sundry avenues. Just as Truth is one, but error is a many-headed monster, so the highway of holiness is a single track in contrast with the numerous pavements in the broad road which leads to destruction. It is "narrow" because those on it are shut in by the Divine commands, which make all else forbidden territory. It is "narrow" because it excludes all fleshly licence and lawless liberty. It is "narrow" because it can only be trodden by faith, and faith is not only opposed to sight but to sense, to self-will and self-pleasing. It is

THE WAY OF SALVATION—CONCLUDED

" narrow " because all other interests have to be subordinated to the pleasing of God. Thus it is a way of difficulty and displeasure to corrupt nature, for our lusts are impatient of any restraint. It is natural to be more concerned about the body than the soul, to be absorbed with things present rather than with things to come, and this natural tendency is fed by habit and custom: "Can the Ethiopian change his skin, or the leopard his spots? then may ye also do good that are *accustomed* to do evil " (Jer. xiii, 23).

Walking along the narrow way denotes a steady perseverance in faith and obedience to God in Christ. It signifies the overcoming of all opposition and the rejecting of all temptations to turn off into what Bunyan terms " Bypath meadow." That narrow way must be followed no matter how much it may militate against my worldly interests. Our minds, our affections, our wills, our speeches and actions have all to be brought within the compass of God's Holy Word, within the compass of both His Law and His Gospel. At ten fundamental points our liberty is circumscribed by the Law, nor is the Gospel any less strict. Our natural desire unto self-confidence and self-sufficiency, self-complacency and self-righteousness is sternly repressed by it. The duties which the Lord has enjoined must be discharged conscientiously and circumspectly. Bounds are prescribed to our thoughts and affections: though certain things be lawful yet they are not expedient, and if things indifferent be used immoderately we sin therein. Good works are to be performed from a holy principle, in a holy manner, and with a holy design, and any failure therein is sin, for sin is a " missing the mark."

The obedience of the Christian is very precise, for not only must the rule be strictly observed but the motive must be pure—the pleasing and glorifying of God. Even our prayers must be according to the Divine will or they are not answered. Those who walk thus are bound to be thought singular and peculiar. Their Lord has faithfully warned them beforehand, " If the world hate you, ye know that it hated Me before it hated you. If ye were of the world, the world would love his own: but because ye are not . . . the world hateth you " (John xv, 18, 19). And mark it well my reader, it was not the profane and heathen world that hated Christ, but the professing and religious world, and so it is still. If by grace you are enabled to tread the narrow way it will be church members, professing Christians, who will say, " Such strictness is not required. I cannot see why you wish to cut yourself from us." If you refuse to imitate their laxity, they will sneer at your " holy preciseness " and mock at such " out-of-date puritanism." Ah, journeying along the narrow way means swimming *against* the tide of popular opinion!

" Narrow is the way which leadeth unto life." By " life " is meant that glorious state of unclouded fellowship with God, the heart's being satisfied with Him, the realization of His unspeakable excellency and the fullness of joy there is in His immediate presence. Even now the real Christian has the promise, yea, the earnest, of it, but life in its fullness, in its unalloyed blessedness, in its ineffable consummation is yet future, as is clear from its being placed over against "destruction." "And few there be that find it." So let not the saint be discouraged because he finds his path so unpopular and a lonely one: his Master declared it would be so. This is one of the surest indexes that he is on the right road. And why is it that so few "find" it? Because so few diligently seek it. The great crowd of religious professors imagine they are already on it, and therefore they heed not that word, "Ask for the old paths, where is the good way, and walk therein" (Jer. vi, 16). We need to *inquire* for it. Where? In God's Word, and then *follow* it, putting into practice what we already know.

Even when a servant of God describes the narrow way to professing Christians they heed him not, but charge him with teaching salvation by works and bringing souls into bondage, knowing not that the Gospel is the handmaid of the Law and not its enemy (Romans iii, 31). Saving faith not only trusts in Christ but follows Him. It not only believes God's promises but obeys His precepts. Saving faith is a fruitful thing, abounding in good works. It enables its possessor to endure trials, resist the Devil, and overcome the world (I John v, 4). None tread the narrow way save those who make vital godliness their chief concern, the main business of life. Hence we see why it is that the vast majority of our fellow men and women, yea, and of professing Christians also, will fail to reach heaven: it is because they prefer sin to holiness, indulging the lusts of the flesh to walking according to the Scriptures, self to Christ, the world to God, the broad way to the narrow. They are unwilling to forsake their sins, destroy their idols, turn their backs on the world, and submit to Christ as *Lord*.

CHAPTER FIFTY

False Prophets

" Beware of false prophets, which come to you in sheep's clothing, but inwardly they are ravening wolves." (Matt. vii, 15.)

IF there be any verse in Holy Writ where it is deeply important to observe (and heed!) *its connection* it is surely the one at which we have now arrived. It may appear to the casual reader that our Lord here began an entirely new subject, having little or no relation to what immediately precedes. It is true our present verse introduces a distinct section of His Sermon, yet it also bears directly on what He had just said. Having described most solemnly and searchingly the way of life, like a faithful Guide Christ went on to warn us against one of the chief impediments to walking in that way, namely false guides; those who under the pretence of offering us Divine directions therein will fatally deceive us if we give heed thereto. In every age, but never more so than in our own, multitudes of gullible souls have been allured into the broad road which leads to destruction by men professing to be teachers of the Truth and ministers of Christ, yet who had not His Spirit and who were none of His: blind leaders of the blind, who with their dupes fall into the ditch.

"Beware of false prophets." The force of this exhortation will be the better perceived if we take to heart what is found in the Old Testament thereon, bearing in mind that history has ever repeated itself since human nature is the same in all ages. "A wonderful and horrible thing is committed in the land: The prophets prophesy falsely, and the priests bear rule by their means" (Jer. v, 30, 31). "Then the Lord said unto me, The prophets prophesy lies in My name: I sent them not, neither have I commanded them, neither spake I unto them; they prophesy unto you a false vision and divination, and a thing of nought and the deceit of their heart" (Jer. xiv, 14) "I have seen also in the prophets of Jerusalem an horrible thing: they commit adultery, and walk in lies; they strengthen also the hands of evildoers, that none doth return from his wickedness; they are all of them unto Me as Sodom. . . . Thus saith the Lord of hosts, Hearken not unto the words of the prophets that prophesy unto you, they make you vain: they speak a vision of their own heart, and not out of the mouth of the Lord " (Jer. xxiii, 14,16). "There is a conspiracy of her prophets in the midst thereof, like a roaring lion ravening the prey; they have devoured souls, they have taken the treasure and precious things, they have made her many widows "

(Ezek. xxii, 25). False prophets were one of the chief factors in the apostasy and destruction of Israel, and these passages are recorded for our admonition and warning.

It must not be supposed that such deceivers passed away with the ending of the Mosaic economy. The Lord Jesus and His apostles announced that there should be false teachers in this Christian dispensation. Christ declared that "many false prophets shall rise and shall deceive many," yea, they would present such imposing credentials that "if it were possible, they shall deceive the very elect" (Matt. xxiv, 11, 24). Paul announced, "I know this, that after my departing shall grievous wolves enter in among you, not sparing the flock. Also of your own selves shall men arise, speaking perverse things, to draw away disciples after them. Therefore watch" (Acts xx, 29-31). And again he said, "Mark them which cause divisions and offences contrary to the doctrine which ye have learned; and avoid them. For they that are such serve not our Lord Jesus Christ, but their own belly; and by good words and fair speeches deceive the hearts of the simple" (Romans xvi, 17, 18). Peter foretold, "But there were false prophets also among the people, even as there shall be false teachers among you, who privily shall bring in damnable heresies, even denying the Lord that bought them, and bring upon themselves swift destruction. And many shall follow their pernicious ways" (II Peter ii, 1, 2). John gave warning, "believe not every spirit, but try the spirits whether they are of God: because many false prophets are gone out into the world" (I John iv, 1).

Immediately after the parable of the Sower Christ declared, "His enemy came and sowed tares among the wheat" (Matt. xiii, 25), the one so closely resembling the other that He commanded, "Let both grow together until the harvest," when it will be seen there is no corn in the ears of the deceitful tares. By placing those parables in juxtaposition the Lord Jesus exposed the method and order of His adversary. "As Jannes and Jambres [the magicians of Pharaoh] withstood Moses" (II Tim. iii, 8) by their imitating his miracles, so when God sends forth His servants to preach the Gospel the Devil soon after prompts his emissaries to proclaim "another gospel": when God speaks the Devil gives a mocking echo. Satan has found that he can work far more effectively by counterfeiting the Truth than by openly denying it, hence in every age "false prophets" have abounded, and therefore we should be neither surprised nor stumbled by their number or success in our own day. We fully agree with Andrew Fuller when he said, "As this word 'beware of false prophets' was designed for Christians of every age, the term rendered 'prophets' must here, as it often is elsewhere, be used of ordinary teachers."

"Beware of false prophets" signifies in this dispensation, Be on your guard against false teachers, heretical preachers. There are no longer any "prophets" in the strict and technical sense of the term, though there are a few of God's servants who in their gifts and special work approximate closely thereto. Those against whom we are here warned are men who have a false commission, never having been called of God to the service they engage in; they preach error, which is subversive of "the doctrine which is according to godliness" (I Tim. vi, 3); and the fruit they bear is a base imitation of the fruit of the Spirit. The chief identifying mark of the false prophets has ever been their saying, "Peace, peace," when there is none (Jer. xxiii, 17; Micah iii, 5; I Thess. v, 3). They heal the wounds of sinners slightly (Jer. viii, 11) and daub "with untempered morter" (Ezek. xiii, 14; xxii, 28). They prophesy "smooth things" Isaiah xxx, 10), inventing easy ways to heaven, pandering to corrupt nature. There is nothing in their preaching which searches the conscience and renders the empty professor uneasy, nothing which humbles and causes their hearers to mourn before God; but rather that which puffs up, makes them pleased with themselves and to rest content in a false assurance.

The general characteristic of "false prophets" is that they make vital godliness to be a less strict and easier thing than it actually is, more agreeable to fallen human nature, and thus they encourage the unregenerate to be satisfied with something which comes short of true grace. So the Pharisees did, notwithstanding all their strict-ness (Matt. xxiii, 25). So the papists do, notwithstanding all their boasted austerities. So Arminians do, notwithstanding all their seeming zeal for good works. So the Antinomians do, notwithstand-ing their pretended superior light and joy, zeal and confidence. This is the common mark of all false teachers: rejecting the Divine way, they manufacture one to suit themselves, and however they may differ among themselves, they all agree to make the practice of piety and the Christian walk an easier thing than the Scriptures do, to offer salvation on cheaper terms, to make the gate wider and the way to heaven broader than did Christ and His apostles. It is this which explains the secret of their popularity: "They are of the world: therefore speak they of the world, and the world heareth them" (I John iv, 5). But of such Christ warns his people to "beware," for they feed souls with poison and not with the pure milk of the Word.

"Which come to you in sheep's clothing, but inwardly they are ravening wolves." In those words Christ emphasized the *danger* of these false prophets: the character they assumed is well calculated to deceive the unwary. The Lord here alluded to a device employed by false prophets in former times who counterfeited the true servants of God by wearing their distinctive attire. Elijah, in regard to his garments, was called "a hairy man" (II Kings i, 8), and therefore when John the Baptist came "in the spirit and the power of Elias" (Luke i, 17) we are told that he "had his raiment of camel's hair" (Matt. iii, 4). When then the agents of Satan posed as the true prophets they counterfeited their attire that they might more easily seduce the people, as is clear from Zechariah xiii, 4, where Jehovah declared that a day would come when the prophet should be ashamed of the vision he had prophesied and should no more wear "a garment of hair to deceive." Thus by this evident reference Christ intimated the plausible pretences of the heretical teachers, the subterfuges which they would employ to conceal their real character and design, thereby stressing what *dangerous* persons they are and how urgent is the need for His people to be constantly on their guard against those who seek their destruction.

"Which come to you in sheep's clothing, but inwardly they are ravening wolves." They pose as being the very opposite of what they really are. They are agents of the evil one, yet claim to be the servants of the Holy One. Their place is on the outside, in the forests and mountains, yet they intrude themselves within the fold. This intimates their great craftiness and seeming piety. People think they are teaching them the way to heaven, when in fact they are conducting them to hell. Often they are difficult to discover, for they "creep into houses and lead captive silly women " (II Tim. iii, 6), yea, even in apostolic times some of them successfully "*crept in* unawares " (Jude 4) into the assemblies of the saints. It was of such Paul wrote when he said, "For such are false apostles, deceitful workers, transforming themselves into the apostles of Christ. And no marvel: for Satan himself is transformed into an angel of light. Therefore it is no great thing if his ministers also be transformed as the ministers of righteousness" (II Cor. xi, 13-15). Though their clothing be "sheep's," yet they have the fierceness and cruelty of wolves.

In addition to their subtlety and plausibility, frequently accompanied by a most winsome personality and an apparently saintly walk, there is a real danger of our being deceived by these false prophets and receiving their erroneous teaching by virtue of the fact that there is that *within the Christian* himself which responds to and approves of their lies. How immeasurably this intensifies our peril! That which flatters is pleasing to the flesh; that which abases is distasteful. Paul complains of this very thing to the Corinthians. Some had evidently resented his plain speaking in the first epistle, wherein he had rebuked their sins, for in his second he wrote, "would to God ye could bear with me a little " (xi, 1). The Galatians first received the Gospel so gladly from him that they would have plucked out their eyes had that advantaged him (iv, 15), yet soon after they imbibed deadly error from the Judaizers, and when the apostle took them to task for this he had to ask them, "Am I therefore become your enemy, because I tell you the truth?" (verse 16). Thus it was with the multitudes in connection with our Saviour: acclaiming Him with their hosannas and less than a week later crying, "Away with Him, crucify Him," so fickle and treacherous is the human heart.

What point does this give to our Lord's command, "take heed *what* ye hear" (Mark iv, 24). Corrupt nature is thoroughly in love with error and will more readily and eagerly receive false than true doctrine. Should any dispute our statement, we would refer them to "the prophets prophesy falsely and the priests bear rule by their means; and My people *love to have it so*" (Jer. v, 31). Said Christ unto the Jews, "because I tell you the truth, ye believe me not" (John viii, 45): what a commentary on fallen human nature—had He preached *lies* they had promptly received Him. Alas, what is man: he will run greedily after something new and sensational, but is soon bored by the old story of the Gospel. How feeble is the Christian, how weak his faith, how fickle and unstable the moment he is left to himself. Peter, the most courageous and forward of the apostles in his profession, denied his Master when challenged by a maid. Even when given a heart to love the Truth, we still have "itching ears" for novelties and errors, as the Israelites welcomed the manna at first, but soon grew weary of it and lusted after the fleshpots of Egypt. Real and urgent then is our need to heed this command, "*Beware of* false prophets."

It is time that we should now proceed to amplify the thought expressed in our opening paragraph. In the previous section of His Sermon Christ had contrasted the broad road and the many who tread it and the narrow way and the few who find it, adding immediately, "Beware of false prophets." Now the narrow way, which leads unto life, is the way of salvation, and therefore the warning given us must have respect to those who teach or present an erroneous way of salvation, thereby placing the souls of their listeners in imminent peril, for to accept their false teachings is *fatal*. Thus the tremendous importance of our present passage is at once apparent. As the verse quoted from II Peter tells us, it is nothing short of "damnable heresies" which these false prophets promulgate. It is about salvation matters they treat, but damnation is the end of those who receive their lies, unless God intervenes with a miracle of grace and disillusions their dupes, which very rarely happens. It therefore behoves each of us seriously to ask, Have I been deceived by these false prophets? Am I treading a way which "seemeth right" unto me but which God declares is the way of "death" (Prov. xiv, 12)? Yea, it behoves us sincerely and earnestly to beseech God to make it unmistakably clear to us *which* "way" we are really treading.

Now it is the duty of God's servants to provide help to exercised souls on this supremely important matter, to expose the lies of these "false prophets," to make plain the way of salvation. This may best be done by defining and showing the relation of *good works* unto salvation, for it is at this point more than any other that the emissaries of Satan have fatally deceived souls. The principal errors which have been advanced thereon may be summed up under these two heads: salvation *by* works, and salvation *without* works. Romanists have been the chief promulgators of the former, insisting that the good works of the Christian have a meritorious value which entitles him to heaven. Thereby they rob Christ of much of His glory, bringing in something of ours in addition to His blood and righteousness to obtain acceptance with God. Romanists do not repudiate *in toto* either the grace of God or the redemption of Christ, but they nullify both by attributing saving efficacy unto the rites of their church, and the performances of the creature. Such an error is expressly repudiated by such scriptures as Romans xi, 6; Ephesians ii, 8 and 9; II Timothy i, 9; Titus iii, 5.

Some of the propagators of the salvation-*without*-works error during the last century have assumed the garb of the orthodox and thereby obtained a hearing from many who had never listened to them had their real characters been suspected. They have gone to the opposite extreme and preached a "gospel" as far removed from the Truth as the Romish lie of salvation *by* works. They teach that while good works from Christians are certainly desirable yet they are not imperative, the absence of them involving merely the loss of certain "millennial" honours and not the missing of heaven itself. They have interpreted those words of Christ's "It is finished" in such a way as to lull multitudes of souls into a false peace, as though He wrought something at the Cross which renders it needless for sinners to repent, forsake their idols, renounce the world before they can be saved; that "nothing is required from them but their simple acceptance of Christ by faith;" that once they have "rested on His finished work"—no matter what their subsequent lives— they are "eternally secure." So widely has this fatal doctrine been received, so thoroughly have these "ravenous wolves" deceived the religious world by their "sheep's clothing," that with rare exceptions anyone who now denounces this deadly evil is to call down upon himself the charge of being a "Legalist" or "Judaizer."

Before we endeavour to show the place which good works have in connection with salvation, let us quote a few sentences from a brief article we wrote in this magazine some years ago. "It is finished: do those blessed words signify that Christ so satisfied the requirements of God's holiness that that holiness no longer has any real and pressing claims upon us? Did Christ 'magnify the Law and make it honourable' (Isaiah xlii, 21) that we might be lawless? Did He fulfil all righteousness to purchase for us an immunity from loving God with all our hearts and serving Him with all our faculties? Did Christ die in order to secure a Divine indulgence that we might live to please self? . . . Christ died not to make my sorrow for and hatred of sin useless. Christ died not to absolve me from the full discharge of my responsibilities unto God. Christ died not so that I might go on retaining the friendship and fellowship of the world. . . . The 'finished work' of Christ avails me nothing if my heart has not been broken by an agonizing consciousness of my sinfulness. It avails me nothing if I still love the world (I John ii, 15). It avails me nothing unless I am a new creature in Christ Jesus (II Cor. v, 17)."

Since then salvation *by* works and salvation *without* works are equally opposed to God's way of salvation, what is the place or

relation which "good works" hold to the saving of a soul? Let us
first define our terms. By "good works" we mean those operations
of our hearts and hands which are performed in obedience to God's
will, which proceed from evangelical principles and which have in
view the Divine glory. By "salvation" we include not only regeneration (which is simply the beginning of it in our experience) but
sanctification and an actual entrance into heaven itself. Thus "godly
sorrow worketh repentance to salvation" (II Cor. vii, 10),
unreserved surrender to the Lordship of Christ (Matt. xi, 29; Luke
xiv, 33), the obedience of faith (Romans xvi, 26; Heb. v, 9), enduring
to the end in sound doctrine (I Tim. iv, 16), love to God (Matt.
xxiv, 12, 13), and the way of holiness (Heb. iii, 15) are all "good
works" and are indispensably necessary if we are to escape the everlasting burnings. The good Shepherd "goeth before" His sheep
(John x. 4) and if they are to join Him on high they must "*follow*
Him*"—"leaving us an example, that ye should follow His steps"
(I Peter ii, 21). There is no reaching heaven except by treading the
only path that leads there—the highway of holiness.

The subject we are now dealing with is far too important to be
condensed into a few brief and general statements, therefore, as our
present space is almost exhausted, we shall conclude with this paragraph and enter into more detail in our next chapter. That good
works are neither the chief nor the procuring cause of salvation is
readily admitted, but that they are no cause whatever, that they
are simply "fruits" of salvation and not a means thereto, we as
definitely deny. On the one hand good works must be kept strictly
subordinate to the grace of God and the merits of Christ: on the
other hand they must not be entirely excluded. It is the corn he sows
which produces the crop, equally true that the fertility of the ground
and the showers and sunshine from heaven are indispensable for a
harvest; but given the finest seed, the richest soil, the most favourable season, would the farmer have anything to reap if he failed to
plough his ground and sow his seed? But does that furnish room
for the farmer to boast? Certainly not; *who* provided him with the
seed and ground, who furnished him with health and strength, who
granted the increase in his labours? Nevertheless, had he remained
inactive there would be no crop.

CHAPTER FIFTY-ONE

False Prophets—Continued

FIRST a brief review of our last chapter. This warning against false prophets or preachers of error forms an appendage to our Lord's teaching on the "strait gate" and "narrow way" in verses 13 and 14. The danger from these false prophets appears in the character they assume—their "sheep's clothing" being thoroughly calculated to deceive the unwary. They are to be found in the circles of "the most orthodox" and pretend to have a fervent love for souls, yet they fatally delude multitudes concerning the way of salvation. It is because there has been so little instruction upon the relation of good works to salvation that people fall such easy victims to these emissaries of Satan. At one extreme there are those (like the papists) who insist that salvation is procured *by* works, at the other extreme are those (boasting most loudly of their "soundness in the Faith") who affirm salvation may be secured *without* works, and rare indeed is it to find anyone today who occupies the middle and true position. That middle position shows that Divine grace does not set aside human responsibility, that the Gospel is no opposer of the Law, and that the "finished work" of Christ has not rendered unnecessary or non-imperative good works on the part of those who are to reach heaven.

Are good works necessary in order to the obtaining of salvation? We answer—and are satisfied the Scriptures warrant our so doing— no and yes. In order to solve that paradox or remove the seeming contradiction we must first define the "good works," then explain carefully what is meant by "necessary" and, last but not least, show what is connoted and included in "salvation." To some of our readers it may appear that entering into such details as these is really a waste of time, as well as rendering complex and difficult that which is really simple and easy. Such people would answer our opening inquiry with a plain and emphatic No, concluding nothing more was required. They would cite "By grace are ye saved through faith; and that not of yourselves: it is the gift of God: Not of works, lest any man should boast" (Eph. ii, 8, 9), and say that *ended* the matter. Yet it is one thing to quote a passage and another thing to have a right understanding of its terms. Nevertheless, the language of Ephesians ii, 8, 9, appears to be so unambiguous and decisive that there seems to be no need to enter upon a laborious study of the subject of which it treats. Why then do we insist upon pressing the inquiry any further?

Why? Because many of the saints are confused thereon and need to have expounded unto them "the way of God more perfectly." Why? Because there is a balance of Truth to be observed here as everywhere, and if one half of it be ignored then the Truth is perverted and souls are deceived. Why? Because it is at this very point that the "false prophets" get in most of their pernicious and destructive work, and unless we are forewarned we are not forearmed. Why? Because it is required of the Christian minister that he should declare "all the counsel of God" and not only favourite portions thereof. Why? Because if on the one hand the exaltation of good works to an unwarrantable place is to repudiate the grace of God, on the other hand the excluding of good works from the place Scripture assigns them is to turn the grace of God into lasciviousness. Why? Because what the Word of God designates "good works" have well-nigh disappeared from Christendom and therefore there is an urgent need for pressing the same. Why? Because vast numbers of professing Christians are fatally deceived thereon, going down to hell with a "lie in their right hand."

The first answer we returned to the question, Are good works necessary in order to the obtaining of salvation? was *No*. Let us now proceed to explain and amplify. Most emphatically we affirm that no descendant of Adam can possibly perform any works which *entitle him* to God's favourable regard. He can no more merit heaven by his own performances than he could create a world. Sooner might the sinner build a ladder which would obtain for him access to the dwelling place of the Most High than he could do any deeds of charity which earned for him an eternity of bliss. He enters this world a fallen and depraved creature and from earliest infancy he has defiled and befouled the garments of his soul: more readily then could he make white the skin of an Ethiopian than cleanse his garments from their stains without having recourse to the blood of Christ. Turning over a new leaf will not erase the blots on the previous pages: if I could live sinlessly today that would not cancel the guilt of yesterday. I am a ten-thousand-talents debtor to God and have not a penny with which to discharge it, and therefore unless His sovereign grace takes pity upon me and gives me everything for nothing there is no hope whatever for me.

No doubt all of our readers would subscribe heartily unto the last paragraph, saying, That is just what I believe; and possibly a few would add: I trust you will not bring in something further that jars against it. Ah, suppose we were writing upon the righteousness of God, and dwelt on His equity and justice. How glorious the contrast between the Lord and most of earth's potentates and authorities: they can be bribed or influenced unto dishonesty, but God is no respecter of persons, giving to each his due, ever doing that which is right. But then I must point out *that* pertains to His office as Judge and His administration of the Law; but He is also sovereign and distributes His favours as He pleases, bestowing a single talent upon one, two on another, and yet five on another. At once the Arminian protests and says I have contradicted myself. Or, suppose I wrote upon the wondrous mercy and love of God, as displayed in creation, in providence and in grace: that His goodness and loving kindness are manifested on every side. But I must also point out that God is holy and hates sin, and will yet consign to the everlasting burnings all who continue defying Him; and at once the Universalist says, Now you have spoilt the whole thing. Probably some will bring the same charge against the remainder of this chapter.

Above we have said that the language of Ephesians ii, 8, 9, appears to be so unambiguous and decisive that there seems to be no need to enter upon a critical examination of its terms—the same may be said of John iii, 16, with like disastrous consequences. Every verse of Scripture requires prayerful and careful consideration, without which no man may expect rightly to apprehend it. " By grace are ye saved " does not stand alone as an absolute statement, but is immediately qualified by the clause "through faith," and thus the salvation there referred to is no more extensive than what is received through faith. This at once shows that "saved" is *not* used in this verse in its widest latitude. Faith itself is a part of God's "so-great salvation," yet faith is not received "through faith." Regeneration is also an essential part of salvation, yet so far from its coming to us through faith, faith is impossible till the soul is born again, Divinely quickened. Again, observe the restriction "by grace *are* ye saved," not "by grace are ye and shall ye be saved through faith." The tense of the verb necessarily limits the salvation here contemplated to that which the believer is in *present* enjoyment of —it does not include his future glorification and entrance into heaven itself.

What has just been pointed out evidences the importance of showing what is connoted and included by the word "saved" or "salvation." First it should be pointed out that it is not used with one uniform sense and scope throughout the New Testament; sometimes it is employed with a wider signification, at others with a narrower. For instance, when we read, "God hath from the beginning chosen you to salvation, through sanctification of the Spirit and belief of the Truth" (II Thess. ii, 13), the term "salvation" is to be understood in its widest latitude as comprehending all the benefits which pertain to redemption, all the gracious works of God toward and within us. But when we read, "Who hath saved us and called us with an holy calling, not according to our works but according to His own purpose and grace, which was given us in Christ Jesus before the world began " (II Tim. i, 9), the word "saved" must be regarded in a more restricted sense, for it is distinguished from our effectual call. "Salvation" is both relative and personal, legal and experimental, what God has done for His people and what He works in them: the former takes in election, adoption, justification, acceptance in the Beloved; the latter embraces their regeneration, sanctification, preservation, and glorification.

As we must not confound what God has done for His people and what He is now doing in them, so we must distinguish between the Christian's having a right or *title to* salvation and his actual *possession of* salvation. Faith in Christ secures an interest in all the benefits of salvation, whether in this world or in the world to come, but it does not convey a present participation in all of them. There is a salvation "in hope" (Romans viii, 24), which is a legal right to that which is yet future in realization: and there is a salvation which is "obtained" now (II Tim. ii, 10). There are certain benefits which the believer has not only a title to, but which he as fully possesses now as he will in the future; such is his justification: he is as righteous now in the sight of the Divine Judge as he will be in heaven, only then there will be a fuller enjoyment of it. Even now we are "the sons of God," but it is not yet made manifest all that favour carries with it (I John iii, 2). Perfect sanctification is prepared by grace in election from all eternity, yet none of the elect now on earth are fully sanctified in their experience. Thus we must distinguish between what is the believer's by title and that which is accomplished by degrees and made good to him in time.

Once more, we must learn to distinguish sharply between the various causes and means of salvation. The *original* cause is the sovereign will of God, for nothing can come into being save that which He decreed before the foundation of the world. The *meritorious* cause is the mediatorial work of Christ, who "obtained eternal redemption" (Heb. ix, 22) for His people, purchasing for them all the blessings of it by His perfect obedience to the Law and His sacrificial death. The *efficient* cause is the varied operations of the Holy Spirit, who applies to the elect the benefits purchased by Christ, capacitating them to enjoy the same and making them meet for the inheritance of the saints in light. The *ministerial* cause and means is the preaching of the Word (James i, 21), because it discovers to us where salvation is to be obtained. The *instrumental* cause is faith, by which the soul receives or comes into possession of and obtains an interest in Christ and His redemption. Such distinctions as these are not merely technicalities for theologians, but are part of the faith once delivered unto the saints, and unless they apprehend the same they are liable to be deceived by any Scripture-quoting false prophet who accosts them.

The Christian's title to salvation, that is to salvation as a whole and complete as it lay in the womb of God's decree, is entirely by grace, for he has done and can do nothing whatever to earn the same. We are not saved *for* our faith, for since it also is the gift of God, wrought in us by the Spirit, it possesses no meritorious worth. We are saved by grace through faith because faith *let in* salvation, being the hand which receives it. Yet there is no salvation without faith: no one is saved until he believes. It is by grace through faith that we obtain deliverance from the curse of the Law and receive title to everlasting life and righteousness. As Thomas Goodwin pointed out in his masterly exposition of Ephesians ii, 8: "We are saved through faith as that which gives us the present *right*, or that which God doth give us as a Judge, when we believe, before faith hath done a whit of works; but we are led through sanctification and good works to the *possession* of salvation." It must not be lost sight of that Ephesians ii, 8, 9, is at once followed by, "For we are His workmanship, created in Christ Jesus *unto good works*, which God hath before ordained that we should walk in them." It is sometimes said, because God has ordained it we *shall* walk in good works. That is true, but it is equally true that we *must* do so if heaven is to be reached.

Are good works necessary in order to the obtaining of salvation? Our answer was no and yes. Perhaps the reader is now better prepared to follow us in such a seemingly paradoxical answer. Certainly no works are required from us in order to induce God to show us favour. Nor are they necessary in order to our justification, for they constitute no part of that righteousness which we have before God. Nor do they procure for us a title to heaven. But it is a great mistake to suppose that because good works are not necessary for one particular end they are not indispensable for any: that because they are not meritorious therefore they are useless. Not so. Good works *are* necessary. They are necessary in order to preserve us from that course and practice which conducts to hell. They are necessary in order to the glorifying of God and the magnifying of His grace. They are necessary in order to keep us in the only way that leads to heaven. They are necessary in order to communion with the thrice holy God. They are necessary in order to prove the quality of our faith and the genuineness of our profession. They are necessary in order to the making of our calling and election sure. They are necessary in order to silence the detractors of the Gospel.

As there is no pardon until we forsake our wicked ways (Isaiah lv, 7), no blotting out of our sins until we repent and turn unto God (Acts iii, 19), so there is no entering into life except by treading the only way that leads thereto, and that is the path of obedience. So long as the Christian remains in this world he is in the place of danger: deliverance from hell is only the beginning of salvation, nor is it completed until heaven is reached. Between justification and glorification there is a fight to be fought, enemies to be conquered, a victory to be won, and the prize is only for the victor. "Conversion is a turning into the right road; the next thing is to walk in it. The daily going on in that road is as essential as the first starting if you would reach the desired end. To strike the first blow is not all the battle: to him that overcometh the crown is promised. To start in the race is nothing, many have done that who have failed; but to hold out till you reach the winning post is the great point of the matter. Perseverance is as *necessary to* a man's *salvation* as conversion" (C. H. Spurgeon).

In *what sense* are good works "necessary" unto salvation—necessary in order to final and complete salvation? First, they are requisite as the *way* in which that final salvation is attained. As a destination cannot be reached without journeying thither, neither can life be entered except through the strait gate and treading the narrow way: it is via the path of holiness that heaven is reached. Second, they are requisite as part of the *means* which God has appointed: they are the means of spiritual preservation. The only alternative to good works is evil ones, and evil works slay their perpetrator—sin is destructive: "if ye live after the flesh ye shall die" (Romans viii, 13; and cf. Gal. vi, 8). Third, they are requisite as *a condition* of the possession of full salvation. Not a condition like a stipulation in a bargain, but as a connection between two things. As food must be eaten for the body to be nourished, as seed must be sown in order to a harvest, so obedience, equally as repentance and faith, precede the crowning. Fourth, as *an evidence* of the genuineness of faith: the fruit must manifest the tree.

Those who deny that good works are in any sense necessary to salvation appeal to the instance of the thief on the cross, arguing that in his case there was nothing more than a simple and single look of faith unto the Saviour. We might dispose of such an appeal by pointing out that his case is quite exceptional—for it is very rarely that God at once removes to heaven him who believes—and that it is not permissible to frame a rule from an exception. Instead, we meet the objector on his own ground and show that his assertion is erroneous. There was far more than a bare looking to the Saviour in his case. (1) He rebuked his companion: "Dost not thou fear God?" (Luke xxiii, 40). (2) He repented of his sins: "we indeed justly, for we receive the due reward of our deeds" (verse 41)—he condemned himself, owning that death was his due. (3) He bore public witness to Christ's sinlessness: "this man hath done nothing amiss." (4) In the face of a hostile mob, he testified to Christ's Lordship and Kingship: "Lord, remember me, when Thou comest into Thy kingdom."

In his sermon on Ephesians ii, 10, Manton says: "Our well-doing is the *effect* of salvation if you take it for our *first* recovery to God, but if you take it for full salvation or our *final* deliverance from all evil, good works *go before it* indeed, but in a way of order, not of meritorious influence. To think them altogether unnecessary would too much deprecate and lessen their presence or concurrence; to think they deserve it would too much exalt and advance them beyond the line of their due worth and value. The apostle steered a middle course between both extremes. They are necessary but not meritorious. They go before eternal life not as a cause but as a way." Let us now summarize it thus: God has made promise of salvation unto His people: Christ has purchased it for them: faith obtains title thereto: good works secure actual admission into the full and final benefits of redemption, and in order to empower the Spirit renews the believer day by day.

CHAPTER FIFTY-TWO

False Prophets—Continued

IT may appear to some of our readers that the preceding chapter of this series had no connection at all with Matthew vii, 15, that instead of giving an exposition of the verse we wandered off to an entirely different subject and entered into a lot of technicalities which few are capable of understanding. Then let us remind such that we gave an exposition of Matthew vii, 15, in the previous chapter, at the close of which we asserted that it is particularly in the matter of the relation of good works unto salvation that the false prophets fatally deceive souls: one school or class of them teaching that salvation is *by* works, another insisting that it is entirely *without* works. The issue thus raised is such an important and vital one that it would be wrong to dismiss it with a few peremptory statements. Moreover, there is now such confusion of tongues in the religious realm, and the method followed by even the orthodox pulpit is so dreadfully superficial—"preaching" having quite supplanted *teaching*—that the Lord's own people are in real need of instruction thereon, and such instruction demands diligence and study on the part of the one imparting, and concentration and patience from those who would receive. Truth has to be "bought" (Prov. xxiii, 23).

In the preceding chapter we sought to define and explain the relation of good works to salvation. First, we pointed out that they possess no meritorious value: by which we mean, they deserve nothing at the hands of God, that in no sense do they earn aught or contribute one mite to our redemption. Second, we insisted that they are necessary, yea, that without them salvation cannot be obtained. Not that any well-doing on our part is required in order to obtain acceptance with God, nor that they can atone for the failures and sins of the past. But rather that the path of obedience must be trod if the realm of unclouded bliss is to be reached. The doing of good works is indispensable in order to the securing of full and final salvation, that is in order to an actual entrance into heaven itself. We are well aware that such language will have a strange sound to some of our friends, that it will savour of "legality," yet if Scripture itself expressly declares that Christ is "the Author of eternal salvation unto all them that *obey* Him" (Heb. v, 9), need we hesitate to employ the same plain language and press the force thereof?

That which we are here advancing is no departure from genuine orthodoxy, but the doctrine propounded by the soundest of God's servants in days gone by. In the last article we quoted from Goodwin and Manton. Hear now the testimonies of other of the Puritans. "If we consider every gracious work of patience, love, meekness, we shall see blessedness is promised to them. Not that they justify, only the justified person cannot be without them. They are the ordained means in the use whereof we arrive at eternal life. I: is faith only that receives Christ in His righteousness, yet this faith cannot be separated from an holy walk" (A. Burgess, 1656). "Freedom from condemnation, from sin, for all the elect, which God Himself so plainly asserts (Romans viii, 32, 33) doth not in the least set thee free from *the necessity of* obedience, nor free thee from contracting the guilt of sin upon the least irregularity or disobedience" (John Owen, 1670). "Christ will save none but those who are brought to resign themselves sincerely to the obedience of His royal authority and laws" (Walter Marshall, 1692). Alas, that there has been so widespread a departure from the teaching of such worthies.

It is just because there has been such a grievous turning away from the Truth as it was formerly so faithfully and fearlessly proclaimed, by men not worthy to blacken their shoes, that so many today are ignorant of the very first principles of Christianity. It is because the pulpit, platform, and pamphlet hucksters of the nineteenth century so wantonly lowered the standard of Divine holiness, and so adulterated the Gospel in order to make it palatable to the carnal mind, that it has become necessary to labour what is really self-evident. Oh, the tragedy of it that at this late day we should have to write chapter after chapter in the endeavour to purge some of God's people of the antinomian poison they have imbibed. As well may writer and reader hope to reach heaven without Christ as without good works: "Whosoever doth not bear his cross, and come after Me, cannot be My disciple" (Luke xiv, 27). Did the Lord Jesus work so arduously that His followers might be carried to glory on flowery beds of ease? Was the Saviour so active that His disciples might be idle? Did he become obedient unto death in order to exempt us from obedience?

Though it will retard our pace, yet because it is necessary to remove stumbling stones out of the way of those anxious to be helped, we must seek to resolve two or three difficulties which may arise in the minds of the Lord's people. (1) It is likely to be objected that by such teachings we are making man in part at least his own saviour. But need we be afraid to go as far as the language of Holy Writ goes? Was the apostle legalistic when he cried, "*save yourselves* from this untoward generation" (Acts ii, 40)? Was the chief of the apostles derogating from the glory of Christ and the grace of God when he bade Timothy, "Take heed unto thyself, and unto the doctrine; continue in them: for in doing this thou shalt both *save thyself*, and them that hear thee" (I Tim. iv, 16)? But was not Timothy already a saved man when thus exhorted? Regenerated and justified, yes: fully sanctified and glorified, no. Because we press the perseverance of the Christian (as well as his Divine preservation) do we make him his own keeper? Suppose we do, are we going beyond Scripture? Did not David say, "By the word of Thy lips *I have kept me* from the paths of the destroyer" (Psalm xvii, 4)? Did not Paul say, "*I keep under* my body" (I Cor. ix, 27)? Does not Jude exhort us, "keep yourselves in the love of God" (verse 21)?

It is against a *dishonest onesidedness* that we so often protest in these pages. The singling out of certain passages and then closing the eyes against others has wrought untold damage. "Is there any doctrine which you almost think is a truth, but your friends do not believe it, and they might perhaps think you heretical if you were to accept it, and therefore you dare not investigate any farther? Oh, dear friends, let us be rid of all such dishonesty. So much of it has got into the church that many will not see things that are as plain as a pikestaff. They will not see, for truth might cost them too dear. They cover up and hide away some parts of Scripture which it might be awkward for them to understand, because of their connection with a church or their standing in a certain circle." If C. H. Spurgeon found it necessary to raise his voice against this reprehensible method of picking and choosing from the Word of God, how much more so is such a condemnation called for in this generation of dishonesty and hypocrisy.

(2) If good works be necessary in order to salvation, is not this putting us back again under the covenant of works, the terms of which were: "Do this and thou shalt live"? No indeed, nevertheless the fact must not be lost sight of that it has pleased God in all ages to deal with His people by way of covenant, and in the same way He will deal with them to the end of the world. It is very largely because *covenant teaching* has been given no place in modern "evangelism" that so much ignorance now obtains. How few preachers today could explain the meaning of "these are the two covenants" (Gal. iv, 24). What percentage of Christians now living understand the "better covenant," of which Christ is "the Mediator" (Heb. viii, 6) and wherein lies the difference between the "new covenant" (Heb. xii, 24) and the old one? How few apprehend the blessedness of those words, "The blood of the everlasting covenant" (Heb. xiii, 20). But let it not be overlooked that there are covenant *duties* as well as covenant blessings: there is a covenant for us to "make" with God (Psalm l, 5) and a covenant to "keep" (Psalm xxv, 10; ciii, 18).

The new covenant or covenant of grace was in its original constitution transacted between God and Christ as the Head of His people. That covenant is published in the Gospel, and the application of its benefits is made when we submit to its terms and fulfil its duties. It is worthy of note that the self-same thing which the apostle calls the "gospel" in Galatians iii, 8, he terms the "covenant" in verse 17. Now a covenant is a compact or contract entered into by two or more parties, the one engaging himself to do or give something upon the fulfilment of a stipulation agreed upon by the other. Thus in the Gospel Christ makes known His readiness to save those who are willing to submit to His Lordship. Hence conversion is termed "the love of thine espousals" (Jer. ii, 2), when the soul as it were signed the marriage contract, vowing to love none other than the Lord and to be faithful to Him unto death. This giving of ourselves to Christ to serve and love Him is designated a "taking hold of the covenant" (Isaiah lvi, 6). And that covenant must be *kept* if we are to receive its benefits.

When defining the essence of the controversy between himself and his opponents, John Flavel stated it thus: "The only question between us is, Whether in the new covenant some acts of ours (though they have no merit in them, nor can be done in our own strength) be not required to be performed by us antecedently to (before) a blessing or privilege, consequent by virtue of a promise; and whether such act or duty, being of a suspending nature to the blessing promised, it have not the true and proper nature of a Gospel *condition.*" Mr. Flavel affirmed, his opponent (Mr. Carey) denied. In proof of the conditionality of certain of the new covenant blessings Mr. Flavel said, "We know not how to express those sacred particles, "if not," "if," "except," "only," and such like (Romans x, 9; Matt. xviii, 3; Mark xi, 26; Romans xi, 22; Col. i, 22, 23; Heb. iii, 6, 14), which are frequently used to limit and restrain the benefits and privileges of the new covenant, by any other word so fit and so full as the word *conditional.*"

In considering the new and better covenant, we must distinguish sharply between the first sanction of it in Christ and the *application* of its benefits to His people. Few men more magnified the grace of God in his preaching and writings than did the Puritan, Thomas Boston, yet we find him saying (in his *View of the Covenant of Grace*): "He gives the rewards of the covenant in the course of *their obedience*. He puts His people to work and labour: but not to work in the fire for vanity as the slaves of sin do. They are to labour like the ox treading out the corn, which was not to be muzzled, but to have access at once to work and to eat. The service now done to Zion's King hath a reward in this life as well as a reward in the life to come. By the *order of* the covenant there is privilege established to follow duty as the reward thereof, the which order is observed by the King in His administration. Accordingly He proposeth the privilege of comfort to excite to the duty of mourning (Matt. v, 4), the special tokens of heaven's favour to excite unto a holy tender walk (John xiv, 21); in like manner to excite to the same holy obedience He proposeth the full reward in the life to come (I Cor. ix, 24; Rev. iii, 21)."

The new covenant requires obedience as really and truly as did the old, and therefore does God write the laws of the covenant on the hearts of those with whom He makes the new covenant (Heb.

x, 16). Those who enter into this covenant with God do approve
of the whole Divine Law so far as they know it, declaring, "I esteem
all Thy precepts" (Psalm cxix, 128). They have an inclination of
heart towards the whole of God's Law so far as they know it, saying:
"I love Thy commandments above gold" (cxix, 127). They heartily
engage to conform to the whole of God's Law so far as they know
it, exclaiming, "O that my ways were directed to keep Thy statutes!"
(cxix, 5). Where the Law is written on a person's heart he will write
it out again in his conversation. Their souls lie open to what of
God's Law they as yet know not, praying "Make me to understand
the way of Thy precepts" (Psalm cxix, 27).

But now if many (we say not all) of the blessings and benefits of
the new covenant are made conditional upon our obedience and
fidelity, wherein does it differ from the old, or Adamic covenant, the
covenant of works? Why, in these respects. First, under the old
covenant, works were meritorious, entitling to the inheritance: had
Adam kept the Law, he and all he represented would have entered
life by legal right, whereas under the new covenant Christ purchased
the inheritance for His people before a single thing was asked of
them. Second, under the old covenant man had to work in his own
strength alone; but under the new all-sufficient grace and enablement are available to those who duly seek it. Third, under the
covenant of works no provision was made for failure: the obedience
required must be perfect and perpetual (Gal. iii, 10): whereas under
the covenant of grace God accepts imperfect obedience, if it be
sincere, because the blood of Christ hath made atonement for its
defects and disobedience is pardoned when we truly repent of and
forsake the same.

(3) If good works be necessary in order to final salvation, how
is a poor soul to ascertain when he has done sufficient of them?
Such a question is not likely to issue from a renewed heart, rather
does he bemoan his unfruitfulness and unprofitableness. He feels he
can never do enough to express his gratitude unto God for the unspeakable gift of His Son. Instead of begrudging any sacrifice he is
called upon to make, or any hardship to encounter, by virtue of his
being a Christian, he deems it the highest honour conceivable to
serve such a Master and endure for His sake. But to the carping
objector, we would say, Scripture declares: "For we are made partakers of Christ if we hold the beginning of our confidence stedfast
unto the end" (Heb. iii, 14). The soldiers of Christ are not granted
any furloughs or "leave" in this life: they cannot take off their
armour until the battle is over. They know not at what hour their
Lord may come, and therefore are they required to have their loins
girded and their lamps trimmed without intermission.

But it should be pointed out that it is not quantity but *quality*
which God requires. A cup of cold water given to one of His little
ones in the name of Christ is infinitely more acceptable to the
Father than a million pounds donated by a godless magnate to

social institutions. On the one hand it is written, "that which is highly esteemed among men is abomination in the sight of God" (Luke xvi, 15), on the other, "man looketh on the outward appearance but the Lord looketh on the heart" (I Samuel xvi, 7). That which issues from love to God, which expresses gratitude for His goodness, is what is well pleasing in His sight. Quality, not quantity. Is not this the point in that saying of Christ's, "if ye have faith as a grain of mustard seed, ye shall say unto this mountain, Remove hence to yonder place; and it shall remove" (Matt. xvii, 20)? What is smaller than a mustard seed and what larger than a mountain? the one seemingly feeble and paltry, the other ponderous and mighty. Ah, but the former is a *living* thing, the latter but a mass of inert matter; the former is energetic and growing, the latter stationary. It is quality versus quantity.

(4) If good works be necessary in order to final salvation, is there not ground thereon for boasting? Yes, if they be perfect and flawless, performed in our own strength, and we bring God into our debt thereby. Before giving the negative answer, consider the case of the holy angels in this connection. When Satan fell he dragged down with him one third of the celestial hierarchy, the remainder remained steadfast in their loyalty to God: did such fidelity puff them up? Throughout their entire history it could ever be said of them that they "do His commandments, hearkening unto the voice of His word" (Psalm ciii, 20), yet nowhere in Holy Writ is there so much as a hint that they are proud of their obedience. On the contrary we find them veiling their faces in the Divine presence and crying one unto another, "Holy, holy, holy, is the Lord of hosts" (Isaiah vi, 3), and falling before the throne on their faces and worshipping God (Rev. vii, 11). How much less then may hell-deserving sinners, redeemed by the blood of the Lamb, find anything in their own performances to afford self-gratulation.

Is there any danger that the doing of good works in order to final salvation will lead to boasting? No, none whatever, if we bear in mind that our best performances are but filthy rags in the sight of Him with whom the very heavens are not clean. No, not if we bear in mind that we are not sufficient of ourselves to think a godly thought (II Cor. iii, 5), still less carry it out into execution; apart from Christ we can "do nothing." No, not if we squarely face and honestly answer the question, "What hast thou that thou didst not receive?" (I Cor. iv, 7). No, not if we heed that word of Christ's, "So likewise ye, when ye shall have done all those things which are commanded you [which none of us ever did], say, We are unprofitable servants: we have done that which was our *duty* to do" (Luke xvii, 10). Yes, "unprofitable servants" so far as making God our Debtor is concerned. The very man who wrought more miracles than any for his Master declared, "yet not I, but the grace of God which was with me" (I Cor. xv, 10).

Again, the reader may be inclined to ask, But what bearing has all

of this on Matthew vii, 15? We answer, Much every way, as we shall
(D.V.) seek to show in our next. Suffice it now to say that what we
have been stressing in this and the preceding chapter is expressly
repudiated by the "false prophets" of our day. They blankly deny
that good works have *any* part or place whatever in our salvation,
that *believing* the Gospel is *all* that is needed to ensure heaven for
any sinner.

CHAPTER FIFTY-THREE

False Prophets—Continued

OUR last two chapters of this series were devoted principally to showing the relation of good works unto final salvation, this being both pertinent and needful, forasmuch as many of the "false prophets" of our day expressly repudiate all that we therein insisted upon. They dogmatically affirm that "believing the Gospel is *all* that is needed to ensure heaven for any sinner." And is it not so? Certainly not. First, it requires to be pointed out that there is an *order* in presenting the Gospel, and it is the business of those who preach to observe that order: unless they do so nothing but disorder will ensue and spurious converts will be the issue of their labours. If due attention be paid to the Word of God, it will not be difficult to discover what that order is: the proclamation and enforcing of the Divine Law *precedes* the publication of the Divine Gospel. Broadly speaking, the Old Testament is an exposition of the Law, while the New Testament sets forth the substance and benefits of the Gospel.

The Gospel is a message of "good news." To whom? To sinners. But to what sort of sinners? To the giddy and unconcerned, to those who give no thought to the claims of God and where they shall spend eternity? Certainly not. The Gospel announces no good tidings to *them*: it has no music in it to *their* ears. They are quite deaf to its charms, for they have no sense of their need of the Saviour. It is those who have their eyes opened to see something of the ineffable holiness of God and their vileness in His sight, who have learned something of His righteous requirements from them and of their criminal neglect to meet those requirements, who are deeply convicted of their depravity, their moral inability to recover themselves, whose consciences are burdened with an intolerable load of guilt and who are terrified by their imminent danger of the wrath to come, who know that unless an almighty redeemer saves them they are doomed, that are qualified to appreciate and welcome the Gospel. "They that are whole need not a physician, but they that are sick."

Now the natural man has no realization of the desperate sickness of his soul. He is quite unconscious of what spiritual health consists of, namely personal holiness. Never having sincerely measured himself by the Divine standard, he knows not how far, far short he comes of it at every point. God has no real place in his thoughts and therefore he fails to comprehend how obnoxious he is in His sight. Instead of seeking to glorify the One who made and sustains him, he lives only to please self. And what is the means for enlightening him? What is the sure "line and plummet" (Isaiah xxviii, 17) for exposing the crookedness of his character? The preaching of God's *Law*, for that is the unchanging rule of conduct and standard of righteousness. "By the law is the knowledge of sin" (Romans iii, 20)— its nature, as rebellion against God; its exceeding sinfulness as contrary to Divine holiness; its infinite evil, as deserving of eternal punishment.

"I had not known sin *but by the law*" (Romans vii, 7) declares one who formerly had prided himself on his integrity and righteousness. God's Law requires inward conformity as well as outward: it addresses itself to the motions of the heart as well as prescribes our actions, so that we are sinless or sinful just in proportion as we conform or fail to conform to the Law both internally and externally. Just so far as we have false ideas of God's Law do we entertain false estimates of our character. Just so far as we fail to perceive that the Law demands perfect and perpetual obedience shall we be blind to the fearful extent of our disobedience. Just so far as we realize not the spirituality and strictness of the Law, that it pronounces a lascivious imagination to be adultery and causeless anger against a fellow creature to be murder, shall we be unaware of our fearful criminality. Just so far as we hear nothing of the awful thunders of the Law's curse shall we be insensible to our frightful danger.

It has been rightly said: "The Gospel has such respect to the Law of God, and the latter is so much the reason and ground of the former, and so essential to the wisdom and glory of it, that it cannot be understood by him who is ignorant of the Law: consequently, our idea and apprehension of the Gospel will be erroneous and wrong just so far as we have wrong notions of God's Law" (S. Hopkins). The excellency of the Mediator cannot be recognized until we see that the Law demands flawless and undeviating obedience on pain of eternal damnation, and that such a demand is right and glorious, and consequently that sin is infinitely criminal and heinous. The essential work of the Mediator was to honour and magnify that Law and make atonement for the wrongs done to it by His people. And they who repudiate this Law, or who view it not in its true light, are and must be totally blind to the wisdom and glory of the Gospel, for while they never see sin in its real odiousness and true ill-desert they are incapable of realizing or perceiving their deep need of the Divine remedy.

That salvation which Christ came here to purchase for His people consists first in the gift of His Spirit to overcome their enmity against God's Law (Romans viii, 7) and produce in them a love for it (Romans vii, 22), and it is by *this* we may discover whether or not we have been regenerated. Second, to bring them to a cordial consent to the Law, so that each genuine Christian can say "So then with the mind I myself serve the law of God" (Romans vii, 25). Third, to deliver them from the curse of the Law by dying for their sins of disobedience against it, Himself bearing its penalty in their stead (Gal. iii, 13). Consequently, they who are experientially ignorant of God's Law, who have never heartily assented to it as "holy, just and good," have never been sensible of sin in its true hideousness and demerits, have never been subject to a supernatural work of grace within them, are yet in nature's darkness, strangers to Christ, still in their sins, having felt neither the strength of sin nor the power of the Gospel.

Again: the order which is to be observed in the presentation of the Gospel is exemplified in the appointment of *John the Baptist*. He was the forerunner of Christ, going before to "prepare His way" (Isaiah xl, 3). John came "in the way of righteousness" (Matt. xxi, 32), crying "Repent ye" (Matt. iii, 2). A saving faith in Christ must be preceded by and accompanied with a heart-felt sense of the true odiousness and ill-desert of sin. An impenitent heart is no more able to receive Christ than a shuttered window is able to let in the rays of the sun. None but the humbled, contrite, broken-hearted penitent is ever comforted by the Lord Jesus, as none but such will ever desire Him or seek after Him. This is the unchanging order laid down by Christ Himself: "repent ye and [then] believe the gospel" (Mark i, 15): ye "repented not afterward that ye might believe" (Matt. xxi, 32) was His solemn affirmation. First "repentance toward God, and [then] faith toward our Lord Jesus Christ" (Acts xx, 21) was what the apostle testified to Jews and Gentiles alike.

It has often been said that nothing more is required of the sinner than to come to Christ as an empty-handed beggar and receive Him as an all-sufficient Saviour. But that assertion needs clarifying and amplifying at two points lest souls be fatally misled thereby. To come to Christ empty-handed signifies not only that I renounce any fancied righteousness of mine, but also that I relinquish my beloved idols. Just so long as the sinner holds fast to the world or clings to any fond sin he cannot thrust forth an *empty* hand. The things which produce death must be dropped before he can "lay hold on eternal life." Furthermore, Christ cannot be received in part but only in the entirety of His person and office: He must be received as "Lord and Saviour" or He cannot be savingly received at all. There must be a submitting to His authority, a surrendering to His sceptre, a taking of His yoke upon us, as well as a trusting in His blood, or we shall never find "rest unto our souls."

"But as many as received Him, to them gave He power to become the sons of God" (John i, 12). This verse is often *quoted* by the self-appointed "evangelists" of our day but it is rarely *expounded*. Instead of throwing all the emphasis on "received," attention rather needs to be directed unto "received *Him*." It is not "received it"— a mental proposition or doctrine—nor even received "His"—some gift or benefit—but "Him," in the entirety of His person as clothed with His offices, as He is proposed in the Gospel. Such a "receiving" as is here spoken of implies an enlightened understanding, a convicted conscience, renewed affections—the exercise of love, an act of the will—choice of a new Master, the acceptance of His terms (Luke

xiv, 26, 27, 33). It is at this last point that so many balk: "why call ye
me, Lord, Lord, and do not the things which I say?" (Luke vi, 46),
and therefore is the inquirer bidden to "sit down first and count the
cost" (Luke xiv, 28). The order is first the person of Christ and then
His gifts (Romans viii, 32): thus God bestows and thus we receive.

Those, then, who declare that a bare believing of the Gospel is all
that is needed to ensure heaven for any sinner are "false prophets,"
liars and deceivers of souls. It also requires to be pointed out that
saving faith is not an isolated act but a *continuous* thing. When the
apostle contrasted genuine saints with apostates, he described them
as "them that believe to the saving of the soul" (Heb. x, 39): note
well the tense of the verb—not "them that believed" one day in the
past, but "them that believe" with a faith which is operative in the
present. In this he was holding fast "the form of sound words"
(II Tim. i, 13) employed by his Master, for He too taught "as Moses
lifted up the serpent in the wilderness even so must the Son of man
be lifted up, that whosoever *believeth* in Him should not perish
but have everlasting life" (John iii, 15, and cf. iii, 18, 36; v, 24).
In like manner another apostle says, "If so be ye have tasted that the
Lord is gracious, to whom [*not*, ye "came," but] *coming*, as unto
a living stone" (I Peter ii, 4)—coming daily, as needy as ever.

Saving faith is not an isolated act which suffices for the remainder
of a person's life, rather is it a living principle which continues in
activity, ever seeking the only Object which can satisfy it. Nor is it a
thing apart, but a *productive principle* which issues in good works
and spiritual fruits. "Faith, if it hath not works, is dead, being
alone" (James ii, 17). A faith which does not bring forth obedience
to the Divine precepts is not the faith of God's elect. Saving faith is
something radically different from a mere mental assent to the
Gospel, believing that God loves me and that Christ died for me.
The demons assent to the whole compass of Divine revelation, but
what does it advantage them? Nor is the "faith" advocated by the
false prophets of any more value or efficacy. Saving faith, my reader,
is one which "purifieth the heart" (Acts xv, 9), which "work*eth*
by love" (Gal. v, 6), which "overcom*eth* the world" (I John v, 4).
And such faith man can neither originate nor regulate. Has such a
faith been Divinely communicated to *you*?

Now it is in their opposition to those aspects of the Truth we have
been concerned with above that the false prophets may be identified.
Not that their preaching is all cast in the same mould: far from it.
As the servants of God are variously gifted—one to evangelize,
another to indoctrinate, another to exhort and admonish—so
Satan accommodates his emissaries to the different types of
people they meet with. On the one hand, Romanists and other
legalists teach that salvation is by obedience to the Law, that
repentance and good works are meritorious; on the other
hand, there are those who insist that the Law is entirely
Jewish, that the Gentiles were never under it and have nothing

to do with it. But just as the Pharisees, the Sadducees and the Herodians differed widely the one from the other yet made common cause in antagonizing Christ, so the false prophets, though far from being uniform in their heterodoxy, nevertheless are one in opposing the Truth. Conversely, whatever be their distinctive gifts and spheres of service, the true ministers of God are always identifiable by their fidelity to the faith once.for all delivered to the saints.

It is particularly the more subtle and less suspected kind of false prophets we are here seeking to expose and warn against. For the last two or three generations "wolves in sheep's clothing" have appeared in circles from which it might be expected that they had been excluded. They have deceived multitudes by their very seeming soundness in the faith. They have denounced "Higher Criticism," and Evolutionism, Christian Science and Russellism. They have affirmed the Divine inspiration of the Scriptures and have made much of the mercy of God and the atoning blood of Christ. But they have falsified God's way of salvation. Christ bade His hearers "strive [agonize] to enter in at the strait gate" (Luke xiii, 24): these men declare such striving to be altogether unnecessary. He affirmed, "except ye repent, ye shall all likewise perish": they say that sinners may be saved without repentance. Scripture asks, "If the righteous scarcely be saved" (I Peter iv, 18): these men aver that salvation is easy for anyone. Scripture uniformly teaches that unless the believer perseveres in holiness he will lose heaven: these men insist that he will merely forfeit some "millennial crown."

As one of the Puritans quaintly yet truly expressed it, "The face of error is highly painted and powdered so as to render it attractive to the unwary." The false prophets, whether of the papist or the Protestant order, make a great show of devotion and piety on the one hand, and of zeal and fervour on the other, as did the Pharisees of old with their fasting and praying and who "compassed sea and land to make one proselyte" (Matt. xxiii, 15). They are diligent in seeking to discredit those truths they design to overthrow by branding them "legal doctrines" and denouncing as "Judaizers" those who are set for the defence of them. "With good words and fair speeches they deceive the heart of the simple" (Romans xvi, 18). They speak much about "grace," yet it is not that Divine grace which "reigns through righteousness" (Romans v, 21), nor does it effectually teach men to deny "ungodliness and worldly lusts" (Titus ii, 11, 12). With "cunning craftiness" they "lie in wait to deceive" (Eph. iv, 14) souls who have never been established in the Truth and beguile with "enticing words" (Col. ii, 4), making a great show of quoting Scripture and addressing their converts as "beloved brethren."

Many of the false prophets of Protestantism have popularized themselves by granting their deluded followers the liberty of preaching. As any reader of ecclesiastical history knows, it has been a favourite device of false prophets in all ages to spread their errors through the efforts of their converts, flattering their conceits by speaking of their "gifts" and "talents": by multiplying *lay* preachers they draw after them a host of disciples. Such incompetent novices are themselves ignorant of the very A B C of the Truth, yet in their egotism and presumption deem themselves qualified to explain the deepest mysteries of the Faith. A great deal safer, and more excusable, would it be to put an illiterate rustic into a dispensary to compound medicines out of drugs and spirits he understands not and then administer the same unto his fellows, than for young upstarts with no better endowment than self-confidence to intrude themselves into the sacred office of the ministry: the one would poison men's bodies, but the other their souls.

"But such are false apostles, deceitful workers, transforming themselves into the apostles of Christ. And no marvel, for Satan himself is transformed into an angel of light" (II Cor. xi, 13, 14). In all opposition to the Truth there is an agent at work which it belongs to the office of the Spirit of Truth to discover and unmask. If "another gospel" (Gal. i, 6) be preached rather than the Gospel of Christ, it is the fruit of satanic energy, the minds and wills of its promulgators being led captive by the Devil. Satan is the arch-dissembler, being the prince of duplicity as well as of wickedness. When he had the awful effrontery to tempt the Lord Jesus he came with the Word of God on his lips saying, "It is written" (Matt. iv, 6)! Though Satan's kingdom be that of darkness, yet his craft is the mimicry of light, and thus it is that his agents work by deception. They claim to be the "apostles [or "missionaries"] of Christ," but they have received no call or commission from Him. Nor should we marvel at their pretence when we remember the hold which the father of lies has over men.

"Therefore it is no great thing if his ministers also be transformed as the ministers of righteousness; whose end shall be according to their works" (II Cor. xi, 15). They are "deceitful workers," for they pose as champions of the Truth and as being actuated by a deep love for souls. As sin does not present itself to us *as sin* nor as paying death for its wages, but rather as something pleasant and desirable, and as Satan never shows himself openly in his true colours, so his "ministers" put on the cloak of sanctity, pretending to be dead to the world and very self-sacrificing. They are crafty, specious, tricky, hypocritical. What urgent need, then, is there to be on our guard, that we be not imposed upon by every mealy-mouthed and "gracious" impostor who comes to us Bible in hand. How we should heed that injunction, "Prove all things" (I Thess. v, 21). Certain it is, my reader, that any preacher who rejects God's Law, who denies repentance to be a condition of salvation, who assures the giddy and godless that they are loved by God, who declares that saving faith is nothing more than an act of the will which every person has the power to perform, is a false prophet, and should be shunned as a deadly plague.

CHAPTER FIFTY-FOUR

False Prophets—Continued

" Beware of false prophets, which come to you in sheep's clothing, but
inwardly they are ravening wolves. Ye shall know them by their fruits. Do men
gather grapes of thorns, or figs of thistles? Even so every good tree bringeth
forth good fruit ; but a corrupt tree bringeth forth evil fruit. A good tree
cannot bring forth evil fruit, neither can a corrupt tree bring forth good fruit.
Every tree that bringeth not forth good fruit is hewn down, and cast into the
fire. Wherefore by their fruits ye shall know them." (Matt. vii, 15-20.)

" BEWARE of false prophets, which come to you in sheep's clothing,
but inwardly they are ravening wolves " (verse 15). No idle or needless warning was this, but one which should be seriously taken to
heart by all who have any concern for the glory of God or value
their eternal interests. Our danger is real and pressing, for "false
prophets" are not few in number but "many" (I John iv, 1), and
instead of being found only in the notoriously heretical sects, have
"crept in" among saints until they now dominate nearly all the
centres of orthodoxy. If we are deceived by them and imbibe their
lies the result is almost certain to be fatal, for error acts upon the
soul as deadly poison does on the body. The very fact that these
impostors assume "sheep's clothing" and pose as the servants of
Christ greatly increases the peril of the unwary and unsuspicious.
For these reasons it is imperative that we should be on our guard.
But to be properly on our guard requires that we should be
informed, that we should know how to recognize these deceivers.
Nor has our Lord left us unfurnished at this vital point, as the
succeeding verses show.

"Ye shall know them by their fruits." Three questions are
suggested by this statement, to which it is necessary for us to obtain
correct answers if this rule here laid down by Christ is to be used
by us to good advantage. First, what sort of knowledge is it that is
mentioned? Is it relative or absolute? Is it the forming of a credible
and reliable judgment of the teachers we sit under and whose
writings we peruse, or is it an unerring discernment which precludes
us from making any mistake? Second, how is this knowledge
obtained? Is it a Divine endowment or a human acquirement? Is
it one of the spiritual gifts which accompanies regeneration, a sense
of spiritual perception bestowed upon the Christian, or is it something after which we must labour, which can be procured only by
our own diligence and industry? Third, what are the "fruits"
brought forth by the false prophets? Are they their character and
conduct, or is something else intended? Really, it is this third

question which is the principal one to be pondered, but we will say a little upon the first two before taking it up.

The answer to the first question should be fairly obvious, for even in this day of human deification we have heard of none laying claim to infallibility except the arch-humbug at Rome. But though the knowledge here predicated be not an inerrant one, yet it is something much superior to a vague and uncertain one. In those words our Lord lays down a rule, and like all general rules we may make mistakes—both favourable and unfavourable—in the application of it. The knowledge which Christ here attributes to His people is such a persuasion as to inform them how they should act toward those who appear before them as preachers and teachers, enabling them to test their claims and weigh their messages. Though it does not always enable its possessor to penetrate the disguise worn by impostors, yet it is sufficient to arouse his suspicion and, if acted on, to preserve him from falling a prey to deceivers. It is a knowledge which fortifies the Christian from being beguiled by religious seducers.

And how is this knowledge procured? It is both obtained and attained: obtained from God, attained by practice. Spiritual discernment is one of the accompaniments of the new birth: necessarily so, for regeneration is a being brought out of darkness into God's marvellous light. In that light the Christian is able to perceive things which previously were hidden from him, yet he must perforce walk with Him who is light if he is not to recede into the shadows. There are degrees of light, and the measure of our spiritual illumination decreases as distance increases between us and "the Sun of righteousness." Moreover, sight is as essential as light for clear vision. The faculty of spiritual perception belongs to each soul renewed by the Spirit, yet faculties unemployed soon become useless to their possessors. When the apostle was contrasting unhealthy saints with the healthy (Heb. v, 11-14) he described the latter as "those who by reason of *use* have their senses *exercised* to discern both good and evil." The more we walk in the light and the more we exercise our spiritual faculties, the more readily shall we perceive the snares and stumbling stones in our path.

"Ye shall know them by their fruits." False prophets are to be identified by what they produce. By their "fruits" we understand, principally, their creed, their character, and their converts. Is it not by these three things that we recognize the true prophets? The genuine servants of God give evidence of their Divine commission by *the doctrine* they proclaim: their preaching is in full accord with the Word of Truth. The general tenor of their lives is in harmony therewith, so that their daily walk is an example of practical godliness. Those whom the Spirit quickens and edifies under their preaching bear the features of their ministerial fathers and follow the lead of their shepherds. Conversely, the ministers of Satan, though feigning to be the champions of the Truth, oppose and corrupt it: some by denying its Divine authority, some by mingling human tradition with it, others by wresting it or by withholding vital portions thereof. Though their outward conduct is often beyond reproach, yet their inward character, the spirit which actuates them, is that of the *wolf*—sly, cruel, fierce. And their converts or disciples are like unto them.

The true prophet accords *God His rightful place*. He is owned as the King of kings and Lord of lords, as the One who "worketh all things after the counsel of His own will." He is acknowledged to be the sovereign Ruler of heaven and earth, at whose disposal are all creatures and all events, for whose pleasure they are created (Rev. iv, 11), whose will is invincible and whose power is irresistible. He is declared to be God in fact as well as in name: One whose claims upon us are paramount and incontestable, One who is to be held in the utmost reverence and awe, One who is to be served with fear and rejoiced in with trembling (Psalm ii, 11). Such a God the false prophets neither believe in nor preach. On the contrary, they prate about a God who wants to do this and who would like to do that, but cannot because His creatures will not permit it. Having endowed man with a free will, he must neither be compelled nor coerced, and while Deity is filled with amiable intentions He is unable to carry them out. Man is the architect of his fortunes and the decider of his own destiny, and God a mere Spectator.

The true prophet gives *Christ His rightful place,* which is very much more than to be sound concerning His person. Romanists are more orthodox about the deity and humanity of Christ than are multitudes of Protestants, yet the former as much as the latter are grossly heterodox upon His official status. The true prophet proclaims the Lord Jesus as *the covenant Head* of His people, who was set up before the foundation of the world to fulfil all the terms of the covenant of grace on their behalf and to secure for them all its blessings. He sets forth Christ as the "Surety" and "Mediator" of the covenant (Heb. vii, 22; viii, 6), as the One who came here to fulfil His covenant engagements: "Lo, I come, to do Thy will, O God"—it was a voluntary act, yet in discharge of a sacred agreement. All that Christ did here upon earth and that which He is now doing in heaven was and is the working out of an eternal compact. Everything relating to the Church's salvation was planned and settled by covenant stipulation between the Eternal Three. Nothing was left to chance, nothing remained uncertain, nothing was rendered contingent upon anything the creature must do. About this glorious and fundamental truth the false prophets are completely *silent.*

It was to fit Him for His covenant engagements that the Surety became incarnate. It was to redeem His people from the curse of the Law that Christ was made under it, fulfilled its terms, endured its penalty in the room and stead of His covenant people. It was for them, and no others, that He shed His precious blood. Because

He faithfully and perfectly discharged His covenant obligations, the Father has sworn with an oath that all for whom He acted shall be eternally saved, that not one of these shall perish, solemnly declaring that "He shall see of the travail of His soul, and shall be satisfied," (Isaiah liii, 11). God has made with Christ, and His people in Him, "an everlasting covenant, ordered in all things, and *sure*" (II Samuel xxiii, 5). But the false prophets reverse all this. They misrepresent the redemptive work of Christ as being a vague, indefinite, general, promiscuous thing, rendering nothing sure. They believe Christ shed His blood for Judas equally with Peter, and for Pilate as truly as Paul. They preach a salvation which is uncertain and contingent, as though it were for anybody or nobody as the caprice of men shall decide: Christ provided it and if we accept of it well and good; if not, He will be disappointed.

The true prophet *puts man in his proper place*. He declares that man is a depraved, ruined and lost creature, dead in trespasses and sins. He points out that man is alienated from God, that his mind is enmity against Him, that he is an inveterate rebel against Him. He shows this to be true not only of those in heathendom, but equally so of those born in Christendom: that "There is none righteous, no not one: There is none that understandeth, there is none that seeketh after God" (Romans iii, 10, 11). He makes it clear that man is a total wreck, that no part of his being has escaped the fearful consequences of his original revolt from his Maker: that his understanding is darkened, his affections corrupted, his will enslaved. Because of what transpired in Eden man has become the slave of sin and the captive of the Devil. He has no love for the true and living God, but instead a heart that is filled with hatred against Him; so far from desiring or seeking after Him, he endeavours by every imaginable means to banish Him from his thoughts. He is blind to His excellency, deaf to His voice, defiant of His authority and unconcerned for His glory.

The true prophet goes still farther. He not only portrays the sinner as he actually is, but he announces that man is utterly unable to change himself or better his condition one iota. He solemnly announces man to be "without strength," that he *cannot* bring himself into subjection to the Divine Law or perform a single action pleasing to God (Romans viii, 7, 8). He insists that the Ethiopian can change his skin or the leopard his spots more readily than they who are accustomed to do evil can perform that which is good (Jer. xiii, 1, 23). In short, he declares that man is hopelessly and irremediably lost unless a sovereign God is pleased to perform a miracle of grace upon him. But it is the very opposite with the false prophets. They speak "smooth things" and flatter their hearers, persuading them that their case is very far from being as desperate as it really is. If they do not expressly repudiate the Fall, or term it (as the Evolutionists) a "fall upward," they greatly minimize it, making it appear to be only a slight accident which may be repaired by our own exertions, that man is little affected by it, that he still has "the power to accept Christ."

According as the fall of man be viewed and preached so will be the conceptions of men concerning the need and nature of redemption. Almost every Gospel truth will necessarily be coloured by the light in which we view the extent of the fall. Take the truth of *election*: which is the deciding factor—God's will or mine? Why, if I be in possession of freedom of will and am now on probation, everything must turn on the use I make of this all-important endowment. But can this be made to square with the Scripures? Yes, by a little wresting of them. It is true that false prophets hate the very word "election," but if they are pressed into a corner they will try and wriggle out of it by saying that those whom God elected unto salvation are the ones whom He foreknew would be willing to accept Christ, and that explanation satisfies ninety-nine per cent of their hearers. The truth is God foreknew that if He left men to their pleasure *none* would ever accept Christ (Romans ix, 29), and therefore He made sovereign and unconditional selection from among them. Had not God eternally chosen me, I certainly had never chosen Him.

The same holds true of *regeneration*. If the sinner be spiritually impotent and his case hopeless so far as all self-effort and help are concerned, then he can no more quicken himself than can a rotten corpse in the tomb. A dead man is powerless, and that is precisely the natural condition of every member of the human race, religious and irreligious alike: "dead in trespasses and sins." The individual concerned in it contributes no more to his new birth than he did to his first. This was expressly insisted upon by Christ when He declared: "which were born not of blood [by descent from godly parents], nor of the will of the flesh [by their own volition], nor of the will of man [by a persuasive preacher], but of God" (John i, 13). There must be an act of Divine creation before anyone is made a new creature in Christ. But the false prophets represent man to be merely "bruised" or at most crippled by the fall, and insist that he may be born again simply by accepting Christ as his personal Saviour—a thing which none can do until he is brought from death unto life.

The genuine prophet trumpets forth with no uncertain sound the grand truth of *justification*. Rightly did Luther declare that "Justification by faith is the doctrine of a standing or falling church," for those who pervert it corrupt the Gospel at its very heart. In view of man's fallen and depraved condition, in view of his being a transgressor of the Divine Law, lying beneath its awful condemnation, the question was asked of old, "How then can man be justified with God?" (Job xxv, 4). To be "justified" is very much more than being pardoned: it is the declaration by the Divine Judge that the believer is *righteous,* and therefore entitled to the reward of the Law, but how is this possible when man has no righteousness of his own and is totally unable to produce any? The answer is that Christ not only bore in His own body the sins of God's elect, but He rendered to the Law a perfect obedience in their stead, and the moment they believe in Him His obedience is reckoned to their account, so that each can say, "in the Lord have I righteousness and strength" (Isaiah xlv, 24). But the false prophets deny and ridicule this basic truth of the imputed righteousness of Christ.

The true prophet gives the *Holy Spirit His rightful place*, not only in the Godhead, as co-eternal and co-equal with the Father and the Son, but in connection with salvation. Salvation is the gift of the Triune God: the Father planned it, the Son purchased it, the Spirit communicates it. The genuine servant of God is very explicit in declaring that the work of the Holy Spirit is as indispensable as the work of Christ: the One serving for His people, the Other acting in them. It is the distinctive office of the Spirit to illumine the understanding of God's elect, to search their conscience and convict of their ruined and guilty condition. It is His office to work repentance in them, to communicate faith unto them, to draw out their hearts unto Christ. The soundest and most faithful preaching in the world will avail nothing else unless the Holy Spirit applies it in quickening power; the most winsome offers and persuasive appeals will be useless until the Spirit bestows the hearing ear. The true prophet knows this, and therefore has he no confidence in his own abilities, but humbly seeks and earnestly prays for the power of the Spirit to rest upon him. But how different is it with deceivers of souls!

The genuine servant of God not only realizes the truth of that word, "Not by might, nor by power, but by My Spirit, saith the Lord of hosts" (Zech. iv, 6) in connection with the fruitage of his labours, but he is also deeply conscious of his own need of being personally taught by the Spirit. He has been made to feel his utter insufficiency to handle sacred things, and to realize that if he is to enter into the *spiritual* meaning of the Word he must be Divinely taught in his own soul. A mere intellectual study of the letter of Scripture cannot satisfy one who longs for a deeper experimental knowledge of the Truth, nor will he be contented with simply informing the minds of his hearers. As it is a tender conscience and a fuller heart-acquaintance with God and His Christ that he covets for himself, so it is to the conscience and heart of his hearers that he addresses himself. It is the opposite with the false prophets: they are occupied solely with the letter of Scripture, with outward profession: there is no deep probing, nothing searching in their messages, nothing to disturb the religious worldling.

Another mark by which many of the false prophets may be recognized is the disproportionate place they give to *prophecy* in their preaching and teaching. This has ever been a favourite device of religious charlatans, as those versed in ecclesiastical history are well aware. Nor should any observer of human nature be surprised at this. God has placed an impenetrable veil upon the future, so that

none can know " what a day may bring forth " (Prov. xxvii, 1). But
man is intensely curious about coming events and gives a ready ear
to any who pretend to be able to enlighten him. If on the one hand
the irreligious will flock to palmists, astrologers and other fortune-
tellers, the religious will crowd around anyone who claims to be
able to explain the mysterious contents of the Apocalypse. In times
of war and national calamity the curious are easily beguiled by men
with charts on the book of Daniel. The express prohibition of our
Lord, " It is *not* for you to know the times or the seasons " (Acts
i, 7), should deter His people from giving ear to those who claim to
have " light " thereon.

In this chapter we have not dealt with false prophets generally,
but have confined ourselves to those who wear " sheep's clothing,"
whose attacks are made upon the flock of Christ. These are men who
boast of their soundness in the Faith, and obtain a hearing among
those who regard themselves as the cream of orthodoxy. Thus far we
have dwelt upon their creed, on what they believe and teach : in our
next we shall describe some of the distinguishing traits of their
characters, and then point out that the type of converts they make
also serves to identify them by the " fruit " they produce. Our design
in entering into such detail is that young Christians may be furnished
with a full-length photo of these deceivers, and to make it clear that
we are not condemning such because they differ from us on one or
two minor matters, but because they are thoroughly corrupt in
doctrine. Furthermore, in all that has been before us it should be
clear that we should labour diligently to become thoroughly
acquainted with God's Word for ourselves—or how shall we be
fitted to detect these seducers of souls? Ponder Acts xvii, 11.

CHAPTER FIFTY-FIVE

False Prophets—Concluded

DURING the days of His earthly ministry the Lord Jesus furnished full proof that He was the perfect Preacher as well as the model Man. That fact has not received the attention which it deserves, especially among those responsible for training the future occupants of our pulpits. We have perused numerous works on homiletics, but never came across one which attempted to analyse and summarize the methods followed by Christ in His public and private discourses. If the believer finds it necessary and beneficial to ponder the prayers of the Saviour in order that his devotional life may be directed and enriched thereby, surely the minister of the Gospel should feel it both essential and helpful to make a close study of how He approached and addressed both sinners and saints. If he does so he will discover the use Christ made of the Scriptures, the wealth of illustration He drew from the simplest objects of nature, the particular aspects of Truth on which He threw the most emphasis, the variety of motives to which He appealed, the different parts of man's complex constitution to which He addressed Himself, the repetitions He deemed needful, the searching questions He so often asked, the homely comparisons He made, and the sharp contrasts He drew.

Even if the student confines his attention to the Sermon on the Mount he will perceive how wide was the range of this single Address, how numerous were the themes covered, how diverse the characters dealt with, and thus how many-sided is the work of the ministry. First the Lord depicted those upon whom the benediction of God rests, describing them according to their character and conduct. Next He defined the function and purpose of His servants: they are the salt of the earth and the light of the world. Then He declared His attitude unto the Law and the prophets and inculcated the basic law of His kingdom (v, 20). Next He expounded the spirituality of the Law and showed it demands conformity of heart as well as of action, displaying the high and holy standard which God will in no wise lower. This was followed by a warning against hypocrisy, especially in connection with prayer and fasting. Treasures in heaven were contrasted with those on earth, and the futility of seeking to serve two masters shown. Expostulation was made against covetousness and carking care. The subject of judging others was opened up, spiritual ambition encouraged, and the golden rule enunciated. The ways of death and of life were faithfully drawn.

This brief summary brings us to our present passage, which opens with a solemn warning. It is not sufficient to enforce the Law and expound the Gospel. Nor has the pulpit completed its task by setting before believers their various duties and calling to the discharge thereof. There are enemies to be warned against. Doubtless it is a far more delightful task to expatiate upon the riches of Divine grace and the excellencies and glories of the Redeemer; but there are also other matters which need attention. If the example of Christ and His apostles is to be followed the saints are to be put on their guard against those who would seduce them, who with " cunning craftiness . . . lie in wait to deceive " (Eph. iv, 14). Salvation is obtained by coming to the knowledge of the Truth (I Tim. ii, 4), and they who are deluded into believing a lie shall be damned (II Thess. ii, 11, 12). The very fact that eternal destiny is involved by what we believe is sufficient to show the deep seriousness of the issue here raised. He who has the care of souls must spare no pains in sounding the alarm.

" Beware of false prophets, which come to you in sheep's clothing, but inwardly they are ravening wolves " (verse 15). Herein we behold their "cunning craftiness." They do not appear in their true colours but are cleverly disguised. They pose as true friends of the Lord's people when in reality they are their deadliest foes. They proclaim themselves to be genuine Christians, whereas in reality they are the emissaries of Satan. They feign themselves to be the teachers of the Truth, but their aim is to instil falsehoods. They work not outside in the profane world, but among the assemblies of the saints, pretending to be deeply taught of God, the champions of orthodoxy, men filled with love, earnestly seeking the good of souls. Beware of them, says the great Shepherd of the sheep, for inwardly they are ravening wolves—fierce, merciless, seeking the destruction of the flock. Let that fact alarm you, arouse you to your danger and make you vigilant in guarding against it. Suffer not yourselves to be imposed upon.

And what is the best course to take in order to heed this solemn warning? What is the wisest policy to follow so as to be safeguarded from these murderers of souls? How shall we obtain the needed wisdom that we may be enabled to detect and identify these subtle dissemblers? Vitally important is it that we should obtain right answers to these questions. First, let us duly note *the place* where this warning occurs in our Lord's sermon. It is found not at the beginning but near its close. Is there not both instruction and comfort in that? Does it not intimate that if we have really taken to heart Christ's teaching in the former sections we shall be fortified against the danger He here warns against? That if we earnestly heed His preceding exhortations, that if we diligently seek to cultivate inward holiness and endeavour to walk according to the rules given by our Master, that if *we* ourselves have a personal and experimental knowledge of what it is to be a real disciple of

His, then we shall have little difficulty in recognizing the false ones?

"The light of the body is the eye: if therefore thine eye be single, thy whole body shall be full of light" (vi, 22). That clearly states the principle to which we have alluded above. Our Lord's language here is parabolic but its meaning is quite clear and simple. The activities of the body are directed according to the light received through the eye, and when that organ is sound and functioning properly, perceiving objects as they really are, the whole body is illuminated and enabled to discharge its duties, for we can then move with safety and circumspection. In like manner the faculties of the soul are principally directed by the dictates of the understanding, and where that is enlightened by the Holy Spirit and dominated by the Truth we shall be preserved from the snares of Satan and the stumbling-stones of the world. A "single eye" has but one object—God, the pleasing and glorifying of Him. "But if thine eye be evil, thy whole body shall be full of darkness." Thus the "single" eye is a *holy* one, being contrasted with that which is evil or carnal.

When the "eye" is occupied with Him who is Light, its possessor is able to distinguish between the things which differ and form a sound and right judgment both of persons and things. Our estimation of values is determined by whether our minds be Divinely illuminated or still in nature's darkness. Where the soul is regulated by the Truth it will be endowed with a wisdom which enables its possessor to distinguish between good and evil; the understanding then becomes a faculty which discerns between the genuine and the spurious. "Thou through Thy commandments hast made me wiser than mine enemies" (Psalm cxix, 98). Habitual submission to the Divine authority brings its own reward in this life—part of which is a spiritual discretion which preserves from impostures. When the understanding is dominated by the Word the whole soul is "full of light," so that all its faculties are under its beneficent influence: the conscience being informed, the affections turned to their legitimate object, the will moved in the right direction. In God's light we "see light" (Psalm xxxvi, 9), perceiving the difference between good and evil, the things to be sought and those to be avoided.

"If any man will do His will, he shall know of the doctrine, whether it be of God" (John vii, 17). The fundamental condition for obtaining spiritual knowledge, discernment and assurance is a genuine determination to carry out the revealed will of God in our daily lives. "A good understanding have all they that do His commandments" (Psalm cxi, 10). Capacity to distinguish Truth from error consists not in vigour of intellect nor in natural learning, but in a sincere willingness and earnest desire to yield ourselves unto the Divine will. Where there is a genuine subjection to the Divine authority and a deep longing to please the Lord, even though it appears to be directly against our temporal interests and worldly prospects, and even though it involves fierce opposition from enemies and ostracism by our professed friends, there will be both spiritual discernment and assurance. Where the heart puts the glory of God before everything else it will be raised above and delivered from the prejudices of pride, self-love, carnal fears, and fleshly aspirations which cloud and bias the understanding of the unregenerate. "Then shall we know, if we follow on to know the Lord" (Hosea vi, 3) is the sure promise.

Bagster's *Interlinear* gives a more literal translation of John vii, 17: "If any one desire His will to practise he shall know concerning the teaching, whether from God it is." The Greek word rendered "desire" signifies no fleeting impression or impulse but a deep-rooted determination. Certainty may be arrived at in connection with the things of God, but in order thereto the heart must first be right toward Him, that is surrendered to Him. Where there is a resolution to perform God's will at all costs, there will be a capacity and an enablement to discern and embrace the Truth and to detect and refuse error. It is the state of our souls which makes us receptive to or repellent against the temptations and lies of the enemy: when the heart is yielded to God and conformed to His will, we have no difficulty in seeing through the deceits of Satan. It is those who are governed by self-will and devoted to self-pleasing who fall such easy victims to "seducing spirits, and doctrines of devils" (I Tim. iv, 1). The Truth frees from deception, but only as the Truth is appropriated and assimilated.

"Ye shall know them by their fruits" (verse 16). Ah, but note well *to whom* this is said. The Lord does not predicate this of all who make a bare profession of faith: it is very far from being a knowledge common to all in Christendom. The "ye" is definitely restricted to God's own people, to those who have entered the strait gate and are walking in the narrow way of the immediate context. True, even they need to be on their guard, but if they give heed to this warning of Christ, as assuredly they will, they shall at once recognize these impostors. *Ye* shall know them: but none other will. It is because the sheep "follow" the good Shepherd that "they know His voice," and because they know His voice "a stranger will they not follow, but will flee from him, for they know not the voice of strangers" (John x, 14, 15). It is the obedient ear, and that only, which distinguishes between the voice of the true and the false shepherds. If the ear be attuned to the precepts of Scripture it will reject the sophistries of religious charlatans.

"Ye shall know them by their fruits. Do men gather grapes of thorns or figs of thistles? Even so every good tree bringeth forth good fruit, but a corrupt tree bringeth forth evil fruit. A good tree cannot bring forth evil fruit, neither can a corrupt tree bring forth good fruit. Every tree that bringeth not forth good fruit is hewn down, and cast into the fire. Wherefore by their fruits ye shall know them" (verses 16-20). In these words our Lord intimates that His people should have no difficulty in recognizing the false prophets: if they do but exercise ordinary precaution they will detect the imposture which is sought to be played upon them. The masqueraders are to be identified by their "fruits." At a distance trees look very much the same, but a closer inspection of them enables us to distinguish the fruitful from the fruitless ones, and whether the fruit be wholesome or injurious. In like manner there needs to be a careful examination of those who appear before us as the servants of God, that the true ones may be distinguished from the counterfeit.

In the preceding chapter we suggested that there is a threefold reference in the "fruits" produced by the false prophets, namely their creed, their character, and their converts. Having dwelt therein at some length on the first, a few words now upon the second and third. The character of these men is clearly indicated by Christ's descriptive words: "inwardly they are ravening wolves." It was none other than the Lord of love who employed what this super-cilious generation would term "harsh language." Love is faithful as well as gentle, and it was love to His own which moved Christ to tear off their disguise and reveal these enemies of His flock in their real character. He who denounced the scribes and Pharisees as "hypocrites" and "blind guides," and termed Herod "that fox" (Luke xiii, 32), hesitated not to brand these subtle deceivers as "ravening wolves." When a bottle of deadly poison is placed among others containing healing lotions it needs to be plainly labelled.

That Christ here left an example for His servants to follow appears clearly from the instance of the apostle Paul. When taking leave of the elders of the Ephesian church, he warned them that "after my departing shall grievous wolves enter in among you, not sparing the flock. Also of your own selves shall men arise, speaking perverse things, to draw away disciples *after them*" (Acts xx, 29, 30). In that last clause we have another mark of the false prophets. They are inveterate proselytizers. They continually obtrude themselves upon people's attention. They are ever creeping into houses, "leading captive silly women led away with divers lusts." They are continually coaxing and wheedling folk to come to their meetings. But the true prophet never attempts guile or presses anyone to attend his services. No, he is content to follow his Master's practice: "he that hath ears to hear let him hear," and there he leaves it. When a place receives them not they "go their way" (Luke x, 10) instead of pleading and arguing and seeking to draw disciples "after them."

"But inwardly they are ravening wolves." What a solemn but suggestive and revealing word is that. The wolf, like the fox, is tricky and treacherous, subtle and sly, hence the words "cunning craftiness" in connection with the purveyors of error who "lie in wait to deceive" of Ephesians iv, 14. They scruple not to employ the most dishonourable tactics and resort to tricks which honest men of the world would scorn to use. The wolf is cruel and merciless:

so are these deceivers of souls. They prate about love, but they are full of hatred toward those who expose them. They are greedy, having voracious appetites, and false prophets are men of insatiable ambition, hungry for applause, avaricious. Jeremiah xxiii, 32, speaks of their "lightness" or irreverence, and Zephaniah iii, 4, also says, "their prophets are light and treacherous." So far from being sober and solemn they are frivolous and frothy: it cannot be otherwise, for the fear of God is not upon them.

"By their fruits ye shall know them." Not by their profession, nor their sanctimoniousness, nor their zeal, but their "fruits" we understand; third, *the converts* they make. Like produces like. The parent is more or less reproduced in his children. In Jeremiah xxiii, 16, it is said of those who give ear to the false prophets, "they make you vain." Egotistical themselves, their disciples are also conceited: proud of their letter-knowledge of the Scriptures, boastful of their orthodoxy, claiming to have light which those in the "man-made systems" are without. But their walk betrays them: no traces of humility, no mourning over sin, no experimental acquaintance with the plague of their hearts. They loudly boast of their assurance, but produce not the evidences on which scriptural assurance is based. They prate about eternal security but refuse to examine their hearts and see whether they be in the faith. They have much to say about their peace and joy, but are strangers to the groanings of Romans vii. They boast that they are "not under the law" and give proof thereof in their characters and conduct.

In conclusion let us anticipate a question: why does God permit these false prophets which work such havoc in Christendom? This is a very solemn question, and we must restrict ourselves to what the Scriptures say by way of reply. "Thou shalt not hearken unto the words of the prophet, or that dreamer of dreams: for the Lord your God proveth you, to know whether ye love the Lord your God with all your heart and with all your soul" (Deut. xiii, 3). From those words it is clear that God suffers teachers of error for the same reason as He does persecutors of His people: to test their love, to try their fidelity, to show that their loyalty to him is such that they will not give ear unto His enemies. Error has always been more popular than the Truth, for it lets down the bars and fosters fleshly indulgence, but for that very reason it is obnoxious to the godly. The one who by grace can say "I have chosen the way of Truth" will be able to add "I have *stuck unto* Thy testimonies" (Psalm cxix, 30, 31), none being able to move him therefrom.

"For there must be also heresies among you, that they which are approved may be made manifest among you" (I Cor. xi, 19). Error serves as a flail, separating the chaff from the wheat. Let some plausible and popular preacher come forward with an old error decked out in new clothes and empty professors will at once flock to his standard; but not so with those who are established in the Faith. Thus, by means of the false prophets, God makes it appear who are the ones who hold the Truth in sincerity: they are faithful to Him despite all temptations to turn away unto a "broader-minded" way. The genuine gold endures every test to which it is subjected. Thus too are the unregenerate "converts" revealed: the counterfeit gold will not withstand the fire. Those who are attracted by a novelty do not wear but are soon carried away by some newer innovation. "They went out from us, but they were not of us; for if they had been of us, they would no doubt have continued with us: but they went out that they might be made manifest that they were *not* all of us" (I John ii, 19). Thus, they who turn away from orthodoxy to heterodoxy must not be regarded as real Christians.

The false prophets are also ordained of God for the punishment of those who receive not the love of the Truth. "For this cause God shall send them strong delusion that they should believe a lie: That they all might be damned, who believed not the truth, but had pleasure in unrighteousness" (II Thess. ii, 10-12). Ahab could not endure Elijah and Micaiah, the servants of God, therefore he was suffered to follow the priests of Baal unto his destruction.

It is very clear from Matthew xxiv, 5, 11, etc., that Israel's rejection of Christ was followed by the appearing of many false christs in their midst who fatally deceived large numbers of the Jews. It was not until primitive and genuine Christianity had been jettisoned that the religious world was plagued by the monster of Romanism. A very large proportion of those found in the false cults of our day were once members of or regular attenders at churches which were more or less sound in the Faith. Beware, my reader, if you despise God's Truth you will fall into love with Satan's lies.

CHAPTER FIFTY-SIX

Profession Tested

" Not every one that saith unto Me, Lord, Lord, shall enter into the kingdom of heaven ; but he that doeth the will of My Father which is in heaven. Many will say to Me in that day, Lord, Lord, have we not prophesied in Thy name ? and in Thy name have cast out devils ? and in Thy name done many wonderful works ? And then will I profess unto them, I never knew you : depart from Me, ye that work iniquity. Therefore whosoever heareth these sayings of Mine, and doeth them, I will liken him unto a wise man, which built his house upon a rock : And the rain descended, and the floods came, and the winds blew, and beat upon that house ; and it fell not : for it was founded upon a rock. And every one that heareth these sayings of Mine, and doeth them not, shall be likened unto a foolish man, which built his house upon the sand : And the rain descended, and the floods came, and the winds blew, and beat upon that house ; and it fell : and great was the fall of it." (Matt. vii, 21-27.)

" Not every one that saith unto Me, Lord, Lord, shall enter into the kingdom of heaven; but he that doeth the will of My Father which is in heaven " (verse 21). With these words our Lord commenced the twelfth and final division of this notable Sermon. It was perhaps the most searching and solemn section in it. Here the One who cannot be imposed upon by any deceit makes known His inexorable demand for reality. Here the One who shall yet officiate as the Judge of all the earth declares that at the Grand Assize all who have deceived themselves and deluded others will stand forth in their real characters. Here the One who knows every thought and imagination of the heart, before whose omniscient eye all things are naked and opened, makes it crystal clear that lip service is worthless and that even the most imposing deeds count for nothing where vital and practical godliness is lacking. The more this passage be thoughtfully pondered the less surprised are we that so many seek to get rid of this Sermon by terming it " Jewish " and insisting " it is not for this dispensation."

If it be true that Matthew v—vii is more hated by our moderns than any other portion of God's Word, it is equally true that none is more urgently needed by them. Never were there so many millions of nominal Christians on earth as there are today, and never was there such a small percentage of real ones. Not since before the days of Luther and Calvin, when the great Reformation effected such a grand change for the better, has Christendom been so crowded with those who have " a form of godliness " but who are strangers to its transforming power. We seriously doubt whether there has ever been a time in the history of this Christian era when there were such multitudes of deceived souls within the churches, who verily believe that all is well with their souls when in fact the wrath of God abideth on them. And we know of no single thing better calculated to undeceive them than a full and faithful exposition of these closing verses of our Lord's Sermon on the Mount.

The relation of this passage to the context is easily determined. Taking the more remote one, this final section forms a fitting conclusion to the whole address, which, be it remembered, was delivered in the hearing of the multitude (v, 1; vii, 28), though more immediately to His "disciples." It was a most suitable climax. Christ had commenced by delineating the character of those who are approved of God, and He finished by describing those upon whom eternal judgment will fall. Herein we may see how the chief of the apostles patterned his ministry after the example of his Master. If on the one hand "love" constrained him, on the other hand it was by "the terror of the Lord," that he sought to persuade men. Thus, when standing before Felix, "he reasoned of righteousness, temperance and judgment" so that the governor "trembled" (Acts xxiv, 25). Alas, how little of this faithful dealing with souls is there in this degenerate day: how little probing of the conscience, how little plain speaking of the awful doom awaiting the ungodly, how little shaking them out of their fatal complacency.

If we look at the more immediate context we shall be increasingly impressed with the appropriateness of this solemn peroration. Our Lord had just uttered warning against the false prophets, who are to be recognized by the "fruits" which they bear, or in other words by the "converts" which they make, the disciples they draw after them. It is the antinomian beguilers who are there more specially in view, as is clear from our Lord's words "which come to you in sheep's clothing," thereby concealing their real character. In like manner their adherents assume a sanctimonious pose and employ the most pious language, carrying a Bible with them wherever they go and being able to quote it freely. They refer to the Redeemer in most reverent terms, being particular to accord Him His title of "Lord." Nevertheless, when weighed in the balances they are found wanting, for they are lacking in vital godliness. Their hearts are not renewed, their wills are not surrendered to God, their conduct corresponds not with their high pretensions.

It is the juxtaposition of Matthew vii, 19, and vii, 20, which enables us clearly to perceive the scope of the latter. Though the Saviour had said in verse 16 "Ye shall know them by their fruits," He repeats this identifying mark of these deceivers of souls in verse 20, and then immediately adds "Not every one that saith unto Me, Lord, Lord, shall enter into the kingdom." The intimate connection then between these two sections of His Address is too plain to miss: the converts made by the false prophets are big talkers but little doers. They claim to be devoutly attached to Christ but their claim is invalid, being unsupported by the evidence which is necessary to give it credibility. Their fine talk is not corroborated by a Christian walk, and therefore it is insufficient to obtain for them an entrance into His kingdom. If the blind follow the blind both fall into the ditch. It takes something more than "sheep's clothing" to make one a servant of Christ, and something more than lip service is needed before He will own anyone as a true disciple of His. It is empty and windy professors whom He here exposes.

"Not every one that saith unto Me, Lord, Lord, shall enter into the kingdom of heaven: but he that doeth the will of My Father which is in heaven." Let us consider first the application of these words to those who were immediately addressed. Many of the Jews were so impressed by the miracles wrought by Christ that they were disposed to be His disciples while ignorant of and in fact strongly opposed to His doctrine concerning salvation and the requirements of the kingdom of God. "When He was in Jerusalem at the passover in the feast day, many believed in His name, when they saw the miracles which He did. But Jesus did not commit Himself unto them" (John ii, 23, 24). Nicodemus expressed the attitude of some of the more influential when he said "Rabbi, we know that Thou art a teacher come from God: for no man can do these miracles that Thou doest, except God be with him" (John iii, 2). But so far from allowing Nicodemus to entertain the idea that an acknowledgment of Him as a "teacher sent from God" would secure for him the blessings He came to bestow, He told him frankly that except he were born again he could neither see nor enter the kingdom of God.

When Christ had fed the great multitude with the five loaves and two small fishes, so deeply were they impressed that we are told: "Then those men, when they had seen the miracle that Jesus did, said, This is of a truth that prophet that should come into the world." Yet "When Jesus therefore perceived that they would come and take Him by force and make Him a king, He departed again into a mountain Himself alone" (John vi, 14, 15). This it was which directly occasioned the searching declaration of the section which is now before us. Very far was He from taking advantage of a temporary and superficial bias of men in His favour: plain speaking and honest dealings characterized the whole of His transactions with His countrymen. It was to prevent them from imagining that their owning Him as Prophet, or even acknowledging Him as the Messiah in the sense that they understood the term, was sufficient that He here impressed upon His hearers that they must be actually and personally *doers* of God's will before they were qualified to participate in the blessings of His spiritual and eternal kingdom.

While the verses before us were addressed first and locally to the Jews of Christ's day, yet it is obvious that they have a far wider application, that they belong to the Gentiles of our day. As we have proceeded through this Sermon section by section, we have endeavoured to point out again and again and make clear the force and relevancy of our Lord's words as they respected His immediate hearers and also their pertinency unto and bearing upon ourselves. There was nothing provincial or evanescent in the teaching of

Christ: it was designed for all nations and for all generations, and by it all men will yet be judged (John xii, 48). This declaration of Christ's then is full of important instruction to all in every country and every age, wherever the Gospel is presented to the examination and reception of men. It was true at the beginning, it is just as true today, and will continue so long as the world lasts, that some, yea, many, will go no farther than a mere lip profession, and consequently will be excluded from the kingdom: and that only those who really perform the Divine will shall enter into the enjoyment of the blessings of Christianity.

This expression "the kingdom of heaven" need not detain us very long, for we have explained its meaning in previous chapters. As it is employed here it is synonymous with "the kingdom of God" in John iii, 3, as a comparison of Matthew xviii, 3, and Luke xviii 17, clearly proves. It had reference to the new order of things introduced by the Messiah, being in contrast with and the successor of Judaism. That new order of things may be contemplated as beginning in this present life and perfected in the life to come, they being two aspects of the one economy: the former we designate the kingdom of grace and the latter the kingdom of glory. Most of the older commentators understood "the kingdom of heaven" in the verse now before us as referring to the second aspect, and therefore as being equivalent to the state of celestial blessedness: but personally we see no reason for this restriction. A mere lip profession fails to secure even a present participation in the peculiar privileges of Christianity, for it obtains neither reconciliation with God, the forgiveness of sins, nor an enjoyment of that holy happiness which is the portion now of those truly converted. It inevitably follows that those who enter not the kingdom of grace on earth will never enter the kingdom of glory in heaven.

"Not every one that saith unto Me, Lord, Lord, shall enter into the kingdom of heaven," or as we find it in Luke vi, 46, "Why call ye Me, Lord, Lord...?" This expression is equivalent to acknowledging Christ as Teacher and Master, even owning Him as the Son of God, the alone Saviour of sinners. There is a designed emphasis in the "Lord, Lord," for it is meant to express not merely profession, but a decided, open, habitual profession. Thus Christ here declares that a mere verbal acknowledgment of the truth concerning His person or a lip profession that we are His disciples, prepared to accept His teaching, however explicit, public, and often repeated that profession be, does not open the way to the enjoyment of the special blessings of His kingdom, unless it is proved to be the result of true repentance and sound conversion, and unless it be accompanied with a corresponding course of conduct in doing the will of the Father. An outward profession of the most orthodox religion is useless if it be joined not with vital godliness and sincere obedience. Even the demons owned Him as the "Son of God" (Matt. viii, 29), but what did it avail them?

It scarcely needs to be pointed out that no entrance into the kingdom of God is possible unless Christ *is* owned as "Lord." Unitarians and those "modernists" who deny that Christ is anything more than the ideal Man are certainly outside the pale of salvation. "The words before us obviously imply, what is very distinctly stated in other parts of Scripture, that a profession of discipleship and acknowledgment of our submission in mind and heart to Christ Jesus is absolutely necessary in order to our enjoying the privileges of discipleship. No person who does not call Christ 'Lord, Lord' can enter into the kingdom of God: no man who is ignorant of His claims, who treats these claims with neglect, who rejects these claims, or who though he may be all but persuaded that these claims are just, yet from worldly motives does not acknowledge them—no such person can participate in the peculiar blessings of His disciples, either on earth or in heaven" (John Brown, to whom we are indebted for some things above and in what follows). "Ye call Me Master and Lord: and ye say well; for so I am" (John xiii, 13). Whosoever transgresseth, and abideth not in the doctrine of Christ, hath not God" (II John, 9).

But while the necessity of owning Christ as Lord is clearly implied in His words here, the truth which they more directly teach is that profession, however necessary in connection with faith and obedience, cannot of itself secure a participation in the spiritual blessings of the new economy. No matter how loudly a man avows his acceptance of the teachings of Christ, unless he be a *doer* of the Word his avowals count for nothing. He who requires the heart will not be put off with shadows for the substance, the mere semblance for the reality, words instead of works. Empty compliments are not worth the breath which utters them. They who trust in a form of godliness which is devoid of its power are building their hopes upon a foundation of sand. Not only is a bare profession insufficient for the saving of the soul, but it is an insult to Christ Himself. It is a horrible mockery to call Him Lord while we continue to do only what is pleasing to ourselves, to profess to obey Him while we treat His commands with contempt. It is *obedience* which marks men as His disciples and distinguishes them from the subjects of Satan.

Let us now describe the different types of professors. First, there are those who are simply *nominal* ones. They bear the name of "Christians" and that is all. They happen to have been born in a country where Christianity is the prevailing religion and where it is regarded as a mark of respectability to give some recognition and assent to it. A few drops of water were sprinkled upon them in infancy by a preacher and possibly they received some kind of instruction in the rudiments of religion during the days of their childhood. But after reaching maturity, excepting for an occasional visit to a church, probably at "Christmas" or "Easter," that is as far as they go. Yet if asked to declare themselves they readily affirm they are "Christians," but that means little or nothing more than that they are not Jews, pagans or open infidels. Such persons usually are grossly ignorant of the very fundamentals of the Faith and often the lives of respectable heathen would put theirs to shame. Surely such people are outside the kingdom of God. They cannot participate in its blessings either on earth or in heaven: if they could, its blessings would not be spiritual ones.

Second, *formal* professors. This class is made up of those who regard themselves as much in advance of the ones in the former. They are able to repeat some catechism, or at least give a fairly intelligent account of both the doctrine and the laws of Christ. If not members of a church they are at least " adherents " and regular attenders at its services. They claim to be submissive to Christ's authority and observe all the outward acts of worship which characterize His followers, but they know nothing of the blessedness of communion with the Lord, nor is His joy their strength. Their religion is but a mental assent to an orthodox creed and going through a round of external observances. They evince no desire for the Truth to have a dominating power over their affections and wills, and most of them regard as deluded enthusiasts and canting hypocrites those who regard experimental godliness as the only genuine Christianity, and pant after a deeper acquaintance with God. It is plain that these, too, are outside the kingdom, being strangers to those operations of the Spirit which alone make us meet for it.

Third, *deceived* professors. " There is a generation that are pure in their own eyes, and yet is not washed from their filthiness " (Prov. xxx, 12). Those in this class look with pharisaical pity upon those described above. These deem themselves better taught. They place no reliance upon infant sprinkling, no subscription to the soundest confession of faith, rather do they pride themselves upon an intellectual assent to the letter of Holy Writ. They are quite sure that Christ died for them and that they have accepted Him as their personal Saviour. None can shake their assurance. Yet meekness and lowliness characterize them not, forbearing one another and forgiving one another they are strangers to, the fruit of the Spirit and practical godliness are missing from their daily lives. Their associates address them as " Brother " or " Sister " and that suffices. But what does it profit me to have the reputation of being a wealthy man if I have not the wherewithal to purchase the necessities of life? What avails it to call me a healthy person if disease be eating away my very vitals? If Christ bars the door of the kingdom against me no personal assurance will give me entrance.

Fourth, *hypocritical* professors. The number in this class, we are fain to believe, is much smaller than in the preceding ones: for them there is some hope while life lasts, but for these we can see none. Hypocritical professors are those who deliberately assume a role: they are consciously playing a part. They know that they are not Christians, but for one reason or other are anxious to make their fellows believe they are so. Some of them belonged formerly to one of the other groups, to the third especially, then they discovered the emptiness of their profession or that they had been deceived; too dishonest to disclaim themselves as Christians they took increased pains to persuade others of their piety. Not content with a dull, formal round of duties, they put on the appearance of a deep interest in the things of God and of zeal in seeking to promote His cause. This is incomparably the vilest of the four classes we have sketched. Such conduct is no less contemptible than irrational. God cannot be imposed upon and no affronts are likely to be more severely punished than dishonour done to His omniscience. The hypocrite's portion will be the " outer darkness " where there is wailing and gnashing of teeth.

Fifth, the *genuine* professor. This is the real Christian, who enjoys the blessings of the kingdom of grace here and will be admitted to the bliss of the kingdom of glory hereafter. He is described here according to his conduct or actions: " but he that doeth the will of My Father which is in heaven." Two points need determining: what is here signified by the Father's will, and what is meant by the doing of it? " The fundamental part of doing the will of God is revealed in these words: ' This is My beloved Son, in whom I am well pleased; hear ye Him ' (Matt. xvii, 5). Where this is complied with, everything else follows " (J. Brown). The will of the Father is perfectly made known by the incarnate Word, for He is the final Spokesman of God (Heb. i, 1, 2), all judgment being committed unto Him (John v, 22). The will of the Father is that we should forsake our sins, trust in His Son, take His yoke upon us, and follow Him; to do less and yet call Him our Lord is most horrible mockery. So perfect and intimate is the oneness of the Father and the Son that Christ goes on to say: " Whosoever heareth these sayings *of Mine*, and doeth them," is like one who builds his house upon a rock (verse 24 and cf. Luke vi, 46).

What is meant by doing the Divine will? Obviously it does not connote a perfect or flawless performance thereof, for there is no Christian who has ever attained to such excellence in this life, though nothing short of this is the standard set before us (Matt. v, 48). It means that I have surrendered my heart and will to the claims of Christ, so that I truly desire Him to " reign over " me (Luke xix, 14) and order my life. It means that I have subjected myself to His authority and that it is the prevailing bent of my mind and constant endeavour to please and honour Him in all things. It means that I genuinely aim to be both internally and externally conformed to His holy image, and that it is my greatest grief when I do those things which displease Him. It means I truly seek that my thoughts, affections and actions are regulated by His precepts. It is not a sin-less obedience which is here in view, but it is a sincere one. It is not a forced one, but prompted by love. It is not merely an external compliance with the Divine commands but a " doing the will of God from the heart " (Eph. vi, 6).

CHAPTER FIFTY-SEVEN

Profession Tested—Continued

" NOT every one that saith unto Me, Lord, Lord, shall enter into the kingdom of heaven; but he that doeth the will of My Father which is in heaven." In the preceding chapter we sought to supply an exposition of this verse: explaining the meaning of its terms, pointing out its bearing upon the Jews of that day, and its application unto our own. On this occasion we propose to deal with it more in a *topical* manner. Obviously the theme of this verse is the inadequacy of a mere lip profession of Christian discipleship, and since so many are fatally deceived at this very point we deem it advisable to devote another chapter to the subject. We shall now endeavour to show something of the attainments possible to the formalist and how near he may come to the kingdom of Christ without actually entering it. It is the third class of professors, the *deceived* ones, that we have chiefly in view. We shall seek to examine and test them at four simple but essential points and show of each one wherein they come short of that which is the experience and portion of the regenerate.

1. *Knowledge.* It is plain from the teaching of Holy Writ that there are two distinct orders or types of knowledge of spiritual and Divine things, and that the difference between them is not merely one of degree but of kind, a radical and vital difference. There is a knowledge of God and of His Word which is a saving one, but there is also a knowledge of the same Objects which—though it may be accurate and extensive—is a non-saving one. Thus it is of vast importance that everyone who values his soul should be properly informed as to the essential differences between these two kinds of knowledge, so that he may diligently examine himself and ascertain *which* of them is *his.* That the above distinction is no arbitrary one, no imaginary one of ours, is evident from many passages. When the apostle declared that the Colossian saints " *knew* the grace of God *in truth* " (i, 6) he was employing discriminating language, for there are others who know the grace of God only *in theory.* " This is life eternal, that they might know Thee the only true God, and Jesus Christ, whom Thou hast sent " (John xvii, 3), which is a saving knowledge. " When they *knew* God they glorified Him not as God," but became idolators and were abandoned of Him (Romans i, 21-24): that was a non-saving knowledge of God.

" Though I have the gift of prophesy, and understand all mysteries, and all knowledge; . . . and have not charity, I am nothing " (I Cor. xiii, 2). Nor is that an altogether unlikely case. Far from it. It is possible for the natural man to acquire a much fuller and more intelligent grasp of the Truth than that which is possessed by the majority of genuine Christians. If he be endowed with a competent intellect, if he has received a good education, if he closely applies himself to the study of Scripture (as he might to one of the arts or sciences), then he may become expertly proficient in a letter know-ledge and notional understanding of the same. By patient industry he may master the Hebrew and Greek languages in which they were originally written. By reading and rereading sound theological works he may secure a comprehension of the whole doctrinal system of Truth. By consulting able commentators he may obtain light upon perplexing passages. He may even arrive at an understanding of the " mysteries " of iniquity and of godliness, so that he is quite sound in the Faith. And if he be a fluent speaker, he may discourse upon Divine things so that none may legitimately take issue with his orthodoxy, yea, many may find his preaching instructive and helpful.

There are also very many unregenerate listeners who by waiting upon the ministry of the Word may obtain a wide knowledge thereof. A considerable number are possessed with an insatiable curiosity, or appetite, for the acquisition of religious information, and, by regular attendance at church, close attention to what they hear and the aid of retentive memories, become well instructed in spiritual things, especially where this be supplemented by the reading of a considerable amount of devotional literature. Though unregenerate they obtain clear views of the whole Gospel scheme and those gifted with clear minds often grasp more of the profounder aspects of Truth than many of God's own children are capable of understanding (for " not many wise men after the flesh " [I Cor. i, 26] are among His elect), and dig more deeply into the mines of Truth and make greater discoveries than do the saved. They may apprehend things so clearly as to satisfy their judgment and express their notions so distinctly to others as to convince, yea, to defend their beliefs so tellingly and argue about the same to such effect as to silence any who differ from them.

Nor is this knowledge limited to the doctrinal side of the Truth. They may attain unto well-proportioned conceptions of the Divine character and perfections and correct views of the person and work of Christ, the office and operations of the Holy Spirit. By sitting under the faithful preaching of God's servants and by reading articles of a searching nature they may secure a good understanding of the experimental side of things. They may be quite clear upon the miracle of regeneration and be able to draw the lineaments of the new creature as true to life as though they had the image thereof in their own souls. They may be able to describe the work of grace as accurately as though they had an experience of it in their own hearts. They may depict the conflicts between the flesh and spirit as though such opposition were taking place within themselves. They may speak as glowingly of the Christian's graces as if they were the possessors of them. They may narrate the actings of certain graces under such and such a temptation as though they were recounting their own history. They may have the exact idea and true notion of all these things in their heads when there is nothing whatever of them in their hearts.

Yet in spite of all that we have predicated above of these unregenerate yet orthodox preachers and hearers, authors and readers, they are those who are "ever learning and never able to come to the knowledge of the truth" (II Tim. iii, 7), that is to say they do not and cannot arrive at the *saving* knowledge of it. And why is this so? Because they lack the necessary faculty for its entrance. "The natural man receiveth not the things of the Spirit of God, for they are foolishness unto him; neither can he know them, because they are spiritually discerned" (I Cor. ii, 14). A saving knowledge of the Truth is impossible unto the unregenerate. There must needs be a suitability between the instrument and its task, between the agent and that which is to be apprehended. An animal is incapable of entering into what the human intellect may comprehend, and one who has no spiritual faculty is unable to receive spiritual things in a *spiritual* way. The natural man may acquire a theoretical and notional knowledge of things, but he cannot obtain a spiritual or saving knowledge of them, for he is totally devoid of spiritual life.

Let us now attempt to answer the question, What is the essential difference between these two kinds of knowledge, wherein does a natural and notional knowledge of Divine things come short of a spiritual and saving knowledge of them? Consider the following: "I have heard of Thee by the hearing of the ear, but now mine eye seeth Thee" (Job xlii, 5): we give not an exposition of those words, but use them illustratively of this contrast. One may listen for years to sermons but when the soul actually has Christ revealed *in* him (Gal. i, 16) he learns the tremendous difference there is between a hearsay knowledge of Him and a spiritual perception as He stands manifested to the soul as a living Reality. Let us endeavour still further to simplify by a human analogy. A child is born with such a filament over his eyes that he is quite blind. He receives a good education and loved ones seek to use their eyes on his behalf and take pains in describing to him some of the beauties and wonders of nature: by their word pictures he obtains clear concepts of many objects. But suppose a specialist performs a successful operation and vision is vouchsafed him: how vastly different his own sight of a glorious sunset from the previous notion he had formed of it!

No matter how carefully and accurately his friends have described a sunset to him, how vivid the contrast when he beheld one for himself! Equally real, equally radical, equally vivid is the difference between a second-hand knowledge of the Truth and a personal acquaintance and experience of its power. Following out the analogy a little farther: while blind, that man may have thought his friends exaggerated the grandeur of a sunset, but as soon as he has seen one for himself he knows that neither poet's tongue nor artist's brush could possibly do it justice. He may even have entertained doubts as to the thing itself, wondering if his friends were but drawing upon their imagination and seeking to amuse him with a fairy tale, but now all uncertainty is at an end. So with the regenerate soul and Christ: once his sin-blinded eyes are opened to behold the Lamb, he exclaims with one of old, "I *know* that my Redeemer liveth." A saving knowledge of Christ ravishes the soul and so draws the heart unto Him as to esteem all else as dross in comparison with the excellency of the knowledge of Him (Phil. iii, 8).

A Laplander may have read about honey, but not until he has eaten some does he really know what it is like. Nor does the soul truly know the Lord until he has "*tasted* that He is gracious" (I Peter ii, 3). The formalist knows God is omniscient, the Christian has an inward experience thereof, by His detecting to him the heart's deceitfulness and discovering secret sins. The former knows God is almighty, but the latter has felt His omnipotency working within him: enabling him to believe (Eph. i, 19), subduing his lusts, overcoming the world. The one kind of knowledge then is speculative, the other practical; the one is merely notional, the other experimental; the one is acquired second-hand, the other is communicated directly. He "hath shined in our hearts, to give the light of the knowledge of the glory of God in the face of Jesus Christ" (II Cor. iv, 6). Natural knowledge puffs up, but spiritual humbles and makes the soul painfully conscious of its spiritual ignorance. Observe how in Psalm cxix David prays no less than eight times "teach me." Natural knowledge produces no spiritual fruit, and it is vain to boast of spiritual learning if it be not accompanied with a holy life.

2. *Repentance.* There are four principal acts and exercises in repentance: confession of sin, hatred of sin, sorrow for sin, resolution against sin; and each of these may be and has been performed by the unregenerate. Cain cried out at the weight and grievousness of his sin saying, "My punishment [or "iniquity"] is greater than I can bear" (Gen. iv, 13). Pharaoh acknowledged his sin and condemned himself for it (Exodus ix, 27), so did Israel when they had provoked the Lord (Num. xiv, 40), so did Saul (I Samuel xv, 14), so did Judas (Matt. xxvii, 3). As to hatred of sin, Jehu detested the idols of Baal and destroyed them, yet his heart was not upright (II Kings x, 26-28, 31). After their lengthy captivity in Babylon Israel were delivered from their love of idolatry, so that the Spirit said "thou that abhorrest idols" (Romans ii, 22). Many there are

who hate injustice and oppression, unmercifulness and cruelty, lying and dishonesty. Concerning sorrow for sin: Israel mourned after their worship of the golden calf (Exodus xxxiii, 4) and "mourned greatly" (Num. xiv, 39) after they had sorely provoked the Lord, and yet continued in their provocations (verse 44). Ahab expressed sore grief for his wickedness (I Kings xxi, 27). As to resolution against sin, a strong case of such is seen in Balaam (Num. xxii, 18, 38).

If the unregenerate may go thus far in a way of repentance, wherein do they fall short? If theirs be not "repentance unto life" (Acts xi, 18), where is it to be found? Saving repentance proceeds from sorrow for sin, whereas the sorrow of the formalist is defective at these points. First, they *mourn not for sin itself*, but over its consequences. Not as their deeds are contrary to God, a violation of His Law, opposed to His holy will, but because they involve unpleasant effects. Second, not for consequences in reference to God, but themselves: not because He is dishonoured, His authority spurned, and the creature preferred above Him. If they mourn because of His displeasure, it is rather for the effects of His anger. They care nothing about Satan being gratified and the cause of Christ reproached so long as they are not afflicted in their persons or estates. Third, they mourn not for all its consequences in reference to themselves: not as it defiles the soul, keeps at a distance from God, hardens the heart and renders it more incapable of holy duties, but only as it deprives of mercies and produces miseries.

Their *hatred of sin* is defective. It is not extended to all sin: they cannot say, "I hate every false way." They may hate gross sins such as the state penalizes, but wink at lesser ones. They may hate open wickedness but not secret faults. They may abominate theft and uncleanness, yet make no conscience of pride and self-righteousness. They may hate those things which are cried down by people among whom they now live, and yet enter into the same heartily if they move to another part of the earth. They may hate an unprofitable sin, but refrain not from those which bring them in a revenue. They may hate a sin which is contrary to their peculiar temperament, but not that which is agreeable to their constitution. They may hate others' sin rather than their own, as Judas complained at the prodigality of Mary; but such hatred is directed rather against the persons than the sins of others. Their hatred is superficial. It is not with all their heart: it reaches not to the corruptions of their nature, nor is it accompanied with mortifying endeavours.

Their *resolutions against sin* are defective. In their *rise*. They issue not from a renewed heart, from a principle of holiness and love to Christ, but from apprehensions of unpleasant effects and future damnation. Or from the restraining power of God, which keeps them from purposing to sin rather than moves them to full resolution against it: so that their resolutions are negative rather than positive. Thus it was with Balaam, who said not "I will not" but "I cannot" (Num. xxii, 18, 38)—he had a mind to, but the Lord prevented him. In their *continuance*. Their good resolutions are not followed out to full execution, but are quickly broken. The cause from which they proceed is not constant, and therefore the effects are evanescent. They flow no longer when the spring from which they issue runs dry. That spring is but a momentary anguish or flash of fear, and when that vanishes their resolutions fail. Their goodness is but as "the morning cloud" and "early dew" (Hosea vi, 4), which quickly disappear. David feared the danger of this when he prayed, "Keep this for ever in the imagination of the thoughts of the heart of Thy people, and *prepare* their heart unto Thee" (I Chron. xxix, 18).

3. *Faith*. We read of those who "stay themselves [rely] upon the God of Israel" (Isaiah xlviii, 2), yet it was "not in truth, nor in righteousness" (verse 1), for they were obstinate and their neck "as an iron sinew." There are those who have a faith so like unto a justifying one that they themselves take it to be the very same and even Christians regard it as the faith of God's elect. Simon Magus, for example, "believed" (Acts viii, 13), and gave such a profession of it that Philip and the local church received him into their fellowship and privileges. Those who received the Seed into stony ground did "for a while believe" (Luke viii, 13), and according to its description it differed nothing from saving faith except in its root—the difference not being evident but lying underground. The unregenerate may have a faith which receives unquestionably the Bible as the Word of God, for the Jews entertained no doubts that the Scriptures were the very oracles of God. Agrippa believed in the veracity of the prophets and received their testimony without question (Acts xxvi, 26, 27). They may have a faith which leads to the owning of Christ as their Lord and worshipping Him as such (Matt. vii, 21). They may even have a faith which produces strong assurance: those who opposed Christ were quite sure they were "Abraham's seed" and not the slaves of Satan (John viii, 33, 34).

Wherein does this faith come short of a saving one? Wherein is it defective? It is merely an intellectual assent to the letter of Scripture and not "with the heart" (Romans x, 10), so as to bring Christ into it (Eph. iii, 17), just as one may read and accredit a historical work and no spiritual effect be produced thereby. It is a faith which is "alone" (James ii, 17), for it is unaccompanied by other graces, whereas a saving faith has as its concomitants love, meekness, holiness, perseverance, etc. Such a faith consents not to take a whole Christ: it will embrace Him as a Saviour, but is not willing for Him to reign over them as King. Those with such a faith desire Christ's pardon but not His sceptre, His peace but not His yoke. They will accept Him to deliver them from hell, but not to sanctify and cast out of their temples whatever God abominates. They are not willing to subscribe to Christ's terms of discipleship, which are the denying of self, the taking up of the cross, and following Him whithersoever He leads: such terms they consider harsh and unnecessary.

The faith of the formalist and empty professor is a lifeless and barren one. " As the body without the spirit is dead, so faith without works is dead " (James ii, 26). In that chapter the apostle points out. first, the worthlessness of a bare profession of charity. To give good words to a brother in need, bidding him, " Depart in peace, be ye warmed and filled," yet withholding those things needful to him, is cruel hypocrisy (verses 15, 16); equally so is such a faith a mockery if we say we believe in the Holy One and a day of judgment and yet live impiously (verse 17). Second, such a faith is inferior to that of the demons, for they " believe and tremble " (verse 19), whereas empty professors are not afraid to mock God. Third, such a faith is radically different from that possessed and exercised by the father of all who believe, for he rendered unreserved obedience unto the Divine commands (verses 21-24). A faith which does not purify the heart (Acts xv, 9), work by love (Gal. v, 6), overcome the world (I John v, 4), and bring forth fruit acceptable to God, will not conduct anyone to heaven.

4. *Good works*. The unregenerate may make an exceedingly fair show on the practical side of religion, that is in their deportment, both in their addresses to God and dealings with men, in public and private alike. They may go far in their external conformity to the rule of righteousness and visible compliance with the revealed will of God, both as to moral and positive precepts. The outward carriage of the Pharisees, by Christ's own testimony, was " beautiful " (Matt. xxiii, 27) and among their fellows they were esteemed as exceptionally holy men. Such may not only abstain from all gross sins but meet all the external requirements of morality and piety. Paul declares that, while unconverted, he was " blameless " as to his observance of the Law (Phil. iii, 6), and the rich young ruler affirmed of the commandments, " all these have I kept from my youth up" (Luke xviii, 21), nor did Christ charge him with idle boasting. They may practise great austerities in order to mortify the flesh, as some of the Gnostics had for their rule, " Touch not, taste not, handle not " (Col. ii, 21). A spirit of fanaticism may induce some of them to suffer martyrdom (I Cor. xiii, 3).

Wherein lies the defectiveness of the works of the unregenerate? First, in the state of the persons performing them. They are not reconciled to God and how can He accept aught from His enemies? The individual must first be reconciled to God before He will receive anything at his hands: " the Lord had respect to Abel *and* to his offering " (Gen. iv, 4). Second, in the root from which their actions proceed: their fruits are but the wild grapes of a degenerate vine: they must be renewed in the inner man before anything spiritual can be borne. Third, in the motive which prompts them, which is either servile fear or a spirit of legality rather than love; a dread of hell, or an attempt to gain heaven instead of from gratitude. Fourth, in the end which they have in view, which is a selfish one instead of seeking to promote the Divine honour: it is to pacify God rather than glorify Him. Fifth, in the absence of Christ's merits: their works are neither wrought for Christ's sake nor offered in His name, and since none may come unto the Father but by Him (John xiv, 6) all their works are refused, as Cain's offering was.

CHAPTER FIFTY-EIGHT

Profession Tested—Continued

THERE are few passages in all the Word of God which are more solemn than Matthew vii, 21-23, and which are more calculated to induce the sober believer to work out his own salvation with fear and trembling. Certainly this writer regards it as much too important to skim over hastily. In these verses the Lord makes it known that there are those who regard themselves as genuine Christians merely because they have certain resemblances to the children of God, and who are even looked upon as such by others simply because of their outward conformity to the principles and ordinances of Christianity, and yet are denounced by Christ as "ye that work iniquity." So presumptuous are they that they are firmly convinced heaven is theirs, yea, they are here represented as complaining to their Judge when He closes the door against them, putting in a plea for their claim at the bar of justice and arguing as though it were unfair that they should be excluded from the everlasting bliss of the righteous. Thus it is clearly implied that they lived and died in the full assurance that they were the objects of God's approbation, that they were completely secured from the wrath to come.

Nor is this fatal delusion cherished by a comparative few, for our Lord here gives plain intimation that there are "many" who have implicit confidence in their salvation, but who will nevertheless hear from His lips those terrible words, "depart from Me." How is their infatuation to be explained? The general answer would be, The deceitfulness of the human heart plus the sophistries of Satan. But on so deeply serious a matter as this we need something more than generalizations. When a thoughtful person learns that some dangerous disease is menacing the community, he wants to learn all he can about its nature, its symptoms, and especially the best means of prevention, of safeguarding himself against it. If we deem no pains and care too much in fortifying ourselves against a bodily disease, will the reader complain at the slowness of the writer's progress if he endeavours to give a more specific and detailed answer to this weighty question: how shall we account for such a fatal confidence? We will seek to point out the grounds on which such a delusion rests, that we may avoid this woeful mistake.

1. *Ignorance.* In our last we showed at some length the insufficiency of a mere intellectual acquaintance with the letter of Scripture, but let it not be concluded therefrom that a notional knowledge of the Truth is of no value because it falls short of a saving

one, still less derive encouragement for slothfulness. It is in the use of means that God is often pleased to meet with souls, and while they are reading and meditating on His Word to shine into their hearts. Scripture places no premium upon ignorance or indolence. Instead of asking, If such knowledge will not bring a man to heaven, to what purpose is it to labour after knowledge? rather say to yourself, How far must I be from heaven if I lack even that knowledge! What we brought out on the subject of a notional knowledge of the Truth in our last, instead of affording comfort to the ignorant should rather strike them with fear and trembling. If so much knowledge will not secure salvation, then how much worse is my case when I am destitute of what even he possesses. If those who come so near to the kingdom as to be able to view it cannot enter, then what hope is there for those who are content to remain far off from it.

So near are the ignorant to hell that they are within the very shadow of it. "Darkness . . . and shadow of death" are joined together in Scripture (Matt. iv, 16). Ignorance is spiritual darkness, the very shadow of eternal death. There is but a thin partition between those immersed in spiritual ignorance and hell itself. Hell is termed "the *outer* darkness" (Matt. viii, 12) because ignorance is the inner darkness, the next room as it were to hell itself. Sad indeed is the condition of such. If those who come so near to Canaan as to obtain a taste of its wondrous fruits yet fall in the wilderness so that they never enter it, how can they expect to enter Canaan who refuse to stir out of Egyptian darkness? One with much knowledge may possibly perish, but one who is quite ignorant of spiritual things shall *certainly* perish. When God makes mention of "a people of no understanding," He at once adds, "therefore He that made them will not have mercy on them" (Isaiah xxvii, 11). "Where ignorance is bliss 'tis folly to be wise" certainly does not hold good here.

We do not have to go as far afield today as what is termed heathendom: there are millions within Christendom, yea, countless thousands of churchgoers and members, who know not what is necessary to bring a soul to heaven. They know not that regeneration is imperative, that "except a man be born again he cannot see the kingdom of God," that as a fish cannot live out of water because away from its own element, so man is totally unfit for communion with the Holy One until he be renewed within. They know not that there must be a new creation, a miracle of grace wrought in the soul to make fallen man a new creature, so that it can be said of him, "old things are passed away; behold, all things are become new" (II Cor. v, 17). The new Jerusalem is for new creatures. They know not that God must communicate to the heart a principle of holiness before there can be any holy affections, motions or fruits. Without holiness no man shall see the Lord (Heb. xii, 14), and by nature man does not have the least grain of it.

So ignorant are the vast majority of those even in places reputed to be sound and orthodox that they know not that there must be the denying of self before anyone can become a follower of Christ: a repudiation of our own wisdom, righteousness, strength, desires, will, and interests. They know not that there must be a renunciation of the world before anyone can be a follower of Him who left the glories of heaven and entered the manger of Bethlehem: that we must be crucified unto the world and the world unto us or we shall never enter into the benefits and blessings purchased by the crucifixion of Christ. They know not that there must be a plucking out of right eyes and a cutting off of right hands, a mortifying of the flesh with its affections and lusts, so that we die daily. They know not that there must be a taking up of the cross if any man will come after Christ, which will cost him the loss of godless companions, the scorn of professors, many a tear and groan. They know not that the Christian life is a fierce wrestling (Eph. vi, 12), a continual fight, a race that has to be run with all our might if the crown is to be obtained. If they really knew these things they would not be nearly so confident of heaven when they are total strangers to the very things required of all those for whom heaven is intended.

2. *Negligence and slothfulness.* Those who *do* have a vague and general idea of the things mentioned above are too indolent to lay them to heart, make them their chief concern and prayerful meditation, that they may understand them more clearly. Even if they know them they will not take the pains seriously to examine their state by them: they will not go to the trouble of comparing their hearts with the Divine rule. So little interested are they in their eternal welfare that they will not spare a few hours to inquire solemnly whether or not they measure up to what the Word of God requires of them. Alas, for the wretched carelessness of the vast majority concerning their souls and everlasting state. They conduct themselves as atheists, acting as though there be no God, no day of reckoning, no lake of fire. They carry themselves as madmen, chasing shadows, playing with dynamite, sporting on the edge of the pit. They are indeed beside themselves (Luke xv, 17), devoid of "the spirit . . . of a sound mind" (II Tim. i, 7). If they were sane they would study God's Word to discover its directions concerning salvation, and would test themselves by those directions.

Their very indifference and carelessness demonstrate the mass of our fellows to be practical atheists and spiritual lunatics. If they were sane they would be deeply concerned whether heaven or hell was to be their eternal abode. They would deem no trouble too great to ascertain which they were journeying unto, which their personal condition fitted them for. They would snatch a few of their swiftly passing hours and devote them to diligent inquiry and self-examination. They would not proffer idle excuses and postpone the task, but would promptly and earnestly set about it. Only those bereft of spiritual sense and reason would neglect a matter the issue of which is either everlasting life or everlasting death. But no; rather than seriously trouble themselves, they will complacently assume all is well with them and take it on trust that they are bound for heaven, when the only grounds they have for such trust are the lies of Satan and that which their own deceitful hearts prompt; and thus they rest the whole weight of eternity upon a cobweb and pin the everlasting concern of their souls upon a shadow.

What makes it more inexcusable is the fact that these same people are quite competent and painstaking over their *temporal* affairs. If a new position be offered them they make careful inquiries before committing themselves. If they purpose making an investment they go to much trouble in ascertaining the soundness of it. If they think of purchasing a property they make full investigations as to its title-deeds and value. But when it comes to eternal things they are dilatory and slipshod, half-hearted and lazy. They make no serious preparation to meet their God, and when His call comes it finds them wanting. They are sluggards and therefore the sluggard's portion and doom will be theirs. Thus, when men and women are so slack and careless about their souls, when they will not make serious and solemn inquiry about their state, we need not wonder that so many are so woefully mistaken as to promise themselves heaven when in reality nothing but hell is reserved for them.

3. *Misapprehensions of God.* Where people are in ignorance and where they are too sottish to make any real and serious effort to dispel their ignorance, false conceptions of the Divine character are certain to obtain. True there are degrees of ignorance and therefore there are considerable differences in the erroneous ideas men form of God. But those formed by the unregenerate, whether they be the gross ones of the heathen or the more refined ones of Christendom, are alike false. Viewing God through the blurred lens of depraved hearts and minds they fashion Him as one suited to their corrupt inclinations. They invent a God who treats sin lightly, who looks with indulgence upon their waywardness, who is willing to accept a few religious performances as sufficient compensation for all their debt. "Thou thoughtest that I was altogether such an one as thyself" is the charge which He prefers against them, but adds: "I will reprove thee, and set them in order before thine eyes" (Psalm l, 21).

They do not believe that God is inexorably just so that He will "by no means clear the guilty," but that every transgression and disobedience must receive a due recompense of reward, unless a sinless Substitute make atonement for them. They do not believe it is impossible to mock God with impunity, that as men sow they reap, so that if they sow to the flesh they must of necessity reap corruption. They do not believe that God is omniscient, that "His eyes are in every place, beholding the evil and the good," for if they did it would act as a curb upon them. They do not believe God is so strict that He will call us to account for "every idle word" and that He "weigheth the spirits" (Prov. xvi, 2)—the springs of action, the motives which prompt. They do not believe He is ineffably holy, so that sins of thought as well as deed, of omission as well as commission, are hateful to Him. They do not believe that God is " a consuming fire " (Heb. xii, 29) so that this world and all its works will be burned up and that everyone whose name is not written in the book of life will be cast into the lake of fire. They do not believe that God is absolute sovereign, so that " He hath mercy on whom He will have mercy, and whom He will He hardeneth " (Romans ix, 18).

Even where there is sufficient light and conviction as to reveal to sinners that they come short of the Divine rule, and where they perceive that what the Word insists is necessary to salvation is not found in them, instead of abandoning their false hopes they persuade themselves that God is more merciful than the Scriptures represent Him to be. It is true, says the sinner, in such a case, that the way to heaven is a narrow one and that God's kingdom can only be entered " through much tribulation " (Acts xiv, 22), but God will save me even though I fail here and there and I be lacking in this and that. It is true that God *is* merciful, yet for one sin He banished our first parents from Eden! It is true that God is merciful, but for one sin His curse descended upon Ham and his posterity. It is true that God is merciful, but for one sin Lot's wife was turned into a pillar of salt, Achan and his family were stoned to death, Gehazi was smitten with leprosy, Ananias and Sapphira became corpses. God *is* merciful, yet He sent the flood upon the world of the ungodly, rained fire and brimstone upon the cities of the plain, sent His angel and slew all the firstborn of Egypt and destroyed Pharaoh and his hosts at the Red Sea.

Though they allow themselves in this sin and that, though they are thoroughly self-willed and self-pleasing, they tell themselves that God is lenient. Though they ignore God's righteous claims upon them and make no effort to meet His holy requirements, they comfort themselves with the thought that He is gracious. They refuse to allow that He is as strict and rigid as His faithful servants declare Him to be. They petulantly ask, Even though I be not so precise and puritanical as some are, shall I not be saved even as they? Though I come not up to their standard, yet God is very pitiful and knows how weak we are, and therefore He will lower the standard for me so that I may be saved as well as the best of them. Poor deluded souls, if that be all their hope, their case is indeed hopeless. Will God be so merciful as to contradict Himself and go contrary to His Word? Must He show them so much mercy as to despise His own Truth and make Himself a liar? What cause have they to tremble who have nothing to bear up their hopes of heaven but downright blasphemy!

4. *Self-love and self-esteem.* This is as prolific and powerful a cause of self-deception as any of those mentioned above. Sinners compare themselves with their fellows and award themselves the

first prize every time. He who is immoral regards himself as better than those who grind the poor and rob the widow. He who is a liar and a thief prides himself that he is no murderer. He who is outwardly religious deems himself vastly superior to the openly profane. Each one discovers some cause or other to say with the self-righteous Pharisee, "I thank God that I am not as this publican." This is because they measure themselves by a wrong standard. Even a soiled handkerchief looks comparatively clean if it be placed on a miry road, but were it laid on newly fallen snow its uncleanness would soon be evident. So it is with those who are blind to their deplorable condition. But men are possessed with such a high estimate of themselves, and entertain such a good opinion of their souls' condition, that even if they can be induced to measure themselves by the rule of God's Word and examine their state they come to the work prepossessed, prejudiced in their own favour. Self-love will not suffer them to deal impartially with their souls.

When they read some condemnatory passage of Scripture they refuse to appropriate it: when they hear a particularly solemn and searching sermon they take it not home to themselves but apply it to some of their fellows. If they be awakened in some measure to the awfulness of sinning against God and alarmed at the fearful punishment reserved for such, this mood is only fitful and fleeting, for they quickly reassure themselves that no such guilt rests upon them. Sudden death may strike down some of their companions, but self-delusion blinds them to their own peril. A manifest judgment from God may fall upon their community, but they persuade themselves that they are in no danger of the wrath to come. The fact is that there are very few indeed who abandon all hope, give way to utter despair and conclude *they will* experience the everlasting burnings, and yet there is only a very little company who will escape them. The multitudes continue defying God, sinning with a high hand, and go on walking along the road which leads to the pit, and yet by one means or another each persuades himself he shall not enter there. "For he flattereth himself in his own eyes, until his iniquity be found to be hateful" (Psalm xxxvi, 2).

Yes, the sinner "*flattereth himself* in his own eyes." If he did not, he would be in terrible distress and anguish. He would not go on so cheerfully and gaily if he really believed himself in danger of hell. But he has too good an estimate of himself for that: he does not think he has ever done anything worthy of such a doom, he is sure he is not bad enough for such a place. Men flatter themselves that they do not live in vice, but are decent citizens and good neighbours. They can see no reason why God should be angry with *them*. They do not take His name in vain nor scoff at religion. Yea, they flatter themselves that they have done much to commend themselves to Him and obtain His approbation. They read their Bibles occasionally and say their prayers. They attend church and contribute to its upkeep. They send their children to the Sabbath school. They resolve that later on they will be even better, out and out for Christ, but meanwhile they want to enjoy the world a little longer, "trust in themselves that they are righteous" (Luke xviii, 9) and are comparatively clean in their own sight, and yet they are not washed from their filthiness (Prov. xxx, 12).

There be others, many such, who flatter themselves that they are genuine Christians. They persuade themselves that they have repented of their past, believed the Gospel, and that their sins are forgiven. Consequently when they hear or read anything solemn it makes no impression upon them. Self-love and self-esteem blind them to their true condition. They are Laodiceans who say, " I am rich [spiritually] and increased with goods [have made considerable progress and grown in grace] and in need of nothing," but as the Lord declares, "and knowest not that thou art wretched, and miserable, and poor, and blind, and naked" (Rev. iii, 17). And nothing shakes them out of their self-complacency. They continue flattering themselves "until their iniquity be found to be hateful" —until they are disillusioned in hell. As a blind man cannot judge of colours, so prejudiced in their own favour are the self-righteous that it is impossible for them to judge of the complexion of their souls, whether the image of God or the image of the Devil be stamped upon it. As one has well said, "Satan blinds one eye and self-love closes the other, and the deceitfulness of sin seals both, and thus they assure themselves that they are on the way to heaven when they are on the high road to hell. Doubtless a number of such will read this very article and be quite unsearched by it, sure that it pertains not to *their* case.

A closing word to Christian readers. Since the four things described above are the principal ones among the more immediate causes of deceit concerning the state of the soul, then how sincerely ought the regenerate to examine themselves at these points and seek to make sure they are not imposing on themselves. How they should "cease from man" and search the Scriptures without bias to ascertain the general tenor of their teaching as to *what God requires* if they are to dwell with Him for ever, not confining themselves to such verses as John iii, 16, and Romans x, 13, but comparing such as Isaiah lv, 7; Acts iii, 19; Hebrews v, 9, so as to obtain a *full* answer to the question, "What must I do to be saved?" How cautiously and conscientiously should we examine ourselves, testing the grounds of our hope, determining whether or not there really is in us that which meets God's terms, whether or not our righteousness exceeds that of the religious formalist (Matt. v, 20). Nor can such a task be discharged hurriedly: "*Give diligence* to make your calling and election sure" (II Peter i, 10)—with what earnestness should we give ourselves to this work!

"Thus saith the Lord, Let not the wise man glory in his wisdom, neither let the mighty man glory in his might, let not the rich man glory in his riches; But let him that glorieth glory in this, that he understandeth and knoweth *Me*, that I am the Lord which exercise lovingkindness, judgment and righteousness in the earth" (Jer. ix, 23, 24). Yes, "knoweth Me," the living God, and not a fantasy devised by your own sentiment. To believe in a God who has no existence save in their own imagination is the case with multitudes in the churches today. "Acquaint now thyself with Him, and be at peace" (Job xxii, 21). To cherish the image of a fictitious god entails a fictitious peace. Eternal life is to "know Thee the only *true God*, and Jesus Christ, whom Thou hast sent" (John xvii, 3): how we should labour after such a knowledge of Him! Finally if self-love and esteem effectually hinder an impartial examination of myself, if it be the case with a host of my fellows that "a deceived heart hath turned him aside, that he cannot deliver his soul nor say, Is there not a lie in my right hand?" (Isaiah xliv, 20), how earnestly should I cry to God to grant me an honest heart which desires to know the truth and nothing but the truth about my case.

CHAPTER FIFTY-NINE

Profession Tested—Continued

WHAT is the relation between our present verses and the one immediately preceding? Matthew Henry gives the following as his analysis of verses 21-23: " (1) Christ here shows by a plain remonstrance that an outward profession of religion, however remarkable, will not bring us to heaven, unless there be a correspondent conversation. (2) The hypocrite's plea against the strictness of this law, offering other things in lieu of obedience. (3) The rejection of this plea as frivolous." Personally we think William Perkins perceived more clearly the connection between verses 22, 23 and verse 21: " In these two verses Christ returns to explain and confirm the first conclusion of the former verse concerning those professors that shall not be saved. The words contain two parts: first, a description of the persons by their behaviour; secondly, a declaration of their condemnation." For our own part we regard the verses which are now to be before us as containing an exemplification and amplification of what had been affirmed in the preceding one, showing that the most gifted and eminent professors will not be treated as exceptions if they fail to meet the fundamental requirement of God's kingdom.

In the previous verse Christ had declared, " Not every one that saith unto Me, Lord, Lord, shall enter into the kingdom of heaven, but he that doeth the will of My Father which is in heaven ": something far more important and radical than a mere lip profession is needed in order to participate in spiritual blessings, even a full surrendering of ourselves unto Christ and a performing of the Divine will from the heart. But now the Lord went on to affirm something still more solemn and searching: " Many will say to Me in that day, Lord, Lord, have we not prophesied in Thy name? and in Thy name have cast out devils? and in Thy name done many wonderful works? And then will I profess unto them, I never knew you: depart from Me ye that work iniquity." Here it is not simply the rank and file of those claiming to be the followers of Christ who are in view, but the most influential ones among them, their *leaders and preachers*. Nor does He single out a few exceptional cases, but declares that there are "many" who have occupied positions of prominence and authority, who wrought mighty works in His name, but so far from enjoying His approbation are denounced by Him as workers of iniquity.

First, it should be pointed out that the gifts and works of these men are described according to the nature of those which obtained in Bible times. Strictly speaking there is no such thing as "prophesying" today, nor has there been for eighteen centuries past. A prophet was the mouthpiece of God. Under an afflatus of the Holy Spirit he gave forth a Divine revelation. In other words, he spoke by Divine inspiration. It was not an ordinary and natural gift, but an extraordinary and spiritual one. It was withdrawn when the Canon of Scripture was completed, for in His written Word we now have the Divine will fully revealed, containing as it does a complete and perfect rule of faith and practice (II Tim. iii, 16, 17). Consequently, any person who now poses as a Divine prophet, claiming to have a special message from God, is either an impostor or a fanatic: an emissary of Satan seeking to beguile the unwary, or a neurotic who suffers his enthusiasm to run away with him, or an egoist who desires to direct attention to himself and occupy the limelight.

Because a man spoke by Divine inspiration in Bible times it was no proof that he was regenerate. Here, as everywhere else, God exercised His sovereignty, employing as His mouthpiece whom He pleased. Thus we find Balaam, the soothsayer, uttered some remarkable predictions concerning Israel, the Messiah Himself, and the judgments which should overtake various nations; all of which were fulfilled. We are told that "the Lord put a word in Balaam's mouth" (Num. xxiii, 5), that he "knew the knowledge of the most High" and "saw the vision of the Almighty" (Num. xxiv, 16), yet he "loved the wages of unrighteousness" (II Peter ii, 15) and perished amid the enemies of the Lord (Num. xxxi, 8). So also of the apostate king of Israel it is written, "the Spirit of God came upon him, and he prophesied," so that it became a proverb: "Is Saul also among the prophets?" (I Samuel x, 10, 11). More remarkable still is the case of Caiaphas, the man who delivered up the Redeemer into the hands of Pilate, for of him we are told: "And this spake he not of himself [but by Divine inspiration]: but being high priest that year, he *prophesied* that Jesus should die for that nation; and not for that nation only, but that also he should gather together in one the children of God that were scattered abroad" (John xi, 51, 52).

"And in Thy name have cast out devils" or "demons." This was another of the supernatural gifts or powers bestowed upon men at the beginning of the Christian era, and yet it was not confined to the regenerate. It is at least open to doubt whether the man mentioned in Luke ix, 49, was such, for there we are told that "John answered and said, Master, we saw one casting out demons in Thy name and we forbade him, because he followeth not with us." But a clearer case to the point is that of the betrayer of our Lord. In Matthew x, 1, we are expressly told that "when Christ had called unto Him His twelve disciples, He gave them power over unclean spirits, to cast them out," and one of that company was Judas Iscariot! Had Judas failed to perform this feat his fellow apostles had at once had their suspicions aroused, and when the Saviour announced, "One of you shall betray Me," instead of asking, "Lord, is it I?" had at once known He referred to Judas. "And in Thy name done many wonderful works" or "works of power," miraculous works—the Greek word occurring again in Matthew xi, 20, in connection with Christ's "mighty works." This power too was conferred upon Judas.

If it should be asked, Why should God so remarkably endow the unregenerate, even using them as His mouthpieces? several answers might be returned. First, as has been intimated above, in order to exemplify God's uncontrollable sovereignty over and ownership of all men. He can employ His creatures as He pleases and select as His agents and instruments whom He will and none can say Him nay. Second, to display His invincible power. "The king's heart is in the hand of the Lord . . . He turneth it whithersoever He will" (Prov. xxi, 1), and if the king's heart, so every man's; but how little is that realized today. Balaam was but a puppet in His hands, unable to resist His will. Caiaphas was the enemy of Christ and yet compelled to utter a remarkable prophecy about Him! Third, to evince that supernatural gifts and endowments—though highly esteemed among men—are not the most precious of His bestowments: something infinitely more valuable is reserved for the objects of His everlasting love. What comparison is there between Balaam's prophecy and the "new song" in the mouths of the redeemed, between the miracles performed by Judas and being made meet for the inheritance of the saints in light?

Our Lord thus plainly intimates that men may conduct themselves as His commissioned servants—acting in His name—that they may be endowed with the most remarkable gifts, that they may perform supernatural works, and yet not be saved. It was so at the beginning of this dispensation; it is so now. It would be a great mistake to draw the conclusion that because our Lord describes these unregenerate professors according to the terminology of the first century, when ministers were endowed with extraordinary gifts and exercised supernatural powers, that it has no direct bearing on leaders among professing Christians in this twentieth century. Because verse 22 depicts conditions which no longer obtain in kind that is no proof that it has no immediate application unto men of prominence in the religious realm today. Rather should we reason that, if such a fearful warning was needed at the beginning of this era, when men were so wonderfully gifted, how much more pertinent is it to those of lesser talents and abilities in this degenerate generation!

The modern equivalent of prophesying in the name of Christ would be *preaching* in His name: the casting out of demons would find its present counterpart in the deliverance of Satan's slaves chronicled by our "city missions"—such as the reforming of drunkards, reclaiming of fallen women, recovering of drug addicts; while the "wonderful works" may be taken as referring to the costly buildings termed "churches" with their huge memberships, and the sensational achievements of "missionaries" in heathen lands. Not that we wish to imply that all engaged in such activities are unregenerate; nevertheless, after close observation and personal contact with many of these workers, we seriously doubt whether more than a small percentage of them have really been born again. Nor should this at all astonish us. Our Lord Himself distinctly declared of "many" of those serving in His name, "I never knew you," and if that were true of those who wrought during the palmiest days of the Christian era, why should it be thought strange that such a state of affairs pertains now that Christendom is so apostate?

Here then is what is most solemn of all in this awe-inspiring passage: that there will be many preachers, Christian leaders and workers—and in view of our Lord's use of the word in verse 13, probably the great majority of them—who will be shut out of heaven. Sad and awful as this is, yet from our observation in many sections of Christendom and from what generally obtains we cannot say it surprises us. Among the young men accepted as students for the ministry is there any larger percentage of regenerate ones than of the young men making a Christian profession who enter not the ministry? We are far from believing they are all hypocrites. Doubtless there are many thousands who select the ministry as their avocation because of the social prestige and financial remuneration it affords. But large numbers of youths who receive the Word "with joy" (Matt. xiii, 20) mistake their religious enthusiasm and fervour for a call from God and love for souls, and having more zeal than knowledge, and friends who encourage rather than counsel caution, they make the great mistake.

Once the young man is accepted as a student for the ministry his regeneration is (with very rare exceptions) tacitly assumed. And what is there then which is in any wise calculated to open his deceived eyes? Some of the denominations require him to spend years at a university in order to obtain a degree, and there his time and energies are strenuously occupied with subjects that contain nothing whatever for the soul, but only that which is apt to foster intellectual conceit. One who has mistaken carnal ambition and enthusiasm for a call from God is not likely to find a course in sociology, psychology, logic, philosophy, etc., likely to disillusion him. And even when the young man is not required to enter a university, he has to take a course in "divinity." In other words he is introduced to the sacred study of theology as a subject on which to exercise his intellectual powers, as a text book over which he must pore and whose contents he must master in order to pass examinations thereon. The result is that in the vast majority of cases he is so sickened therewith that after his ordination he never again opens a theological treatise.

Nor is there any more hope, humanly speaking, that his eyes may be opened to his lost condition after he has been ordained and called to a charge. If he is to " make good " therein such a multitude of duties demand his attention that there is little opportunity for the careful examination of his own soul. There are so many departments of the church he has to superintend, so many sermons and addresses he must prepare each week, so many calls to make, that he has little leisure for self-introspection. He is so occupied with the concerns and needs of others that attention to the ministerial injunction "take heed *unto thyself*" (I Tim. iv, 16) is crowded out. It is greatly to be feared that thousands of ministers today have ground to lament " they made me the keeper of the vineyards; but *mine own vineyard* have I not kept " (Song of Sol. i, 6). But whatever be the contributing causes and occasions of this tragic fatality, the fact remains that the Divine Judge is yet going to say unto many of those who preached and wrought in His name, " I never knew you."

"And then will I profess unto them, I never knew you: depart from Me ye that work iniquity" (verse 23). There are five things here which claim our attention, though utterly insufficient is any mortal to do them justice. First, the time-mark: " then." Second, the character in which Christ is here viewed: as the Judge of men. Third, the solemn verdict announced: " I never knew you." Fourth, the fearful sentence imposed: "depart from Me." Fifth, the real character of religious formalists: " ye that work iniquity." It would not be possible to assemble together five things of greater gravity and moment than these. And what human pen is competent to comment upon subjects so awesome? Oh, that both writer and reader may approach the same with becoming reverence and solemnity.

"And *then* " looks back to the ' in that day ' of the previous verse. It is the day of final retribution, when " every man's work shall be made manifest: for the day shall declare it, because it shall be revealed by fire; and the fire shall try every man's work of what sort it is " (I Cor. iii, 13). It is " the day of wrath and revelation of the righteous judgment of God " (Romans ii, 5), " because He hath appointed a day, in the which He will judge the world . . . by that Man whom He hath ordained " (Acts xvii, 31). Who can conceive of the consternation which will possess the hearts of impenitent rebels, of unmasked hypocrites, of disillusioned formalists, as they are compelled to stand with an assembled universe before the dread tribunal? Then will the books be opened, the secrets of all hearts disclosed, the hidden things of darkness brought to light. Then shall each one who has trampled upon the Divine Law, rejected the only Mediator, and done despite to the Spirit of grace, stand forth in his true colours, stripped of the disguise with which he imposed upon his fellow creatures. " The heaven shall reveal his iniquity; and the earth shall rise up against him " (Job xx, 27). They will be speechless with guilt, utterly overwhelmed, unable to "stand in the judgment " (Psalm i, 5).

"And then will *I* profess unto them, I never knew you, depart from Me, ye that work iniquity." The Speaker is the Lord Jesus, yet not as presenting Himself as the Saviour of sinners, but rather officiating as their Judge, pronouncing their doom. In this solemn passage our Lord gave plain intimation that He was more than man, that He is none other than the Arbiter of every man's eternal state, from whose decision there can be no appeal. Amazing indeed was the contrast between His lowly appearance and external circumstances and this language of conscious majesty and power. While delivering this sermon on the mount Christ appeared before men's eyes as a Galilean peasant, yet both the tone and tenor of it proclaimed Him to be none other than Immanuel, God manifest in flesh. No wonder we are told that "when Jesus had ended these sayings, the people were astonished at His doctrine: For He taught them as one having authority and not as the scribes" (verses 28, 29). And it is before this very Judge that both writer and reader must yet appear!

"I never knew you." This does not mean that Christ was totally unacquainted with their persons, that He was not cognizant of their character and conduct. No, rather does it signify that He did not approve of or accept them. When it is said, "The Lord *knoweth* the way of the righteous" (Psalm i, 6), it is to be understood that He is pleased with the same. Here then is the awful verdict: "I never knew you"; no, not even when you were preaching and working in My name. You may have deceived yourselves and those to whom you ministered, but it was impossible to impose upon Me. In His "I will *profess* unto them," He seems to speak ironically: *you* have professed much, made free use of My name, maintained your standing as leaders in the Church—so now hear *My* profession! "I *never* knew you" makes it quite clear they were not such as had fallen from grace, as it also looks back to eternity past: they had never been born again, never evangelically repented, never believed savingly, and had not been among the favoured company upon whom His approbation rested before the foundation of the world.

"Depart from Me." Here is the fearful sentence imposed. They may have been highly respected in the churches, but they are objects of abhorrence to the Lord Christ. They frequently had His name on their lips, but since He dwelt not in their hearts they are totally disqualified for the celestial courts. "If the most admired and useful preacher on earth had no better evidence of his conversion than his abilities and success as a preacher, he would preach to others and be himself a castaway" (T. Scott). "Depart from Me" is the announcement of their just condemnation. They had been near to Him by their profession and by the position they held in the Church, but now they must go to the only place for which they are fitted, which is banishment from the Holy One. Herein we discover the force of that terrible expression "the second death" (Rev. xxi, 8): it is not extinction of being or the annihilation of the soul, but eternal separation from Christ, alienation from the life of God; it is a being "punished with everlasting destruction *from* the presence of the Lord, and from the glory of His power" (II Thess. i, 9), cut off for ever from the Bestower of blessing, tormented in the lake of fire.

"Ye that work iniquity." How different is the Divine estimate from the human! These preachers and leaders pleaded that they had wrought many "wonderful works," but because they had not proceeded from renewed hearts, because they had been done to win the applause of their fellows, rather than for the glory of God, the One who cannot be imposed upon declares they are "works of iniquity." Ah, my reader, we may look upon and admire the outward show, but the One who will yet judge us "looketh on *the heart*" (I Samuel xvi, 7), and therefore "that which is highly esteemed among men is abomination in the sight of God" (Luke xvi, 15)—even the righteousnesses of the natural man are but "filthy rags" in His sight.

> "Deeds of greatness as we deemed them
> He will show us were but sin;
> Cups of water we'd forgotten
> He will tell us were for Him."

Not only the gross external crimes, but pride and presumption and the religious performances of hypocrites are "works of iniquity."

In view of the chapters preceding this one there is no need for us to make a lengthy application here. The chief lesson for us to take to heart from the above is the utter insufficiency of the most imposing gifts. Yet how many there are who suppose that the exercise of unusual abilities in the church is evidence of great spirituality. As uncommon natural endowments are by no means always accompanied by moral worth, so the presence of abnormal powers is no proof of regeneration. We must learn to distinguish between the performing of wonderful works and the possession of spiritual graces, for the former is no guarantee of the latter. Showy talents may raise a man above his fellows, even above genuine Christians, but unless he is indwelt by the Spirit of God what are they worth? "Though I have the gift of prophecy, and understand all mysteries . . . and have not charity, I am nothing" (I Cor. xiii, 2). Then let us search ourselves and see whether or not we have something better than those to whom Christ will yet say, "I never knew you." A principle of holiness within evidenced by a godly walk without is infinitely to be preferred above the power to cast out demons and heal the sick. To commune with God in private is an inestimably grander privilege than to speak with tongues in public.

CHAPTER SIXTY

Profession Tested—Continued

VERSES 24-27 form the conclusion of our Lord's Address. Upon them Spurgeon said, "These were the closing words of our Saviour's most famous sermon upon the mount. Some preachers concentrate all their powers upon an effort to conclude with a fine thing called a peroration, which being interpreted means a blaze of rhetorical fireworks, in the glory of which the speaker subsides. They certainly have not the example of Christ in this discourse to warrant them in the practice. Here is the Saviour's peroration, and yet it is as simple as any other part of the address. There is an evident absence of all artificial oratory. The whole of His hill-sermon was intensely earnest, and that earnestness was sustained to the end, so that the closing words are as glowing coals, or as sharp arrows of the bow. Our Lord closes not by displaying His own powers of elocution, but by simply and affectionately addressing a warning to those who, having heard His words, should remain satisfied with hearing, and should not go forth and put them into practice."

"Therefore whosoever heareth these sayings of Mine, and doeth them, I will liken him unto a wise man, which built his house upon a rock: and the rain descended, and the floods came, and the winds blew, and beat upon that house; and it fell not: for it was founded upon a rock" (verses 24, 25). Simple as that language is, many have misunderstood its meaning and missed its import. No two of the commentators give a uniform exegesis of these verses, and though there is more or less substantial agreement with the older and soundest expositors, yet even among them there is considerable difference of opinion. When we consult more recent writers thereon, especially those who may be broadly classed as belonging to the "fundamentalist school," while there is much more of a saying of the same thing, yet we are personally convinced it is a saying of the *wrong* thing. A critical examination of the view they have taken obliges one to point out that they have read into this passage what is not there, that they have utterly failed to bring out what is there, and this because they have missed the scope of our passage through ignoring its context.

According to the antinomian interpretation of this passage our Lord ought to have said, "Whosoever believeth the Gospel and trusts in My atoning blood, I will liken him unto a wise man who built his house upon the rock; and everyone who endeavours to heed My precepts and then trusts in his own good works to obtain for him acceptance with God, I will liken unto a foolish man who built his house upon the sand." But in the verses before us, Christ said nothing of the sort. And why? Because He was dealing with something more solemn and searching than what constitutes the ground of a sinner's acceptance with God. It is perfectly true, blessedly true, that every sinner who exercises a saving faith in the sacrifice of Christ is a wise man, and that he is eternally secure; as it is equally true that anyone who relies upon his own obedience to the Divine commandments in order to obtain a passport into everlasting bliss is a fool, as he will prove in the day of testing. But we say again, Christ is not here speaking of either the object or ground of saving faith, but of something far more probing and revealing, and we throw everything into the utmost confusion if we confound the two things.

Before we are ready to weigh the *terms* of our passage we must first ascertain and determine its *scope,* and that calls for a careful noting of its context. In the verses immediately preceding it is clearly the testing of profession which is in view, the making evident of the reality which lies behind all surface appearances, and in this closing section Christ continues to show what it is which distinguishes the genuine and living Christian from a nominal and lifeless one. In some passages the "house" or home is a figure of the place of affection and rest, but here it is viewed as a shelter and refuge from the storm. The stability and security of a house depend ultimately on the strength of its foundation. For if *that* be faulty, no matter how good the materials of which it is composed or how reliable the workmanship of those engaged in its construction, when a hurricane strikes it will fall. This obvious fact has been grasped by all the commentators, but as to *what* our Lord signified by the "rock" foundation there is wide difference of opinion.

Probably the passage which occurs most readily to the minds of many of our readers in this connection is Isaiah xxviii, 16, "Thus saith the Lord God, Behold, I lay in Zion for a foundation a stone, a tried stone, a precious corner stone, a sure foundation," and from Acts iv, 11 and I Peter ii, 5-7, we know that that precious "stone" and "sure foundation" is Christ Himself. Yet we make a great mistake if we suppose that *every* New Testament passage containing the word "foundation" looks back to Isaiah xxviii, 16, or refers to the same thing. Not so. "The foundation of God standeth sure, having this seal, The Lord knoweth [loveth, and therefore preserveth] them that are His" (II Tim. ii, 19): as the contrast with the preceding verse denotes, the "foundation" here signifies the Divine decree or fore-ordination, which cannot be overthrown. "Built upon the foundation of the apostles and prophets, Jesus Christ Himself being the chief corner stone" (Eph. ii, 20) refers to the ministerial foundation, the Truth proclaimed. Hebrews vi, 1, speaks of "the foundation of repentance from dead works," for one has not made a start in practical godliness until that has been laid. Thus there is a need for the teacher here who is qualified to distinguish between things that differ.

There is one other passage which it is important to consider in this connection, namely "Charge them that are rich in this world, that they be not highminded, nor trust in uncertain riches, but in the living God, who giveth us richly all things to enjoy; That they do good, that they be rich in good works, ready to distribute, willing to communicate; Laying up in store for themselves a good foundation against the time to come, that they may lay hold on eternal life" (I Tim. vi, 17-19). Why is this passage so infrequently cited and still more infrequently expounded and enforced? For every time allusion is made to it, "For other foundation can no man lay than that is laid, which is Jesus Christ" (I Cor. iii, 11) is quoted twenty times. Is that handling the Word honestly? No, it is not, and the churches have suffered greatly because of such unfaithfulness in the pulpit. This passage, be it noted, is addressed to the minister of the Gospel, specifying one of the duties his office obligates him to perform, but has one preacher in a hundred, during the past fifty years, conscientiously discharged it? Have not the vast majority toadied to their wealthy members and withheld from them that which they most needed?

But does this passage teach that we are required to perform deeds of charity for the purpose of acquiring "merit" before God and thereby purchase for ourselves His favourable regard, or, as one has expressed it, "raise a cloud of gold-dust which will waft us to heaven"? Certainly not: there is nothing here which fosters the fatal delusion of papists. Nevertheless, there is important instruction which we cannot afford to ignore. It is *Christians* that are "rich in this world" who are to be thus charged: "Be not high-minded," affecting yourselves to be superior to the poor of the flock, "nor trust in uncertain riches," which may speedily disappear, "but in the living God," who changes not, and is your true Portion; "Who giveth us richly all things to enjoy," but not to squander on over-indulgence; "That they do good" with what God has loaned to them, faithfully discharging their stewardship; "Laying up for themselves a good foundation" in their conscience, a reliable basis for their hope, a sure ground of assurance, thereby confirming their personal interest in Christ, for "good works" are the evidences of the genuiness of our faith.

"Laying up in store for themselves [not "before God"!] a good foundation against the time to come": whether it be adversity that overtakes you through financial reverses, so that those you have aided will be the readier to assist you; or a bed of lingering illness, so that you may not have the additional anguish of a conscience accusing you of selfishness and callousness; or the hour of death itself, that you may have the comfort of knowing you have discharged your stewardship faithfully and that the poor call you blessed; or the day to come, when "they that have done good" will

come forth "unto the resurrection of life" (John v, 29) and their
"good works" will be owned and rewarded by the Judge of all the
earth. "That they may lay hold on eternal life": obtaining a firmer
conscious grip on the same, for the "good works" of the Christian
are so many testimonies of his portion in heaven. Having our affections set upon Christ and our true riches in Him, let us act like wise
merchants, not grasping at shadows and uncertainties, but using for
His glory and the good of our fellows what He has entrusted to us,
thereby laying up for ourselves "treasures in heaven" (Matt. vi, 20)
and acquiring additional confirmation that we already possess the
"earnest" of "eternal life." The "house" of *such* a one is built
upon a "*rock*"!

It will be seen from the last four paragraphs that the term "foundation" is found in different connections, that it is not always used
to denote precisely the same thing, and therefore that its significance
in a particular verse must be sought by ascertaining the scope and
meaning of the passage in which that verse occurs; and that is no
task for the "novice," but rather for the experienced expositor.
What, then, is the *scope* (the dominating subject and design) of
Matthew vii, 24, 25? As already stated, it is the *testing of profession*,
a furnishing proof of the reality or worthlessness of the same.
Rightly did Andrew Fuller point out: "Our Lord is not discoursing
on our being justified by faith, but on our being judged according to
our works, which, though consistent with the other, is not the same
thing, and must not be confounded with it. The character described
is not the self-righteous rejecter of the Gospel, but one who, though
he may hear it and profess to believe it, yet brings forth no corresponding fruit. It is not a passage suited to expose the errors of
Romanists, but one which needs to be pressed upon Antinomians
—they who hold "only believe, and all is well."

Our passage opens with the word "Therefore," which indicates
our Lord was drawing a conclusion from what He had just been
saying. In the preceding verses He was certainly not describing work-
mongers, those who trusted in their good deeds and religious performances to gain them acceptance with God. Rather is He there
calling upon His hearers to enter in at the strait gate (verses 13, 14),
warning against false prophets (verses 15-20), denouncing an empty
profession. In the verse immediately before (23), so far from presenting Himself as the Redeemer, tenderly wooing sinners, He is seen
as the Judge, saying to the hypocrites "depart from Me, ye that
work iniquity." Thus to say the least, this would be a very strange
point in His discourse at which to abruptly introduce the Gospel
of the grace of God and announce that His own finished work is
the only saving foundation for sinners to rest their souls upon:
this would give no meaning whatever to the opening "therefore."
Moreover, in what at once follows, instead of speaking of our need
of trusting in His atoning blood, Christ shows how indispensable
it is that we render obedience to His precepts.

John Brown, the renowned Scottish expositor, brought out quite clearly the force of our Lord's "Therefore" both in reference to what preceded and to what follows. "Surely, if not every one who calls Christ 'Lord, Lord' shall enter into the kingdom of heaven; but he only who does the will of His Father which is in heaven'; if to all workers of iniquity, even although they shall have 'prophesied and cast out devils, and done many wonderful works in the name of Christ,' it shall at last be said by our Lord, declaring by His judgment the final state of men, 'depart from Me: I never knew you'; then it certainly follows that he who hears and does our Lord's sayings is a wise man, and that he who hears them and does them not is a fool. The one saves, the other loses, the salvation of the soul, the happiness of eternity." As Matthew Henry also pointed out, "The scope of this passage teaches us that the only way to make sure work for our souls and eternity is to hear and do the sayings of the Lord Jesus." They who think they are savingly trusting the blood of Christ while disregarding His commands are fatally deceiving themselves.

In many respects Matthew vii, 24-27, is closely analogous to xxv, 1-12. Both passages treat of professing Christians. In each case those professors are divided into two classes, called the "wise" and the "foolish." In each case these radically different characters had something in common: in the former, both are likened unto builders and each erects a house: in the latter, both are termed "virgins" and both go forth to meet the Bridegroom with lamps in their hands. In each case the latter is found wanting when put to the proof and meets with irretrievable disaster: in the former when the storm bursts the house of the fool falls, in the latter when the Bridegroom arrives the fool faces a closed door. In each case the difference between the two classes was nothing external, but that which lay *out of sight*—the faulty "foundation" of the former and the lack of oil "in their vessels" with the latter. We have compared these two passages together not only to note the interesting correspondence which exists between them, but chiefly because the latter throws light upon the former and helps to fix its interpretation.

Let us duly note what Christ does *not* here say of the one He terms wise, "he that heareth these sayings of Mine and *understandeth* them," nor even "he that heareth these sayings of Mine and *believeth in Me*": what He *did* say goes much farther than that. There are multitudes who believe in Christ who do not put His precepts into practice. In the same way that there are millions in India who believe in Buddha, millions in China who believe in Confucius, millions in Africa who believe in Mohammed, so vast numbers in Christendom believe in Christ. And because "they believe in Christ" they suppose that all is well with them and that when they die they will go to heaven. Nor are there many now left on earth who are likely to disillusion them. The great majority of the preachers in this apostate age are only adding to the number of

the deceived, by telling them that all God requires of them is to
believe in the Gospel and receive Christ as their personal Saviour.
They quote such passages as John iii, 16, and Acts xvi, 31,
which contain the word "believe," but are guiltily silent on the
many verses which insist on repentance, forsaking of sins, denying of
self, and which call to obedience.

How often, for example, we hear quoted, "For in Christ Jesus
neither circumcision availeth any thing, nor uncircumcision, but a
new creature [or creation]" (Gal. vi, 15), especially by those who
(rightly) wish to show that neither the ceremonial ordinances of
Judaism nor baptism and the Lord's supper of Christianity are of
any worth in the justifying of sinners before God. So, too, though not
quite so frequently, we are reminded that "For in Jesus Christ
neither circumcision availeth any thing, nor uncircumcision; but
faith which worketh by love" (Gal. v, 6), that is out of gratitude
to God for His unspeakable Gift and not from a legal motive which
works only for what it may obtain. But how very rarely is this
one ever mentioned: "Circumcision is nothing. and uncircumcision
is nothing, but the *keeping of the commandments of God*"
(I Cor. vii, 19). That which concerns our submission to the Divine
authority, our walking in subjection to His will, is studiously
kept in the background: such partiality is most reprehensible. It is
only by placing these three verses side by side that we obtain a complete and balanced view. We are not vitally united to Christ
unless we have been born again; we are not born again unless we
possess a faith which "worketh by love"; and we have not this
saving faith unless it is evidenced by a "keeping of God's commandments."

No wonder there is now so much dishonesty among those in the
pew when there has been such dishonesty in the pulpit. The unsaved
are frequently told, "Whosoever shall call upon the name of the
Lord shall be saved" (Romans x, 13), but who is faithful enough to
tell them that none ever did or could savingly "call upon" Him
out of an *impenitent heart*? Fewer still will remind them that Christ
is "the Author of eternal salvation unto all them that obey Him"
(Heb. v, 9). In like manner, when addressing those who profess to
be Christians, how many preachers give great prominence to the
comforting promises of God, but say little about His holy requirements. There is also a certain class of Calvinists who are fond of
citing "Greater love hath no man than this, that a man lay down his
life for his friends," but they fail to add "ye are My friends, if ye *do*
whatsoever I command you" (John xv, 13, 14), which is the surest
identifying mark of those for whom Christ died. There are
thousands who glibly talk of their love for Christ, but how rarely
are they reminded. "And hereby we do know that we know Him, if
we *keep* His commandments. He that saith, I know Him, and
keepeth not His commandments, is a liar, and the truth is not in
him" (I John ii, 3, 4).

In the passages before us Christ continues to insist upon the imperative necessity of practical godliness. The regard or disregard which we pay to His precepts in this life He likens unto building our house on a sound or a worthless foundation, and the issue thereof in the Day of testing is compared to a tempest which puts to the proof our labours. Only those who have actually done that which He enjoined, who have rendered sincere obedience to His laws, will endure the test. He who has heard Christ's sayings and talked about repentance but has never repented, he who has admired the statutes issued by Christ but never rendered personal submission to them, shall be put to utter confusion in the hour of crisis. For the last time in this sermon our Lord enforced what may be termed its text: "except your righteousness shall exceed that of the scribes and the Pharisees, ye shall in no case enter into the kingdom of heaven." It is not sufficient to eulogize the practical righteousness which He taught: it must be embodied and expressed in our personal character and conduct. Saving faith is a practical persuasion of the truth of Christ's teaching which is followed by a wholehearted obedience to His authority.

CHAPTER SIXTY-ONE

Profession Tested—Continued

A PONDERING of Matthew vii, 24-27, suggests the need of our seeking to supply answers to the following questions. First, what is the force of the opening "Therefore"? Second, who are represented by the "wise" and the "foolish" men? Third, what is denoted by the "rock" and the "sand" on which they build? Fourth, what is signified by the "house" which each one erects? Fifth, what is portrayed by the hurricane which bursts upon the "house" and tests its security? Simple as these questions are, the replies returned thereto will determine the soundness or unsoundness of any exposition given to the passage. In seeking our answers recourse must also be had unto the parallel passage in Luke vi, 47-49, which supplies a number of additional details. The best analysis of these verses we have met with was furnished by one of the earliest of the Puritans, W. Perkins, 1590. He focused attention on three things: the duty inculcated—obedience; the property of this duty—wisdom; the reward—security. The three parts of this wisdom lay in digging deep, in securing a rock foundation, and in building thereon.

First, the force of the opening "Therefore." In addition to the more general remarks made thereon in the previous article let us now point out that Christ was here drawing a plain but searching conclusion from His solemn statement in verses 21-23. There He had declared that not everyone who renders lip-service to His Lordship shall enter into the kingdom of heaven, but only he who does the will of the Father as made known by the Son; yea, that the many who substitute preaching and performing wonderful works for actual obedience to His commands, He will yet say unto such, "Depart from Me, ye that work iniquity." Then He at once added, "*Therefore* whosoever heareth these sayings of mine and doeth them, I will liken him unto a wise man, which built his house upon a rock." Is not the connection, then, between the two passages unmistakably indicated? Is not our Lord's design and meaning in the verses now before us crystal clear? In verses 21-23 Christ is viewed in His office of Judge, testing professors, making known unto us who it is that will survive the fiery trial of that dread Day; and in verses 24-27 He reveals the path which must be trod if that Day is to be wisely and successfully anticipated.

In the Day of testing, not what we have said but what we have *done* in obedience to the Divine will shall alone be accepted as evidence: not the profession we have made, but the verification we have given of it in our Christian walk; not the doctrines we believed, but the fruits they bore in our daily lives. It will be useless to plead that we possessed extraordinary gifts and employed them in "Christian service," that we were leaders in the churches and did much in the name of Christ, if we wore not His yoke and followed not the example He has left us. Real practical godliness is the only thing which will be approved in that Day. Personal holiness is little esteemed here, but it will be everything there (Hebrews xii, 14). In that Day the Judge of all the earth will "give to every man according as his *work* shall be" (Rev. xxii, 12). Therefore, the man who acts wisely now is the one who makes conscience of the commandments of Christ, who regulates his conduct by them; conversely, the one who disregards the revealed will of God and follows a course of self-pleasing, no matter what garb of religion he wears, is playing the part of the fool, as he will yet discover to his eternal undoing.

The answer to our second question has largely been anticipated in what we wrote in the preceding chapter. The "wise" man is the one who "heareth these sayings" of Christ, who "cometh to" Him (Luke vi, 47), which involves turning his back upon the world and forsaking the service of Satan, and who "doeth them." "These sayings of Mine" are emphatic, having particular reference to the principles Christ had enunciated and the precepts He had inculcated in the previous sections of this Sermon on the Mount. We have to go unto other parts of the New Testament to learn Christian *doctrine*, but here we have described Christian *practice*. Some, like Tolstoi, have magnified this Sermon to the disparagement of the Epistles; others, like the Dispensationalists, have exalted the Epistles above the Sermon: the one is as reprehensible as the other. One part of Scripture must not be pitted against another part. Both this Sermon and the Epistles are essential parts of the revealed will of God. "Who have, in every age, uprightly and unreservedly, obeyed these sayings of our Lord, except they who have firmly believed the doctrines of the Gospel as more clearly and fully revealed in the apostolic epistles?" (T. Scott).

The "wise" man, then, is the one who comes to Christ, hears His instructions and does them. To *do* that which He has commanded includes, first, a believing of them, that is a definite appropriation of His precepts, a taking of them home to myself. It involves an understanding of them, and that calls for humility and meekness of mind rather than keenness of intellect; a meditation upon Christ's words and a crying unto Him, "that which I see not teach Thou me." It involves a making conscience of them, the realization that these sayings of Christ contain not only good counsel which it is my wisdom to heed, but that they are His imperative requirements which I disregard at my peril. It involves an actual putting of them into practice so that I abstain from those things which He forbids and perform those duties which He specifies: "If ye know these things, happy are ye if ye do them" (John xiii, 17). "*All* the sayings of Christ: not only the laws He has enacted, but the truths He has revealed must be done by us. They are a light not only unto our eyes, but to our feet, and are designed not only to *in*form our judgments but to *re*form our hearts and lives" (Matthew Henry).

We regard the word "doth" as the all-important one in our present passage, and care needs to be taken lest we improperly limit its meaning. To "do" our Lord's sayings includes very much more than the mere outward performance of those actions which He requires. Our whole inner and outer man must be conformed to them; our character must be moulded by them, our affections must be regulated, our wills governed, and our habits of thought dominated by them, as well as our actions being in accord with them. The Word of Christ must "dwell in" us, and that "richly" (Col. iii, 16), and that calls for a definite process of spiritual horticulture. We must "lay apart all filthiness and superfluity of naughtiness" if we are to "receive with meekness the engrafted Word which is able to save our souls" (James i, 21). Note well that expression "the *engrafted* Word": that which is addressed to us must be rooted in us, planted in the soul, drawing all the sap of the stock to itself— "all that is within us" serving the Word. Thereby ye are "transformed by the renewing of your mind" (Romans xii, 2). This, and nothing short of this, is what constitutes a genuine "conversion."

From what has been said above it will appear how intimately related are the several answers unto those questions we formulated in the opening paragraph, how that they necessarily grow naturally out of each other. Cannot the reader now decide for himself what is denoted by this "rock" on which our Lord represents the wise man as building his house? Bearing in mind the scope of our passage and its relation to the context, does not the first half of verse 24 furnish a decisive index to the meaning of the second half? It is "these sayings" of Christ, understood, believed and obeyed, which are the "rock" here. "These sayings are the dictates of eternal truth and righteousness, and the everlasting mountains shall be sooner rooted up than any one of these shall be falsified. This is the foundation on which the wise builder places his edifice: not his own conjectures or reasonings, nor the arguments and reasonings of other men, but the 'true and faithful sayings of God'" (J. Brown) —to which may be added, and not following the carnal desires of our own hearts. If the reader still insists that the "rock" here is Christ Himself, we reply, If so, Christ considered as Prophet and not as Priest, as Lord and not as Saviour, as *Teacher* and not Redeemer.

There should be little difficulty in determining *what* is signified by the "house" which the builder here erects upon the "rock" or "sayings" of Christ, though a certain latitude should be allowed as to *how* it be stated. The principal definitions made by the best of the expositors are: the *profession* he makes, the *character* that is formed, the *hope* which is cherished. When analysed these three expressions or things differ little in essence. The profession made is valid only if it be verified by a character which is formed by the whole range of Christ's teaching in this Sermon, a character which is displayed by conduct in accordance therewith. So too the hope cherished by the believer, the assurance he possesses, that God has accepted him in the Beloved, is but presumption, a mere carnal confidence, unless it be grounded upon this "rock," that is unless the one claiming such a hope be possessed of that character which alone warrants the expectation of everlasting bliss. Furthermore, the cherishing of a good hope, the possession of a peaceful assurance that I am a child of God, is an essential part of a character which is formed by an appropriation and assimilation of the "sayings" of Christ.

This figure of the building of a house to represent the formation of a Christian character under the teaching of Christ is employed frequently in the Acts and Epistles. When taking leave of the elders of Ephesus Paul commended them to God and the Word of His grace "which is able to *build you up*" (Acts xx, 32). The Colossian saints were exhorted, "As ye have therefore received Christ Jesus the Lord, so walk ye in Him: Rooted and built up in Him" (ii, 7, 8); while Jude bade the saints be "building up yourselves on your most holy faith" (verse 20). The same word here rendered "built" is also translated "edify." Thus, "Follow after the things which make for peace and things wherewith one may edify another" (Romans xiv, 19); "Let every one of us please his neighbour for his good to edification" (Romans xv, 2). "Let no corrupt communication proceed out of your mouth, but that which is good to the use of edifying" (Eph. iv, 29). "Wherefore comfort [or "exhort"] yourselves together, and edify one another, even as also ye do" (I Thess. v, 11). Timothy was instructed, "Neither give heed to fables and endless genealogies which minister questions, rather than godly edifying which is in faith" (I Tim. i, 4). How careful we should be in our converse with each other that what we say be of a spiritually constructive character and not destructive.

The "house," then, may be taken first for the profession made, which is yet to be put to the proof in the day of testing. Or more definitely it represents the character of the one making a Christian profession; and by "character" we include the whole frame of his beliefs, sentiments, affections, and active habits. Having by the faith of the Truth found the only sure foundation, he erects on it an edifice of thoughts, feelings and volitions. He is moulded according to "that form of doctrine which was delivered you" (Romans vi, 17). He is not regulated by his own carnal desires, nor the opinions and examples of his fellows, but by the sure and authoritative precepts of Christ. Accordingly he cherishes a "hope of eternal life" (Titus i, 2) and it is a "good hope through grace" (II Thess. ii, 16), for it is based upon a reliable foundation, grounded on the precepts and promises of the Lord; which precepts have been laid hold of and translated into practice, and which promises have been mixed with faith and made our own. Such a hope will prove both "sure and stedfast" in the hour of testing.

From all that has been before us on the different points it will be seen that everything goes back to and turns upon the word "doeth": *that* strikes the keynote of the verse, and therefore its dominant theme is our practical compliance with the Divine will. The importance which God attaches to and the value which He places upon *obedience* comes out plainly in the words of His prophet, "Behold, to obey is better than sacrifice, and to hearken than the fat of rams" (I Samuel xv, 22). To keep strictly to the path of the Divine commandments is more pleasing unto God than any of the outward forms of religion or the most liberal contributions to His earthly cause. Well did T. Scott point out with regard to the Levitical sacrifices, "their value was entirely from the appointment of God, and they were not acceptable except offered in obedience to Him, and with a penitent, believing and pious mind. When therefore they were substituted in the place of true piety or trusted in as meritorious when the means were used to compensate for the neglect of the end, they became an abomination, however costly and numerous they were." So now.

The same insistent emphasis upon obedience was made by Christ. When interrupted in His talking to the people by one who informed Him that His mother and brethren stood without, desiring to speak with Him, He made answer by stretching forth His hand "toward His disciples" and saying, "Behold My mother and My brethren. For whosoever shall *do* the will of My Father which is in heaven, the same is My brother and sister and mother" (Matt. xii, 46-50). It was as though He said, Those that are nearest and dearest to Me, spiritually speaking, are My "disciples," and they are described as the ones who *comply* with the Divnie will. Again, when a certain woman said to Him, "Blessed is the womb that bare Thee and the paps which Thou hast sucked," He replied, "Yea, rather, blessed are they that hear the Word of God and keep it" (Luke xi, 27, 28). The ones on whom the benediction of God rests are they who *keep* His Word—in their hearts, as their most precious possession; in their minds, by frequent meditation; in their lives, as the rule of practice.

Conscientious souls are likely to be troubled at this point, sensible that their obedience is so imperfect and faulty. It remains therefore that we should endeavour to set their fears at rest and attempt to show more definitely what Christ did *not* signify and what He *did* imply by "whoso heareth these sayings of Mine and *doeth* them." Our Lord did not mean that His disciples perpetually and flawlessly perform His precepts, for He does not remove from them the carnal nature at their regeneration, nor does He grant them such a measure of His grace in this world as to enable them to render a sinless obedience. God could have done both had He thought well, but it has pleased Him to exalt imputed righteousness rather than inherent in this life. Not only does every saint fail to render that obedience which is required by God's Law as a whole, but he does not obey any single commandment perfectly, for every duty we perform, yea, our highest act of worship, is marred by sin. In the most holy men corruption deprives them of the purity that ought to be there, and lusts fight against the perfect holiness they desire and strive after (Romans vii, 18-21; Gal. v, 17).

Christians perform the sayings of Christ *sincerely* though not perfectly, in spirit and in truth, though not in the letter and full execution. When Christ said to the Father of His apostles, "They *have kept* Thy word" (John xvii, 6), He did not mean they had done so as flawlessly and excellently as He had Himself done. And when we read "hereby we do not know that we know Him if we keep His commandments" (I John ii, 3), consistency requires us to understand it that as we only "know Him" in part in this life (I Cor. xiii, 12) so we only "keep His commandments" *in part*. Where there is a *genuine willingness* (Romans vii, 18; Heb. xiii, 18; I Tim. vi, 18), God accepts it for the deed (II Cor. viii, 12). Because His people have His Law written in their hearts (Heb. x, 16), because they delight in it with their inner man (Romans vii, 22), because they truly desire to obey it fully (Psalm cxix, 5), and pray earnestly to that end (Psalm cxix, 35), and repent of and confess their disobedience (Psalm xxxii, 5), God is pleased—according to the terms of the covenant of grace, and for Christ's sake—to accept their imperfect obedience and account it as a keeping of His Law.

To prevent wrong conclusions being drawn from the last paragraph two things need to be pointed out. First, it must *not* be inferred that God has lowered His standard in order to meet our infirmities: that standard is *par excellence* and shall never be altered. But the Surety of God's people fully conformed to it and His perfect obedience is reckoned to the account of those who savingly believe on Him, so that imputatively they are flawlessly righteous in the sight of the Law. Inherently they are righteous in the sense that they fully approve of the Law, delight in it, and sincerely set themselves to an unreserved obedience of the whole of it; and thus "the righteousness of the law *is* fulfilled *in* them" (Romans viii, 4). Yet because of their remaining depravity they fail to realize their desires (Phil. iii, 12), mourn over and confess their sinful failures, and are forgiven for Christ's sake. In this life they are more active in seeking from God the remission of their failures than they are in offering to Him that which is faultless. Some of the old writers were wont to say that the present perfection of a Christian consists in a penitential acknowledgment of his imperfection.

Second, the nature and scope of this sincere but imperfect obedience needs to be amplified and honestly stated. (1) The Christian's compliance with "these sayings" of the Lord is *internal and spiritual* as well as external. If any man should respond to every positive and negative precept of Christ in his outward conduct and yet his inner man be not affected and influenced by them, it would be like a body minus a soul—a corpse. As someone has aptly expressed it, obedience of soul is the soul of obedience. It is at this point, especially, that the righteousness of the saints exceeds that of the scribes and Pharisees, for while they rested wholly on their outward obedience of the Law, within they were full of unmortified lusts. The Law is "spiritual" (Romans vii, 14) and requires spiritual compliance thereto. The only worship God will accept is that which is " in spirit and in truth " (John iv, 24). Nevertheless, our obedience is not to consist solely of spiritual meditation and contemplating the mortification of our lusts and the cultivation of our graces: there must be an external walking in the Truth also.

(2) Sincere obedience is *impartial*, extending to the whole Law as it is explained in the precepts and exhortations of both the Old Testament and the New. To affect much devotion unto the things pertaining to God and then evince an utter lack of conscience and equity in things pertaining to men is horrible hypocrisy. The Pharisees were notorious in this: they made long prayers, yet devoured widows' houses; they fasted twice a week, yet laid burdens on their disciples grievous to be borne; they tithed, yet taught that neither father nor mother was to be relieved if men had placed their substance under a vow to God. Oh, my reader, your attendance at "early morning communion" or "the breaking of bread" is a vile mockery if you are unscrupulous and grasping in your dealings with men. Your psalm singing and lauding of the person and perfections of Christ are a stench in God's nostrils if you lie and thieve. On the other hand, however honest and truthful with your fellows, if you rob God of the submission, devotion and praise which are His due, your heart is rotten. Of the parents of the Baptist it is written, "They were both righteous before God, walking in *all* the commandments and ordinances of the Lord blameless" (Luke i, 6).

(3) Sincere obedience is *universal*, by which we mean it includes things to be believed as well as practised, and hence it is termed " the obedience of faith " (Romans i, 5). God's commandments must not be limited to the prohibition of wickedness, but extended also to false doctrines. If the Epistles be read attentively it will be found that the apostles were as emphatic and stern in their denunciation of teachers of errors as of lascivious livers, and that they pressed the necessity of a sound and holy faith as vehemently as they did a good and pure conscience. A sincere heart is set against heresies as definitely and diligently as against sinful conduct, and sinful conduct as heresies. One who is opposed to ungodliness but indifferent about false doctrines may justly suspect the soundness of his heart; while one who denounces false doctrine but tolerates wickedness in himself or his family has serious reason to question the validity of his profession. Christians are given no more licence in matters of faith

than of deportment. Stubborn heretics are to be cast out of the church equally with the openly immoral.

This chapter is already long enough, so we must postpone our answer to the fifth question—What is portrayed by the hurricane which bursts upon the "house" and tests its security?—till we consider verse 27.

CHAPTER SIXTY-TWO

Profession Tested—Continued

"AND every one that heareth these sayings of Mine, and doeth them not, shall be likened unto a foolish man which built his house upon the sand: And the rain descended, and the floods came, and the winds blew, and beat upon that house; and it fell: and great was the fall of it" (verses 26, 27). It is scarcely necessary to point out that our Lord was here using parabolic language, but what is the force of the figure He employed? What is signified by this building a house upon the sand? Clearly He had in view those who claim to be His followers, but whose profession has no reality behind it: a class of people who expect to go to heaven, but whose hopes rest upon a faulty foundation; those who trust in something which will fail them in the hour of testing. Unspeakably solemn, then, are these verses, containing that which should cause every reader who values his soul to tremble at them, and to re-examine himself with sevenfold thoroughness, to discover whether or not they describe his own perilous condition.

For the last time in this Sermon our Lord enforced the text on which it is based: "For I say unto you, That except your righteousness shall exceed the righteousness of the scribes and Pharisees, ye shall in no case enter into the kingdom of heaven" (v, 20). Wherein lay the defectiveness of their "righteousness"? First, there was a total neglect of their internal condition: "Woe unto you, scribes and Pharisees, hypocrites! for ye are like unto whited sepulchres, which indeed appear beautiful outward, but are within full of dead men's bones, and of all uncleanness" (Matt. xxiii, 27) —there was no mortification of their lusts. Second, they failed to put first things first: "Ye pay tithe of mint and anise and cummin, and have omitted the weightier matters of the law, judgment, mercy and faith" (xxiii, 23). Third, they wrought for their own glory, from a principle of self-interest: "But all their works they do for to be seen of men" (xxiii, 5) and not for the purpose of obeying and honouring God. Fourth, they practised not what they preached: "they say, and do not" (xxiii, 3)—their talk was all right, but their walk was all wrong.

Spirituality of soul, purity of heart, integrity of conduct, the scribes and Pharisees had no regard for. They were forward in fasting, praying at street corners, and giving of alms ostentatiously, but it was all done with the object of enhancing their reputation among men. And in *their* religion we have an exemplification of what is the natural persuasion of men the world over, namely that a religion of external performances will suffice to ensure a blissful eternity. Undoubtedly there are many who would in words deny this, but who in their works substantiate it. They bring their bodies to the house of prayer, but not their souls; they worship with their mouths, but not "in spirit and in truth." They are sticklers for immersion or early morning communion, yet take no thought about keeping their hearts with all diligence. They boast of their orthodoxy, but disregard the precepts of Christ. Multitudes of professing Christians abstain from external acts of violence, yet hesitate not to rob their neighbours of a good name by spreading evil reports against them. They contribute regularly to the "pastor's salary," but shrink not from misrepresenting their goods and cheating their customers, persuading themselves that "business is business." They have more regard for the laws of man than those of God, for *His* fear is not before their eyes.

After dwelling at such length in the previous chapter on the "wise" builder, there should be little difficulty in identifying the various groups which are commonly classified as the "foolish." They are all those, no matter what their profession and pretensions, who *do not* the "sayings" of Christ. Even F. W. Grant, in his brief notes on this passage, said: "He who puts His sayings livingly into practice shall build a house that will endure the storm. None else and nothing else will": though we are very much afraid that scarcely two out of a hundred of those wont to read his *Numerical Bible* really believe any such thing. In Luke's account of the "wise" builder an additional item is added: "Whosoever cometh to Me, and heareth My sayings, and doeth them, I will shew you to whom he is like: He is like a man which built an house, and *digged deep*, and laid the foundation on a rock" (vi, 47, 48). The "foolish" ones *failed* to "dig deep." As this is the vital point which distinguishes the two classes let us endeavour to show what is signified by this "digging deep."

If ever there was a time when these words "digged deep" needed to be pressed upon the notice of professing Christians it is today. We are living in an age characterized by superficiality and shallowness, when religion itself has degenerated into a mere surface thing. There is no deep ploughing, no spade work, no foundation exercises, no brokenness of heart. If I have never mourned over my waywardness, I have no solid ground for rejoicing. "Want of depth, want of sincerity, want of zeal in religion—this is the want of our times. Want of an eye to God in religion, lack of sincere dealing with one's soul, neglect of using the lancet with our hearts, neglect of the search-warrant which God gives out against sin, carelessness concerning living upon Christ; much reading about Him, much talking about Him, but too little feeding upon His flesh and drinking of His blood—these are the causes of tottering professions and baseless hopes." If Spurgeon found occasion for making such complaint as far back as 1870, how sadly conditions have worsened since then!

A saving apprehension or laying hold of Christ is not the simple thing so many suppose. Man must be humbled into the dust before he will, as a beggar, betake himself to the Redeemer. The Divine Law is the appointed schoolmaster to drive sinners to Christ, but so many people play truant—run away from school. Not a few attempt to build upon Christ, but there has been no proper foundation-work, and so in the day of testing the floods of opposition and perse-cution come in between their hearts and Christ, and temptations part them to the overthrow of their profession. By nature our hearts are so filled with self-love and self-pity that there is no room for Christ. Many are willing to receive Him for His benefits who have no love for His person and no resolution to bow to His Lordship, which is like a woman marrying a man solely for his money. Observe Paul's order: "For whom I have suffered the loss of all things, and do count them but dung, that I may win Christ, And be found in Him, not having mine own righteousness which is of the law, but that which is through the faith of Christ, the righteousness which is of God by faith" (Phil. iii, 8, 9)—first Christ Himself and then His righteousness!

1. He "digs deep" who does not enter upon a Christian pro-fession hurriedly and lightly, but instead "sits down and counts the cost" (Luke xiv, 28). There are some who say they are saved before they have any feeling sense that they are lost. There are others who profess to receive Christ who yet have no realization of the claims of His sceptre. There are those who present themselves for baptism who know nothing about the terms of Christian discipleship. Such people rush into a profession of religion, and in most cases rush out of it again. They receive the Word "with joy" rather than with painful convictions of sin, but they have "not root in themselves" and so "dureth for a while" only (Matt. xiii, 20, 21), Hence it was that when one said unto Him, "I will follow Thee whithersoever Thou goest," Christ told him that he had not "where to lay His head"; and when another lightly said, "I will follow Thee," He answered, "No man, having put his hand to the plough [and ploughing is no easy work!], and looking back, is fit for the kingdom of God" (Luke ix, 58-62); while to His apostles He gave the warn-ing "Remember Lot's wife" (Luke xvii, 32).

2. He "digs deep" who labours to be emptied of self-righteous-ness, self-esteem, and self-sufficiency. The sinner needs first to be convicted of his utter inability *to come* to Christ—that God must give him a heart which is willing to receive Him as King to rule over him. Observe how the Lord Himself pressed this fact upon His hearers: "No man can come to Me, except the Father which hath sent Me draw him" (John vi, 44)—but who believes that today when the "free will" of man is so much cried up! "They that be whole need not a physician, but they that are sick" (Matt. ix, 12).

Why should I seek unto the great Physician for strength when I have no consciousness of my weakness, for cleansing while I am quite unaware of my foulness? Only God can subdue our innate pride and self-complacency, and in order thereto there must needs be ardent wrestlings of soul with Him that He would graciously put forth His power and overcome that in me which rises up against Him.

3. He "digs deep" who strives after an experimental and inward knowledge of the Truth. A mere notional or theoretical acquaintance with it will not suffice him. He longs to have a practical knowledge of the Truth so that it becomes deeply rooted within him, so that it finds a home in the "hidden parts" (Psalm li, 6). Truth has to be bought (Prov. xxiii, 23), and the wise builder is quite willing to pay the necessary price—sacrificing worldly interests so to do. As Spurgeon said, "Seek an inwrought experience of Divine Truth. Ask to have it burnt into you. Why is it that people give up the doctrines of grace if they fall in with eloquent advocates of free will? Why is it that they renounce the orthodox creed if they meet with smart reasoners who contradict it? Because they have never received the Word in the power of the Holy Spirit so as to have it sealed in their hearts. . . . It is one thing to have a creed, it is quite another thing to have the Truth graven upon the tables of the heart. Many fail here because Truth was never made experimentally their own."

4. He "digs deep" who balks not at the work of mortification, who follows Christ as the grand Exemplar of mortification. What the Saviour suffered in His pure flesh by way of expiation, those who would be saved must suffer in their corrupt flesh by way of mortification. It is true the flesh in us is reluctant, as was the holy humanity of Christ, saying, "let this cup pass from Me," but the spirit is willing, crying "Father, Thy will be done" even in the crucifixion of my dearest lusts. Christ died a violent death, and sin must not die an easy and comfortable one. His body was nailed to the tree till His soul was separated from it, and the body of sin must be so nailed till the soul of sin—the will and love of it— depart. Christ died a tormenting death, in pains and agonies, and we must so die to sin that we "suffer in the flesh" (I Peter iv, 1). Christ died a lingering death, and so does sin languish little by little, mortification upon mortification, dying "daily." Alas, how few dig deep enough to come to the denying of self!

5. He "digs deep" who endeavours to hide God's Word in his heart so that he may be kept from sinning against Him (Psalm cxix, 11). By "hiding" is not here meant concealing but treasuring, so that it may be preserved. To so "hide" means, first, to obtain a spiritual understanding of it—and for that, diligence and labour are required (Prov. ii, 1-4). Only then does "wisdom" enter the heart and knowledge become pleasant unto the soul (Prov. ii, 10). Second, when it is assented unto by faith, otherwise it will quickly

vanish: "The word preached did not profit them, not being mixed with faith in them that heard it" (Heb. iv, 2). Third, when it is kindly entertained: Christ complained to the Jews, "ye seek to kill Me, because My word hath no place in you" (John viii, 37). Fourth, when it is deeply rooted, settled in the affections, so that it becomes the "engrafted word" (James i, 21). The Word must not be studied out of curiosity, or for the object of teaching others, nor for our comfort, but with this prime end in view: that it may deliver us from sin—storing our minds with what is holy, resisting Satan's temptations with an, "It is written," its promises sustaining us in times of trial.

6. He "digs deep" who sincerely endeavours to have his heart sensibly affected by the exceeding sinfulness of sin. Since sin be that abominable thing which God hates, that which occasioned the death of Christ, and that which is the cause of all his own misery, the believer seeks to obtain a deeper horror for and hatred of sin. To this end he frequently reminds himself of and meditates upon the fearful tragedy which the first sin introduced into Eden, how that it corrupted at its source the stream of human nature. He constantly ponders the fact that all the sorrow and suffering in the world is the immediate effect of sin. He essays to view sin in the light of eternal punishment. "When I meet with professors who talk lightly of sin, I feel sure that they have built without a foundation. If they had ever felt the Spirit's wounding and killing sword of conviction, they would flee from sin as from a lion. Truly forgiven sinners dread the appearance of evil as burnt children dread the fire. Superficial repentance always leads to careless living. Pray earnestly for a broken heart" (Spurgeon).

7. He "digs deep" who makes diligent search and thorough examination within to make sure that God has written His Word on his heart (II Cor. xiii, 5; II Peter i, 10). He is so concerned about his eternal welfare, so aware of the deceitfulness of the human heart, that he dare not take anything for granted. He is determined to prove his own self, that a supernatural work of grace has been truly wrought within him. He spares no pains to measure himself by the Word to see whether the fruits of regeneration are really being brought forth in the garden of his soul. He earnestly seeks the Divine assistance in the all-important matter, crying to God, "Examine me, O Lord, and prove me; try my reins and my heart" (Psalm xxvi, 2): let me not be mistaken, but graciously make known to me my real condition, and if I be one of Thy redeemed cause Thy blessed Spirit to bear witness with my spirit that I am a child of Thine. And if the seeker be sincere and importunate his quest will not be in vain, neither will his request fall upon deaf ears.

Let us now describe several kinds of "foolish" builders. First, they build "upon the sand" whose hope is based upon a round of religious performances. The one who counts upon church membership, church attendance, the saying of prayers and the reading of the Bible as being all that is needed to ensure for him an entrance into the everlasting kingdom is resting on a broken reed. That was the case with the Pharisees. They fasted and tithed, made long prayers and were most punctilious in attending to ceremonial rites, but they were outside the pale of God's mercy. "Except a man be born again, he cannot see the kingdom of God" (John iii, 3) no matter how zealous he be in attending "communions," how liberal in supporting "missionaries," or how "faithful to the cause." Until I have a heart which receives Christ as my Prophet, Priest and King, which unfeignedly loves Him, which obeys Him, there is no hope for me.

Second, they build "upon the sand" whose hope is based on visions, dreams and happy feelings. There is a class in Christendom, larger than some suppose, whose trust reposes in those very things. Ask them to tell you their experience, inquire what ground they have for concluding that God has met with them in saving grace, and they will relate to you some mysterious vision, some remarkable dream, some voice which spoke to them, many years ago, saying "thy sins be forgiven thee," which produced an ecstasy of joy and assurance which nothing can shake. Now we will not positively affirm that they were deluded into imagining such things, yet we would point out that Satan transforms himself as an "angel of light" and can produce remarkable impressions. Whatever remarkable experience you met with in the past, unless you are *now* trusting in the blood and righteousness of Christ and sincerely endeavouring to *perform* His precepts, you are trusting in what will fail you in the Day to come.

Third, they build "upon the sand" whose hope is based on a "faith in Christ" which produces no obedience to Him. Unto such He searchingly says, "Why call ye Me, Lord, Lord, and do not the things which I say?" (Luke vi, 46). A mere intellectual assent to the Gospel or a belief in the historical Christ is worthless, for it brings forth no spiritual fruits. To hear and acquiesce and then perform not is a mocking of God. As there were many who "believed in His name when they saw the miracles which He did" to whom the Saviour "*did not* commit Himself" (John ii, 23, 24), so there are thousands today who non-savingly "believe in Christ" yet have not "the root of the matter" (Job xix, 28) within them. The faith of God's elect is one which in a vital and practical way is "the acknowledging the truth which is after godliness" (Titus i, 1), which issues in "purifying their hearts" (Acts xv, 9), which "worketh by love" (Gal. v, 6) and which "overcometh the world" (I John v, 4). Only *such* a faith will suffice for time and eternity.

Fourth, they build "upon the sand" whose hope rests on a merely intellectual knowledge of the Truth. The difference between theoretical and practical knowledge is one both of kind and of degree. Theoretical knowledge is fluctuating and evanescent, constantly subject to alteration; but practical knowledge is deep-rooted and permanent. Once I have experienced the burning effects of fire no sophistical arguments can persuade me it is harmless. Once I have tasted that the Lord is gracious none can convince me that He is not. The difference between the two is apparent also from the effects produced. Pilate had a theoretical knowledge that it was contrary to the evidence before him to condemn Christ to death, but when the issue of his own interests with Caesar was raised (John xix, 12) his practical judgment determined him to save his prestige. One who has a theoretical acquaintance with the precepts may talk well about them, but only one with a practical knowledge will walk according to them. One with a theoretical knowledge of the Truth may admire it, but only one with a practical knowledge thereof would die for it.

Fifth, they build "upon the sand" who make not conscience of confessing sin. There is a radical difference between the unregenerate and the regenerate in this matter. The former, being dead toward God and having but light thoughts upon sin, are not weighed down by it; but to the latter it is their heaviest burden, and therefore are they thankful to unbosom themselves unto the Lord. Christ has bidden them pray to their Father "forgive us our sins" (Luke xi, 4). Scripture warns them, "he that covereth his sins shall not prosper" (Prov. xxviii, 13), and so David proved: "When I kept silence, my bones waxed old through my roaring all the day long"; but eventually he said, "I will confess my transgressions unto the Lord; and Thou forgavest the iniquity of my sin" (Psalm xxxii, 3, 5). After his sad fall, Peter went out and "wept bitterly." Read through the second half of Romans vii and observe how keenly distressed Paul was by indwelling corruption. The believer has a sensitive conscience and keeps short account with God; but the conscience of the unbeliever is calloused, and he neither mourns over nor confesses his sins.

To sum up. No matter what experience I have had, or what be the character and strength of my faith, or how deep and steady be my assurance, or how eminent my gifts, unless any or all of these issue in a life of practical obedience to Christ they will avail nothing when death overtakes me. And that is no harsh verdict of ours, but the decision of the Son of God: "every one that heareth these sayings of Mine, and *doeth them not*, shall be likened unto a foolish man who built his house upon the sand." Not that the Christian will "do" them perfectly—"For in many things we offend all" (James iii, 2)—though he ought to, and must not excuse but rather mourn over and confess his failure. No, the obedience of the Christian is not a faultless one, yet it is real and actual. It is not flawless, yet it is sincere. It is the genuine desire, resolution and endeavour of the Christian to please Christ in *all* things, and it is his greatest grief when he displeases Him. Lord, "*Make me to go in the path of Thy commandments; for therein do I delight*" (Psalm cxix, 35).

CHAPTER SIXTY-THREE

Profession Tested—Concluded

It now remains for us to ascertain what is signified by the hurricane which struck the "house" of the "wise" and of the "foolish" builder. Concerning that of the former it is said, "And the rain descended, and the floods came, and the winds blew, and beat upon that house; and it fell not: for it was founded upon a rock" (verse 25). Identically the same thing is narrated in connection with the latter, except in regard to the outcome: "it fell, and great was the fall of it." After having entered into such detail concerning the "wise" and the "foolish" man, the "digging deep" of the former and this fatal omission by the latter, the foundation of "rock" and that of "sand," and the "house" which each one erected, there should be little difficulty in discovering the general drift of what is denoted by the storm: though the language used be figurative, its purport is obvious. By means of the storm the strength and stability or the weakness and insecurity of the "house" was demonstrated.

The hurricane was that by which the work of each man was put to the proof and his wisdom or folly made evident. Thus it is clear that once more what is here before us is the *testing of profession* and the making manifest of its worth or worthlessness. This had been the dominating theme of our Lord's Sermon from vii, 13, onwards. The "strait gate" and "the narrow way" correspond to the digging deep and the foundation of rock, while the "wide gate" and "broad way" correspond to the omission of digging deep and the foundation of sand. In like manner we may see in the "wise" builder the "good tree" which brings forth "good fruit," and in the "foolish" builder the "corrupt tree" with its "evil fruit." In the "he that doeth the will of My Father which is in heaven" we have the one whose house stands firm, while in the many to whom Christ will say, "I never knew you, depart from Me, ye that work iniquity" we have those whose building is overthrown by the storm.

We must not, however, conclude that nothing more is signified by our Lord in this figure of the storm bursting upon the house than the testing of Christian profession, though scarcely any of the commentators seem to have seen anything further in it. Surely due attention to the immediate setting, to say nothing of the more remote or general context, requires us to enlarge our viewpoint. Consider the *outcome* of the storm. In the case of the "wise man" it beat upon his house in vain: in spite of all its fury, his building stood firm. And why? Because it was founded upon a "rock." And what did that purport? Why, that the wise man was something more than a hearer of the Word, namely a *doer* of it, one who heeded its warnings, who responded to its exhortations, who performed its precepts, whose character and conduct were moulded and regulated by its teachings. This, and nothing but this, is what Christ insists upon at the beginning of our passage: "Whosoever heareth these sayings of Mine and *doeth* them, I will liken him unto a wise man which built his house upon a rock."

Among the "sayings" of Christ are some peculiarly distasteful to flesh and blood, yea, at direct variance with the inclinations of fallen human nature. To pluck out right eyes and cut off right hands, to love our enemies, bless them which curse us, do good to them that hate us, and pray for them which despitefully use and persecute us, is not so simple as it may sound—see, then, the appropriateness of our Lord's similitude of "digging deep" when portraying such tasks. To distribute our alms and perform our devotions in secret, to expressly ask the Father to forgive us our debts *as we* forgive our debtors—being told that if we forgive not neither shall we be forgiven—to take no anxious thought for the morrow but to have a heart freed from carking care, to have such confidence in the providential bounty of God that we trustfully count upon Him supplying our every need, are duties which will tax our abilities to the utmost. True, but we shall not be the losers by practising such precepts.

"And it *fell not,* for it was founded upon a rock": that is what we desire to lay hold of in this connection. Here is *encouragement* indeed. Instead of being so occupied with the narrowness of the way, cast your eye forward to the glorious goal to which it conducts you—even life. Instead of being so concerned about the painfulness of the work of mortification, think rather of what it is the appointed means of saving you from—even from being "cast into hell" (v, 29). Instead of complaining about the difficulties of obedience, consider its rich compensation. God has definitely assured us that in the keeping of His commandments "there is great reward" (Psalm xix, 11), such as "the answer of a good conscience," peace of soul, the enjoyment of His approbation. It is *this* aspect of the Truth which Christ is here pressing upon our attention: the one who *does* His "sayings" is assured of *safety* in the day of testing and trial. The "house" of such a one will not, cannot, be overthrown by the storm. Is not *that* a recompense well worth striving for?

Throughout this Sermon on the Mount the Lord Jesus had presented a most exalted and unique standard of morality and spirituality, one which calls for real self-sacrifice on the part of those who sincerely endeavour to measure up to it and perform the duties it enjoins. But here He shows how great is the reward of those who submit themselves unto His yoke. In the stability and security of the wise man's "house" we have depicted one of the principal fruits of an obedient walk: the actual doing of these "sayings" of Christ delivers from the fatal assaults of the Devil, the world and the flesh. This consideration ought to move us to perform obedience readily and gladly, for this is a benefit which no human monarch can bestow. Neither wealth, education nor social prestige can confer security on the soul—rather do such things generally occasion destruction to their possessors. Neither human wit nor strength of resolution can procure preservation in the hour of trial and tribulation: nothing but the keeping of Christ's Word will obtain it, but that *does*. How this promise should encourage us and stimulate unto unreserved obedience!

The force of the figure which was here used by Christ would be more impressive to His immediate hearers than to those of us who live in strong houses and in those parts of the earth where devastating floods and tornadoes are seldom or never experienced. "In Judea, as in other oriental countries, the rains are periodical. When they descend, they often descend in torrents, and continue to do so, with unabated violence, for a number of days. In consequence of this, the most trifling mountain brook becomes a mighty river—a deluge rushing down with dreadful impetus from the high grounds to the plains, converting them into one wide waste of waters. The huts of the inhabitants, generally formed of clay hardened in the sun, are exposed to great danger. They are often literally melted down by the heavy rains or overturned by the furious gusts of wind; and, when not founded on the solid rock, undermined and swept away by the resistless torrent. In such a country, it is the part of a wise man to take good care that the foundation on which he builds his habitation be solid. He who attends to this precaution is likely to find the advantage of doing so, and he who neglects this precaution is likely to pay dear for his folly" (J. Brown).

Spurgeon was right when he said, "Whether your religion be true or false, it will be *tried;* whether it be chaff or wheat the fan of the great Winnower will surely be brought into operation upon all that lies on the threshing floor. If thou hast dealings with God, thou hast to do with a 'consuming fire.' Whether thou be really or nominally a Christian, if thou comest near to Christ He will try thee as silver is tried. Judgment must begin at the house of God, and if thou darest to come into the house of God, judgment will begin with thee." It is God's will that whosoever takes upon him the profession of His name shall be tried and proved. Adam and Eve were tempted and tried by Satan. God made trial of Abraham when He bade him take his only and dearly loved son and offer him up for a burnt offering on mount Moriah (Gen. xxii). For the trial of his faith and patience He gave Job and all that he had, except his life, into Satan's hand. God left Hezekiah to himself to try him and make known what was in his heart, when the ambassadors of Babylon came to inquire of him what wonders God had done in the land of Israel (II Chron. xxxii, 31).

It will be gathered from the above that we do not accept the view of those who *restrict* this trial of the "house" to the hour of death or the day of judgment. It is true that at death "the spirit shall return unto God who gave it " (Eccles. xii, 7) and that it then enters paradise or is consigned to the abode of the damned. At the Grand Assize the worth or worthlessness of the profession will be made manifest to an assembled universe. But we can see nothing in our present passage which requires us to limit the meaning of this storm unto the final testing, while on the other hand there is much in Scripture which makes it clear that both real and empty profession is, in a variety of ways but in different degrees, put to the proof in *this* life. When our Lord announced of His apostles "Satan hath desired to have you, that he may sift you as wheat " (Luke xxii, 31), which desire was granted, He expressed that which applies to all His people. It is as requisite that the faith of the saints should be tried by afflictions as gold is tried in the fire (I Peter i, 7).

When the apostle said to believers, "Beloved, think it not strange concerning the fiery trial which is to try you, as though some strange thing happened unto you" (I Peter iv, 12), he was referring unto an experience which is met with in this life, and one which, as his language denotes, is by no means exceptional. For example, for a Jew belonging to an orthodox family to make public profession of the Christian faith has always involved dishonour and disgrace; his family disinherit and disown him, and in the sight of all his brethren he is regarded as "the offscouring of all things." In the first two centuries A.D., being a Christian frequently involved forfeiture of citizenship, the "spoiling of his goods " and being cast unto the lions, or at least living in caves "destitute and afflicted." Yet notwithstanding such trials the faith of God's elect remained unshaken. During the past century the Lord's people, and especially His servants, have been tested in a more subtle manner: they have had to suffer the reproach of credulity and simple-mindedness, of being hopelessly behind the times, because they refused to believe the agnostic scientists and the theories of "modern scholarship"—sensitive natures find such reproaches harder to bear than physical sufferings. In this day, the test is to resist the seductions of an alluring world, to refuse to compromise.

Having generalized so much upon the verses before us, it is time that we turned to examine more closely their several details. First, "And the rain descended." This may be taken as a figure of the providential trials and adverse dispensations by which those bearing the name of Christ are put to the proof. "These rains typify *afflictions from heaven*. God will send you adversities like showers, tribulations as many as the drops of the dew. Between now and heaven, oh, professor, you will feel the pelting storm. Like other men, your body will be sick; or if not, you shall have trial in your house: children and friends will die, or riches will take to themselves wings and fly like an eagle. You must have trials from God's hand, and if you are not relying on Christ, you will not be able to bear them. If you are not by real faith one with Christ, even God's rains will be too much for you" (C. H. Spurgeon). The response of the heart, the manner in which we act in times of adversity, reveals our state; if unregenerate, our unbelieving heart will betray itself by acting as the worldling does—seeking to drown our sorrow amid carnal pleasures, or sinking in despair.

Second, " and the floods came," or as Luke vi, 48, says, " the floods *arose.*" Thus it is a thing of the earth which is here in view, namely *opposition from the world.* By this also must the professor be tested, to demonstrate whether or not his claim to being a Christian is genuine. It is true that in former days the floods of persecution raged more furiously than they do now; nevertheless, they are far from having totally subsided. The world's opposition assumes many forms: sometimes it is ridicule—and how often have the gibes and sneers of the ungodly tumbled down the " houses " of those who made a fair show in the flesh! Cruel mockings are still used against the people of God. In other cases it is reproach and slander, the " cold shoulder," boycotting, and only those who have a rock foundation will bear up under them. Not that the ones exposed always drop their profession entirely: far from it—often they retain the *name* of Christian, but compromise and walk arm-in-arm with the world to escape its persecutions.

Third, " and the winds blew and beat upon the house." Here it is " the prince of the power of the air " (Eph. ii, 2) who is at work: in other words, it is *Satan assaulting* the one who claims to be saved. At times he will cast a cloud of despondency over the human spirit, assailing with artful insinuations and blasphemous suggestions, particularly so when God's providences seem to be all against us, seeking to fill the soul with doubts of the Divine goodness and faithfulness. At other times he seeks to beguile with error, and only those established in the Truth will withstand him. He employs various tactics, according as he approaches in the form of a serpent or seeks to terrify as the roaring lion. He attracts by the world, appeals to the carnal nature, and only those whose "treasure " is really in heaven scorn his gilded baubles. He suggests a compromise, the making the best of both worlds, the serving of two masters, and none save they who have truly "received Christ Jesus *the Lord*" (Col. ii, 6) resist him.

The Lord plainly teaches us in this passage that he who takes upon him the Christian profession must expect a stormy passage through this world. He who is Truth incarnate painted no false and flattering picture of what Christian discipleship involves, but faithfully warns us that severe testings and trials await those who profess to be His followers. So far from being carried to heaven on " flowery beds of ease," they may expect to meet with fierce opposition from the world, the flesh and the Devil. He who was despised and rejected of men, tempted of the Devil, hated by the world, opposed

SERMON ON THE MOUNT

by the religious leaders, deserted by those who should have stood
by Him, has said, "the disciple is not above his Master." "We must
through much tribulation enter into the kingdom of God" (Acts
xiv, 22), and they who deny this are false prophets. "All that will
live godly in Christ Jesus shall suffer persecution" (II Tim. iii, 12),
yet that very persecution shall be made to work together for their
good.

"And it fell not." Here are consolation and compensation indeed.
Severely assaulted and shaken their "house" may be, but overthrown it shall not be. And why? "For it was founded upon a rock,"
that is to say the profession was a *genuine* one, and, therefore, one
which endures and survives every testing. It is no comfortable thing
to live through such an experience as this hurricane: ah, but dwell
upon the happy issue. It is no pleasant experience to meet with the
sneers of acquaintances, the loss of friends, the opposition of the
world and the enmity of Satan, but is it not worth all these and
much more if, like the three Hebrews, we come forth from the fires
unharmed? While I *do* Christ's "sayings," Satan can gain no
advantage over me: while I tread the path of obedience the "flesh"
is denied and cannot bring about my ruin. Neither in this life, the
hour of death, nor the day of judgment will the "house" of such a
one fall.

"And the rain descended, and the floods came, and the winds
blew, and beat upon that house; and it fell; and great was the fall
of it" (verse 27). Here is the solemn contrast. Here is the fearful
outcome for the one who erects his house upon the sand. Here
is the certain fate of all who rest their hope and base their
confidence on a worthless foundation. Here is the fearful ruin which
overtakes the empty professor. He who makes no conscience of
Christ's "saying," joins not practice to profession, who refuses to
walk in the path of the Divine commandments, is headed for eternal
damnation. An empty professor may withstand the lighter gusts of
opposition in days of peace and prosperity, but he is not at all likely
to survive the temptations of the times in which our lot is cast, as
witness the multitudes now making shipwreck of the faith they once
affirmed. And even those who continue to call themselves Christians
but refuse the Master's yoke will find in the hour of death that they
have no refuge from the judgment awaiting them.

Sometimes God exposes those who have made an eminent profession by sending them such anguish of conscience and foretastes of
hell that at the end they are exposed to all around them. A notable
example of this was Francis Spira in the seventeenth century. For
weeks he lay groaning on his couch, not from physical pain but from
anguish of soul, and though numbers of God's servants spoke to
and prayed with him, no relief was obtained. Said he to the ministers
and friends around his bed, "Take heed of relying on that faith
which worketh not a holy and unblamable life, worthy of a believer.
Credit me, it will fail. I have tried it. I presumed I had gotten the

right faith. I preached it to others. I had all places of Scripture in memory that might support it. I thought myself sure, and in the meantime lived impiously and carelessly. And behold now the judgment of God hath overtaken me: not to correction, but to damnation." He felt the fires of God's wrath burning in his soul as few have ever experienced them in this world, and expired thus. His house "fell" and great was the fall of it.

What has been before us should dispel the influence of the world, move us to self-judgment, and warn us against a superficial use of God's Word. If we allow Satan's world so to ensnare us that, for the sake of enjoying it, we consent to ignore Christ's rules for separation from evil and holiness of life, then dire will be the consequences. Such a passage as this ought to bring home to us both the heinousness and madness of our acts of disobedience, cause us contritely to confess the same, and entreat the Lord's pardon while it may yet be obtained. Finally, we would press upon our readers that the will of God, the standard He has appointed, cannot be known by mere casual and occasional glances at the Bible. Too many are but textmongers, singling out favourite passages which appeal to them. It is only by carefully and earnestly searching the Scriptures, by a systematic and continuous pondering of them, that we can discover "all the counsel of God." Those who do so will have their souls sustained by grace and upheld by the power of Christ in the day of trial, and will have no regrets for so employing their time and energies when the hour of death is upon them.

CHAPTER SIXTY-FOUR

Conclusion

"And it came to pass, when Jesus had ended these sayings, the people were astonished at His doctrine: For He taught them as one having authority, and not as the scribes." (Matt. vii, 28, 29.)

ONCE more we have been permitted and enabled to complete a lengthy though pleasant task, for after writing sixty-three chapters on Matthew v—vii our present business is to pen the closing one. Those three chapters record what is commonly designated our Lord's Sermon on the Mount. Really, it is far more than a sermon, being what might well be termed the Messiah's manifesto, the magna charta (or "constitution") of His kingdom, for therein He unfolded the laws and conditions under which alone we can enter His kingdom. In our second chapter we pointed out that, in keeping with its character and design, this address had twelve divisions—the *governmental* number. They may be expressed thus: 1. The character of those on whom the Divine blessing rests (v, 3-11). 2. The ministerial office (v, 12-16). 3. The spirituality and authority of the Moral Law (v, 17-48). 4. Practical righteousness or good works (vi, 1-19). 5. Warning against covetousness (vi, 20-34). 6. Unlawful judgment (vii, 1-5). 7. Unlawful liberality (vii, 6). 8. Seeking grace (vii, 7-11). 9. The golden rule (vii, 12). 10. The way of salvation (vii, 13, 14). 11. False prophets (vii, 15-19). 12. Profession tested (vii, 20-27).

In the verses which are to be before us we are informed of the effect which our Lord's sermon had upon the large concourse that heard it. This writer often closes his eyes and seeks to visualize the various scenes presented in Holy Writ. On this occasion the incarnate Son of God, but known only as "Jesus of Nazareth" to the Jews at that time, sat down upon the mountain side—perhaps on some slight eminence, that all might see and hear Him the better. Follow Him then throughout the whole of Matthew v-vii and attempt to enter into the feelings of His audience. Remember there was no halo of glory about His head, that to their eyes He appeared simply as a Galilean peasant. Yet again and again He sets over against "Ye have heard that it was said by them of old time" His imperative and imperial "But *I* say unto you." He denounced the Pharisees as "hypocrites." He declared that in the Day to come He would say unto the empty professors, "I never knew you: depart from Me, ye that work iniquity." He closed by insisting that men's eternal destiny

436

would be regulated by how they complied with "these sayings of Mine."

"And it came to pass, when Jesus had ended these sayings, the people were astonished at His doctrine: For He taught them as one having authority, and not as the scribes" (vii, 28 and 29). Here is made known to us the impression which our Lord's discourse produced upon its auditors. They were amazed, and well they might be. The Speaker had not graduated from the rabbinical schools, nor had He been granted a "preaching licence" by the Sanhedrin; yet He declared, "Think not that I am come to destroy the law, or the prophets: I am not come to destroy, but to fulfil." Then He added, "For I say unto you, That except your righteousness exceed the righteousness of the scribes and Pharisees, ye shall in no case enter into the kingdom of heaven." He went on to declare that causeless anger was incipient murder and that those who indulged in lustful glances were guilty of adultery. He bade them, "Love your enemies, bless them that curse you, do good to them that hate you." He made it evident that it was not merely good advice or salutary counsel He was offering them, but rather was issuing peremptory demands. It was as the King of righteousness He spoke.

The crowd was astonished both at the matter and manner of His preaching, for He spoke with weight, a majesty, an earnestness which carried conviction. They were filled with a temporary wonderment: yet it is not said that they repented or believed on Him or became His disciples. We too admire the matchless wisdom of His discourse, maintaining as it did throughout a perfect balance of Truth. We are made to marvel at its scope: that He covered so much ground in so brief a space, containing that which was suited to all classes and conditions of men, be they lost or saved, babes or fathers in Christ. We are made to tremble at the fearful solemnity of its utterances: the repeated reference to "hell" and "hell fire." We are solemnized as we learn from its final section that in the Great Assize the Preacher of this sermon will personally officiate as the Judge of men, pronouncing sentence of doom upon those who conform not to the Divine will. No wonder that, on another occasion, the officers sent by the Pharisees to arrest Christ returned without Him, saying "Never man spake like this man" (John vii, 46).

"The people were astonished at His doctrine." Have we not good reason to be astonished that they were not much more than "astonished"? Ought they not to have been brought to His feet in worship, perceiving it was more than man who addressed them? Ought they not to have been convicted and converted by His teaching: made deeply sensible of how far, far short they fell of such a standard of holiness, turning to Him in contrition and crying out for mercy? Alas, what is man, even when he hears the Truth from the lips of Truth incarnate! Capable of being impressed by a Divine message when it falls on his ears from without, but incapable of perceiving his own inward depravity and wretchedness in the

light of that message. How true it is that "except a man be born
again, he cannot see the kingdom of God" (John iii, 3), no, not
even when it is brought nigh to him by the King Himself. Then
let us not be surprised when only temporary effects are produced
under the most faithful and earnest preaching; rather let us be
deeply thankful if the message has found an abiding home in *our*
heart.

It may be asked, Why did not Christ put forth His Divine power
and turn the hearts of His hearers unto Himself? If three thousand
were converted under the Pentecostal sermon of Peter (Acts ii, 41),
why were not a similar number at least brought from death unto
life by this address of the Saviour's? Most certainly He could, had
He so pleased, have imparted to the whole of that multitude a
saving knowledge of the Truth. Then why was He not pleased to do
so? Why should the apostles perform "greater works" (John xiv,
12) than He wrought? Because He had taken upon Him the "form
of a *servant*" (Phil. ii, 7), and therefore did He aver, "I came down
from heaven not to do Mine own will, but the will of Him that
sent Me" (John vi, 38). The exercise of His Divine attributes was
entirely subordinated unto the will of the Father. Not only did He
refuse to work miracles on His own behalf (Matt. iv, 3, 4), but He
only put forth His power for the good of others as He had orders
to do so from above. This lovely perfection of Christ's, which is the
glory of His mediatorial holiness, has not received anything like the
attention which it justly calls for.

The obedience of Christ was the absolute conformity of His
entire spirit and soul to the mind and will of the Father, His ready
and cheerful performance of every duty and every thing which God
commanded Him. As He Himself declared, "My meat is to do the
will of Him that sent Me" (John iv, 34). Familiar as are these words
to the saints, how few have perceived the *fullness* of Christ's obedience or recognized that His *every act* during the thirty-three years
He tabernacled among men was distinctly and designedly an act
of submission to God. But this will be the more plainly seen if the
reader traces through the four Gospels that oft-repeated expression,
"that it might be fulfilled which was spoken by —— the prophet," and
then ponders the import of those words. The whole of Christ's
course had been marked out for Him. Thus it was that "He came
and dwelt in Capernaum" (Matt. xii, 12-14). It was not the force
of circumstances which drove the Lord Jesus to select that place as
His ministerial headquarters, nor was it out of personal inclination:
that town had been selected by God for Him long before He came
to earth, and it was in subjection to the Divine will that He went
there. Christ made obedience to the Father the one great business
of His life.

His miracles of mercy were wrought in obedience to the Father's
revealed will. "When the even was come they brought unto Him
many that were possessed with devils: and He cast out the spirits

with His word: and healed all that were sick: *That it might be ful-filled* which was spoken by Isaiah the prophet" (Matt. viii, 16). How striking is the particular aspect of Truth here made known to us! Christ was tender, sympathetic, full of compassion, yet the first and deepest motive which moved Him to heal the sick was that the will of God might be done. In the volume of the Book it was written of Him, and therefore did He say, "I delight to do Thy will, O my God" (Psalm xl, 7, 8). A striking and beautiful illustration of this is found in John xi. Lazarus was taken seriously ill, and his sisters sent the Saviour an urgent message, saying: "Lord, behold, he whom Thou lovest is sick" (verse 3). Then we read, "Now Jesus loved Martha, and her sister, and Lazarus," yet the very next thing recorded is "when He had heard therefore that Lazarus was sick, He abode two days still in the same place where He was." Mysterious delay! But the mystery was solved by His own declara-tion, "this sickness is not unto death, but for the glory of God" (verse 4). Not even His affection for those sorely tried souls would move Him to respond to their appeal until the Father's hour had arrived.

In like manner, Christ's saving of sinners was in order to the rendering of obedience to God. "All that the Father giveth Me shall come to Me and him that cometh to Me I will in no wise cast out. *For* I came down from heaven, not to do Mine own will, but the will of Him that sent Me" (John vi, 37, 38). What a view does this present to us of the redemptive work of Christ! How it magnifies His blessed submission unto the One who had commissioned Him! Here then is the explanation why He put not forth His own Divine power to convert the whole of His hearers by this Sermon on the Mount: because He had no word from the Father so to do. Admire then and adore the Lord of glory as He so perfectly discharged His office as Servant. What an example of entire submission to God has He left us. Does the reader desire that we press the question a stage farther back and ask, Why was it the Father's pleasure that His incarnate Son should so often suspend the exercise of His Divine attributes and restrain from putting forth His own power? Surely if no other answer was available than what has been pointed out above, *it* would be sufficient: to display the perfect oneness between the Son and the Father, to evidence that the Former would not act independently of the Other, to manifest His moral perfections and thereby leave His people an example.

But there were other reasons why it was fitting that a veil should be cast over the Divine glory of the incarnate Son. This was the season of His humiliation, when He came not to rule over the earth as King of kings and Lord of lords, but to have "not where to lay His head." He had entered the place of subserviency, of obedience, yea, He had become "obedient unto death, even the death of the cross" (Phil. ii, 8). And in order thereto it was necessary that He should come unto His own and that His own receive Him not

(John i, 11), yea, that He should be " despised and rejected of men."
He had descended from heaven to earth in order that He should be
" taken, and by wicked hands crucified and slain " (Acts ii, 23), yet
at the same time offer Himself as a sacrifice to God, as a sin-offering
on behalf of His people. It was not then the season for Him to
convert men *en masse*, to overthrow Satan's kingdom and deliver
his captives. The corn of wheat must fall into the ground and die
before the fruit thereof is brought forth (John xii, 24). In due time
God would exalt Him "with His right hand to be a Prince and a
Saviour, for to give repentance to [the spiritual] Israel, and forgiveness of sins " (Acts v, 31), for then would " the rod of His strength "
go out of Zion and His people be made willing " in the day of His
power " (Psalm cx, 2, 3).

Again, by cloaking His Divine power, yet at the same time acting
as a Minister of the circumcision for the Truth of God, to confirm
the promises made to the fathers and that the Gentiles might glorify
God for His mercy (Romans xv, 8, 9) an admirable test was made
of men. Though He stopped short of renewing their hearts, yet by
acting as the final Spokesman of God (Heb. i, 1, 2), by speaking to
men as they had never been spoken to before, Christ addressed Himself to the responsibility of His hearers. The Light shone in midday
splendour, but the darkness comprehended it not. And why?
Because men loved darkness rather than light. Thereby their real
character was unmistakably revealed: as incorrigibly and inveter-
ately opposed to God, steeled against Him even when speaking to
them through His own Son. Nor could they plead lack of clear
evidence that Christ was the Messiah Himself, for the miracles He
wrought unequivocally established His credentials. Thus, in their
not being converted by such a Sermon as this, they were left " without excuse." Christ, then, put not forth His power to regenerate
them, first, because He had no commission from the Father so to
do; second, because it was not the time for Him to exercise His royal
prerogative; third, because by leaving His auditors to the exercise of
their own wills, their accountability was put to the proof and their
utter depravity demonstrated.

But further: the Father was pleased that His Son should restrain
the power of His Godhead even from His public ministry that it
might be more clearly evidenced when His term of obedience had
expired, that He was vested with all-sufficient unction and invincible might. After His resurrection Christ affirmed " all power is
given unto Me in heaven and in earth " (Matt. xxviii, 18), and on
the day of Pentecost after the public descent of the Holy Spirit
Peter announced, " Let all the house of Israel know assuredly, that
God hath made that same Jesus, whom ye have crucified, both Lord
and Christ " (Acts ii, 36), where " made " has *not* the force of " constituted " but signifies *made manifest*, for it was from Christ that the
Spirit had been given (verse 33). God would have it made known
unto His people that the Mediator, being ascended, was not only

"set down on the right hand of the Majesty on high," where He is "upholding all things by the word of His power" (Heb. i, 3), ruling as King in His royal office, but also that He governs His Church by His Word and Spirit (Rev. iii, 1). It was for this reason, when promising the apostles that they should do "greater works" than He had wrought, that He added by way of proof "because I go unto My Father" (John xiv, 12)—there to rule His people and remain until His enemies are made His footstool.

Finally, there appears to us to be yet another and more solemn reason why (so far as the inspired narrative informs us) not one soul was born again through the instrumentality of this Sermon. We cannot shake off the conviction that here in Matthew v-vii we have, as it were, a miniature tableau, a typical representation and anticipation of the Great Assize. Christ seated on the mount was a figure of His taking His place on the throne of judgment. Encircled by His disciples and the "multitudes" before Him gives a picture of the dread Day to come. The contents of this Sermon reveal both the order of procedure which will then be followed and the grounds on which the verdicts will be passed: "His own" vindicated by the benediction (the "Blessed are ye" pronounced upon them) and all the others weighed and found wanting in the balance of the very laws which He here enunciated. The effect upon the people will be the same. For though the visible appearance of Christ in that day will be very different, though He will be seen with "His eyes as a flame of fire" and wearing "many crowns" (Rev. xix, 12), yet none shall be brought to repentance and faith by such a sight. "Astonished" they may well be as they learn *who* it is they despised and rejected, overwhelmed with horror they will be as they hear His "Depart from Me ye cursed into everlasting fire," but saved by such a spectacle and sentence none will be.

"For He taught them as one having authority and not as the scribes." Apparently no deeper impression was made on the people than a sense of wonderment, which caused them to draw an invidious distinction between Christ and the scribes, who dwelt mainly on "the traditions of men" and such matters as tithing mint and cummin and the ceremonial washings of pots and pans. That Christ should teach with authority was intimated in prophecy, when it was announced that Jehovah would put His own words in His mouth and that He should speak unto Israel all that had been commanded Him (Deut. xviii, 18). It is remarkable that even His enemies bore witness, "Master, we know that Thou art true, and teachest the way of . . . Truth, neither carest Thou for any man" (Matt. xxii, 16). "Though Christ were here in a mean and base state, yet He would not suffer His calling to be condemned, but gets grace thereto" (W. Perkins, 1590, to whom we have been indebted in the course of these expositions). Herein Christ has left His servants an example, for the minister of the Gospel is bidden to "exhort and rebuke with all *authority*" (Titus ii, 15), which he can do only as he cleaves closely to the Word and exhorts in the name of Christ.

Let our closing reflection be this: the words of "authority" in Matthew v-vii are addressed as directly *to us* as to those who first heard them! By its precepts and rules our conduct must be directed: by its promises and encouragements our souls are to be sustained, for in these very scales shall *we* be weighed in the Day of testing and adjudication. To us this Sermon comes with even greater authority than to those who heard it preached in Palestine, for in moving His apostle by the Spirit to register the same as a permanent record of His will He speaks to us from heaven. Hence the force of that exhortation, "See that ye refuse not Him that [not "hath spoken" but] *speaketh*. For if they escaped not who refused Him that spake on earth, much more shall not we escape, if we turn away from Him that speaketh from heaven" (Heb. xii, 25). Then let us earnestly seek grace to be something more than "astonished" with this Sermon, namely receive it into our hearts and minds and incorporate it into our daily walk.

Index of Scripture

Genesis
1:11 237, 240
1:21 170
1:26, 27 139
1:31 228
2:7 241
2:25 238
3:5, 6 148
4:4 390
4:6 72
4:13 20, 387
chapter 9 89
11:5 265
14:14–16 118
15:1 189, 192
18:21 265
chapter 19 89
21:19 194
21:23, 24 105
chapter 22 431
22:16 105
24:8, 9 105
27:41 195
31:53 106
32:7, 9–11 195
32:26 306
39:7 82
41:42 238
47:31 106

Exodus
2:14 287
5:2 148
5:11 41
9:27 387
11:2 129
14:11 41
14:15 308
16:2 41
17:2 41
17:12 308
18:16 130
20:6 216
20:7 98, 103

20:16, 17 130
chapter 21 111
21:1, 24 110
21:23–25 111
22:11 108
22:11, 12 99
22:21 320
23:2 331
23:4 322
23:4, 5 130
32:10 38
33:4 388

Leviticus 186
5:1 99
10:3 23
10:10 289
10:12–15 290
chapter 18 54
19:12 99
19:16 267
19:17 263, 281, 282, 283
19:18 129, 322
19:18, 34 130
19:33, 34 129
23:29–32 174
24:19, 20 111
25:35 146

Numbers 186
5:19–21 99
7:89 156
12:3 24
12:13 31, 170
14:39, 44 388
14:40 387
16:47, 48 38
20:10 72
22:18, 38 388, 389
23:5 401
23:21 271
24:16 401

31:8 401
32:11 216

Deuteronomy
6:5 216
6:7 233
6:13 98, 99, 106
8:18 187, 192
12:8–11 209
13:3 375
15:7, 8 146, 322
18:18 330, 441
19:18, 21 110
19:19, 20 111
19:19–21 112
21:15 92
22:5 234
23:3, 18 289
23:20 92
24:1, 4 93
24:1–4 92
29:19 207

Joshua
7:6 180
14:8 216

Judges
1:6, 7 111
9:45 45
16:1 82
20:26 174

Ruth
3:3 182
3:13 108

I Samuel
2:7 232
3:18 23
chapter 6 89
7:5, 9, 12 308
8:5 41
10:10, 11 401

15:14 387
15:22 418
15:30 195
16:7 33, 63, 80,
   355, 406
17:43 289
chapter 21 268
22:18 268
24:17 170
25:17 290
25:36, 37 287
30:6 195

II Samuel
6:11 258
7:25 299
chapter 10 265
11:2 82
12:1–11 264
12:16 174, 177
16:9 289
18:33 155
23:5 366
24:14 38

I Kings
8:31, 32 108
13:2 236
17:19, 20 155
18:10 108
18:17 41
18:26 157
18:43 306
19:2 41
21:27 181, 388

II Kings
1:8 339
8:13 289
9:30 83
10:26–28 387
10:31 387

I Chronicles
16:29 235
29:11 251
29:18 389

II Chronicles
18:17 41
20:1–13, 17 308
20:3, 4 174
20:22–24 308
32:31 431

Ezra
4:8 61
7:1, 5, 6 61
8:21 174
9:3 180

Nehemiah
1:4 174
2:2 180
chapter 4 41

Esther
4:16 177

Job
1:8–11 264
10:8 225
11:12 120
14:5 226
19:28 427
20:27 404
21:14 255
22:21 38, 399
22:25 190
23:10 314
25:4 367
29:16 146
31:1 82
31:12 81
33:4 184
36:24 227
38:41 228
42:5 386
42:12 192

Psalms
1:2 334
1:5 404
1:6 329, 405
2:11 365
4:6 203
10:4 197
15:1, 4 99
15:2 257
16:5, 6 190
16:8 35
17:4 352
17:14 157
17:14, 15 192
17:15 35
18:25 32
19:7 321
19:11 430
20:1 162

21:26 25
22:6 23
25:9 22
25:10 352
26:2 426
27:14 306
30:5 21
32:3, 5 428
32:5 419
34:10 224
35:13 174
36:2 397
36:9 206, 284, 372
37:3 224
37:5 223
37:11, 16 24
37:21 31
39:9 23
40:7, 8 439
40:17 17
41:1 146
42:1 26
45:13 63, 236
49:18 186
50:5 352
50:21 395
51:5, 6 33
51:6 69, 425
51:9, 10, 13 286
55:22 223
62:10 188
66:16 293
66:18 75, 82, 286
69:10 177
69:33 17
72:13 18
73:25 194
75:5–7 232
78:30, 31 304
78:36, 37 181
81:10 304
82:4 27
82:5 199
84:7 240
84:10 191
84:11 258
89:30–32 271
90:12 208
90:17 236
92:4, 5 228
103:13 249, 311
103:18 352
103:19 251
103:20 355

104:15 182
104:24 227
104:25, 27 228
107:41 18
109:16 31
110:2, 3 440
111:2, 4 227
111:10 203, 372
112:5 126
112:9 147
chapter 119 157, 387
119:5, 27 354
119:5, 35 419
119:6, 31 217
119:11 294, 425
119:16 216
119:30, 31 375
119:35 428
119:37 83
119:45 277
119:47, 54 216
119:50, 54 294
119:53 20
119:67, 71 224
119:69 216
119:72, 127 194
119:92 195
119:96 13, 81, 101, 103, 132
119:97 216
119:98 372
119:98, 105 203
119:105 294
119:127, 128 354
119:127, 140 216
119:159, 167 216
119:174 299
123:1, 2 214
126:5 21
127:1, 2 231
127:2 223
132:15 18
139:14 227
139:17, 18 197
139:21, 22 131
139:23, 24 284
140:3 72
141:5 269
143:5 228
145:4, 5, 15 228
147:6 25
147:9 228
149:4 23

Proverbs
2:1–4, 10 425
2:3–5 194
3:5 334
3:13–15 294
3:27 126
4:19 209
4:23 62, 80
4:25 89
4:26 331
4:27 334
6:6 220
6:6–8 187
8:1, 11 203
8:17 257
8:20, 21 203
9:8 269, 290
11:13 267
11:17 32
13:10 38
13:18 287
14:7 293
14:10 21
14:12 329, 341
14:21 32, 147
15:3 207
15:16 24
15:32 287
16:2 395
16:3 223
16:32 170
18:10, 11 195
18:13 265
19:17 147, 195
20:22 116, 121
21:1 402
21:13 147, 171
21:21 32
22:9 199
22:21 293
23:5 189, 192
23:6, 7 199
23:9 290
23:23 350, 425
24:17 322
24:17, 18 130
24:29 121, 170
25:11 287
25:12 269
25:21 130, 322
25:21, 22 116, 121
27:1 369
27:19 201
28:9 296

28:13 286, 428
28:27 147
30:12 382, 398

Ecclesiastes
3:7 12
5:1, 2 154, 279
7:5 287
7:13 227
7:16 265
7:21, 22 319
7:29 62
12:7 432

Song of Solomon
1:6 404
2:16 190

Isaiah 110
1:2 236
1:11, 15 74
1:15, 17 316
1:16 35
5:20 200
6:3 355
9:15 59
9:16 200
11:6–9 120
chapter 14 148
17:12 329
19:18 104
22:12, 13 176
22:12–14 182
24:15 162
26:9 197
26:20 155
27:11 393
28:16 408
28:17 358
29:19 25
30:10 339
30:18 306
32:5–8 199
33:15, 16 224
35:3 15
35:4–6 10
37:15–20 308
37:35, 37 308
40:1 15
40:3 359
42:3 242
42:21 57, 282, 342
44:20 399
45:8 25

45:23 106
45:24 368
46:12, 13 25
48:1, 2 389
49:15 311
51:5 25
53:11 366
55:2 188, 202
55:7 327, 348, 398
55:7–9 168
56:1 25
56:6 353
58:5, 6 74, 176
58:6, 9 316
59:2 34, 309
61:1 23
61:3 21
61:10 25, 253
62:6, 7 305
64:3–8 161
66:2 18

Jeremiah
2:2 353
4:2 105
5:7–9 108
5:24 309
5:30, 31 337
5:31 341
6:16 336
7:9, 10 74
8:6 285
8:11 339
9:23, 24 399
10:2 217
10:3 334
12:11 38
12:16 106
13:1, 23 366
13:17 20
13:23 335
14:14 337
15:19 289, 292
17:9 33
21:8 330
22:29 236
23:14, 16 337
23:16, 32 375
23:17 339
29:13 254, 300, 306

Lamentations
3:26 306
3:40 284

Ezekiel
3:26 12
6:3 236
9:4 20
13:14 339
13:18 270
13:22 292
16:25–28 93
22:25 338
22:26 289
22:28 339
22:30, 31 38
33:6 88
33:22, 23 12
33:31 197
44:23 289

Daniel
6:10 155
9:3 175
10:2, 3 177
10:3 175

Hosea
4:6 97
6:3 373
6:4 389
13:11 304

Joel
1:13, 14 180
1:14 174, 177
2:13 176, 184
2:15, 16 175

Amos
2:6 147
4:7 142
5:12 147
6:1, 3–6 218

Jonah
chapter 3 178
3:5–10 173

Micah
3:5 339
4:3 120

Zephaniah
2:3 25
3:4 375

Haggai
1:5 178
1:6, 9 231

Zechariah
3:1 48
4:6 368
5:4 108
7:5 176
7:9, 13 316
9:17 236
12:10 19
13:4 339

Malachi 9
2:9 46
2:10 160
3:2 136
3:17 311
3:18 289

Matthew 9, 10, 333
1:1 9
chapter 2 9, 10
2:23 10
3:2 59, 359
3:4 339
3:15 145
chapter 4 182
4:3, 4 438
4:6 362
4:12, 13 10
4:16 46, 393
4:16, 17 10
4:17 13, 327
4:19 43
4:23 255
4:23–25 10
chapters 5–7 377,
   436, 441, 442
chapter 5 108, 154,
   321
5:1 11, 298, 378
5:1, 2 10, 13, 292
5:1–12 43
5:1–11, 13 44
5:3 16, 18
5:3, 4 22
5:3–11 15
5:3–16 59
5:4 18, 353
5:5 22
5:5–12 41
5:6 25

5:7 29, 31, 171, 277
5:7, 9 37
5:8 32, 80
5:9 36
5:10 39
5:11, 12 41
5:13 45
5:13–16 43
5:14 46
5:14–16 47
5:16 141, 293
5:17 50, 51, 281, 289
5:17, 18 49, 52, 53, 107
5:17–19 56, 57
5:17, 19 58
5:17, 19, 20 65
5:17–20 55, 79
5:17–48 68, 135
5:17–7:5 298
5:18–20 66
5:18–48 50
5:20 61, 62, 63, 261, 317, 370, 398, 422
5:20–30, 44 295
5:20, 47 145
5:20–48 79
5:21 69, 80
5:21, 22 73
5:21–26 67, 79, 85
5:21–48 133
5:22 71, 75
5:23, 24 73, 74, 170
5:24 76
5:24–26 78
5:25, 26 77
5:27, 28 80
5:27–30 91
5:27–32 79
5:28 81, 83
5:28, 30 85
5:29 85, 430
5:29, 30 117, 324, 333
5:30 88
5:31 92
5:31, 32 91
5:32 93, 95
5:33–36 99
5:33–37 97, 98, 103, 106, 107
5:34 108, 119

5:34–36 101
5:34–37 100
5:34, 42 220
5:37 102
5:38 110, 113
5:38, 39 121
5:38–42 109, 110
5:39 115, 122
5:39–42 114
5:40 123
5:41 125
5:42 126
5:43 129
5:43–48 127, 134, 139
5:44 132, 170
5:44, 45 141
5:44, 48 136
5:45 139, 142
5:45, 47 140
5:46, 47 142, 143
5:48 144, 383
chapter 6 186, 296
6:1 146, 148
6:1, 2 149
6:1–4 145
6:1–18 145, 152, 179
6:2–4 150
6:2–21 205
6:3 173
6:5 153
6:5–8 152, 157
6:6 154, 156, 166
6:9 160, 161, 162
6:9–13 159
6:10–12 163
6:13 164
6:14, 15 166, 167
6:15 117, 319
6:16–18 172, 179
6:17, 18 182
6:18 184
6:19 186, 187, 192
6:19, 20 188, 193, 213
6:19–21 185, 196, 201
6:19–30 246
6:19–34 199, 212, 219, 220
6:20 189, 410
6:21–24 200
6:22 372

6:22, 23 198, 205, 206
6:23 207, 208, 210
6:24 206, 212
6:25 219
6:25, 31 226, 233, 243
6:26 227
6:26, 27 226, 230
6:26, 30 241
6:26, 31, 32 249
6:28, 29 233, 239
6:28, 30 235, 240
6:29 237
6:30 248
6:32–34 246
6:33 26, 163, 250, 252, 253
6:33, 34 259
7:1 260, 261, 267
7:1, 15 263
7:1–4 281
7:1–5, 20 262
7:1–11 295
7:2 32, 111, 171, 277
7:2–4 274
7:3 284, 285
7:3, 4 278, 283
7:3–6 290
7:5 281
7:6 288, 292, 294
7:6, 7 296
7:6–8 298
7:7, 8 295, 308
7:7, 8, 11 304
7:7–11 302, 310, 316
7:9, 10 312
7:9–11 309
7:11 169, 249, 299
7:12 50, 316
7:13 403
7:13, 14 323, 331, 332, 344
7:13–20, 23 310
7:13–27 429
7:14, 15 330
7:15 337, 350, 356, 371
7:15–20 363
7:16, 19, 20 378
7:16–20 373
7:21 389

7:21–23   392,   400,
    414
7:21–27   377
7:22   402
7:22, 23   404
7:24   383, 416
7:24, 25   410
7:24–27   407,   411,
    414
7:25   333, 429
7:26, 27   422
7:27   434
7:28   298, 378
7:28,   29   12,   13,
    405, 436, 437
8:12   393
8:16   439
8:29   332, 380
8:31, 32   304
9:11   142
9:12   424
10:1   401
10:25   333
10:34   37
10:42   196
11:5, 29   17
11:9   142
11:12   59, 326
11:20   402
11:23, 24   279
11:28   20
11:29   22, 343
12:12–14   438
12:26   251
12:33   87
12:37   270
12:46–50   418
13:8, 9, 11   291
13:19   255
13:20   403
13:20, 21   424
13:22   222
13:25   338
13:36   11, 291
13:43   239
13:52   61
15:4–6   81
15:8   207
15:14   293
15:19   93
15:26   288
15:28   306
16:23   283
16:24   324, 333

17:1–8   11
17:5   383
17:20   355
17:21   177
18:3   65,   255,   331,
    353, 380
18:15   170
18:15–17   117,   122
18:20   154
18:23–35   168
19:3, 7, 9   93
19:9   95
19:9, 29   94
19:16   69
19:21   187
19:23   332
19:23, 24   188
19:29   196
20:15   199
21:32   359
21:43   252
22:5   325
22:16   441
22:32   241
22:37   216
22:37, 39   132,   134
22:39   321
chapter 23   15, 97
23:2   11, 61
23:3, 5   422
23:5–7   62
23:13   153,   255,   326
23:15   361
23:16   99
23:23   62
23:23, 27   422
23:25   62, 339
23:25, 26   80
23:26   87
23:27   390
23:27, 28   62
23:34   278
chapter 24   291
24:3   11
24:5, 11   376
24:11, 24   338
24:12, 13   343
24:13   333
24:26   155
24:29   285
chapter 25   270, 291
25:1–12   411
25:10   326
25:34   256

26:55   11
26:63, 64   107
27:3   387
27:29   72
28:6   11
28:18   440

Mark 333
1:15   49, 359
2:4, 5   301
2:13   291
3:5   71
4:24   340
7:17   291
7:22   199
9:50   46
10:26   333
11:15–17   117
11:26   353
15:21   125

Luke 333
1:6   420
1:17   339
2:37   175
2:51   294
3:1–6   327
4:16–22   65
4:28–30   10
6:17   11, 291
6:27   170
6:35   141
6:46   360,   380,   383,
    427
6:47   415
6:47, 48   423
6:47–49   414
6:48   433
7:38   19
7:43   261
7:46   182
8:13   389
8:37   188
9:49   401
9:58–62   424
10:10   374
10:25   69
10:29   129
10:39, 42   190
11:1, 2   159, 311
11:1–13   302
11:4   169, 428
11:5–8, 13   303
11:5–13   307

11:7–9, 13 311
11:9, 10 304
11:12 314, 315
11:20 255
11:27, 28 418
12:1 153
12:27 284
12:30 248
12:32 324
12:33 190, 196
12:34–36 198
12:47, 48 278
12:57 262
13:24 325, 361
13:32 374
14:26, 27 359
14:26–28 360
14:27 351
14:28 334, 424
14:33 343, 359, 360
15:15 216
15:17 394
15:18 19
16:15 16, 355, 406
16:16 50
16:25 21
16:26 330
17:3, 4 171
17:10 355
17:32 424
18:2 112
18:9 261, 398
18:12 148, 179
18:13 19
18:17 380
18:18 69
18:20 285
18:21 390
19:8 124, 142
19:14 383
21:34 177
22:31 432
22:32 286
22:39 155
chapter 23 168
23:40, 41 349
24:25 72, 283

John 333
1:11 440
1:12 359
1:12, 16 190
1:13 367
1:16 333

2:13–17 117, 122
2:23, 24 379, 427
2:23–25 311
2:27 209
3:2 379
3:3 380, 427, 438
3:3, 5 201
3:5 255
3:15, 18, 36 360
3:16 346, 398, 412
3:36 35
4:18 91, 92
4:21, 24 156
4:24 420
4:34 438
5:22 383
5:24 271, 360
5:29 410
5:44 333
6:14, 15 379
6:27 193
6:37 292
6:37, 38 439
6:38 438
6:44 424
7:17 13, 372, 373
7:24 262, 265
7:46 437
7:51 261
8:4, 5 81
8:12 284
8:33, 34 389
8:37 426
8:39 323
8:41 328
8:45 341
8:56 210
10:4 334, 343
10:9 327
10:14, 15 373
11:3, 4 439
11:41 153
11:51, 52 401
12:24 440
12:27, 28 163
12:31 254
12:48 380
13:13 381
13:17 415
14:6 391
14:12 438, 441
14:18 81
14:21 353
15:13, 14 412

15:18, 19 335
15:19, 20 41
16:2 40
17:3 384, 399
17:6 419
17:9, 10 15
17:14 249
17:15 164
18:11 23
18:22, 23 118
18:31 261
18:37 291
19:11 279
19:12 428
20:17 160

Acts
1:7 369
1:14 154
2:23 440
2:33, 36 440
2:37 19
2:40 351
2:41 438
2:42 154
3:19 348, 398
4:11 408
4:25 247
5:31 440
5:41 42
6:4 154
7:60 170
8:13 389
8:22 298
9:1, 4 279
10:30 175
11:11 152
11:15 313
11:18 388
11:29, 30 150
12:5 154
12:23 149
13:3 175, 177
14:22 324, 396, 434
14:23 175, 177
15:9 33, 143, 360,
    390, 427
16:13 154
16:15 261
16:25 42
16:31 412
16:35–37 24
17:11 71, 369

17:24, 27 156
17:31 404
19:34 157
20:21 359
20:26 88
20:29, 30 374
20:29–31 338
20:32 417
23:6 61
24:25 88, 378
25:23 238
26:5 62
26:18 46
26:26, 27 389
27:35 153
28:31 255

Romans
1:5 420
1:18 87
1:19, 20 237
1:21–24 384
2:1 264
2:2, 11 270
2:5 186, 404
2:14, 15 140
2:22 387
3:10 26
3:10, 11 366
3:17 208
3:19, 20, 31 137
3:20 358
3:21 53
3:22 253
3:31 281, 316, 336
4:6 62
4:16 323
4:18 242
4:20 241
chapter 5 63
5:9, 10, 15 227
5:10 76
5:17 253
5:21 119, 167, 275, 361
6:6 214
6:13 89
6:14 60
6:17 417
chapter 7 375
7:6 214
7:7 358
7:12 299
7:12–25 428

7:12, 14 282
7:14 321, 420
7:18–21 419
7:21, 23, 25 32
7:22 281, 419
7:22, 25 64, 139, 358
chapter 8 63
8:1 271
8:3 282
8:4 53, 419
8:5 190
8:7 64, 136, 358
8:7, 8 366
8:13 324, 349
8:14, 16 141
8:18 42
8:19 39
8:20 193
8:23 19, 33
8:24 347
8:24, 25 314
8:26 159
8:32 225, 242, 250, 360
8:32, 33 351
9:1 107
9:18 396
9:29 367
10:4 53
10:9 353
10:10 332, 389
10:13 398, 412
10:15 38
11:6 342
11:18–20 88
11:22 88, 353
12:2 249, 416
12:8 31, 199
12:10 32
12:11 187
12:15 20
12:17, 20 116
12:18 37
12:19 123
12:20 133
12:21 170, 281
13:3, 4 112
13:8 52
13:10 128
13:14 183
14:3 261
14:4 264
14:10, 11 272

14:11 106
14:17 40, 253
14:19 417
15:2 417
15:8, 9 440
15:30 48, 310
16:17 263
16:17, 18 338
16:18 361
16:26 343

I Corinthians
chapter 1 16
1:26 385
1:30 202
2:8, 9 190
2:14 208, 386
2:15 202
3:6, 7 231
3:11 195, 409
3:13 404
3:13–15 272
3:21, 22 24
4:3 269
4:5 151
4:7 355
4:13 42, 270
4:15 189
6:1–7 119
6:1–8 124
6:9, 10 81
7:2, 15, 39 95
7:3 96
7:5 175
7:19 412
8:2 302
9:22 108
9:24 353
9:25 325, 326
9:27 175, 352
10:13 259
10:15 260
11:13 261
11:19 375
11:21 284
11:31 149
chapter 13 270
13:2 385, 406
13:3 390
13:12 34, 419
14:34 293
15:10 355
15:36 72
16:2, 3 126

II Corinthians
1:1 141
1:11 48
1:12 198, 200
1:20 242
1:23 107
3:5 355
3:18 240
4:4 254
4:6 209, 387
5:10 272
5:11 88
5:17 250, 342, 393
5:17, 18 64
5:20 76
5:21 190
6:10 21, 24
6:17, 18 140, 141
7:1 35, 84
7:10 313, 343
8:2–9 199
8:11, 13 199
8:12 419
8:13, 14 126
9:6 317
9:9 147
10:1 22
11:1 340
11:13–15 340, 362
12:8 157
12:14 187, 220
13:5 426

Galatians
1:6 137, 362
1:16 247, 386
1:20 107
3:8 110
3:8, 17 352
3:10 354
3:13 358
3:19 67
3:29 323
4:6 160
4:15, 16 340
4:24 352
4:29 72
5:6 143, 360, 390,
    412, 427
5:17 419
5:19 93
6:1 23, 170, 287
6:2 32
6:7 111

6:7, 8 88
6:8 349
6:15 412

Ephesians
1:19 387
2:2 251, 254, 328,
    433
2:8, 9 342, 344, 346
2:8–10 348
2:10 349
2:11 19
2:12 209
2:16 76
2:20 408
3:8 190
3:17 389
3:20 299
4:1, 2 22
4:2, 3 38
4:14 361, 371, 374
4:18, 23 205
4:24 62, 140, 254
4:26 71
4:28 126
4:29 417
4:31, 32 72
4:32 166, 167, 168
5:1 230, 317
5:1, 2 141
5:3, 4 83
5:5 217
5:11 263
5:21 287
6:1 142
6:6 383
6:8 317
6:12 394
6:12, 18 310
6:18 305, 307
6:18, 19 12
6:19 48

Philippians
1:6 33, 314
1:8 107
1:9, 10 202
2:5–11 190
2:7 438
2:8 439
3:2 294
3:6 390
3:8 194, 203, 387
3:8, 9 424

3:8, 14 27
3:10 315
3:12 144, 419
3:19 173
3:21 256
4:6 223
4:6, 7 259
4:11 248
4:13 144
4:19 224

Colossians
1:6 384
1:21 76
1:22, 23 353
2:3 190, 202
2:4 361
2:6 433
2:7, 8 417
2:20–23 265
2:21 390
2:23 175, 183
3:2 208
3:3 190, 194
3:5 87, 188, 217
3:10 140
3:12 32
3:13 319
3:16 416
3:23 272
3:24, 25 273
4:6 45
4:12 307, 310, 326

I Thessalonians
1:6 21
2:2 42
2:15, 16 131
3:4 334
4:11 263
5:3 339
5:11 417
5:21 362
5:27 293

II Thessalonians
1:9 406
2:10–12 376
2:11, 12 371
2:13 346
2:16 417
3:6 263
3:10 126, 148, 244

I Timothy
　1:4　417
　1:16　169
　2:4　371
　2:8　153, 168
　3:6　148
　3:9　294
　4:1　373
　4:8　258
　4:10, 15, 16　46
　4:12　48
　4:16　60, 189, 343,
　　351, 404
　5:8　187, 220
　5:22　283
　6:3　339
　6:11　46
　6:12　326
　6:17–19　195, 409
　6:18　419

II Timothy
　1:6　282
　1:7　394
　1:9　342, 346
　1:13　360
　1:16, 18　32
　1:18　276
　2:10　347
　2:15　292
　2:19　408
　3:6　340
　3:7　386
　3:8　338
　3:12　39, 434
　3:16, 17　401
　4:1–5　276
　4:2　287
　4:18　256

Titus
　1:1　427
　1:2　417
　1:16　217
　2:11, 12　297, 361
　2:12　248
　2:15　441
　3:2　22, 267
　3:3　36, 37, 168
　3:5　33, 342

Hebrews
　1:1, 2　322, 383, 440
　1:3　441

2:1　322
2:11　39
3:1　107
3:6, 14　353
3:12　211
3:14　354
3:15　343
4:2　110, 426
5:9　343, 350, 398,
　412
5:11–14　364
5:14　262
6:1　408
6:10　150, 190
6:16　99, 104, 107
7:2　327
7:22　365
8:6　352, 365
8:10　140
9:10　57
9:19, 20　53
9:22　347
10:16　353, 354, 419
10:26–30　88
10:29　279
10:34　196
10:39　360
chapter 11　110
11:1, 13　210
11:7　242
11:16　39
11:25, 26　143
12:11　19, 21
12:14　37, 393, 415
12:16　188
12:23　184
12:24　352
12:25　322, 442
12:29　396
13:4　81
13:18　419
13:20　39, 352

James
　1:3　306
　1:5　303
　1:5, 27　199
　1:6, 7　299
　1:20, 21　22
　1:21　347, 416, 426
　1:23　285
　2:1–5　277
　2:9–11, 13　277
　2:10　58

2:12　276
2:13　21, 32, 171
2:15–17, 19　390
2:17　360, 389
2:19　314, 332
2:21–24, 26　390
3:1　131, 278
3:2　33, 428
3:17　37
4:3　296
4:4　213
4:11　265
5:5　218
5:12　102, 106

I Peter
　1:4　196
　1:7　432
　1:13　276
　1:16　48
　1:24　235
　2:3　387
　2:4　360
　2:5–7　408
　2:9　284, 293
　2:12　141
　2:21　107, 343
　2:23　117
　3:3, 4　236
　3:7　96
　3:15　35, 293
　4:1　425
　4:7　310
　4:12　432
　4:15　264
　4:15, 16　40
　4:17　271
　4:18　361
　4:19　225
　5:5　149, 238, 263
　5:7　223, 241, 325
　5:10　275

II Peter
　1:4　65, 160
　1:5–7, 10　195
　1:10　398, 426
　1:10, 11　256
　1:19　46
　2:1, 2　338
　2:14　82
　2:15　401
　2:20　211

I John
  1:8 32
  1:9 20, 271, 275
  2:3 419
  2:3, 4 412
  2:15 215, 342
  2:19 376
  2:28 273
  2:29 254
  3:1 160
  3:2 27, 347
  3:12 40
  3:14 195, 307
  3:17 31, 126
  4:1 338, 363
  4:5 114, 339

  5:4 143, 336, 360, 390, 427
  5:14 160, 305
  5:20 190, 208

II John
  9 381
  10 143

Jude
  4 340
  13 208
  20 417
  21 32, 352
  22 30, 293

Revelation
  1:6 40

  1:14, 15 272
  2:20, 22 93
  3:1 441
  3:16 148
  3:17 285, 398
  3:18 209
  3:21 353
  4:11 365
  7:11 355
  7:16 27
  10:4–6 107
  chapter 17 234
  19:12 441
  21:8 405
  22:12 415
  22:15 294